A Free Society Reader

RELIGION, POLITICS, AND SOCIETY IN THE NEW MILLENNIUM

Series Editors: Michael Novak, American Enterprise Institute, and Brian C. Anderson, Manhattan Institute

For nearly five centuries, it was widely believed that moral questions could be resolved through reason. The Enlightenment once gave us answers to these perennial questions, but the answers no longer seem adequate. It has become apparent that reason alone is not enough to answer the questions that define and shape our existence. Many now believe that we have come to the edge of the Enlightenment and are stepping forth into a new era, one that may be the most religious we have experienced in five hundred years. This series of books will explore this new historical condition, publishing important works of scholarship in various disciplines that help us to understand the trends in thought and belief we have come from and to define the ones toward which we are heading.

Political Memoirs, by Aurel Kolnai, edited by Francesca Murphy
Challenging the Modern World: Karol Wojtyla/John Paul II and the Development of Catholic Social Teaching, by Samuel Gregg
The Scepter Shall Not Depart from Judah: Perspectives on the Persistence of the Political in Judaism, by Alan L. Mittleman
In the World, But Not of the World: Christian Social Teaching at the End of the Twentieth Century, by Andrew L. Fitz-Gibbon
The Surprising Pope: Understanding the Thought of John Paul II, by Maciej Zieba, O.P.
A Free Society Reader: Principles for the New Millennium, edited by Michael Novak, William Brailsford, and Cornelis Heesters
Meaninglessness: The Solutions of Nietzsche, Freud, and Rorty, by Michael A. Casey

A Free Society Reader

Principles for the New Millennium

Edited by Michael Novak,
William Brailsford, and Cornelis Heesters

LEXINGTON BOOKS
Lanham • Boulder • New York • Oxford

LEXINGTON BOOKS

Published in the United States of America
by Lexington Books
4720 Boston Way, Lanham, Maryland 20706

12 Hid's Copse Road
Cumnor Hill, Oxford OX2 9JJ, England

Copyright © 2000 by Lexington Books

All rights reserved. No part of this publication may be reproduced, stored in a retrieval system, or transmitted in any form or by any means, electronic, mechanical, photocopying, recording, or otherwise, without the prior permission of the publisher.

British Library Cataloguing in Publication Information Available

Library of Congress Cataloging-in-Publication Data

A free society reader : principles for the new millennium / edited by Michael Novak, William Brailsford, and Cornelis Heesters.
    p. cm. — (Religion, politics, and society in the new millennium)
  Includes bibliographical references and index.
  ISBN 0-7391-0143-9 (alk. paper) — ISBN 0-7391-0144-7 (pbk. : alk. paper)
    1. Sociology, Christian (Catholic). 2. Economics—Religious aspects—Catholic Church. 3. Democracy—Religious aspects—Catholic Church. 4. Christianity and culture. 5. Catholic Church—Doctrines. I. Novak, Michael. II. Brailsford, William. III. Heesters, Cornelis. IV. Series.

BX1753.F73   2000
261—dc21   00-029645

Printed in the United States of America

∞™ The paper used in this publication meets the minimum requirements of American National Standard for Information Sciences—Permanence of Paper for Printed Library Materials, ANSI/NISO Z39.48-1992.

Dedicated to

Pope John Paul II

Who personified a past century of Catholic Social Thought and led the way into its Third Millennium

Contents

Acknowledgments	xi
Introduction *Michael Novak*	xiii

Part I: Preliminaries: John Paul II on Liberty

1	*Centesimus Annus*: The Architecture of Freedom *George Weigel*	3
2	Behind *Centesimus Annus* *Rocco Buttiglione*	25
3	The Liberalism of John Paul II *Richard John Neuhaus*	29
4	The Philosophy of John Paul II *Michael Novak*	40

Part II: Economics and the Free Society

5	The Temple in the Polis: Faith Is Not Ideology *Maciej Zieba*	51
6	The Monk and the Market: What Does a Priest Need Economics For? *Maciej Zieba*	60
7	Property and Creativity *Richard John Neuhaus*	68
8	Christian Economics 101 *Rocco Buttiglione*	83

| 9 | How Christianity Changed Political Economy
Michael Novak | 91 |
| 10 | The Love That Moves the Sun
Michael Novak | 98 |

Part III: Democracy and the Free Society

11	Christianity and Democracy (Part I) *Pierre Manent*	109
12	Christianity and Democracy (Part II) *Pierre Manent*	116
13	The Church Embraces Democracy *Alain Besançon*	126
14	A New Order of Religious Freedom *Richard John Neuhaus*	133
15	Catholicism and Democracy: Parsing the Other Twentieth-Century Revolution *George Weigel*	141
16	The Trouble with Toleration *Ryszard Legutko*	166
17	The Catholic Moment *Richard John Neuhaus*	179
18	The Pope and the Liberal State *Russell Hittinger*	185

Part IV: Culture and the Free Society

19	John Paul II and the Priority of Culture *George Weigel*	201
20	Modern Individualism *Pierre Manent*	213
21	The Liberal Paradox: Might Religion Have an Answer? *Thomas L. Pangle*	219
22	True and False Tolerance *Philippe Benéton*	231
23	Law and Liberty in *Veritatis Splendor* *Russell Hittinger*	237

24	Against the Adversary Culture *Michael Novak*	246
25	Truth and Liberty: The Present Crisis in Our Culture *Michael Novak*	274

Part V: Documentation

Introduction to The Federalist	291
The Federalist Papers James Madison et al.	293
Introduction to Democracy in America	313
Democracy in America Alexis de Tocqueville	315
Introduction to *Centesimus Annus*	331
Centesimus Annus John Paul II	333
What Freedom Is: Homily in Orioles Park at Camden Yards	387
John Paul II on the American Experiment	392
Letter to the National Prayer Breakfast	395
Index	399
About the Contributors	413

Acknowledgments

The editors would like to thank the following editors and publishers for granting permission to reprint selections which first appeared in their pages. More exact information is provided in each chapter.

America, for chapter 4.
Crisis, for chapters 2, 5, 6, 8–13, 20–23.
First Things, for chapters 3, 13, 14, 17, 18, 19.
Partisan Review, for chapter 16.
The Review of Politics, for chapter 25.

Doubleday Publishing for *Doing Well and Doing Good: The Challenge to the Christian Capitalist*, by Richard John Neuhaus.
Harper & Row for *The Catholic Moment: The Paradox of the Church in the Postmodern World*, by Richard John Neuhaus.
Wm. B. Eerdmans Publishing Company for *Soul of the World: Notes on the Future of Public Catholicism*, by George Weigel.
The Free Press for *The Catholic Ethic and the Spirit of Capitalism*, by Michael Novak.

Introduction

Michael Novak

This Reader provides a vigorous introduction to the problems of building and maintaining free societies in the new millennium.

The free society is constructed by three liberties: as system of *political* liberty from torture and tyranny; of *economic* liberty from poverty and coercion; and of liberty of *spirit*—moral, cultural, religious—a liberty of conscience, inquiry, and communication.

To construct any one of these systems takes time, experimentation, and a suitable base in social and individual habits and *mores*. To build all three systems at once is three times as hard. And to keep all three functioning in tolerable balance and harmony is, again, difficulty squared.

Accordingly, this Reader is organized into three parts, one for each of the three liberties. Throughout, the historical lessons from which these systems took shape are stressed, and so are current difficulties and dilemmas. No one ever promised that human liberty would be easy to gain, only that it is possible—and as necessary to humans as adulthood to adolescents.

This Reader was first assembled in the caldron of the reconstruction of whole societies in Central and Eastern Europe after the fall of the Berlin Wall in November 1989. Before thirty months had passed, a summer institute for students from that region (together with a smaller number of American students) was up and running, and has been perfecting the Reader ever since. For those so interested, perhaps a few words about that institute will help shed light on the concrete problems this Reader addresses.

The key person in the founding of the summer institute for which this Reader gradually took shape is Rocco Buttiglione, an extraordinary Italian Catholic philosopher, the only living philosopher John Paul II has quoted in one of his own addresses. Before Bishop Karol Wojtyla ever became Pope, Buttiglione had gone to Krakow to study with him and other phenomenologists; and the Pope, after his election, invited Professor Buttiglione to come back to Rome to counsel with him from time to time.

Early in 1991, Pope John Paul II sent Professor Buttiglione on an informal mission to the United States to gather ideas about papal social thought. In May of that year, an encyclical (everyone expected) would be issued on the hundredth anniversary of the launching of papal social thought in Leo XIII's *Rerum Novarum* (May 1891). The Pope was determined, Professor Buttiglione later confirmed, that Americans should recognize their own social experience in the new encyclical. The encyclical *Centesimus Annus* did then appear early in May 1991 and many American writers, whether Catholic or not, saw in it an American resonance they had not seen in its predecessors. This resonance rang out not only from the passages on invention, discovery, know-how, human capital, and community, but also from the passages on the rule of law, the separation of powers, the social decadence of the welfare state, the creation of new wealth through enterprise, and the importance of the subjectivity of (that is, the personal responsibility of individuals in) society.

About a month after *Centesimus Annus* appeared, Professor Buttiglione telephoned me at a hotel in Interlaken, Switzerland, where I was attending a conference, and set up a luncheon meeting the next day. He wanted to introduce me to Josef Seifert, the president of the International Academy of Philosophy in nearby Liechtenstein; in fact, they invited me to come give a lecture to the students there. The three of us spoke of the great grace given us in *Centesimus Annus*, and of the desirability of forming an international study group for European/American dialogue on the intellectual questions that lie ahead of modern societies. Professor Seifert, author of important books in phenomenology, had considerable experience teaching in America, and Professor Buttiglione had lectured there often and was, besides, an American by second-nature. Both worried about the growing cultural and intellectual gap between the continents, especially among Catholics. To all of us, it seemed as though the generation before ours, following World War II, had enjoyed far closer spiritual bonds than seemed nowadays being formed. We tried to imagine a corrective.

Professor Buttiglione, for instance, had been among the founding fathers of a vastly successful youth movement in Italy, Communione e Liberazione, and had seen that organization veer off in new directions, one wing of it expressing strong anti-American sentiments. Younger philosophers, social thinkers, and theologians seemed to lack knowledge of things American; few read Acton, Tocqueville, or the American founders, Madison, Adams, and Jefferson. The Americans seemed to know too little of Continental experience and traditions. The three of us concurred that it is not good for our nations, or for the universal church, that such fissures are widening.

To make a long story short, we decided that the next year we would develop a month-long program at the International Academy of Philosophy, which Rocco and I would direct, and invite a handful of other scholars, American and European, to join us on the faculty, and to come to know one another as colleagues. We all felt a special responsibility to the young people of Central Europe, cut off from contact with the world ever since September 1, 1939. Therefore, we would invite some twenty students from Eastern and Central Europe (the lands until recently behind the Iron Curtain) to a setting—the Academy grounds in Liechtenstein—already shared by Western students, and in addition recruit about ten American graduate students each year. In this way, we thought, we could raise some additional funds for the Academy through rental fees for a month in which it is not normally in use, bring together American and European leaders of the next generation, and together study the principles of the free society, in its political, economic, and cultural dimensions. *Centesimus Annus* and the agenda and uncompleted work it set before us would provide an ideal cross-cultural text.

And so we did. It was my responsibility to raise the money and to call upon the assistance of American faculty members, as well as to recruit the first class of ten American students; I would also invite my friend, the splendid Polish Dominican priest, Father Majiec Zieba, O.P., to join the faculty and to use his extensive contacts in Central Europe to recruit the European students. Professors Seifert and Buttiglione and I were able to provide him with contacts of our own in Prague and Bratislava, Budapest, and a few other places. The Bradley and Olin Foundations, joined in some years by some farsighted individuals or smaller foundations such as John Galvin of Motorola, Elizabeth Lurie of the Brady Foundation, Heather Richardson Higgins of the Randolph Foundation, Anthony Sullivan of the Earhart Foundation, Carl Gershman of the National Endowment for Democracy, and Tim Donner of the Donner Foundation, showed constant and steady support. Thus, the summer institute has been able to continue right up to the millennium and beyond.

Between 1992 and 1999, more than 240 students completed the program. With every year that goes by, graduates fill higher and higher positions: a member of Parliament in Italy; editors of magazines in Poland, Ukraine, Italy, and the Czech Republic; heads of organizations in several countries; and, among others, foundation officers, lawyers, professors, administrators, members of the military, priests and ministers, and one cofounder of a publishing house.

Over the years, the faculty have included Rocco Buttiglione, Russell Hittinger, Jaroslaw Kupczak, O.P., Mark Henrie, William Klimon, Michal Semin, Paul Ballantyne, Graham Walker, Derek Cross, Brian Anderson, James Neuchterlein, Rev. Robert Sirico, Robert Royal, and Jody Bottum. Year after year, the regulars have been Maciej Zieba, O.P., Richard John Neuhaus, George Weigel, and myself.

During 1992 and 1993, the institute was held in Liechtenstein, at the invitation of Prince Nicholas. Then Professor Buttiglione brought us a message that Pope John Paul II, who had been well informed about the institute and had sent his greetings to us from its beginnings, suggested that Central Europe—specifically, Poland—might be a needier location. As the 1992 meeting concluded, Derek Cross, who was then the administrator of the institute, traveled to Krakow with Fr. Zieba, and reported back that the Dominican monastery in Krakow, built on the site of one of the oldest Catholic chapels in Poland (dating back to the tenth century) and boasting through St. Hyacinth a lineage going back to the first generation of Dominicans in the thirteenth century, would be an ideal center for us, and would be available each summer when the seminarians left. Such a move would also, of course, help us to cut our costs. Most of all, it would involve all of us in the profound experience of the transition from Communism and the quiet, confident power of the faith that had overthrown Communism. We have been meeting in Krakow every July since 1993.

The learning and sophistication of Polish Catholic faith, and the palpable piety and regular practice of its people, have deeply influenced all of us. The experience of the institute, summer after summer, has become one of intense spiritual and intellectual renewal. The lives of most of us have been changed far more than we ever imagined they would be. Each weekend in the Dominican church the masses are crowded, sometimes to overflowing, and the lines outside the confessional are as long as lines at movie theaters. The stream of devotions and study groups and choral groups at the monastery flows like a river.

The city square of Krakow is full of vitality. In the evenings, our students drink beer and watch many street theater performances. The Cybernet Café has become a favorite hangout. But there are others. We generally take our noon and evening meals together at one or another restaurant with which we have contracted for the session. Breakfasts are at the monastery. Although attendance is optional, we participate in the Eucharist every evening before the dinner hour.

Each Saturday we have a chartered bus to take us on day trips, and on at least one afternoon each week we take shorter bus excursions, often including dinner away. These day trips, longer or shorter, usually include Czestochowa, Auschwitz, rafting on the Dunajec River or an excursion into the Tatra Mountains, a visit down into an underground salt mine and its ancient and contemporary sculptures, and an evening of Renaissance music in a restored manor house in the country. George Weigel has also organized a very popular walking tour of the key sites of the life of Karol Wojtyla in Krakow. Other scheduled walking tours include the Jagiellonian University, Wawel Castle, and the Jewish Quarter.

From year to year, various distinguished Polish intellectuals and civic leaders have offered lectures and discussion periods to the group. A perennial favorite has been Ryszard Legutko, a collection of whose essays one alumnus of the institute—Brian Anderson—has organized for publication in the United States.

The intellectual work of the seminar is divided into one segment for each of the three weeks: the economics, politics, and culture of the free society. Yet these questions require some introduction and some foundational investigations. Thus, during the opening days of the institute, in addition to the daily lectures, we have also scheduled small-group seminars in the late afternoon to discuss the text of *Centesimus Annus* and at least a few pivotal texts from *The Federalist* and *Democracy in America*. One purpose of these small-group sessions is to offer the European students a chance to accustom themselves to speaking in English and to get a taste, at least, of two American classics. (In some years, we have been able to provide them free copies of the entire texts for their personal libraries.) A more important purpose is to give the faculty an early idea of some of the main concerns, strengths, and needs of the students. A third purpose is to help the Americans and the Europeans to bond together intellectually.

The readings for the institute, which have varied slightly from year to year, bring together both European and American writers. Mostly, they represent the work of the faculty, or works the faculty intend to rely upon in their lectures, as a ground for student disagreement and questioning. (It cannot be assumed that the students, coming from such varied backgrounds, have had access to such papers.) The two morning lecture periods are ninety minutes in length, separated by a thirty-minute coffee break, in order to allow ample time for discussion.

The intellectual context of the institute is, on the practical side, the twofold struggle: the struggle of Central and Eastern European peoples to build free societies in the spiritual desert left by forty (or—in the former USSR—seventy) years of Communism, and the struggle of American (and other Western European societies) to develop cultures worthy of the political and economic liberties they have inherited. On the theological side, the context is *communio* theology, that is, the theology of the love of the Persons of the Trinity that is shared with human beings and that endows in each of them a vocation for liberty, since their Creator wants from them the love and thanksgiving of humans who are not slaves, but free.

The problems of the free society are many. There are cultural and moral problems, problems of political structure and action, and problems of economic structures and actions. Many of these problems are, first of all, conceptual. Many of the insights necessary for building up worthy free societies are counterintuitive; they are learned from experience rather than from logic, from the way things actually work in practice rather than from geometric deduction from principles. In part, this is because of the irrationality sown into human affairs by human sins (which are deeds of darkness, turning away from the light), and in part simply because of the contingencies written into human events, which seldom fall out exactly as planned, and suffer from many unintended consequences of prior actions and many unforeseen (even unforeseeable) hazards strewn across the trajectory of our actions.

In other words, practical intellect is always acting partially, and in large measure, in the dark and is epistemically unmatched to the complexity of concrete reality. It is a "fatal conceit" (Friedrich Hayek) to boast that we can understand the future unfolding of concrete events. There are innumerable slips between the cup and the lip. We can learn from experience, take precautions, build in checks and balances, and devise auxiliary fallbacks. But we cannot pretend to be masters of history. We proceed best by trial and error, and the practical wisdom that comes from being close and prudent students of human experience. This is the approach of *The Federalist*, for instance, as it is of Aristotelian prudence and Thomistic *caritas*. It is one of the inner secrets of Catholic social thought, and one key to the Catholic genius of Tocqueville and Acton, Maritain and Pieper.

Thus, from a merely theoretical and logical point of view, it seems that a monarchical or dictatorial society would work best—lines of authority and accountability absolutely clear—but experience shows how many defects monarchies and dictatorships over time are prey to. Similarly, it seems that markets are clumsy and wasteful and that authoritative planning would make for a more efficient and fairer economy, more helpful to the poor; but experience shows the opposite. The insuperable problem of socialism is this, one sufferer under it quipped: Who in a collective will stay up all night with the sick cow? (The private owner of the cow would.) From the time of Aristotle, the case for private property has never been argued from logical deduction, but rather from experience of the abuses of its absence. The case for the market is not argued from logical deduction either, but from experience with its absence upon the incentives of those who are able to serve one another freely. In cities in which markets are free, there are taxis available at four in the morning to take one to the airport—and to compete with one another to do so better than others. In general, where there are incentives, more people freely look to serve others than where there are not. In this counterintuitive way, the unplanned market harnesses centripetal energies of mutual coordination and freely chosen efficiency—that is, puts practical intellect to work—in ways that soar far beyond the powers of rational planners deploying coercive measures.

During the first third of the twentieth century, dictators persuaded many intellectuals and peoples that dictatorship was better for the poor than democracy, which results (they said) in too much yak-yak-yak. For the first three-quarters of the century, socialists persuaded many, many intellectuals, not least among theologians, that "socialization" was the wave of the future and that socialism is better for the poor than capitalism. Then the Iron Curtain fell down, and the light flooded in. Then people saw how desperate, in fact, was the level of life in East Germany as opposed to West Germany, and how mean were the conditions of the poor throughout the Soviet Empire—at about, Gorbachev himself said, not the Third World but the Fourth. China, too, like India before it, faced with the immense practical problem of feeding its growing population, was rudely awakened from its dogmatic slumbers, abandoned socialist methods in economics (but not in politics), and turned to private property, markets, and incentive systems, and then experienced very positive economic results. Experience rather than logical deduction is the best teacher of economic, as of other practical, wisdom.

Yet even when experience leads whole peoples to unprecedented levels of liberty and prosperity in political and economic systems, experience further teaches that humans do not live by political economy alone; their spirits are not satisfied, and their moral habits soon begin to fall into decadence. Free societies are inherently unstable, since any single generation can freely choose to abandon the hard-won principles on which they are built, learned from long ordeals of history. Thus, the more mature democratic and capitalist countries are suffering from a spiritual and moral crisis in the cultural sector that cuts to the heart of the free society. There is an "ecology" to the free society, a moral and cultural ecology, every bit as significant as the ecology of the biosphere, yet much less widely recognized.

Introduction

In addition, there are many unresolved problems arising from the very nature, structure, and history of modernity. If once (a century or so ago) there seemed to be a question whether the church could survive in a democratic era, there now appears to be a question whether democracy can survive without a healthy and vigorous church—in particular, without Christian and Jewish religious institutions. For are not Judaism and Christianity the source, even the only source, of the world's current belief in the sanctity and inviolability of personal liberty and dignity? According to Hegel, history is a butcher's bench, and from a scientific point of view, the viewpoint of Darwinian survival, it is not obvious that the human being will survive longer, or is of any greater intrinsic worth, than the cockroach and some other vile and lowly creatures of proven durability.

The current Reader does not pretend to deal with all, or even most, of the problems of the free society today. But it does, we believe, make available in a multicultural Euro-American environment a coherent and compelling point of view that is much discussed around the world today, and raises for discussion most of the salient issues on which critics of this point of view assail it. If these selections do not do justice to all such critics, neither do they do full justice to the point of view they roughly represent. The covers of a single volume impose unavoidable limits. Within those limits, however, I am certain that this is a meaty, challenging, mind-expanding collection—certain, because it has been so for me—and continues to be so, and because it raises further questions, each time I consult it.

Allow me to express my gratitude to all my colleagues—and to the French authors we all admire but who did not actually take part in the institute except through their essays, Pierre Manent, Alain Besançon, and Philippe Benton—for permission to reprint their contributions. On another page, please note, we also thank in detail the journals and publishers to whose cooperation we are also indebted for permission to reprint works which they first brought to the public.

Washington, D.C.
January 2000

Part I
PRELIMINARIES: JOHN PAUL II ON LIBERTY

1

Centesimus Annus:
The Architecture of Freedom

George Weigel

"We live, my dear, in a time of transition." Adam's legendary comment to Eve on their way out of the Garden of Eden seems particularly apt for the years since the collapse of European Communism. Yet for some, this period has been less a time of mere transition than a time of final settling: a time when the West has achieved the "end of history" by demonstrating beyond doubt the unsurpassable superiority of liberal democratic polities and market economies. On this provocative understanding of our situation, first argued by Francis Fukuyama, all that remains to do is to fine-tune Western political and economic systems in order to solve "technical problems," assuage "environmental concerns," and satisfy "sophisticated consumer demands."[1]

In central and eastern Europe, however, the collapse of Communism has meant not the "end of history" but rather the return of history to its normal patterns and rhythms. And the victory of the West in the Fifty-Five Years' War against totalitarianism, welcome as it was, has not seen the inauguration of the kingdom of righteousness, truth, and justice here among us. Indeed, historians of the late twenty-first century may well record that the crisis of Communism was followed in short order by the crisis of liberal democracy or democratic capitalism. Moreover, and to illustrate the venerable axiom that there are many ironies in the fire, the crisis of liberal democracy, if it descends upon us with full fury, will be similar to the crisis of Communism in one crucial respect: it will be an "anthropological" crisis, in which a false idea of the human person and human community leads to tremendous stress, and ultimately to breakdown, within our political and economic systems.

Reprinted from *Soul of the World: Notes on the Future of Public Catholicism* (Grand Rapids, Mich.: Eerdmans, 1996), pp. 125–149.

Communism failed for many reasons: it was economically inefficient, technologically backward, culturally stultifying, politically cruel. But above all, it failed because it was a heresy, a congeries of false teachings about the nature of man and human community, about human history and human destiny. Those false teachings provided the ideological rationale for the political and economic institutions that Communist societies created. And the failures of those institutions—in governance, production, distribution, and consumption—were foreshadowed by the errors of Communism as a doctrine. Marxist-Leninist theory, following a Hegelian dialectic, stressed the impact of "internal contradictions" on the rise and fall of pre-socialist societies. In yet another irony, the Marxist-Leninist project itself failed because of the "internal contradictions" of Marxism-Leninism.[2]

Similarly, the crisis of liberal democratic society that may soon be upon us (if it has not already arrived) has an "anthropological" root in a great debate over the nature of the human person. That debate is publicly focused, in the United States, on the meaning of human freedom. And on this question, a culture war of potentially explosive consequence has broken out.

THE AMERICAN CULTURE WAR

In one corner, we have those who would agree with an assertion made by Professor Rocco Buttiglione, a careful and sympathetic student of the American scene, a distinguished Italian philosopher, and an adviser to Pope John Paul II: "Nothing good can be done without freedom, but freedom is not the highest value in itself. Freedom is given to man in order to make possible the free obedience to truth and the free gift of oneself in love."[3] On this understanding of freedom and its relation to the nature of the human person, democracy is a substantive moral experiment. The procedures of democracy grow out of, and depend upon, the *ethos* of the democratic society. And if those procedures are to serve human goods, that *ethos* must reflect the truth about the human person. Thus democracy depends on an ongoing process of moral-cultural revitalization. Democratic self-governance is never finally secured; each generation must face Lincoln's question as to whether nations conceived in liberty and dedicated to equality before the law can long endure.

In the opposing corner are those who argue that freedom is constituted by the liberty to pursue one's personal gratifications, self-defined, so long as no one else (or at least no one in which the state asserts a "compelling interest") gets hurt. This anorexic conception of freedom is not confined to the groves of academe, where tenured radicals celebrate the joys of debonair nihilism; it was succinctly formulated by the U.S. Supreme Court in a joint opinion by Justices Kennedy, O'Connor, and Souter, in June 1992: "At the heart of liberty is the right to define one's own concept of existence, of meaning, of the universe, and of the mystery of human life."[4]

On this understanding of things, democracy is merely an ensemble of procedures, largely legal, by which we regulate the pursuit of our personal satisfactions. Democracy has no substantive moral core. No civil society, no community of republican virtue, no public moral conversation sustains democracy; there are only the Rules of the Game. The gratification of the unencumbered, self-constituting, imperial Self is the end toward which the American democratic experiment is ordered.

Those of us who have been writing about an American *Kulturkampf* (or "culture war") in recent years have sometimes been accused of exaggeration, even by colleagues sympathetic to our views on specific issues. But with the Kennedy/O'Connor/Souter dictum in *Casey v. Planned Parenthood*, the culture war was defined with unmistakable clarity, its gravity underscored beyond anything that any sound-bite publicist could have proposed.

For in a decision celebrated by the prestige press, the elite culture, most of the academy, and many religious leaders, the so-called moderate center of the U.S. Supreme Court declared that republican virtue, understood as a broad communal consensus on the moral coordinates of our common life, is no part of the inner constitution, the moral architecture, of "freedom" in America. Why? Because to define such a consensus and to embody it in law would, according to Kennedy, O'Connor, and Souter, be an act of "compulsion" that would deny citizens the "attributes of personhood."[5] And yet there are tens of millions of Americans who, with the Founders and Framers, believe the opposite: who believe that rights and laws ought to be grounded in prior understandings of rights and wrongs (the alternative being governance through sheer coercion); who believe that familial and public responsibility has a higher moral status in a civilized conscience than private satisfaction; who believe that the common good is a nobler horizon against which to conduct one's life than the narrow infinity described by the pursuit of the self-actualized, self-constituting self.[6]

These battle lines in the American *Kulturkampf* are, admittedly, broadly described. And if we are honest with ourselves, we might concede that the trenches in the war run through our own hearts, as well as between ourselves and others. But that there is a culture war in America today, and that the resolution of that war will determine the future of the American democratic experiment, we need not doubt. The power of ideas in history has been decisively demonstrated by the course of events in the twentieth century. How we *conceive* freedom will have much to do with how we construct and operate the political and economic *institutions* through which freedom is mediated and publicly expressed. Wise Americans since colonial days have understood that those institutions can so decay that the result is social chaos, and ultimately oppression. Whether that chaos unfolds in our time is the outcome being contested in the American *Kulturkampf*, and in the crisis of liberal democratic society that seems, ironically, to be following hard on the heels of the collapse of Communism.

JOHN PAUL II ON HUMAN FREEDOM

In May 1991, Pope John Paul II issued a social encyclical that quickly established itself as a landmark event in contemporary religious thought. Issued to honor the centenary of Pope Leo XIII's pioneering encyclical *Rerum Novarum*, *Centesimus Annus* ("The Hundredth Year") offers both a look back at the *res novae*, the "new things" that seized the attention of Leo XIII, and a look ahead at what we might call the "new new things," the new facts of public life at the end of the twentieth century and the turn of the third Christian millennium. Like other papal documents, *Centesimus Annus* reaffirms the classic themes of Catholic social thought. But John Paul II's creative extension of the tradition makes *Centesimus Annus* a singularly bold, and singularly relevant, document—one that reconfigures the boundaries of the Catholic debate over the right ordering of culture, economics, and politics under the conditions of modernity, and one that provides a badly needed framework for the debate over the future of ordered liberty in these United States.

Centesimus Annus is not a matter for Catholics only, for the encyclical addresses itself to "all men and women of good will." Pope John Paul II understands himself to be making *public* moral arguments, in which he invites others to engage. Moreover, and as if to prove the point, non-Catholic scholars, religious leaders, and politicians have been showing an increasing interest in modern Catholic social teaching as perhaps the most well-developed and coherent set of Christian reference points for conducting the argument about how Americans should order their lives today. Indeed, John Paul II's witness to Christian orthodoxy has sometimes been more appreciated outside his church than within it. As a prominent Southern Baptist once put it to a group of Catholic colleagues, "Down where I come from, people are saying, 'You folks finally got yourself a pope who knows how to pope.'"

For these reasons, *Centesimus Annus* should be of particular interest to citizens of the United States. As a nation "conceived in liberty," as the leader of the party of freedom in world politics, and as a country involved in a grave public debate over the very meaning of freedom, the United States might well pay careful attention to what the most influential moral leader in the contemporary world has to say about the many dimensions of freedom, and about the intimate relationship between freedom and truth, particularly the "truth about man" that has been such a prominent theme in the teaching of this pope.

What John Paul II means by "freedom," of course, is not exactly what America's cultural elites have had in mind since the fevered "liberations" of the 1960s. And so an argument is upon us: What *is* this freedom that, in Miami in 1987, the Pope called a "great gift, a great blessing of God"? How is it to be lived by free men and women in free societies that must protect individual liberty while advancing the common good?

Here the Pope's concerns directly intersect the most basic issues in the American *Kulturkampf*, and so *Centesimus Annus* can shed some much needed light on our national debate over rights, responsibilities, and republican virtue.

The Problem of Freedom

Centesimus Annus is a profound meditation on man's quest for a freedom that will truly satisfy the deepest yearnings of the human heart. In this sense, *Centesimus Annus* is theology long before it is political science and economics. The encyclical is an exercise in Christian anthropology and, more specifically, a reflection on human nature as it expresses itself in history through political and economic action. John Paul II does not regard the human quest for true freedom as something peripheral to the concerns of the Church. Quite the contrary: the quest for freedom is "built in" to the very nature of man's way of being in the word, and "built in" by a God whom we are to find and worship, in freedom. Thus a Christian anthropology of freedom necessarily engages questions of the theology of freedom. For history, as Hans Urs von Balthasar reminds us, is "unfolded before us" because of the "art of the world-architect," who is God.[7]

Centesimus Annus begins with a review of the teaching of Leo XIII in *Rerum Novarum*. There, in 1891, the Church began to grapple with the new problem of freedom that had been created by the upheavals of the Industrial Revolution in economics and the French Revolution in politics: "Traditional society was passing away and another was beginning to be formed—one which brought the hope of new freedoms but also the threat of new forms of injustice and servitude."[8] That threat was particularly grave when modernity ignored "the essential bond between human freedom and truth."[9] Leo XIII understood, his successor argues, that a "freedom which refused to be bound to the truth would fall into arbitrariness and end up submitting itself to the vilest of passions, to the point of self-destruction."[10] In the last decade of this bloodiest of centuries, it is difficult to suggest that Leo XIII was unduly pessimistic about certain aspects of the modern quest for freedom.

From Leo XIII on, Catholic social teaching's answer to the "problem" of freedom has begun with a theologically and philosophically grounded moral reflection on man himself: with an insistence on the dignity and worth of each human being as a creature endowed with intelligence and will and thus made in the "image and likeness" of God (Gen. 1:26). Therefore the beginning of the answer to the rapaciousness of Manchesterian liberalism in economics was to assert, on the basis of man as the *imago Dei*, "the *dignity of the worker* . . . [and] the *dignity of work*."[11] And the beginning of the answer to the massive repression and injustice of the twentieth-century tyrannies was Leo XIII's insistence on the "necessary limits to the State's intervention" in human affairs.[12] Why are those limits "necessary"? Because "the individual, the family, and society are prior to the State, and . . . the State exists in order to protect their rights and not stifle them."[13]

The Catholic human-rights revolution of the late twentieth century thus owes a large debt of gratitude to the last Pope of the nineteenth century. For it was Leo XIII who first pointed toward Christian *personalism* as the alternative to socialist collectivism (which subsumed human personality into the mass) and to radical individualism (which locked human personality into an auto-constructed prison of solipsism).

Deepening the "Rights" Debate

Since he took office in October 1978, John Paul II has been a vigorous proponent of basic human rights, particularly the fundamental right of religious freedom. This pattern continues in *Centesimus Annus*, in which the Pope decries the situation in those countries "which covertly, or even openly, deny to citizens of faiths other than that of the majority the full exercise of their civil and religious rights, preventing them from taking part in the cultural process, and restricting both the Church's right to preach the Gospel and the right of those who hear this preaching to accept it."[14]

For that reason, it is all the more striking that the human-rights language is a bit more muted in *Centesimus Annus* than in John Paul's earlier encyclicals—and far more muted than it was in Pope John XXIII's famous 1963 letter, *Pacem in Terris*. John Paul II has not suddenly become less interested in the problems of human rights. Rather, he seems determined to deepen (and, in some respects, to discipline) the debate over "rights" by linking rights to *obligations* and to *truth*.

On this latter point, John Paul argues forcefully that conscience is not some kind of moral free agent, in which an "autonomous self" declares something to be right because it is right "for me." No, conscience is "bound . . . to the truth."[15] And the truth about man is not to be confused with "an appeal to the appetites and inclinations toward immediate gratification," an appeal that is "utilitarian" in character and does not reflect "the hierarchy of the true values of human existence."[16]

Nor are "rights" simply a matter of our immunities from the coercive power of others, important as such immunities are. Rights exist so that we can fulfill our obligations. Thus, to take an example from one sphere of life, a man should be free economically so that he can enter into more cooperative relationships with others and meet his obligations to work in order to "provide for the needs of his family, his community, his nation, and ultimately all humanity."[17] Ownership, too, has its obligations: "Just as the person fully realizes himself in the free gift of self, so too ownership morally satisfies itself in the creation, at the proper time and in the proper way, of opportunities for work and human growth for all."[18]

By harking back to the Christian personalism of Leo XIII, while at the same time thickening, so to speak, the concept of rights in the Catholic tradition, *Centesimus Annus* provides a powerful example of Christian anthropology at work, probing the mystery of man as it reveals itself in the many dimensions of human community. But this is no abstract philosophical exercise. For, having set the proper framework for thinking about public life, the Pope immediately brings his analysis of the "truth about man" to bear on one of the most stunning events in this century of the unexpected—the Revolution of 1989 in central and eastern Europe.

Revolution of the Spirit

"The fundamental error of socialism," says John Paul II, "is anthropological in nature":

Socialism considers the individual person simply as an element, a molecule within the social organism, so that the good of the individual is completely subordinated to the functioning of the socioeconomic mechanism. Socialism likewise maintains that the good of the individual can be realized without reference to his free choice, to the unique and exclusive responsibility he exercises in the face of good or evil. Man is thus reduced to a series of social relationships, and the concept of the person as the . . . subject of moral decision disappears, the very subject whose decisions build the social order.

From this mistaken conception of the person there arise both a distortion of law . . . and an opposition to private property. A person who is deprived of something he can call "his own," and of the possibility of earning a living through his own initiative, comes to depend on the social machine and on those who control it. This makes it much more difficult for him to recognize his dignity as a person, and hinders progress toward the building up of an authentic human community.[19]

Western political scientists and international-relations specialists have had a hard time agreeing on the primary cause of the dramatic events that took place in central and eastern Europe in 1989. "Delayed modernization" is one frequently encountered answer: the economic systems of the Communist world could not compete, and the only way to change them was to get rid of the political regimes that had imposed collectivism in the first place. It is, in truth, a deliciously (if depressingly) Marxist "answer" to the utter collapse of Marxism—and a worrisome indication of how deeply quasi-Marxist themes have sunk into the collective unconscious of the new knowledge class.

Pope John Paul II, however, is not persuaded by this materialistic analysis of modern history.

Centesimus Annus would be well worth careful study for its marvelous third chapter alone. For in "The Year 1989," the Pope offers a succinct, pointed, and compelling analysis of the roots of the Revolution of 1989—an analysis whose implications for Western societies we ignore at our peril. The fundamental problem with Communism (or what the Pope calls "Real Socialism") was not its economic decrepitude. Rather, Communism failed because it denied "the truth about man." Communism's failures were first and foremost failures in the order of ideas. Its faith was misplaced, and so its hope was utopian and its charity non-existent. "The God That Failed" was a false god whose acolytes murdered tens of millions of human beings and led societies and economies into terminal crisis.

Pope John Paul begins his historical analysis of 1989 in 1945, with the Yalta Agreements. "Yalta," in fact, has loomed very large indeed in the vision of the Polish pontiff. World War II, "which should have re-established freedom and restored the right of nations, ended without having attained these goals"—indeed, it ended with "the spread of Communist totalitarianism over more than half of Europe and over other parts of the world."[20] Yalta, in other words, was more than a diplomatic accommodation; it was a moral catastrophe and a betrayal of the sacrifices of the war, a betrayal rooted in incomprehension of (or indifference to) the nature of Marxist-Leninist totalitarianism. A failure of moral intuition or of will led to a failure of politics.

Thus the first truth about central and eastern Europe was that the "Yalta arrangement" could not be regarded as merely a historical datum: regrettable, perhaps, but nonetheless an unchallengeable fact of life with which one had to deal. Dealing had to be done; not for nothing did Pope John Paul spend his early priesthood in a Polish Church dominated by Cardinal Stefan Wyszyński of Warsaw, the tenacious prelate who gained Catholicism—and the remnants of Polish civil society—crucial breathing room in the 1950s. But there should be no illusions amidst such negotiations, no false expectations of a gradual "convergence" between East and West.[21] The only "dealing" that would contribute to a genuine peace would be based on the conviction that no peace worthy of the name could be built on the foundations of Yalta.

Facing Down Fear

As it began, so it would end. The origins of this bizarre and suffocating empire found their parallels, forty-four years later, in the ways in which the empire fell.

The moral catastrophe of Yalta was attacked at its roots by "the Church's commitment to defend and promote human rights," by a confrontation with Stalin's empire at the level of ethics, history, and culture. Communism, and particularly Communist atheism, the Pope said time and time again, was "an act against man."[22] And the antidote to the false humanism of Marxism-Leninism came from a truly Christian humanism in which men and women once again learned the human dignity that was theirs by birthright.

That understanding had never been completely snuffed out in central and eastern Europe. But there was fear—the pathology that bound the Yalta imperial system together. Breaking the fever of fear was thus the crucial first step in addressing the calamity of Yalta.

First in Poland, then elsewhere, millions of people in the region began to face down their fear during John Paul II's first, dramatic return to Poland in June 1979. His message during that extraordinary pilgrimage was decidedly "pre-political." It was a message about ethics, culture, and history devoted to explicating "the truth about man" that Poles knew in their bones—the truth that their regime had denied for two generations. But although it was not a message about "politics" in the narrow sense of the struggle for power, it was high-octane "politics" in the more venerable sense of the term: "Politics" as the ongoing argument about the good person, the good society, and the structure of freedom. And that upper-case Politics led, over time, to the distinctive lower-case politics of the Revolution of 1989, the revolution that reversed Yalta.

John Paul II believes that, among the "many factors involved in the fall of [these] oppressive regimes, some deserve special mention." The first point at which "the truth about man" intersected with politics was on the question of the rights of workers. The Pope does not hesitate to drive home the full irony of the situation:

> It cannot be forgotten that the fundamental crisis of systems claiming to express the rule and indeed the dictatorship of the working class began with the great upheavals

which took place in Poland in the name of solidarity. It was the throngs of working people which foreswore the ideology which presumed to speak in their name. On the basis of a hard, lived experience of work and of oppression, it was they who recovered and, in a sense, rediscovered the content and principles of the Church's social doctrine.[23]

That reappropriation of "the truth about man" led to another of the distinctive elements of the Revolution of 1989—its non-violence. Tactical considerations surely played a role in the choice of non-violence by those whom we used to call "dissidents": the bad guys had all the guns, and the good guys knew it. But it is hard to explain why the mass of the people remained non-violent—particularly given the glorification of armed revolt in Polish history and culture—unless one understands that a moral revolution, a revolution of conscience, had preceded the political revolution of 1989.

The Pope was fully aware that the economic systems of central and eastern Europe were a shambles by the mid-1980s, and that this played its role in the collapse of Stalin's empire. But John Paul also argues that the economic disaster of command economies was not a "technical problem" alone; it was, rather, "a consequence of the violation of the human rights to private initiative, to ownership of property, and to freedom in the economic sector."[24] Marxist economics, just like Leninist politics, refused to acknowledge "the truth about man."

State atheism in the Eastern bloc also carried the seeds of its own destruction, according to John Paul. The "spiritual void" the state created by building a world without windows "deprived the younger generation of direction and in many cases led them, in the irrepressible search for personal identity and for the meaning of life, to rediscover the religious roots of their national cultures, and to rediscover the person of Christ himself as the existentially adequate response to the desire in every human heart for goodness, truth, and life."[25] The Communists had thought they could "uproot the need for God from the human heart." They learned that "it is not possible to succeed in this without throwing the heart into turmoil."[26]

And Communism onto the ash heap of history.

John Paul II's carefully crafted discussion of the Revolution of 1989 makes no claims for the Church's role as agent of the Revolution that would strike any fairminded reader as implausible or excessive. The Holy See was well aware of the many other factors that conspired to produce the peaceful demolition of Stalin's empire: the Helsinki process, which publicly indicted Communist regimes for their human-rights violations and created a powerful network of human-rights activists on both sides of the Iron Curtain; the fact of Mikhail Gorbachev; and the Strategic Defense Initiative (SDI), which a number of Vatican officials consider, privately, to have been decisive in forcing a change in Soviet policy.[27]

But in *Centesimus Annus*, John Paul II was determined to teach a more comprehensive truth about the Revolution of 1989—that a revolution of the spirit, built on the sure foundation of "the truth about man," preceded the transfer of power from Communist to democratic hands. The Revolution of 1989, viewed through this wide-angle lens, began in 1979. It was a revolution in which people learned first to throw off fear, and only then to throw off their chains—non-violently. It was a revolution of conservation, in which people reclaimed their moral, cultural, and historical identities. It was a revolution "from the bottom up," the bottom being the historic, ethical and cultural self-understandings of individuals and nations.

Which is to say, it was a revolution that reminded the West that a vital civil society was the essential foundation of a democracy.

The Free Economy

John Paul II's analysis of the dynamics and structure of freedom then turns to the question of how the free society ought to organize its economic life in light of the "truth about man":

> Not only is it wrong from the ethical point of view to disregard human nature, which is made for freedom, but in practice it is impossible to do so. Where society is so organized as to reduce arbitrarily or even suppress the sphere in which freedom is legitimately exercised, the result is that the life of society becomes progressively disorganized and goes into decline.
>
> Moreover, man, who was created for freedom, bears within himself the wound of original sin, which constantly draws him toward evil and puts him in need of redemption. Not only is *this doctrine an integral part of Christian revelation*; it also has great hermeneutical value insofar as it helps one to understand human reality. Man tends towards good, but he is also capable of evil. He can transcend his immediate interest and still remain bound to it.
>
> The social order will be all the more stable, the more it takes this fact into account and does not place in opposition personal interest and the interests of society as a whole, but rather seeks to bring them into a fruitful harmony. In fact, when self-interest is violently suppressed, it is replaced by a burdensome system of bureaucratic control which dries up the wellsprings of initiative and creativity. When people think they possess the secret of a perfect social organization which makes evil impossible, they also think that they can use any means, including violence and deceit, in order to bring that organization into being. Politics then becomes a "secular religion" which operates under the illusion of creating paradise in this world. But no political society . . . can ever be confused with the Kingdom of God.[28]

Perhaps the most striking "new thing" about *Centesimus Annus* is the way in which John Paul II draws out the implications of his Christian anthropology of human freedom, and his analysis of the dynamics of the Revolution of 1989, in the field of economics. In fact, *Centesimus Annus* contains the most striking papal endorsement of—and challenge to—the "free economy" in a century. The endorsement comes in the form of the answer to a pressing question:

> Can it be said that, after the failure of Communism, capitalism is the victorious social system, and that capitalism should be the goal of the countries now making efforts to rebuild their economy and society? Is this the model which ought to be proposed to

the countries of the Third World which are searching for the path to true economic and civil progress?

The answer is obviously complex. If by "capitalism" is meant an economic system which recognizes the fundamental and positive role of business, the market, private property, and the resulting responsibility for the means of production, as well as free human creativity in the economic sector, then an answer is certainly in the affirmative, even though it would perhaps be more appropriate to speak of a "business economy," "market economy," or simply "free economy." But if by "capitalism" is meant a system in which freedom in the economic sector is not circumscribed within a strong juridical framework which places it at the service of human freedom in its totality, and which sees it as a particular aspect of that freedom, the core of which is ethical and religious, then the reply is certainly negative.[29]

In other words, if by "capitalism" is meant what the West at its best means by capitalism—a tripartite system in which democratic politics and a vibrant moral culture discipline and temper the free market—then that is indeed the system that the Pope urges the new democracies and the Third World to adopt, because it is the system most congruent with a human freedom that is truly liberating.

Latin American liberation theologians, western European social democrats, east-central European traditionalists, and the defenders of the liberal status quo in American Catholicism insist that this endorsement carries many conditions with it. Of course it does and of course it should: those conditions are neither new nor surprising nor unwelcome. No thoughtful defender of the market would deny the need for its careful regulation by law, culture, and public morality.[30] What is new about *Centesimus Annus* comes in passages like these:

> The modern *business economy* has positive aspects. Its basis is human freedom exercised in the economic field, just as it is exercised in many other fields.[31]

> It is precisely the ability to foresee both the needs of others and the combinations of productive factors most adapted to satisfying those needs that constitutes another important source of wealth in modern society. Besides, many goods cannot be adequately produced through the work of an isolated individual; they require the cooperation of many people working towards a common goal. Organizing such a productive effort, planning its duration in time, making sure that it corresponds in a positive way to the demands which it must satisfy, and taking the necessary risk—all this too is a source of wealth in today's society. In this way, the *role* of disciplined and creative *human work* and, as an essential part of that work, *initiative and entrepreneurial ability* becomes increasingly evident and decisive.[32]

> Another task of the State is that of overseeing and directing the exercise of human rights in the economic sector. However, primary responsibility in this area belongs not to the State but to individuals and to the various groups and associations which make up society. The State could not directly ensure the right to work for all its citizens unless it controlled every aspect of economic life and restricted the free initiative of individuals.[33]

> Indeed, besides the earth, man's principal resource is *man himself*.[34]

Centesimus Annus thus marks a decisive break with the curious materialism that had characterized aspects of modern Catholic social teaching since Leo XIII. Wealth-creation today, John Paul II readily acknowledges, has more to do with human creativity and imagination, and with political and economic systems capable of unleashing that creativity and imagination, than with "resources" *per se*. And that, he seems to suggest, is one of the "signs of the times" to which Catholic social thought must be attentive.

In fact, one of the most distinctive characteristics of *Centesimus Annus* is its empirical sensitivity. John Paul II has clearly thought carefully about what does and what does not work in exercising what has come to be known as a "preferential option for the poor" in the new democracies, in the Third World, and in impoverished parts of the developed world. The "preferential option," the Pope seems to suggest, is a formal principle; its content should be determined, not on the basis of ideological orthodoxy (that is what was rejected in the Revolution of 1989), but by empirical facts. And for John Paul, the evidence is in. What works best for the poor is democratic polities and properly regulated market economies. Why? Because democracy and the market are the systems that best cohere with human nature, with human freedom, with "the truth about man."

It will take some time for this new direction in Catholic social thought to register on the compasses of those still committed to what the Pope calls the "impossible compromise between Marxism and Christianity,"[35] as well as by those who continue to search for a chimerical Catholic "third way" between capitalism and socialism. (At a meeting in Rome shortly after the encyclical was published, for example, the dean of the social science faculty at the Pontifical Gregorian University told me that "Capitalism A [i.e., the capitalism the Pope endorses] exists only in textbooks." I suggested to the dean, a Latin American Jesuit, that if he really believed that, he had no business running a faculty of social science.) But the text of *Centesimus Annus* itself is plain; the authoritative teaching of the Catholic Church is that a properly regulated market, disciplined by politics, law, and culture, is best for poor people. It works. It allows the poor to participate in economic life, to enter what Richard John Neuhaus has called the "circle of productivity and exchange."[36] And thus it gives the poor an "option" to exercise their freedom and creativity as economic actors that is available in no other system.

The moral implications of this analysis for U.S. social welfare policy are not difficult to define. We best exercise our responsibility for and to the poor by efforts to include them in the free economy and in democratic public life. Empowerment, rather than dependency, is the goal.

Culture Wars, Revisited

If man does not live by bread alone, neither does the free society. And so *Centesimus Annus* next turns to the question of how the explosive energies of the market are made to serve a freedom that finds its fulfillment in goodness rather than in ephemeral goodies:

> It is not possible to understand man on the basis of economics alone, nor to define him simply on the basis of class membership. Man is understood in a more complete way when he is situated within the sphere of culture through his language, history, and the position he takes toward the fundamental events of life, such as birth, love, work, and death. At the heart of every culture lies the attitude man takes to the greatest mystery: the mystery of God. Different cultures are basically different ways of facing the question of the meaning of personal existence. When this question is eliminated, the cultural and moral life of nations are corrupted.[37]

Understandably enough, much of the debate in the immediate aftermath of *Centesimus Annus* focused on the encyclical's careful endorsement of the "free economy." But the truth of the matter is that John Paul II is rather more concerned about the "culture" leg of the politics-economics-culture triad than about the argument between market economists and those still defending state-centered schemes of development. The latter debate has been settled. The real issue remains the ability of a culture to provide the market with the moral framework it needs to serve the cause of integral human development.

The lessons of 1989, for both East and West, are once again on the Pope's mind. Can the new democracies develop societies that provide for the free exercise of human creativity in the workplace, in politics, and in the many fields of culture without becoming libertine in their public moral life? Will "consumerism"—that is, consumption as an ideology, not the reality of "consumers" as a natural part of what dissidents used to call a "normal society"—replace Marxism-Leninism as the new form of bondage east of the Elbe River? Has it already done so in the West? If not, how can we prevent its triumph? If so, how can we repair the damage and put the free society on a firmer moral foundation?

The Pope is not persuaded by libertarian arguments. "Of itself," he writes, "the economic system does not possess criteria for correctly distinguishing new and higher forms of satisfying human needs from artificial new needs which hinder the formation of a mature personality." The market cannot be left on its own. "*A great deal of educational and cultural work* is urgently needed" so that the market's remarkable capacity to generate wealth is bent toward ends that are congruent with "the truth about man"—which is not, John Paul continually urges, an economic truth alone, or even primarily.[38]

In fact, the Pope seems convinced that consumerism-as-ideology ought to be blamed, not on the market system, but on the moral-cultural system's failures to discipline the market:

> These criticisms [of consumerism in its hedonistic form] are directed not so much against an economic system as against an ethical and cultural system. . . . If economic

life is absolutized, if the production and consumption of goods become the center of social life and society's only value . . . the reason is to be found not so much in the economic system itself as in the fact that the entire socio-cultural system, by ignoring the ethical and religious dimension, has been weakened, and ends by limiting itself to the production of goods and services alone.[39]

As should be abundantly clear by now, *Centesimus Annus* is no dreary exercise in papal scolding. John Paul II knows that the things of this world are important, and that material goods can enhance man's capacity for living a freedom worthy of a creature made in the image and likeness of God. "It is not wrong to want to live better," he says. "What is wrong is a style of life which is presumed to be better when it is directed toward 'having' rather than 'being,' and which wants to have more, not in order to be more but in order to spend life in enjoyment as an end in itself." Self-command, in economic life as well as in interpersonal relationships, is the hallmark of a freedom being lived in a truly liberating way.[40]

Reconstructing Civil Society

So what is to be done to construct (or reconstruct) the moral-cultural foundations of the free society? On this front, John Paul is not inclined to look first toward the institutions of the state. Indeed, another "new thing" in *Centesimus Annus* is the Pope's severe criticism of the excesses of the welfare state, which in its extreme form he styles the "social assistance state." Here, the Pope argues, is another abuse of human freedom: "By intervening directly and depriving society of its responsibility, the Social Assistance State leads to a loss of human energies and an inordinate increase of public agencies, which are dominated more by bureaucratic ways of thinking than by concern for serving their clients, and which are accompanied by an enormous increase in spending."[41]

John Paul's preference, which is an expression of the classic Catholic principle of "subsidiarity," is for what in the American context would be called "mediating structures": "Needs are best understood and satisfied by people who are closest to [the poor, the weak, the stricken] and who act as neighbors to those in need."[42] Such mediating structures—religious institutions, voluntary organizations, unions, business associations, neighborhood groups, service organizations, and the like—are the backbone of what Václav Havel's "Chapter 77" and the Solidarity movement worked to resurrect in central and eastern Europe throughout the 1980s under the rubric of "civil society." The reconstruction of this civil society is the first order of business in setting the foundations of democracy—a message that ought to be taken to heart by those in the West, too, especially those who have read their Tocqueville and have pondered the Frenchman's identification of the voluntary association as *the* distinctive and essential institutional foundation of democratic culture in America.[43]

In sum, what is needed is a public moral culture that encourages "lifestyles in which the quest for truth, beauty, goodness, and communion with others for the sake of common growth are the factors which determine consumer choice, savings, and investments."[44] We do not live in hermetically sealed containers labeled "economic life," "politics," and "lifestyle." John Paul insists that it is all of a piece. There is only one human universe, and it is an inescapably moral universe in which questions of "ought" emerge at every juncture; or as the Pope puts it, "Even the decision to invest in one place rather than another, in one productive sector rather than another, is always *a moral and cultural choice*."[45]

As with economics, so with politics. I have stressed here the importance of "1989" in the Pope's historical vision. But by 1989, the Pope means a set of events fraught with meaning for the West as well as for the East. John Paul II has vigorously positioned the Church on the side of the democratic revolution throughout the world, not because he is a geopolitician, but because he is an evangelist, a moral teacher, and a pastor. On the threshold of the third millennium, the post-Christendom Church, he insists, "has no models to present." But, as an expression of its fundamental concern for "the truth about man," the Church "values the democratic system inasmuch as it ensures the participation of citizens in making political choices, guarantees to the governed the possibility of both electing and holding accountable those who govern them, and of replacing them through peaceful means when appropriate."[46]

Truth and Consequences

There are no guarantees about the future of the free society, particularly given the mistaken attitude toward the relationship between rights and obligations, between rights and the truth, common among Western cultural elites. It was not as Cassandra but as a friend of democracy that John Paul II laid down the challenge noted previously about the importance of a horizon of truth for the democratic experiment:

> Nowadays there is a tendency to claim that agnosticism and skeptical relativism are the philosophy and the basic attitude which correspond to democratic forms of political life. Those who are convinced that they know the truth and firmly adhere to it are considered unreliable from a democratic point of view, since they do not accept that truth is determined by the majority, or that it is subject to variation according to different political trends. It must be observed in this regard that if there is no ultimate truth to guide and direct political activity, then ideas and convictions can easily be manipulated for reasons of power. As history demonstrates, a democracy without values easily turns into open or thinly disguised totalitarianism.[47]

Still, the Pope continues, "the Church respects *the legitimate autonomy of the democratic order*," and the Church "is not entitled to express preferences for this or that institutional or constitutional solution." Rather, the Church is the Church, and thus "her contribution to the political order is precisely her vision of the dignity of the person revealed in all its fullness in the mystery of the Incarnate Word."[48] But that vision itself, as we have seen, has public consequences, not least in terms of civic education and democratic legitimation.

Centesimus Annus is an extraordinary statement of faith and hope. At the end of a century of tyranny, the Pope speaks a word of hope in freedom. At the end of a century of fear in which the human family has become afraid of what it might be capable of, the Pope speaks of hope in man's capacity to order his public life in ways that serve the cause of human flourishing. And those expressions of hope are not fragile optimism, because the worldly hopes expressed in *Centesimus Annus* are grounded in a transcendent hope, born of faith in the God who created man with intelligence and free will.

Given the breadth of the issues it addressed, the depth at which questions were probed, and the empirical sensitivity John Paul II shows to the "signs of the times" as they illuminate freedom's cause at the end of the twentieth century, this encyclical may well be regarded, in time, as the greatest of the twentieth-century social encyclicals. With *Centesimus Annus*, the "Pope of Freedom" did far more than mark the centenary of a great tradition: he brilliantly scouted the terrain for the next hundred years of humanity's struggle to embody in public life the truth that makes us free. His is a vision of the possibilities and the crisis of freedom that Americans, especially in this season of *Kulturkampf,* most certainly ought not to ignore.

AN AMERICAN EPILOGUE: WOJTYLA MEETS MURRAY

To my knowledge, John Courtney Murray, S. J., never spoke of a public Church "after Christendom." But his call for Catholicism to contribute to the formation of a religiously informed public philosophy that would ground, discipline, and direct the American experiment in ordered liberty has many affinities with John Paul II's "public" ecclesiology. Indeed, in Murray's critical analysis of the modern American circumstance, we may find an anticipation of some of the key themes in *Centesimus Annus's* critique of merely "proceduralist" democracy. And in Murray's prescription for a revitalization of American democracy through a retrieval of the classic moral and political understandings from which the United States was born, we may find a notable example of how the social doctrine of the Church can be "translated" into a historic American idiom without losing its moral cutting edge.

Murray believed, with Lincoln (and not unlike John Paul II), that America was a "proposition country"—a political community gathered together by certain ideas and ideals, whose very future rested on the capacity of those ideas and ideals to shape its people's lives. The "American proposition" was composed of truths that the American Founders held in common; these truths were the "inner architecture" of the American experiment in ordered liberty. Moreover, the contemporary vitality of those truths was the key to the successful working out of our national experiment today.[49]

Five Foundational Truths

Forty years after Murray wrote *We Hold These Truths*, it is precisely these foundational truths that are being contested in the American culture war. Murray believed, and I think John Paul II would agree, that the degree to which these truths are "received" in contemporary America and inform the life of the American political community is *the* crucial index of the health of the civil society that sustains our democracy. For unless there is some consensus on the moral architecture of the American experiment, there can be no disciplined public discourse over the ways in which we order our common life. As Murray put it, if "barbarism threatens when men cease to live together according to reason . . . [barbarism] likewise threatens when men cease to talk together according to reasonable laws."[50]

What are these truths? Five of them seem to me most basic, and most urgently in need of reiteration today.

1. The first "truth" on which the American experiment is built, in terms of the ontology of the experiment as well as its functional aspects, is that *God is sovereign over nations as well as over individuals.*

This truth distinguishes the American tradition—a conservative tradition, in the sense of maintaining continuity with the central political tradition of Christian Europe—from the Jacobin/laicist tradition of late-eighteenth-century continental Europe and its nineteenth- and twentieth-century epigones. In the latter tradition (which gave rise, as we have seen, to the Reign of Terror as practiced by both Robespierre and Lenin), the "autonomous reason of man" was "the first and the sole principle of political organization."[51] In the American revolutionary tradition, by contrast, the sovereignty of God, which necessarily stands in judgment on all our works, is the first principle of political organization.

This theological affirmation has critical public consequences. First, it establishes, on as secure a foundation as possible, the penultimacy of the political. The affirmation of God's sovereignty over the nation as well as over the individuals who compose it sets limits on the boundaries of the political, even as it invests politics with its own proper dignity.

Moreover, because God is sovereign, all the works of our hands—and especially those that have to do with the exercise of power—are under judgment. When Americans pledge allegiance to the flag today and affirm "one nation, under God," we reaffirm the Founders' notion that the nation, this American experiment in ordered liberty, is under judgment. The organization of the experiment, and the laws by which it is conducted, are to be judged against a wider moral horizon than that of immediate political expediency or interest.

This is not a truth that is well understood in, say, the Supreme Court today. The recovery of it is the key to a revitalization of the American experiment that is in moral continuity with the Founding.

2. The second truth on which the American experiment is built is that *the human person has the God-given capacity to be self-governing.*

The God who gave us life and liberty also gave us the capacity to reflect on our nature and our circumstances, and to discern from that reflection our moral obligations. The social embodiment of this truth about the human person is, Murray argued, the notion of a "free people under a limited government"—the best shorthand formula, he believed, for the essence of the American experiment.

According to that familiar formula, government is not simply coercion. Government is "the right to command"; government is authority, and this authority is both derived from law and limited by law.[52] Thus the notion of the rule of law should not be understood, Murray wrote, in the positivist sense that the law is simply what the law says it is. No, the law, too, is under judgment. The law is to be judged by moral criteria that transcend it.

Here, too, is an issue on which a renewed conversation is imperative in contemporary America, most especially in terms of the controversies over abortion and euthanasia. The fact that a right-to-life movement is thriving in the United States, twenty years after the principal culture-forming institutions of our society pronounced the issue settled on behalf of a radical abortion license, is powerful testimony to the "reception" of Murray's second truth by millions of Americans. And the resistance to that movement in the academy, the media, many churches, and much of the permanent political class (a resistance increasingly mounted on the basis of "autonomy" claims) illustrates the depth and gravity of the culture war.

3. The third truth undergirding the American experiment, in Murray's analysis, is that *just governance—governance that is congruent with the dignity of human beings as persons, as moral agents—is by, through, and with the consent of the governed.*

This was, Murray argued, an ancient principle, with deep roots in the political thought of Christian medieval Europe (which, of course, was shaped by Roman law and Greek political philosophy). But in the American experiment, the ancient principle of consent was married to another principle that looms large in the social vision of John Paul II: the principle of popular participation in governance.[53]

Thus Lincoln's phrase at Gettysburg, "government *by* the people," was no mere rhetorical flourish. The people adopted their basic law, the Constitution, through elected representatives. The people made the laws of the land through other elected representatives and rotated the executive power such that the Constitution "came alive" in the rhythms of our national life. In short, as Murray put it, "the people are governed because in a true sense, they govern themselves."[54]

All of this raises serious questions today, of course, about the rise of a permanent political class, the role of the media in public life, and the conditions of civic education, and these questions bear heavily on the conduct of the American *Kulturkampf.*

4. Murray's third truth involves a real act of faith in the capacity of the people, not to settle technical minutiae, but to wrestle seriously with great issues. That faith was, in turn, built on Murray's fourth truth, the fourth building block in the intellectual/moral foundations of the American experiment: "*there is a sense of justice inherent in the people*" by which they are "*empowered to judge, direct, and correct the processes of government.*"[55]

This truth, medieval in root, took concrete political form in the First Amendment's guarantees of free speech and a free press. In Murray's view, these freedoms were not rooted in the thin individualistic claim that someone has a right to say what he thinks just because he happens to think it. Rather, these freedoms had a thicker reality; they were social, *public* necessities. For, as Murray argues, people who are required to obey have the "right to be heard" about the matters on which their obedience is to be required; and people who bear burdens and make sacrifices have the right to debate and pass judgment on whether the policy requiring those sacrifices in fact serves the common good.[56]

These rights give concrete reality to the fundamental distinction between *society* and the *state*, and embody the traditional Western Christian understanding that "society" is *prior* to the state. This means, in practical, daily terms, that the state exists to serve society, not the other way around. As we have seen, that understanding of "civil society" played a crucial role in the collapse of Communism. But it is also the foundation, in our American context, of the freedom from governmental control enjoyed by the academy, the means of communication, the family, and religious institutions. It is no accident that legal encroachments on the independence of those "prior" institutions (especially church/synagogue and family) are among the most fevered issues in the American *Kulturkampf*—which, yet again, shows itself to be an argument down to first principles.

5. The fifth truth on which the American experiment was grounded was the classic claim that "*only a virtuous people can be free.*"[57]

Like the Founders, and like Pope John Paul II, Father Murray understood that free government in a free society is not inevitable, only possible, and that its possibility can be realized *publicly* only when the people are governed *inwardly* by the "universal moral law." Or, as Lord Acton put it, freedom is "not the power of doing what we like, but rather the right of being able to do what we ought."[58]

On this understanding, of course, and to come straight back to the beginning, democracy is more than a political experiment, more than the "Rules of the Game." Democracy is a spiritual and moral enterprise, and its success (or failure) depends upon the virtues (or lack thereof) of the people of the enterprise. As Murray argued, men and women who would be free must learn to discipline themselves, and the governing institutions of a free society must be self-governing "from within" if they are to serve the ends of virtue—and of freedom.[59]

NOTES

1. Francis Fukuyama, "The End of History?" *The National Interest* (Summer 1989): 16. Fukuyama has refined his position and now argues that the replenishment of "social capital" is essential to the survival of democracy and the market. See his 1995 book *Trust: The Social Virtues and the Creation of Prosperity* (Free Press).

2. A brief interpolation: I do not mean to argue here, in the manner of the unrepentant left and the isolationist/libertarian right, that since Communism would eventually have

failed anyway, containment (and its revivification by Ronald Reagan, Margaret Thatcher, and Helmut Kohl) was unnecessary and wasteful. The grave "anthropological" errors of Communism would ultimately have led to the failure of the Communist experiment in social engineering. But absent containment, the immense human suffering that Communism caused would have been extended even further, and the demise of the Communist system would have been delayed long into the future. Communism collapsed when it did, and the way it did, because of the intersection (and interaction) of Western foreign and military policies with a moral-cultural revolution that made possible the re-creation of civil society in central and eastern Europe.

3. Rocco Buttiglione, "The Free Economy and the Free Man," in George Weigel, ed., *A New Worldly Order: John Paul II and Human Freedom* (Washington: Ethics and Public Policy Center, 1992), 70.

4. *Casey v. Planned Parenthood of Southeastern Pennsylvania*, 112 Sup. Ct. 2791, at 2807.

5. Ibid.

6. The concept of a "narrow infinity" is a variant on G. K. Chesterton's description of the "madman":

> His mind moves in a perfect but narrow circle. A small circle is quite as infinite as a large circle; but, though it is quite as infinite, it is not so large.... There is such a thing as a narrow universality; there is such a thing as a small and cramped eternity; you may see it in many modern religious. [*Orthodoxy* (New York: Doubleday Image Books, 1959), 20]

Including, I might add, the religion that worships the imperial autonomous Self.

7. Hans Urs von Balthasar, *A Theology of History* (San Francisco: Ignatius Press, 1994), 133. And here, too, in this matter of the interior structure of freedom, we may be reminded that Christians are a people "ahead of time":

> ... for the Christian [the] freedom [brought about by the messianic intervention in history] is already present. It is present in a fullness that can never be improved upon, and human progress can proceed now only in reference to this being-at-hand (*parousia*) of the Last, the Absolute, the *eschaton* of history. No upward advance can ever even draw near to that, let alone catch it up and pass it.... There can, therefore, be no question of a convergence or harmonizing of the history of the world and the history of the Kingdom; but as the parable says, the wheat and the tares grow *together*, because the increasing responsibility toward himself of historical, cultural man, and the increasing responsibility toward God of the believers who administer the inheritance of Christ both equally lead to ever-sharper alternatives and decisions. [139–40]

John Paul and Balthasar seem agreed that the eschatological horizon of Christian faith creates a singular Christian optic on history (and thus on politics and economics). But while Balthasar stresses the parallel growth of "wheat and tares," John Paul's emphasis in *Centesimus Annus* and elsewhere seems to be on the post-Christendom Church as a leaven in the world, witnessing to the relationship between the "truth about man" and the exercise of freedom, and thus helping build a culture of freedom and a civilization of love.

8. *Centesimus Annus*, 4. John Paul refers here to the "new conception of society and of the State, and consequently of authority itself" that emerged in the French Revolution. One of the intriguing aspects of *Centesimus Annus*, however, is the way in which the Pope's reflection on the free society at the end of the twentieth century tacitly brings the American revolutionary experience of 1776—which was, as we have seen, a different expression of the eighteenth-century quest for freedom—into the dialogue.

9. Ibid.
10. Ibid.
11. Ibid., 6.
12. Ibid., 8.
13. Ibid., 11.
14. Ibid., 29.
15. Ibid.
16. Ibid.
17. Ibid., 43.
18. Ibid.
19. Ibid., 13.
20. Ibid., 19.
21. See my book *The Final Revolution* (New York: Oxford University Press, 1992), chapters three and four, for the dramatic (and yet subtly executed) difference John Paul II made in the *Ostpolitik* of the Holy See.
22. *Centesimus Annus*, 22.
23. Ibid., 23.
24. Ibid., 24.
25. Ibid.
26. Ibid.
27. On the role of these various factors in 1989, see my book *The Final Revolution*, chapter one.
28. *Centesimus Annus*, 25.
29. Ibid., 42.
30. As, for example, Michael Novak has argued in *The Spirit of Democratic Capitalism* (New York: Simon and Schuster, 1982) and *The Catholic Ethic and the Spirit of Capitalism* (New York: Free Press, 1993).
31. *Centesimus Annus*, 32.
32. Ibid.
33. Ibid., 48.
34. Ibid., 32. The Pope continues:
Man's intelligence enables him to discover the earth's productive potential and the many different ways in which human needs can be satisfied. It is his disciplined work in close collaboration with others that makes possible the creation of ever more extensive *working communities* which can be relied upon to transform natural and human environments. Important virtues are involved in this process, such as diligence, industriousness, prudence in undertaking reasonable risks, reliability and fidelity in interpersonal relationships, as well as courage in carrying out decisions which are difficult and painful but necessary, both for the overall working of a business and in meeting possible setbacks.
35. Ibid., 26.
36. See Richard John Neuhaus, *Doing Well and Doing Good: The Challenge to the Christian Capitalist* (New York: Doubleday, 1992).
37. *Centesimus Annus*, 24. This section of the encyclical follows the Pope's dissection of the failures of Marxist economics, and thus constitutes another challenge to the "materialistic" interpretation of 1989.
38. Ibid., 36.
39. Ibid., 39.

40. Ibid., 36.

41. Ibid., 48. It would not offend against charity to suggest that this critique has not been seriously engaged by the major Catholic social-welfare agencies in the United States.

42. Ibid.

43. See Alexis de Tocqueville, *Democracy in America,* trans. George Lawrence, ed. J. P. Mayer (New York: Harper & Row, 1966), 513–24.

44. *Centesimus Annus,* 36.

45. Ibid.

46. Ibid., 46.

47. Ibid.

48. Ibid., 47.

49. John Courtney Murray, *We Hold These Truths: Catholic Reflections on the American Proposition* (New York: Doubleday Image Books, 1964), 47.

50. Ibid., 25.

51. Ibid., 40.

52. Ibid., 43.

53. Ibid., 45.

54. Ibid.

55. Ibid.

56. Ibid., 46.

57. Ibid., 47.

58. Ibid.

59. Ibid., 48.

2

Behind *Centesimus Annus*

Rocco Buttiglione

It seems that one of the many merits of the new encyclical *Centesimus Annus* is that it has fostered a much needed step forward in the dialogue between the Catholic Church and the American spirit. This step forward is the consequence of carefully drawn distinctions which make some of the usual misunderstandings of the Holy Father's intentions difficult or impossible and which compel those willing to criticize the Church's social doctrine to come to grips with the encyclical's contents rather than battling over words whose meaning is often different and which are charged with different emotions on this or that side of the Atlantic, in the northern or in the southern hemisphere.

One of these often misunderstood words is *capitalism*.

In the United States capitalism is a thoroughly positive and respectable word. It implies free enterprise, free initiative, the right to work out one's own destiny through one's own efforts. In short: it is a bastion of the American liberty.

In Europe, as a rule, we have a different perception of the same word. Here capitalism implies rather the exploitation of large masses through an élite of tycoons who dispose of the natural and historical resources of the land and expropriate and reduce to poverty large masses of peasants and artisans.

In Latin America the situation is even darker: there, at least among the intellectuals and a large section of the masses, capitalism is simply synonymous with social injustice.

A detailed analysis is needed in order to understand why the same word resounds with so different, even contradictory meanings. In the Anglo-Saxon countries, the free market economy experienced an organic growth. On the European continent, however, the industrial revolution was often the result of the activity of small groups,

First published in *Crisis*, July-August 1996.

organized and led by banking rather than by industrial entrepreneurs, and possessing the decisive support of the state. This means that freedom of enterprise was restricted to a privileged social group and capitalism, from the beginning, was a *monopoly* capitalism. Even worse was the situation in many Third World countries, where control over all the resources of the country was concentrated in the hands of foreign companies and of corrupted local power élites.

Shall we speak, then, of different models of capitalism? In part the formal rules of the system were (and are) the same in all these continents. The concentration of power in the hands of a privileged group, however, causes the rules to produce different effects. In Italy, for instance, only in recent years have we had the significant development of a large class of small entrepreneurs, which has resulted in the social acceptance of freedom of enterprise and in a growing legitimation of the market. We may perhaps say that, in a certain measure, it is always possible that power groups possessing a monopoly of natural or cultural or political or economic resources try to close the mark to make it impossible for other men to acquire the means necessary to enter into the market which they dominate.

It is not so important whether we say that this monopoly really deserves the name of capitalism or whether we are convinced that this is a form of badly concealed socialism (as perhaps Michael Novak would say). What is important is that we share the same positive judgments on "capitalism" in the first sense and the same negative judgment on "capitalism" in the second sense.

This leads us to a second, equally important point. The market is not a natural state of affairs; it is a social institution. As such, it must be created and it must be defended; it may be enlarged and it may be restricted. In order to enter into the market, to be able to sell and to buy in the market place, there are many necessary assumptions. Some of these assumptions are of a legal and objective nature. For example, we need laws defending the freedom of individuals and their property, and we need a law of contracts. It is impossible to buy and sell if somebody can take forcefully what he wants. We need efficient communications and transportation systems, in order to take our commodities to market. We need information concerning the kinds of commodities in demand; we need educational and technical skills in order to produce them. Those who will take the responsibility of production need a minimum of capital to allow them the chance to expose their good ideas to an intelligent and active banker who can provide them with needed capital.

In some countries these market prerequisites are available, in other countries only a small minority of persons stand within the market, while the great majority have no access to these prerequisites. Here the market does not exist, or at least is severely restricted. Large masses have no choice but to accept whatever conditions are offered them by those who have a monopoly of access to the market. Under such circumstances, something just short of a social revolution is required to create a market: a peaceful revolution of freedom.

We reach here a third point that is equally important.

Even in countries where the market works, many persons remain out of the market because of natural and social handicaps. It is a moral duty of solidarity to supply these persons with the material help needed to rehabilitate them, if possible, or otherwise to preserve their life and their human dignity. This duty does not fall, however, only upon the state. The new encyclical defends the necessity of welfare politics but warns against the deviations and the bureaucratization of the welfare state. The state should rather, insofar as it is possible, enhance the activity of society, allocating resources in order to help families and other social institutions to meet social needs. Money channeled through such agencies is as a rule more effective than money channeled through bureaucratic institutions, and different social groups are thereby encouraged to meet social needs by satisfying their social responsibilities. The expansion of large bureaucratic state agencies, which have a tendency to expansion without corresponding to the needs and the satisfactions of the needy, is to be restricted.

A fourth point, strongly stressed in the encyclical, regards the connection between market and culture. If the market is a social institution which needs to be constituted and enhanced through a corresponding institutional framework, then the market cannot exist and function alone. The market has legal, cultural and social presuppositions: it enters into a necessary alliance with different cultural and philosophical positions. In our societies there is a certain alliance between markets and libertinism. This alliance is called in the encyclical *consumerism*: market values are the only values which are socially considered and everything is considered as a commodity, even things (like sex, the human body, human dignity, truth, culture, and religion) which according to their very essence are not and may not become merchandise.

In criticizing consumerism the encyclical makes it clear that this connection between market and libertinism is not essential. It does not arise necessarily out of the nature of the market: it is rather a consequence of a certain historical development. For this reason it is possible to work to substitute this alliance with another one: between free markets and an adequate philosophy of man.

The encyclical even goes so far as to suggest that the alliance between the market and libertinism cannot, in the long run, work. Free market society needs not only consumers but also responsible individuals, capable of hard work and creative action. It does not need consumers who are willing to consume without working. Strong, responsible, and reliable individuals are not produced, for example by sexual revolution, but rather are born and educated in morally healthy families. It seems, then, that the alliance between an adequate philosophy of man and a free market economy corresponds more to the true essence of a market economy than does an alliance with libertinism.

These considerations lead us to a final point, which should perhaps have been the first, since it is the most important point, namely, the extraordinarily positive evaluation of human freedom in the economic field and the function of the entrepreneur.

The free economy presupposes the free man. In order to have a market we need two free individuals, whose wills meet on the conditions of a contract. In a slave society we cannot have a market economy but must rather have a command economy. Already this simple fact shows us that there is a certain specific value to a free economy. Our perception of this value grows if we consider that the principal cause of the wealth of nations is human intelligence and human will seeing the needs of other men, seeing the natural resources and human skills that could satisfy them, organizing them, and taking the risks involved in the enterprise of bringing resources in contact with needs. Very seldom has the role of entrepreneurship as the creative side of human work been so clearly seen and so highly evaluated as in this encyclical. It is even qualified as a particular human virtue, which of course implies a particular responsibility to the common good.

This corresponds, however, to a general principle which underlies not only this encyclical but also the whole teaching of this pope: nothing good can be done without freedom, but freedom is not the highest value in itself. Freedom is given to man in order to make possible the free obedience to truth and the free gift of oneself in love. Truth and love are the measure of freedom and of the rules of the self-realization of freedom, in the field of economics as well as in all others.

# 3

The Liberalism of John Paul II

Richard John Neuhaus

It is no secret that when *Centesimus Annus* appeared in 1991 some of us viewed it not only as an important teaching moment, but also as a vindication of our understanding of Catholic social doctrine. There was a great temptation to declare triumphantly, "I told you so." That temptation was not always resisted as it should have been. This contributed to a degree of polarization over the encyclical. Liberals who paid any attention at all to the document were not convinced of the demise of socialism and lifted up passages that they thought supportive of their collectivist dream. But, for the most part, liberals paid little attention. As with the other great teaching documents of the pontificate of John Paul II, the appearance of *Centesimus Annus* was for most liberal Catholics a nonevent.

The stronger polarization developed between certain conservatives and those called neoconservatives, the former accusing the latter of hijacking this pontificate, and *Centesimus Annus* in particular, in order to gain magisterial legitimation for what is called democratic capitalism or liberal democracy. The neoconservatives are described, and sometimes describe themselves, as advancing "The Murray Project," referring to the effort of the late Father John Courtney Murray to square Catholic teaching with the American democratic experiment. The conservative critics—for instance, Professor David Schindler of the John Paul II Institute in Washington, D.C.—accuse Murray and those like him of selling out authentic Catholic teaching to a desiccated and desiccating liberalism.

Schindler writes in his recent book, *Heart of the World, Center of the Church*: "My argument, then, offered in the name of de Lubac and Pope John Paul II as authentic interpreters of the Second Vatican Council, has two main implications. First, it demands that we challenge the regnant liberalism which would claim that it (alone)

First published in *First Things*, May 1997.

is empty of religious theory in its interpretation of the First Amendment and indeed of Western constitutionalism more generally. Secondly, it demands that we seek a truly 'Catholic Moment' in America [as distinct from Richard John Neuhaus' 'Catholic Moment'], understood, that is, not as another Murrayite moment but as a truly Johannine (John Paul II) moment. This means that we must expose the con game of liberalism which enables it, precisely without argument, to privilege its place in the public order."

In his book, and repeatedly in the pages of the English edition of *Communio*, of which he is the editor, Schindler assaults the liberal "con game" in which he thinks some of us are complicit. I confess that I find this somewhat frustrating. In my experience, David Schindler is a friendly fellow. We have engaged our differences in both private and public exchanges, after which he ends up agreeing that there is no substantive disagreement between us. I always look forward to our next amicable conversation, and brace myself for his next public attack.

I do think there is an important difference between us. It is not, or at least it is not chiefly, a difference over Catholic theology. The difference, rather, is that Prof. Schindler and those who are associated with his criticism tend to put the worst possible construction upon the liberal tradition, and on the American cultural, legal, and political expression of that tradition. In doing so, I believe Prof. Schindler and his friends hand an undeserved victory to those who interpret the liberal tradition in ways that we all deplore. With John Courtney Murray, I suggest that our task is to contend for an interpretation of liberalism that is compatible with the fullness of Catholic truth.

There is no doubt that the American experiment is constituted in the liberal tradition. Since we cannot go back to the eighteenth century and reconstitute it on different foundations, we must hope that the foundations on which it is constituted are not those described by Ronald Dworkin, John Rawls, Richard Rorty—and David Schindler. Toward the end of understanding the liberal tradition as consistent with Catholic truth, *Centesimus Annus* is an invaluable guide.

Liberalism, needless to say, is a wondrously pliable term. There is the laissez-faire economic liberalism condemned by Leo XIII in *Rerum Novarum*, and also by John Paul II. In American political culture that liberalism goes by the name of libertarianism, and, despite its many talented apologists, including Charles Murray (no relation to John Courtney), it has never acquired many adherents beyond what Russell Kirk called its "chirping sectaries." In the American context, libertarianism remains in the larger part a thought experiment for college sophomores of all ages.

The liberalism so fiercely criticized today is not limited to libertarianism. At the hands of the critics, the republican liberalism of virtue and the communitarian liberalism of Tocquevillian civil society come off little better than libertarianism. David Schindler has good ecumenical company in attacking liberalism *tout court*. Stanley Hauerwas, a Methodist theologian at Duke University, has in books beyond number been assaulting, hammering, pummeling, and battering it with magnificent aplomb. Liberalism and all its ways and all its pomps have more recently taken a severe beating from Oliver O'Donovan, Regius Professor of Theology at Oxford. Despite his Anglican bias against what he calls "papalism," I most warmly recommend his book, *The Desire of the Nations: Rediscoving the Roots of Political Theology* (Cambridge University Press). It is not only a devastatingly convincing critique of a certain version of liberalism, but also a fascinating examination of what the idea of "Christendom" might mean in our moment of modernity's discontent.

We can summarize some of the salient points in the indictment offered by the Christian critics of liberalism and modernity (the two terms usually being more or less interchangeable). Whether it be the enchanted G. K. Chesterton, the near-magisterial Alasdair MacIntyre, the caustic George Grant, the swashbuckling Stan Hauerwas, the daring O'Donovan, or the melancholic David Schindler, the indictment tends to be much the same. Lest there be any misunderstanding, let me say that I find myself in warm agreement with the indictment of a certain kind of liberalism. The contention turns on what we mean by liberalism.

The first charge is that Christian thinkers have been too ready to trim the Christian message in order to accommodate the ruling cultural paradigm of liberalism. I definitely agree. That, however, is more accurately seen as an indictment of Christian thinkers, not of liberalism. If we are hesitant to declare in public that Jesus Christ is Lord, the fault is in ourselves. We cannot plead the excuse that liberalism made us do it. John Rawls or Richard Rorty or the Supreme Court, claiming to speak in the name of liberalism, may have intimidated us, but the fault is with our timidity.

Other points in the indictment of liberalism are variously expressed. It is charged that liberalism is purely procedural. Excluding the consideration of ends, liberalism claims to be only about means, but in fact disguises its ends in its means. Thus Father Murray's construal of the First Amendment as "articles of peace" is in fact—or so the indictment reads—a surrender to the inherently antireligious bias of liberalism. In short, the claimed "neutrality" of liberalism is anything but neutral. Liberalism, it is charged, is premised upon the fiction of a "social contract" that is, in turn, premised exclusively upon self-interest. Liberalism denies, or at least requires agnosticism about, transcendent truth or divine law, recognizing no higher rule than the self-interested human will. Liberalism's idea of freedom is freedom from any commanding truth that might impinge upon the totally voluntaristic basis of social order.

These liberal dogmas, it is further charged, are inextricably tied to the dynamics of capitalism. Liberal dogma and market dynamics are the mutually reinforcing foundation and end of a social order that is entirely and without remainder in the service of individualistic choices by the sovereign, autonomous, and unencumbered Self. The wages of liberalism is consumerism, and consumerism is all-consuming. The end result is what some critics call "liberal totalitarianism." It is an impressive indictment, and it is supported by impressive evidence. Against each of the distortions mentioned, I have written at length, as have others who are favorably disposed toward liberal democracy or, as some prefer, democratic capitalism. But that is just the point: one may argue that the indictment is an indictment of the distortions of liberalism. If that is the case, we are contending for the soul of the liberal tradition.

A personal word might be in order. In the 1960s I was very much a man of the left. Not the left of countercultural drug-tripping and generalized hedonism, but the left exemplified by, for instance, the civil rights movement under the leadership of Dr. Martin Luther King Jr. In the latter half of the 1960s this began to change with the advent of the debate over what was then called "liberalized" abortion law. By 1967 I was writing about the "two liberalisms"—one, like that earlier civil rights movement, inclusive of the vulnerable and driven by a transcendent order of justice, the other exclusive and recognizing no law higher than individual willfulness. My argument was that, by embracing the cause of abortion, liberals were abandoning the first liberalism that has sustained all that is hopeful in the American experiment.

That is my argument still today. It is, I believe, crucially important that that argument prevail in the years ahead. There is no going back to reconstitute the American order on a foundation other than the liberal tradition. A great chasm has opened between the liberal tradition and what today is called liberalism. That is why some of us are called conservatives. Conservatism that is authentically and constructively American conservatism is conservatism in the cause of reappropriating and revitalizing the liberal tradition.

Toward that end, *Centesimus Annus*, as I said, is an invaluable guide. The document is often described as an encyclical on economics, but I suggest that is somewhat misleading. Certainly it addresses economic questions in considerable detail. One reason for that is that the encyclical is commemorating and developing the argument of *Rerum Novarum*, which was much and rightly concerned about the problems of the worker and the threat of class warfare in an earlier phase of capitalism. Another reason for the focus on economics is that the Pope is addressing the situation following the Western-assisted suicide of the Soviet empire, and that empire had justified itself by a false ideology that reduced the human phenomenon to the economic dimension. In explaining why that ideology is false and in pointing the way toward a more promising future, it was necessary for the encyclical to pay close attention to economics.

It is more accurate, however, to say that *Centesimus Annus* is about the free society, including economic freedom. The discussion of *Rerum Novarum*, of the right understanding of property and exchange, and of the circumstances following the momentous events of 1989, culminates in chapters 5 and 6, "State and Culture," and "The Person Is the Way of the Church." When we consider the encyclical in relation to American liberalism, several cautions are in order. *Centesimus Annus* is not a freestanding text. It must be understood within the large corpus of this most energetic teaching pontificate, and, beyond that, in the context of modern Catholic social doctrine dating from *Rerum Novarum*. Even further, it must be understood in continuity with the Church's teaching ministry through the centuries. Then too, we must always be mindful that the Pope is writing for and to the universal Church.

Keeping these and other cautions in mind, however, one cannot help but be struck by how much *Centesimus Annus* is a reading of "the signs of the time" with specific reference to the world-historical experiences of this century. The encyclical is not historicist, in the narrow sense of that term, but it is firmly and determinedly located in a historical moment. And, while it is not a freestanding text, one can through this one text trace the controlling themes of this teaching pontificate. Although it is written to and for the universal Church, the Church in each place is invited and obliged to read the encyclical as though it were addressed to its own specific circumstance.

Moreover, I am confident that we as Americans make no mistake when we think that the American experiment is a very major presence in *Centesimus Annus*. After all, the Western democracies, and the United States most particularly, are the historically available alternatives to the socialism that so miserably failed. I think it true to say that in this pontificate, for the first time, magisterial teaching about modernity, democracy, and human freedom has a stronger reference to the Revolution of 1776 than to the French Revolution of 1789. It is, then, neither chauvinistic nor parochial to read *Centesimus Annus* with particular reference to the American experiment. On the contrary, it is the course of fidelity, made imperative by the duty to appropriate magisterial teaching to our own circumstance, and by the powerful awareness of the American experiment in the mind of the encyclical's author.

There is no more common criticism of the liberal tradition than that it is premised upon unbridled "individualism." *Centesimus Annus* (*CA*) speaks of the "individual" and even of the "autonomous subject" (13), but most typically refers to the "person." Citing the earlier encyclical *Redemptor Hominis*, John Paul writes that "this human person is the primary route that the Church must travel in fulfilling her mission . . . the way traced out by Christ himself, the way that leads invariably through the mystery of the Incarnation and Redemption." He then adds the remarkable statement, "This, and this alone, is the principle which inspires the Church's social doctrine" (53).

This, and this alone. He writes, "The Church has gradually developed that doctrine in a systematic way," above all in the past century. Very gradually, we might add without disrespect. In the later encyclical *Veritatis Splendor*, John Paul pays fulsome tribute to modernity and its development of the understanding of the dignity of the individual and of individual freedom. Individualism is one of the signal achievements of modernity or, if you will, of the liberal tradition. Nor should we deny that this achievement was effected in frequent tension with, and even conflict with, the Catholic Church. One important reason for such conflict, of course, was that the cause of freedom was perceived as marching under the radically anticlerical and anti-Christian banners of 1789. It is a signal achievement of this pontificate that it has so clearly replanted the idea of the individual and of freedom in the rich soil of Christian truth from which, in its convoluted and conflicted development, it had been uprooted. Only as it is deeply rooted in the truth about the human person will the flower of freedom flourish in the future.

It is a mistake to pit, as some do pit, modern individualism against a more organic Catholic understanding of community. Rather should we enter into a sympathetic liaison with the modern achievement of the idea of the individual, grounding it more firmly and richly in the understanding of the person destined from eternity to eternity for communion with God. The danger of rejecting individualism is that the real-world alternative is not a Catholic understanding of *communio* but a falling back into the collectivisms that are the great enemy of the freedom to which we are called. As *CA* reminds us, "We are not dealing here with humanity in the 'abstract,' but with the real, 'concrete,' 'historical' person." The problem with the contemporary distortion of the individual as the autonomous, unencumbered, sovereign Self is not that it is wrong about the awesome dignity of the individual, but that it cuts the self off from the source of that dignity. The first cause of this error, says *CA*, is atheism (13).

"It is by responding to the call of God contained in the being of things that man becomes aware of his transcendent dignity. Every individual must give this response, which constitutes the apex of his humanity, and no social mechanism or collective subject can substitute for it" (13). The great error of both collectivist determinism and of individualistic license is that their understanding of human freedom is detached from obedience to the truth (17). Culture is a communal phenomenon, but it is in the service of the person's response to transcendent truth. In one of the most suggestive passages of the encyclical, John Paul writes, "At the heart of every culture lies the attitude a person takes to the greatest mystery: the mystery of God. Different cultures are basically different ways of facing the question of the meaning of personal existence" (24).

We are brought back to the remarkable proposition about the flourishing of the human person. "This, and this alone, is the principle which inspires the Church's social doctrine." This is not individualism in the pejorative sense, but it is commensurable with the modern achievement of the idea of the individual. It is commensurable with the constituting ideas of the American experiment, in which the state is understood to be in the service of freedom, and freedom is understood as what the Founders called "ordered liberty"—liberty ordered to the truth. And there are, as the Declaration of Independence declares, "self-evident truths" that ground such freedom and direct it to the transcendent ends of "Nature and Nature's God."

The theistic references of the Declaration are not, as some contemporary commentators claim, simply crowd-pleasing asides but are integral to the moral argument of the document—and the Declaration is, above all, a moral argument. Moreover, such references must be understood in the context of the innumerable statements by all the Founders that this constitutional order is premised upon moral truths secured by religion. The American experiment is constituted by a Puritan-Lockean synthesis that in recent decades has been bowdlerized to fit the secularist prejudices of our academic elites. It is imperative that we challenge the bowdlerized version of the founding that has been fobbed off on several generations of students, from grade school through graduate school, and take our American history straight.

It will be protested by some that this is mere "civic religion." But we have missed the point of *CA* if we think there is anything "mere" about sustaining a public order that acknowledges the transcendent source and end of human existence. Of course such formal acknowledgment provides only a very thin and attenuated theology, but it creates the condition within which the Church can propose a rich and adequate account of the human story. But that, it is objected, is just the problem: In a liberal society the Church can only propose its truth, putting the gospel on the marketplace as one consumer item among others.

This is a frequently heard objection, and we have to wonder what people mean by it. Are they suggesting that the Church should coerce people to obey the truth? In the encyclical on evangelization, *Redemptoris Missio*, the Pope says, "The Church imposes nothing, she only proposes." She would not impose if she could. Authentic faith is of necessity an act of freedom. If we fail to understand this, it is to be feared that we fail to understand what John Paul calls the principle which alone inspires the Church's social doctrine. The Church is to propose—relentlessly, boldly, persuasively, winsomely. If we who are the Church are not doing that, the fault is not with liberalism but with ourselves. Although the Church's message provides a secure grounding for liberalism, liberalism is not the content of the Church's message. It is simply the condition for the Church to invite free persons to live in the *communio* of Christ and his Mystical Body, which communion is infinitely deeper, richer, and fuller than the liberal social order—or, for that matter, any social order short of the right ordering of all things in the Kingdom of God.

Few things are more important to the free society than the idea and reality of the limited state. However much the courts and secular intellectuals may have denied it in recent decades, the American order is inexplicable apart from the acknowledgment of a sovereignty higher than the state. As in "one nation under God," meaning a nation under judgment. Christians understand and publicly declare that higher sovereignty in the simple proposition, "Jesus Christ is Lord." It is not necessary for the state to declare that Jesus Christ is Lord. Nor, at least in the American circumstance and any foreseeable reconfiguration of that circumstance, is it desirable that the state declare that Jesus Christ is Lord. The role of the limited state is to respect the political sovereignty of the people who acknowledge a sovereignty higher than their own. As the encyclical states, "Through Christ's sacrifice on the cross, the victory of the Kingdom of God has been achieved once and for all" (25). That victory denotes the highest sovereignty by which the state is limited, and the proclamation of that victory is the most important political contribution of the Church. In a democratic society that has been effectively evangelized, citizens do not ask the state to confess the lordship of Christ. Their only demand is that the state be respectful of the fact that a majority of its citizens confess the lordship of Christ. We affirm not a confessional state but a confessional society, always remembering that the state is the servant of society, which is prior to the state.

The Church also makes an invaluable political contribution by insisting upon the limits of politics. The great danger, says *CA*, is that "politics becomes a 'secular religion' which operates under the illusion of creating paradise in this world. But no political society... can ever be confused with the Kingdom of God.... By presuming to anticipate judgment here and now, people put themselves in the place of God and set themselves against the patience of God." The power of grace "penetrates" the political order, especially as the laity take the lead in the exercise of Christian public responsibility, but there can be no pretensions that earthly politics will create the final right order for which our hearts yearn (25).

As in the liberal order the ambitions of the state are checked by the democratic assertion of a higher sovereignty and by the limits of politics itself, so those ambitions are checked by diverse "sovereignties" within society itself. With Leo XIII, John Paul declares that "the individual, the family, and society are prior to the State." The state exists to serve and protect individuals and institutions that have priority (11). Human persons and what I have elsewhere described as the mediating institutions of society "enjoy their own spheres of autonomy and sovereignty," according to *CA* (45). These spheres of sovereignty are smaller than the state, but they are not lower than the state.

The striking modernity of the encyclical's argument is evident also in its understanding of the state. Unlike earlier formulations, the state is not situated within a hierarchy of authorities, descending from the rule of God to the rule of the lord of the manor. The argument of *CA* is profoundly democratic. Christ is sovereign over all, and that sovereignty is asserted by those who acknowledge the sovereignty of Christ. The unlimited state, whether based on Marxist atheism or the engineering designs of Enlightenment rationalism, aspires to totalitarian control. "Thus there is a denial of the supreme insight concerning man's true greatness, his transcendence in respect to earthly realities, the contradiction in his heart between the desire for the fullness of what is good and his own inability to attain it and, above all, the need for salvation which results from this situation" (13). The limited state is kept limited by the democratic assertion of the transcendent aspiration of the human heart.

In this connection, John Paul infuses the doctrine of subsidiarity with new vitality by the use of a most suggestive phrase, "the subjectivity of society." "The social nature of man... is realized in various intermediary groups, beginning with the family and including economic, social, political, and cultural groups which stem from human nature itself and have their own autonomy, always with a view to the common good" (13). In the free society, the state is one institution, one player, among others. It is an indispensable player in its service to all the other players, but it is subject to the subjectivity of society, and the subjectivity of society consists in free persons and free persons in community living in obedience to God and solidarity with one another. There is in *CA* and in other writings of this pontificate, I believe, a fresh and compelling theory of democracy that awaits systematic development by the next generation.

There must be a cultivated skepticism about the state if it is to be kept limited. "To that end, it is preferable that each power be balanced by other powers and by other spheres of responsibility which keep it within proper bounds" (44). Skepticism regarding the power of the state does not mean, however, skepticism about the purposes that the state is to serve. Quite the opposite is the case. Only when those purposes are clearly and unambiguously asserted can the state be held accountable. Section 45 of *CA* clearly and unambiguously challenges the point at which contemporary liberalism has most severely distorted the meaning of democracy in the liberal tradition. Here is the crucial paragraph:

> Authentic democracy is possible only in a state ruled by law, and on the basis of a correct conception of the human person. It requires that the necessary conditions be present for the advancement both of the individual through education and formation in true ideals, and of the "subjectivity" of society through the creation of structures of participation and shared responsibility. [Then comes the vital passage.] Nowadays there is a tendency to claim that agnosticism and skeptical relativism are the philosophy and the basic attitude which correspond to democratic forms of political life. Those who are convinced that they know the truth and firmly adhere to it are considered unreliable from a democratic point of view, since they do not accept that the truth is determined by the majority, or that it is subject to variation according to different political trends. It must be observed in this regard that if there is no ultimate truth to guide and direct political activity, then ideas and convictions can easily be manipulated for reasons of power. As history demonstrates, a democracy without values easily turns into open or thinly disguised totalitarianism.

The importance of this paragraph, and its pertinence to our American situation, can hardly be overestimated. The dogmatic insistence upon agnosticism in public discourse and decision making has created what I have called "the naked public square." People who, like the Founders, hold certain truths to be self-evident are today "considered unreliable from a democratic point of view." In a usurpation of power that indeed threatens a "thinly disguised totalitarianism" the courts have presumed to declare that the separation of church and state means the separation of religion and religiously grounded morality from public life, which means the separation of the deepest convictions of the people from politics, which means the end of democracy and, in fact, the end of politics. Thank God, we are not there yet. But it is the direction in which we in the United States have been moving these last several decades, and it is the real and present danger requiring those of us called conservatives to rally to the defense of the liberal tradition.

In contending for the soul of liberalism, we must be sympathetically alert to some of our fellow citizens who honestly believe that any appeal to transcendent truth poses the threat of theocracy. John Paul recognizes how widespread that misunderstanding is, and therefore immediately follows the above passage with this:

> Nor does the Church close her eyes to the danger of fanaticism or fundamentalism among those who, in the name of an ideology which purports to be scientific or religious, claim the right to impose on others their own concept of what is true and good. Christian truth is not of this kind. Since it is not an ideology, the Christian faith does

not presume to imprison changing sociopolitical realities in a rigid schema, and it recognizes that human life is realized in history in conditions that are diverse and imperfect. Furthermore, in constantly reaffirming the transcendent dignity of the person, the Church's method is always that of respect for freedom.

Let it be candidly said that that has not always appeared to be the Church's method. We should not leave it to others to point this out. In *Tertio Millennio Adveniente* (*As the Third Millennium Nears*) and on many other occasions, the Pope has candidly called upon Christians to acknowledge the ways that, individually and corporately, they have failed to respect the dignity and freedom of others. That acknowledgment must, however, be joined to two other propositions. First: When, in the name of democracy, transcendent truth is excluded from the public square, the result is "open or thinly disguised totalitarianism." Second: Democratic totalitarianism, which recognizes no higher truth than majority rule, creates a treacherously dangerous circumstance for minorities.

We could go on to examine other themes of *Centesimus Annus* that can be correlated with the liberal tradition, rejuvenating that tradition and turning it in more promising directions. There is, for instance, the connection between freedom and virtue, both personal and public, which must evoke intensified effort toward the evangelizing and reevangelizing of society. The stakes in that effort are very high, as John Paul sets forth with such urgency in *Evangelium Vitae*'s dramatic portrayal of the conflict between "the culture of life" and "the culture of death." But these and other questions are for another time. Indeed, as I have suggested, it will be the work of generations to systematically unfold and disseminate the remarkable teaching ministry of this pontificate.

I began with some comments on *Centesimus Annus* and what some call "The Murray Project." Nobody should try to usurp the authority of magisterial documents in order to advance particular intra-Catholic partisan arguments. Before the magisterium of the Church we are all learners. Our purpose must be *sentire cum ecclesia*, to think with the Church. I know that I have learned from and have been changed by *Centesimus Annus*, and I trust that will continue to be the case. In no way should the encyclical be interpreted as an unqualified affirmation of the American experiment. In many ways, it is a searing criticism of what that experiment has become under the influence of contemporary liberalisms. Yet I do believe *CA* is commensurate with the American liberal tradition, and in critical continuity with the great work of John Courtney Murray. I believe that is the case, and I hope that is the case, for we have not the luxury of imagining the reconstitution of this social and political order on foundations other than the liberal tradition.

As sympathetic as we may be to some of the determined critics of liberalism, we do well to remind ourselves that all temporal orders short of the Kingdom of God are profoundly unsatisfactory. When we survey the depredations and ravages of our social, political, and religious circumstance, it is tempting to look for someone or something to blame. It is easy to say, "Liberalism made us do it." But liberalism is freedom, and what we do with freedom is charged to our account. For American Christians, and for Catholics in particular, there is nothing that has been done wrong that could not have been done differently. Amidst the depredations and ravages of an American experiment that once exalted the human spirit, and may do so again, *Centesimus Annus* invites us to reappropriate and rebuild the liberal tradition.

4
The Philosophy of John Paul II

Michael Novak

Unless many recent conversations around the country mislead me, intelligent Catholics in significant numbers seem not to be on the same wavelength as Pope John Paul II. In some ways this is odd, because intelligent Catholics usually like an intelligent and articulate pope, and this one is perhaps the most intellectually original, articulate and prolific pope of the past 100 years. Some of this discordance results (those who don't cotton to him sometimes suggest) from their very different reading of the Second Vatican Council. Some of it results, they say, from very strong feelings of disagreement about particular questions such as women's ordination, contraception and celibacy. Many are willing to admit, however, that they simply do not see what this pope is up to—do not follow, and cannot recount, his arguments. To a remarkable extent, in rather wide circles of U.S. Catholicism a certain resistance to John Paul II seems to be the expected attitude. It is sad, I think, to be alive during one of the great pontificates in history and to be in passive opposition to it.

This general lack of insight into why the Pope teaches and acts as he does is apparent in two popular recent biographies, one by Tad Szulc and another by Carl Bernstein and Marco Politi, as well as in the recent account *American Catholic* by Charles R. Morris, not to mention the running commentaries of the late Peter Hebblethwaite.

Nonetheless, it should be possible to set out an account of John Paul II's method, and to assist readers in grasping the originality of several of his conceptual achievements, even without attempting to close the disagreements on particular questions that some Catholics express. I hope that even those who do not go along with the Pope may find such an effort of service.

First published in *America*, vol. 17, October 25, 1997.

It has often been pointed out that the Pope was a professional philosopher before he became a bishop, and that he is probably better identified as belonging to the school of phenomenology than, say, as a Neo-Thomist. People often said that Pope Paul VI, for example, was an admirer and even follower of Jacques Maritain, but while there are points of contact with Maritain in Karol Wojtyla's work, one could not readily understand him within Maritain's framework.

One key to understanding Karol Wojtyla, I think, is that he is first of all a poet and dramatist. His sensibility is that of an artist. He is sensitive, feels things deeply, responds instantly to persons and situations through his emotions, takes things in as wholes and learns quickly from concrete experience. He trusts experience more than words. He likes to reflect on concrete wholes, as an artist would, in order to allow their inner form to emerge subtly and slowly. He is not in a rush to channel or contort parts of these concrete wholes into concepts or systems. These dispositions led him at a very young age to find both release and congenial techniques in phenomenological method, particularly as he found it in Max Scheler (d. 1928), the philosopher par excellence of the feelings.

It is a rare American who is helped by hearing the term phenomenology. I have seen even professional philosophers blanch on being asked to offer a thumbnail sketch of phenomenology, and listened as well-travelled journalists approached even the pronunciation of the term the way they would approach a three-foot-wide ditch: back up a few steps, take a deep breath and lunge.

Simply put, phenomenology is a sustained effort to bring back into philosophy everyday things, concrete wholes, the basic experiences of life as they come to us. It wishes to recapture these quotidian realities from the empiricists, on the one hand, who analyze them into sense data, impressions, chemical compositions, neural reactions, etc., and from the idealists, on the other hand, who break them up into ideal types, categories and forms.

When girl meets boy (as Rebecca, in the Book of Genesis, first sees Isaac coming toward her across the field), the psychologist may be interested in her prior relation to her father, and Kant may be concerned that her attachment to the categorical imperative may be going wobbly in the face of teleological hedonism. But the phenomenologist is interested in her experience of love as a concrete whole, in the many strands that there move her. How much is involved? How many elements make up the whole? How does this whole of experience differ from others she has known? What does her own heart tell her is lacking—or fulfilling—within it? This example suggests why, despite its cumbersome name, phenomenological method has had some of its greatest successes in the arts and aesthetics, as in the work of Wojtyla's friend from Krakow, the philosopher Roman Ingarden. A certain dramatic texture is inherent within it, and it has a taste of "the real."

As an actor who had played men moved by both great and tender passions on the stage, and as a dramatist and poet who had tried to create scenes in which powerful emotions and rich experiences could be relived by others, Wojtyla found Max Scheler to be in part a wonderful guide to the panoply of meanings and values embodied in the rich world of human feelings. Perhaps a contemporary parallel on the American scene today might be the recent book by James Q. Wilson, *The Moral Sense*. In the end, though, Wojtyla found Scheler not a complete guide to human experience and feeling; in his own life there were elements Scheler did not know of or explain.

I am not able to read the Polish texts of Wojtyla's Lublin lectures, in which as a young professor he recounted both his appreciation of and disappointments in Scheler's work. But I have been enormously helped by a brilliant doctoral thesis produced at Catholic University last year by a young Dominican from Krakow, Jaroslav Kupczak. According to Kupczak, Scheler was allergic to feelings of obligation, and determined to show that Kant was wrong in grounding morals in duty rather than in feelings. Wojtyla knew from his own experience that feelings are very important to the moral life and wonderfully subtle teachers; they often lead us to insights to which the intellect itself is at first blind or resistant. On the other hand, he had himself experienced moments when he felt the heavy hand of duty upon reluctant feelings, and knew he had to act even when he was afraid and experiencing dread.

More to the point, perhaps, feelings are something that "happen" to us; in a way, we are receivers of feelings, we suffer them, they come unbidden. But Wojtyla had also known moments when it was clear he had to take charge of his own life, to will something, to make something new happen, to become the agent of his own decisions. Here, too, he found Scheler too passive.

Before studying Scheler, Wojtyla had also—during World War II and just afterward—been introduced to the writings of Thomas Aquinas, through a textbook produced by a transcendental Thomist who had studied at Louvain with Cardinal Désiré Mercier and the Jesuit Joseph Maréchal. For two long months Wojtyla struggled with the density and abstraction and complexity of the thing. What a way to meet both Aquinas/Aristotle and Kant, at the same time—under Nazi occupation and after some years of hard manual labor and work in the clandestine theater!

When Wojtyla had climbed high enough through the thickets to see where he was and get a sense of the terrain, he had two very strong feelings. First, he had found a way of articulating some of his most important experiences—for example, of inner searching and conversion, of will, of agency, of call and obligation, of growth and becoming. Second, he saw that Thomism was stronger on nature than on human nature—it lacked a full theory of consciousness, of interiority and even of the feelings. It had strengths the moderns lack, but it was weak in some places where modernity demands strength. He thought it might be his task to contribute to bringing to the Thomistic patrimony a sense of interiority, a theory that included consciousness in its full range: somatic, vegetative, neural, emotional, passional, imaginative, intellectual, volitional.

At Lublin in the mid-1950s, then the freest and most independent university in the entire East behind the Iron Curtain, Wojtyla lectured on Hume, Kant, Scheler and other figures in the history of ethical thought, while slowly developing his own thesis on human agency and creativity, which was eventually published (more as notes-in-progress than as the rounded book he would have wished to produce) under the title *The Acting Person*. He was working on it even during sessions of Vatican II.

If we now imagine Wojtyla at his desk in St. Peter's as a young bishop during the years 1961 to 1965, this might be a good moment to pause to introduce one other major strand in his way of thinking. During his earlier stay in Rome for doctoral studies at the Angelicum (1946–48), where he wrote a thesis on St. John of the Cross and St. Thomas Aquinas on faith, Karol Wojtyla had been much taken with the argument in favor of Christian philosophy launched by Etienne Gilson. According to Gilson, while maintaining its own methodological autonomy, philosophy had been and could continue to be enriched by questions posed for it by Christian faith. For example, the concept of "person" had first been developed in the context of the doctrine on the Trinity, and the concept of will arose from questions posed in the New Testament about doing what we will not, and not doing what we will. The notion of "conscience" arose from reflections on Christian experience to which secular theories proved inadequate.

For Wojtyla, the most impressive problem posed for him by Christian experience in our time—a problem arising directly from biblical texts and from his own experience—is the question of freedom. For him, the question is first of all interior, but under the Nazis and the Communists he could not help noticing that freedom also has a political, even an economic, dimension, and a cultural as well as a personal dimension. It is not easy to explain how some people seem to yield up their freedom to threats or even to the mass sentiment surrounding them, while others, like St. Maximilian Kolbe, are able to remain fearless masters of their own decisions. Wojtyla has always been fascinated by the agency open to humans, the ability to—and the call to—take charge of one's own life. Ironically, of course, this "taking charge" often means remaining receptive to calls of grace, keeping oneself out of comfortable ruts so as to be disposed to going wherever God calls, even if one feels one has not the strength.

The point is that, unlike the lives of kittens or dogs, human lives are not bound by iron circles of instinct and routine; our minds and wills are always open to fresh and immediate inspirations of grace, new calls to conversion and action, even if only in the manner and intensity with which we attend to everyday duties. In each staccato second the human spirit is open, free, creative, receptive and ready to act in fresh ways.

Twice in his life, Wojtyla requested permission to enter the Carmelites, the order that nourished St. John of the Cross, St. Teresa of Avila and St. Thérèse of Lisieux, three of the greatest doctors of the interior life, especially the life of inner darkness of spirit and naked, abandoned faith. All three, too, each in a different way, stressed the utility of humble daily routines and humdrum quotidian activities for poverty of spirit and acts of love for God and others. To fail to see the extent to which Wojtyla's soul is Carmelite is to miss a great deal indeed. This means that he sees grace in all the things of nature, and all the things of nature as whisperers of grace.

He tries always to be in the presence of God, even when (perhaps especially when) sharing a good joke. Like most Poles, he likes being made to laugh; and his friend the Rev. Josef Tischner, for example, has a reputation of being one of the best joke tellers in a nation of joke tellers. Laughter, even more than sorrow, is part of the splendor of being; Poland knows more than its share of both.

At the Second Vatican Council, Wojtyla worked closely with Henri DeLubac, and he and the famous Jesuit became good friends, as the latter testifies in his memoirs. Wojtyla also shares with DeLubac the conviction that the concept of pure nature—apart from the fall and grace—is a merely hypothetical category, which does not and never did exist. Today everything that is is graced, wounded though it be by the fall. Both also share a vision of the church as a communion, a "we." It would not be right to say that the views of Wojtyla and DeLubac on these questions are identical, but Wojtyla's views on them are closer to DeLubac's than to those of any other theologian. This helps to explain why the Pope sees so much sacramentality and grace in every land, historical event and monument—as his talks in every part of the world demonstrate. He reads history and nature sacramentally.

To those brought up thinking about natural law in the way, say, that the great John Courtney Murray did, the Pope's habit of insisting that the human being cannot be understood apart from Jesus Christ may at first seem disconcerting. Yet the Pope is always thinking about the enormous impact of Jesus Christ upon concrete history, including huge geological shifts, so to speak, in the terrain of philosophy itself. To choose English and American examples, even philosophers as disparate as Bertrand Russell and Richard Rorty have candidly admitted that key concepts absolutely central to their own philosophies—compassion, for the former, and solidarity, for the latter—derive from the heritage of Jesus Christ, not from Greece or Rome or even the Enlightenment. Even such concepts as person, conscience, the dignity of every individual without exception and individual liberty, Wojtyla notes, arose from sustained reflection on the Gospels. In the Pope's thought, the realm of "nature" is thin and hypothetical indeed, compared to the actual workings of the fall and of grace in real history.

On the other hand, Wojtyla has never hesitated to speak a secular language to those who are secular. As a philosopher, he is quite accustomed to discussing problems without appeal to the language or premises of faith. In the old days during his debates with Marxist philosophers, he found it quite possible to turn the Marxist doctrines or labor inside-out through a purely philosophical (phenomenological) examination of the concrete experience of the steelworker in Nova Huta and the fisherman in Gdansk. He is not one of those Christians who cannot think unless he quotes biblical texts. When, as on his recent visit to Poland, the Pope spoke privately to the Communist president of the nation, one imagines that he was able to speak man-to-man in terms the president had no difficulty understanding, terms that did not require Christian faith.

In other words, it is not merely that Wojtyla has an unusual facility with many national languages; he also feels at home in and can communicate in a large number of quite different intellectual traditions and disciplinary contexts. One might say that in this way, by a different route, he also observes the protocols of the two different languages of nature and of grace.

The letters of advice that Bishop Wojtyla sent to the Preparatory Commission of the Second Vatican Council may have been the first to suggest the two axial concepts that later were to run through every document of the council as if lettered in crimson, a kind of conceptual spine: *person* and *community*. These became the axial concepts not only of the document on religious liberty but also of *Lumen Gentium* (on the church) and *Gaudium et Spes* (on the church in the modern world). Wojtyla remembers with special fondness his intimate collaboration on the drafting of this last. Yet Paul VI gave credit to the interventions of Wojtyla on behalf of the document on religious liberty for his last-minute decision that the document must be voted on before the council closed, when the tactic of the opposition had been to work for irretrievable delay. Paul VI could not turn down the appeal of those suffering behind the Iron Curtain for a strong word about liberty; and the interventions of Wojtyla proved, he told the conservatives, that the issue arose not solely from restless bishops in the secular countries of the West.

As bishop and as pope, Wojtyla has been consistent in his belief that Vatican II was an immense grace and marks out God's will for the church in our time. He rejects projective readings of the council, however, by which some read into it their own wishes or even fantasies. He asks for a full, balanced, nonselective reading of its documents, rich in their balance and measured reflection. Many in the advanced countries, it seems, have an image of what Vatican II meant that is not based upon actual meditation on the written text. He urges serious inquirers to study the documents in a spirit of prayer and learning. He is not afraid to recommend an attitude of obedience to God, obedience of the sort that led many thousands of priests in his generation to accept martyrdom. The so-called "spirit of Vatican II," I have found myself, is no substitute for getting the doctrine of Vatican II straight from the texts. Rereading those documents brings surprises on virtually every page.

In the July issue of *Crisis* (1997), John Crosby points out how much the Pope's teachings on sexual ethics have in common with those of many "progressives"—but also the unnoticed premise that differentiates his teaching from theirs; namely, the phenomenological analysis of action that stresses the unity of body and spirit, and uncovers in consciousness pain at their separation. I do not wish to enter into these controversies here, for my aim is not to argue such matters of content, but rather to call attention to the originality of the Pope's way of analyzing matters. Too many, I find, are reacting with resistance to something they do not recognize, without having any guide to help them clarify further the area of dispute. It is not right to allow unnecessary obscurity to persist. Some effort is required, but Wojtyla's reasoning is far more interesting and original than he is being given credit for. Some are judging him entirely within their own categories, a tactic they do not like when others use it against them.

A resident assistant at a supposedly sedate Ivy League university told me how, at freshmen orientation week, representatives of the university threw handfuls of condoms out into the gathered assembly of young men and women, fresh from their homes and eager to learn about the university experience, and how they scrambled around on the floor picking up the condoms. Everyone was expected to carry one away, as a ticket to the university experience. Instructions were also passed out for a variety of sexual acts that some of them, at least, did not even care to know about.

The rationale for the distribution of condoms was "safety." It was assumed that they would be having sex with people they did not know and could not trust, and probably with multiple partners. In other words, the university expected them to experience a radical separation between their bodily acts and their souls. The weeks to follow were made endurable by the ingestion of large quantities of alcohol and drugs before sex. (During that term, three women in the dorm—a mixed dorm, naturally—were found nude and unconscious in various rooms, including common bathrooms, and in one case outside on the grounds.) Hearing this story, others from other universities have matched it.

Yes, some will say, but within the bonds of matrimony and within a loving permanent relationship, the use of contraceptives is different. No doubt. Yet, Wojtyla points out, the alienation between body and soul remains detectable. However one finally resolves this question in one's own mind, one must say that Wojtyla's analysis hits a worrisome nerve. (It reminds one, too, of the empirical research describing young women who sometimes do not use contraceptives, not because they want to conceive, but because they do not want anything to come between them and the one they actually love; sometimes tragically, they intend this as a sign to him.)

On the question of a celibate clergy, too, it is useful to ask what Wojtyla thinks the priesthood is. When he became a priest, and during the forty years afterward, Wojtyla knew that thousands of Polish priests were being killed, sent to labor cramps, beaten and jailed for years at a time, simply for being priests. To be a priest was to be a marked man. In such circumstances, the fact that priests did not have families to support was a blessing. To become a priest was regarded as a brave and manly act. The life to be led was one of poverty, uncertainty, physical discipline and mortified flesh. A significant part of one's work would be clandestine. One would need to go out at all hours and in all weather. One priest would be clubbed by an anonymous band of thugs, in circumstances that made the act seem not unplanned; another would be approached after mass and struck on the head by a rock swung by a "madman," who would go unpunished. To see the large number of vocations to the priesthood in Poland today, and to witness the manly bearing and high morale of those who enter, is to see the harvesting of countless acts of courage and fidelity.

On matters of social ethics, one well-known U.S. theologian likes to describe Catholic social thought as a triad of "three S's"—solidarity, subsidiarity and social justice. To these, John Paul II has added subjectivity—the human person as subject, as agent, as center of imagination, initiative and determined will. Against collectivism of all sorts, the Pope counterpoises the self-conscious human subject who pours herself into all that she does.

Here, too, he sees the ground for defending rights to private property and to private initiative; and, more basic still, rights to religious and moral liberty. Further, because he sees social justice as rooted in individual subjects, he is also able to defend it as a virtue, a habit of a new and specific sort proper to free men and women, a new seat of social responsibility.

In this vein, too, the Pope now places on families—what he calls, following Vatican II, the domestic church—the new locus of the royal power that the church once vested in kings, the royal obligation of building up the civilization of love. For him, the new *civis* is the husband and wife; and it is they, not the state, who are the prime bearer of civilizing responsibilities. (Russell Hittinger of the University of Tulsa has best tracked this turn in papal thought.)

Those who wish to pursue further studies in the thought of John Paul II will now be tremendously helped by the magisterial, clear and profound book of Rocco Buttiglione, *Karol Wojtyla* (Eerdmans), the best study in any language. Buttiglione learned Polish and worked with Wojtyla before the latter became pope. He is much loved and trusted by the Pope, who asked Buttiglione to write the brilliant introduction to the third Polish edition of *The Acting Person* (1994), which is reprinted in this handsome volume.

Many American Catholics, I believe, will be stunned by the intellectual achievement recorded in Buttiglione's study. Like Wojtyla, Buttiglione also shares a great love for America and its tradition of practicality and common sense, and is able to show connections between phenomenological method and typically American habits of thought.

Since Pope John Paul II has the large vision of a philosopher, he is a little like Leo XIII (1878–1903) in the broad range of the subjects he writes about. It looks now, too, as if his papacy may run as long, or longer. Indeed, if John Paul lives as long as Leo (93 years), he will celebrate Easter of the year 2013 in the papacy. Beyond sharing years and range of views, however, I think it can be fairly argued that John Paul II is more professionally trained in a variety of contemporary disciplines than Leo XIII was, more penetrating, more original and—perhaps for that reason—more disturbing.

I hope all my progressive friends will forgive me if I close with the ancient Polish prayer, on behalf of Karol Wojtyla: *"May he live a hundred years!"*

Part II
ECONOMICS AND THE FREE SOCIETY

5

The Temple in the Polis: Faith Is Not Ideology

Maciej Zieba

> Nor does the Church close her eyes to the danger of fanaticism or fundamentalism among those who, in the name of an ideology which purports to be scientific or religious, claim the right to impose on others their own concept of what is true and good. Christian truth is not of this kind. Since it is not an ideology, the Christian faith does not presume to imprison changing sociopolitical realities in a rigid schema, and it recognizes that human life is realized in history in conditions that are diverse and imperfect. Furthermore, in constantly reaffirming the transcendent dignity of the person, the Church's method is always that of respect for freedom.
>
> —John Paul II

Fervent Christians, in the name of love and freedom, have sometimes been guilty of shedding human blood. Faithful believers, invoking the Gospel, have drafted laws to segregate their fellow citizens into different classes. From the lips of the same people who declare that love of neighbor must extend even to one's enemies, one can nonetheless hear words of contempt for those who profess different views. Why? The more we seek a "new evangelization" or (to use the formulation of John Paul II) the louder we say with the whole Catholic community to all those outside it, "Do not be afraid to open the door to Christ," the more insistently we should pose this question.

To be sure, the Church has a human dimension, and to be "human" is to be born into sin. Although people of the church have written many beautiful pages in the chronicle of world events, ecclesiastical history is also a teacher of humility. The Vatican Council reminds us that "in the life of God's people pilgriming through the

---

First published in *Crisis*, January 1994.

vicissitudes of human history, a way of acting often appears which is not quite conformable with the evangelizing spirit and even is opposed to it."

The fact that the Church is made up of people who can be *disloyal* to their professed values is only one objection that can be urged against its public influence. Many outside the Church rather fear that fervent believers, in the *name* of Christianity, will resort to force of law in order to burn heretics at the stake, teach contempt for others, or hinder freedom of conscience.

The post-Enlightenment epoch has largely been marked by a spirit of hostility towards the Church. Modern politics was itself partially constituted by the intention to free public life from religious influence. In public discussion, scientific research, and common opinion, Christianity is often considered merely a religious variant of the dangerous secular ideologies.

Yet according to John Paul II, there is a distinct difference between ideology and Christianity, and in *Centesimus Annus* he unequivocally separates the one from the other. He cites as typical features of an ideology that: (1) it contains a conception of truth and goodness; (2) its followers believe that they are free to impose their conception upon others; (3) it expresses the whole of reality in a simple and rigid scheme. The Pope maintains that Christian truth does not fulfill the second and third conditions, and so Catholicism is not an ideology.

Theologians in the Middle Ages did not articulate the distinction between faith and ideology. One should not be astonished at this, for the theoretical difference between ideology and faith is not obvious, whereas the practical temptation to ideologize the faith is extremely strong. Nor did the modern philosophers who opposed the influence of Christianity on politics comprehend this distinction. The burden of their thought was antireligious, rather than anti-ideological. As a consequence, their teaching fostered yet more lethal ideologies. Only today, after many sad experiences of history, have we come to consider the problem of the difference between ideology and faith.

What is at stake here is more than Church complaints about the imposition of unwelcome limitations on its activity or about the biased presentation of moral and religious topics in the popular media. A whole culture now believes that both ethics and religion are, at most, private matters; consequently, it finds itself embroiled in self-destructive conflicts. This topic has been precisely and penetratingly described by outstanding secular thinkers, including Arendt, Bell, Camus, Nisbet, Bloom, Kristol, and also such Poles as Kolakowski, Milosz, Dorosz, and Michnik.

"POSSESSION": A NECESSARY CONDITION OF IDEOLOGY

What distinguishes Christianity from ideology? The key to the matter is the notion of "possessing" the truth. Ideologists and their followers (whether they be Muslims, Marxists, Christians, Freudians, or positivists) believe that they possess a truth which explains reality. They believe that they possess an objective truth which other people, for reasons such as class, race, lack of intelligence, blindness of sin, caste, or nation, are not able to perceive. The attitude of the "possessor of truth" may manifest itself in the form of lofty contempt for the rest of mankind, but it is usually only a step away from imposing objective truth on the "subjectively" lost. (Those who are "objectively" lost, history teaches us, one may try to eliminate.)

Fundamentalism is connected with this attitude of *possessing* the truth, not with faith in the *existence* of absolute truth. Unfortunately, the view that faith and fundamentalism are precisely coincident is deeply embedded in contemporary culture. Each believer is regarded as at least a potential fanatic, whereas fanatical positivists or relativists (that is, people convinced that they have discovered an ultimate truth: that there is no absolute) are regarded as enlightened and tolerant humanists.

When John Paul II states that the Christian truth is not an ideology he means something more than that the Church today understands very well that it is not possible to embrace the complexities of the world in simple and rigid forms, or that the Church has no wish to impose its conception of truth and good by force. The Pope here says that *by its nature* Christian truth has the character that it cannot be "possessed." Not only is fundamentalism not an integral profession of the Catholic faith, but it is an abuse of Catholicism. For Christian truth by its very essence has a complex, not to say a dialectical, character. It is absolute and revealed to the Church, but at the same time the Church is not its "possessor." The truth surpasses the Church immersed in history—for it is above man, above reason, above philosophy, above theology.

As Hans Urs von Balthasar put it: "the incomprehensible love of God, acting through the event of Christ, extols Him highly above all . . . philosophical images of God." One of the most important challenges for the Church is to prevent this truth, revealed by God and not fully comprehensible to our intellect, from becoming simply an ideological version of Catholic dogma. The incomprehensibility of the biblical God has a meaning only as long as—again we quote von Balthasar— "dogmatic formulas prevent it from renewed rationalization . . . surround like cherubs with blazing swords, shocking for the Jews and Greeks, the madness of God's love, not permitting any cabalistic or Hegelian storm of gnosis." That is why negative theology is important: to judge what one cannot say about God. Even positive theology, when it predicates attributes of God through analogy, maintains that "although the similarity between the Creator and the creature is so great, the difference will always remain greater" (Erich Przywara).

The relation, therefore, between the truth proclaimed by the Church and the subsistent truth, God, is of this kind: First, the Church merely preserves the revealed truth, of which God is the only possessor. Second, this truth surpasses the Church, one of whose important tasks is to defend this truth from being enclosed in purely human categories. Third, the Church continues to grow in the knowledge of this truth, meditating on it with love, at the same time aware that never in the course of history, while time and space exist, will this truth be known completely. As the Vatican Council teaches, "The Church in the course of time constantly aspires to the full truth of God." Von Balthasar articulates this from a personal perspective: "a Catholic may claim the right to the title of being a Catholic provided that . . . he does not talk himself or others into believing that he has already achieved this."

God's truth, therefore, by its very nature is anti-ideological. It cannot, without being crippled, be treated as a closed conception which one may impose upon other people. Cardinal Joseph Ratzinger reached a similar conclusion by considering the difference between the Magisterium of the Church and the ideological apparatus of the Marxist party:

> That the teaching authority can come in danger of behaving like a party organ cannot be doubted. But that structurally it is something of this kind and thus an instrument of party constraint that is alien to learning must be disputed. The difference between the structure of a party constituted on ideological grounds and the Church lies precisely in the question of truth. Materialism . . . presupposes that what we have at the beginning is not reason but the irrational—matter. . . . Reason does not precede man but only comes into being as a human construct. . . . This means that truth is absorbed in the construct of the party and is totally dependent on it. The fundamental conviction of the Christian faith, on the contrary, is that at the beginning we have reason and with it truth; it brings forth man and human reason as capable of truth. . . . The community of the Church is admittedly necessary as the historical condition for the activity of reason, but the Church does not coincide with the truth. It is not the constructor of truth but is constructed by it and is the place where it is perceived. *Truth therefore remains essentially independent of the Church and the Church is ordered towards it as a means.*

This basic fact—that Christian truth is first in relation to the Church and not embraced by it—is the source of the anti-ideological character of Christian faith.

One of the fundamental principles of the modern state is the detachment of religion from public life. This is probably the only feature which communism, Nazism, and liberal democracy possess in common. Totalitarianism attempts to supplant religion with its own ideology. In liberal democracy, religion is treated as a matter of private opinion. Together with ideologies, conceptions of morality, and superstitions of all kinds, religion has no access to the public sphere, which in a modern state is supposed to remain "naked."

Following an epoch of religious wars and persecutions, it is difficult not to admit that there was some justification for this stratagem. Nevertheless, based as it is on naïve Enlightenment atheism (deism), this prescription is incoherent in theory and unfeasible in practice. A public square never remains naked. Even if religion sometimes (and the Catholic Church always) disturbed the founders of modern democracy, paradoxically enough, a "naked public square" meant for them a square in which Christian criteria of good and evil were in play and Christian institutions and customs were established. In other words, the founders of liberal democracy wanted Christianity without Christ and the Church. After eighteen or nineteen centuries during which Europe had been formed by the teaching of the Scriptures, how could these thinkers have imagined a completely different world? Yet, from the point of view of intellectual cohesion, theirs was a breakneck construction. Despite the intentions of the founders of the modern state, it is not true that the public square is naked, that it has been cleansed from all ideologies, philosophical systems, and religions.

The offensive propaganda initiated by the Enlightenment élite, "whose only pabulum was anti-clericalism, who from anti-clericalism made only one program, who believed that anti-clericalism is sufficient in order to change governments, to perfect societies and to bring about happiness" (Paul Hazard) provided justification for the use of the most brutal methods. In practical life, the postulate of the "naked square" has been realized sometimes through executions, more often through administrative force (annulment of monastic orders, destruction of the educational system) or confiscations.

The Church, deeply rooted in the culture, politics, and economics of the Middle Ages, found itself suddenly attacked on all fronts and often responded nervously, aggressively, and without understanding the essence of the changes which were occurring. A serious discourse about the place of religion in social life is impeded to this day, owing to the fact that the public square has been built upon antireligious and anticlerical foundations. As a result, it has become a place of mutual accusation and debate between clericalists and anticlericalists.

DEVASTATION OF THE PUBLIC SQUARE

The argument for the naked public square presupposes two axioms: (1) the only real being is the individual; (2) there is no absolute. The contention behind these two axioms is this: If the individual were to achieve his fulfillment only as a member of society, it would be appropriate for society to cancel individual freedom, to constrain man. If a social group were to think that it possessed an absolute truth, it would be only a small step away from creating a totalitarian ideology.

These axioms seemed to provide an effective panacea for the bloodthirstiness of religious wars, as well as the peremptoriness of Church authorities. At the same time, however, these postulates have encouraged the erosion of family life, the loosening of social ties, a weakening of national identity, and the elimination of religion and morality from social life. The social philosophy on which the liberal democracies were built has already passed its period of fertility. Its creative tenets—the equality of citizens, protection of individual freedom, respect for various convictions in the public square—have been absorbed. Nowadays, with ever greater force, the tendency of liberalism to destruction is manifesting itself.

If the only real being is the individual and there is no important general norm of morality, value-in-itself is reduced to value-for-me. Ethics is a more or less enlightened egoism—in the best case, pragmatism. Since debate about public morality is impossible (for there is no such morality), moral discourse becomes political discourse. "Justice" depends entirely upon the number of adherents which can be mustered to support a given conception. Since the only real being is the individual, society is a collection of interest groups.

Because this is not an external disturbance in the functioning of liberal democracy but its natural effect, liberal democracy cannot effectively counteract the erosion of social communication and social consensus. Increased legislation is the only means of self-defense. It specifies with full particulars the rights of husbands in relation to wives and vice versa, protects children and parents from each other, adjudicates quarrels between the faithful and the hierarchical Church, legalizes business transactions with particular countries, regulates the conditions of employment, work, and pay, and determines immigration quotas, racial quotas, and sexual quotas.

The battle for favorable legislation becomes the highest norm of public life. Society is a congeries of pressure groups, factions, and political parties who account a law moral when it expands their power and immoral when it limits their entitlements. Instead of preventing harm and protecting the innocent, this use of the law precipitates the destruction of the public square. Laws which are not based on a persistently conserved and continually renewed moral consensus possess no authority.

When people regard the proclaimed law as the highest norm of social life, they begin to perceive themselves and others as simply allies or enemies. *What* someone talks about is unimportant. Instead, one asks whether the speaker is a man or a woman, black or white, Catholic or Protestant, a pensioner or a government representative, a member of some party, or a homosexual. Politics becomes the art of winning over the majority amongst all possible "minorities."

SOCIAL CONCLUSION

The time may be slowly approaching for the breakdown of inherited resentments. The Church has a deeper awareness that at times when it ideologized its faith, this constituted a real danger to public life. The fact that it usually acted in good faith did not reduce the problem in the slightest but made it even more dramatic. Religious resentments do not assist the proper development of liberal democracy but rather destroy it completely.

On the threshold of a new and dangerous millennium, it is an anachronism to repropose 200-year-old solutions to the problems of the relation between Church and state, ethics and politics, education and social communication, or Christianity and public life. For a long time, public dispute has been dominated by people with a leaning towards either religious or relativistic fundamentalism, but the majority today opposes a fundamentalist approach, and dialogue in search of a new consensus is possible.

Both sides of the dialogue can endorse the view of John Paul II that

> the postulate of neutrality connected with people's outlook on life is correct mainly in this domain, that the state should guard the freedom of conscience and beliefs of all

its citizens, regardless of which religion or outlook they avow. But the postulate not to permit under any circumstances the dimension of holiness to social and national life is a postulate of an atheistic state and social life, and it does not have much in common with the neutrality connected with people's outlook of life. Mutual kindness and good will is necessary to obtain such forms of the presence of what is holy in social and national life which will injure nobody and make nobody an alien in their own land.

Without a broad social imagination, a significant dose of patience, the breaking down of many stereotypes and prejudices, and openness to mutual understanding, kindness, and good will, this not unreasonable expectation does not have much chance of being realized. The creation of "forms of the presence of what is holy in social and national life, which will injure nobody" is very difficult, but badly needed both for the Church and for the democratic state.

POLITICAL CONCLUSION

To promote this new consensus, a clear definition of the political role of the Church in a democratic society is necessary. The Church may opt to become the subject of a political game, participating in the mechanisms of legislation, exercising power in the state. But it could also consciously resign from a share in concrete legal solutions and political games and concentrate on the *metapolitical* sphere. The Church's proper action in this sphere would be the renewal and building of social consensus, in the light of moral values and the vision of the human vocation proclaimed by the Gospel.

The Church cannot fulfill both a strict political role and a metapolitical one, that is, it cannot claim the right to be one of the elements in a democratic game and at the same time contest this game, stressing that it is a community of a different category. Out of loyalty to the Good News, the role of the Church in the sphere of politics must be precisely defined and limited. "The Church's political stance must not be directed simply at the Church's power," Cardinal Ratzinger stresses. "This can become a direct contradiction of the Church's true nature and would consequently go directly against the moral content of the Church's political stance. It is guided rather by theological perception and not simply by the idea of increasing influence and power."

In the light of what has been said, the most realistic solution seems to be to insist on the clear division of lay and clerical vocations. This division of vocations is not a reaction to a special political context, but flows directly from the hierarchical structure of the Church. (The assertion that the Church can serve contemporary democracy better by stressing its hierarchical structure than by succumbing to pressures for "democratization" might be surprising to some.)

The laity has full right to political activity, but only to act on its own account, without involving the authority of the Church. For the good of the evangelizing mission of the Church—even if they are operating in a party which calls itself

"Christian"—politicians should recognize, as Cardinal Hoeffner puts it, that "such a party is neither a Church institution nor religious party nor a clerical one but is a political party responsible for the good of the entire nation. When it defines itself as Christian, that does not mean that it finds itself under the care of the Church, but simply that it acquaints itself with the Christian principles of social teaching."

At the same time, the clergy, representing the hierarchical Church, does not participate in the procedures of establishing law and political mechanisms. As the Pope puts it in *Centesimus Annus*, "the Church respects the legitimate autonomy of the democratic order." The Church requires a kind of asceticism in the manifestation of its political sympathies. Even more, it requires a constant distancing from all party games, legislative processes, and electoral campaigns.

Any loss which the Church might suffer because of the reduction of its direct influence on politics is compensated by the clear demonstration that the Church is above politics. It is thereby manifest that the Church is opposed to the ideologizing of faith and to its transformation into a collection of political solutions. Only in this way can the contemporary world observe and understand that the Christian faith is not an ideology. In seeking "new forms of the presence of what is holy in social and national life," the Church does not aspire to ownership of the public square. To yearn for a religious state is a simple contradiction of the mission of the Church.

ECCLESIASTICAL CONCLUSION

To better grasp its identity, the Church has recourse to the contemplation of biblical images, such as the sheep and its shepherd, the vineyard and the landowner. Each of these images presents a different aspect of the mystery of the Church. To set forth the proper relation of the Church to the democratic state, one may employ another great scriptural image, the temple. The image of the temple standing in the democratic city-state, the polis, brings to light features of the Church to which the symbols of the mystical body of Christ and the people of God do not advert. The latter emphasize the supernatural dimension and integration of Christ with the Church, on the one hand, and the earthly dimension and human community on its pilgrimage to a New Earth, on the other. But the image of the temple in the town—a clearly marked sphere of the *sacrum* is more the issue here than a separated, specifically built region—*situates* the Church in the world.

The Church is present in the world, where the powers of the hierarchy and the laity remain structurally divided, and the hierarchy respects the due autonomy of lay power. But the temple clearly cuts itself off from the town and is not subject to its laws. This does not mean that only the clergy have a right to enter the temple. Anyone may enter the temple, but then he is on nonpolitical grounds. To paraphrase St. Paul: there is neither Pole nor Jew, feminist nor antifeminist, Christian democrat nor social democrat, for all are one in Jesus Christ. The Church as a temple in a democratic city-state is the place of the real presence of God, the place of offering sacrifice, the place of teaching and prayer. The temple is also a special place for the dwelling of people who strictly identify their work and activities with the Church.

To acknowledge the relative autonomy of the political does not eliminate the tension between the *profanum* and the *sacrum*. The Church is in the world as well as above it: it serves the inhabitants of the polis, but is not subordinated to the political order. At times the most important form taken by its ministry to the world is to be "a sign which they will reject." The Church serves the world best when it is fully itself.

6

The Monk and the Market: What Does a Priest Need Economics For?

Maciej Zieba

Not so long ago, I was sharply criticized by a priest during a public debate. "Isn't it paradoxical," he said, "that a member of a begging order promotes free enterprise in his writing and speech? What is more, that he is a confrère of Saint Thomas of Aquinas, who was so critical with regard to economics?" I tried to refute the first charge with the help of logic: "Before I start to beg, I must do my best to win over the person, whom I may then ask for alms." I tried to refute the other charge with the help of history: "Another saint, Saint Anthony of Florence, whom Schumpeter called 'presumably the first man who formulated a holistic vision of an economic process in all its aspects,' was a member of my order. Moreover, the famous school in Salamanca founded by a Dominican, Francesco de Vittoria, where my confrères played an important part, acquired its fame not only by constructing a theory of human rights, but also by having come out with a subjectivist theory of the value of currency, the external entitlement to interest, and the principles of credit."

It is clear, though, that the problem posed by my questioner is serious. Why does a priest need to pry into economic matters? Such prying is approved neither by liberal economists and entrepreneurs, nor by the Church community. For the former, it violates the autonomy of the free market and tends to a naïve sentimentality, or else a supposedly totalitarian interference with somebody else's business.

To many fervent members of the Church, being involved in economic matters is a deviation from the proper course, the preaching of the Gospel, or a waste of priests' energy for the secularization of Christianity. Since each of these charges is supported by serious arguments, and both the dangers of clericalizing the economy and of selling Christianity off are equally threatening, I would like to give some thought to the issue of why, as a Dominican who works in the Poland of the 1990s, I write and talk a lot about economic matters.

First published in *Crisis,* July-August 1994.

A DISTORTED UNDERSTANDING OF ECONOMIC REALITY INCREASES POVERTY AND SOCIAL FRUSTRATION

This statement, trivial in its obviousness, is of enormous social importance. Within a democratic system and a free-market economy there can never be a community able to make full use of the capabilities of all its members. However, it is extremely important how big a part of the population will feel put outside the pale of society and rejected by the system. If a large part of society feels outside the pale, it poses a threat to democratic harmony. By contrast, in the free market—an institution more stable than democracy—such a phenomenon means, first, an increase in the range of poverty.

Poverty and related unemployment are only to some extent the reflection of the economic conditions. They result also from misunderstanding the mechanisms of the free market or from assuming them to be inhuman, "cold," or even dehumanizing powers, within which a human being cannot realize himself without the loss of his identity. Thus, first of all, the inability to operate, or the rejection of operating, in the free market should not lead to the social marginalization of man. The Church should always remind the rest of society about this fundamental truth through the preaching of the Gospel and its living testimony.

The free market is the institution that is the fastest and the most effective generator of goods (according to statistical data, within the last 200 years the population of Europe increased fourfold, while workers' salaries rose about fifteen times, with the work time shrunk by half). Thus, showing people the possibility of growing rich in an honest way is strongly connected with the charity work of the Church. I would call it a precharity activity. Saint Augustine reasoned in his *Commentary on the Letter of Saint John*: "We should not wish that the poor and the unhappy exist for us to perform acts of charity. You give bread to the poor, but it would be better that nobody hungered for it and that no one was needed to give it. You dress the naked. May everyone be dressed and may there be no such need!" Poverty always provokes social ills. The increase of poverty always means an increase of alcoholism, drug addiction, abortions, and crime.

If the above statements are generally true, the situation in the post-communist countries is, without a doubt, much more serious. In a couple of years it will become dramatic. The widespread misunderstanding of the logic of economic, political, and cultural changes, the fear of an unpredictable and dangerous future, as well as nostalgia for the stability of the past will constitute a huge social pressure which may make the process of change in Poland, Hungary, the Czech Republic, and Slovakia extremely difficult and slow. As for the remaining countries of the region, such misunderstandings, fears, or nostalgia may pose the threat of a renewed nationalist socialism.

In popular belief there exists a deeply rooted conviction that the basic means for solving economic problems is the intervention of the state (such a belief is not completely groundless if, as minister Jan Maria Rokita says, 88 percent of the national budget income is distributed by the government). This is strongly connected with the opinion that the remedy for poverty is a strongly progressive system of taxes, together with the control of the economy in a tight network of laws, which make any abuse impossible. Add to this public ignorance of such mechanisms of the market as the laws of accumulation and credit, or public fear of capital investment, and you have a horrifying picture of a country that may become stuck in the corset of post-socialist precapitalism. Clearly these sorts of problems, which should be the subject of education on the scale of the whole society, should first of all be of interest to the state, which is the owner of a significant majority of the mass media and of almost the whole system of education. Next, they should concern local governments and certain foundations.

I should add that, as a priest, I cannot be indifferent to the political and economic system in which the people to whom I come to preach the Gospel will live. And postsocialist precapitalism means a system in which people's talents and abilities are to a large degree wasted. The system squanders honest work and evokes a wave of emigration, especially of the most gifted individuals. It also means a system of widespread corruption, bribery, populist hatred, and aggression, and brings about the likely introduction of an autocratic regime. None of these things is unimportant from the moral point of view.

THE ABSENCE OF MORAL REFLECTION IN THE ECONOMIC LIFE

A few decades of irrational and amoral "socialist economics" have resulted in a lack of moral evaluation of economics in terms of human cost. Throughout these decades a "semi-moral" behavior was characteristic of the lives of millions of people. Naturally, this caused the escalation of essentially immoral attitudes, such as common theft, called an "extra salary," "damages," or "a dispensation of justice." In Czechoslovakia—which was believed to be the next country after the German Democratic Republic in which all the middle-class virtues were most deeply rooted—according to the Czechoslovakian Chief Board of Supervision about 40 percent of salesmen cheated their clients in the mid-1970s. Ten years later, this number had increased to 55 percent. The numbers in Poland were comparable, to say nothing of the USSR, where probably they were higher.

The lack of respect for property is particularly acute in the domain of intellectual property. It could not be otherwise, for I can remember that in the '70s, when I was a young physicist, I might spend my whole salary on an American handbook of quantum mechanics, or I might buy an "official" but copyright-violating version printed in the USSR. Since this was, supposedly, a promotion of Russian culture, the price of the copy amounted to half the price of a cinema ticket. It is hard to expect that the problem of paying taxes should be easily found within the sphere of moral evaluation, for, until recently, it was very difficult to identify with the state, which was run by "them." Indeed, the taxes of the majority of citizens of the Polish People's Republic were paid by the state itself. It may also be added that various systems of irreclaimable loans, coupons, and interest-free credits to be paid back by social funds effectively undermined the notion of reliable credit taking and credit repaying.

Today, when we live in a free state of participatory democracy, this decay of public morality is a grave disease which undermines the health of the society. The Church cannot remain indifferent.

CAPITALISM AT THE COST OF SECULARIZATION?

Numerous authors, from Berger to Dawson, from Tawney to Kolakowski, and from Guardini to Arendt, have paid attention to the links between the evolution of capitalism and the weakening of religion. Countless hypotheses have been constructed and a multitude of analyses and comparisons concerning that matter have been made. The essence of this process may be summarized as making economics autonomous and religion private. The free market excuses itself on grounds of efficiency. It has its own laws and criteria, to which religion is redundant. The forms of behavior inspired by religion cannot facilitate anything in economics, while they may make matters worse. Such a view is now deemed axiomatic. The view is shared by both theorists and practitioners, by atheists and believers. Another conviction is that religion is a private affair.

It is hard to deny the reason in such views: it did sometimes happen that theological theories either formulated the rules of management, or they provided a moralizing critique of economics, without the knowledge of such rules. Undoubtedly, religion is first of all a personal encounter with God; undoubtedly, too, the clericalization of social life may pose a threat to individual freedom. While we understand this anxiety, we have to state clearly, as Cardinal Ratzinger did, that "the Church is not going to impose anything like a new *respublica Christiana*. It would be absurd to return to the past and to a system of politicized Christianity."

At the same time, to leave the whole sphere of social life—in which economics plays such an important part—outside the scope of Christian reflection and the fulfillment of Christian vocation would mean the erosion and, consequently, the decay of faith. To deem religion only a private matter means, in fact, its destruction. As Romano Guardini noted,

> there is a growing demand that different aspects of life, such as politics, economics, sociology, science and art, philosophy and education develop and are derived from their own internal norms. Thus arises a way of life which is non-Christian and frequently anti-Christian . . . while, when the Church demands that life be guided by the truths of Revelation, it is considered to exceed its competences. . . . Just as we cultivate purely scientific science and purely economic economics, religion, too, is to be purely religious. Thus, religion is less and less connected with actual life.

To avoid an erroneous interpretation of this quotation, it should be stressed that Guardini does not mean to negate either the inner laws or the specific autonomy of science, politics, art, or economics. What he opposes is the principle that a Christian, operating in the world of politics, science, and economics, should put his Christianity aside, for secularization is not a process of closing down empty churches or unnecessary seminaries. Nor does it begin with the diminishing of the number of practicing believers. Secularization begins the moment religion loses touch with actual, real human life, when in the lives of individuals and societies there disappear the patterns of behavior inspired by faith; and, even more precisely, when the religious description of reality which evokes such patterns of behavior is no longer adequate.

It is true that the truths of Revelation when brought to bear upon public affairs may result in conflict with people who do not identify themselves with Christianity (let us call them the "liberal party"). Yet, such a conflict is unavoidable only between the religious and the liberal fundamentalists. Apart from the fundamentalists' standpoint, there exists the possibility of a fruitful, though admittedly difficult dialogue. I believe that this dialogue lies not only within the scope of interest of the Church; it is needed by both sides.

From the perspective of the Church, it should be noted that the Church's basic mission of evangelization is connected with the working out of a realistic Christian view of economics, as well as of politics, mass media, and education. However, it should be kept in mind that what is meant here is a realistic Christian approach to modern economics, which adequately describes specific human experience and is not an attempt to create a Christian economics. For if the Church does not adopt such an attitude, it will mean that a huge sphere of human activity will be acknowledged as non-Christian, implying that a Christian can fulfill his vocation through prayer, family life, or charity work, but not through running a business, administering services, or performing any other activity in the free market.

A danger of another kind is possible (and there are, in fact, many advocates of such a viewpoint), namely, the free market may be recognized as an anti-Christian institution, an institution based on egoism and the lust for profit, which will destroy the common welfare and interpersonal solidarity. In such circumstances, if an orthodox Catholic enters the sphere of free-market economics, which to some extent involves every man, he will continually experience an inner conflict. Thus, if the Church does not offer its worshippers an "alternative" vision of economics, this will mean a consent to rapid and widespread secularization. This is why the question whether and how a Christian who operates in the free market may fulfill his vocation is such an important one.

A BEAUTIFUL STRANGER

For the centennial of *Rerum Novarum* I wrote a text entitled "A Beautiful Stranger." I made Catholic social education the heroine. Over two years later, I may define this "beautiful stranger" in a more specific way: she is the encyclical *Centesimus Annus*, a document that is underappreciated by the Polish Church. As a matter of fact, the question of "the Christian in the free market" already has been powerfully formulated by John Paul II. This was done within the context of the changes in Middle and Eastern Europe. "Can we say," asks the Pope, "that the defeat of communism means the triumph of capitalism as a social system? And, thus, should it be aimed at by all the countries which undertake the task of social and economic restructuring?" And though his answer is complex, at the same time it is explicit: "If the term 'capitalism' denotes an economic system which recognizes the fundamental positive role played by businesses, the market, and private property, as well as by responsibility for the means of production, which results from the above, the answer to this question should definitely be positive. . . . Yet, if capitalism be understood as a system in which economic freedom is not restrained through a framework of legal systems, which would make it serve the integral human freedom and treat it as just one aspect of this freedom, which is first of all of ethical and moral nature, then the answer is definitely negative." In other words, there exists a capitalism in which a Catholic should feel a stranger, but there also is a variant of the free-market economy in which he should feel at one with the Church.

The whole of *Centesimus Annus* is devoted to the specification of this distinction. The great innovative power of the encyclical consists in the fact that, until now, the popes who wrote social encyclicals were only describing and evaluating the social reality. *Centesimus Annus* is the first document whose author gives up the judge-and-witness attitude, since the encyclical includes also a positive exposition of how a Christian may fulfill his vocation through being engaged in the free market. The Pope avoids making a moralizing evaluation of economics, which has sometimes happened in Church documents. He stresses the positive part played by the principal institutions and mechanisms of liberal economics, such as the free market, enterprise, profit, and private property. Moreover, the Pope concentrates on delineating "anthropological compatibility," as I would call it; that is to say, a concurrence of the teaching of the Church and the vision of man as an individual operating in the free market, which is implied.

A person, understood as a free, reasonable, and creative individual cooperating with others for the common good, both belongs to the Christian tradition of understanding human beings and is a subject capable of creative activity within the free-market economy. This does not mean that there are no differences between Catholic anthropology and the "anthropology of the free market," but, as John Paul II stresses, that the differences appear not on the level of free economics or the democratic political system, but on the level of culture. This is why the Pope, choosing the positive aspects of the free market and democracy, writes also about the possible dangers and degeneration of democratic capitalism, which may result from overvaluing such phenomena as production (as the only measure of development), market (as the mechanism which automatically solves all the problems), and property (which does not come under any restrictions). The dangers may also result either from "anthropological reductionism," the assumption that man is solely *Homo Oeconomicus* and so counts mainly as a producer or a consumer of goods, or from treating a human being like an atomized set of separate sensations.

To conclude, John Paul II cites serious dangers in the modern world which may be caused by economic and political liberalism. Yet, he stresses that these dangers are rooted in liberal ideology, rather than in the functioning of the free market and democracy itself. He also shows a positive vision of fulfilling a Christian vocation in the world of democratic capitalism. This positive exposition is not an attempt to "baptize" liberalism in order to hold back secularization; it is the result of an anthropological reflection rooted in theology.

WHAT DO LIBERALS NEED THEOLOGY FOR?

For a reader who is not connected with the Church, the fulfillment of vocation, which concerns Catholics so much, may be an unfamiliar problem; for him the process of secularization may seem to be a positive phenomenon: "this is how a strange empire slowly ceases to exercise its influence." For this point of view, a dialogue with Catholicism or, more generally, with Christianity, is unnecessary. But the matter is not that simple. One more question should be answered, namely, whether the free-market economy is a self-sufficient system and whether it is in possession of all the indispensable means to reproduce itself over a longer period of time. The majority of liberal thinkers are very doubtful of this. That is why, beginning with Adam Smith and ending with Friedrich Hayek, thinkers have stressed the importance of non-economic motivation in human life, as well as the significance of the moral component in economics. As was rightly noticed by Hayek, "the system [of free enterprise] itself is not more than a means, and its countless advantages must serve to achieve the goals which exist outside of it.... A society which does not have any norms other than effectiveness is definitely going to lose its effectivity."

Thus, although the free market itself is an amoral institution, it still may function effectively only within a moral environment. It demands justice, honesty, and basic social agreement with respect to right and wrong, as well as a theory of the human being in society. For liberals at the turn of the eighteenth century, the conviction that liberalism could develop only on the grounds of Christianity was firm. Later, the belief in an evolutional moral self-development of the human species became more and more widespread. But, as Lord Ralf Dahrendorf stressed, the Hayek who is profound and precise when he analyzes a free society and the free market stands in sharp contrast with the naïve and doctrinaire Hayek who puts forward hypotheses about the evolutionary development of morality.

More and more observations and arguments support another thesis, and a growing circle of thinkers is prone to agree with Wilhelm Roepke, who wrote in his *Crisis of Modern Times* that it "has long been believed that the economy of the market, based on competition and the division of labour, is an excellent educational institution. Through an appeal to egoism, it may push people into peace, decency and all the civil virtues. Today, however, we know something that may have always been known, namely that an economics based on free competition is a consumer of morality. You must be really blind to facts to consider it a purveyor of morality. The existence of a free-market economy assumes the existence of moral reserves outside of it."

What is more, the liberal institutions are "cold," that is, they do not promote the feeling of identity, community, or of being rooted. They need the complement of the "warm" institutions, such as family, the Church, neighborhoods, and the nation. This is a new element in liberal thinking and another possible meeting point with Christian thought and the Church. If Eric Voegelin was right when he criticized liberals in *From Enlightenment to Revolution* for not being "intelligent enough to understand the issue of institutionalizing spiritual matters," we still have to admit that years ago we, within the Church, also lacked the intelligence to understand the problems of the spiritual dimension of social institutions. Yet after nearly two centuries of struggle and evolutions the time has come, I think, for a difficult but inevitable dialogue. The underground press author "Jdrzej Branicki" (who turned out to be the future minister Janusz Lewandowski) observed half a century ago that there were differences between the liberal understanding of economics and the social teaching of the Church, differences which apparently could not have been overcome.

Today, after *Centesimus Annus* and in the face of all the changes connected with modern democratic capitalism, we can see the wide plane of their constructive confrontation. "The aim of the dialogue of all political and intellectual powers, to which I urge everyone, is a definition of a common economic minimum," said Joseph Cardinal Ratzinger in his conversation with Henri Tinque. "We want the basic Christian values and the liberal values, which dominate in the contemporary world, to have a chance to meet and fertilize each other." Because of unfortunate previous encounters, there are many opponents of such an encounter, and there are still more circles that do not perceive the need for such a dialogue.

Still, I am convinced, and this view is shared by more and more people towards the close of our century, that the discussion about what separates us and what unites us is necessary for the efficient functioning of democratic capitalism. The discussion is indispensable also for the Church, to help her in the fruitful accomplishment of her mission. Thus, this is one more reason for which I, being a monk, read and try to talk about the free-market economy.

7

Property and Creativity

Richard John Neuhaus

In 1840 the socialist-anarchist Pierre-Joseph Proudhon wrote *Qu'est-ce que la Propriété?* His answer to the question of what is property was unambiguous: "Property is theft!" For a century and a half that answer has possessed the ring of truth for many, firing resentment and anger in the hearts of the propertyless and striking guilt and fear in the hearts of the propertied.

Leo XIII intended to meet the challenge of Proudhon's question head-on. "By defining the nature of the socialism of his day as the suppression of private property," writes John Paul, "Leo arrived at the crux of the problem." If Proudhon was right, then the socialist remedy would seem logically to follow. That many were to follow that remedy is now a fact of history. As John Paul ruefully remarks (in *Centesimus Annus* [1991]), "The remedy would prove worse than the sickness" (12).

Private property is not entirely private. That is, it is not something to be grasped entirely for itself, or for oneself. Ownership can be *legally* free and clear, but it is not *morally* free and clear. There is always, so to speak, a social entailment that comes with property. Commenting on *Rerum Novarum*, John Paul writes, "The amount of space devoted to [private property] in the encyclical shows the importance attached to it. The Pope is well aware that private property is not an absolute value nor does he fail to proclaim the necessary complementary principles such as the universal destination of the earth's goods" (6).

The Psalmist declares, "The earth is the Lord's and the fullness thereof, the world, and those who dwell therein" (Psalm 24). If everything belongs to the Lord, it is obvious that our ownership of anything cannot be absolute. John Paul observes that the freedom to say that something is "my own" is necessary to personal identity. But

---

Reprinted from *Doing Well and Doing Good: The Challenge to the Christian Capitalist* (New York: Doubleday, 1992), pp. 187–208.

it identifies a person less as an owner than as an acting person who is an administrator. And that, of course, brings us back to the familiar biblical concept of being a steward or caretaker.

The "universal destination of goods" means that the fullness of the earth is to benefit all God's children. In the Christian view of things, that will one day be the case. There is, as it were, an eschatological proviso attached to all private property. But the "universal destination" is not just a matter of future promise. There is a present imperative to seek the ways in which the fullness of the earth can best benefit all. On this there would seem to be no big difference between socialists and the proponents of the free economy. It is just that "the simple and radical" of socialism has been tried and found wanting. We have seen the socialist future, and, to put it very gently, it does not work. A better way is needed.

The better way, according to John Paul, is found by reading the signs of the times thrown up by the historical experience of freedom and creativity. "The type of private property that Leo XIII mainly considers is land ownership," he writes (6). In many parts of the world, the ownership of land and natural resources is still the main form of property. But today, John Paul argues, property must be understood not in static but in dynamic terms. Property is not so much a matter of what happens to be there and who claims it first. Property is the product of work and creativity. The "origin of material goods" is, finally, in the continuing creativity of God.

"The original source of all that is good is the very act of God, who created both the earth and man, and who gave the earth to man so that he might have dominion over it by his work and enjoy its fruits . . . This is the foundation of the universal destination of the earth's goods." So both the originating foundation and the eschatological destination are in place. What is needed in between is "the human response to God's gift." Through work, a person "makes part of the earth his own" and this is "the origin of individual property." The response to God's gift is blessed by God, and with that blessing comes also the obligation "not to hinder others from having their own part of God's gift." More than not hindering others, we are to "cooperate with others so that together all can dominate the earth" (31). This, then, is John Paul's proposal for a dynamic and creative understanding of property. In this view, private property is not the enemy of the common good but an essential instrument for realizing that common good.

DESIRES RIGHT AND WRONG

Without work there will be no economic creativity, and without incentives there will be no work. One would like to think that the incentive to work exists because people recognize that work is a part of their dignity as acting persons who contribute to the common good, and all this to the glory of God. Although they may express it in a confused and inarticulate manner, perhaps that really is the reason why most people work most of the time. Witness the resistance of so many people to the prospect of retirement, and the resentment of the "indignity" of unemployment, even when material needs are secured. At the same time, however, incentives to work certainly include the desire for material gain. As we have seen, John Paul does not despise that desire, but generously affirms self-interest as natural and good.

In that connection, he affirms the role of profit in business enterprise. If they allow themselves to be influenced by John Paul's teaching, it will be more difficult in the future for religious activists to style themselves as "prophets against profits." He writes, "The Church acknowledges the legitimate role of profit as an indication that a business is functioning well." That may seem a little odd. Most people think of profit less as an "indicator" than as good in itself. The Pope's formulation puts one in mind of the Texas billionaire who, when asked why he still wanted to make more money, answered, "It's a way of keeping score."

But John Paul is not unaware of the usual reason for profit. His concern is to underscore the intimate connection between profits and people. "It is possible," he writes, "for the financial accounts to be in order, and yet for the people—who make up the firm's most valuable asset—to be humiliated and their dignity offended." In thinking about "goods" to be valued, people come first. This is not simply an idealistic or rhetorical flourish. The Pope is not asking people to run their businesses on the basis of disinterested altruism. His point is that the "human and moral factors . . . are at least equally important for the life of a business" (35).

So it is also for the sake of business itself—it is in the self-interest of business—that the "human and moral factors" must be taken very seriously. Once again, John Paul highlights the sometimes curious ways in which "how the world works" can work to the benefit of all. If one believes that the origin of all goods and creativity is in the conjunction of divine grace and human freedom, it should not come as a surprise that there is a benign pattern in how the world works. The Church, he seems to be saying, is on friendly terms with how the world works—except when human sin and stupidity get in the way of its working.

The possession of property can be and should be put to a moral testing. The test is whether it expands the circle of exchange and productivity. Does it contribute to the vibrancy of an economy of "free work, of enterprise, and of participation"? Does it progressively expand the "chain of solidarity"? John Paul lays down the following rule: "Ownership of the means of production, whether in industry or agriculture, is just and legitimate if it serves useful work. It becomes illegitimate, however, when it is not utilized or when it serves to impede the work of others in an effort to gain a profit that is not the result of the overall expansion of work and the wealth of society, but rather is the result of curbing them or of illicit exploitation, speculation or the breaking of solidarity among working people. Ownership of this kind has no justification and represents an abuse in the sight of God and man" (43). The most fervent advocate of the market economy should have no argument with that. The nonutilization of resources and the exclusion of others from the circle of exchange and productivity are dumb ways of conducting business. Exclusionary and protectionist measures may sometimes seem to be in the short-term interests of the advantaged, but they end up by undercutting the very system by which such advantage was gained.

WHEN GAIN IS ILLICIT

At the beginning of the section where he offers that rule about the ownership of property, the Pope observes that "the Church has no models to present." What the rule means in application has to be worked out "through the efforts of all those who responsibly confront concrete problems in all their social, economic, political, and cultural aspects as these interact with one another." A question to be answered, for example, is what is meant by the criticism of "illicit speculation." At another point (48), he refers to the corrupting influence of "purely speculative activities." Since he repeatedly affirms the importance of capital and exchange, he obviously is not criticizing the trade in stocks, bonds, and other securities. Perhaps "illicit speculation" refers, in the East European context, to black-market exchanges or old-guard bureaucrats who made speculative gains on the basis of their positions in the party.

Coming closer to home, however, language about "illicit speculation" and "purely speculative activities" is not uncommon in American business and finance. One thinks, for example, of the controversy over the trade in "junk bonds" in the 1980s. Junk bonds are high-risk corporate bonds that, quite predictably, attracted highfliers on the financial markets. In financial circles there is lively dispute over whether junk bonds constitute "illicit speculation" or are an important contribution to economic vitality. Widely condemned in the 1980s, junk bonds seem to be making a comeback in the 1990s. The defenders of the trade in high-risk bonds claim that they make available billions of dollars to capitalize entrepreneurial ventures that would otherwise languish. While many criticize the corporate takeovers financed by junk bonds, others contend that such takeovers typically improve management and make corporations more accountable to stockholders. The public view of such high-risk activity as "illicit speculation" has been greatly influenced by the rather astonishing sums of money made by some who engage in the trade.[1]

The most infamous, or famous, of dealers was a young man named Michael Milken. Later successfully prosecuted for technical violations of trading rules, Milken was reputed to have made more than $500 million in personal income in one year. The newspapers were full of it at the time, and one of them interviewed prominent financial figures to find out what they thought. Donald Trump, a New York financier who was riding high then, allowed that he had read about it and was somewhat puzzled. You don't need $500 million a year, he opined, in order to be happy. Mr. Trump was reportedly getting by on $50 million a year.

Americans have conflicting feelings about such financial goings-on.[2] Some are morally outraged, others wish the superrich well and hope that they or their children will get a crack at the same opportunities. Most people seem not to care very much. Despite the conventional talk about America being an incorrigibly materialistic society, surveys over the years tend to confirm that Americans are relatively devoid of envy and not terribly interested in being rich. A bookkeeper making $30,000 per year would undoubtedly like to make $20,000 more, but the prospect of $500 million does not keep him awake at night. The Robin Hood stratagem of robbing the rich to give to the poor has seldom had great appeal in the American political culture. Most people seem to feel that it might ruin the economic game by which they and their children stand to gain.

The more ideologically minded, however, have no doubt that a Michael Milken is engaged in "illicit speculation." His "earnings," they readily judge, are "unjust" and "obscene." The latter would seem to be more an aesthetic judgment than a moral one, but perhaps the line between the two is not as clear as one might suppose. In any case, comparable indignation is not usually expressed about sports figures, rock and movie stars, and others in entertainment who take in millions of dollars per year. A discussion of whether Michael Jackson or Madonna receives "a just wage" could make for an interesting seminar. When the Mets sign a player for a guaranteed $4 million per year, people mumble about its "ruining the game," and they may be right. But it is hard to know what is the *right* amount to pay, say, Dwight Gooden.

The idea that there is a right amount or a "just" amount always runs up against the question, Compared to what? The conventional answer is that one pays what the market demands, or what the market will bear. From Athens to Elizabethan England to the Great Terror of the French Revolution, societies have experimented with "sumptuary laws" setting limits on people's income and expenditures. The experiments have never worked out very well, the obvious reason being that it is almost impossible to agree on standards. Few egalitarians, even among the well-to-do, propose a top income limit that is less than what they themselves receive. At the same time, the average middle-class man or woman in America is living in incredible opulence compared with the majority of humankind. Yet they, who are already rich, are likely to think that "being rich" means making twice or three times what they do at present. It is all very confusing.

WHOSE POVERTY? WHOSE RICHES?

Since people think of poverty and riches in comparison with their own life situation, clergy are inclined to hold a peculiar view of what constitutes great, even "obscene," wealth. Clergy are among the lowest-paid professionals, and Catholic priests and religious are devoted to poverty or simplicity of life. A priest who received $15,000 a year, plus room and board, might understandably have a keen eye for the obscene wealth that surrounds him. But again, it is difficult to say what is obscene or unjust. Unless, of course, we have available to us some moral principle mandating equality. *Égalité*, it will be recalled, is the name of the dog that does not bark in *Centesimus*. And, in fact, there is almost nobody who thinks absolute equality of income or wealth is a good idea. Yet innumerable religious statements on economic justice are haunted by the suspicion that there should be something like equality, more or less, and that somebody should be in charge of seeing to it.

Centesimus, like earlier papal statements, does speak about a "just wage" (8, 15). In the Catholic tradition this is frequently referred to as a "family wage," meaning that it is enough for a man to support his family in dignity. (The assumption that it is the husband and father who will be the "breadwinner" is implicit also in *Centesimus*.) Many free-market economists scorn the idea that there is such a thing as a just wage. Wages are determined by the market, and whatever wage the market sets is, if one insists upon using the term, just. One may, however, suggest that at least at the bottom end of the scale, it is meaningful to speak of a just wage. If an employer pays below what his business can afford and what would not disrupt the market, one might say that he is behaving unjustly. If workers are unnecessarily kept at a mere subsistence level of income, it would seem to be a clear case of what John Paul means by offending the dignity of the person.

We need not be entirely speculative, however, about the abuses criticized by John Paul. The daily financial pages supply ample instances of gross injustices in which people exploit the free market. It is no secret that some champions of capitalism are much more effective in undermining the ethos of the free market than are its declared enemies. For example, corporate executives give themselves millions of dollars in benefits while forcing a company into bankruptcy. Such behavior both deprives people of jobs and cheats the stockholders, while contributing absolutely nothing to economic productivity.

One need not believe that capitalism is driven by nothing more than greed in order to recognize the ugly dynamics of greed that both drive and corrupt the free economy. To recognize such wrong is not the same thing as having a remedy for it. *Centesimus* underscores in many ways the danger of remedies for the abuse of freedom that turn out to destroy the free economy itself. Contrary to libertarian ideology, John Paul knows that the market is not always self-correcting. The answer to abuses of the free market is not always to be found in the economic system, he says, but is finally moral and spiritual. Those who want a technical or legal fix for human sinfulness will find that answer unsatisfactory. In important respects, they are right. The moral and spiritual ethos required for the free economy will never be satisfactorily secured. That is why guidance, admonition, and encouragement such as that provided by *Centesimus* will always be necessary.

In making moral discernments we are always returned to specific circumstances of concrete cases. For instance, the statement that workers should not necessarily be kept at a wage below what is required for a life of dignity depends upon contingent judgments about business and market realities that determine what is and is not "necessary." At the upper end of the income scale, moral discernment is still more difficult. The Church, it would seem, has a serious obligation to warn the super-rich about the moral perils of great wealth, and to remind them of the duties of philanthropy and charity (on which more in due course). But should a Michael Milken make $500 million a year? Is what such people do an instance of "illicit speculation"? It would appear that the only answer *in principle* proposed by John Paul is that property and economic activity "is just and legitimate if it serves useful work."

Perhaps that is the only answer that can be given. Whether, in fact, trading in junk bonds and similar activities do contribute to expanding economic opportunity for all is, the Pope would seem to suggest, a question best left to "those who responsibly confront concrete problems" in the economic arena. John Paul does not pretend to be an expert on the operations of Wall Street. Were he to know about, for example, the discussion of junk bonds, he might well share the moral uneasiness generated by a case such as Milken's. The Church has effective ways of giving expression to that uneasiness. A good many of those who deal with these "concrete problems" in the market are in parish pews on a regular basis. Certainly there is a pastoral requirement to press them on their moral responsibilities.

THE INESCAPABLE QUESTION

Equally, there is a pastoral requirement to listen and to learn. The "self-denying ordinances" observed by John Paul caution against squandering Christian moral authority by indulging in ignorant judgments or, worse, self-righteous posturing. The Church has many searching, even painful, questions to ask of everybody. The more important questions have to do with the ordering of loves and allegiances to the truth revealed in Christ. Few of those questions are substantively affected by whether one is rich or poor. Our loves and allegiances, however, emphatically do encompass, for rich and poor alike, the world of work. Nobody can escape the question of whether his work enhances or impedes, expands or contracts, the human circle of freedom characterized by those key words in *Centesimus*—enterprise, exchange, productivity, participation, and solidarity.

Among the new developments in John Paul's examination of "new things," few are more striking than what he has to say about the "sources of wealth." Here Catholic teaching moves dramatically ahead of former attachments to assumptions that were appropriate to traditional societies and zero-sum economics. Section 32 of the encyclical in particular richly repays our careful attention. When we speak of property and ownership, John Paul says, we must give our attention to "the possession of know-how, technology, and skill." And then this: "The wealth of the industrialized nations is based much more on this kind of ownership than on natural resources."

Fans of Adam Smith are no doubt warranted in drawing some satisfaction from the implied reference in that sentence to *The Wealth of Nations*. (It seems unlikely that it is an accident.) At the very time the American Founders were launching this experiment in political and cultural freedom, Smith was laying out the rationale for a free economy that could benefit all. As becomes evident in John Paul's treatment of global poverty, his hope, like Smith's, is that "the wealth of the industrialized nations" will indeed become, through expanding the circle of exchange and productivity, the wealth of all nations.

The origins of the word "capital" are in a traditional economy, when *capita* referred to heads of cattle as a measure of wealth. As Michael Novak is fond of urging, however, the same word suggests *caput*, meaning the human head. The thinking, responsive human being is the source of the creativity and initiative that the Pope calls "creative subjectivity." This is the source of what he calls "know-how, technology, and skill," and therefore of wealth. The process involving "initiative and entrepreneurial ability," John Paul says, is one that "Christianity has constantly affirmed [and] should be viewed carefully and favorably." Land and what is in the earth are indeed resources, but "man's principal resource is man himself." That insight, as we shall see, has everything to do also with the Pope's understanding of "the potential of the poor."

Most of us assume that we know the difference between rich nations and poor nations, and which nations today are which. That knowledge has about it a taken-for-granted character. Japan is rich, Bangladesh is poor. Taiwan is rich, China is poor. And so forth. *Centesimus* invites us to consider *why* some nations are rich and others are not. It is not "natural." Something happened, and what happened didn't "just happen." There are studies beyond number on the causes of poverty, both domestically and globally. Some are no doubt useful, but one may be permitted to be mildly skeptical. If somebody came up with *the* definitive study on what causes poverty, what would we do with it? Nobody in his right mind wants to cause poverty. The Pope focuses our attention on the much more interesting and promising question of what ends poverty, of what produces wealth.

Some of the richest nations in the world today are not rich in what we ordinarily call natural resources. Were natural resources the only or even the most important key to prosperity, Japan would be a very poor country and most of the countries of Latin America would be rich. Peter Berger has brilliantly analyzed the factors that make for development in *The Capitalist Resolution: Fifty Propositions about Prosperity, Equality, and Liberty*. Berger certainly agrees with John Paul's judgment that "on the level of individual nations and of international relations the free market is the most efficient instrument for utilizing resources and effectively responding to needs" (34). But he would even more strongly underscore the Pope's focusing of attention on "concrete problems in all their social, economic, political, and cultural aspects as these interact with one another" (43).

Berger has given currency to the concept of "economic culture"—the attitudes, dispositions, institutions, patterns of behavior, and ways of being-in-the-world that make for development. It is in the possibility of influencing the economic culture that the Catholic Church can play such a powerful role. Stalin, who fancied himself a realist, foolishly asked how many divisions the Pope has. So some equally foolish souls today might derisively ask how many billions of dollars the Church has for Third World development work. If that is the right question, the Catholic Church is almost entirely irrelevant to world development. The relatively modest operation of the Vatican itself runs an annual deficit of many millions. But that way of evaluating the role of the Church quite thoroughly misses the point about economic culture.

THE WEALTH OF THE CHURCH

This may be the place to address briefly the perennial canard that the Church is wealthy and, if it were really serious about poverty, it would sell its immense holdings and give the proceeds to the poor. The Holy See and probably every diocese in the worldwide Church regularly run a deficit. In 1991 the Holy See had to call upon the bishops, mainly those in America and Western Europe, to make up a shortfall of more than 100 million dollars. Would the sale of the art treasures of, for instance, the Vatican Museum and Sistine Chapel bring in billions of dollars? Almost certainly. Would the world be better off were those treasures privately owned by billionaires in Zurich or Tokyo? Certainly not. Being a careful steward of the artistic patrimony of the West is a service that the Vatican renders to the entire world. Selling off the holdings of the Metropolitan Museum would no doubt produce revenue enough to support the entire government of New York City for several years. There is no end to the good uses to which the money could be put, especially for the poor. To our knowledge, however, nobody has suggested that selling the art and turning the Metropolitan into, say, a vocational high school for the underprivileged would be a just and wise course of action.

But some critics point to the Church's huge investment in buildings—churches, rectories, convents, hospitals, and so forth—in almost all our major cities. In fact, such buildings generally represent liabilities more than assets. They house service-giving, not profit-making, institutions. Churches, for instance, are entirely dependent upon free-will offerings by those whom they serve. Further, even were they sold, they are often worth very little. In recent years in Detroit and Chicago, more than fifty churches have been closed because they were no longer effectively serving their inner-city communities. In many cases churches that would cost millions of dollars to build today were sold to other denominations, such as black Baptist or Pentecostal groups, and sometimes for as little as a token payment of one dollar. The claim that the Catholic Church—or, for that matter, most other churches—has great economic wealth is a fantasy that has demonstrated remarkable endurance. The Church's contribution to the poor is not in distributing its physical property but in creating a moral and spiritual ethos in which the poor can benefit more fully from "the new meaning of property." The distinctive task of the Church in this connection is cultural.

At the heart of culture, we again recall, is religion, and with *Centesimus* the Church's influence is decisively thrown on the side of the economics of freedom and productivity. In large parts of the world, notably in Latin America, the attitudes and disciplines of entrepreneurship have in recent years been generated by evangelical Protestants, usually in conscious opposition to the cultural influence of Catholicism. Not tomorrow and probably not in the next year or two, but the teaching of *Centesimus* could significantly change that situation over time. In conventionally distorted views of reality, something like the economic influence of the Church is thought to be a "soft" factor, while, say, a change in the interest rates by the Federal

Reserve Board is taken to be a "hard" factor. It is further assumed that hard factors have more impact than soft. This is almost certainly a great mistake. What is naturally complex we tend to call soft, and what we artificially simplify we tend to call hard. In a more nuanced understanding of how the world works, the religiocultural transformation proposed by *Centesimus* could turn out to be the greatest economic development of the next century.

OVERTHROWING MATTER

Old and familiar ideas about wealth and resources, then, are no longer helpful. Technology, know-how, and the things that make for economic culture have come to the fore. In short, "man's principal resource is man himself." The acting, thinking, creating person-in-community has become, far and away, the chief source of wealth. George Gilder, the author of *Wealth and Poverty* and a sometimes controversial seer who peeks around corners that most people don't even know are coming up, calls this new understanding of wealth and resources "the overthrow of matter." "The overthrow of matter reached its climax in the physical sciences when quantum theory capsized the rules that once governed and identified all solid objects. Physicists now agree that matter derives from waves, fields, and probabilities. To comprehend nature, we have to stop thinking of the world as basically material and begin imagining it as a manifestation of consciousness." According to Gilder, the computer is at the heart of this revolution. "By collapsing the computer to invisibility and imbedding it in the matter of everyday life, man may impregnate the world with his mind and waken it to the sound of its master's voice."[3]

Gilder is an enthusiast, and it may be objected that others made similarly grandiose projections from the invention of, for example, the wheel, the printing press, and electricity. But that is not much of an objection, since those and other events were in fact revolutionary in their impact. The theologian might raise the more serious objection that "the overthrow of matter" is a problematic expression, since Christianity is rather firmly attached to matter, beginning with the Genesis account where God pronounces it good and centered in "God became man." But Gilder's essential point is an elaboration of John Paul's insight that "man's principal resource is man himself." In other words, the resources for the production of wealth to meet human needs are only as limited as are human imagination, initiative, and creativity. Which is to say, we live in a world of unlimited resources.

Resources are not simply given by nature. Resources are themselves the product of human ingenuity. To take an obvious example, oil was nothing but gunk in the ground until "know-how, technology, and skill" turned it into a valuable resource. Even more dramatic is the revolution of the microchip. Next to oxygen, silicon is the most abundant item in the earth's crust. There is so much of it that it is not even worth pennies per ton. Barring the end of the world, the supply is inexhaustible. Yet the development of the semiconductor has produced wealth that beggars by comparison all the wealth produced from "valuable" resources such as gold, diamonds, and copper. Natural resources are, by virtue of human ingenuity and enterprise, as inexhaustible as the Sahara or Gobi Deserts. The useless sand that once covered what became, by ingenuity and enterprise, the natural resource of oil is now much more important than the oil it covered.

Moreover, *Centesimus* underscores the fact that *business itself* is a source of wealth. "A person who produces something other than for his own use generally does so in order that others may use it after they have paid a just price mutually agreed upon through free bargaining. It is precisely the ability to foresee both the needs of others and the combinations of productive factors most adapted to satisfying those needs that constitutes another important source of wealth in modern society" (32). This insight is crucial to John Paul's argument. It is not the case that creativity is limited to geniuses who make great inventive breakthroughs. There is a genius to knowing what to do with those breakthroughs. It requires the "ability to foresee" how they can be brought to the market in order to meet human needs and desires. Business people who, like Anatole France's juggler, are embarrassed by the modesty of their talent not only give pleasure to Our Lady, but participate in the continuing creativity of God himself. It does, one might observe, give new meaning to taking care of business.

WEALTH AND WHIMSY

Business that is itself a source of wealth does not only require know-how, technology, and skills. It also requires *virtues,* disciplined habits of perception and behavior. The Pope writes: "Important virtues are involved in this process, such as diligence, industriousness, prudence in undertaking reasonable risks, reliability and fidelity in interpersonal relationships, as well as courage in carrying out decisions that are difficult and painful, but necessary both for the overall working of a business and in meeting possible setbacks" (32). He might have added that it takes a sense of humor, an appreciation of *homo ludens*—man as a player of games. There is undoubtedly a gamelike quality to economic enterprise, and a closer connection between wealth and whimsy than is ordinarily thought.

This author was recently in conversation with an entrepreneur in post-Communist Czechoslovakia who has made a stunning success of things. He started with a travel agency, expanded it into several, and then moved into computers, office equipment, and brokering loans for other entrepreneurs. One thing seemed to follow naturally from another. A devout Catholic, he explains what he has done in terms of promoting free enterprise, building democracy, providing useful work, supporting his family, and so forth. Then he pauses, and says with just a touch of embarrassment, "The one thing that has really surprised me is that doing business is so much fun."

True, *Centesimus* does not explicitly refer to the fun of the thing, but one expects that John Paul would approve. Of course, there are always people for whom their work is not fun. Sometimes because the work is onerous, backbreaking, degrading, and miserably paid. But all too often because they have not perceived the dignity and worth of what they are doing. There are drones who drag themselves to work at a brokerage house or retail business, just as there are drones writing books, directing graduate studies, and preaching sermons. The fault, in most cases, is not in our work but in ourselves. "God loveth adverbs; and cares not how good, but how well." A job that cannot be done adverbially to the glory of God and benefit his children should, in all likelihood, not be done at all.

There is frequently loose talk in our political culture about "meaningless and dead-end" jobs. All too often such talk reflects a class-based snobbery. Because we and "our kind" would not want to do a particular job, we say it is meaningless. As to dead-end employment, in the case of younger and basically competent workers, no job is dead-end in a free economy. Especially for the poor in the urban underclass, the challenge is not to move directly into the middle class but to move into any employment. Once that entry-level job is secured, the cultivation of the habits of reliability and initiative will, with a regularity that makes it almost inevitable, lead to other employment opportunities. To say this is not to subscribe to the much-derided Horatio Alger myth of limitless opportunity. It is simply to agree with social experts who point out that the great difference today is not between dead-end and open-ended jobs but between those who do and those who do not develop the habits appropriate to steady work.[4]

Once again, however, the market, in and of itself, is hardly the answer to all our problems. The creativity that makes the market a source of wealth is also to be employed in making the market work better for everyone. As people are economically creative, so they have a capacity for political creativity. Some of the reforms of primitive capitalism, John Paul notes, "were carried out by states" through political means. The labor movement was and still can be a creative instrument of reform. Then he focuses on reforms brought about by "an open process by which society organized itself through the establishment of effective instruments of solidarity that were capable of sustaining an economic growth more respectful of the values of the person" (16).

INVITING OTHERS INTO THE CIRCLE

Creativity that is fully human is not captive to the market. Precisely as a resource, the market is an instrument. Things can be done that have yet to be imagined in order to make it a more effective instrument. But people will never do the creative things that might be done with the market unless they clearly assert who is in charge—human beings. The market was made for human beings, not human beings for the market. That means recognizing the limits of the market, and indeed of economics itself. As the Pope says, "There are many human needs that find no place on the market" (34). Part of the answer to that is to make the market work better, which means more inclusively.

The goal is to help "needy people to acquire expertise, to enter the circle of exchange, and to develop their skills in order to make the best use of their capacities and resources" (34). But there are also needs and goods that while they can find a place in the market, they *should not* be in the market. Here John Paul mentions drugs and pornography as examples (36). The list could be extended to include prostitution, the marketing of dead fetuses and human body parts, the renting of the wombs of poor women in surrogate motherhood, and so forth. John Paul is not pitting the market and morality against one another. His attention fixes on the *acting person*. The same creativity, initiative, and enterprise that make the market work can help direct the workings of the market to worthy ends, knowing full well that it will also and always be used for unworthy ends.

The generativity of the market may be beyond comprehension and seem almost magic at times, but the real mystery is in the human mind and spirit. An economic system in itself, the Pope says, "does not possess criteria" for determining what is worthy of human beings (36). The risk in becoming too impressed with the semimagical qualities of the market is that human beings abdicate their own responsibility for choices made. "The market made me do it" becomes another version of "The devil made me do it." When, for instance, John Paul criticizes the "consumerism" of developed societies, he is not criticizing the market, *he is criticizing us*. "The economy in fact is only one aspect and one dimension of the whole of human activity." Consumerism is like Marxism in that it constitutes a surrender of the human to economic determinism. The reason for the social decadence of the consumer society "is to be found not so much in the economic system itself as in the fact that the entire sociocultural system, by ignoring the ethical and religious dimension, has been weakened" (39).

Whether we clean streets, teach school, trade stocks, or sell computer software, the business that we are each given to take care of is but a small part of the whole. At the same time, we are not *wholly* defined by the business that is ours. Each of us is, above all, an acting person capable of and responsible for decisions. For those in business, says the Pope, "even the decision to invest in one place rather than another, in one productive sector rather than another, is always a moral and cultural choice" (39). The "business logic" of the decision is not the only determinant. It may, in the long run, be good business to "do the right thing" morally, just as we saw John Paul argue earlier that pitting profits against people turns out to be bad for business.

To that, many business people might respond with the very cynical Lord Keynes, "In the long run we're all dead." So John Paul offers another reason for doing the right thing. Making the moral decision, he writes, "is also determined by an attitude of human sympathy and trust in providence, which reveals the human quality of the person making such decisions" (36). The virtues required for business, including "courage in carrying out decisions that are difficult and painful," are only virtues if people accept responsibility for the decisions they make. The suggestion is that it is seldom true that we have no choice; those who say they have no choice are often saying that they have no imagination or courage.

IN THE COURAGE OF OUR UNCERTAINTIES

Of course, we may be more certain about the outcome of one decision than another. But courage is only courage in the face of uncertainty. At the core of this question is the Pope's adamant insistence upon the acting person. We are not ciphers but free moral agents. Having dispensed with socialist oppression, John Paul is not prepared to accept capitalist pusillanimity. Surrender of personal responsibility to the laws of the market can be as much a denial of freedom as surrender to the myth of collective ownership of the means of production. Between the socialist lickspittle to economic determinism and the capitalist lickspittle to economic determinism, there is little difference, except the latter has less excuse.

Toward the end of *Rerum Novarum* Leo declared, "Everyone should put his hand to the work that falls to his share, and that at once and straightway, lest the evil that is already so great become through delay absolutely beyond remedy." In a similar vein, toward the end of *Centesimus* John Paul asks everybody to take care of the business that they discern to be theirs. Throughout Christian history, people have had different vocations or callings. He refers to the early Christians who distributed their goods to the poor, and to those in religious vocations over the centuries who "devoted themselves to the needy and to those on the margins of society, convinced as they were that Christ's words 'as you did it to one of the least of these my brethren, you did it to me' were not intended to remain a pious wish, but were meant to become a concrete life commitment."

Centesimus proposes that every acting person, whatever his or her vocation, is called to a concrete life commitment. On the last day, the judgment will be adverbial, less attention being paid to what people did than how they did it. Christians hope so to live that they will hear the words of the Lord, "Well done thou good and faithful servant" (Matthew 25).

NOTES

1. For a blistering popular treatment of junk bonds and other high-risk speculation, see *Den of Thieves* by James B. Stewart, Simon and Schuster, 1991. Although debunked by many financial experts, the book was for many weeks at the top of the *New York Times* best-seller list.

2. Data on most Americans not caring very much about being rich are from the Gallup Organization, *Emerging Trends*, vol. 12, no. 9, February 1991. For further comment on this phenomenon, see "Numbers and the Numinous," *First Things*, April 1991.

3. George Gilder, *Microcosm: The Quantum Revolution in Economics and Technology*, Simon and Schuster, 1989.

4. On "dead-end" employment see, for instance, Lawrence M. Mead, *Beyond Entitlement: The Social Obligations of Citizenship*, Free Press, 1985. In thinking about unemployment, Mead urges, the relevant distinction today is between the "competent" and the "incompetent" unemployed. It is the latter, together with those who have voluntarily quit a job in order to look for a better one, who make up the great majority of people counted as unemployed in America today.

8

Christian Economics 101

Rocco Buttiglione

ON DOCTRINE VERSUS TEACHING

Christian social doctrine is not immediately the same as Christian social teaching. The doctrine is rather a specific, scientific elaboration of the teaching. It is developed when the application of the teaching to a changing and more and more complicated reality becomes problematic. The foundations of Christian social teaching lie in the gospel of Jesus Christ and in Christian anthropology. They are rooted therefore in the very trinitarian life of God and are not subject to change.

On the other hand in the doctrine there is not only this Christian anthropology (which is at the same time a philosophical and a theological anthropology), but also a relation to a more or less clearly defined historical and social situation.

Now this situation may change in time; some aspects which were in a certain time secondary and scarcely deserved to be mentioned, may with time become principal; others, which were decisive, may become less important. Our understanding of a situation, under the impulse of the very activity of Christians engaged in worldly affairs, may grow. For these reasons the doctrine may change while the *teaching* in itself does not change.

ON LIBERTY VERSUS *COMMUNIO*

John Paul II has revindicated recently the theological nature of Christian social doctrine. This means that the core of this doctrine is the human person, with her dignity and rights, with her specific structure, as she becomes known to us through

---

First published in *Crisis*, July-August 1992.

revelation, through the person of Jesus Christ. Jesus is an individual; He possesses an individual human substance. At the same time He lives for both communion with other men, and above all for communion with God. In this *communio*, mediated by His obedience to truth and to the Father, He accomplishes His destiny. As son of God and God Himself, Jesus continually receives His Being from the Father and exists as free gift of Himself to the Father.

Similarly, the destiny of all men, who accept regeneration through grace, is to participate in the inner life of God, through their incorporation into the Body of Christ, realized through a free act of self-giving to Christ through their brothers. All of this is of course Christian theology, and non-Christians are free not to believe it. Nevertheless they should not dismiss all of it as sheer nonsense. There is at least a part of it that makes perfectly good sense from a purely philosophical point of view. The concept of the person, originally developed in order to understand the relation of Christ to the Father and the intertrinitarian relations of the divine Persons, has also become a cornerstone of human philosophy. It seems that this concept, even if its root remains theological, can nevertheless be brought to evidence with the means of pure phenomenological philosophy. We may say that, philosophically considered, the person has two sides.

On the one hand, a person is an individual substance and like all individual substances aims at self-preservation. On the other hand, the person possesses a rational nature, that is, he can grasp the objective truth and the truth about the good. He is therefore called to realize his own specific good within this framework of the universal objective good and may even be free to sacrifice himself for the objective good. The person, indeed, realizes himself through the free gift of himself in truth and love.

To make a free gift of oneself one needs, first of all, the possession of oneself, that is, *liberty*. Only a free being can give his property, or his life, or himself. This is the reason why Christianity (all temptations of clericalism notwithstanding) is essentially a religion of freedom.

Freedom is not, however, the highest value, at least if we understand freedom exclusively as the faculty to choose between alternative options. The highest value is love or, rather, *communio* as the free encounter of individual liberties in love, or freedom accomplished and perfected in love.

ON PRIVATE PROPERTY

Man is, however, endowed with a human body, which not only belongs to him but is himself and enters into the essential constitution of his substantial being. The body can subsist only in a relation of organic exchange with nature and the environment. This relation is mediated by human labor. We work in order to live and to be able to satisfy our needs. It belongs to the teleology of work that we should possess the product of our work or its equivalent.

Our freedom implies the possibility to satisfy through our activity our basic needs. In order to be free we need a certain measure of control over our environment. In the language of law this control over ourselves and over our environment is called "property." Hegel once wrote that property is the external sphere of the realization of freedom, and whatever we may think of Hegel's philosophy in general, in this definition there is much truth. If we have no money in our pocket, our freedom to fly to Rome, or even just to take the bus, must remain unrealized.

A man completely dependent upon others lives every moment out of their grace, and therefore is not free. There is of course an interior dimension of freedom, which is quite independent of the exterior conditions of human existence. Man is, however, a being joining in himself an exterior and an interior dimension. Human freedom stands therefore as a rule at the junction of interior and exterior freedom, and these two dimensions of freedom in man condition each other so that, as a rule, one of them cannot develop itself or even subsist without the other. As we have seen, the exterior dimension of freedom is property. For these reasons property has always been seen by the Christian social doctrine as a natural right of man.

ON MARXISM AND COLLECTIVISM

The connection between personalistic philosophy, Christian religion, private property, and entrepreneurial spirit has been very clearly explained by Marx. In his *Economical-Philosophical Manuscripts* Marx explains that it is very difficult to erase from the consciousness of an empirical human being the idea of God, because the empirical subject always adopts as a starting point for his thought his own empirical existence. He is worried about the salvation of *his* soul, about the meaning of *his* life, about the origin of *his* being. He does not see things from the point of view of the Absolute in itself, or of the human essence as such.

This is the reason why religion does not seem to suffer very much under the attack of the Hegelian Left, for instance of Feuerbach. In his own existence as an individual every man finds the starting point of his search for God. My existence is particular and contingent; I do not find in myself the necessary foundation of my being; I am therefore compelled to admit of a similar ground for my existence outside of myself, and that is God. The necessity of this argument, and its evidence, derives from the fact that my *particular* existence is not existence in general.

Marx links this state of consciousness with a specific social and economical situation. Since he lives in a society in which he must take care of himself through his own work, applying his force to those instruments which belong to him, and since he is made responsible for the success of his work and for his own survival and that of his family, man is compelled to develop an individual consciousness. The real demonstration of the atheist thesis cannot therefore take place through theoretical argumentation. Only a drastic change in the economic structure can produce a new kind of man, who does not experience himself as individual but rather immediately as a collective universal being, because he has no property, does not exercise any individual responsibility, and his individual conscious existence has an immediately social character.

This thesis is of course directly linked to a general presupposition of Marx's system: the dependence of consciousness upon the forms of economic organization. The thesis maintains, however, a certain value, even if we reject its systematic foundation in Marx's thought.

Even if we refuse to agree that the forms of consciousness are dependent upon the forms of economic organization, we may still admit that the forms of economic organization can make the perception of a certain truth either easier or more difficult.

In our case it seems to be true that a collectivist system makes it more difficult for men to perceive the unicity and the special value and responsibility of their individual existence. In so far as the individual does not so clearly experience himself as "I," he does not so clearly experience the desire for a personal salvation or for a transcendent meaning of his existence. If it were possible to produce a completely collectivized man, he would have only a collective consciousness and no existential longing for personal salvation or for God.

Our thesis of an essential connection obtaining between free initiative and private property on the one hand and personal, religious consciousness on the other, seems to be confirmed by the testimony of Marx, even if, of course, our evaluation of this matter of fact opposes his. It is not difficult to show how Marx arrives at the idea of socialism starting from the research of a practical atheism. His collectivist political economy and his atheism cannot be separated from one another so easily as some left-wing Catholics suppose, because the abolition of private property is essentially connected to the idea of the abolition of the private person, that is, of the subject of a religious feeling and of the search for God.

ON ENTREPRENEURSHIP

One of the distinctive features of a free-market economy is that it presupposes free men. The main instrument of this economy is the contract, and the contract is an agreement of two free wills.

This situation does not obtain when there is too strong a disproportion between the two partners of the contract, as in the case of a monopoly. In this situation there is really no free market but rather a situation of slavery, and this is the situation denounced by Christian social doctrine in *Rerum Novarum*. In addition to this, the monopoly capitalism of the European continent at the end of the nineteenth century was to a large extent dominated by an anti-Catholic ideology, stressing not so much human freedom but rather technology and science. What was emphasized was the technical nature of economic activity, which is therefore exempt from any ethical or theological control. As a consequence, the teaching of the Church concentrates on distribution rather than on production, and underrates the ethical meaning of work as such (production) and of the entrepreneurial activity that spurs it.

This leads to some shortcomings of traditional Christian social doctrine, which have been exaggerated by her critics, but which do nonetheless exist. They can easily be explained by the general situation of the time in which this doctrine was formulated. In an agrarian society the fundamental force of production is the natural fertility of the soil, and this had been thought the main source of the riches of nations by the physiocrats. Just for this reason, they concentrated their attention on the forms of circulation of wealth rather than on its production. The situation did not change very much with the industrial revolution. With the industrial revolution, the cause of riches was seen in the steam engine, in the machine, or in "capital," understood as the whole of the material instruments of economic consideration. It was a matter pertaining to engineering, which applies to the productive process the knowledge of the natural sciences.

If we consider this background, it is easier for us to understand why the original formulation of Catholic social doctrine does not enter very deeply into the problem of the creation of wealth and has not very much to say, for instance, on the function of the entrepreneur. After all, this doctrine was formulated first of all in relation to European continental experience in Belgium, France, Germany, and Italy.

I do not mean that the Anglo-Saxon experience remains completely foreign to these developments. It should not be forgotten, however, that the Catholics in England were only a tiny minority. Meanwhile, in the United States their number began to grow only at the end of the nineteenth century, and a certain amount of time was needed before they could be completely integrated into American society and contribute to the formation of its ruling political, cultural, and economic élites. There is no reason to be surprised, then, if the capitalism which is mainly criticized in the first documents of Christian social doctrine is the monopoly capitalism of the European continental type.

ON CONSUMERISM AND LIBERTINISM

In affluent Western societies, it seems that a free economy goes hand in hand with the dissolution of the family and of traditional moral values and with a growing estrangement from Christian religion. This is the well-known phenomenon of "consumerism." We must now answer the question: Is consumerism necessarily and essentially connected with a free-market economy? If the alliance between the free market and libertinism is essentially necessary, then between the free society and the Catholic Church there must be an opposition in principle. On the other hand, if it can be shown that this alliance is due to particular circumstances and that it can be broken, then it is possible to substitute for the old connection of libertinism and free market a new connection of the free market and solidarity.

In considering this problem we must start from a turn in Western political culture in the 1960s. In this period the struggle against communism began not so much from the point of view of a Christian civilization but rather from that of a more coherent materialism. The capitalist system is more successful in satisfying material human needs and desires, it was said, and in this and exclusively in this consists its superiority to Marxism. This economic success makes moral virtues superfluous; society is not based anymore on a certain set of virtues but rather on the good functioning of the economic machinery and on the fact that individuals are satisfied in their private sphere, well-fed and well-clothed. The only public values generally acknowledged are vital values, the right to the satisfaction of instinctive drives and impulses. So capitalism is deemed to be superior to Marxism within materialism, because it is economically more effective. The idea of the person, in this context, becomes superfluous.

This new trend is closely linked to the myth of automation. The free-market society, as it is described for instance by Tocqueville, is a society of workers and producers. Their ethics is an ethics of work and production. Now it seems that new technical advances will make the old virtues of work and production superfluous. The automated machines—so it is supposed—will take up all work and leave to humans the task of consuming the goods so produced.

We have here the transition from a society of producers and of workers to a society of consumers. This has tremendous ideological and sociological consequences. A society of workers and producers stresses the virtues of self-control and self-discipline that are acquired within a family. A society of consumers does not need these virtues. As Herbert Marcuse put it, the new society can get along with a weaker ego and allow more scope for instinctive satisfaction and irresponsibility. The result comes very close to what Marx wanted: the abolition of the Christian subject and his replacement by a new mass-individual, whose drives and instincts, whose longing and desires are no more unified by a conscious responsible center in the person.

In the '60s the social analysts dreamed of an organized capitalism with a limited number of extremely large corporations that would have almost no internal competition, be faced with the problem of underproduction, and thus be ready to finance an expanding state expenditure in order to support the demand for their own goods and to avoid social tensions. In this context, a utopia could arise of a society without work or with a limited role for human work.

This same mentality, to some degree, can be found in today's so-called yuppies, or young urban professionals. Here an extremely competitive standpoint is combined with moral permissiveness. Self-discipline in one dimension of life is the condition for self-indulgence in the other. This implies an attitude which is conservative in economic matters and permissive in the educational and cultural field. But it seems that this mentality does not work. As a rule, one cannot stand the stress of struggle for life without the support of a family and of a well-established set of morals. The ethic of the free society is not marked only by competition. Cooperation is an equally important part of it. Cooperation requires rules that bring to a coincidence the interests of the individual and of the larger human group to which he belongs. Without cooperation and rules it becomes difficult to make a distinction between competition and criminal behavior.

ON THE JAPANESE EXAMPLE

Even those businessmen who like to act as uncompromising supporters of a business ethic that excludes any state intervention in the economy often ask for state support or restraints on competition in the face of fast-growing Japanese exports. The opinion is widely accepted that competition with the Japanese is impossible today and will also be impossible tomorrow without structural changes in our economies and in our societies. Why?

Japanese competition—says U. Agnelli—is not a competition of individuals or of corporations. It is a competition of systems. I would add: it is a cultural competition.

Japan has fostered a workers' and producers' mentality rather than a consumers' mentality. This does not mean of course that there has not been a tremendous increase in consumption. But the fundamental truth has never been forgotten that in order to consume one has to work. This is already a fundamental comparative advantage against societies where the consumer mentality has prevailed. The educational system educates men and women who will be responsible for themselves and who will work.

The second comparative advantage is that these citizens are not atomized individualists. They can cooperate with one another. They have families. They do not want to become rich tomorrow in order to indulge in a life of pleasures. Rather, they want to construct on a solid basis the future of their families and of their society. They know that if their individual success ruins their society, in the long run they will pay the price for it together with the others.

Extremely hard competition, then, does not contradict cooperation for a common interest. In Europe (and to a lesser degree also in the United States) a large part of the energy and creativity of the people has not been invested in the productive process, but rather in an attempt to overthrow it, or at least to defend against it the rights and the living conditions of the exploited masses. The entrepreneurial class did not succeed in winning the heartfelt cooperation of the workers—or even did not want this cooperation—and organized work in the factories on the principle of control from above, rather than on cooperation and shared responsibility. The right balance between competition and cooperation was not found. The result is a tremendous competitive disadvantage in relation to Japan, where the workers' organizations wanted to second and not to oppose the integration of the worker in the productive process.

I do not suggest that we should imitate Japan, and I do not consider Japan a perfect model. I do not underrate the present difficulties of the Japanese model, its flaws, the fact that it is not a fixed model but a work in progress whose evolution is not easy to foresee. I only want to attract attention to the fact that many presuppositions of the consumer society are shaken, that Japanese competition (and that of the Third World countries entering in the world market) will shake them even more in the future, that we need an ethic of work, connected with an ethic of the free person. The ethic of work and the alliance of competition and solidary are the factors that propelled the development of the United States and later on of all Western economics, and propitiated an alliance of religion and freedom.

ON *CENTESIMUS ANNUS*

I have tried to propose some elements of criticism of the conventional thesis that sees a natural alliance between libertinism and the free-market economy. I did this by offering a hypothesis on the historical genesis of this connection. I suggested that another alliance is possible, that of free market and solidarity. Just this alliance stands at the center of the Pope's new encyclical *Centesimus Annus*. In giving due attention to production and to the human virtues implied in productive action, this encyclical fills the gap between Christian social doctrine and modern economics. By pointing out the possibility of a new alliance between the free-market economy and solidarity, the same encyclical tries to influence future developments. This alliance is a possibility, not a necessity. It is possible to refuse it in the name of the "animal spirits" of capitalism, which do not accept limitation by an ethical, religious, or legal system. Those who refuse this alliance, however, forget that the free-market economy is not an omnipotent and self-sufficient natural force. It is an institution of the free society and can grow only in connection with a balanced growth also of the other institutions, which give to the free market the indispensable anthropological, political, and cultural preconditions. The economic sphere by itself cannot create these preconditions. Economics develops human rationality in our fundamental sphere of human life, in relation to one fundamental but particular good. The science concerned with the good of man as such is not economics but ethics. Without negating the legitimate autonomy of economical considerations, the last decision governing the whole system must be ethico-political. Not by chance according to Aristotle (but also according to Adam Smith), economics is a science subordinated to ethics.

9

How Christianity Changed Political Economy

Michael Novak

What did Jesus Christ add to Athens and Rome that altered the human conception of political economy? The question is a little odd to the ear. It is not a question usually asked. Yet it turns out to suggest, for all its novelty, a fresh way of looking at political history.

Permit me to propose for your consideration the following thesis: At least seven contributions made by Christian thinkers, meditating on the words and deeds of Jesus Christ, altered the vision of the good society proposed by the classical writers of Greece and Rome, and made certain modern expectations possible. Be warned that space is lacking to support each assertion with clinching argument. I present a horizon, a way of thinking to be explored, not an airtight argument in its defense.

It should also be noted that history does not proceed as logic. Many of the implications of the teaching of Jesus—especially the implications for politics, economics, and culture—were not immediately apparent, and some may still not be. Sometimes, as in the case of human rights and even democracy, attention is drawn to these implications not by logical deduction, but by the shocking impact of events arising from outside the Christian community. Catholic social thought proceeds dialectically, that is, by way of reflection on experience as well as logic, and by prudence much more than by logical deduction. Nonetheless, the yeast of Christ's teaching does work darkly in the dough of history even through crooked and contingent byways. Even the devil serves God's purposes.

Be warned, also, that I want to approach this subject in a way satisfying to honest secular thinkers. You shouldn't have to be a believer in Jesus Christ in order to grasp the plausibility of my argument. In fact, Richard Rorty, the self-described atheist

---

First published in *Crisis*, February 1995.

and nihilist, opened up this approach in criticizing the Platonism of the revered Czech philosopher and martyr Jan Patocka (1907–1977):

> Jerusalem should share the credit with Athens for making Europe what it has become. The Christian suggestion that we think of strangers primarily as fellow sufferers, rather than as fellow inquirers into Being, or as fellow carers for the soul, should have a larger role than Patocka gives it. The waves of joy of 1989 cannot plausibly be traced to the sense that judgment had been rendered on Socrates' judges, as opposed to the belief that a lot of people who had been humiliated and shamed would now be able to stand up and to speak. Separating out the roles of Socrates and Christ in the history of Europe is a notoriously tricky business, but surely Patocka oversimplifies things when, like Heidegger, he approvingly quotes Nietzsche's comment that "Christianity is Platonism for the people." Might not a sense that charity and kindness are the central virtues have caught on, and helped make Europe what it became, even if some eager Platonists had not grabbed control of Christian theology?

Analogously, in his book, *Why I Am Not a Christian*, Bertrand Russell concedes that, although he takes Jesus Christ to be no more than a humanistic moral prophet, modern progressivism is indebted to Christ for the ideal of compassion.

I. *The first contribution of Jesus was to bring Judaism to the Gentiles; and in at least three key respects, Judaism changed Mediterranean ideas about political economy.* First, from Jerusalem, that crossroads between three continents open to the East and West, North and South, Jesus brought recognition of the One God, the Creator.

Second, the term "Creator" implies a free person; it suggests that creation was a free act, an act that did not flow from necessity. It was an act of intelligence; the Creator knew what He was doing, and He willed it; that is, "He saw that it is good." From this notion of the One God/Creator, some practical corollaries for human action follow.

- Made in the image of God, we should be attentive and intelligent. *Inquire relentlessly.*
- As God loved us, so it is fitting for us to respond with love. Since in creating us He knew what He was doing and He willed it, we have every reason to trust His understanding and His will. Since He made us in His image, well ought we to say with Jefferson: "The God who gave us life gave us liberty." *Trust liberty.*
- At a certain moment, time was created by God, and given a direction toward "building up the Kingdom of God . . . on earth as in heaven." *Understand that history has a beginning, and an end—and that our vocation is progress, in both personal and social pilgrimmage.*

Third, then, following from this last point, as many scholars have noted the idea of "progress," like the idea of "creation," is not a Greek idea—nor is it Roman. The Greeks preferred notions of the necessary procession of the world from a First Principle. They viewed history as a cycle of endless return. The idea of history as a category distinct from nature is a Hebrew rather than a Greek idea.

What are the implications for political economy of the fact that history begins in the free act of the Creator, who made humans in His image, and who gave them with their first breath both existence and an impulse toward liberty and communion? In this act of creation, in any case, Jefferson properly located—and it was the sense of the American people—not only the origin of the inner core of human rights (" . . . and endowed by their Creator with certain inalienable rights . . ."), but also the perspective of providential history ("When in the course of human events . . ."). The early Americans were aware of creating something "new": a new world, a new order, a new science of politics, a new republic. As children of the Creator, they felt no taboo against originality; on the contrary, they thought it their vocation.

II. *The revelation that God is Three: Father, Son, and Holy Spirit.* When Jesus spoke of God, He spoke of the communion of three persons in one. Unlike the Greeks (Parmedides, Plato, Aristotle), who thought of God or the *Nous* as One living in solitary isolation, the Christian world was taught by Jesus to think of God as a communion of three. In other words, the mystery of community is one with the mystery of being.

Thus, the West wondered at the fact that we are part of a long procession of the human community in time; and that we are, by the grace of God, one with one another and with God. To exist is already something to marvel at; universal communion is even more so.

Recognition of the Trinity is not without significance for the relation between person and community, in political economy as well as in theology. (This is a point frequently made by Catholic writers, but admittedly little noted by Protestant or secular writers.) First, it establishes an ideal of community in which each person is separate, distinct, and independent, and yet one with others. Christians should not simply lose themselves in community, having their personality and independence merge into an undifferentiated mass movement. On the contrary, Christianity teaches us that in true community the distinct independence of each person is crucial.

The communal side of this point taught the West that persons reach their full development only in community with others. No matter how highly developed in himself or herself, a totally isolated person, cut-off from others, is regarded as something of a monster. Catholics, Jews, and socialists have emphasized this half of the truth. The personalistic side of this point taught the West that a community that refuses to recognize the personhood of individuals often uses them as means to "the common good," rather than treating persons as ends in themselves. Such communities are coercive and tyrannical. Protestants, Catholic personalists, and liberals have emphasized this half of the truth.

III. *The equality-uniqueness* (not *the equality-sameness*) *of the children of God.* In Plato's *Republic,* citizens were divided in this way: A few were of gold, a slightly larger body of silver, and the vast majority of lead. The last had the souls of slaves, and it was fitting that they be enslaved. Only persons of gold are truly to be treated as ends in themselves. For Judaism and Christianity, on the contrary, the God who made every single child gave worth and dignity to each of them, however weak or vulnerable. "What you do unto the least of these, you do unto me." God identified Himself with the most humble and most vulnerable.

Our Creator knows each of us by name, and understands our own individuality with a far greater clarity than we ourselves do; after all, He made us. Each of us reflects a small fragment of God's identity. If one of us is lost, the image of God intended to be reflected by that one is lost, and His image in the entire race is distorted.

Judaism and Christianity grant a fundamental equality in the sight of God to all humans, whatever their talents or station. This equality arises because God penetrates *below* any artificial rank, honor, or station that may on the surface differentiate one from another. He sees past those things. He sees *into* us. He sees us as we are in our uniqueness, and it is that uniqueness that He values. We may call this *equality-as-uniqueness*, not because we are *the same*, but because each of us is *different*.

This conception is quite different from the modern "progressive" or socialist conception of *equality-sameness*. The Christian notion is not a levelling notion. Neither does it delight in uniformity.

For most of its history, Christianity like Judaism flourished in hierarchical societies. While recognizing that all humans are equal in this: that each single person lives and moves under God's Judgment, Christianity has also rejoiced in the differences among us. God did not make us equal in talent, ability, calling, office, fortune, or graces.

Equality-uniqueness is not the same as equality-sameness. The first recognizes our claim to a unique identity and dignity. The second desires to take away what is unique and to submerge it in uniformity. Thus, modern movements such as Socialism have disfigured the original Christian impulse of equality. Like Christianity, modern Socialist movements reject the Platonic stratification of citizens into gold, silver, and lead. But their materialistic impulse led them to pull people down, to place all on the same level. This was an ugly program.

IV. *Compassion*. It is true that virtually all peoples have traditions of care for those in need. However, in most religious traditions, these movements of the heart are limited to one's own family, kin, or nation. In some ancient cultures, young males in particular were taught to be hard and insensitive to pain, so that they could be sufficiently cruel to enemies. Terror was the instrument intended to drive outsiders away from the territory of the tribe. In principle (though not always in practice), Christianity opposed this limitation by encouraging the impulse to reach out, especially to the most vulnerable, to the poor, the hungry, the wretched, those in prison, the hopeless, the sick, and others. It told humans to love their enemies. This is the "solidarity" whose necessity for modernity Rorty perceives.

In the name of compassion, Christianity tries to humble the mighty, and to prod the rich into concern for the poor. It does not turn the young male away from being a warrior, but it does teach him to model himself on Christ, in order to become a new type of male: The knight bound by a code of compassion, the gentleman. It teaches the warrior to be meek, humble, peaceable, kind, and generous. It introduces a new and fruitful tension between the warrior and the gentleman, between magnanimity and humility, between kindness and fierce ambition. Nietzsche falsely complained that Christianity brought about the feminization of the male. It did bring about the making of gentlemen.

V. *Universal community, incarnate (local) community.* Christianity has taught human beings that an underlying imperative of history is to bring about a law-like, peaceable community, among all people of good will on the entire earth. This was the impulse behind the Holy Roman Empire, however naively conceived that empire was. For political economy, Christianity proposed a new ideal: the entire human race is a universal family, created by the one same God, and urged to love that God.

Yet at the same time, Christianity (like Judaism before it) is also the religion of a particular kind of God: Not the Deist who looks down on all things from an olympian height but the God of one chosen people and, in Christianity's case, a God who became *incarnate*. The Christian God was carried in the womb of a single woman, among a particular people, at a precise intersection of time and space, and nourished in a local community then practically unknown to the rest of the peoples on this planet. Christianity is a religion of the concrete and the universal. It pays attention to the flesh, the particular, the concrete, and each single intersection of space and time; its God is the God of the "dapple-dawn-drawn" poems of Gerard Manley Hopkins, the "prudence" of St. Thomas Aquinas, and the respect for the *nationes* of the University of Paris. Its God is the God of singulars, the God who Himself became a singular man. At the same time, the Christian God is the Creator of all.

With Edmund Burke, Christianity sees the need for proper attention to every "little platoon" of society, to the immediate neighborhood, to family. At the same time, Christianity directs the attention of these little communities toward ever larger communities. Christianity forbids them to be merely parochial or xenophobic, but it also warns them against becoming premature universalists, one-worlders, gnostics pretending to be pure spirits detached from all the limits of concrete flesh. Christianity instructs us about the precarious balance between the concrete and the universal in our own nature. This is the mystery of catholicity. In this sense, Christianity goes beyond contemporary conceptions of "individualism" and "communitarianism."

VI. *"I am the Truth." The defense of intellect. Truth matters.* The Creator of all things has total insight into all things. He knows what He has created. This gives the weak and modest minds of human beings the vocation to use their minds relentlessly, in order to penetrate the hidden layers of intelligibility that God has written into His creation. Meditation on this theme over many centuries, Alfred North Whitehead suggested, prepared the ground for modern science. Everything in creation is in principle understandable: In fact, at every moment everything is understood by Him, who is eternal and therefore simultaneously present to all things. (In God there is no history, no past-present-future. In His insight into reality, all things are as if simultaneous.)

John Adams, our second president, wrote that in giving us a notion of God as the Source of all truth, and the Judge of all, the Hebrews laid before the human race the possibility of civilization. Before the undeceivable Judgment of God, the Light of Truth cannot be deflected by riches, wealth, or worldly power. Armed with this conviction, Jews and Christians are empowered to use their intellects and to search without fear into the causes of things, their relationships, their powers, and their purposes. This understanding of Truth makes humans free. For Christianity does not teach that Truth is an illusion based upon the opinions of those in power, or merely a rationalization of powerful interests in this world. Christianity is not deconstructionist, and it is certainly not totalitarian. Its commitment to Truth beyond human purposes is, in fact, a rebuke to all totalitarian schemes and all nihilist cynicism.

Moreover, by locating Truth (with a capital T) in God, totally beyond our poor powers to comprehend, Christianity empowers human reason. It does so by inviting us to use our heads as best we can, to discern the evidences that bring us as close to Truth as human beings can attain. It endows human beings with a vocation to give play to the unquenchable eros of the desire to understand—that most profoundly restless drive to know that teaches human beings their own finitude and yet, as well, their participation in the infinite.

The notion of Truth is crucial to civilization. As Thomas Aquinas held, civilization is constituted by conversation. Civilized persons persuade one another through argument. Barbarians club one another into submission. Civilization requires citizens to recognize that they do not possess the truth, but must be possessed by it, to the degree possible to them. Truth matters greatly. But Truth is greater than any one of us. Therefore, humans must learn such civilizing habits as being respectful and open to others, listening attentively, trying to see aspects of the Truth that they do not as yet see. Because the search for Truth is vital to each of us, humans must argue with each other, urge each other onward, point out deficiencies in one another's arguments, and open the way for greater participation in the Truth by every one of us.

In this respect, the search for Truth makes us not only humble but also civil. It teaches us *why* we hold that every single person has an inviolable dignity. Each is made in the image of the Creator to perform such noble acts as understanding, deliberating, choosing, loving. These noble activities of human beings cannot be repressed without repressing in them the Image of God. Such repression is doubly sinful. It violates the other person, and it is an offense against God.

One of the ironies of our present age is that the great philosophical carriers of the Enlightenment no longer believe in reason. They have surrendered their confidence in the vocation of Reason to cynics such as to the postmodernists and deconstructionists. Such philosophers (*Sophists,* Socrates called them) hold that there is no Truth, that all things are relative, and that the great realities of life are power and interest. So we have come to an ironic pass. The children of the Enlightenment have abandoned Reason, while those they have considered unenlightened and living in darkness, the people of Jewish and Christian faith, remain today Reason's best defenders. For believing Jews and Christians ground their confidence in reason in the Creator of all reason, and their confidence in understanding in the One who understands everything He made—and, besides, loves it.

There can be no civilization of reason (or of love) without faith in the vocation of reason.

VII. *Judgment/Resurrection.* Christianity teaches realistically not only the glories of human beings—their being made in the image of God—but also their sins, weaknesses, and evil tendencies. Judaism and Christianity are not utopian; they try to understand humans as they are, as God sees them both in their sins and in the graces that He grants them. This sharp awareness of human sinfulness was very important to the American founding.

Without ever using the term "original sin," the authors of *The Federalist* are eloquent about the flaws, weaknesses, and evils to which humans are prone. They designed a republic that would last, not only among saints, but also among sinners.

Christianity teaches that at every moment the God who made us is judging how well we make use of our liberty. And the first word of Christianity in this respect is: "Fear not. Be not afraid." For Christianity teaches that Truth is ordered to mercy. Truth is not, thank God, ordered first of all to justice. For if Truth were ordered to strict justice, not one of us would stand against the gale.

God is just, yes, but the most accurate name for Him is not justice, but mercy. (The Latin root of this word conveys the idea more clearly: *Misericordia* comes from *miseris + cor*—give one's heart to *les miserables*, the wretched ones.) This name of God, *Misericordia,* according to St. Thomas Aquinas, is God's most fitting name. Toward our misery, He opens His heart. "At the heart of Christianity lies the sinner," Charles Péguy wrote.

Judgment Day is the Truth on which civilization is grounded. No matter the currents of opinion in our time, or any time; no matter what the powers and principalities may say or do; no matter the solicitations pressing upon us by our families, friends, and larger culture; no matter what the pressures may be—we will still be under the Judgment of One Who is undeceivable, knows what is in us, and knows the movements of our souls more clearly than we know them ourselves. In His Light, we are called to bring a certain honesty into our own lives, and into our respect for the Light that God has imparted to every human being.

On this basis human beings may be said to have inalienable rights, and dignity, and infinite worth.

SUMMARY

These seven recognitions lie at the root of Jewish-Christian civilization, the one that is today evasively called "Western civilization." From them are derived our deepest notions of truth, liberty, community, person, conscience, equality, compassion, progress, and judgment. These are the most powerful energies working in our culture, as yeast works in dough, as a seed falling into the ground dies and becomes a spreading mustard tree.

10

The Love That Moves the Sun

Michael Novak

In one of the two greatest lines of world poetry, Dante bows gently toward "The Love that moves the sun and all the stars." Many moralists speak of love as the one fundamental and universal moral principle, the golden rule honored in all traditions. But what do we mean by love? In English we are hampered by having but one word for many kinds of loves. In Latin at least five different terms are available for five different loves.

The most general term is *amor*—the term that Dante used for the force that moves the sun and choreographs the stars in their millennial dance across the skies. *Amor* means pull, attraction, being driven together. One can use it of Earth's gravity, the passions that pull the sexes to cohabitate, and "the force that through the green grass drives" (e. e. cummings).

A more limited term is *affectus*—a term referring to those movements of our feelings that kindle within us admiration for our beloved and a desire to be with her, feelings of compatibility and comfort, feelings that tend to have a longer run than the hotter passions, and yield in daily life a quieter security.

The term *dilectio* introduces a more restricted notion still, that of a love born of deliberation and reflective choice; it comes from, but intensifies, the root *electo* (choose) and means a love of commitment: "You are the one I choose to love forever." That love can be relied upon, because it is deliberate; it follows from a weighing of the consequences. I am not swept off my feet. I mean it. It is the love on which friendship is built.

The term *amicitia* adds to *dilectio* the note of mutuality. If (perhaps as a teenager) you have ever loved anyone who did not reciprocate that love, you know the pain caused by the lack of mutuality. All the more, you appreciate the gift of love

---

Reprinted from *Crisis*, December 1995.

that someone freely makes when she returns the love you offer. Mutual love—*amicitia* (friendship)—is far more powerful than any love, save one.

That love is a special form of *amicitia*, but its origin does not lie in us. We would not dream of pretending to it. We would not know how. It exceeds our powers utterly. It is *caritas*. It is God's own love, the love that is the fire of his nature, that in him is so strong it generates another Person, and then their mutual love generates a third. *Caritas* is the inner action of the Trinity.

Now when we Christians speak of the Trinity, the inner being of our God, we know not whereof we speak. The point we seize upon, however, is that our God has spoken of himself in such a way that we are to imagine him—not as one in eternal solitude, as Plato, Aristotle, and many of the ancients imagined him, but rather as more like a community of love and friendship than like any other phenomenon of our experience. No one has seen God. Strictly, no one knows what he is like. Yet he himself points our minds in these directions: He is to be thought of as a Communion of Divine Persons—radiating his presence throughout creation, calling unworthy human beings to be his friends, and infusing into them his love so that they might love with it. *Caritas* is our participation in a way of loving not our own. It is our participation—partial, fitful, hesitant, imperfect—in his own loving.

We can even say, in a certain way of speaking, that our Creator's whole point in making the world was that some of his creatures should share in his love. The Love that moves the sun and all the stars is ours to give to others.

To make us able to share in his love, he had to make us capable of reflection, deliberation, choice, and commitment. He had to make us in his image. He had to make us provident of our own destiny, as he is provident. He had to make us free. Responsible, too. Capable of saying "no." And capable of evil.

WHY DID THE CREATOR CREATE?

It is a law of being that being is good, and that good is diffusive of itself. You can see this when you hear a good joke and can hardly wait to tell it to others; or when you surmise, by the happiness and generosity she is suddenly showing to others, that your usually uncommunicative teenage daughter has fallen in love.

Thus, we may surmise that when God thought to create the world, he could not quite show us the fullness of his loving merely by creating the world in its splendor and goodness, although he did that. He also had to show us a special characteristic of his love, one that St. Thomas Aquinas called the most divine characteristic of his being, His mercy. That is, God had to make us capable of evil, so that in our wretchedness he could show us the power of a love that sees it quite realistically, but wipes it away and gives us to share in his own power of loving. Mercy—*misericordia*=*miseribus* + *cor*—God gives his heart to the miserable ones, even when they have turned against him. His is, in Dostoyevsky's favorite term, "humble charity," the most powerful force in the universe.

Not only in the glory of creation—these mountains, this lake, this great night sky of the Alps—and not only in his *misericordia* did God share with us insight into the special characteristics of his love, but also in sending us a human model of it in sending us his Son, who called us his friends, and sacrificed his life for us. Divine love is as glorious as a summer day high in the Alps; it is merciful and makes our sins, though they be as scarlet, vanish into insignificance, replacing them with his own action in us; it is, finally, self-sacrificial unto death, for it seeks not its own. It is in being lost that it is found. It is in dying that it gains life.

In short, love is no simple thing. It is not what we might at first think it is. We spend a lifetime being instructed in its secrets. It is shallow enough for ants to walk safely across, deep enough for elephants to drown in. Saints of great soul endure many torments being inflamed by it.

In this vast cosmos, such as science knows it, we humans (even as an entire race, from beginning to end) are barely a speck in silent space, unimportant, less enduring than galaxies and stars—less so even than many plants, insects, and viruses—here today like the grass of the field, tomorrow gone. Yet for us in our unimportance God wished to show what he is made of, to let us look behind the veil at the Love that moves the sun and all the stars, and to draw us into acts of *caritas*.

CARITAS AS REALISM

One thing should perhaps be stressed about *caritas*. It is realistic. To love is to will the good of the other as other. To will, not what you wish for the other, nor what the other wishes, but the *real* good—which neither of you may yet recognize. Love is not sentimental, nor restful in illusions, but watchful, alert, and ready to follow evidence. It seeks the real as lungs crave air.

If we try, then, to imagine a civilization based upon *caritas*, we must be careful to think realistically. For *caritas* shows itself as mercy to sinners, and it is love aimed at the real, not the apparent, good of the other. One almost infallible sign of the presence of *caritas* is the steady experience of realistic judgment. Love based upon appearances, illusions, and sentimentality is the opposite of *caritas*. A civilization of *caritas* is a civilization acutely aware of, and provident for, human sinfulness.

The first step in such providence is to differentiate the three fundamental human systems, thus separating the three great human powers: economic, political, and cultural. Since every person sometimes sins, we wish to prevent any one person (or group) from coming into possession of all three powers. The point of differentiation into three is to check the errant ambition, each of the orders.

Put another way, the point of differentiation is to bring about three liberations. The first is liberation from torture and tyranny through civil and political liberties. The second is liberty from poverty and want through economic liberties. The third—and most basic—is liberty of the human spirit, through religious liberty, liberty of the press, the liberties of inquiry in the arts and sciences, and the free exercise of the moral authority of conscience.

Liberty of spirit is fundamental, since the free society is founded on respect for truth—specifically, upon openness to the light of evidence. If it were based merely upon opinion (unhinged from evidence), or upon relativism, the free society would have no footing on which to stand against raw power. Truth is its defense against wealth and power. One word of truth has more power than all the wealth of earth and all the armies of the world together. The dignity of the powerless and the vulnerable is rooted in truth. This is why our forebears said: "The truth shall make you free."

CARITAS: ECONOMICS FOR SINNERS

In the civilization of *caritas*, what sort of economic system must there be? (Let us set aside for another time consideration of the political system and the moral system.)

First of all, such an economic system must be aimed at liberating all the poor of the earth from the prison of poverty. This implies that it must have an international vision and international institutions and also that it must have a theory and practice of development—that is, of wealth creation of universal reach. In short, it must be an economic system better at raising up the poor of the world—and more quickly—than any known alternative.

Second, it must have institutions that rest upon, and nourish, voluntary cooperation. Such cooperation will manifest *caritas* only to the extent that it wells up from below, and is not coerced from the top down. A maximum of worldwide coordination (possibly even instantaneous) based upon a minimum of control from above will be one sign of its good functioning. It will exhibit a sort of universal solidarity, married to the healthy practice of subsidiarity. Most of its decisions, initiatives, and energies will originate in vital local communities.

Third, an economy of *caritas* will respect the human person as the originating source of human action, the *imago Dei, homo creator*, the chief cause of the wealth of nations. It will, accordingly, afford constitutional protection (or the equivalent, among the rights tacitly retained by the people) to the fundamental human right to personal initiative, including economic initiative. For the state without due process to repress that right is a grave offense against human rights, a disfigurement of the image of God in humans, and a serious step in social retardation.

Fourth, the economy of *caritas* must provide the necessary (but not sufficient) cause for the polity of *caritas*, whose best approximation in history so far is democracy under the rule of law. It must help conspicuously to defeat envy, the greatest of the social sins (worse even than hatred, because more often invisible, and itself one of the causes of hatred). It must also help to divide the material interests of people, so as to help prevent democracy from degenerating into a tyranny of the majority (its abiding deformation).

Fifth, the economy of *caritas* must take realistic precautions against the besetting economic sins of all eras and times, but particularly its own. For example, in order to promote innovation and openness to creativity, it needs to avoid concentrations of economic power. It checks monopolies by promoting peaceable competition.

Sixth, the economy of *caritas* must be based upon the presupposition that humans often fail in love, and only rare ones among them base all their actions thoroughly upon realistic love. *Caritas* is the ideal in whose light economic practices are judged, and it is the magnetic lode drawing ever more actions to itself. In all realism, the institutions of this world must presuppose mercy and forgiveness, not the expectation of perfect love. To ask too much of human beings is not fair to them; it is to fall short of *caritas*. For this reason, Charles Péguy wrote, at the heart of Christianity is the sinner. *Caritas* is the light that attracts all things to itself, from whose brilliance all of us sometimes turn away. That is what sin is. For the economics of *caritas*, therefore, the perfect must not be allowed to become the enemy of the good. The economics of *caritas* is realistic, not utopian.

HELPING THE POOR

Democracy, Winston Churchill once said, is a poor form of government, except when compared to all the others. Much the same might be said of capitalism. Especially in Europe, capitalism is a term supposed to be spoken with faint—or not so faint—moral disapproval. It is what all are supposed to be opposed to, not only Marxists, who spent more than a century vilifying (and misdefining) the term, but also humanists, poets, playwrights, churchmen, journalists, and all sensitive spirits. In Britain, even more than half the Tories appear to be opposed to it. European conservatives tend to dislike it as much as socialists. Such universal disapprobation is often a good sign. It is typically from among the rejected and despised things of men that God chooses to draw humble good.

My friend Irving Kristol writes of *Two Cheers for Capitalism*. That may be excessive. One cheer is quite enough. The other economic systems known to history have done far worse. Especially for the poor.

What do I mean by capitalism? It is not a term accurately defined by (a) private property, (b) market exchange, and (c) private accumulation or profits. That is the way Marx defined it, and that definition applies to virtually every economic system in history, even in biblical times. It is not sufficient to distinguish capitalism from the precapitalist systems that prevailed everywhere until the end of the eighteenth century and still prevail in most of what is called "the third world." Max Weber, R. H. Tawney, and many others noted that something *new* entered the economic world some time after the Protestant Reformation. (*Post hoc*, of course, is not *propter hoc*.)

What is new about capitalism is that it is the first mind-centered system. It is the system constituted by social institutions that support human creativity, invention, discovery, enterprise. In this new economy, the most important form of capital is not land, as it was in feudal times (that is, most of human history); nor the cold instruments of production referred to as "capital goods"; nor even financial assets. The most important form of capital is human capital. The best resource a country has is its own people. The human person is the chief cause of the wealth of nations, deploying human skill, knowledge, know-how, inventiveness, and enterprise.

In Poland, for example, capitalism did not begin when in 1990 the socialist planning board was abolished and market exchange began; or when private property rights were again respected in law; or when private profit was again regarded as a social good. All these were insufficient. Capitalism was born in Poland when the Polish people began looking around to *see* what needed doing, and began to *do* it. Capitalism only begins with *acting persons*. Its constitutive act is the activation of the habit (virtue) of enterprise—the act of discovering and doing what must be done—an act of creativity, innovation, and invention.

The moral principles that inspire capitalism, therefore, are three: creativity, community, and personal initiative. Capitalism is first of all a fruit of the human spirit. It depends upon, and nourishes, a special (and demanding) moral ethos. The formerly socialist countries are discovering how high and how difficult its moral standards are. (It depends, for example, on the rule of law and on respect for the free voluntary consent of persons. In nations where law does not rule and persons are treated as means or obstacles, capitalism withers.)

The most distinctive invention of capitalism is not the lonely individual, as is often charged, but social: the stock association, the business corporation (independent of the state and transgenerational, potentially international), the social market itself, practices of teamwork, brainstorming, and consensus building, and voluntary cooperation. The capitalist vision was the fist to imagine the possibility (and moral imperative) of lifting every single person on earth out of poverty, to set the goal of universal economic development, and to bring about the embourgeoisement of the poor.

In the U.K. during the nineteenth century, standards of living for the working class rose by 1,600 percent. Poor vision began to be treated with eyeglasses, dental care began to be supplied. As late as 1832, the poor of France were described by Victor Hugo as *Les Miserables*; in 1789, Jefferson had written that a majority in France lived in conditions worse than American slaves. In 1800, only duchesses had access to silk stockings; by 1900, nearly all women in France did. By 1900, the poor were drinking coffee and tea, to which before they had no access, and meat was replacing bread as the chief staple. Famines, common before on a regular basis, disappeared. Decade by decade, new discoveries in medicine and hygiene kept extending human longevity. (This is the real cause of the "population explosion.")

Concomitant with the rise of the middle class came a marked decline in alcoholism, crime, and births out of wedlock. In the U.K., France, and the United States, such indices hit all-time lows about 1850, where they remained with amazing steadiness through the 1930s. *Post hoc* is not *propter hoc*, but with the decline of personal responsibility and the rise of the welfare state, such indices have now formed a remarkable U-curve, except that new heights are being reached in all of them.

After some 150 years of distortion about the actual record of capitalism, and correcting for the failure of economists to analyze the moral springs of capitalism—its inner ethos and internal ideals and necessary standards—we need today to grasp this system's great internal moral possibilities. The vast majority of Christians in the world today, as well as those of other religions, find their calling within this system. It is crucial for moral progress to diagnose this system's moral origins and inner dynamism accurately, rather than lazily to accept its systematic denigration by its hostile critics, on the right as on the left. Traditionalists hate it because it is not aristocratic; socialists hate it as the *bête noire* they use to terrify themselves.

Space is limited, yet I want to mention two indications that the critics of capitalism have missed its essence. One of these concerns the poor, the other democracy under the rule of law.

The first empirical test about the nature of capitalism you might wish to employ is to watch the poor of the world. To which systems do they migrate? Which do they line up by the millions to enter—Third World, precapitalist economies? Socialist economies? Or the relatively few truly capitalist economies, which trust, respect, and support the capacity of human persons to be creative? The facts speak for themselves.

In the United States today, for example, 99.9 percent of us derive from families that came to the United States in utter poverty—the "wretched refuse" of the earth, as the poem on the Statue of Liberty said of our grandparents. By official statistics, 13 percent of Americans are poor today—many of them immigrants of the last few years who will not long remain poor, and measured by a standard that counts as poor families with cash income (*not* income in kind, from welfare benefits, for example) up to about $15,000 for a family of four. By this standard, some 87 percent of Americans who started poor have already moved out of poverty, and 13 percent have still to do so. For the poor, capitalism has no rival in offering the opportunity to move out of poverty in a very short time. The poor show by the millions that they know this.

The second empirical test is to examine which economic system is present in every successful democracy in the world. (I mean genuine democracies, which respect the rights of individuals and minorities, live under the rule of law, have separated powers and limited government. These are to be distinguished from fraudulent pretenders to the title such as Colonel Qaddafi's Popular Democratic Republic, the "Democratic Republics" of the old USSR, etc.) The sociologist Peter Berger, against his own earlier predilections, has shown in *The Capitalist Revolution* that among all existing nations capitalism is a necessary (but not sufficient) condition for democracy. A free political system appears to require a free economic system. For example, respect for the initiative and responsibility of the person is common to both, as is a preference for voluntary cooperation, teamwork, and self-guiding coordination.

A civilization of *caritas* is not based on sentimentality, but on checks and balances and other remedies for human weakness. It is one of today's most urgent tasks that people of good will continue to explore the ways in which capitalism serves this function in working democracies.

Part III
DEMOCRACY AND THE FREE SOCIETY

11

Christianity and Democracy (Part I)
Some Remarks on the Political History of Religion, or, on the Religious History of Modern Politics

Pierre Manent

Whoever compares the relations that obtain today between democracy and Christianity, particularly the Catholic Church, with what they were during the greater part of their common history, has the feeling that each one of the two protagonists has ceased to resemble itself, that it has become wholly other than it was. Democracy consents to the presence in its bosom of a numerous mass of believers. With the exception of a very small number of "rationalists" without an audience, it no longer plans "to destroy the infamous thing" (i.e., Christianity); and the famous proclamation of Viviani today sounds like an amusing curiosity from the Belle Époque: "Together, and with a magnificent gesture, we have extinguished in heaven stars which will never again be relit."

The change accomplished, or suffered, by the Catholic Church, however, is even more striking. The Cardinal Archbishop of Paris, and the Holy Father himself, ask Christians to discover in their religion the true, although long-hidden source, of the most precious good which is at the heart of modern democracy: the rights of man. The Catholic Church today celebrates the sacred character of religious liberty, of the liberty of conscience that it formerly denounced with thunderous indignation. In the encyclical *Mirari Vos* (15 August 1832) directed against Lamennais, Gregory XVI speaks of this "very fecund cause of the evils that today so deplorably afflict the Church, to wit indifferentism, the vicious opinion which, by the perversity of the wicked, gains credit everywhere and according to which the salvation of the soul can be obtained by whatsoever profession of faith, provided that morals conform to the rule of the just and the honorable . . . and from this poisoned source of indifferentism has come the false and absurd opinion, or rather delirium, according to which the liberty of conscience of each ought to be affirmed and defended." As late as the

---

First published in *Crisis*, January 1995. Translated by Daniel J. Mahoney and Paul Seaton.

beginning of this century, Saint Pius X, in the encyclical *Vehementer Nos* (11 February 1906) addressed to the people and clergy of France, condemned the separation of the Church and state as "supreme injustice" done to God, and also as contrary to natural right and to the law of nations, contrary to the fidelity due to oaths, contrary finally to the divine constitution and the liberty of the Church.

What happened? How are we to understand so complete a change of appreciation on the part of the supreme heads of an institution which loves to underscore the centuries-old, even, millenary, immutability of its thoughts and words? Must one follow the historians who, in order to explain past conflicts, are prone to invoke an enormous "misunderstanding" bound to "historical circumstances," follow them into the still doubtful combat in which the parties are drawn irresistibly beyond the natural and reasonable limits of their opinions? Before concluding in such an irenic manner one at least must determine the intellectual content of the debate, that is, the motives advanced by the Church when she condemned the principal propositions of modern politics. If the Church initially, and for so long, declared herself against democracy, it is because she had the sentiment, or rather the conviction, that the modern democratic movement was directed fundamentally against her, that is, against the true religion and thus against the true God. It is impossible even to enter into the great subject of the relations between democracy and the Church if we do not first clarify this central fact.

THE MODERN MOVEMENT OR THE EMANCIPATION OF THE WILL

The movement of the Enlightenment, the vector of modern politics, had for its goal, and result, the establishment of the lay, liberal state, "without opinion," particularly without religious opinion—of what was called "the neutral and agnostic state." The dominant Catholic opinion was that this agnosticism of the state was in fact state agnosticism, and that this state agnosticism was in fact a state atheism. In this judgment the Roman magisterium itself joined the Catholic writers of the so-called "reactionary" school such as de Maistre and de Bonald who were so influential at the beginning of the nineteenth century.

What is true in the Catholic affirmation that the liberal state is not neutral, or "agnostic," but rather atheist? It is the fact that the liberal state, in its first project, or primary purpose, wants to institutionalize the sovereignty of the human will. Recognizing only free and equal individuals, it has no legitimacy except that founded on their will: the institutions of this state have for their raison d'être the manifesting of this will through suffrage, then the putting of this will into action by a representative government.

Such a project certainly does not affirm, with "the foolish" of Scripture, that "there is no God." Not only does it say nothing about God, but it says nothing, or very little, about the world, and even about man. However, by positing that the political body has for its only rule or law the will of the individuals who compose it, it deprives the law of God of all political authority or validity, whether the latter is conceived as explicitly revealed, or solely inscribed in the nature of man. It refuses all authority to that which has by definition, naturally or supernaturally, the highest authority. The man of the Enlightenment implies, or presupposes, that there is no God, or that He is unconcerned with men, since he rejects, or at most considers as "private," as optional, obedience to the law of God.

One might add: if there is a God, the human will cannot be "autonomous," or "sovereign"; to affirm this "autonomy" or "sovereignty," is to deny the existence of God.

Certainly, the atheism of presupposition or of implication is too exactly the atheism of affirmation, or atheism simply. Few men truly know what they think and what they want, and many will be liable to affirm simultaneously the divine law and human sovereignty; as was often said at the time of the second Vatican Council, many will believe "in God and in man." But one does not judge a political and spiritual situation according to the idea of it that the least enlightened members of the community make for themselves. Moreover, the intention, and to speak truly, the anti-religious passion, of the great men who in the seventeenth and eighteenth century elaborated these new doctrines, was clearly enough avowed. The Church therefore judged in its wisdom, let us say from 1791 to 1907, from the brief *Quod Aliquantum* condemning the Civil Constitution of the Clergy to the encyclical *Pascendi* reproving modernism, that the modern political and intellectual movement *willed* the eradication of the true religion.

Keeping in view the motives behind the original conflict, we foresee also the motives behind the later reconciliation. After all, this insurrection, this revolt of the human will—to continue to speak the language of the Church of the nineteenth century—by the effect of its progress and its triumph, is going to transform itself into institutions, habits, sentiments—into "human things" where human nature and the divine law necessarily will find, in some form, their place. After all, if God exists, the human nature created by Him, that even without the support of the secular arm retains awareness of the exigencies of His law, will inhabit and humanize, that is, Christianize, the state created by the sovereign or human will in its revolt. Whatever the successes of the "Revolution," the moment of some "restoration" always comes. Even if we admit that the modern will essentially revolted against God, God is necessarily stronger than it, and this means that the nature of man is stronger than the human will. Hence, at the end of some generations, the satanic pride of the Enlightenment, duly humbled by reality, gives way to the firm resolution to organize a rational society full of solicitude for human needs and where the Church can live, speak, and exercise her influence: our society. The Church, which has concern for men, cannot curse such a society.

Things did happen in this manner to a certain extent, but only to a certain extent. The will of the Enlightenment, humiliated by democratic reality, by bourgeois prose, revolted against the bourgeois democratic society which it took to be a humiliation. The revolutionary spirit, the spirit of sovereignty, revolted in the form of socialism and communism against its first incarnation. The Church, to be sure, explicitly condemned these revolts, at least in the case of communism. They acted on her, however, in two contrary senses. These demonic revolts encouraged her to reconcile herself with the very democracy that the revolutionaries wanted once again to overturn, and with which she henceforth shared responsibility for the things that are. But they also confirmed her hostility to modern democracy, which appeared to engender endlessly ever more radical revolts against the Church. It is in this way, precisely as a fatal sequence, that the encyclical *Quanta Cura* (8 December 1864) condemned as a single ideological and political series: Naturalism (we would say: liberalism), Socialism, Communism.

The historical landscape would be clear if we did not have to take account of a third possibility. Certain quarters of Catholic opinion agreed with socialism and communism in their hostility to democracy, which as Catholics they had learned to detest. And while some reconciled with democracy in order to confront the communist threat, others were favorable to communism out of hatred for democracy. This last reaction was particularly observable during the twenty years that followed the Second Vatican Council, which, moreover, quite curiously did not renew the condemnation of communism. In this manner were realized all the possible theological-political dispositions or arrangements subsequent to the French Revolution.

Perhaps one will grant such a summary presentation a certain plausibility. But, it will be said, it is too dependent not only on the point of view of the Church but also, less excusably, on the most immoderate of Catholic rhetoric. What is this "demonic" will to institutionalize the sovereignty of the human will, to substitute the latter for the law of God or for the finalities, aptitudes, and necessities of the nature of man? Is not this a way of speaking which is perhaps acceptable in the heart of a bitter conflict of vast import, but incapable of establishing an historical explanation? I believe on the contrary that we have here the guiding thread of the correct explanation; if not that, we have at least an exact description.

Three massive facts must here be taken into consideration. First, the history of modern philosophy, from Machiavelli to Nietzsche, appears as oriented to and animated by the elaboration of the concept of will. Next, the intellectual center of modern democracy is constituted by the notion of the rational will, elaborated, at the center of this history, by Rousseau, Kant, and Hegel. Finally, the first and decisive affirmations of the will, of man as will, were conceived and formulated in an explicitly polemical relation with the ecclesiastical institution and the Catholic understanding of the world—to which one can add, as culmination and superfluous proof, that Nietzsche at the end of this spiritual history, joined the unlimited affirmation of the human will to the unlimited polemic against Christianity. It is difficult to find in human history a closer representative linkage.

Let us look first at the third point. The modern project to establish political legitimacy on the will of the human individual has been led to its completion. It has been transformed into the institutions, mores, and sentiments of our democracy. This reality satisfies us, and we no long perceive the extraordinary audacity of the original project of establishing the human world on the narrow point of the human will. A fact however must help us experience the astonishment indispensable for understanding. This invention was neither necessary, nor even probable. The *proof* is that one can describe very well the human world, particularly political existence, that one can conceive and institutionalize very well political liberty, without having recourse at all to the notion of the free individual endowed with a sovereign will.

Aristotle's *Politics* gives a description and analysis of political life which in a certain way is exhaustive—in any case more complete and subtle than any subsequent description or analysis. The bringing to light of the elements of the city, the critical and impartial analysis of the claims of the different parties, the exploration of the problem of justice, of the relations between liberty, nature, and law: the phenomenology of political life is presented without either prejudice or lacuna. Whoever wants to orient himself in the political world, either for the sake of action or understanding, finds in Aristotle's *Politics* a complete teaching. It is therefore the case that only a historical *accident* could have obliged us to dismiss Aristotle, and given us a reason to invent the notion of the sovereign will.

According to Aristotle, every human association has for its end a certain good; and every human action is done in view of a certain good. Therefore, when Aristotle studies the elements which constitute the city, he only encounters groups and "goods," each group defining itself by the type of good it seeks and can attain, and on which it ordinarily bases its claims for power. At no time does the individual with his will appear: Aristotle does not even have a word to name him (more exactly, the sovereign individual will). The landscape is reversed with the founders of modern politics. Henceforth only one element enters into the composition of the legitimate city, the one for which Aristotle did not even have a word, the sovereign individual. Next to the *Politics*, the book of the ancient city, let us put the *Social Contract*, the book of modern democracy. Not only does Rousseau say very different things from those that Aristotle says, not only does he contradict him frequently, but quite strikingly the tone, the movement, the very principle of the thought are wholly different: something has happened that places thought under an unprecedented law of attraction, or repulsion.

The Aristotelian analysis of human action and association had been received and formally ratified by the Catholic Church. In the eyes of the latter, however, a new community has appeared, among those of which the human world is constituted: the Church herself—*vera perfectaque respublica*, or *societas*, the perfect republic, or society, because its object, its raison d'être, its end, even its Author, is the perfect Being, the Sovereign Good, God Himself. Henceforth a supernatural community, the Church, was added to the natural communities. Its dignity necessarily was incomparably superior to theirs, as eternal salvation and eternity are incomparably more important than temporal well-being and time. Assuredly, this posed some problems.

Aristotle had envisaged the case of a man, or a group, whose virtue was incomparably superior to that of the rest of the political body. He concluded that one must either give him total power, or ostracize him. And medieval Europe, in its relation to the Church, oscillated between these two positions. In accord with the first line of reasoning, the "plentitude of power"—not only spiritual but also temporal—was granted to the Church, and she claimed it for herself. In accord with the second, she was excluded completely from temporal power. The human world was constituted as though it was closed upon itself and self-sufficient, under the sole power of the emperor. This is what Dante and Marsilius of Padua wanted. In this way Aristotle was of no help in resolving the new theological-political problem: certainly it cannot be said that one is in a position to resolve a problem when the principle of the solution can engender two strictly contradictory solutions with equal plausibility or legitimacy; when the premises, that is, imply two contradictory conclusions. An accident that Aristotle had not foreseen, and could not have foreseen, obliged western man to renounce Aristotle's philosophy.

In order to have a chance of finding a solution, it was necessary to make oneself independent both of nature and of the accident which is not natural—what Marsilius of Padua calls "this cause [that] neither Aristotle nor any other philosopher of his time or before him could have observed," this "miraculous effect produced a long time after Aristotle's time by the Supreme Cause beyond the possibilities of inferior nature and of the habitual action of the causes found in things." It was necessary to sever oneself from the complexity of groups and goods, both natural and supernatural, to decompose human sociability, both natural and supernatural, and then to finally reconstruct the political body from the element which survives at the end of this effort of abstraction: the free individual. The new political body, neither natural like the city nor supernatural like the Church, is created by human will in order to effect what it wants.

The movement of modernity is structured by the stages of the will's emancipation. However, even as philosophy properly speaking pursued the radicalization of this notion, one can see throughout the nineteenth century in the order of action and of political theory, beginning from a certain date, a contrary movement, or a counter-movement. The French Revolution is the moment when the movement of Enlightenment (we can also say: "liberalism") experienced fright at the results of its action. It became fearful especially before the notion of the sovereignty, or the will, of the people. The latter had become a terrible reality as a result of the action of the French revolutionary Convention. According to the quite striking formulation of Benjamin Constant: "There are weights too heavy for the hands of men." While as a consequence of the aggressively antireligious action of the Revolution the Catholic Church in the nineteenth century was going to clarify and harden its opposition to the political movement of modernity, a part of that movement, the part properly liberal, was willing to join with, if not always the Church, at least Christianity, or with "religion" in general. It is at the moment of, and as the result of, the French Revolution—and with reference to the problem of the will—that the partisan arrangements with which we have lived so long were determined.

On the right, the conservatives, or reactionaries, reacting expressly to the Revolution, reject the will; they see in the exercise of it and in the affirmation of its free exercise, the source of all disorder. Man is only worthy in his position as heir or inheritor. It is by inheritance, or in the attitude of the heir, that man receives the most precious goods of which he is capable. Such is Burke's conviction, determined from the first moment of the revolutionary tempest. With some, reaction goes so far that they are led to maintain two extreme and perfectly contradictory positions, precisely on the problem of the will. Joseph de Maistre affirms on the one hand that nothing of what man expressly has willed can be good, that good can only come to him from what he has not willed. Simultaneously, he posits the necessary existence of a sovereign will to hold together society—and, one can assume, in order to repress the efforts of revolutionary wills—in short, a sovereign will that has the task of repressing the rebellious human will. On the left, on the side of the revolutionaries, later the socialists and the communists, they continued to affirm the human will. They even promised themselves "next time" not to let it be captured by "Thermidor."

It is in the center that the intellectual situation is the most complex and interesting: as I just noted, the liberals are caught between their doctrinal heritage and their new fear in the face of the revolutionary event, which their doctrines had perhaps caused, or in any case had accompanied and facilitated. It is then that religion finds again, or rather finds, since it had never before truly appeared in this light, its specifically modern political and moral credibility. What had been its defect becomes its merit. It is now praised for the very reason it was formerly and even recently criticized: it is something *above* the human will. Evoking the Convention's attack on the Church, Constant writes, with gratitude and approval: "The smallest saint, in the most obscure hamlet, resisted successfully against the entire national authority drawn in battle against him." Quite a remarkable affirmation on the part of this anticleric who, by birth, education, and conviction belongs to the eighteenth century, and whose Huguenot ancestors—like the soldiers of the revolutionary army in 1793—used hammers to flatten saints' images on the facade of churches, even those found "in the most obscure hamlet." However, it is to Tocqueville that we must turn for the most precise analysis of the difficulties and contractions of the new political and religious situation.

12

Christianity and Democracy (Part II)
Some Remarks on the Political History of Religion,
or, on the Religious History of Modern Politics

Pierre Manent

DEMOCRACY AND RELIGION ACCORDING TO TOCQUEVILLE

Tocqueville, like most liberals of the nineteenth century, has the feeling that there was something artificial and violent, artificially violent, if it can be put that way, in the hostility that the eighteenth century exhibited towards Christianity and the Church. It is necessary to return to a more "natural" situation: "It is by a kind of intellectual aberration, and assisted by a sort of moral violence exercised on their own nature, that men distance themselves from religious beliefs: an invincible penchant leads them back to them. Unbelief is an accident: faith alone is the permanent state of mankind." Tocqueville does not concern himself to justify such considerable propositions, but their political import is clear. If religion has its anchor or support in nature, it can do without the support of political institutions. Therefore, the dismantlement of the Old Regime, and even the separation of Church and state, contrary to what most French Catholics think, are not at all contrary to the interests of religion. Better yet—and here we have one of the principal assertions of his argument and of postrevolutionary liberalism in general—it is by being separated from the political order that religion can best exert its political beneficence: "Religion which, among the Americans, never mixes itself directly in the government of society, must therefore be considered as the first of their political institutions; for, if it does not give them the taste for liberty, it singularly facilitates for them its use."

How does religion so singularly facilitate the use of liberty? The answer lies with the relationship that religion has with the will.

Modern democracy—this theme is the guiding line of my exposition—is founded on the emancipation of the will. This emancipation, leading to the idea of a total

First published in *Crisis*, February 1995.

liberty of man to decide his destiny, has two opposite but equally disastrous consequences. The first is fear before this unlimited liberty. Under the empire of this fear, the modern individual is tempted to renounce this liberty, this sovereignty of the will that modern democracy proposes to him, and presents to him as legitimate and even as sacred. "There are weights too heavy for the hands of men . . ." Not only does he recoil before this new liberty, but he even risks abandoning his former liberties: "When there no longer exists any authority in religious matters, as well as political affairs, men soon are quite frightened at the sight of this independence without any limits. The perpetual agitation of all things renders them anxious and exhausts them. Since everything is in motion in the intellectual order, they desire that at least in the material order everything should be firm and stable. And, no longer able to accept their former beliefs, they give themselves a master." Paradoxically, the emancipation of the will in this way can move men to consent more easily to despotism, because of the intellectual and moral uncertainty in which they are obliged to live.

But it has another consequence which is basically its opposite, and which is perhaps more natural. Instead of giving rise to fear, it can give men the desire to exercise this will in all its new amplitude. Democratic man spontaneously has the feeling that the human will, in the form of the will of the people, has the right to will everything and anything; it willingly approves that "impious maxim" that "in the interest of society all is permitted." Thus modern democracy gives rise to a new passivity and a new activism. These two contrary consequences of the new liberty together and equally foment a new despotism.

Now religion, by determining and fixing the moral order, by putting order in the soul, renders less pressing the democratic desire for "material" order, all the while, to be sure, rejecting the impiety that "all is permitted." "At the same time that the law allows the American people to do everything, religion stops it from conceiving of everything and forbids it from trying to do everything." Simultaneously tempering the new activism and the new passivity, religion helps democratic man to keep his balance. The coin, however, has another side.

In the United States, religion is separated from the state, from the political order; but it has a power of influence and opinion in society. It exhibits therefore the disadvantages inseparable from all power of opinion, in particular that of hampering liberty. Tocqueville goes so far as to write: "The Inquisition never was able to inhibit the circulation in Spain, in large number, of books contrary to religion. The rule of the majority does even better in the United States: it has taken away even the thought of publishing such books." Even in the United States religion does not escape from the fatality of power: it no longer has political power, no longer is a state religion, but it has become a "social" power, a "social religion," if one may put it that way. And it appears from Tocqueville's acknowledgment that "liberty" has not gained in the process.

We find ourselves, then, before a strange contradiction. Tocqueville seems to be suggesting that religion in the United States singularly facilitates the use of liberty by singularly diminishing the quantity of liberty. This in fact is his thought, but we must immediately state it more exactly: Religion in the United States singularly facilitates the use of political liberty by singularly diminishing the extent of intellectual liberty. So put, there is no contradiction. We understand easily in fact that the dangers of political liberty are decisively limited when—contrary to what happens, alas, in Europe—citizens do not entertain "revolutionary ideas" concerning man and the world, but rather are content with ideas transmitted by the religious tradition for the essentials of their moral life.

In truth, however, this social power of religion is more a social power than a religious power. The shocking comparison with the Spain of the Inquisition runs the risk of leading us into an error: there is no question here of religious fanaticism. Americans themselves basically share Tocqueville's analysis; the latter only reproduces for us the awareness that Americans have of themselves. Religion is a part of their social habits: it is in this light that they are attached to it. It is a matter then of conformism and not fanaticism. Tocqueville writes: "It is also in this light [that of utility] that the inhabitants of the United States themselves consider religious beliefs. I do not know if all Americans believe their religion, for who can fathom the depths of hearts? But I am sure that they consider it necessary for the maintenance of republican institutions. This opinion is held, not by a class of citizens or a party, but by the entire nation; it is found among all ranks."

To be sure, we are left with a great difficulty. How can religion be truly useful if it is viewed by the faithful from the point of view of utility? Certainly the utilitarian conception of religion is as old as politics, but it assumes at Rome, according to Machiavelli, for example, the class difference between an unbelieving patriciate and believing, even superstitious, plebs. But is it possible for this difference to pass into the interior of the soul of each citizen, so that each American should be simultaneously the unbelieving patrician and the sincere plebeian? This is what Tocqueville assumes. This, obviously, is inconceivable, unless the American citizen allows what he truly believes and what he truly thinks to fall into a propitious penumbra. Such a social and religious situation presupposes as one of its necessary conditions a general absence of intellectual rigor.

Tocqueville, we recall, claimed that religious belief is inscribed in the nature of man, that therefore it did not need the support of the state, and that contrary to what French Catholics and even the Church herself thought, a separation of Church and state is both desirable and possible. But what happens to this fundamental assertion if it appears that men thought to believe "naturally" in fact believe "socially"? The religion of Americans is founded in principle on the rigorous—because natural—separation of faith and politics; it appears in fact, however, as the most political of religions. The separation of religion and the state produces a confusion of religion and society. If political liberty benefits as a result, religion loses in sincerity, and intellectual life loses in clarity and honesty. One sees that the very reasons Tocqueville advances to justify and promote the *rapprochement* between the old religion and modern democracy also provide motives for the refusal, so long maintained, by the Roman Catholic Church to lend itself to this reconciliation.

The most important lesson we can and must draw from this examination of the Tocquevillian analysis is to bid farewell definitively to the opinion, advanced and refuted by Tocqueville, that there is a "natural," hence apolitical, state of religion. Now we are in a position to envisage the political history of Christianity in an impartial fashion, as a succession of theological-political arrangements, of solutions to the theological-political problem, no one of which can claim to close that history, on the ground that it would be, finally, "conformed to the nature of things" or "conformed to reason." The solutions are linked not because history is increasingly more rational, but because each solution always ends by revealing itself to be as unsatisfactory as the one which it succeeded. I would like to try to sketch the history of these solutions.

A BRIEF POLITICAL HISTORY OF RELIGION

Let us begin by considering the first theological-political solution, the medieval one. The Church is the true republic, the perfect society, the association par excellence in which man finds his ultimate end. All other associations have, so to speak, an ontologically inferior rank. They are therefore logically and "naturally" subordinated to the perfect association which in the person of its head holds the plenitude of authority or power (*plenitudo potestatis*). This plenitude of power can be conceived as being direct or indirect in character. The direct plenitude is hardly practicable, and, moreover, it is contrary to the divine commandment which enjoins the disciples of Christ to leave to Caesar the things that are Caesar's. Creation in itself is good, human nature capable of tolerably organizing the earthly city by the means of reason alone, as the pagan politics and philosophy of Greece and Rome evidence. One can envisage seriously only an indirect authority which leaves a subordinate but very large place for autonomous politics, for the Empire. From this, however, is unleashed a permanent division and uncertainty since two loyalties necessarily share the heart of each Christian. Moreover one of the two great protagonists, the Empire, does not succeed in fulfilling its idea with even a minimum of plausibility. Another solution must be found.

The second solution is that of the absolute national monarchy. Each King wants to be, and acts as if he were, "emperor in his Kingdom." A plurality of perfect republics emerge, the national monarchies, whose members, first of all their heads, have religious opinions: they are either Catholic or Protestant. The perfect Christian republic, the seamless cloth, which, to be sure, never had existed as such but whose notion had had such a power over the minds of men, henceforth was dismembered. Earlier, one had in an inchoate way Christendom; in its place now there are Christian state religions.

The new historical compromise is the following: religion remains a command, but this command is essentially administered by the temporal sovereign: *cujus regio eius religio*. That which motivates the adoption of this system, however, is also what renders it intrinsically untenable, because contradictory. A lay or profane human will declares *ex officio* and obliges his subjects to recognize that the state religion is superior to every human will. In the case of absolutism the prince simultaneously is superior and inferior to the Church that he enthrones. This introduces certain uncomfortable paradoxes such as was already the case with Queen Elizabeth I of England who, although Head of the Anglican Church, is doubly incapable—both as a lay person and female—of distributing the sacraments, i.e., of performing the acts that constitute the life of the Church. This specific form of the difficulty, or contradiction, characterizes in each case the national history.

The national monarchy was intended to overcome the medieval duality of the priesthood and the emperor, "to reunite the two heads of the eagle," to bring it about that Christian subjects ceased "to see double." On the contrary, the identity of the body-politic was disturbed at the same time as the identity of the theological-political head, the prince, was ever more divided: ever more absolute, and thus "more superior" to the Church, but in order to be more Christian. This escalation obviously could not continue indefinitely.

The most interesting case in this context is undoubtedly Louis XIV; the revocation of the Edict of Nantes simultaneously reveals the sublimity and the precariousness of his position. Certainly the monarch's faith was its first cause, but the revocation was more a monarchical than a Catholic act. The monarch who is now proclaimed as the new Constantine or Theodosus has been for some years close to schism with the Papacy. In addition, Innocent XI will let it be known that the Revocation pleases him little. This episode contributed to the contrary movement of the English Glorious Revolution; it rendered complete and definitive the opposition of enlightened European opinion to the system of absolutism. The sovereign of the age of absolutism proved his sovereignty by giving religious commands. By more and more subordinating religion to himself, he increasingly weakened the rationale and vigor of his sovereignty. Another solution then must be sought.

One can distinguish three ways of leaving absolutism. The English solution is entirely unique. It is a simultaneously caricatural and weakened absolutism, which doubtlessly is why it is called "liberal." At the time of the Glorious Revolution and the subsequent Act of Settlement, the English aristocracy imposed upon the King and the people a state religion, or rather, perhaps, a national religion. This religion guaranteed that England would not return to Catholicism and that it also would not espouse too ardent a version of Protestantism. The force of the state was put behind the weakest religion. I say the weakest religion because, of all the versions of Christianity that divided and still divide Europe, the only one that strictly speaking is "unbelievable" is Anglicanism, unless one admits—according to the epigram of Joseph de Maistre—that God became man for the English exclusively. Clearly this version left dissatisfied what remained of the Catholics, as well as the fervent Protestants. The latter readily had recourse to the American solution.

The English Protestants dissatisfied with the state religion since the beginning of the 1620s had acquired the habit of emigrating far from the Old World and of founding in the New World self-governing communities which were homogenous in matters of religion, the townships of Puritan New England. Puritanism is characterized by a certain confusion of religion and politics. Tocqueville observes: "Puritanism was not only a religious doctrine; it merged on several points with the most complete democratic and republican theories." While absolutism tended, without being able to succeed, toward the exclusive affirmation of political command, while religious commands became the material, the occasion, or the pretext, Puritanism, fleeing absolutism, recognized as legitimate only religious commands. In Protestantism, however, the entire community was alone empowered to make these commands observed. This arrangement is remarkably ambiguous. If, in American Puritanism, religion regulates all the details of social and even personal life, it does so in a special way. This religious power or authority is exercised "democratically" by all the members of the body on each one, and by each one on all. Thus, one can describe this power, not as that of religion over society, but as that which society exercises over itself by means of religion. This equivocation and indetermination contains the subsequent history of America.

Each day there are occasions when society governs itself, when democracy is at work for reasons other than the putting into practice of religious commands. Americans progressively experience that their society is securing its hold on itself, that it acts on and by itself. It remains sincerely religious but religious commands, which, at the beginning constituted the entirety of life, occupy a more and more restrained place. No one wants to abandon them, and they still are held to be respectable, and useful. But the center of gravity of social life is henceforth elsewhere: democracy, understood as the working of society upon itself, becomes self-sufficient. At this point, religion can be completely separated from politics—the situation observed and appreciated by Tocqueville, and which I commented on above.

Now, what happens in continental Europe during this same period? Absolutism, because of the contradiction I underlined, exasperates and hampers the search for an absolute sovereignty of the political order over the religious. It was this search which gave to the movement of continental Enlightenment its political wedge. After the expulsion of the Jesuits—which was heavy with political significance—this movement will culminate in the Civil Constitution of the Clergy. With the latter, a theological-political cycle is closed. The Nation is born; it takes upon itself the attributes of the Church; thus it is the *vera perfectaque respublica* found at last. To be sure, the Nation-form did not put an end to political-religious conflicts. On the contrary, it stirred up new ones, the first, and greatest, as a result of the Civil Constitution of the Clergy. Let us think also of the *Kulturkampf* in Bismarckian Germany, of Combism and the expulsion of the religious congregations from France.

But beyond its properly political power the Nation exercises such a spiritual power that it succeeds in being—much more so than the national monarchies—both Empire and Church. It is the Nation, even when anticlerical, which more than the Most Christian King "reunites the two heads of the eagle."

In August 1914, French Catholics, including Jesuits, rushed forward to die with joy for the France whose republican regime a few years before had rather wickedly persecuted them. The Nation inspired throughout Europe sacrifices that no King and no Church had ever obtained.

From the nineteenth century onward, moreover, in each country historians and philosophers saw in the construction and development of nations, particularly of their own nation, the meaning or sense of European history. In this way *the* theological-political problem no longer appeared except as enveloped in a national context. It was more of a French or German problem than a universal problem, *the* theological-political problem. The Nation truly was the human association par excellence, the sole true *respublica*. But there were several nations in Europe, and August 1914 marks the beginning of the end of the nation. The wars of the twentieth century have worn away the charm of the sacredness of the nation. And in Europe today, the nation, which triumphed over the Church as a perfect republic, is now in the process of taking a back seat in turn.

We are, therefore, at the end of a cycle. The situation seems rather satisfactory in western Europe; at least it is peaceful. The protagonists are weak and tired. The Church has been completely domesticated by the nation; the nation, for its part, is exhausted. Its effacement is inscribed in the dual development whose irresistibility is underscored by authoritative voices: on the one hand, the massive immigration of non-Christian populations; on the other, the construction of a so-called supranational Europe. The instrument and the framework for the solution to the West's theological-political problem, this Nation-form which for so long appeared as the ultimate political and spiritual horizon, no longer owns the future. Because of this, one can conjecture that there will be a resurrection of the theological-political problem in an unprecedented form. To be sure, the legitimacy of democracy is self-evident today throughout Europe, and the "privatization" of religion, largely accomplished, has suppressed almost all occasions of conflict. However, since the context for the exercise of democracy, i.e., the nation, is on its way out, the problem of the definition of a new framework will swiftly become a problem of the first order. Democracy—understood as the autonomy of individuals and groups—hardly suffices, in fact, to define the public space. Religion is necessarily interested in the increasingly urgent problem of the "self-definition" of Europe.

On the other hand, at the end of this cycle, uncertainty also attaches to religion. The quite visible diminution of religious practice should not lead us to the dogmatic conclusion that this tendency is destined to continue indefinitely. Bossuet perfectly formulated one of the two reasons for our uncertainty on this point: "Religious sentiments are the last thing to be effaced in man, and the last that man consults. . . ."

Whatever the future holds, we can at least try to analyze more precisely the present situation.

THE PRESENT SITUATION

What defines the Church as an agent in the human world, as a "spiritual body," is that she bears a specific, proper thought or doctrine: she says *something* about man. She thereby, as Tocqueville noted, limits the arbitrariness of the democratic will, of democratic sovereignty, by reminding the latter that man cannot do whatever he wills. At the same time, the Church's thought or doctrine contains commands, which is its nature, indeed its duty to want to have respected. The Church necessarily tends, therefore, to usurp the role of the solitary instance of legitimate command in democracy, the government.

It is said that this problem has been resolved precisely by the separation of Church and state, the sole viable solution to the theological-political problem. In reality, however, it is when one considers the question of government, or of command, that one sees how much separation—far from being a stable situation which leaves the two protagonists intact—is an endless process which implies the growing and indefinite domestication of the Church.

The political, juridical, and moral foundation of separation is that religion is a *private matter*. Now this idea—polemically decisive in the process of the disestablishment of the Church—is much less consistent than is generally thought. It claims to say that I have the right to observe or not to observe Easter, as I have the right to end my meal with cheese or dessert: *Privatsache*. The decisive question is avoided: Does or does not the Church have the right to command me? The liberal, and seemingly reasonable response, will be: yes, if you have consented beforehand to its command; no, if not. So be it—but then the question arises, how are the seeking out and obtaining of this consent organized and institutionalized? One cannot speak of consent as if it were a given existing by itself, and simply available or not. It only appears by means of an institution which manifests it, and sometimes produces it. How can the Church make individuals agree with her commands? What facilities does she have, what obstacles does she encounter, when obtaining it? After all, an elected democratic government, founded in principle on consent, requires the obedience even of those who did not vote for it, even if they hate it as Voltaire hated the Church. Does the Church have the right to avail herself of consent of this sort? In short, the separation of Church and state, of the private and the public, is founded on an essential inequality of consents, which gives a decisive advantage to the public institution over the private one. The inequality of the consents demanded or required translates into the essential superiority of the state over the Church in the regime of separation.

In this extremely disadvantageous situation, the Church, the religious institution, basically has the choice of two ways of proceeding. She can accept literally the "regime of separation," and give the appearance of believing in the *Privatsache*. Down this path, she then seeks to govern men as much as she can within the context of the limits permitted her by the regime of separation. This is pretty much what the Catholic Church attempted to do in France between the "rally" to the Republic and the Second Vatican Council. However, to govern is to govern. To govern in civil society is *not so* different from governing in the state. Because the reality of governing undermines the constitutive convention of the regime of separation, the Church's conduct is very difficult. It is difficult practically, because the state is necessarily hostile, or at least not terribly sympathetic. It is difficult morally, because the Church must now play a role that is structurally hypocritical. She can only fully play her role in civil society by exercising "governing energy," which gives her a quasi, or parapolitical role—in truth, a political role—a role which she must necessarily deny. I am tempted to say that it is only when she accepts it grudgingly that the Church can play well the exclusively private role conceded to her under the regime of separation. This situation is so uncomfortable, and exposed to so many inconveniences, that the Church embraces with relief the second way of proceeding, the one followed for the most part by the postconciliar Church. She no longer presents herself as the most necessary and most salutary *government*, doing her best in a political situation contrary to the good of souls. She becomes simply the *critic* of all governments, including that which was for centuries the government of the Church. She becomes the collective "beautiful soul," presenting herself to men as "the bearer of ideals and values." An "ideal," or "value," in contrast to a law, cannot be commanded, but is left solely to the free initiative, and "creativity" of each individual—because man is the "creator of values." The Church escapes from the discomfort of its political situation by substantially transforming the character of her message. For the past generation, the churches propose "Christian values," which, unlike the old Decalogue and also unlike democratic law, are impossible either to obey or to disobey. The Church repeats, in a more emphatic way, what democracy says about itself. Under the rubric of "values," it is hopeless to make "the gospel message" listened to, or at least heard, except by engaging in humanitarian and egalitarian overbidding. Assuming, along with Tocqueville, that democracy needs a brake or restraint to facilitate the good use of liberty, religion, once arriving at the truly "ideal" state, certainly cannot provide it. It simply accompanies democracy as much in its reasonable as in its foolish conduct.

 After this long survey, must we therefore conclude that the first, strongly negative reactions of the Church confronted by democracy were basically well founded? Must we say that after two centuries of an often confused and conflicted history, democracy as the institutionalization of human sovereignty seems to have completely subjected the Christian Churches, and even the long resistant Catholic Church? This conclusion would be rash. As I indicated while considering the destiny of the nation, the foundation of modern democracy—human sovereignty—is not the immediate author of the framework or written code by which it exercises itself. It cannot be so. Whether it busies itself within the framework of the city, the kingdom, the empire, or even the whole Earth, it does not immediately make decisions by itself: determination is not contained in the principles of democracy.

The political momentum, primarily territorial, of democracy is essentially indeterminate. It depends upon historical inheritance, on the action of great men without a mandate, and on simple chance. The actualization of human sovereignty simultaneously manifests human impotence and ignorance, the disproportion between wills democratically registered and the sum of wills. Democracy appears then as a partial and contingent agent, quite brilliantly illuminated, but severed from the fabric of all humanity. For the latter includes the dead, the living, and those yet to be born. This complete Humanity, without a possible political expression but out of which democracy necessarily operates, where can it be found? In which ledgers does it write itself? That of Nature? But it is precisely modern humanity that desires to be the sovereign over nature, creator of its own nature. By affirming its indeterminate sovereignty over itself, democratic humanity basically declares that it wills itself, without knowing itself.

Yesterday's Church denounced, and with indignation, the impiety of this will. Today's Church, or its most astute representatives, make known with a benevolence tinged with irony, the import of this lack of self-knowledge.

Thus, the political submission of the Church to democracy is, perhaps, finally, a fortunate one. The Church willy-nilly conformed herself to all of democracy's demands. Democracy no longer, in good faith, has any essential reproach to make against the Church. From now on it can hear the question the Church poses, the question which it alone poses, the question *Quid sit homo*—What is man? But democracy neither wants to nor can respond to this question in any manner or form. On democracy's side of the scale, we are left with political sovereignty and dialectical impotence. On the Church's side, we are left with political submission and dialectical advantage. The relation unleashed by the Enlightenment is today reversed. No one knows what will happen when democracy and the Church become aware of this reversal.

13

The Church Embraces Democracy

Alain Besançon

We have entered into a new time in which democracy has become the sole legitimate regime. Alternatives to democracy either offer nothing better or suffer from utopian aspirations. This means that the Catholic Church at this moment is leaving one political epoch and entering into another.

Long ago, the Church left the Constantinian political context which the Roman Empire and its successors, the old monarchical regimes of Europe, provided for it. The Church had formally accepted this context. She saw in it the natural political form within which she was to carry out her various missions. It was natural because the human city, while inclined towards evil, nonetheless recognized God as Lord, and accepted that the emperor or king received his power—*potestas*—from the Lord. It also affirmed that the human law guided itself in theory by the principles of the natural law, and that the natural law modeled itself structurally on the eternal law.

Within this assumed context, the Church was as happy as one can be with one's family, that is to say, not very happy. The innumerable conflicts between the Church and the State, however, remained exactly that, family quarrels, and did not create a fundamental insecurity. As a member of a family, the Church had to make itself recognized. It had to acquire a status. In the East, she developed the rather suffocating theory of "symphony." In the West she developed the more quarrelsome and separatist theory of the "two swords." By its means, she could assure for good, or evil, her liberty as a body and her mission of salvation. Across a thousand often dramatic conflicts, and a thousand often shameful compromises, "the ship continued."

The Church, however, also passed through this intermediate period of which there still remain many consequences. The long period which extends from the ruin of

---

Translated from *La Pensée Politique* (#2, 1994) by Paul Seaton and Daniel J. Mahoney. First published in *Crisis*, September 1995.

the old regime to the definitive establishment of the new regime is that of democracy. The period lasted at least four centuries: the seventeenth century witnesses the preparation and accomplishment of the English Revolution; the eighteenth and nineteenth the French Revolution; the nineteenth and twentieth the German, Spanish, East European revolutions and, finally, the still ongoing Russian Revolution.

All these different routes end at the same point—democracy. We know its principles: all legitimacy is founded on individual or collective consent; men enjoy equal rights; law is sovereign; the state is the representative instrument of a society distinct from it. An artificial mechanism is put in place so that the conflicts between men may be resolved by observing the rules of the game.

The intellectual fathers of the new system—Machiavelli, Hobbes, Locke, Montesquieu, Rousseau—agreed that the Church was the principal obstacle blocking the arrival of the new regime. The Church therefore was attacked both for its dogma and its place in the city. The first battle was quickly won. From the end of the seventeenth century almost the entirety of the intellectual elite no longer felt themselves bound by the dogmatic teaching of the Church. The second battle was more difficult, and we cannot here trace its history. But through all the democratic revolutions, be they by violent means (as happened in France several times), or by imperceptible ones, the Church in practice was expelled from the State. After so many centuries this was such a cruel defeat that it is only recently, one could say only in my generation, that the Catholic Church has taken stock and has resigned itself to the new situation.

THE UTOPIAS OF THE CHURCH

Thus the Church is in the process of leaving a period of its intellectual life which corresponded to these intermediate centuries, and which was marked by utopias of its own.

The first utopia is simply reactionary: it is the hope of a return to the *Ancien Régime* and a head-to-head struggle against the democratic attack. This utopia was not dogmatically affirmed by the Magisterium, which has never affirmed that the Church was bound to any particular political system. But since the Church underwent the full brunt of the struggle for the new regime, she found herself thrown back on the old regime in which she reclaimed her old habits and, one hesitates to add, her home. In France, in Spain, in Italy, throughout the nineteenth century, she found herself in the party of resistance. This, moreover, was not necessarily a utopian mistake, except to the extent to which the Church, effectively attacked from all sides, underestimated the irresistible force of the democratic process and missed several occasions to make peace with the new order. In this way the French episcopate sabotaged the "rally" to the republic proposed by Leo XIII, and the papacy took some time in coming to an agreement with the Italian State (to the great despair of Cavour) on the status of Rome.

A second series of utopias was born of the search for alternative solutions to representative democracy. In fact, during this age-old transition from the old to the new regime, some transitory political forms appeared which, on the one hand, were opposed to representative democracy and suspended certain political liberties, but, on the other hand, favored economic development, social egalitarianism, and the destruction of ancient elites. In this way, they worked toward the establishment of the equality of conditions, an important page of the democratic program. Among what could be termed antidemocratic democratizations, we should cite Napoleon III, Mussolini, Franco, Pilsudski, and even Pétain.

These political formations sought the support of the Church. For its part, the Church had no reasons to refuse the negotiated accord, which could culminate in the Concordat. She fell into utopia only when she considered these movements a stable solution to the political problem, and a better solution than democracy because they were more organic, less individualistic, more protective of the poor, capable of eliminating class struggle, while attaining harmony in the social body. When all that proved illusory and the democratic process took new force, the Church found itself compromised with the losers. She was included in the malediction which struck them.

The third series of utopias, much more dangerous for the Church because with them she was not only compromised but tempted, developed in contact with the socialist idea. They can be enumerated in the chronological order of its principal elements.

- The underlying theme of the entire episode is the old millenarian heresy, seen in medieval Joachimism, revived by Romanticism, which dreamt of a perfect society, regulated by love and not by law, by gift and not exchange, with the absolute sharing of goods and the disappearance of conditions.
- This deception was provoked by those conservatives nostalgic for the *Ancien Régime* and those merely looking for a reactionary stance towards what was new. Among conservative clerics and laymen, this deception provoked a mutation into and a leap toward the revolutionary hope of the left. The prototype of these transformations is Felicité de Lamennais. An entire posterity will imitate him, sometimes beyond progressivism, but always irreconcilable without bourgeois democracy and a free market economy.
- The tremendous impact of Marxist-Leninism, with its almost age-old duration, its worldwide extent, its intensity, cannot be analyzed in a few words. In many respects Marxism was a perverse imitation of Christianity, and represented one of the most mortal attacks in its history. The Catholic Magisterium quickly sized it up, as witnessed in the encyclicals and attitudes of Pius XI and Pius XII. But after the death of Pius XII, because of circumstances of war which had weakened the moral position of the Church, the effect of the irresistible terror which discouraged even calling the enemy by his name, the Christians living under communist domination, and, finally, because of the infiltration of communist

ideas into the clergy, the Magisterium kept a silence for which the Church without doubt will have to pay the price.

Benefitting from this silence, three utopias were able to develop. The first was the attempt to baptize communism, by admitting its vision of the world and adding to it a dose of spiritualism and idealism of a Christian tint. This was characteristic of progressivism and, later, liberation theology.

The second was the search for a third way between the real alternatives. This is the most utopian of the utopias. One begins by admitting that the socialist utopia exists, that is, that there exists a *socialist society*. Then one accepts the Leninist definition of our society as *capitalist*. Finally, one imaginatively places oneself outside of this double reality which is already imaginary.

The third utopia is *apoliticism*. However, since it continues in the new state in which the Church is entering, it should be treated in the next section of exposition—the Church in the context of an uncontested and incontestable democracy.

THE STRATEGY OF BABEL

Since 1946 the Church has decided in favor of democracy. Despite all the consequences and wounds of former times, this line has been confirmed and is no longer seriously contested within the Church herself. However, does this suggest that in addition the Church has converted, or ought, or can convert to the democratic ideal? Nothing is less certain.

Relative to the Church's mission, which is to conduct human beings to eternal salvation, the new regime does not enjoy any superiority vis-à-vis the old. The democratic principle asserts that the citizen obeys himself when it comes to interests and preferences he himself defines. In this sense, the democratic ideal is inferior to that of the ancient cities and monarchical regimes which did not, in principle, lose sight of the education of the citizen in virtue nor the search for a common good transcending individual interest. The prevalence of the human will over the divine will, the acceptance of a divide between the civil law, natural law, and eternal law have no reason to elicit the enthusiastic adherence of the Church.

More exactly, the democratic regime in principle discredits the idea of truth, of an absolute truth, revealed and then transmitted by the Church's tradition. This is inscribed in the foundation of the first and most exemplary of modern democracies, the United States.

Many Americans crossed the Atlantic in order to gain shelter from religious conflict: English dissidents, Dutch Arminians, German Lutheran antipietists, French Huguenots, and Jews. When they thought of establishing a free government, the American constitutionalists evidently thought of how to establish the right of religious liberty. They sought an "artificial" mechanism to forestall religious conflict and persecution. Madison's solution was to multiply rights and the subjects of rights, that is, to assimilate religious convictions to the multiplicity of interests. "In a free government the security for civil rights must be the same as that for religious rights. It consists in the one case in the multiplicity of sects. The degree of security in both cases will depend on the number of interests and sects."

Madison's point of view is doubtless connected with the idea of tolerance as it had been developed by Locke and the Anglo-French Enlightenment. But it also contains a trace of biblical influence. American Calvinism retained, against the optimism of the European Enlightenment, the consciousness of original sin. Madison did not seek to render man good, nor did he count on his goodness. He knew man's corruption and, thus, deployed what I will call the strategy of Babel. Following the Eternal, who had dispersed men so that they could not unite in the project of a fatally bad goal, Madison dispersed citizens into innumerable interest groups and religious denominations, in order to render them incapable of building the totalitarian city, of persecuting and oppressing one another, which would happen if a denomination became powerful enough to impose its will politically. Since men, because of original sin, see their most sublime enterprises (and especially those) turn to disaster and to crime, let us divide them so that they will only be capable of partial and localized evils. Since the government of the United States is to abstain forever from legislating in religious matters, the denominations fragmented and as numerous as possible (the more, the better), see withdrawn the power of the State, the instrument par excellence of their malignant will. The strategy of Babel marvelously attains its goal. The different denominations were able to disdain, to hate, to compete with one another. They never were able to enter into warfare nor seriously oppress each other. What is the situation today, after two centuries of living under this strategy?

The different religious groups found things with which to be satisfied in the generalized *apartheid*. Tranquil, sheltered from one another, they have organized and prospered. God, introduced afterwards in the redaction of the Constitution, is today the object of a devotion and reverence more sincere and widespread than in most European countries. This God presides over a sort of child's garden of religions, a vast playpen in which all the denominations can play together, without harming each other, under the gentle surveillance of constitutional rule. Since no one can cause his claim to the truth to prevail, the search for the truth has become in each something that is secondary. Religion has become a *community affair* devoted to the prosperity of the community, to charitable works, to the moral health of the faithful. But no religious truth can assume for itself a status superior to that of a *persuasion*, of a legitimate opinion which the constitution authorizes as *opinion* but not as truth. The political benefit of such an arrangement is evident and immense. But not everyone is equally happy as a result.

The happiest were the Jews, who, for the first time were recognized as full citizens, entirely free to lead a decent and productive life; for this they rejoiced. Then the Protestants who had fled Europe in order to be able to lead a decent, productive private life. They were habituated to individual religion, to the interior illumination, to a religious community of small proportions, to the fragmentation of the churches and the variations of dogma.

It could not be the same with Catholics. While they have done very well and shown an irreproachable loyalty, they retained a discomfort. American democracy did not have complete confidence in them, and with some reason. To begin with, the Catholic Church has attained a size a little too large for the spirit of the Madisonian constitution. She is twice as large as the denomination which comes after her, the Baptists, who are fragmented. If, as one can fear, there occur schisms, one must acknowledge the part of the "constitutional" factor, that is the lines of fracture that Madison foresaw and hoped for the sake of the public well-being.

In addition, the Catholic Church could not completely renounce its claim to possess the truth. To be sure, in America she put it between parentheses as much as she could, and she was hardly preoccupied with dogmatic theology. But the renunciation could not be total.

Finally, the Church is hierarchical and this hierarchy is designated by the Roman monarchy. This goes against not only the principle but also the mores of American democracy, where the election of the superior by the community is the unique source of his legitimacy.

The effective renunciation of its claim to the truth weakens the Church. As a result, she loses her title to define the rule of conduct. In democracy, mores are like political power. They belong to the domain of the human will. Like religions, they are relative to the human group which, enjoying democratic legitimacy, grants them consequently a moral legitimacy. The demand for equality for women overturns the fragile barrier surrounding the ecclesiastical hierarchy. The demand for the moral legitimacy of divorce, of abortion, or of homosexuality are equally authorized by the democratic principle and from the relativism which flows from it. In order to resist, the Church is obliged to attest to a divine authority in matters of moral truth which democracy cannot but deny. In this situation of comfortable disease, which can turn fatal, what can the Catholic Church do now that it is willingly immersed in democratic society?

THE SPLENDOR OF THE TRUTH?

The Church is often tempted by an apoliticism of principle. Apoliticism is a way of taking note of the political errors where the Church went astray in predemocratic times. Since her interventions were rarely crowned with success, isn't it tempting no longer to intervene at all? Apoliticism is also a way of taking stock of the situation circumscribed by democracy for religion: it is to remain a private affair. But it is still a utopia. The Church must engage in politics in order to assure her existence and her status in the city. She must do so because she cannot concern herself with men without taking into account their nature, which is, as one has known since Aristotle, political. There would be something ridiculous about legislating with so much care and to the last detail sexual conduct, while leaving the faithful without guidance in what constitutes an essential domain of their life. Finally, because of the doctrine of the Incarnation, the Church cannot leave her teaching to float in the domain of the ideal and interiority of individual life without any hope of seeing it incarnate itself in the real, concrete, social world.

Another temptation is to confuse her preaching with the discourse of democracy. Many sermons today enjoin the Christian to be "nice," "fraternal," to be responsible and egalitarian, to be solicitous for the "excluded," the immigrants, the handicapped, even the animals. But all this is only the development of democratic discourse. Democracy contains an indefinite program of including all human beings—and soon the animals—in an egalitarian community. Communism was a perverse imitation of Christianity which lured many Christians. But there is also an imitation, less perverse no doubt, and more livable, in the democratic ideal, which from the beginning envisaged a society of a Christian or Evangelical type, once the Church, its principal obstacle, had been placed in a condition where it could do no harm.

However, the confounding of democratic discourse and Christian preaching does nothing for modern man in his deepest ill, the deprivation of the truth. In communism, the contrary of the truth was the lie, and the lie was the very nature of communism. In democracy, the contrary of the truth is the meaningless, and the meaningless is a menace of democratic life. The relativity of truth, its reduction to opinion, the progressive weakening of opinion, create a metaphysical void of which modern man suffers, and if it doesn't cause him suffering, it diminishes and mutilates him, which is worse. This is what such diverse minds as Tocqueville, Flaubert, Nietzsche, and Péguy have seen and denounced.

For a full century the Church has attempted to promote the social spirit. In this she has rendered great services to democracy and for this democracy no longer persecutes her. But she does not help democracy to heal itself from this deficit of truth which is its secret and deep ill. The Church's effort would be better employed in healing herself from the intellectual deficit which inhibits her from spreading the truth she believes is her privilege from fructifying, shining, and convincing.

One of my friends, an old Spanish diplomat, having looked over this text, returned it to me, sighing: "Therefore one cannot put one's confidence in either History or the Church!" And in fact, if democracy is inevitable and the Church cannot subsist within it, the temptation of nihilism presents itself. In the Church it takes the form of millenarianism. To overcome this temptation, the Church can do no better than to make available to democratic man the pleasure of intelligence seeking faith and faith seeking understanding. It is this salubrious pleasure which democratic man gropes for in the dark, and which causes him often to end up in inferior religions or murderous ideologies. If, herself capable of a well-ordered charity, the Church renders this eminent service to democratic man, democracy itself will become livable and acceptable to her. But for this to occur she must continue to think about thinking.

14

A New Order of Religious Freedom

Richard John Neuhaus

More than he wanted to be remembered for having been president, Mr. Jefferson wanted to be remembered as the author of the Virginia "Bill for Establishing Religious Freedom." In his draft of that bill he wrote: "The opinions of men are not the object of civil government, nor under its jurisdiction." In a republic of free citizens, every opinion, every prejudice, every aspiration, every moral discernment has access to the public square in which we deliberate the ordering of our life together.

"The opinions of men are not the object of civil government, nor under its jurisdiction." And yet civil government is ordered by, and derives its legitimacy from, the opinions of the citizenry. Precisely here do we discover the novelty of the American experiment, the unique contribution of what the Founders called this *novus ordo seclorum*, a new order for the ages. Never before in human history had any government denied itself jurisdiction over that on which it entirely depends, the opinion of its people.

That was the point forcefully made by Lincoln in his dispute with Stephen Douglas over slavery. Douglas stubbornly held to the Dred Scott decision as the law of the land. Lincoln had the deeper insight into how this republic was designed to work. "In this age, and this country," Lincoln said, "public sentiment is every thing. *With* it, nothing can fail; *against* it, nothing can succeed. Whoever moulds public sentiment, goes deeper than he who enacts statutes, or pronounces judicial decisions. He makes possible the inforcement of these, else impossible."

The question of religion's access to the public square is not first of all a question of First Amendment law. It is first of all a question of understanding the theory and practice of democratic governance. Citizens are the bearers of opinion, including opinion shaped by or espousing religious belief, and citizens have equal access to

---

First published in *First Things*, February 1992.

the public square. In this representative democracy, the state is forbidden to determine which convictions and moral judgments may be proposed for public deliberation. Through a constitutionally ordered process, the people will deliberate and the people will decide.

In a democracy that is free and robust, an opinion is no more disqualified for being "religious" than for being atheistic, or psychoanalytic, or Marxist, or just plain dumb. There is no legal or constitutional question about the admission of religion to the public square; there is only a question about the free and equal participation of citizens in our public business. Religion is not a reified "thing" that threatens to intrude upon our common life. Religion in public is but the public opinion of those citizens who are religious.

As with individual citizens, so also with the associations that citizens form to advance their opinions. Religious institutions may understand themselves to be brought into being by God, but for the purposes of this democratic polity they are free associations of citizens. As such, they are guaranteed the same access to the public square as are the citizens who comprise them. It matters not at all that their purpose is to advance religion, any more than it matters that other associations would advance the interests of business or labor or radical feminism or animal rights or whatever.

For purposes of democratic theory and practice, it matters not at all whether these religious associations are large or small, whether they reflect the views of a majority or minority, whether we think their opinions bizarre or enlightened. What opinions these associations seek to advance in order to influence our common life is entirely and without remainder the business of citizens who freely adhere to such associations. It is none of the business of the state. Religious associations, like other associations, give corporate expression to the opinions of people and, as Mr. Jefferson said, "the opinions of men are not the object of civil government, nor under its jurisdiction."

It is to be feared that those who interpret "the separation of church and state" to mean the separation of religion from public life do not understand the theory and practice of democratic governance. Ours is not a secular form of government, if by "secular" is meant indifference or hostility to opinions that are thought to be religious in nature. The civil government is as secular as are the people from whom it derives its democratic legitimacy. No more, no less. Indeed a case can be made—and I believe it to be a convincing case—that the very founding principle that removes opinion from the jurisdiction of the state is itself religious in both historical origin and continuing foundation. Put differently, the foundation of religious freedom is itself religious.

"We hold these truths," the Founders declared. And when these truths about the "unalienable rights" with which men are "endowed by their Creator" are no longer firmly held by the American people and robustly advanced in the public square, this experiment will have turned out to be not a *novus ordo seclorum* but a temporary respite from humanity's penchant for tyranny. Yet in the second century of the experiment, secularized elites in our universities and our courts became embarrassed by the inescapably religious nature of this nation's founding and fortune.

These secularized elites have devoted their energies to explaining why the Founders did not hold the truths that they said they held. They have attempted to strip the public square of religious opinion that does not accord with their opinion. They have labored assiduously to lay other foundations than those laid in the beginning. From John Dewey to John Rawls, and with many lesser imitators in between, they have tried to construct philosophical foundations for this experiment in freedom, only to discover that their efforts are rejected by a people who stubbornly persist in saying with the Founders, "We hold these truths." A theory of democracy that is neither understood nor accepted by the democracy for which it is contrived is a theory of democracy both misbegotten and stillborn. Two hundred years ago, and even more so today, the American people, from whom democratic legitimacy is derived, are incorrigibly religious. This America continues to be, in the telling phrase of Chesterton, "a nation with the soul of a church."

And yet there are those who persist in the claim that "the separation of church and state" means the separation of religion from public life. They raise the alarm about "church-state conflicts" that are nothing of the sort. There are conflicts, to be sure, but they are the conflicts of a robust republic in which free citizens freely contend in the public square. The extreme separationists will tolerate in public, they may even assiduously protect, the expression of marginal religious opinion, of opinion that is not likely to influence our common life. But they take alarm at the voice of the majority. In that voice it is the people that they hear; it is the people that they fear; it is democracy that they fear.

Mr. Jefferson did not say that the civil government has no jurisdiction over opinion *except* when it is religious opinion. He did not say that the civil government has no jurisdiction over opinion *except* when it is expressed through associations called churches or synagogues. He did not say that the civil government has no jurisdiction over opinion *except* when it is majority opinion. He said, "The opinions of men are not the object of civil government, nor under its jurisdiction."

Many worry about the dangers of raw majoritarianism, and well we all should worry. The Founders worried about it, and that is why they devised a constitutional order for *representative* governance, and for the protection of minority opinion and behavior. But, without the allegiance of the majority to that constitutional order, such protections are only, in the words of James Madison, "parchment barriers" to tyranny. As Lincoln observed, without the support of public sentiment, statutes and judicial decisions—including those intended to protect citizens who dissent from public sentiment—cannot be enforced.

In our day, minorities seeking refuge in the protections of the Constitution frequently do so in a manner that pits the Constitution against the American people. That is understandable, but it is a potentially fatal mistake. We must never forget the preamble and irreplaceable premise of the Constitution: "We the people . . . do ordain and establish this Constitution for the United States of America." That is to say, the Constitution and all its protections depend upon the sentiment of "we the people." Majority rule is far from being the only principle of democratic governance, but it is a necessary principle. In the Constitution, the majority imposes upon itself a self-denying ordinance; it promises not to do what it otherwise could do, namely, ride roughshod over the dissenting minorities.

Why, we might ask, does the majority continue to impose such a limitation upon itself? A number of answers suggest themselves. One reason is that most Americans recognize, however inarticulately, a sovereignty higher than the sovereignty of "we the people." They believe there is absolute truth but they are not sure that they understand it absolutely; they are, therefore, disinclined to force it upon those who disagree. It is not chiefly a secular but a religious restraint that prevents biblical believers from coercing others in matters of conscience. For example, we do not kill one another over our disagreements about the will of God because we believe that it is the will of God that we should not kill one another over our disagreements about the will of God. Christians and Jews did not always believe that, but, with very few exceptions, we in this country have come to believe it. It is among the truths that we hold.

Then too, protecting those who differ is in the self-interest of all. On most controverted issues in our public life, there is no stable majority, only evershifting convergences and divergences. Non-Christians, and Jews in particular, sometimes see an ominous majoritarian threat in the fact that nearly 88 percent of the American people claim to be Christian. As a matter of practical fact, however, that great majority is sharply divided along myriad lines when it comes to how civil government should be rightly ordered. Furthermore, a growing number of Christians, perhaps most Christians, have a religiously grounded understanding of the respect that is owed living Judaism. Those Christians who argue that "Christian America" should be reconstructed in conformity with a revealed biblical blueprint for civil government are few and marginal, and are likely to remain so.

Father John Courtney Murray observed that, while in theory politics should be unified with revealed truth, "it seems that pluralism is written into the script of history." Some of us would go further and suggest that it is God who has done the writing. Pluralism is our continuing condition and our moral imperative until the End Time, when our disagreements will be resolved in the coming of the Kingdom. The protection against raw majoritarianism, then, depends upon this constitutional order. But this constitutional order depends, in turn, upon the continuing ratification of the majority who are "we the people." Among the truths these people hold is the truth that it is necessary to protect those who do not hold those truths.

It is a remarkable circumstance, this American circumstance. It is also fragile. We may wish that Lincoln was wrong when he observed that "In this age, and this country, public sentiment is every thing." But he was right, and in the conflict over slavery he was to see public sentiment turn against the constitutional order and nearly bring it to irretrievable ruin. We are dangerously deceived if we think that Lincoln's observation about our radical dependence upon public sentiment is one whit less true today.

The question before us, then, is not the access of religion to the public square. The question is the access, indeed the full and unencumbered participation, of men and women, of citizens, who bring their opinions, sentiments, convictions, prejudices, visions, and communal traditions of moral discernment to bear on our public deliberation of how we ought to order our life together in this experiment that aspires toward representative democracy. It is of course an aspiration always imperfectly realized.

II

I noted at the start that the question before us is not first of all a question of First Amendment law. It is a question, first of all, of understanding the origins, the constituting truths, and the continuing foundations of this republic. That having been said, the question before us is also and very importantly a question of the First Amendment, and of the first liberty of that First Amendment.

The first thing to be said about that first liberty is that liberty is the end, the goal, and the entire rationale of what the First Amendment says about religion. This means that there is no conflict, no tension, no required "balancing" between free exercise and no-establishment. There are not two religion clauses. There is but one religion clause. The stipulation is that "Congress shall make no law," and the rest of the clause consists of participial modifiers explaining what kind of law Congress shall not make. This may seem like a small grammatical point, but it has far-reaching jurisprudential significance.

The no-establishment part of the religion clause is entirely and without remainder in the service of free exercise. Free exercise is the end; no-establishment is a necessary means to that end. No-establishment simply makes no sense on its own. Why on earth should we need a no-establishment provision? The answer is that no-establishment is required to protect the rights of those who might dissent from whatever religion is established. In other words, no-establishment is required for free exercise. It is, one may suggest, more than a nice play on words that Mr. Jefferson's bill of 1779 was called the "Bill for *Establishing* Religious Freedom." The purpose of the non-establishment of religion is to establish religious freedom. It follows that any interpretation of no-establishment that hinders free exercise is a misinterpretation of no-establishment.

In recent history, especially in the last four decades, the priority of free exercise has been dangerously obscured. Indeed, one must go further. The two parts of the religion clause have been quite thoroughly inverted. One gets the distinct impression from some constitutional scholars and, all too often, from the courts that no-establishment is the end to which free exercise is something of a nuisance. To take but one prominent example, Laurence Tribe writes in his widely used *American Constitutional Law* that there is a "zone which the free exercise clause carves out of the establishment clause for permissible accommodation of religious interests. This carved-out area might be characterized as the zone of permissible accommodation."

There we have the inversion clearly and succinctly stated. Professor Tribe allows—almost reluctantly, it seems—that, within carefully prescribed limits, the *means* that is no-establishment might permissibly accommodate the *end* that is free exercise. This is astonishing, and it is the more astonishing that it no longer astonishes, for Professor Tribe is hardly alone. Scholars and judges have in these few decades become accustomed to having the religion clause turned on its head.

Once we forget that no-establishment is a means and instrument in support of free exercise, it is a short step to talking about the supposed conflict or tension between the two provisions. And from there it is a short step to the claim that the two parts of the religion clause are "pitted against one another" and must somehow be "balanced." And from there it is but another short step to the idea that the no-establishment provision protects "secular liberty" while the free exercise provision protects "religious liberty." When the religion clause is construed according to this curious inversion, it is no surprise that religious liberty comes out the loser. Any impingement of religion upon public life is taken to violate the "secular liberty" of the nonreligious. Thus has no-establishment become the master of the free exercise that it was designed to serve.

We need not speculate about the practical consequences of this curious inversion of the religion clause. The consequences are plainly to be seen all around us. In the name of no-establishment, wherever government advances religion must retreat. And government does inexorably expand its sway over the entire social order. In education, social services, and other dimensions of public life, it is claimed that, for the sake of the non-establishment of religion, Americans must surrender the free exercise of religion. Those who insist upon the exercise of religious freedom in education, for example, must forego the government support that is available to those who do not so insist. Thus is religious freedom penalized in the name of a First Amendment that was designed to protect religious freedom. Thus has the constitutionally privileged status of religion been turned into a disability. Thus has insistence upon the free exercise of religion been turned into a disqualifying handicap in our public life.

The argument that public policy should not discriminate against citizens who are religious is said to be an instance of special pleading by those who have an interest in religion. That seems very odd in a society where over 90 percent of its citizens claim to be religious. It is more than odd, it is nothing less than grotesque, that we have become accustomed to the doctrine that public policy should not benefit religion. What is this "religion" that must not be benefited? It is the individually and communally expressed *opinion* of a free people. To say that government should not be responsive to religion is to say that government should not be responsive to the opinion of the people. Again, the argument of extreme separationism is, in effect, an argument against democratic governance.

Once more, Mr. Jefferson: "The opinions of men are not the object of civil government, nor under its jurisdiction." The state of current First Amendment jurisprudence is such that the opinions of men and women, when they are religious, have been placed under the jurisdiction of the government. According to the inverted construal of the religion clause, wherever the writ of government runs the voice of religion must be silenced or stifled—and the writ of government runs almost everywhere. No-establishment, the servant of the free exercise of religion, has become the enemy of the free exercise of religion.

To contend for the free exercise of religion is to contend for the perpetuation of a nation "so conceived and so dedicated." It is to contend for the hope "that this nation, under God, shall have a new birth of freedom; and that government of the people, by the people, for the people, shall not perish from the earth." Despite the perverse jurisprudence of recent decades, most Americans still say with the Founders, "We hold these truths." And, with the Founders, they understand those truths to be religious both in their origin and in their continuing power. Remove that foundation and we remove the deepest obligation binding the American people to this constitutional order.

The argument here is not for an unbridled freedom for people to do whatever they will, so long as they do it in the name of religion. That way lies anarchy and the undoing of religious freedom in the name of religious freedom. There are of necessity limits on behavior, as distinct from opinion. But the constitutionally privileged and preferred status of religious freedom is such that, when free exercise is invoked, we must respond with the most diligent caution. The invocation of free exercise is an appeal to a higher sovereignty. The entire constitutional order of limited government is premised upon an acknowledgment of such higher sovereignty.

Sometimes—reluctantly, and in cases of supreme and overriding public necessity— the claim to free exercise protection for certain actions must be denied. Where such lines should be drawn is a matter of both constitutional law and democratic deliberation. It is a matter that engages the religiously grounded moral discernments of the public, without whose support such decisions cannot be democratically implemented. In other words, in this age and this country, the limits on the free exercise of religion must themselves be legitimated religiously.

A morally compelling reason must be given for refusing to allow people to do what is morally compelling. Those who seriously invoke the free exercise of religion claim to be fulfilling a solemn duty. As Madison, Jefferson, and others of the Founders understood, religious freedom is a matter less of rights than of duties. More precisely, it is a matter of rights derived from duties. Denying a person or community the right to act upon such duty can only be justified by appeal to a yet more compelling duty. Those so denied will, of course, usually not find the reason for the denial compelling. Because they may turn out to be right about the duty in question, and because, even if they are wrong, religion bears witness to that which transcends the political order, such denials should be both rare and painfully reluctant.

We have in this last half-century drifted far from the constituting vision of this *novus ordo seclorum*. The free exercise of religion is the irreplaceable cornerstone of that order. In his famed *Memorial and Remonstrance*, James Madison wrote: "It is the duty of every man to render to the Creator such homage, and such only, as he believes to be acceptable to Him. This duty is precedent, both in order of time and in degree of obligation, to the claims of Civil Society."

The great problem today is not the threat that religion poses to public life, but the threat that the state, presuming to embody public life, poses to religion. The entire order of freedom, including all the other freedoms specified in the Bill of Rights, is premised upon what Madison calls the precedent duty that is religion. When the American people can no longer publicly express their obligations to the Creator, it is to be feared that they will no longer acknowledge their obligations to one another—nor to the Constitution in which the obligations of freedom are enshrined. The free exercise of religion is not about mere "access." The free exercise of religion is about the survival of an experiment in which civil government has no jurisdiction over the expression of the higher loyalties on which that government depends.

Debates over the niceties of First Amendment law must and will continue. We should not forget, however, that our real subject is the constituting vision of a constitutional order that, if we have the wit and the nerve for it, may yet turn out to be a new order for the ages.

15

Catholicism and Democracy: Parsing the Other Twentieth-Century Revolution

George Weigel

In a conversation in the mid-1980s, Sir Michael Howard, then the Regius Professor of Modern History at Oxford, suggested that there had been two great revolutions in the twentieth century. The first had taken place when Lenin's Bolsheviks expropriated the Russian people's revolution in November 1917. The other was going on even as we spoke: the transformation of the Roman Catholic Church from a bastion of the *ancien régime* into perhaps the world's foremost institutional defender of human rights. It was a fascinating reading of the history of our century. I also sensed, in Sir Michael's telling of the story, just a *soupçon* of surprise: fancy that— the Vatican as defender of the rights of man!

There are, to be sure, reasons to be surprised by the contemporary Vatican's aggressive defense of human rights, and by Pope John Paul II's endorsement of democracy as the form of government that best coheres with the Church's vision of "integral human development." In the worlds of political power, those surprised would have to include the Brezhnevite and post-Brezhnevite generations of Communist leaders in central and eastern Europe, as well as Ferdinand Marcos, General Augusto Pinochet, and General Alfredo Stroessner. Yet in another way there should be no surprise. Key themes in classic Catholic social ethics—personalism, the common good, and the principle of subsidiarity—are not simply congruent with liberal democratic forms of governance: they would seem to require democratic polities for their effective embodiment, at least under today's circumstances.

That would come as news indeed to Pope Gregory XVI or Pope Pius IX, whose attitudes toward liberal democracy in the nineteenth century were decidedly chilly. What has happened between then and now, between the mid-nineteenth and late

---

Reprinted from *Soul of the World: Notes on the Future of Public Catholicism* (Grand Rapids, Mich.: Eerdmans, 1996), pp. 99–123.

twentieth centuries, between an official Catholic skepticism bordering on hostility about democracy and a Catholic endorsement of democracy that not only threatens tyrants but actually helps to topple them? And where might the encounter between Catholicism and democracy be headed in the twenty-first century?

CATHOLICISM AGAINST SECULAR LIBERALISM

The hostility of the mid-nineteenth-century papal magisterium to certain liberal concepts of the rights of man (as defined, for example, in the creed of the French Revolution) and the Church's deep skepticism about the liberal democratic state in its teething phase are well known to students of the period. The general position was neatly summed up in Pius IX's 1864 Syllabus of Errors, whose last condemned proposition was that "the Roman Pontiff can and should reconcile himself to and agree with progress, liberalism, and modern civilization." Eighteen years earlier, however, Giovanni Maria Mastai-Ferretti had been elected as Pius IX in part because he was thought to have a more tolerant attitude toward modern thought and institutions than his predecessor, Gregory XVI (1831–46), who in the 1832 and 1834 encyclicals *Mirari Vos* and *Singulari Nos* had flatly condemned liberalism (including "this false and absurd maxim, or better this madness, that everyone should have and practice freedom of conscience") as essentially irreligious.[1]

But events—particularly the Italian *Risorgimento*, whose liberal anticlerical leadership made no pretense about its intention to dislodge traditional ecclesiastical authority throughout Italy—hardened Pius IX in his views. By the time of the First Vatican Council (1869–70), the pope who had been elected twenty-three years earlier as something of a reformer had become, throughout the world, the very symbol of intransigent resistance to the ideas and institutions of modernity.[2]

Reasons for the Resistance

Personal factors and the churnings of Italian politics undoubtedly bore on the retrenchment strategy of Pius IX. But it seems more fruitful to focus on the substantive reasons why official Catholicism in the nineteenth century found itself in resistance to the Continental liberal project.

First, there were the enduring effects of the shock that the French Revolution sent through European Catholicism—a shock of greater intensity than any other the Church had absorbed since the Reformation. There was, to be sure, the crazed bloodiness of the Terror itself. Beyond that, however, and even beyond Napoleon's persecution of Pope Pius VII, the leadership of Roman Catholicism saw the lingering specter of Jacobinism as an ideological force that threatened the very foundations of European civilization.[3] That civilization in its public aspects had been rooted in the notion that states, as well as individual men, were accountable to transcendent moral norms, generally held to be revealed by a God who was sovereign over states as well as over individuals. By its defiant insistence on the autonomous reason of man as the first, and indeed only, principle of political organization, Jacobinism threatened more than the position of the Church as mediator between the sovereign God and his creatures. In the Church's view, the Jacobin spirit would inevitably lead to the implosion of civilization and its subsequent collapse into mobocracy, or what J. R. Talmon has called totalitarian democracy,[4] and events in France and elsewhere made it clear that this hard judgment was not unfounded. Thus in the minds of a church leadership that had long identified, not merely its institutional prerogatives, but civilization itself with the moral understandings that (in however attenuated a form) underlay the structures of the *ancien régime*, a damning equation formed: liberalism = Jacobinism = (anticlericalism + The Terror + anarchy). Discriminating or not, fair or not, the brush of Robespierre tarred the revolutionaries of 1848, the leaders of the Italian *Risorgimento* (Cavour, Mazzini, Garibaldi, and the like), and in fact the entire Continental liberal project.[5]

The second factor that colored the mid-nineteenth-century Church's appraisal of liberalism and democracy was the Church's own internal situation. The answer that Roman Catholicism devised to the political threat posed by the rise of postmonarchical states in Europe and to the advance of liberal ideas was centralization: the concentration of effective authority over virtually all matters, great and small, in the person (and, of course, staff) of the Roman pontiff. The pope would be the judge of orthodoxy and orthopraxis; the pope would manage the Church's affairs with sovereign states through an expanding network of papal diplomats, concordat arrangements, and so forth. *Ubi Petrus, ibi ecclesia* ("Where Peter is, there is the Church") is an ancient theological maxim. But it was given new breadth in the nineteenth century in response to the ideological (and indeed physical) threats posed by the forces of what the Syllabus called "progress, liberalism, and modern civilization."

There is, of course, an irony, here: the Church's answer to the threat of "progress, liberalism, and modern civilization" was to adopt a quintessentially modern (i.e., highly centralized and bureaucratically controlled) structure. Nonetheless, the new emphasis on centralized authority, coupled with the traditional understanding of the divinely given prerogatives of the Roman pontiff, and further complicated by the dependence of the Papal States (pre-1870) on European monarchs for physical security, created a situation in which the Church's leadership was rather unlikely to feel much affinity with liberal democracy.

A third obstacle that kept the Church from looking kindly on liberal democracy was that liberalism in the latter part of the nineteenth century was widely perceived in Vatican circles as a package deal that included Darwinism, which seemed to threaten the distinctiveness of human beings in creation; "higher criticism" or the "historical-critical method," which seemed to challenge the integrity of the Bible and its status as the revealed word of God; and socialism, which seemed to threaten the Church's traditional teaching on the right of private property. To these perceived threats in the order of ideas must be added the physical threat of revolutionary Marxism as it showed itself in, say, the 1870 Paris Commune.

The most fundamental reason for the Church's resistance to the liberal democratic project in the nineteenth century should not, though, be located on this institutional/ideological axis. The threats noted above were real, in both institutional and personal terms (ask Pius VII or Pius IX), and those threats did act as a lens through which ideas and events were, in some cases, misperceived. All that can be conceded. But beneath it all lay, I believe, an evangelical concern.

Rightly or wrongly, the central leadership of nineteenth-century Roman Catholicism truly believed that religious freedom—a key plank in the platform of liberal democracy—would inevitably lead to religious indifference and, given the right circumstances, to government hostility toward religion. The secularization of western Europe in the nineteenth century was a complicated business,[6] and it would be a serious mistake to attribute it solely (or even primarily) to the collapse of the old altar-and-throne arrangements that had been obtained since the Peace of Westphalia ended the European wars of religion in 1648. On the other hand, and from the Vatican's point of view at that time, secularization had proceeded apace with the collapse of those arrangements. Those of us with the luxury of hindsight should perhaps be less quick to dismiss as mindless the inferences that were drawn. There was, after all, at the beginning of the nineteenth century, the Napoleonic persecution of the Church; and after 1870 there was the pressing problem of the violently anti-clerical Third French Republic. This government hostility toward religion made it all too easy to read the historical record backwards, from the depredations of the Commune and the later anticlericalism of the Third Republic, to the *Déclaration des Droits de L'Homme et du Citoyen.*

We should not, in short, dismiss Roman resistance to the liberal democratic project as merely institutional self-interest. Some liberal democratic states did put grave difficulties in the path of the Church's evangelical and sacramental mission, and larger conclusions were shortly drawn.

On the other hand, the Roman authorities were slow to seize the opportunities presented by what might be called the Catholic Whig tradition, which looks to Thomas Aquinas for its inspiration and which had, in Lord Acton, a powerful spokesman in the mid- and late-nineteenth century. But given Acton's negative views on the utility of the definition of papal infallibility at the First Vatican Council (itself, *inter alia*, an act of defiance against the epistemological spirit of the age), the British historian was an unlikely broker between this tradition, which taught the possibility of genuine progress in history when that progress is mediated through rightly ordered public institutions holding themselves accountable to transcendent moral norms, and the Roman Curia.

In any case, the Catholic Whig tradition, a revolutionary liberal tradition in its own right, if in sharp contrast to the Jacobinism with which the Vatican typically associated liberalism, would not have all that long to wait, as history goes, for its moment to arrive.

THE TURN TOWARD DEMOCRACY BEGINS

What accounts for the shift in official Catholic teaching between 1864 and 1965, between the rejection of the modern constitutional state in the Syllabus of Errors and the Second Vatican Council's acceptance of the juridical state in *Dignitatis Humanae* (the Declaration on Religious Freedom) and *Gaudium et Spes* (the Pastoral Constitution on the Church in the Modern World)?[7] Many factors were in play, of course, but one has received relatively little attention in most church histories: the fact of America.

In the United States the Church was confronted with a genuine *novum*: a liberal, pluralistic society and a liberal democratic state that were good for Roman Catholics. Religious liberty and the constitutional separation of the institutions of church and state in America had led, not to religious indifference, but to a vibrant Catholicism that unlike its western European counterparts still held the allegiance of the working class. Moreover, while anti-Catholicism was a fact of life in the United States and Catholic immigrants not infrequently received a rough welcome, the U.S. government had never conducted an overt program of persecution on the basis of religious conviction.[8]

This was, as can be imagined, somewhat difficult to handle for those in Rome who were still committed to a restoration of the *ancien régime*, or were simply skeptical about the American experiment. A bold, public attempt to press the argument for religious freedom and the democratic state took place in Rome on March 25, 1887, when the newly created Cardinal James Gibbons of Baltimore took possession of his titular Church of Santa Maria in Trastevere, and preached to his Roman congregation in these terms:

> Scarcely were the United States formed when Pius VI, of happy memory, established there the Catholic hierarchy and appointed the illustrious John Carroll first Bishop of Baltimore. This event, so important to us, occurred less than a hundred years ago.... Our Catholic community in those days numbered only a few thousand souls ... and were served by the merest handful of priests. Thanks to the fructifying grace of God, the grain of mustard seed then planted has grown to be a large tree, spreading its branches over the length and width of our fair land.... For their great progress under God and the fostering care of the Holy See *we are indebted in no small degree to the civil liberty we enjoy in our enlightened republic.*
>
> Our Holy Father, Leo XIII, in his luminous encyclical on the constitution of Christian States, declares that the Church is not committed to any particular form of civil government. She adapts to all; she leavens all with the sacred heaven of the Gospel. She has lived under absolute empires; she thrives under constitutional monarchies; she grows and expands under the free republic. She has often, indeed, been hampered in her divine mission and has had to struggle for a footing wherever despotism has cast its dark shadow ... but in the genial air of liberty she blossoms like the rose!
>
> For myself, as a citizen of the United States, and without closing my eyes to our defects as a nation, I proclaim, with a deep sense of pride and gratitude, and in this

great capital of Christendom, that I belong to a country where the civil government holds over us the aegis of its protection without interfering in the legitimate exercise of our sublime mission as ministers of the Gospel of Jesus Christ.

Our country has liberty without license, authority without despotism. . . . But, while we are acknowledged to have a free government, we do not, perhaps, receive due credit for possessing also a strong government. Yes, our nation is strong, and her strength lies, under Providence, in the majesty and supremacy of the law, in the loyalty of her citizens to that law, and in the affection of our people for their free institutions.[9]

Gibbon's proud assertions sound mild to our ears, but in their own day they were intended as a challenge and were understood as such, by celebrants and detractors alike. As Gerald Fogarty, S. J., puts it, "Here was the gauntlet of the benefit of American religious liberty thrown down by the new world to the old. . . ."[10]

Pope Leo XIII (1878–1903) was happy to acknowledge the practical benefits of the American arrangement in the American circumstance. But he was not yet prepared to concede the moral superiority of the liberal (i.e., confessionally neutral) state over the classic European arrangements. In his 1895 encyclical letter to the American hierarchy, *Longinqua Oceani*, Leo cautioned against any temptation to universalize the American experience and experiment:

> . . . the Church amongst you, unopposed by the Constitution and government of your nation, fettered by no hostile legislation, protected against violence by the common laws and the impartiality of the tribunals, is free to live and act without hindrance. Yet, though all this is true, it would be very erroneous to draw the conclusion that in America is to be sought the type of the most desirable status of the Church, or that it would be universally lawful or expedient for State and Church to be, as in America, dissevered and divorced. The fact that Catholicity with you is in good condition, nay, is even enjoying a prosperous growth, is by all means to be attributed to the fecundity with which God has endowed his Church, in virtue of which unless men or circumstances interfere, she spontaneously expands and propagates herself; but she would bring forth more abundant fruits if, in addition to liberty, she enjoyed the favor of the laws and the patronage of the public authority.[11]

Thus the situation in the late nineteenth century: the American arrangement and the liberal democratic, confessionally neutral state it represented *tolerari potest* (could be tolerated). Indeed, the accomplishments of the Church under such a new arrangement could be gratefully acknowledged. This was a large step ahead of the rejectionist posture of Pius IX and the Syllabus. But it still stopped considerably short of the stage at which the confessionally neutral state—i.e., the state that acknowledges religious freedom as an inalienable right grounded in the nature of the human person and reflecting the inherent limits of the state's competence—is preferred to a benign altar-and-throne (or altar-and-desk) arrangement.

The path to that more developed position, which is the basis of the contemporary Catholic rapprochement with democracy, would be traversed over the next sixty years. The vigor of American Catholicism continued to play an exemplary role in ensuring that the issue remained alive. And the providential loss of the Papal States also meant that popes from Leo XIII on were able to consider, from a far less encumbered political and theological position, the relative merits of various forms of modern governance.

The Pressures of History

As the nineteenth century gave way to the twentieth, other realities of modern life began to influence the Church's perspective. One was the rise of totalitarianism in both its Leninist and Fascist forms, and the threat posed to Roman Catholicism by both of these modern political movements. Confronted by raw political power in the service of demonic ideology, the Church was led, not only to look toward the democracies for protection, but to look toward democracy itself as an antidote to the totalitarian temptation. This was particularly true in the immediate post-World War II period, when Vatican diplomacy, often in cooperation with U.S. diplomats and occupation forces, worked to strengthen Christian Democratic parties in Germany and Italy. In the Italian case, this represented a shift indeed, for Pope Pius XI (1922–39) had summarily ended the proto-Christian Democratic experiment led by Don Luigi Sturzo in the early twentieth century—with unfortunate results.[12] Now, in a world where even constitutional monarchy was clearly on the wane, Christian Democracy both in theory and in practice seemed to many Vatican minds (including that of Giovanni Battista Montini, later Pope Paul VI) the best available alternative to either Leninist or Fascist totalitarianism. Montini was influenced in this judgment by his regard for the philosophical work for the French neo-Thomist Jacques Maritain, whose *Christianity and Democracy*, written during the summer of 1942, became a kind of theoretical manifesto for the Christian Democratic movement.[13]

The Church's turn toward Christian Democracy was also facilitated by the decline of anticlericalist bias among European liberals, and by the difference between liberals and radicals that was horribly clarified by totalitarian persecution. The Vatican may still have had its differences with liberals, but after the ruthless persecution of Christianity under Lenin and Stalin, the Ukrainian terror famine, and the Holocaust, it was no longer possible even to suggest that modern radical dictators such as Stalin and Hitler were but exceptionally virulent forms of a general liberal virus. In the French situation, cooperative efforts during World War II between Catholic intellectuals and a few religious leaders, and the wider Resistance movement (with its secularist and Marxist leaderships), helped break down some of the stereotypes that had plagued life under the Third Republic.[14] In Italy, the tradition of Don Sturzo, embodied in such major postwar figures as Alcide de Gasperi and Aldo Moro, could be reclaimed, just as in Germany Konrad Adenauer was able to tap the Christian Democratic tradition of the old Catholic Center party.[15] In the post-World War II period, then, there were new facts of national and international life that validated Gibbons's thesis beyond the borders of the United States. These new facts created the sociological conditions for retrieving Pius VII's views on the potential compatibility of Catholicism and democratic political institutions.

Finally, and perhaps most significantly for the history of ideas, the evolution of Catholic social teaching itself pushed the Church toward a more positive appraisal of liberal democracy. The key development here was Pius XI's emphasis on *subsidiarity*, a principle that was central in the encyclical he issued in 1931 for the fortieth anniversary of Leo XIII's groundbreaking social encyclical *Rerum Novarum*. The key passage in Pius XI's letter, *Quadragesimo Anno*, was the following:

> It is true, as history clearly shows, that because of changed circumstances much that formerly was performed by small associations can now be accomplished only by larger ones. Nevertheless, it is a fixed and unchangeable principle, most basic in social philosophy, immoveable and unalterable, that, just as it is wrong to take away from individuals what they can accomplish by their own ability and effort and entrust it to a community, so it is an injury and at the same time both a serious evil and a disturbance of right order to assign to a larger and higher society what can be performed successfully by smaller and lower communities. The reason is that all social activity, of its very power and nature, should supply help [*subsidium*] to the members of the social body, but may never destroy or absorb them.
>
> The state, then, should leave to these smaller groups the settlement of business and problems of minor importance, which would otherwise greatly distract it. Thus it will carry out with greater freedom, power, and success the tasks belonging to it alone, because it alone is qualified to perform them: directing, watching, stimulating, and restraining, as circumstances suggest or necessity demands. Let those in power, therefore, be convinced that the more faithfully this principle of subsidiary function is followed and a graded hierarchical order exists among the various associations, the greater also will be both social authority and social efficiency, and the happier and more prosperous too will be the condition of the commonwealth.[16]

The Elements of Subsidiarity

As it has worked itself out in subsequent Catholic social teaching, the principle of subsidiarity has consisted of the following substantive elements:

1. The individual human person is both the source and the end of society: *civitas propter cives, non cives propter civitatem* ("The city exists for the benefit of its citizens, not the citizens for the city").
2. Yet the human person is "naturally" social, and can achieve the fullness of human development only in human communities. (This is sometimes referred to, particularly in the writings of John Paul II, as the principle of *solidarity*.)
3. The purpose of social relationships and human communities is to give help (*subsidium*) to individuals as they pursue, freely, their obligation to work for their own human development. The state or society should not, save in exceptional circumstances, replace or displace this individual self-responsibility;

society and the state provide conditions for the possibility of exercising self-responsibility.
4. There is a hierarchy of communities in human society; larger, "higher" communities are to provide help (*subsidium*), in the manner noted above to smaller or "lower" communities.
5. *Positively*, the principle of subsidiarity means that all communities should encourage and enable (not merely permit) individuals to exercise their self-responsibility, and larger communities should do this for smaller communities. Put another way, decision-making responsibility in society should rest at the "lowest" level commensurate with the effective pursuit of the common good.[17]
6. *Negatively*, the principle means that communities must not deprive individuals, nor larger communities deprive smaller communities, of the opportunity to do what they can for themselves.

Subsidiarity, in other words, is a formal principle "by which to regulate competencies between individual and communities and between smaller and larger communities." Because it is a formal principle, its precise meaning in practice will differ according to circumstances; because it is rooted in "the metaphysics of the person, it applies to the life of every society."[18]

There is both a historical and a substantive connection between the identification of the principle of subsidiarity and the Roman Catholic Church's increasingly positive appraisal of democracy in the mid-twentieth century. Historically, the very concept of subsidiarity was developed in the German *Königswinterer Kreis*, a group of Catholic intellectuals interested in questions of political economy. This group had a deep influence both upon the author of *Quadragesimo Anno*, the Jesuit Oswald von Nell-Breuning, and upon the evolution of Christian Democracy in pre- and postwar Germany.[19]

The substantive connection was closely related to the historical connection. *Quadragesimo Anno* was written under the lengthening shadow of totalitarianism. If its predecessor encyclical, *Rerum Novarum*, had been issued at least in part to warn against the dangers inherent in Manchesterian liberalism, *Quadragesimo Anno* was written in response to the threat posed by the overweening pretensions of the modern state:[20] thus the importance of the principle of subsidiarity, which tried to set clear boundaries to state power. The question then arises: Under modern circumstances, what form of governance is most likely to acknowledge, in practice as well as in rhetoric, the limited role of the state, the moral and social importance of what Edmund Burke called the "small platoons," and the principle of *civitas propter cives*?

In contemporary practice, liberal democracies have best met the test of these moral criteria. That was not quite what Pius XI, with his corporatist vision, had in mind in 1931, but it was certainly what Pope Pius XII (1939–58) had in mind by the mid-1940s. Pius XII was not a "global democrat," in any romantic sense of the term. He did seem to think, however, that democracy provided the best available modern form of government in the developed world, not least because it would provide a powerful barrier against the totalitarian temptation.

VATICAN II ON CHURCH AND STATE

The proximate origins of what I have elsewhere called the "Catholic human rights revolution,"[21] which led to the Church's overt support of the democratic revolution in world politics, should be located in the Second Vatican Council's Declaration on Religious Freedom (*Dignitatis Humanae*). The Declaration, issued in 1965, reflected aspects of the American experience and experiment, and a brief sketch of that background is in order.

One of the chief intellectual architects of *Dignitatis Humanae* was the U.S. Jesuit theologian John Courtney Murray. Beginning in the late 1940s, Murray conceived and orchestrated a creative extension of Catholic church/state theory. The official Roman position, when Murray first took up the topic, was precisely where Leo XIII had left it in *Longinqua Oceani*: the "thesis," or preferred arrangement, was the legal establishment of Catholicism on either the classic altar-and-throne or the modern Francoist model; the American arrangement, i.e., religious freedom for all in a confessionally neutral state, was a tolerable hypothesis. Moreover, in a confessionally neutral state, the Church ought (according to the official position) to work for the day when it would enjoy the benefits of state support. The "thesis," with its rejection of religious freedom as a fundamental human right, was grounded on the moral-theological maxim that "error has no rights." This meant, in public terms, that "erroneous" religious communities, such as the sundry forms of Protestantism in America, should not, under "ideal" circumstances, receive the tolerant (if tacit) blessing of the state, a view defended by prominent American Catholic theologians like Joseph Clifford Fenton and Francis Connell, C.S.S.R., of the Catholic University of America and the *American Ecclesiastical Review*.[22]

Murray's challenge to this position, and his creative extension of Catholic church/state theory, involved the retrieval and development of a largely forgotten current in Catholic thought that antedated the altar-and-throne model. Murray found the *locus classicus* of this forgotten current in a letter sent by Pope Gelasius I to the Byzantine emperor Anastasius in 494, in which the pope had written, "Two there are, august emperor, by which this world is ruled on title of original and sovereign right— the consecrated authority of the priesthood and the royal power." This "dualism," Murray argued, was not a radical "two kingdoms" construct so much as a declaration of independence for both Church and state. The Church's freedom to exercise its ministry of truth and charity was a limit on the powers of government; the state's lack of authority in matters spiritual "desacralized" politics. And this, as we have seen above, helped open up the possibility of a politics of consent, in place of the politics of divine right or the politics of coercion. The Gelasian tradition, Murray concluded, frowned on a unitary church/state system for the sake of the integrity of both religion and politics.

After considerable theological and ecclesiastical-political maneuvering, and in no small part because of the witness of the persecuted Church in central and eastern Europe, Murray's Gelasian retrieval prevailed at Vatican II. Enriched by a personalist philosophical approach that taught that persons had rights, whether their opinions were erroneous or not, Murray's view was incorporated into *Dignitatis Humanae*, with a palpable effect on the Church's subsequent stance toward democracy.

The Nature of Religious Freedom

Just how is the definition of religious freedom as a fundamental human right connected to the affirmation of democratic forms of governance? The connection has to do with the very nature of religious freedom, which has both an "interior" meaning and a "public" meaning. Its interior meaning can be stated in these terms: Because human beings, as persons, have an innate capacity for thinking and choosing and an innate drive for truth and goodness, freedom to pursue that quest for the true and the good, without coercion, is a basic human good. This innate quest for truth and goodness, which is the basic dynamic of what John Paul II has called the "interior freedom" of the human person, is the object or end to be protected by that human right we call the right of religious freedom. The right of religious freedom, in other words, is, in the juridical order, an acknowledgment of a basic moral claim about the constitutive dynamics of human being-in-the-world. As the Council put it, religious freedom means that "all men are to be immune from coercion on the part of individuals or of social groups and of any human power, in such wise that in matters religious no one is to be forced to act in a manner contrary to his beliefs."[23] Therefore religious freedom can be considered the most fundamental of human rights, because it is the one that corresponds to the most fundamentally human dimension of human being-in-the-world.

This, then, is the interior or personalist meaning of religious freedom. There is also a public meaning. According to the analysis above, religious freedom can be considered a crucial aspect of civil society: religious freedom is a basic condition for the possibility of a *polis* structured in accordance with the inherent human dignity of the persons who are its citizens. The right of religious freedom, as we have had occasion to note before, establishes a fundamental barrier between the person and the state that is essential to a just *polis*. The state is not omnicompetent, and one of the reasons we know that is that, in acknowledging the right of religious freedom, the state gives juridical expression to the fact that there is a *sanctum sanctorum*, a privileged sanctuary, within every human person, where coercive power may not tread.

In *Gaudium et Spes*, for example, the bishops of the Second Vatican Council describe conscience as "the sanctuary of man, where he is alone with God whose voice echoes in him."[24] This affirmation of the sanctuary of conscience is not to be understood in relativist terms as endorsing a putative "right to be wrong"; nor did the council fathers have in mind some "right to *do* wrong," based on the individualist notion that a human being has the right to think whatever he likes, and to behave accordingly, simply because he thinks it. The free man of conscience is also and always obliged to listen to the "voice of God"—the voice of truth—echoing within him. Thus John Paul II notes that the dialogue of conscience is always a dialogue "with God, the author of the [natural moral] law, the primordial image and final end of man."[25] Religious freedom, in other words, is not dependent on epistemological skepticism or indifferentism.[26] And the state, by acknowledging the "prior" right of religious freedom, also acknowledges its own inability to write or edit the script of the dramatic dialogue that takes place within the sanctuary of human conscience.

The right of religious freedom includes, as the Council taught, the claim that "within due limits, nobody [should be] forced to act against his convictions in religious matters in private or in public, alone or in association with others."[27] This claim is also helpful in establishing that distinction between society and the state which is fundamental to the liberal democratic project. As we have seen, in both theory and practice democracy rests upon the understandings that society is prior to the state, and that the state exists to serve society, not the other way around. Social institutions have a logical, historical, and one might even say ontological priority over institutions of government.[28] Among the many social institutions that have persistently claimed this priority are religious institutions and, in the Gelasian tradition, the Christian Church.

Thus the public dimension of the right of religious freedom is a crucial barrier against the totalitarian temptation, in either its Leninist or its mobocracy forms. Some things in a democracy—indeed, the basic human rights that are the very building blocks of democracy—are not up for a vote, in the sense that their truth is not to be measured by majority acquiescence.[29] Democratic politics is not merely procedural politics; democracies are substantive experiments whose successful working out requires certain habits (virtues) and attitudes, in addition to the usual democratic procedures. The public meaning of the right of religious freedom reminds us of this, in and out of season. And thus the importance of the right of religious freedom for unbelievers as well as believers, for the secularized U.S. new-class elite as well as for the 90 percent of the American people who remain stubbornly unsecularized.[30]

In short, and as Murray himself put it, at Vatican II and in *Dignitatis Humanae* Roman Catholicism embraced "the political doctrine of . . . the juridical state . . . [i.e.] government as constitutional and limited in function—its primary function being juridical, namely, the protection and promotion of the rights of man and the facilitation of the performance of man's native duties."[31] The juridical or constitutional state is ruled by consent, not by coercion or by claims of divine right. The state itself stands under the judgment of moral norms that transcend it, moral norms whose constitutional and/or legal expression can be found in bills of rights. Moreover, religious freedom, constitutionally and legally protected, desacralizes politics and thereby opens up the possibility of a politics of consent. Where, in the modern world, could such constitutionally regulated, limited, consensual states be found? The question, posed, seemed to answer itself: in democratic states.

Thus the path to an official Roman Catholic affirmation of democracy had been cleared, and the obligatory ends of a morally worthy democratic *polis* specified, in this American-shaped development of doctrine on the matter of the fundamental human right of religious freedom.

The Contemporary Discussion

Pope John Paul II has deepened and intellectually extended the Catholic human-rights revolution during his pontificate: first, by explicitly connecting it to the democratic revolution in world politics, and then by undertaking a searching evaluation and critique of democratic theory on the edge of the third millennium.

It is interesting to remember that the pope who has effected this decisive extension of Catholic social doctrine has never lived under a fully democratic regime (interwar Poland having been something of a truncated democracy, especially after 1926). Yet in a sense his intense interest in questions of democracy reflects his experience in Poland, where the "parchment barriers" (as James Madison would have called them) of Communist constitutions illustrated how important it is that rights be secured by the structure of governmental institutions, as well as by the habits and attitudes of a people. Here, again, we see how the totalitarian assault on human rights in the twentieth century has been, paradoxically, a prod to the extension of Catholic human-rights teaching.

In the first ten years of his pontificate, though, John Paul II also had to contend with various theologies of liberation, and it was in his dialogue with liberation theology that the new Catholic "theology of democracy" began to take distinctive shape.

Whether liberation theology represents a genuinely distinctive phenomenon in Catholic history, or merely the old Iberian fondness for altar-and-throne arrangements in a unitary state moved from right to left on the political spectrum, is an intriguing question. In any event, and while liberation theology was and is more complex than what has typically been presented in the secular media, the sundry theologies of liberation have tended to share a pronounced skepticism, at times verging on hostility, toward what they consider the bourgeois formalism of liberal democracy. Thus by the early 1980s these theologies had taken a sharply different path, in defining the nature and purposes of public Catholicism, than that taken by the Roman magisterium.

In an attempt to close this widening breach between official Catholic social teaching and the theologies of liberation, the Congregation for the Doctrine of the Faith issued two documents on liberation theology, one in 1984 and the other in 1986. The 1984 Instruction on Certain Aspects of the "Theology of Liberation," issued by the Congregation with the Pope's personal authority, acknowledged that liberation was an important theme in Christian theology. It frankly faced the overwhelming facts of poverty and degradation in much of Latin America and argued that the Church has a special love for, and responsibility to, the poor. But the Instruction rejected a number of key themes of the various theologies of liberation: the locating of sin primarily in social, economic, and political structures; the class-struggle model of society and history and related analyses of structural violence; subordination of the individual to the collectivity; the transformation of good and evil into strictly political categories, and the subsequent loss of a sense of transcendent dimension to the moral life; the concept of a partisan Church; and an "exclusively political interpretation" of the death of Christ.[32]

For our purposes here, though, the most crucial passage in the 1984 Instruction was this:

> One needs to be on guard against the politicization of existence, which, misunderstanding the entire meaning of the Kingdom of God and the transcendence of the person, begins to sacralize politics and betray the religion of the people in favor of the projects of the revolution.[33]

Against the core dynamic of the Catholic human-rights revolution, the theologies of liberation seemed to be proposing a return to the altar-and-throne arrangements of the past—this time buttressed by the allegedly "scientific" accomplishments of Marxist social analysis. With this new monism came, inevitably, the use of coercive state power against individuals and against the Church. The politics of consent was again being threatened by the politics of coercion. In short, the theologies of liberation had broken with the modern retrieval of the Gelasian tradition as it had evolved in the teaching of the Second Vatican Council and the social teaching of John Paul II.

The 1986 Instruction on Christian Freedom and Liberation pushed the official Roman discussion even further toward an open endorsement of the moral superiority of democratic politics:

> [T]here can only be authentic development in a social and political system which respects freedoms and fosters them through the participation of everyone. This participation can take different forms; it is necessary in order to guarantee a proper pluralism in institutions and in social initiatives. It ensures, notably by a real separation between the powers of the State, the exercise of human rights, also protecting them against possible abuses on the part of the public powers. No one can be excluded from this participation in social and political life for reasons of sex, race, color, social condition, language, or religion. . . .
>
> When the political authorities regulate the exercise of freedoms, they cannot use the pretext of the demands of public order and security in order to curtail those freedoms systematically. Nor can the alleged principle of national security, or a narrowly economic outlook, or a totalitarian conception of social life, prevail over the value of freedom and its rights.[34]

The politicization of the Gospel—its reduction to a partisan, mundane program—and the resacralization of politics were decisively rejected by the 1984 Instruction. The 1986 Instruction taught that participatory politics was morally superior to the politics of vanguards, whether aristocratic or Marxist-Leninist. The link between these themes and the positive task of democracy building was made in late 1987 by John Paul's encyclical *Sollicitudo Rei Socialis.*

The Case for Participation

Sollicitudo's portrait of the grim situation of Third World countries was based on a more complex historical, social, and economic analysis than could be found in the encyclical it was written to commemorate, Paul VI's *Populorum Progressio* (1968). Where Paul tended to assign primary (some would say, virtually exclusive) responsibility for underdevelopment to the developed world, John Paul II argued that responsibility for the condition of the world's underclass was not unilinear. For the development failures of the postcolonial period certainly involved "grave instances of omissions on the part of the developing countries themselves, and especially on the part of those holding economic and political power."[35] In a more positive vein, John Paul II extended the Catholic human-rights revolution in explicitly political-cultural terms, teaching that sustained economic development would be impossible without the evolution of civil society: "the developing nations themselves should favor the self-affirmation of each citizen, through access to a wider culture and a free flow of information."[36]

Yet the enhanced moral and cultural skills of a people, important as they were, were not enough, the Pope continued. "Integral human development" could not take place if the peoples in question remained the vassals or victims of inept, hidebound, ideologically rigid, and/or kleptocratic dictatorships. Thus, true development required that Third World countries "reform certain unjust structures, and in particular their political institutions, in order to replace corrupt, dictatorial, and authoritarian forms of government by *democratic and participatory ones.*"[37] In short, in *Sollicitudo Rei Socialis*, the formal leadership of the Roman Catholic Church reconfirmed its support for the democratic revolution in world politics. As John Paul II said of this striking phenomenon of the 1980s,

> This is a process which we hope will spread and grow stronger. For the health of a political community—as expressed in the free and responsible participation of all citizens in public affairs, in the rule of law, and in respect for and promotion of human rights—is the *necessary condition and sure guarantee* of the development of the whole individual and of all people.[38]

Sollicitudo thus brought Catholic social theory into congruence with Catholic social practice during the first decade of the pontificate of John Paul II. Whether the locale was El Salvador, Chile, Nicaragua, Paraguay, Poland, the Philippines, South Korea, or sub-Saharan Africa, John Paul II was, throughout the 1980s, a consistent voice of support (and, in Poland, the Philippines, and Chile, far more than that) for replacing "corrupt, dictatorial and authoritarian forms of government" with "democratic and participatory ones." As for criticism that his preaching on behalf of human rights and democracy constituted an unbecoming interference in politics, the Pope, en route to Chile and Paraguay in 1987, had this to say to a reporter who asked him about such carping: "Yes, yes, I am not the evangelizer of democracy, I am the evangelizer of the Gospel. To the Gospel message, of course, belong all the problems of human rights, and if democracy means human rights it also belongs to the message of the Church."[39] From religious conversion, to moral norms, to institutions and patterns of governance: the Pope's sense of priorities was clear, but so too was the connection between Catholic social teaching and the democratic revolution then unfolding dramatically throughout the world.

A Critique from "Inside"

None of this should be taken to suggest that the Church had become an uncritical or naïve celebrant of the democratic possibility. As John Paul II made clear during his pastoral visit to the United States in 1987, democratic societies have to remind themselves constantly of the moral standards by which their politics are meant to be judged. The Pope put it this way, speaking, in Miami, of the United States:

> Among the many admirable values of this country there is one that stands out in particular. It is freedom. The concept of freedom is part of the very fabric of this nation as a political community of free people. Freedom is a great gift, a blessing of God.
> From the beginning of America, freedom was directed to forming a well-ordered society and to promoting its peaceful life. Freedom was channelled to the fullness of human life, to the preservation of human dignity, and to the safeguarding of human rights. An experience of ordered freedom is truly part of the history of this land.
> This is the freedom that America is called upon to live and guard and transmit. She is called to exercise it in such a way that it will also benefit the cause of freedom in other nations and among other peoples.[40]

Thus did the Bishop of Rome endorse the moral intention of the American experiment in categories reminiscent of the Catholic Whig tradition—but emphasizing Acton's postulate that freedom is not a matter of doing what you want, but rather having the right to do what you ought.[41]

This line of development in the magisterium of John Paul II displayed a particularly sharp edge, of course, in the Revolution of 1989 in central and eastern Europe: a political revolution that was, as the Holy Father has insisted, made possible by a moral revolution, a revolution of conscience and of the human spirit, in the countries of the old Warsaw Pact.[42] The experience of 1989 and the struggles of democracies both old and new in the 1990s have, in turn, driven the social doctrine of the Church under John Paul II into a new reflection on the philosophical and moral foundations of democracy. The question for the late 1990s and beyond will be, it seems: How can democratic societies foster the flourishing of human life in its many dimensions, not merely the political or economic?

The Church's encounter with democracy, from the days of Gregory XVI and Pius IX to the present, can be described as a process of transition from *hostility* (Gregory XVI and Pius IX) to *toleration* (Leo XIII and Pius XI) to *admiration* (Pius XII and John XXIII) to *endorsement* (Vatican II and John Paul II), and now, in the late 1990s, to *internal critique*. Prior to the Council, the Church was speaking to democracy from "outside"; since the Council, the Church has, in a sense, spoken to democracy from "within" the democratic experiment as a full participant in democratic life, committed, through its own social doctrine, to the success of the democratic project.

To describe the relationship in these terms is by no means to subordinate the Church to politics; it is to note, however, that as the Church's understanding of democracy has evolved, so has the Church's understanding of itself vis-à-vis democracy. Because of the teaching of the Council and of John Paul II, an "exterior" line of critique has given way to an "interior" critique. Far from being a neutral observer, and without compromising its distinctive social and political "location," the Church now believes that it speaks to democracy from "within" the ongoing democratic debate about the democratic prospect.

John Paul II has developed this "internal line" of analysis—which now constitutes the world's most sophisticated moral case for, and critique of, the democratic project—in a triptych of encyclicals: *Centesimus Annus* (1991), *Veritltis Splendor* (1993), and *Evangelium Vitae* (1995).

In *Centesimus Annus*, John Paul challenged the notion, prominent in the American academy and in certain intellectual circles in post-Communist east central Europe, that democracy was necessarily hollow in its philosophical core, so that the democratic project could be reduced to a matter of "democratic" legal and political procedures:

> Nowadays there is a tendency to claim that agnosticism and skeptical relativism are the philosophy and the basic attitude which correspond to democratic forms of political life. Those who are convinced that they know the truth and firmly adhere to it are considered unreliable from a democratic point of view, since they do not accept that truth is determined by the majority, or that it is subject to variation according to different political trends. It must be observed in this regard that if there is no ultimate truth to guide and direct political activity, then ideas and convictions can easily be manipulated for reasons of power. As history demonstrates, a democracy without values easily turns into open or thinly disguised totalitarianism.[43]

The question of the relation between truth and democracy, and the papal critique of the idea of the merely procedural republic, continued two years later in *Veritatis Splendor*. "The Splendor of Truth" is not a "social encyclical" but rather a lengthy reflection on the current situation of Catholic moral theology. Nonetheless, John Paul II was at pains to draw out, at some length, the public implications for democratic societies of one of the encyclical's key teachings: that there are "intrinsically evil" acts, acts that are always and everywhere wrong, irrespective of circumstances or the intentions of individuals.

This might seem, at first blush, an abstract point, or at best one that engages the private decisions of individuals. Yet John Paul argues that the reality of objective evil is a public truth with public consequences. The "truth," in this instance, is that there is a moral logic "hard-wired" into human persons, which we can discern through a careful reflection on human nature and human action. And that "truth" is, in turn, a crucial structural component of the inner architecture of civil society and democracy. Why? Because, the Pope suggests, the foundations of democratic politics can be secured only when society possesses a common moral "grammar" that disciplines and directs the public debate about public life. Truth and freedom, in short, have a lot to do with each other; and so do truth and democracy.

John Paul intensified his "internal critique" of the democratic project in *Evangelium Vitae*, his 1995 encyclical on the "life issues" of abortion and euthanasia. If *Centesimus Annus* opened the question of truth and democracy, and *Veritatis Splendor* specified the ways in which moral truth sets the cultural foundations for substainable democratic societies, *Evangelium Vitae* discusses several of the ways in which "real existing democracies" can betray their own core values, setting in motion processes that lead to their decay and, ultimately, to their dissolution.

John Paul recognizes that "decisions that go against life"—i.e., decisions to take an innocent human life through abortion or to terminate a life through euthanasia—often reflect "tragic situations of profound suffering, loneliness, a total lack of economic prospects, depression, and anxiety about the future." These circumstances can mitigate "subjective responsibility and the consequent culpability of those who make . . . choices which in themselves are evil." But that has always been the case. What is different, indeed ominously different, today is that these choices "against life" are being described as "*legitimate expressions of individual freedom, to be acknowledged and protected as actual rights.*"[44] Wrongs have become rights.

The modern quest for freedom, in the politics of nations and in the social witness of the Church, has frequently been articulated in the language of "human rights." Now, the Pope argues, a decisive turning point has been reached, and the entire edifice of freedom has been jeopardized in consequence:

> The process which once led to discovering the idea of "human rights"—rights inherent in every person and prior to any Constitution and State legislation—is today marked by a *surprising contradiction*. Precisely in an age when the inviolable rights of persons are solemnly proclaimed and the value of life is publicly affirmed, the very right to life is being denied or trampled upon, especially at the more significant moment of existence: the moment of birth and the moment of death.
>
> On the one hand, the various declarations of human rights and the many initiatives inspired by these declarations show that at the global level there is a growing moral sensitivity, more alert to acknowledging the value and dignity of every individual as a

human being, without any distinction of race, nationality, religion, political opinion, or social class.

On the other hand, these noble proclamations are unfortunately contradicted by a tragic repudiation of them in practice. This denial is still more distressing, indeed more scandalous, precisely because it is occurring in a society which makes the affirmation and protection of human rights its primary objective and its boast. How can these repeated affirmations of principle be reconciled with the continual increase and widespread justification of attacks on human life? How can we reconcile these declarations with the refusal to accept those who are weak and needy, the elderly, or those who have just been conceived? These attacks go directly against respect for life and they represent a *direct threat to the entire culture of human rights.*[45]

When democracies use the language of "rights" as a tool to justify laws permitting objectively evil acts—indeed, when those objectively evil acts are described as "rights"—more has been lost than precision of language: something has happened to the character of democratic practice. And that defect of character quickly shows up in public policy. As the contemporary American experience illustrates, democracies, when they abandon the central moral principles that give meaning to self-governance, begin to take on some of the attributes of tyrannies. For when those moral principles are abandoned or traduced, says the Pope,

> The State is no longer the "common home" where all can live together on the basis of principles of fundamental equality, but is transformed into a *tyrant State*, which arrogates to itself the right to dispose of the life of the weakest and most defenseless members, from the unborn child to the elderly, in the name of a public interest which is really nothing but the interests of one part. The appearance of the strictest respect for legality is maintained, at least when the laws permitting abortion and euthanasia are the result of a ballot in accordance with what are generally seen as the rule of democracy. Really, what we have here is only the tragic caricature of legality; the democratic ideal, which is only truly such when it acknowledges and safeguards the dignity of every human person, *is betrayed in its very foundations.* . . .
>
> To claim the right to abortion, infanticide and euthanasia, and to recognize that right in law, means to attribute to human freedom a *perverse and evil significance*: that of an *absolute power over others and against others*. This is the death of true freedom.[46]

It may seem a harsh judgment. But examples of this process of democratic decay are not hard to find in the contemporary United States. When, for example, judicial ukase and congressional legislation combine to prevent pro-life Americans from exercising their free-speech rights, or when pro-life Americans are required by law to provide tax support for procedures that they deem to be grave moral evils, then consciences are being coerced by force in a way that threatens the integrity of the democratic experiment. Democracy is also imperiled when certain misconstrued "rights" become the pretexts for circumventing the normal legislative processes of democratic government by handing over all power on issues of life and death to "shadow governments" such as courts, regulatory agencies, and professional associations, which by their nature are less open to scrutiny, and less susceptible to change by democratic persuasion.[47]

If a single sentence could sum up the main thrust of this new "internal critique" of democracy in the social magisterium of John Paul II, it might be this: Culture is "prior" to politics and economics. In this sense, John Paul II is a "postmodern" pope. Since *Sollicitudo Rei Socialis*, he has become markedly less interested in the old structural questions of politics and economics (democracy vs. *ancien régime* vs. totalitarianism, capitalism vs. socialism vs. the "Catholic third way"). Those questions, the Pope seems to suggest, have been largely answered. If, under the conditions of modernity, you want a free and prosperous society that protects basic human rights while advancing the common good, you choose democracy and the market (or, in the Pope's preferred phrase, the "free economy"). The really interesting and urgent questions today have to do with culture: with the habits of heart and mind that make democracy and the market work to promote genuine human goods.

In the second decade of John Paul II's pontificate, the "other twentieth-century revolution"—the emergence of the Catholic Church as the world's premier institutional defender of human rights—has been both deepened and amplified. In the name of human rights, the Church still challenges tyrants. But it now challenges democrats, too, and on the basis of the same core moral principles that form the basis of the Catholic human-rights revolution.

All of which suggests that the twentieth century's "other revolution" will continue long into the twenty-first.

NOTES

1. From *Mirari Vos*, as cited and discussed in Roger Aubert et al., *History of the Church*, vol. 8: *The Church between Revolution and Restoration* (New York: Crossroad, 1981), 286–92. The historical and sociological context of Gregory XVI's condemnation is well summarized by Rodger Charles, S.J.:

> Gregory XVI was a temporal ruler faced with a revolt in his own dominions, a revolt which was in the name of a liberalism which ... was in practice anti-clerical and anti-Christian.... The Pope could not accept state indifferentism in matters of religion, nor grant liberty of conscience while these implied positive anti-clerical and anti-Christian attitudes. Liberty of the press and separation of the Church and the state were likewise rejected absolutely because of their secularist implications. *This was the essence of the papal dilemma: popes, as vicars of Christ, could hardly recommend policies which, if put into practice in their own states, would link them [i.e., the popes] with men and ideas both anti-clerical and anti-religious.* Only when the question of temporal power of the papacy had been solved ... could the situation satisfactorily be resolved. [*The Social Teaching of Vatican II* (San Francisco: Ignatius Press, 1982), 239, emphasis added]

2. For a portrait of Pius IX that usefully complexifies many of the regnant stereotypes, see E. E. Y. Hales, *Pio Nono: A Study in European Politics and Religion in the Nineteenth Century* (London: Eyre & Spottiswoode, 1954).

3. The Holy See was not alone in this judgment, though the logic of concern varied from institution to institution. See Henry A. Kissinger, *A World Restored: Metternich, Castlereagh and the Problems of Peace, 1812–1822* (Boston: Houghton Mifflin, 1973).

4. For a discussion of this point, see John Courtney Murray, *We Hold These Truths: Catholic Reflections on the American Proposition* (Garden City, N.Y.: Doubleday Image Books, 1964), 40 ff.

The danger in question was encapsulated in the Abbe Sieyes's defense of the replacement of the old States-General by the revolutionary National Assembly: "The nation exists before all, it is the origin of everything, it is the law itself." Cited by Conor Cruise O'Brien in "A Lost Chance to Save the Jews?" (*New York Review of Books*, April 27, 1989, 27). O'Brien correctly identifies the Jacobin current as the forerunner of twentieth-century totalitarianism, and chillingly cites the German theologian Gerhard Kittel (a "moderate"), who wrote in 1933, in *Die Jüdenfrage*, that "'Justice' is not an abstraction but something which grows out of the blood and soil and history of a *Volk*." O'Brien could, of course, have cited any number of Leninist *mots* to this effect, too.

Murray was not inclined to back off this hard judgment on the Jacobin tradition in the wake of the new "spirit of Vatican II." Thus, in a 1966 commentary on the evolution of the Declaration on Religious Freedom (*Dignitatis Humanae*), he condemned

> ... that desire to deny and destroy the past which was the very essence of Enlightenment rationalism (whereby it aroused the bitter antipathy, for instance, of Edmund Burke). What appeared on the surface ... was not progress but simply revolution. Society as civil was not simply being differentiated from society as religious; the two societies were being violently separated, and civil society was being stripped of all religious substance. The order of civil law and political jurisdiction was not simply being differentiated from the order of moral law and ecclesiastical jurisdiction; a complete rupture was made between the two orders of law and the two authorities, and they were set at hostile variance, each with the other. Society and the state were not invested with their due secularity; they were roughly clothed in the alien garments of continental laicism. [John Courtney Murray, "The Declaration on Religious Freedom," in J. Leon Hooper, S.J., ed., *Bridging the Sacred and the Secular* (Washington, D.C.: Georgetown University Press, 1994), 191]

5. Pope Pius VII (1800–23) was something of a countercase. Despite his personal suffering at the hands of Napoleon, Pius VII was not so thoroughly soured on the liberal political project as his successors Leo XII, Gregory XVI, and Pius IX. As Cardinal Luigi Barnaba Chiaramonti, Pius VII was a compromise candidate at the conclave of 1800, but one who had shown his moderate colors at Christmas 1797, when he shocked his conservative congregants with a sermon in which he declared there was no necessary conflict between Christianity and democracy. As pope, Pius VII and his secretary of state, the brilliant Cardinal Ercole Consalvi, tried to "blend administrative, judicial, and financial reforms on the liberal French model with the antiquated papal system"—an effort at cross-breeding that "exasperated reactionaries and progressives alike, and led to serious revolts" (J. N. D. Kelly, *The Oxford Dictionary of Popes* [Oxford: Oxford University Press, 1986], 302–4). Pius VII's

modest reforms were rolled back by his successor Leo XII (1823–29), who also took up again the rhetorical cudgels against liberalism. Thus ended what might be called the Chiaramonti/ Consalvi experiment in rapprochement between Roman Catholicism and the liberalizing political reforms of the day. For the next fifty years, retrenchment would dominate Vatican policy, and the notion of conservative reform pioneered by Pius VII and Consalvi would fall by the wayside.

6. See Owen Chadwick, *The Secularization of the European Mind in the Nineteenth Century* (Cambridge: Cambridge University Press, 1975).

7. It is worth noting that these were the two conciliar documents on which the archbishop of Kraków, Karol Wojtyla, worked most intensively during the third and fourth periods of Vatican II.

8. Arthur Schlesinger Sr., once told the dean of American Catholic historians, John Tracy Ellis, that "I regard the prejudice against your Church as the deepest bias in the history of the American people." Cited in John Tracy Ellis, *American Catholicism*, 2d ed., rev. (Chicago: University of Chicago Press, 1969), 151. Some Mormons might contest the claim that the U.S. government had never conducted an overt program of religious persecution.

9. "Cardinal Gibbons on Church and State," in John Tracy Ellis, ed., *Documents of American Catholic History*, vol. 2 (Wilmington: Michael Glaxier, 1987), 462–63 (emphasis added).

10. Gerald P. Fogarty, S. J., *The Vatican and the American Hierarchy from 1870 to 1965* (Wilmington: Michael Glazier, 1985), 41.

11. *Longinqua Oceani*, in Ellis, *Documents of American Catholic History*, vol. 2, 502.

12. See Anthony Rhodes, *The Vatican in the Age of the Dictators, 1922–1945* (New York: Holt, Rinehart and Winston, 1973), 14–15.

13. See Jacques Maritain, *Christianity and Democracy* (San Francisco: Ignatius Press, 1986). Maritain had an interesting historical perspective on the events through which he was living, in exile in the United States:

> We are looking on at the liquidation of what is known as the "modern world" which ceased to be modern a quarter of a century ago when the First World War marked its entry into the past. The question is: in what will this liquidation result? . . . [T]he tremendous historical fund of energy and truth accumulated for centuries is still available to human freedom, the forces of renewal are on the alert and it is still up to us to make sure that this catastrophe of the modern world is not a regression to a perverted aping of the Ancient Regime or of the Middle Ages and that it does not wind up in the totalitarian putrefaction of the German New Order. It is up to us rather to see that it emerges in a new and truly creative age, where man, in suffering and hope, will resume his journey toward the conquest of freedom. [Pp. 11, 17]

14. The divisions in prewar French society are well captured, in fictional form, in Piers Paul Read, *The Free Frenchman* (New York: Ivy Books, 1986).

15. Note also the connection between these national Christian Democratic movements and the movement for West European integration that eventually led to the Common Market and the European Parliament. This raises an interesting question in terms of the debate, in the 1990s, over the future of European integration. Post-World War II Christian Democratic parties in western Europe have traditionally been "pro-European." Will this position be sustainable as the institutions of the European Community show themselves as suscep-

tible to gross bureaucratization and ideological manipulation as the institutions of the United Nations? The new democracies of east central Europe are also raising interesting questions about the use of "Christian" in the name of a political party or faction.

16. Cited in Joseph A. Komonchak, "Subsidiarity in the Church: The State of the Question," *The Jurist* 48 (1988): 299.

17. Is there a connection between the principle of subsidiarity and the American concept of federalism here? It would be going considerably out of bounds to suggest that Madison's concept of federalism, as suggested in *Federalist 10* and *Federalist 51*, was informed by the classic Catholic social theory that eventually evolved the principle of subsidiarity; Madison should not be taken as a kind of proto-Pius XI. Indeed, *Federalist 10* and *Federalist 51* endorse decentralized decision making not as an expression of human possibility, but as a remedy for human defects (the defect of faction). On the other hand, one can argue that federal arrangements (irrespective of their political-philosophical rationale) are one possible expression, in history, of the principle of subsidiarity. One could possibly go further and suggest that the principle of subsidiarity establishes a firmer moral-cultural and indeed philosophical foundation for federal arrangements than Madison's "let a thousand factions bloom" (so to speak) so that no one of them may become oppressively dominant. Grounded as it is in an ontology of the person that links *being* and *acting*, and that regards human community as rooted in the social nature of the human person, the principle of subsidiarity might provide a more satisfactory basis for federalism than the voluntarism with which Madison is (wrongfully, in my view) often charged, but of which some of his successors in American political theory (principally the "progressivist" historians of the Parrington/Beard school) are surely guilty.

18. These definitions, as well as the schema above, are adapted from Komonchak, "Subsidiarity in the Church."

19. On the Königswinter Circle, see Franz H. Mueller, *The Church and the Social Question* (Washington, D.C.: American Enterprise Institute, 1984), 116–17.

20. On this distinction between the two encyclicals, cf. Mueller, *The Church and the Social Question*, 114.

21. See George Weigel, "John Courtney Murray and the Catholic Human Rights Revolution," *This World* 15 (Fall 1986): 14–27.

22. For a detailed examination of the Murray/Fenton/Connell controversy, see Donald Pelotte, *John Courtney Murray: Theologian in Conflict* (New York: Paulist Press, 1975).

23. *Dignitatis Humanae*, 2.
24. *Gaudium et Spes*, 16.
25. *Veritatis Splendor*, 58.
26. Thus *Dignitatis Humanae*:

It is in accordance with their dignity that all men, because they are persons, that is, beings endowed with reasons and free will and therefore bearing personal responsibility, are both impelled by their nature and bound by a moral obligation to seek the truth, especially religious truth. They are also bound to adhere to the truth once they come to know it and [to] direct their whole lives in accordance with the demands of truth. But men cannot satisfy this obligation in a way that is in keeping with their own nature unless they enjoy both psychological freedom and immunity from external coercion. Therefore *the right of religious freedom has its foundation not in the subjective attitude of the individual but in his very nature.* For this reason the right to this immunity continues to exist even in those who do not live up to their obligation of seeking the truth and adhering to it. The exercise of this right cannot be interfered with as long as the just requirements of public order are observed. [2, emphasis added]

27. Ibid.
28. Chief among these "prior" social institutions and the fundamental values they incarnate are what Murray called the *res sacrae in temporalibus*, those "sacred things in man's secular life" of which the Church had been the traditional guardian:

... man's relation to God and to the Church, the inner unity of human personality as citizen and Christian but one man, the integrity of the human body, the husband-wife relationship, the political obligation, the moral values inherent in economic and cultural activity as aspects of human life, the works of justice and charity which are the necessary expressions of the Christian and human spirit, and finally that patrimony of ideas which are the basis of civilized life—the ideas of law and right, of political power and the obligations of citizenship, of property, etc. [John Courtney Murray, "Paul Blanshard and the New Nativism," *The Month* [new series] 5, no. 4 (April 1951): 224]

29. And in the further sense that, should a democracy "subtract" such basic human rights as religious freedom from its roster of essential constitutional and/or legal protections for the human person, that state would cease to be a democracy in any morally meaningful sense of the term: as was made manifest by the spurious "people's democracies" of the late Warsaw Pact.
30. Murray summed up the personal/public connection in *Dignitatis Humanae* in these words:

The foundation of the [human and civil right to free exercise of religion] ... is the truth of human dignity. The object of the right—freedom from coercion in religious matters—is the first debt due in justice to the human person. The final motive for respect of the right is a love [or] appreciation of the personal dignity of man. Religious freedom itself is [thus] the first of all freedoms in a well-organized society, without which no other human and civil freedoms can be safe. [Murray, "The Declaration on Religious Freedom," 199]

31. John Courtney Murray, S. J., "The Issue of Church and State at Vatican Council II," *Theological Studies* 27, no. 4 (December 1966): 586.
32. For a fuller discussion of the Instruction, and references, see my *Tranquillitas Ordinis: The Present Failure and Future Promise of American Catholic Thought on War and Peace* (New York: Oxford University Press, 1987), 291ff.
33. Instruction on Certain Aspects of the "Theology of Liberation," 17.
34. Instruction on Christian Freedom and Liberation, 95.
35. *Sollicitudo Rei Socialis*, 16.
36. Ibid., 44.
37. Ibid. (emphasis added).
38. Ibid.
39. Cited in *New York Times*, April 6, 1987.
40. Cited in *Origins* 17, no. 15 (September 25, 1987).

41. John Paul returned to this Actonian theme in his 1995 pastoral pilgrimage to the United States; see his homily at the papal Mass at Camden Yards and his remarks at the Cathedral of Mary Our Queen in Baltimore, October 8, 1995.
42. See John Paul II, *Centesimus Annus,* chapter three, "The Year 1989."
43. *Centesimus Annus,* 46.
44. *Evangelium Vitae,* 18.
45. Ibid.
46. *Evangelium Vitae,* 20.
47. I am indebted for this analysis to Russell Hittinger.

16

The Trouble with Toleration

Ryszard Legutko

There is something sacrosanct about toleration in modern political folklore: Without much exaggeration, it can be said that the triumph of liberalism has elevated this category into the ultimate and almost the only generally acceptable litmus test of morality. At the very least, no other single category—not justice, not equality, not even freedom—has won such wide moral support in the Western world. What the radical philosopher Robert Paul Wolff wrote almost thirty years ago would probably arouse little controversy today; just as the basic value of a monarchy is loyalty and that of a military dictatorship is honor, so the basic value of the modern pluralist democracy is tolerance. The common wisdom permeating modern political theory has it that one can get away with anything as long as one is tolerant. Intolerance is more to be feared than all traditional sins. Human vices are deplorable, yet within the framework of toleration they can be tamed and civilized. When this framework is missing, it is believed that our social and political life suffer from mortal disease.

Not surprisingly, the question of whether the concept of toleration deserves such high esteem is rarely taken up today, although the limits of toleration are recognized and few thinkers or politicians would profess a doctrine of absolute toleration, a concept hardly defensible to any nondoctrinaire mind. Yet whenever conflict arises and a new idea or movement challenges the status quo, a call for toleration usually outweighs any demand that such an idea or movement should justify its dissenting position. In fact, to make such a demand is frequently interpreted precisely as an expression of intolerance. Most of those who write about or defend toleration ignore the cost, primarily intellectual and moral, of the puzzling omnipotence which has been given to a category that originally occupied a far more modest position. Logically, it would seem that since the contemporary Western world is much more

---

First published in *Partisan Review*, vol. 61, no. 4, 1994.

human—"tolerant," one might say—than Europe of the seventeenth and eighteenth centuries, there should be less need to talk about toleration. What has occurred within our philosophical and moral outlook to keep us preoccupied with a concept which we apparently have been very successful in implementing? Stalin once said that the closer the socialist paradise, the more numerous and more powerful its enemies. Can it be that a similar fear haunts the modern liberal conscience?

In the classical formulations of toleration, those of Bayle, Locke, and Voltaire, the first problem one stumbles upon is to what extent toleration has a distinct meaning of its own and to what extent it can be reduced to other notions. Voltaire's *Traite sur la tolerance*, for example, was occasioned by the unjust sentencing to death of Jean Calas, a French Protestant accused of killing his own Catholic son. One wonders to what degree the famous *philosophe* was entitled to speak of toleration in this context. Is justice, fairness, rule of law not enough to prevent similar cases from happening again? Will our judicial system work better if to good laws, good legal institutions, and good judges we add "toleration"? Was Jean Calas sentenced to death because the judiciary system in France did not function properly and because the French did not respect the elementary requirements of justice, or did he die because the French Catholics lacked tolerance?

One of the reasons why these and similar doubts arise is that the intolerance, the opposite of toleration, of which Bayle, Locke, and Voltaire spoke was most often identified with violence of the most brutal kind, as in Locke's "persecute, torment, destroy, and kill other men upon pretence of religion." It is even more strongly illustrated by Voltaire, who wrote of Irish Catholics

> sacrificing, as an acceptable offering, the lives of their Protestant brethren, by burying them alive, hanging up mothers upon gibbets, and tying their daughters round their necks to see them expire together; ripping up women with child, taking the half-formed infant from the womb, and throwing it to swine or dogs to be devoured; putting a dagger into the hands of their manacled prisoners and forcing them to plunge it into the breasts of their fathers, their mothers, their wives, or children, thereby hoping to make them guilty of parricide, and damn their souls while they destroyed their bodies.

The consequence of identifying intolerance with violence, persecution, and cruelty was the conviction that anything lessening the risk of violence, persecution, and cruelty counted as toleration. Thus a call for toleration was, in Locke's *Letter Concerning Toleration*, a call for "charity," "faith which works . . . by love," "meekness," "good-will." To these could be added other virtues and rules of behavior to make people's interactions more harmonious: good manners, a sense of justice, tact, knowledge, honesty, respect for others, open-mindedness. It was also asserted that toleration was linked to self-preservation and self-interest: the first manifesting itself in the need for social peace rather than civil wars to which anyone could fall victim; the second in the beneficent connection between toleration and trade, which soon became evident to many observers of social life. Yet not only virtues and natural dispositions contributed to neutralizing intolerance and building toleration; various vices could also serve the aim. For instance, hypocrisy, one of those undoubtedly and often condemned human frailties, nevertheless could be useful. Voltaire's treatise gives us a telling anecdote about a Dominican and a Jesuit who had fiercely quarrelled:

> The mandarin being informed of this scandalous behavior ordered them both to be sent to prison. A submandarin asked His Excellency how long he would please to have them remain in confinement. Until they are both agreed, said the judge. Then, my lord, answered the submandarin, they will remain in prison all their days. Well, then, said the mandarin. Let them stay until they forgive one another. That they will never do rejoined the deputy; I know them very well. Indeed, said the mandarin; then let it be until they appear to do so.

The scope given to the concept of toleration in the classics is intriguing. Is there anything specific in toleration that distinguishes it from other apparently related but far more tangible notions and phenomena like kindness or disinterestedness? What will be left of toleration if we deprive it of tact and justice, of love and meekness, of charity and good manners, of knowledge and curiosity, of instincts for self-interest and self-preservation, of hypocrisy and other private vices which are public virtues? If we possess most of these qualities, is it necessary to invoke the concept of toleration? What would be gained?

One plausible answer is that toleration, whatever its precise meaning, is attached to all these virtues, vices, instincts, and habits. Without them, or in opposition to them, or abstracted from them and treated separately as an autonomous quality, toleration is empty and meaningless. Possibly, there is nothing conceptually faulty with insistently relating toleration to other practices of moral behavior; pure toleration, distilled of all related notions, may be dubious and—if separated from related practices—even harmful. Advocating toleration without love, justice, rule of law, self-interest, hypocrisy, and so on may be like advocating courage without the training of character, at best an arid exercise in philosophical speculation and at worst a form of subversion aimed at the most vital and widely shared values of social life. Therefore, such "pure" toleration might well bring results hardly compatible with the ordinary sense of the concept. A tolerant individual could thus be either someone who lives peacefully with his philosophical and religious adversaries, or someone who antagonizes people by ordering them to obey an abstract rule, which he claims will bring peace and harmony to all, unrelated to experience. In the first case, tolerance is a virtue of an individual human character; in the second, a principle to which human habit should conform.

Voltaire himself perfectly illustrated both of these attitudes. There were in fact two Voltaires: the first is the author of *Traite sur la tolerance*, a good Christian (at least pretending to be one), defending toleration as the culmination of many moral components. The other is the Voltaire of *Ecrasez l'infame*, the visionary of the

Enlightenment who sought to elevate toleration on the ruins of Christianity, the extirpation of which he regarded as the major mission of his life. In his struggle against *l'infame*, Voltaire committed precisely the error that the idea of toleration was meant to prevent. He fell victim to intellectual hubris: armed with his philosophical humanism, he set out to eradicate the evil and falsehood that people—because of the inertia of tradition and ignorance—still allegedly harbored in themselves.

John Locke was more cautious. His *Letters* spelled out a case for toleration that was based on an attitude of humility toward truth. To generalize his insight, one can say that if there is some specificity in the idea of toleration, irreducible to other ideas and habits, it reveals itself in the acceptance of human imperfection; it expresses the effort to put into practice the ultimate moral standards—truth being the most vital one. Locke formulated his argument against the magistrates who claimed the power to punish the false religion and to defend the true one. We need toleration, he argued, when we do not have the knowledge or certainty of what is true, or when the nature of controversy is such that it precludes the establishment of any common ground. The latter case clearly applies to religious conflicts which, as Locke repeatedly emphasized, are to a considerable degree a matter of faith and cannot be settled through rational argument. The purpose of toleration was to draw the attention of all parties involved to the danger of arrogant and hasty transformation of true or seemingly true concepts into political instruments.

Such a rendering of toleration was clearly modest, and there was not much philosophy in it, except perhaps an implied empiricist distrust of abstract and aprioristic formulas functioning as criteria in political life. This version of toleration is often called negative: it usually limits itself to negative qualifications. Contrary to what Voltaire the prophet of the Enlightenment (in contrast to the Voltaire of *Traite*) thought, it neither indicates truth nor promotes it, nor even helps intellectually in the process of establishing truth. Toleration does not presuppose any identifiable metaphysics or ethics or political philosophy. Locke and Voltaire (in his *Treatise*), while stressing that toleration and truth are in practice related, did not say that truth as such is a repressive notion. They did not therefore suggest that in the name of toleration we should avoid or suspend truth. They did not even allow that there could be several truths of equal validity and that therefore no truth could enjoy superiority. Locke believed that his religion was the true one. Voltaire saw nothing reprehensible in the fact that some religions were dominant in certain societies, and that those who belonged to these religions were given leading political positions. He thought it natural that certain government functions were thus not accessible to some people because of their religious beliefs. By modern standards this does not seem a particularly libertarian position, but it is reconcilable with the general idea of toleration. Hierarchy and intolerance are two different things. The aim of toleration is not to be a substitute for equality, justice, and other moral and political qualities. Toleration cannot make any positive claims such as that a certain category of persons should be given certain political or social positions, specifically on the grounds of toleration.

From the beginning, however, it was obvious that the advocates of toleration were tempted to transcend the narrow limits of the negative version. The temptation was to make it more committed in the struggle for a better world, more partisan, more positive. The decisive step toward a positive interpretation was to neutralize certain points of view and to promote others; to oppose those philosophies, religions, and social norms which are coercive, dominating, authoritarian, monolithic; and to support other philosophies, religions, and social norms that do not have these unpleasant characteristics. Thus, toleration would no longer be blind, uncommitted, indifferent to the final result of the dispute between contending parties. On the contrary, it would be a major actor in the dispute, strengthening one party and withdrawing its support from the other. It would consist not in refraining from doing certain things, but in acting in a certain way, in choosing and committing oneself to the cause of freedom. By being passive, by not choosing and committing oneself, one ran the risk of becoming an unwitting accomplice to the intolerant party.

The history of the last two hundred years of Western political philosophy may be interpreted, among other things, as a gradual decline of negative toleration and a simultaneous growth of its positive counterpart. Most of these efforts have aimed at no less than the discovery of the final key to the tolerant world, that is, the creation of a framework of ethical guidelines which effectively present intolerance. To put it yet differently, there has been the hope that the forces of toleration could finally achieve victory in the war against the forces of intolerance, or—even if reality proves resistant—that at least we will have a clear formula of the strategy and the general goal. This tradition extends from John Stuart Mill—who located the source of oppression in the customs and social stereotypes which, understandably, made him attribute a special role to eccentrics constantly undermining our thoughtless sense of stability—to Herbert Marcuse—who came to a somewhat baffling conclusion in *A Critique of Pure Tolerance* that "liberating tolerance" meant "intolerance against movements from the Right, and toleration of movements from the Left."

During the last decade or so, another solution of how to make the world safe for toleration has come from a group of thinkers who like to label themselves as postmodern. In spite of important differences among them, they seem to share a conviction that we can, we should, and we have already begun to liquidate the intellectual basis of intolerance. Negative tolerance was defective because—it is maintained—with respect to truth it preached only humility. It is truth as such, regardless of the degree of arrogance or humility with which it is professed, that is responsible for intolerance. Whatever we regard as true, be it in philosophy, morals, ways of life, criteria of permissiveness, is always exclusive. It inevitably relegates some people outside the sphere of what is normal and respectable. For example, by stressing one's heterosexuality one may be suspected of implying that there is something objectively wrong with homosexuality, which in turn makes one susceptible to the charge of depriving homosexuals of their dignity and consequently of inciting discrimination against them.

From truth to persecution there is then a straight and logical transition. Hence the obvious implication is that in order to secure toleration we must abandon the traditional criteria of evaluation, and in more ambitious projects, we must abandon traditional metaphysics and the epistemology from which the criterion of truth derived its strength. We must eradicate once and for all the sense of philosophical certainty that permitted some to look down on others, a sense of certainty stemming from the assumption that our world has an essence or foundation reachable by the cognitive faculties of the wise, who then impose it on the ignorant. Once we annihilate the assumption of philosophical essentialism and foundationalism, the sting of intolerance will be cut off.

Truth, wrote Michel Foucault in *Power/Knowledge*, is not something to be discovered but rather "a regime": "the ensemble of rules according to which the true and the false are separated and specific effects of power attached to the true." For the old followers of the truth-as-regime theory, for Marx, Lenin, and their disciples, the power-holders were explicit: the bourgeoisie, capitalists, the industrial-military complex. For the following generations of the philosophers of suspicion—for poststructuralists, postmodernists, deconstructionists—the enemy who holds truth through power is more obscure. We usually see only the effects, not the perpetrators: a frame of mind, a system of concepts, a philosophy. This power has become thus even less visible than a dictatorship of customs and opinion, so feared by nineteenth-century liberals, and more harmful to the human mind. For Derrida it would be "phallogocentrism," a domination of human consciousness and behavior by male rationalism. The cause of toleration has been given a new target, more deeply hidden than previous ones. Where once it was the Catholic Church, then political authoritarianism, then customs and prevailing opinion, now it is philosophy, language, intellectual education.

This program of liberation amounts to a virtual abolition of philosophy in the form in which it has existed for two and a half millennia. Along with the concept of truth, other basic notions and distinctions have been divested of their philosophical legitimacy and come to be viewed as the potential carriers of oppression: essence, nature, subject-object dichotomy, reason, good, evil. Until recently conceived of as "strong thinking," philosophy must be replaced by something far less demanding, less authoritarian and patronizing, in short, by "weak thinking" characterized by Gianni Vattimo as *il pensiero debole*. What will it be like? Some call up the ancient quarrel between rhetoric, championed by the sophists, and philosophy, whose greatest defenders were Socrates, Plato, and Aristotle. They argue that we are witnessing today the decline of strong philosophy, inhumanely objective and hierarchical, and the triumph of essentially weak rhetoric: the criteria of social coexistence, adaptable and malleable, have begun to play a more important role than the suprahuman criteria of truth. As Richard Rorty put it, democracy has become prior to philosophy.

What philosophers once interpreted as a disinterested pursuit of truth has now been replaced by social praxis; by dialogue and communication; by deconstruction and hermeneutics; by play and spontaneous expression; by individual or collective therapy. The abolition of philosophy has to lead to the abolition of the distinction between the center and the periphery. In the new world there are no peripheries, or—what amounts to the same thing—there are nothing but peripheries. Some enthusiasts of "weak thinking," like G. B. Madison, do not hesitate to speak of the new era in human relations:

> The politics of postmodernity, like postmodern philosophy itself, will . . . no longer be one of opposites. Oppositional thinking goes along with metaphysical hierarchies, and it is precisely these which are being undermined by the new postmodern, global civilization now coming into being. The new era has the potential of being one not of metaphysical, essence-bound homogeneity and modernistic uniformity but of difference, particularity, plurality, and heterogeneity. In regard, for instance, to the new geo-economic order, we are witnessing the emergence of a complex, interlocking, and decentered network of institutions in which there is no longer any identifiable source, origin, or centre.

Those who live in such a world will no longer be troubled by the metaphysical horror or the specter of nothingness; on the contrary, a sense of Kundera's "lightness of being" will produce in them what Rorty has called "the air of light-minded aestheticism," an attitude which the American philosopher has openly welcomed and approved:

> The encouragement of light-mindedness about traditional philosophical topics serves the same purposes as does the encouragement of light-mindedness about traditional theological topics. Like the rise of large market economies, the increase in literacy, the proliferation of artistic genres, and the insouciant pluralism of contemporary culture, such philosophical superficiality and light-mindedness helps along the disenchantment of the world. It helps make the world's inhabitants more pragmatic, more tolerant, more liberal, more receptive to the appeal of instrumental rationality.

On a popular level, this frame of mind, as well as the hope attached to it, is illustrated by the kind of postmodernist fiction which in many cases is built on one symptomatic pattern: the protagonist (and with him the reader) is forced by circumstances or by manipulation to repeatedly reorganize his interpretation of reality and to pass through heuristic trials which reveal to him the arbitrariness of his former philosophical self-assured seriousness.

A somewhat different version of positive toleration expresses itself in an attitude rendered by one Polish author as "sympathetic openness." Since, as Goethe put it, "to tolerate is to offend," we cannot, following his indication, confine ourselves to negative toleration which others might find patronizing and humiliating. To the modern liberal British philosopher R. M. Haire, man acknowledges the ideal of toleration if he acknowledges "a readiness to respect other people's ideals as if they were his own."

Those who champion this form of toleration do not maintain—and such possible misunderstanding must be made clear—that sympathetic openness should prevail only in the initial stages of contacts with unknown individuals, groups, and opinions. It thus excludes the possibility of being sympathetically open to something as yet unknown, of then encountering it, finding it repulsive, and ultimately deciding to treat it neither with sympathy nor with openness. Rather, sympathetic openness must be present at all stages of contact with other people's opinions and ideals. Haire argues for the plausibility of his thesis and tells us how expansive the limits of liberals' respect for other points of view ought to be:

> It is part of the liberal's ideal that a good society, whatever else it is, is one in which the ideals and interests of all are given equal consideration. It is, to use Kantian language, a kingdom of ends in which all are, at least potentially, legislating members. . . . He may even think that a diversity of ideals is in itself a good thing . . . because it takes all sorts to make a world. If the liberal's ideal is of any of these kinds, he is not betraying it but following it if he tolerates other people's pursuit of their ideals, provided that, where the pursuit of one ideal hinders the pursuit of another, there shall be . . . a just distribution of advantages and disadvantages. It is only the last proviso which prevents the liberal from allowing even the fanatic to pursue his ideals without impediment; but the liberal is not required by his own ideal to tolerate intolerance.

In practice, it "might be difficult to be sympathetically open to all points of view. This, however, does not discredit the sympathetic attitude itself, since what matters here is not infinite sympathy to an infinite number of opinions but a certain disposition which reveals itself in contacts with new phenomena and consists in encouraging and welcoming diversity in human life. On the other hand, sympathetic openness modifies our definition of "the fanatic." In this view, the fanatic is transformed. The fanatic is no longer a person with excessive, religious or quasi-religious, and usually mistaken enthusiasm for a certain system of beliefs. Since the sympathetically open person is self-defined as one who approves and works for diversity, then by contrast, the fanatic is someone who acts and speaks against diversity as an organizing principle, someone who does not necessarily hold one set of opinions and launch a crusade to impose it on others but who opposes egalitarian diversity in principle and who chooses some form of hierarchy in social life as a necessity.

Because both tolerance and fanaticism reveal themselves, in real life, as tendencies and dispositions (the first for milder and the second for stricter criteria of selection of acceptable societal ideals), it is reasoned that all those who cherish the value of diversity must perceive those even merely considering the subjection of the plurality of ideals to selection and hierarchical organization to be intolerant. According to such reasoning, one does not have to try very hard to be vulnerable to the charge of intolerance to diversity. Thus, the growth of the pluralistic order is likely to increase the number of suspicions of fanaticism. The more diverse the world, the greater the probability that any statement, act, thought, or idea will be regarded as an expression of the intention to exclude, patronize, limit, subject, discriminate.

The pluralistic liberal who is enchanted with diversity, despite repeated declarations that the pluralistic world serves the cause of truth better than any other system, paradoxically has no difficulty in accepting the assumption shared by Marx, Lenin, Foucault, and many others: truth is primarily a partisan weapon; it is power or a regime rather than a theoretical concept. Therefore dispersing truth is a matter as urgent as dispersing power. In their struggle against the concentration of truth, pluralist liberals argue that analogous to the plurality of the centers of power there are just as many possible versions of truth. Their argument is undoubtedly ingenious, and it serves the same purpose as the postmodern assault on the concept of the center itself. The ultimate aim of those who resort to this argument is not to facilitate the exchange of ideas in order to have a better and truer understanding of the world but, in their view, to prevent the emergence of any dominant truth-power structure, to fight fanaticism.

Contemporary toleration has ceased to be what it once was—a practical skill that enabled people to live together—and has become a complex theoretical issue. Just as negative toleration was in theory and practice insolubly linked with several human virtues and vices, so positive toleration seems closely connected with several political ideals—justice, diversity, equality, liberty, fraternity. Yet this latter association is a most dubious one. It is relatively easy to demonstrate that negative toleration can humanize political order, but it is a much greater challenge to posit a complex theory of a superior political system built on the idea of positive toleration. Since it is agreed that negative toleration has indeed humanized political order, then it must also be agreed that it is possible to settle essential questions and differences about political order and philosophy irrespective of the problem of positive toleration (although toleration, naturally, may add to the value of particular solutions). Yet in the face of such evidence, efforts to connect positive toleration with actual political ideals continue to imply that the concept of positive toleration itself contains a comprehensive set of fundamental philosophical assertions.

There would be nothing obviously wrong in maintaining a political philosophy serving the cause of toleration, were it not that it involves a deception. If we fail to keep in mind the distinction between negative and positive toleration, we may easily be misled into believing that both make the same demands of us. The deception lies in the assertion that a political philosophy of toleration or, more precisely, *the ideology of toleration*, conveys nothing more than a minimal requirement. Its supporters want to persuade us that only a minor concession related to an outer form of behavior—as negative toleration is—is necessary: we should be civilized, compassionate, open, flexible, well-mannered. In fact, their requirement is maximalist, and the expected concessions are anything but minor. It is no trifle that, as postmodernism teaches, we are to renounce basic philosophical categories and to throw traditional belief in the essential meaningfulness of the world into the dustbin of history. It is no trifle that, as pluralist libertarians insist, we are forbidden to discriminate between different ideals and that in case of their conflict we must distribute them equally.

The deception is that the advocates of positive toleration make sweeping philosophical statements while at the same time refuse to admit they are making them. Postmodernism, for example, blurs the distinction, to use Rorty's phrase, between democracy and philosophy. One does not know whether the postmodernists propound a highly controversial philosophical thesis that objective truth does not exist, or whether they are arguing that toleration and pluralism require that there *be* no objective truth. In the first case, the thesis cannot be proven, since the criterion of truth on which such a proof could be built has been destroyed. In the second case, the argument becomes irrelevant because toleration is a form of behavior, not a philosophical hypothesis favoring one model of metaphysics rather than another. Uneasiness about the antimetaphysical revolution is countered with the assertion of the world's pluralistic nature. Any defense of some form of hierarchy in social life is met with the idea of a centerless metaphysics.

The essential trouble with positive toleration (especially in its "sympathetic openness" version) is that it attempts to combine two attitudes which are extremely difficult to reconcile. First, it implies that one can have one's own point of view; second, that one must accept a world of diversity where all points of view are equal (except those that are "fanatical"). Logically, such a combination leads to insoluble conflicts. The possession of a point of view presupposes a certain hierarchy; certain ideas and attitudes have been found right and deserving of sympathy; others found to be tolerable; still others to be wrong, dangerous, and repulsive. The supporters of sympathetic openness imply that one is not entitled to such hierarchies. The absence of effective hierarchies implies that one is forbidden to do two things. First, one is virtually prohibited to make any negative judgments about other points of view because such negative evaluations could be considered discriminatory. (In the case of negative toleration, certain critical evaluations were also discouraged or prevented but for different reasons: out of hypocrisy, humility, good manners, intellectual honesty, and so on.) One is forced to respect something which, contrary to his deepest convictions, he finds distasteful. One is also prohibited strong self-identification. To be true to the demands of sympathetic openness or postmodern anti-foundationalism, one should not identify oneself without simultaneously adding a list of qualifications to dispel any suspicion or harboring an exclusive or closed character. For instance, a truly tolerant Christian would be bound to affirm: "Yes, I am Christian, but I am nevertheless sympathetically open to an artist who puts the Crucifix in urine."

Can we—one must ask—live with those two prohibitions? I think the answer is, "No." One cannot be, for example, a Catholic and not feel outrage at a view of the Crucifix in urine. I see, however, one possible way for both prohibitions to be accepted. One would have to develop a certain frame of mind, or even a certain worldview, detached from any traditional hierarchical points of view such as Judaism, Islam, Protestantism, Catholicism, nationalism, conservatism, socialism, and so on. To put it briefly, one would have to become a *homo liberalis*, whose first and foremost loyalty in public as well as in private is to the order of diversity, not to any one particular creed; someone who strongly believes in the equality of cultures, moralities, ideals, usually because he feels they are authentic expressions of human existence; someone who compensates for the lack of hierarchy (that is, egalitarianism) by resolutely and vehemently opposing all forms of hierarchical outlooks, defined as "fanaticism"; someone who compensates for the indefiniteness of his creed by espousing different causes at different times (those that are currently fashionable, as his adversaries would not hesitate to remark). One day he will defend AIDS victims; another day he will speak against the oppression of women in Muslim countries; another day he will sign a petition against the antiabortion law in Ireland.

Homo liberalis constitutes a distinct conception of humanness, and as with every such conception, good and bad things can be said about it. Whether it is preferable to other conceptions of the human person is here beside the point. What is important is that *homo liberalis* is the only embodiment of humanity that can satisfy the requirements of and conditions for toleration (understood as sympathetic openness), as the particular conception of man advocated by the postmodern version. This is the major and, I would say, irredeemable weakness of sympathetic openness and postmodernism. The principal merit of toleration in the original sense was that a Protestant was not compelled to renounce his Protestantism, and a Jew was not compelled to renounce his Jewishness. It appears now that to earn the honor of being counted among the tolerant we must all become *homines liberales* and substantially transform our worldviews. Moreover, we must do so not because those worldviews have been proven false but because they are believed to be socially and politically offensive. In short, toleration entails a program of profound social reeducation. Of course, such a program may be a good thing in itself or may lead to beneficial results, but why call it toleration? A society which consists of *homines liberales* may be more tolerant than any of the actually existing societies. This does not mean, however, that it is better than those societies; or that it in the end is worth pursuing at all cost; or that the means which lead to such an end are those of tolerance.

Positive tolerationists ignore the role of strong identities and of strong thought in the functioning of social order. Like Mill, they think that stable identities and stable thought are enemies of freedom. Sometimes—it would be hard to deny—they undoubtedly are. On the other hand, however, they give us a sense of security and self-assuredness which are necessary ingredients of responsible and predictable social behavior. There is certainly some correlation between self-confidence, deriving from an awareness of the opportunity to rely on norms believed to be stable and valid, and civility, with which one may approach other points of view. Similarly, rootlessness, instability, and identity crises often jeopardize the harmony of political coexistence of groups and individuals. The most dangerous form of nationalism, for example, xenophobic and intolerant (in the original sense), is the one that feeds itself on self-doubt and confusion. For this reason, well-integrated communities, just as well-integrated individuals, are better partners of coexistence than those whose sense of integration has been weakened. Temporary stability founded on such weakness may very well collapse under the pressure of untamed longings, first thwarted and then reborn, for distinct collective identities and for strong philosophies that would give them a relatively durable legitimacy.

Strong identities and strong thought should not be put in radical opposition to toleration for another reason. The category of toleration was conceived precisely for handling the problems that arise out of the clash of strong identities and strong *Weltanschauungen*. Toleration was not a solution to these problems but a way of life where no such solution—on a theoretical as well as on a structural level—seemed at hand. With the abolition of strong identities and strong thought toleration ceases to be necessary, because it is asserted that the original problem it was proposed to cope with no longer exists. If we agree with such enthusiasts of the postmodern weakening such as Zygmut Bauman, who claims that in our times "the universal existential mode" is "the experience of estrangement" and that rootlessness and strangeness have become universal to the point of dissolution ("if everyone is a stranger, no one is"), then the question of toleration becomes immaterial. What can intolerance consist of, if we are all not only rootless, homeless, estranged, but also satisfied with our new existential condition, having lost the illusions of traditional metaphysics? Where in the new world of thin, provisional, easily changeable and pluralistic identities would it be possible to find a source of discrimination?

Here we are once again confronted with the paradox: in a world constructed so that there should be less and less intolerance, the obsession with its danger increases. The postmodernists and the pluralists, as one might suspect, have not called off their crusade for toleration, nor are they willing to modify its maximalist ambitions. No less than their predecessors, convinced of the imminence of the new era of ultimate toleration, they perceive the danger that supposedly comes from those who do not share their belief in weak identities and weak thought. It would, however, never occur to them that those enemies of the new civilization—"neofascisms" and "new archaisms," as G. B. Madison called them, still exist. Fortunately the real world continues to frustrate, as it has so often in the past, the expectations of enlightened minds. Obviously we do not know what will be, if there is such a thing, the final outcome. Perhaps those enemies—absolutists, foundationalists, essentialists, traditionalists, monists—will lose the battle and be heard from no longer. Perhaps they will become a tiny minority in a world of universal rootlessness and ever increasing diversity and perform the role of eccentrics, which the old liberals thought would be perennially performed by anticonservatives. Perhaps their importance will grow. Perhaps the postmodernists and the pluralists tend to be somewhat hysterical about fanaticism precisely because they have never really believed that their ideal of openness and centerlessness will materialize.

No matter what happens, one thing seems unquestionable. With the continuing struggle for positive toleration in our ways of thinking, of writing, of teaching, of transmitting knowledge, of using certain words and avoiding others; with the continuing emphasis on disenchanted rootlessness and diversity as the metaphysical (or rather antimetaphysical) safeguard of toleration; with the continuing suspicion and fear of partisanship in philosophy and knowledge in general, it may very well be that the world will indeed become more tolerant. At the same time, the things that will be said or allowed to be said about the world will be less and less interesting.

17

The Catholic Moment

Richard John Neuhaus

The argument and presuppositions here can be brought together in thesis form. (The reader may be pleased to note that there are not ninety-five theses.)

1. THIS IS THE CATHOLIC MOMENT

There are of course many moments in two millennia of Christian history and more than four centuries of Roman Catholicism as a church among the churches in the West. Each moment in time is equally close to God's purpose, and God's purpose equally close to each moment. But we are to read the signs of the times to discern the obligations, limits, and opportunities of our moment. This, I have argued, is the moment in which the Roman Catholic Church in the world can and should be the lead church in proclaiming and exemplifying the Gospel. This can and should also be the moment in which the Roman Catholic Church in the United States assumes its rightful role in the culture-forming task of constructing a religiously informed public philosophy for the American experiment in ordered liberty. The first obligation and opportunity is much more important. Indeed the achievement of the second is entirely dependent upon giving careful priority to the first. The specifically Christian proposition, and the community of faith that it brings into being, must be held in relentless and dynamic tension with all other propositions, including the American proposition. Pope John Paul is this historical moment's most public witness to the truth that if this tension is relaxed, the Church has nothing distinctive or ultimately helpful to offer the world.

Reprinted from *The Catholic Moment: The Paradox of the Church in the Postmodern World* (New York: Harper and Row, 1978), pp. 283–288.

2. THE MOST IMPORTANT OPENING EFFECTED BY VATICAN COUNCIL II IS THE OPENING TO THE CHURCH

This opening to the Church is, above all, an opening to the Gospel by which the Church is created and sustained. This is the Gospel that forms and integrates what Joseph Cardinal Ratzinger calls "the structure of faith." In the Council's further development of the tradition, it is made much clearer than it was before that the Roman Catholic Church is vulnerable to the Gospel and to the entire community that is claimed by the Gospel. In subsequent official teaching the primacy of the Gospel is asserted with a force unprecedented in Roman Catholic history. In truth, the Reformation understanding of the Gospel as God's justifying grace centered in the scriptural *kerygma* of cross and resurrection is today more boldly proclaimed by Rome than by many of the churches that lay claim to the Reformation heritage.

3. THE CATHOLIC MOMENT IS TO ALERT THE WORLD TO THE TRUE NATURE OF ITS CRISIS

The greatest threat to the world is not political or economic or military. The greatest problem in the Church is not institutional decline or disarray. *The* crisis of this time and every time is the crisis of unbelief. With a sense of urgency that the world, and much of the Church, find embarrassing, Rome persists in asking, "When the Son of Man comes, will he find faith on earth?" This Pope is exercised not about dissent but about apostasy. He is attempting to chart a Christian course that is not so much against modernity as it is beyond modernity. The only modernity to be discarded is the debased modernity of unbelief that results in a prideful and premature closure of the world against its promised destiny. This Pope is giving voice to the Christian correlate to the opening to the transcendent that in culture, philosophy, and science is the great intellectual and spiritual event of our time. The Christian correlate, of course, is Christ. In this respect, John Paul is far ahead of those Christians, including many Roman Catholics, who are only now learning to accommodate the faith to a debased modernity that history is fast leaving behind. It is said that John XXIII opened the windows of the Church to the modern world. John Paul has entered the modern world to help open the windows of the modern world to the worlds of which it is part.

4. ECUMENISM, INHERENT AND IRREVERSIBLE, IS ESSENTIAL TO THE REALIZATION OF THE CATHOLIC MOMENT

The Roman Catholic decision to pursue the more visible unity of the Church is irreversible because it is based upon the understanding that Christian unity is inherent in *being* the Church. The only Christ and the only Gospel by which a community can be the Church is the Christ and Gospel of the entire Church. The only unity that is lasting and worth pursuing is a unity rooted in a shared confession of Christ and the Gospel. Theological integrity is therefore not an obstacle to unity but the servant of unity. Ecumenism is not so much a program with a timetable as a way of living together in the one Church. Unity is to be achieved not by ecclesiastical conquest but by reconciled diversity in obedience to the Gospel. The Roman Catholic Church has a singular ecumenical calling to take the lead in healing the breach between the churches of the East and those of the West. In the West, the foremost obligation and opportunity is the healing of the breach of the sixteenth century between Rome and the Reformation. In America and especially in the developing world, the forces of greatest Christian vitality are Roman Catholicism and evangelical Protestantism. In many parts of the world, notably in Latin America, these forces are at war with one another. Although the obstacles are daunting, the Catholic Moment requires that the ecumenical mandate of Vatican II be extended to evangelical and fundamentalist Protestantism. An ecumenical commitment indomitable and full-orbed is required if Christianity is believably to represent hope for the unity of humankind.

5. THE CATHOLIC MOMENT REQUIRES A RENEWED DEMONSTRATION OF UNITY IN DIVERSITY

Pluralism is not a fault. It is evidence of the incompleteness of the world and of the Church within the world. Pluralism in the Church should not be the result of dissent from the Gospel but of diverse forms of radical obedience to the Gospel. The Roman Catholic Church is by far the most diverse of churches. With its discrete orders of ministry, its monastic communities, its myriad works of mercy, its multifarious national and cultural traditions, its political and ideological inclusiveness, and even its different patterns of theological reflection, the Roman Catholic Church is the paradigmatic instance of the unity in diversity that other churches should emulate and to which the world aspires. John Paul now declares that unity in diversity is in jeopardy—not because a few dissent from juridical authority but because many have been led astray from the Gospel. He is engaged in a project of restoration that some view as a renewed oppression and others as an effort to restore coherence to a tradition shattered by the assaults of modernity. In Vatican II the Roman Catholic Church kept its long-delayed appointment with modernity. The future of Christianity in the world will be powerfully influenced by whether Catholicism emerges from this meeting with a unity that is not uniformity and a diversity that is not division.

6. THE CATHOLIC MOMENT REQUIRES A RENEWAL OF THEOLOGY IN SERVICE TO THE COMMUNITY OF FAITH AND ITS MISSION IN THE WORLD

There are inevitable tensions between the magisterium, or official teaching authority, and the theological enterprise. The basic relationship between the two, however, is not one of tension but of mutual service under the Gospel. That at least is the argument of Joseph Cardinal Ratzinger. Theology is a continuing conversation in which the magisterium plays the essentially pastoral part of guiding but not controlling the discourse. This ecclesial understanding of the theological enterprise is radically at odds with patterns of academic theology that have emerged since Vatican II. Like liberal Protestant theology before it, Roman Catholic theology increasingly finds itself torn between two communities competing for loyalty: academe and the church. This competition engages a strong element of class conflict, for most theologians belong to what is accurately described as the new knowledge class whose interests are preeminently served by academe. Continuing disputes about intellectual freedom are typically not about intellectual freedom. They are disputes over which community and which tradition is given priority by the theologian. In a "postliberal" understanding of cultural-linguistic traditions, it is seen that academic freedom is also an imposed discipline, that putative universalisms are also particularistic, and that release from orthodoxies is yet another orthodoxy. The Catholic Moment depends in large part upon whether Roman Catholic theologians move toward a postliberal position of service to the Gospel and the community that bears the Gospel, or, as in most of Protestantism, become stalled in sterile contests between liberalism and traditionalism.

7. IF THE CATHOLIC MOMENT IS REALIZED, IT WILL ENHANCE THE PROSPECT FOR FREEDOM AND JUSTICE IN THE WORLD

Among world figures today, John Paul is the foremost champion of freedom as the first component of justice. He proclaims the truth that "the free adherence of the person to God" is both the font and foundation, the source and safeguard, of all human rights. Without that transcendent referent, all talk about human rights is, as Bentham declared it to be, nonsense on stilts. Against the propensities of all states, and against the ideology of some states and movements, the Church must contend to secure social space for the personal and communal "aspiration to the infinite." In order to be more effective, however, Roman Catholic social teaching must more thoroughly integrate the moral and political wisdom of specific experiments in ordered freedom and justice. John Courtney Murray's long-neglected exploration into the meaning of the American proposition should be taken up again, and the Council's "Declaration on Religious Freedom" should be further elaborated to illumine the choices facing the modern world.

8. THE CATHOLIC MOMENT CHALLENGES THE IMPERIOUSNESS OF THE POLITICAL

This thesis follows closely upon the last. The freedom of the person and of persons in community must be secured by right political order. Right political order requires setting sharp limitations upon the political, if political is understood as state power. A wide array of associations, including religion, are "public" institutions and essential to the vitality of the earthly *polis*. The Church makes its greatest public contribution when it is most true to its own nature and mission. In a democracy, the primary political contribution of church leadership is to "equip the saints" for the exercise of their ministry in the public arena. The Church itself is called to be a community of virtue and a zone of truth in a political world of viciousness and mandacity. A "partisan church" is an apostate church. The Church has a theology of politics, not a political theology. A theology of politics requires that pastoral leadership both affirm the political project while, at the same time, keeping all political proposals under moral judgment. The Church in all times and places has never done this very well. Religious leadership, including Roman Catholic leadership, in America today sometimes seems hardly to be trying. The results are that the Church is perceived as but one political actor among others, political discourse is inflamed rather than informed, and the integrity of both Church and political order are grievously violated.

9. THE CATHOLIC MOMENT WILL REDIRECT THE WORLD'S PASSION FOR LIBERATION

With love for its proponents and even greater love for its victims, Christians must repudiate the proposal that politics is salvation and salvation is politics. With John Paul, and invoking Saint Paul, we must reject the now dominant forms of liberation theology as "another gospel." Contrary to certain ideologies, eternal destiny and temporal duty are not opposed to one another. It is empirically probable and logically persuasive that human development is best advanced by transcendent hope. It is historically undeniable that, where transcendent hope is denied, all development leads only to new forms of bondage. Because it is the only Gospel we have been given, and because it is the deepest truth about humanity, the Church must boldly proclaim our vocation to the radically "new politics" of the heavenly city. Short of the Kingdom Come, we are alien citizens. In contending against the idolatry of the political, the Roman Catholic Church is today contending on behalf of the Gospel and therefore on behalf of all Christians.

10. THE CATHOLIC MOMENT IS FOR THE DURATION

Even when, please God, all the churches are in full communion in the one Church Catholic, there will likely still be a Roman Catholic Church. By virtue of its size, tradition, structure, charisms, and energies, the Roman Catholic Church will have a singular part in shaping the world-historical future of Christianity. And if the Gospel is true, Christianity bears witness to the future of the world, who is Christ. Therefore the Catholic Moment is encompassed by an eschatological horizon. Before that final consummation the relationship between Church and world will always be problematic. The world is ever prone to premature closure, turning in upon itself and against its transcendent destiny. The Church is ever tempted to join the world in that fatal turning. This is the temptation represented by Dostoyevsky's Grand Inquisitor, and the Grand Inquisitor takes many forms—theological, philosophical, spiritual, political. The Grand Inquisitor would persuade the prodigal sons of earth that they can be at home in a world that is still far from the home of the waiting Father. Resisting that temptation, the Church must often appear to be against the world, but it will always be against the world for the world. The Church's view of reality is premised upon a promise and is therefore in tension with all views of reality premised upon the present alone. The Church too lives in the present, but it lives by a promise that is also the ultimate truth about the present. Thus the Church's relationship to the world is essentially paradoxical. It is a relationship of yes and no, now and not yet. The Church will endure until the End Time, but along the way it is ever being tested as to whether it has the courage to live in paradoxical fidelity. Nowhere is that testing so severe, nowhere is the outcome of that testing so ominous, as in the Roman Catholic Church. This Pope, we all have reason to believe and reason to hope, knows that the paradox cannot be resolved and must not be relaxed. It can only be superseded by the coming of the One who is both the consummation and companion of our common pilgrimage.

18

The Pope and the Liberal State

Russell Hittinger

It is not hard to understand why when *Centesimus Annus* was issued in 1991, its economic teachings almost immediately received the most attention. For with respect both to substance and emphasis, *Centesimus* does represent a considerable development in papal social thought on economic matters.

In *Rerum Novarum* (1891), Leo XIII defended what he called the "stable and perpetual," "inviolable," and "sacred" right to private property (RN 6, 15, 46). Yet he was less interested in understanding the phenomenon of economic freedom on its own terms than he was in asserting moral and juridical principles necessary for answering the twin evils of unrestricted laissez-faire and state socialism. Pope John Paul II, however, evinces a more direct interest in the entrepreneurial spirit and in the moral value of "the modern business economy" (CA 32).

Moreover, John Paul II's stiff criticism of centralized command economies and his admonitions about the dangers of the welfare state have important implications for how papal social teaching must now be brought to bear upon economic policies in Eastern Europe, the Third World, and even in the developed nations where these issues are debated by prelates and the laity.

Though this revision in the papal approach to economic issues is undeniably important, nevertheless it is the Pope's view of the political state that represents the more important evolution in papal teaching since *Rerum Novarum*. *Centesimus*, indeed, is the first papal encyclical that treats the modern state as what recent history has taught us to recognize it to be: namely, a potentially dangerous concentration of coercive power requiring the most exacting juridical and structural limitations. Simply put, the political state depicted in *Centesimus Annus* is no longer the classical or medieval *civitas* assumed by John Paul II's predecessors.

First published in *First Things*, December 1992.

The encyclicals of the Leonine papacy, for example, typically treated the state as a kind of prodigal child of Christendom that needs to be summoned once again by the Holy See to its proper responsibilities, albeit in the face of certain modern crises. But the state visualized by Pope Leo is still the premodern state, pictured as an organic *communitas perfecta*—in Leo's words, "some likeness and symbol as it were of the Divine Majesty, even when it is exercised by one unworthy" (*Sapientiae Christianae*, 1890, 9).

This conception of the political state is not John Paul II's. Not that, for him, the political state has no moral task, much less that the state is bereft of God-given norms. The state is repeatedly called to its moral responsibilities in *Centesimus*. Nonetheless, the Pope regards the state as more of an artificial construct, whose end it is to serve the legitimate economic and cultural interests of individuals and corporate entities that are not reducible to the state. This does not merely accommodate liberal political and legal institutions. Rather, it bespeaks a decisive, normative turn toward the liberal state. The key here is not whether the state has moral responsibilities, but the institutional and juridical limits on how the state may rightfully exercise those responsibilities.

II

At the very beginning of *Centesimus*, the Pope takes note of the historical context in which *Rerum Novarum* was promulgated. "In the sphere of politics the result of these changes was a new conception of society and of the state, and consequently of authority itself. A traditional society was passing away and another was beginning to be formed—one which brought the hope of new freedoms, but also the threat of new forms of injustice and servitude" (CA 4). The problem underscored here was not just Pope Leo's response to the economic crises engendered by industrialization, but a wider and deeper change in the relation between the state and society, and indeed in the understanding of authority itself. And the problem of "limits inherent in the nature of the state" (CA 11) is not only central to the Pope's exegesis of *Rerum Novarum*, but also to his assessment of the contemporary situation.

Pope Leo's treatment of the state relied upon the traditional language of natural law, that is, the Thomistic concept of natural law as a participation in the eternal law. All power of governance, Leo asserts, "emanate[s] from God" (*Diuturnum*, 1881, 12). It does not derive from consent or contract, much less from human rights, but from God "as from a natural and necessary principle" (D 5; but also in *Libertas Praestantissimum* [1888, 13, 17]; *Immortale Dei* [1885, 3–4]; RN 7, 52). Pope Leo describes the "necessary principle" as the eternal law, of which the natural law is our first participation in divine governance. This participationist scheme, moving from eternal to natural to human laws is, in its essentials, Thomistic. The first and most important limit upon the state is, as it were, from above rather than below.

The broad metaphysical and theological picture here is that of a divine commonwealth in which the political state can properly be described as under an imperative to imitate (however imperfectly) God (LP 33). And because the state is a "likeness and symbol as it were of the Divine Majesty" (SP 9), Pope Leo does not shrink from calling its ruling powers "sacred" (ID 18). The reference in *Rerum Novarum* to property rights as *iura sancia* notwithstanding, the principle *sanctum* in the order of political theory remained, for Pope Leo, the state as a participator in divine governance—even, as he says, when the power is exercised "by one unworthy." When citizens submit to the civil authority, they submit to divine authority (ID 18).

This point of view persisted, more or less explicitly, in papal encyclicals up to the present time—including what many would regard as the most modern of encyclicals, Pope John XXIII's *Pacem in Terris* (1963). Citing Pius XII, Pope John maintained that "the dignity of the state's authority is due to its sharing to some extent in the authority of God himself" (47).

While Pope John Paul is certainly correct when he says that the author of *Rerum Novarum* faced radical changes in the notion of authority, it is equally important to bear in mind that Pope Leo did not give an inch on the older formulation of the authority of the state. While he did have a keen appreciation for the potential tyranny of some modern states—incorporating the modern language of individual rights as one way to counter the tyranny of an unjust or disordered political regime and putting forth the notion of property as a *ius sanctum*—*Rerum Novarum* evinces no approval of what could be called (either then or now) "liberalism." It is worth recalling that the encyclical was issued less than forty years after Pope Pius IX's *Syllabus of Errors* (1854), which declared: "It is an error to believe that the Roman pontiff can or should reconcile himself to and agree with progress, liberalism, and modern civilization" (69).

From all available evidence, Leo XIII regarded the *ius sanctum* of property as something implicit in the traditional moral and political theory of Thomas Aquinas. The right could be recognized, and indeed emphasized, without in any way conceding a "liberal" doctrine of the state. His main response, therefore, was to reassert the model of a divine commonwealth: in *Rerum Novarum* (27) he expressly calls European peoples back to the "primal constitution" of Christian order, by which he means Christendom as a political entity, like "the institution of the Holy Roman Empire, [which] consecrated the political power in a wonderful manner" (D 22).

III

Centesimus Annus bespeaks a distinctly different historical and philosophical view. For one thing, the "image of God" in *Centesimus* is reserved for human persons, in contrast to the powers of the state:

> The root of modern totalitarianism is to be found in the denial of the transcendent dignity of the human person who, as the visible image of the invisible God, is therefore by his very nature the subject of rights which no one may violate—no individual, group, class, nation, or state. Not even the majority of a social body may violate these

rights by going against the minority, by isolating, oppressing, or exploiting it, or by attempting to annihilate it (CA 44).

The important point here is John Paul II's refusal to drape any kind of theological mantle over the state. Nowhere in *Centesimus* is there any reference to the political state as in the image of divine governance. On the contrary, the political state tends to be described in forbidding terms. John Paul speaks pejoratively, for instance, of the "national security state," the "social assistance state," "state administration," "state capitalism" as "bureaucratic control" and as "secular religion" (CA 19, 48, 49, 35, 25). To be sure, this language is intended to refer to degraded and disordered aspects of the modern state. Still, Pope John Paul is extremely critical of the power of the political state—not so much as an abstract entity in political philosophy, but as a concrete historical reality.

Thus whereas Leo XIII was generally sanguine about the positive role of the political state, but cautious about modern economic developments, John Paul II is generally optimistic about the creative dynamism of the modern business economy, but palpably suspicious of the state. The reason for the divergence between them is hardly mysterious: Leo lived at the end of an era in which the authority of Christian princes was being challenged by secular ideologies and in which both socialism and radical laissez-faire practices were threatening the *civitas* as Leo knew it. John Paul, on the other hand, witnessed the emergence of totalitarian states that conducted a policy of "total war" within and without (CA 14). They obliterated, along with Christian culture, the conditions of economic development and the rule of law.

From John Paul's perspective, the modern state has not so much defaced the political image of divine governance vested in the civil authority as it has assaulted that image as it subsists in human persons. Hence where Leo was interested in reconnecting the civil authority to the proper understanding of divine governance under the eternal law, John Paul emphasizes the need to connect the state to a proper understanding of the human person. Whether in the areas of economics, law, or politics, he emphasizes and reemphasizes the teaching that the root cause of totalitarianism is a false anthropology (CA 11, 133).

How, in the view of John Paul, is the state to be limited? His most critical remarks about the welfare state are made in light of the principle of subsidiarity (CA 48, and also in 10, 15, 49), drawn not from Leo XIII but from Pius XI. He is exceedingly critical of top-heavy bureaucracies that, however well-intentioned, undermine local initiatives and responsibilities in economic matters. Interestingly, when *Centesimus* addresses the problem of the relation between the state and those who are poor and/or vulnerable, it speaks mainly of the responsibility to protect juridical rights (CA 10)—a notion markedly different from a responsibility to engage in administrative interventions. While the state has a responsibility to oversee and direct the exercise of economic rights, the "primary responsibility in this area belongs not to the state, but to individuals and to the various groups and associations which make up society" (48). Significantly, the Pope maintains that the decentralization of power and responsibility promotes greater productivity and efficiency, "even though it may weaken consolidated power structures" (CA 43).

When he speaks of the "rule of law," however, he goes beyond the principle of subsidiarity. John Paul writes approvingly that Pope Leo XIII

> presents the organization of society according to the three powers—legislative, executive, and judicial—something which at the time represented a novelty in church teaching. Such an ordering reflects a realistic vision of man's social nature, which calls for legislation capable of protecting the freedom of all. To that end, it is preferable that each power be balanced by other powers and by other spheres of responsibility which keep it within proper bounds. This is the principle of the "rule of law" in which the law is sovereign, and not the arbitrary will of individuals.

Interestingly, sections 32–33 of *Rerum Novarum*, cited as evidence for this "novel" teaching, contain a quite different approach. Here, Pope Leo quotes Aquinas's dictum: "As the part and the whole are in a certain sense identical, so that which belongs to the whole in a sense belongs to the part." Read in context, this is not even remotely similar to John Paul's notion of limiting the state by means of pragmatic allocation and division of its powers, much less an equation between such an arrangement and the rule of law.

The check upon the power of the state is not drawn simply from an understanding of the hierarchical and organic distinction between the parts of the whole, but from a "realistic" understanding of structural limitations imposed upon institutions of the civil *potestas*. While the division of powers can be interpreted as something complementary to the older organic model, the equation of such structural limits with the "rule of law" is modern. It is modern not only with respect to its historical pedigree in eighteenth-century republicanism, but also with respect to its function: one speaks of the division of powers not to provide a picture of how the individual members are distinguished and fitted to the body but to ameliorate the potential abuses of power.

The structural division of the civil *potestas* is not a necessary metaphysical principle. It does not, as was claimed for the Marxist state, flow from a knowledge of "deeper laws," but has been learned by trial and error. Among the many philosophical errors John Paul attributes to modern totalitarians is that they took themselves to be "exempt from error." And in exempting themselves from error, they erected no structural safeguards to the misuse of civil power.

This is not for one moment to suggest either that John Paul II sees in the structural elements of the rule of law merely extrinsic compensation for human failure or that he recommends a merely neutral and proceduralist rule of law shorn of substantive notions of justice. "Authentic democracy," he warns, "is possible only in a state ruled by law and on the basis of a correct conception of the human person" (CA 46). Nor would his understanding of what is entailed in the "correct conception" be apt to satisfy a liberal proceduralist. Milton Friedman's remark that the Pope's emphasis upon obedience to the truths about God and man "sent shivers down my back" speaks for itself.

Even so, it is important not to lose sight of the fact that, however adamant about the importance of timeless truths, the encyclical clearly introduces the note of human fallibility with regard to political institutions. In the light of recent history, two problems in particular emerge in somewhat sharpened focus: the need, in economics, to protect nongovernmental initiatives, and the even more pressing need to set juridical limits to the power of the state. The Pope's turn toward a liberal model of the state is not shaped by any conscious aversion to the theories of Locke, Madison, or any of our great constitutional jurists. Forged in the crucible of a very different history, *Centesimus* nevertheless recommends both structural and rights-based limits on the state that are remarkably similar to those achieved in Anglo-American institutions.

There remains the question of how to reconcile the Pope's sense of the state with the ideal of "solidarity" that is so evident in the pages of the encyclical. Is it possible to espouse a liberal, or at least quasi-liberal, view of the state and at the same time speak, as he does, of the "expanding chain of solidarity" (43)? (This is, of course, a question that has led to fervent debate among liberal theorists themselves: can liberal political institutions accommodate the communitarian ideals of modern citizens?)

One thing this Pope has learned is the inevitability of conflict. For him, conflict in the economic and social sectors is not necessarily an evil or a disordered phenomenon. Indeed, he appears to assume that some states will be religiously pluralistic and will thus have to negotiate religious differences according to juridically recognized rights. It is important to remember that Marxist and socialist states claimed to have as their principal goal the elimination of self-interest and societal conflict by subsuming all activities into the power of the state. For John Paul, the main problem is not the stress and strain of either religious pluralism or economic markets. Rather, it is conflict not "constrained" by ethical or juridical considerations"—a "total war" in which force is put above the rule of law (CA 14). The state's principal task, then, is to determine the "juridical framework" of economic and social activities.

In contrast to the classical or medieval conception of the *civitas*, the state in *Centesimus* is not the locus or principal expression of cosmic harmony. It is not empowered to smooth over the rough and tumble of economic and religious difference. Nor is it to sacrifice the shaggy and incomplete dynamisms of economic activity to consolidated state power. John Paul recognizes that once it is submitted to proper limits, the power of the state will be weakened. It is interesting that the reference to the "progressively expanding chain of solidarity" in 43 is set in the context of a discussion of limits upon state power.

In the encyclical *Sollicitudo Rei Socialis* (1987), solidarity denotes various kinds of "collaboration" among individuals and states (SR 39). Yet in *Sollicitudo* solidarity also stands in tension with freedom: "In order to be genuine, development must be achieved within the framework of solidarity and freedom, without ever sacrificing either of them under whatever pretext" (SR 33). Here, the Pope distinguishes between the principle of social and affective unity whereby persons or groups collaborate toward common ends, and the principle of freedom. And it is the latter principle that constitutes the reason for political rights.

In *Centesimus* the cultural, familial, economic, and religious activities are ordained to "solidarity" of various sorts, while the state, on the other hand, has the obligation to protect the rights of citizens to engage in such activities. Throughout the encyclical the Pope invariably reserves juridical language for application to the state's dealings with its citizens and reserves for the societal and cultural spheres the language of solidarity. For instance, he writes that:

> According to *Rerum Novarum* and the whole social doctrine of the church, the social nature of man is not completely fulfilled by the state, but is realized in various intermediary groups, beginning with the family and including economic, social, political, and cultural groups which stem from human nature itself and have their own autonomy, always with a view to the common good. This is what I have called the "subjectivity" of society which, together with the subjectivity of the individual, was canceled out by "real socialism" (CA 13).

This is but one piece of evidence of John Paul's clear distinction between the structures of the state and the "subjectivity" of society. Indeed, even though the Pope regards religion as the center of culture, and hence the preeminent locus for solidarity, he nevertheless insists that juridical right to religious liberty is the "primary foundation of every authentically free political order" (CA 29).

In *Catholic Social Thought and Liberal Institutions* (1989), Michael Novak has pointed to a chief difference between "solidarist methods" (whether of the left or right) and the institutional procedures of liberal regimes. Whereas solidarist approaches to the common good envisage the public authority "suffused throughout the society from *above*," the liberal approach emphasizes multiple and coordinate perspectives. In this light, the traditional papal doctrine of subsidiarity is amendable to two quite different views of institutions. If we take the older understanding of organic hierarchies, the principle of subsidiarity reemphasizes the notion of those proper analogies that obtain between the various levels of the body politic. Solidarity could be said to suffuse the entire body, but be enacted in analogically different ways. If, however, we take the perspective of liberal institutions, the sectors are more sharply differentiated. Even the powers of the state are to be divided. In *Centesimus Annus*, the organic idea of one power subsisting in another is jettisoned in favor of the idea of externally coordinated powers. Throughout the encyclical there is no hint of Aristotelian organicism, at least not with respect to the state. This allows the Pope to emphasize the nature of solidarity in the social, religious, and cultural spheres.

Centesimus Annus is not a "liberal" account of the destiny of man, but it does reflect the hard-won lessons of liberal political institutions. John Paul's stringent attention to the structural limits of the state, his careful efforts to distinguish its sphere from the social, economic, and religious life, and his persistent endorsement of individual rights against the state must be regarded as a rejection of those liberation theologians like Gustavo Gutierrez who deny the "distinction of planes" (e.g., between politics, law, religion, and culture). *Centesimus*, therefore, not only represents a considerable change from the older "conservative" model of organic hierarchies, it also stands adamantly opposed to the "leftist" reduction of *praxis* to an undifferentiated notion of politics. It would also seem that *Centesimus Annus* settles the much-debated business about a Catholic "third way." On the eightieth anniversary of *Rerum Novarum*, Pope Paul VI issued *Octogesima Adveniens* (1971). The encyclical appeared to suggest a third way between the Marxist and liberal models, both of which Pope Paul put under the rubric of "ideology." Concerning liberalism, Paul wrote:

> [I]t asserts itself both in the name of economic efficiency, and for the defense of the individual against the increasingly overwhelming hold of organizations, and as a reaction against the totalitarian tendencies of political powers. . . . But do not Christians who take this path tend to idealize liberalism in their turn, making it a proclamation in favor of freedom? They would like a new model, more adapted to present-day conditions, while easily forgetting that at the very root of philosophical liberalism is an erroneous affirmation of the autonomy of the individual in his activity, his motivation, and the exercise of his liberty.

While *Centesimus* does not disagree on the point about liberalism as an "ideology," the events of 1989 seem to have led John Paul to render a quite different verdict about the historical and institutional issues. Bluntly put, John Paul takes more seriously than did his predecessors the practical need to limit totalitarianism. He takes more seriously the practical, lived experienced of peoples who have suffered under these states.

IV

The prominence of rights language in the postwar encyclicals and pronouncements represents a considerable change form the prewar encyclicals running from Leo XIII to Pius XII. Of course, Pope Leo XIII insisted upon the importance of natural rights, and may fairly be credited with making the idea a more or less permanent fixture in papal social encyclicals. Yet something important did change after the Second World War. Papal and ecclesial documents began for the first time to speak of rights in terms of an ideal of modern constitutionalism. Indeed, both *Dignitatis Humanae* (1965, 1) and *Pacem in Terris* (1963, 27) explicitly refer to rights in the context of constitutional and juridical limits upon the political state.

No doubt there are a number of reasons for this. The Church appropriated the language used not only by international bodies like the United Nations, but also by the Western allies who subdued Hitler and Mussolini. As Maritain wrote in 1951, the "great achievement" of the eighteenth century had been "to bring out in full light the rights of man as also required by the natural law." The wars in Europe brought the Church to see the good sense of this historical judgment. Hence, there was at least one thing about the Enlightenment that the Church could embrace, for both philosophical and practical reasons. The new *Codex Iuris Canonici* (1983) maintains that: "To the Church belongs the right always and everywhere to announce moral principles, including those pertaining to the social order, and to make judgments on any human affairs to the extent that they are required by the fundamental rights of the human person [*quatenus personae humanae iura fundamentalia*] or the salvation of souls" (canon 747/2). These *iura fundamentalia* might include natural rights, or for that matter, particularly important legal and constitutional rights. In any case, the Code explicitly refers to the Church's authority to address *iura fundamentalia*, rather than to interpret the *lex naturalis*.

What are these rights? In *Centesimus* the Pope does not clearly distinguish among their different genera and species, but appears rather to use an all-purpose language of natural rights. In some places, he speaks of *iura fundamentalia* (fundamental rights, CA 6), *iura hominis* (rights of man, CA 22), and of *iura . . . ab ea abalienari* (inalienable rights, CA 7). Elsewhere, he refers to one or another right as a *ius naturae* (right of nature, CA 7), or a *ius ad autoniam* (a right to autonomy, CA 30). Of course, a fundamental right need not be the same as a natural right, and all natural rights need not be seen as inalienable ones. The language does not have the same kind of precision that we would expect in an academic treatise on legal and political rights. That problem notwithstanding, it is generally clear what the Pope has in mind: natural rights that are in one or another sense antecedent to political society.

There is no need here to extract a complete list of these rights; they are enumerated in more than one place in the encyclical. Sometimes the Pope refers to the rights enunciated in *Rerum Novarum*, while in other places he refers to rights in the light of the events of 1989. But he also refers to rights affirmed by various international bodies, as well as those mentioned in one or another papal encyclical or conciliar document. Taken together, and edited somewhat for brevity, a short list includes the following:

—"right and duty to seek God, to know him and to live in accordance with that knowledge" (29, 47);
—"rights to private initiative, to ownership of property, and to freedom in the economic sphere" (24);
—"right to express one's own personality at the workplace without suffering any affront to one's conscience and personal dignity" (15);
—"right to private associations" (7);
—"right to life" (47);
—"right to live in a united family and in a moral environment conducive to the growth of the child's personality" (47);
—"right to develop one's intelligence and freedom in seeking and knowing the truth" (47);
—"right to share in the work which makes wise use of the earth's material resources" (47).

Again, there is no explicit reference to "natural law." Pope Leo XIII might have been surprised to discover that the encyclical celebrating and recapitulating the hundredth anniversary of *Rerum Novarum* had nothing to say about natural law. *Pacem in Terris*, which contains the most extensive papal compilation of natural rights, was careful to claim that the rights are derived from God via the natural law: "And rights as well as duties find their source, their sustenance, and their inviolability in the natural law which grants or enjoins them" (PT 28, and also 4–7). Even the conciliar decree on religious liberty, *Dignitatis Humanae*, retained the traditional language of the eternal and natural laws (DH 3). Whether or not Leo XIII would have approved of *Dignitatis*, he certainly would recognize its philosophical vocabulary.

How are we to interpret *Centesimus* in this regard? Does the absence of explicit reference to natural law represent a rhetorical anomaly or oversight, or does it bespeak a substantive position? Having jettisoned the older participationist model of the political state, has the Pope taken the next step, which is to drop the metaphysical language of natural law associated with that model, in favor of natural rights?

An alert reader can find bits and pieces of natural law language in *Centesimus*. In paragraph 29 the Pope refers to "truth, both natural and revealed." But he seems more interested here in showing the conformity of rights to the Helsinki Accords than to any scholastic notion of reason and faith on matters of law. In paragraph 13, he refers to the various intermediary groups as stemming "from human nature," but immediately introduces his own philosophical language of the "subjectivity" of the individual and society. Indeed, where Leo XIII gave a natural law analysis of the right to human association—"all striving against nature is in vain" (RN 17)—Pope John Paul II enunciates the social dimension of "personalism" (CA 38). There can be no question but that the Pope wants to discuss these things in the light of a theocentric anthropology. The truth about man is a central theme to which the issues of rights, markets, and the state are subordinated. Inasmuch as one believes that there is an objective morality based upon the truth about human nature, one could be said to have a natural law position. But this could be claimed for any species of moral objectivism.

While the text of *Centesimus Annus* simply does not provide us with a sure way to answer the question about natural law, there are three things we do know. First, since the pontificate of John XXIII, the popes have been sensitive to the danger that the term "natural law" may be construed to mean the subhuman regularities and predictabilities of physical nature—that is to say, "natural laws" as they are understood by the modern sciences. While Americans are perhaps more liable to recognize the connection between "natural law" and the so-called "higher laws," this is not necessarily so for Europeans. For us, natural law as a "higher" law is evident in our Declaration of Independence, in the discussion leading to the adoption of the Thirteenth and Fourteenth Amendments, in Martin Luther King's "Letter from Birmingham Jail," and in the almost continuous judicial use of the concept (for good or for ill) since the late nineteenth century. Indeed, there is something distinctively American in John Courtney Murray's case for natural law in *We Hold These Truths*

(1960). Murray believed that Americans can return to the commonplace of natural law as a source of consensus about basic political and legal values because our regime was founded in the eighteenth century upon that consensus. But, as the Pope points out in *Centesimus*, Europeans "are closely united in a bond of common culture and an age-old history" (27). The culture of Europe was not founded upon a consensus about the rather abstract doctrine of natural law. In fact, for Europeans, natural law can suggest either an ahistorical order of physics and biology, or the tradition of revolutionary Jacobinism, which is hardly suited to a defense of first things in the political order.

Moreover, it must be remembered that the Vatican was stung by the criticism that *Humanae Vitae* (1968) reduced the moral norms concerning birth control to a kind of biologism. Cardinal Ratzinger, who is more comfortable with the scholastic language of natural law than is Pope John Paul II, has nonetheless taken great pains to explain that natural law pertains to a "rational order" rather than to biological necessities. Hence, we can speculate that the absence of natural law language in *Centesimus* reflects a rhetorical strategy to avoid a reductionist construal of the terms.

In the second place, *Centesimus Annus*, like many other of the Pope's writings, gravitates toward the historical, cultural, and religious intelligibility of human nature. For example, the Pope writes:

> Man is understood in a more complete way when he is situated within the sphere of culture through his language, history, and the position he takes toward the fundamental events of life such as birth, love, work, and death. At the heart of every culture lies the attitude man takes to the greatest mystery: the mystery of God. Different cultures are basically different ways of facing the question of personal existence. When this question is eliminated, the culture and moral life of nations are corrupted. (CA 24)

Of course, the culturally and linguistically situated agent is reconcilable with *some* theories of natural law. Yet it remains true that this Pope is more interested in discussing the universal and transcendent characteristics of man through the realms of culture and history, and ultimately theology, than he is in terms of either scholastic or Enlightenment versions of natural law.

Finally, and most importantly, the subject of natural rights is a ready-made and widely accepted way to address the problem of limits upon the political state. A. P. d'Entreves once said that "the real significance of natural law must be sought in its function rather than in the doctrine itself." Although this does not recommend itself as good advice for one who wishes to understand the philosophical issues, it is a shrewd way to cut through the often bewildering verbal protocols about natural law. Functionally speaking, discourse based on natural law of rights has had a readily identifiable purpose, viz., the limitation of state power. This best explains the Pope's use of natural rights language. It fits hand in glove with his interest in liberal political institutions.

On this score, paragraph 29 is important, for it summarizes very clearly the functional purpose of rights. Referring to modern totalitarian regimes, the Pope maintains that: "Man was compelled to submit to a conception of reality imposed on him by coercion and not reached by virtue of his own reason and the exercise of his own freedom. This principle must be overturned and total recognition must be given to the rights of the human conscience, which is bound to the truth, both natural and revealed. The recognition of these rights represents the primary foundation of every authentically free political order."

The Pope gives three reasons for the urgency of the rights-based approach to the political order. First, the older forms of totalitarianism are not completely vanquished. In effect, the Pope recommends that rights be juridically established while the opportunity is at hand. Second, even in developed countries there is what the Pope calls "an excessive promotion of purely utilitarian values." Because of the tendency to enlist the state to resolve social, economic, and political crises on a merely utilitarian basis, it is crucial to erect rights-based limits to governmental power. Third, and perhaps most interesting, the Pope worries about the problem of "religious fundamentalism" denying "to citizens of faiths other than that of the majority the full exercise of their civil and religious rights."

Paragraph 29 is one of the most extraordinary discussions in the entire encyclical. Among the kinds of mischief that rights are supposed to guard against, the Pope underscores those caused by political majorities—either in the name of utility, or in the name of religion. This bespeaks the ideal of the liberal rule of law rather than the ideal of the medieval *civitas*, or for that matter the ideal of solidarity. In addition to the division of governmental powers, it is necessary to provide for individual rights as checks against what majorities can effect through the government. In 44, where he discusses the rule of law, the Pope expressly says that rights must be understood as inviolate against "even the majority of a social body."

It would be wrong, of course, to insinuate that the convergence between the Pope's discussion of rights and the standard liberal accounts of rights means that he operates from the same philosophical premises. The Pope's sense of urgency for the rights-based limits upon the state is shaped by his reading of historical events. It is not taken from a thin account of the human good, nor from the premise that individual liberty is the highest good—or even the highest political good. In paragraph 29, after all, the Pope insists that protection against utilitarian values is needed in order to "recognize and respect the hierarchy of the true values of human existence." Properly understood, the Pope says that we need rights not to protect ourselves against a "hierarchy of true values," but rather to protect ourselves against a state-sponsored preemption of those values. We can imagine a civil situation in which basic issues of justice and human flourishing are not treated in this language of juridical rights. But that is not the world that *Centesimus Annus* has in mind.

V

The clearest achievement of *Centesimus*, then, is the Pope's reckoning with the problem of the modern state. Whether we view the problem from our own historical experience, or whether we see it from the standpoint of the Pope's view of the events of 1989, it is clear that liberal political and legal institutions are a good (though not perfect) way to limit the power of the state. John Paul is the first modern Pope fully to come to terms with this issue. He sees clearly that the older notion of the state as the image of divine authority does not square with modern political realities. Most Catholics have lived in this century under the yoke of despotic political regimes that bear not the slightest resemblance to the classical or medieval conception of the *civitas*.

Although we can only speculate about this, it might be that the Pope is making a bid to return to what he takes to be the original source of European unity—the religious vision of human nature—while at the same time endorsing liberal political structures to protect the recovery of that vision. We should take the Pope seriously when he says that religion is the key to culture. Whereas Pope Leo XIII never gave an inch on his understanding of the political *civitas*, John Paul does not compromise on his vision of a religious principle for cultural unity. The principle of individual rights against political majorities, the division of the organs of state power, and the warning about the welfare state are for this Pope things that need to be in place if the Church is to go about its mission of creating religiously centered cultures. He realizes that, even in Europe, the Catholicizing of the culture is a long-term project. Whatever inherent merits there are to liberal political institutions, they are (perhaps like the *Pax Romana*) instrumentally valuable to the Church.

But there is a gamble in all of this. The Pope has put behind him a philosophical approach that is not only familiar to Catholics, but has much in its favor. *Centesimus Annus* does not reflect the elegant metaphysical scheme of *Rerum Novarum*. Nor does it maintain the scholastic language that shaped the thought of both conservative and progressive pontiffs over the past century. Whether this Pope's approach to issues of human nature, law, and political society can match the level of theoretical integration achieved in the older method and language is yet to be seen.

On this score, the rights-based strategy of limiting the power of the state harbors a number of potential problems that this encyclical does not address. It is one thing to set aside the older natural law account of the state, but it is quite another thing to argue for natural rights without some grounding in a doctrine of natural law. Although the Pope wants to avoid the scholastic and Enlightenment versions of natural law, it must be recalled that the American founders did not. We may ask whether the liberal state can be defended, at least on terms acceptable to Catholics, without some kind of natural law theory. *Centesimus Annus* seems to ground these rights in a personalist-theological view of the human person, but without any of the intermediate analysis traditionally associated with natural law. Among other things, there is the danger that if the ground of these rights resides *only* in revealed theology, that ground will be summarily dismissed, with the result that there remains no intellectually defensible ground between Scripture and antiperfectionist liberalism (as espoused, e.g., by Rawls, Dworkin, et al.). While this Pope seems more interested in the practical rather than the theoretical issue of rights, these practical considerations will never be sufficient to keep rights properly focused.

Furthermore, it should go without saying that the most important moral teachings of Catholicism cannot be encapsulated in the language of rights. Rights language inevitably tends to overflow from its limited political and legal functions and to infiltrate all levels of moral analysis and every sector of cultural life. It remains uncertain whether the Pope's strong affirmation of the correct hierarchy of values can be effectively interrelated with the rights-based personalism. In Western constitutional democracies, this move toward a rights-based personalism has not achieved a congruence between law and a correct hierarchy of values. In fact, secular versions of this approach have brought about the very opposite of what the Pope has in mind.

We can understand why the recently emancipated peoples of Europe are so eager to vindicate the ideal of rights. Immediately after the failed coup d'état of August 1991, the Soviet Congress of People's Deputies adopted a "Declaration of Human Rights and Freedoms." The first article states: "Every person possesses natural, inalienable, and inviolable rights and freedoms." In a similar vein, the former Czech president, Václav Havel, recently said at Lehigh University that he is "in favor of a political system based on the citizen, and recognizing all his fundamental civil and human rights in their universal validity." The state, he said, must be based upon rights rather than "nationality" or "religion." As Americans, we cannot but approve of this aspiration. But we also understand that even a modern, liberal polity involves more than individual rights.

In this respect, the Pope might learn from our historical and institutional experience, in which all-purpose and vague notions of natural rights have sometimes tended to subvert the appreciation of the common good. Given the Pope's strong endorsement of the rule of law, there is the problem of how to litigate, balance, and enforce all of these rights. While *Centesimus* reflects a keen appreciation of institutional limits upon the power of the state, the encyclical is not very illuminating on the institutional problems that attend the expansion of rights claims by individuals. What, for instance, are the judicial and administrative implications of a right to "express one's personality in the workplace"? Whatever meaning such a right might have in Warsaw, it is apt to have a quite different one in Malibu, California.

In any case, the historical career of the Marxist state in Eastern Europe is closed; the history of how these peoples can forge an appropriate political and legal order is still to be written. *Centesimus* takes the gamble of recommending new institutional ways to engage that project—ways concerning which the Church has had relatively little experience. But given its much longer historical experience, and its capacity to resist the degraded ideological baggage that frequently goes under the name of "liberalism," the Church could prove to be a crucial force for the project of limited government. Whoever is Pope in 2091 will no doubt take stock of the new lines opened by *Centesimus Annus*. He will be able to evaluate whether, in fact, the cultural and religious mission of the Church thrived under liberal political institutions, and whether the Catholic version of a rights-based personalism was able to distinguish itself from the debased secular versions that seemed triumphant in the closing decades of the twentieth century.

Part IV
CULTURE AND THE FREE SOCIETY

19

John Paul II and the Priority of Culture

George Weigel

That no good deed goes unpunished is nicely illustrated by the terms in which several biographers have recognized Pope John Paul II as a seminal figure in the Revolution of 1989.

Thus Carl Bernstein and Marco Politi, in their 1996 book, *His Holiness: John Paul II and the Hidden History of Our Time*, argue that, yes, the Pope played a large role in the collapse of European communism—as coconspirator with the Reagan administration in a "holy alliance" that wedded the diplomacy of the Holy See to the anti-Communist passions of conservative Republicans and the wiles of the CIA. Jonathan Kwitny agrees with the basic proposition that "1989" cannot be understood without taking account of the Polish pontiff, but his 1997 biography, *Man of the Century*, inverts the Bernstein/Politi proposition by arguing that the Pope, a nonviolent revolutionary on the model of Gandhi and Martin Luther King Jr., pulled the whole thing off against the machinations of the Reaganites and the CIA.

What these and similar journalistic accounts tend to discount, unfortunately, is the Pope's own reading of "the history of our time," whose locus classicus is the 1991 encyclical, *Centesimus Annus*. There, John Paul argued that "1989" could not be understood through the conventional analytic categories of Realpolitik. Rather, "1989" was made possible by a prior moral and cultural revolution, which created the conditions for the possibility of the nonviolent political upheaval that swept Marxism-Leninism into the dustbin of European history. The Pope was hardly unaware of the political, military, and economic factors that contributed to the breach of the Berlin Wall on November 10, 1989. But, he suggested, if we want to grasp why "1989" happened when it did and how it did, a deeper reading of the dynamics of history and a more acute analysis of the twentieth-century crisis of European

---

First published in *First Things*, February 1998.

civilization are required. Against the Realist school of historiography and international relations theory, in both its left- and right-wing forms, John Paul argued for the priority of culture over politics and economics as the engine of historical change; and at the heart of culture, he proposed, is cult, or religion.

In the years after *Centesimus Annus*, John Paul II has insisted that what was true of the epic changes we call "1989" is also true for the consolidation of free societies in Central and Eastern Europe, and for the well-being of the established democracies of the West. Democratic polities and free economies, he argues, are not independent variables; absent the habits of mind and heart that make people democrats and that channel their economic energies to good ends, the free society risks becoming a "thinly-disguised totalitarianism" (as he put it in the most controversial section of *Centesimus Annus*). The tendency, even among some celebrants of the Pope's role in "1989," has been to dismiss this as so much pontifical rodomontade; and the tone-deaf Western media have generally agreed that these are the cranky protestations of an angry old man incapable of understanding the world he helped create (see, for example, Tad Szulc in his 1995 effort, *Pope John Paul II: The Biography*).

But two papal pilgrimages in mid-1997—to Poland in June, and to the 12th World Youth Day in Paris in August—provided ample evidence that John Paul II's reading of contemporary history has not lost its salience, nor has it been blunted in its capacity to generate historical change. Moreover, the Pope's reorientation of Catholic evangelism and social doctrine toward the conversion of culture has given him a distinctive understanding of the requirements of freedom in the third millennium— which he insists, against the backdrop of this fast-closing century of unprecedented wickedness, can be a "springtime of the human spirit."

II

The Pope's June 1997 journey through his Polish homeland took place under two shadows. The first was the memory of his 1991 Polish pilgrimage, the first after the Communist crack-up, which was widely (and accurately) regarded as the least successful of his visits to his native country. In retrospect, it is possible to see just how difficult the situation was in those heady days. Poles were still intoxicated with their new freedom and wanted to celebrate it with the man to whom they gave credit for their deliverance; but the prescient Pope, who had quickly decoded the new threats to freedom implicit in the value-neutral notion of democracy being exported to east central Europe from the West, wanted to talk about the dangers he saw ahead. The Polish hierarchy had not found an appropriate voice to make its presence felt in the new circumstances of democratic pluralism, particularly on the heated issue of abortion; neither had Catholic politicians who wanted to think with the Church, but who resented being instructed in their duties by bishops who seemed unable to distinguish their episcopal role from that of party bosses. The net result was a tense visit, full of controversies, in which the fervor and the sense of national unity demonstrated in the Pope's 1979, 1983, and 1987 pilgrimages was often absent. This unhappy memory hung heavily over anticipation of the Pope's June 1997 return home.

The second shadow was Poland's recent political history. In September 1993 a coalition led by ex-Communists won the national parliamentary elections and took power in the Sejm. Two years later, on November 19, 1995, Alexander Kwasniewki, the youthful (and, some might say, Clintonesque) founder of the Democratic Left Alliance, defeated Lech Walesa for the presidency of Poland. Walesa's erratic behavior in the years since 1989 made his dismissal by the electorate understandable; but the fact that it was understandable made it no less disconcerting. The icon of the Solidarity revolution had been displaced by a former Communist party apparatchik: what had happened to the brave dreams on which "1989" had been built? Is this what happened in a "normal society"?

The combination of these two factors, and concerns about John Paul's health, made for considerable nervousness prior to the Pope's arrival. Would a pilgrimage that might turn out to be the Pope's farewell fail?

In the event, the pilgrimage was a triumph; as one exuberant Polish Dominican put it, "He's done it again; it's like 1979." But what, precisely, had he done?

The eleven days between John Paul's arrival on May 31 and his departure on June 10 were, to be sure, full of emotion and drama. The Pope struck a sympathetic chord and immediately reconnected with his countrymen when he said, at the arrival ceremony in Wroclaw, that he had come to them "as a pilgrim . . . filled with profound emotion," because "every return to Poland is like a return to the family home, where the smallest objects remind us of what is closest and dearest to our hearts." Three days later, at Gorzow Wielkopolski, John Paul reminded an immense throng that the late primate, Cardinal Stefan Wyszynski, had told him just after he had been elected Pope that "You are to lead the Church into its Third Millennium," and requested that they "ask God on your knees . . . that I am able to meet this challenge." (The crowed chanted back, "We will help you!"—a phrase that conjured up memories of strikers in 1970 responding to the pleas of the new Communist prime minister, Gierek; the Pope answered the chant with a moment of papal whimsy: "I recognize the words but I hope it will be better this time.")

Then there was Mass at Zakopane, the ski resort in the Pope's beloved Tatra Mountains. The mayor, in traditional Polish highlander dress, knelt before John Paul on June 6 to thank him for "freeing us from the 'red slavery' and for teaching us how to eradicate from our Polish homeland all that is degrading, humiliating, and all that enslaves us." After Mass, when the tough, craggy Polish mountain people began to sing to John Paul an old folk song about a highlander going into exile ("Mountaineer, why do you leave your beautiful hills and silvery brooks?"), one would have been hard put to find a dry eye among the half-million present, including the Pope.

For eleven days, John Paul (who seemed to get stronger as the visit unfolded) worked the crowds masterfully. When hundreds of thousands of youngsters in Poznan began to chant *Sto lat!* ("May you live a hundred years!"), he was quick to reply, "Don't flatter the Pope so much; you'd better think about Paris [the upcoming World Youth Day]." And, more poignantly, when an enormous congregation at the shrine of Czestochowa, home of the Black Madonna, began to chant, "Long live the Pope," John Paul wryly responded, "He does, he does, and he grows older...."

But the meaning of the Pope's Polish pilgrimage should not be measured simply by the colossal crowds, with over 1.2 million in Krakow alone on June 8, when the Pope canonized Blessed Queen Jadwiga, cofoundress of the Jagiello dynasty. As in any papal event, what ultimately counts—what historians must finally deal with— are the texts. And the twenty-six major texts of this pilgrimage, taken together, spelled out John Paul's distinctive vision of the priority of culture over politics and economics and his Vatican II-driven sense of the "public Church" as, essentially, the shaper of culture.

The June pilgrimage was deliberately filled with images of Poland's Christian past: a pan-Central European celebration of the millennium of the martyrdom of St. Adalbert, held in Gniezno; the canonization of Jadwiga; the commemoration in Krakow of the 600th anniversary of the Jagiellonian University's theology department. But this constant evocation of the past was not an exercise in pious nostalgia; rather, it was anamnesis in the service of the present and the future. As the Pope put it at the departure ceremony on June 10, "Fidelity to roots does not mean a mechanical copying of the patterns of the past. Fidelity to roots is always creative, ready to descend into the depths, open to new challenges, alert to the 'signs of the times.'... Fidelity to roots means above all the ability to create an organic synthesis of perennial values, confirmed so often in history, and the challenge of today's world: faith and culture, the Gospel and life." And that, he said, was why he had wanted to celebrate the canonizations of Jadwiga and John of Duka, as well as two beatifications, during his pilgrimage: because "the Church's saints are a particular revelation of the loftiest horizons of human freedom."

The canonization of Jadwiga afforded perhaps the greatest temptation to forget present and future in a binge about Poland's glorious past. But the Pope stoutly resisted this, and his canonization sermon focused on the fourteenth-century queen as a model for Poland today and tomorrow: Jadwiga the queen, for whom power was a question of public service; Jadwiga the diplomat, working to build a community of nations in east central Europe; Jadwiga the patroness of culture, "aware that faith seeks rational understanding," who endowed the university that bears her dynastic name with a gift of her golden scepter; Jadwiga, born to wealth and privilege, whose "sensitivity to social wrongs was often praised by her subjects." The message to Poland's new democracy could not have been clearer: you are the inheritors of a great cultural tradition, and it is that tradition that will enable you to build a genuinely free society worthy of the half century of sacrifice you made in the name of freedom.

At the commemoration of the 600th anniversary of the Jagiellonian University faculty of theology, held in the collegiate church of St. Anne later that same day,

John Paul sent another signal about the Church's relationship to politics. As it happens, Karol Wojtyla was the last student to receive a doctorate form the Jagiellonian University theology faculty before it was shut down by the Communist regime in early 1954; and the struggle to sustain serious theological scholarship in Krakow had been one of the hallmarks of his time as cardinal-archbishop of the city. So it might have been expected that the Pope would take the occasion of this anniversary celebration to say something about Poland's upcoming parliamentary elections, in which the heirs of the suppressors of the Jagiellonian faculty of theology were contestants. John Paul minced no words about "the dramatic struggle for existence" that that faculty had gone through "at the time of the Communist dictatorship." And he reminded the congregation (composed of Poland's leading intellectuals and educators, many of them his old friends) that the Church had "never resigned herself to the fact of a unilateral and unjust suppression" of the theology faculty by the Communist regime.

But this was not, he said, a matter of the Church's offended *amour propre*. Rather, in terms reminiscent of Newman's *Idea of a University*, he insisted that the defense of the theological faculty was a defense of the integrity of the intellectual life, a defense of culture, and a defense of the nation. The Church was not protesting the abuse of an ancient ecclesiastical privilege; by fighting for theology's place in the academy, the Church "did everything in her power to ensure that the university environment of Krakow was not deprived of an academic *studium* of theology" that had made its own "contribution to the development of Polish learning and culture." And a culture cut off from transcendent reference points could not serve the human good, because it could not know the truth about man.

Indeed, the Pope's richly textured address at St. Anne's, in which the politics of the present moment was not mentioned once, seemed to be saying to all concerned (within and without the Church), that while politics was undoubtedly important, the nurturance of culture, especially in the life of the mind, was far more important. You think that parliamentary elections will decide Poland's future? No, the Pope suggested, Poland's future really depends on "a lively awareness" that "man does not create truth; rather, truth discloses itself to man when he perseveringly seeks it." That is what universities are supposed to do. That is why universities are, over time, of far more consequence to a nation than parliaments. And that is why the Church, embodied in her supreme pontiff, is reflecting with you on the meaning of true humanism, that "integral notion of the human person" that is a "condition for the sound development" of the intellectual life, rather than telling you for whom to vote.

Five days before, at Gniezno, John Paul had delivered a similar message about the free society's dependence on a vibrant public moral culture to the presidents of Poland, the Czech Republic, Slovakia, Hungary, Lithuania, Ukraine, and Germany: all new (or newly reunified) democracies. Politics was not just a matter of winning elections, he reminded them, nor was the success of economic reform to be measured solely by the indices of gross national product. Rather, "the greatness of the role of political leaders is to act always with respect for the dignity of every human being, to create the conditions of a generous solidarity which never marginalizes any citizen, to permit each individual to have access to culture, to recognize and put into practice the loftiest human and spiritual values, to profess and to share one's religious beliefs." The Realpolitik of amoral power had given Europe "this sorely tried century." The birth of a new Europe capable of responding "to its age-old vocation in the world" depended on a European rediscovery of the continent's ancient "cultural and religious roots."

Prior to the Pope's arrival, the scent of a valedictory was in the air. Eleven dramatic and intellectually challenging days later, speculation had already begun about a papal visit in 1989, this time to the Baltic region (where Solidarity was born) and to the Mazurian Lakes where Father Karol Wojtyla loved to kayak. It may not have been "1979 again," as my enthusiastic Polish friend suggested. But John Paul's politics of culture (combined with terminal ex-Communist incompetence in the face of catastrophic floods in Poland in July) had their effect: in September, the voters threw out the ex-Communists and elected a new parliament led by a reconfigured Solidarity coalition.

That parliament is now the steward of Europe's fastest growing economy and east central Europe's most stable polity. And so the great Polish experiment will continue: can democratic pluralism and a free economy be built and sustained on the basis of an intact Catholic culture? That John Paul II gave Poles and Polish culture a living past rather than a nostalgic past during his June 1997 pilgrimage bodes well for a positive answer to that historic question.

III

The evangelical potency of the Pope's "culture first" approach to the "Church in the modern world" was also on display in Paris during the 12th World Youth Day in August 1997.

On his first pastoral visit to France in the spring of 1980, John Paul II, whose affection for the Gallic "Eldest Daughter of the Church" and her culture dates back to his student days, shocked a congregation of 350,000 at LeBourget Airport by bluntly asking, "France . . . are you faithful to the promises of your baptism? France, Daughter of the Church and educator of peoples, are you faithful, for the good of man, to the covenant with eternal wisdom?" Seven months later, the Pope acted on his judgment that the revitalization of French Catholicism was an urgent pastoral need by making what has been, arguably, the boldest episcopal nomination of his pontificate: the appointment of Jean-Marie Lustiger, son of Polish-Jewish parents, as archbishop of Paris.

Lustiger, who converted to Catholicism as a teenager, had been an innovative student chaplain at the Sorbonne and a Parisian pastor before being named Bishop of Orléans, where he spent a mere thirteen months before his translation to Paris. During his years as chaplain and pastor, Lustiger and a group of young lay intellectuals developed a distinctive analysis of the historical and cultural situation of the French Church. Prior to the French Revolution, the Church in France had been a "Church of power," allied to the political order and in some sense dependent on it. Then came 1789 and the subsequent Terror, during which French Catholicism took the first and (until the twentieth century) hottest blast from secular modernity. Reeling from that massive and bloody assault, the Church divided. A restorationist faction sought the return of the *ancien régime*—at first tout court; later, when the monarchist option became politically untenable, culturally. This faction produced, over time, the extremism of Action Française, Petainism during World War II, and, ultimately, Lefebvrism in the post-Vatican II period. The counter-faction sought an accommodation with secularity and the political left, and eventually gave birth to the bizarre phenomenon of "Christian Marxism." The bitter contestation between these two factions had divided French Catholics for over 150 years and had drained the Church of its evangelical vigor.

The creativity of the Lustiger group's analysis lay in its claims that these two factions, far from being the polar opposites they claimed themselves to be, were in fact two variants on the same false option: the determination to be a "Church of power." The two factions differed, of course, on what form of political power was preferable as a partner for the Church. But both agreed (although they could never admit it to each other) that to be the Church in France *must* mean to be a "Church of power."

Lustiger and his friends disagreed. It was the marriage with power, they believed, that had made the Church so vulnerable to the assault of secular modernity. Nor was there any way to mediate between the claims of the accommodationist and restorationist factions: the restorationists regarded *Dignitatis Humanae*, Vatican II's Declaration on Religious Freedom, as heresy (for declaring the state theologically incompetent), while the accommodationists had mistaken the Council's opening to the modern world (in *Gaudium et Spes*) an an invitation to cohabit with Marxism and, later, postmodernist deconstruction, both of which led in short order to the dissolution of Christian orthodoxy.

In these circumstances, the Lustiger group proposed, the only option was the evangelical option: to abandon the pretense of power, to eschew alliances with any political force, and to bring France back to her baptismal promises, not through the mediation of politics but through the reconversion of culture. And this, in turn, meant taking the evangelical proposition straight to the molders and shapers of culture: the by-now thoroughly secularized French intelligentsia. After his accession to Paris, Lustiger began implementing this pastoral strategy of reevangelization "from the head down" in a dynamic fashion: in a slew of best-selling books, many of them addressing the possibility of faith amidst modernity; by refounding a seminary (and thus personally encouraging a more evangelically assertive Parisian presbyterate); and through a direct, personal, weekly outreach to students and the professorate in a Sunday evening Mass and homily at his cathedral of Notre-Dame.

World Youth Day 1997 fit well into this strategy of reconversion through culture. World Youth Day would not simply happen in Paris. In the strategic vision of

Cardinal Lustiger and his associates, shared by John Paul II, World Youth Day would be an integral part, perhaps even a turning point, in the reconversion of France through the evangelization of culture. Thus the Pope's contacts with the French authorities were kept to the minimum required by protocol and good manners; there was a brief welcoming meeting with President Chirac and a brief predeparture meeting with Prime Minister Jospin. But whenever John Paul appeared in public in Paris it was in an explicitly ecclesial context: his was not a "Church of power," but a Church of the Gospel whose witness to Christ compelled a defense of the rights of man.

The rhythm of the 12th World Youth Day was deliberately set by a model of pilgrimage that Lustiger had first encountered in his days as chaplain at the Sorbonne. There, Monsignor Maxim Charles, later the rector of Sacré Coeur, was reviving the French tradition of student pilgrimages with a group of young intellectuals who would later become close friends of Father Lustiger and, later, his informal advisors as archbishop. These pilgrimages, first to Notre-Dame, later to Chartres, were inspired by the theology of Louis Bouyer and his teaching that every significant Christian event should, in some fashion, recapitulate the Paschal Triduum, the core of Christian experience. Thus on every student pilgrimage, no matter at what time of the year, the retreatants would "relive" Holy Week, from Palm Sunday through the Easter Vigil.

The Bouyer-Charles paschal template was adapted to World Youth Day 1997 to great effect. Thus the first official day of the youth festival (which happened to be a Tuesday) "was" Palm Sunday: the Holy Year cross, given by John Paul II to the participants in the first World Youth Day in 1985, was solemnly carried in procession by a dozen youngsters from around the world, through a crowd of perhaps 500,000 young people stretched from the Eiffel Tower along the Champ de Mars to the front lawn of the Ecole Militaire, where a great platform had been built for the opening Mass. Thursday, when John Paul II arrived in Paris and first met the young people, was "Holy Thursday"; the Gospel read during the welcoming ceremony was John 13:1–15, the washing of the disciples' feet, which the Pope explicated to the youngsters in a text read in their language-based catechetical groups the next day. On Friday, hundreds of thousands of teenagers and young adults relived Good Friday by making the Way of the Cross at dozens of venues all over Paris. On Saturday night, a candlelight baptismal vigil was celebrated by a congregation of 750,000 at the Longchamp racecourse, as the Pope baptized twelve young catechumens from every continent. And then, after this re-creation of the Easter Vigil, came the closing Eucharist on Sunday morning, which turned out to be the largest attendance at one Mass in French history, with more than a million gathering at Longchamp.

The massive turnout far exceeded the expectations of the event's planners, who, as things got under way, were anticipating perhaps 250,000 youngsters all week, and a crowd of 500,000 for the closing Mass. At least twice that number of young people turned out, and the outpouring of interest from French teenagers stunned the Paris press, which spent the better part of the week editorially wondering what on earth was going on. One also had the sense that it stunned those French bishops who, having internalized a sense of their own marginality, were unsympathetic to Lustiger's pastoral strategy and its forthrightly evangelical approach to the keepers of the French cultural flame.

When John Paul II visited Reims in September 1996, similar skepticism about public interest was expressed but another massive turnout ensued. Then, the focus was on the Christian roots of the French nation, the occasion being the 1,500th anniversary of the baptism of Clovis. At World Youth Day, the two "icons" proposed for reflection were drawn from the modern history of French Catholicism: St. Thèrése of Lisieux, and Frederick Ozanam, founder of the worldwide St. Vincent de Paul societies, whom the Pope beatified at Notre-Dame on August 22. This choice of patrons for the papal pilgrimage to Paris was not accidental. Both were young Catholics (Thèrése died at twenty-four, Ozanam at forty). Thèrése, perhaps the most popular of modern saints, was a contemplative woman who made original contributions to theology. Ozanam was an intellectual in an age of radical skepticism, a democrat detached from the *ancien régime* fantasies of many of his coreligionists, a servant of the poor, a devoted husband and father, and an original thinker whose writings on the just society prefigured and influenced the birth of modern Catholic social doctrine in Leo XIII's *Rerum Novarum*. The message being sent through this iconography was unmistakable: sanctity is possible in modernity; youthful enthusiasm can be drawn to Christ; Catholic faith can nurture a free society (liberty), human dignity (equality), and human solidarity (fraternity).

Cardinal Lustiger drove this point home on French national television the night World Youth Day concluded. Asked by a middle-aged interviewer how he explained such an extraordinary response to World Youth Day, the cardinal suggested that it was a question of generations. The reporter belonged to a generation that had grown up in the Church, had lost its faith (circa 1968), and had been fighting its parents, so to speak, ever since. These young people, the cardinal said, grew up empty; they have found Jesus Christ; they want to explore all that that means. Do not, he concluded, read their lives through your experience. They do not think that being Christian and being engaged, intelligent, compassionate, dedicated people are antinomies.

Or, as the Pope put it to the young in his closing homily at Longchamp: "Go forth now along the roads of the world, along the pathways of humanity, while remaining ever united in Christ's Church. Continue to contemplate God's glory and God's love, and you will receive the enlightenment needed to build the civilization of love, to help our brothers and sisters to see the world transfigured by God's eternal wisdom and love." In the capital of a particularly skeptical and anticlerical Enlightenment, a new enlightenment of culture, leading to a new concept of the free society, was being proposed. The response suggested that World Youth Day 1997 may one day be remembered as a turning point in the modern history of France.

IV

Professor Stefan Swiezawski, the distinguished Polish historian of philosophy who was instrumental in bringing young Father Karol Wojtyla to the faculty of the Catholic University of Lublin, once said that the post-Conciliar Church was "living in a new epoch." "Vatican II was not just one Council: it marked the end of the Constantinian epoch, thank God. Now the Church has no army, no state. It is a quite different situation." Working out the implications of this post-Constantinian ecclesiology with an eye toward the third millennium of Christian history has been one of the principal leitmotifs of the pontificate of John Paul II, who played such an important role in drafting *Gaudium et Spes*, the Council's Pastoral Constitution on the Church in the Modern World.

In some respects, of course, the Church will always be engaged with "power," as the world defines power. Vatican diplomacy continues; the Holy See exchanges diplomatic representatives with 166 states and is an active participant in international legal and political institutions. What the pontificate of John Paul II has done, in fulfillment of the promise of Vatican II and its seminal Dogmatic Constitution on the Church (*Lumen Gentium*), is to locate this inevitable engagement with the principalities and powers in an explicitly evangelical context. The Church's defense of human rights (and especially the first human right of religious freedom), like its groping toward an ethic of "humanitarian intervention" in the post-Cold War world, its efforts to mediate ethnic and nationalist conflict in the Middle East and elsewhere, and its proposals for securing the moral foundations of the free society, cannot be understood merely as the Church's dealings with the "real world." In the ecclesiology and social doctrine of John Paul II, the witness of the "public Church" is an expression of the Church's essential task, which is the proclamation of the Gospel of Jesus Christ—a Gospel with many things to say about the nature of man, of human community, and of human destiny.

The "real world" is the human universe that has been redeemed and transformed by the atoning death of the Son of God. The Church is not "here" and the "real world" there; the story of the Church is the world's story, rightly understood. This belief is what grounds the public ministry of John Paul II and directs his attention, as teacher and witness, to the realm of culture: that dimension of the human universe in which the self-understanding of individuals and peoples is formed and is transmitted to new generations. Because the Church is first and foremost evangelical, the Church must, in this post-Constantinian epoch, be the evangelizer of cultures.

This steady insistence on the priority of culture is difficult to grasp for those who read John Paul II as another great figure on a world-historical stage whose dramatic action is defined by politics. He has been that, of course. But he is that precisely because, not in spite, of the fact that he is a Christian, a priest, and a bishop who insists that politics is not all there is. Thus there are not two John Pauls: in conventional media terms, the "social progressive" and the "doctrinal conservative." There is only one John Paul II, as there is only one Karol Wojtyla.

Jonathan Kwitny's *Man of the Century* is less woodenheaded in its wrestling with the complex simplicity of the life of Karol Wojtyla than were Tad Szulc and the authorial dyad of Carl Bernstein/Marco Politi. But Kwitny, who deserves full marks for demolishing the Bernstein/Politi "holy alliance" fiction and who avoids the worst of Szulc's gaucheries about the angry old man fighting vainly against the world he helped create, also tries to force Wojtyla's life and accomplishment onto the Procrustean bed of his own political preferences: in this instance, the Pope becomes the last great twentieth-century exponent of democratic socialism and pacifism.* The public accomplishment, Kwitny rightly claims, is a large one: Wojtyla was crucial in the destruction of the totalitarian option that caused such immense human suffering throughout the century. But is John Paul II the "man of the century" because of a political achievement?

The crisis of the twentieth century, which gave birth to totalitarianism in its sundry forms, has been in the first instance a crisis of culture: a crisis in the order of ideas and morals. This has been Karol Wojtyla's conviction since he helped lead a clandestine cultural resistance to the Nazi occupation of Poland during World War II. The will to power, the hallmark of the politics of this century, was a direct consequence of the collapse of a publicly available concept of human freedom that was tethered to truth and ordered to an objectively knowable human good. A modernity that could not give a persuasive account of the truth of its highest aspiration—freedom—was a modernity in which freedom necessarily came to be understood as a neutral faculty of choice. And, absent any agreed and publicly accessible standards by which the goodness of various choices could be judged and adjudicated, the reduction of social life to a raw contest for power necessarily ensued. Nietzsche, in other words, was right; and seeing what was coming, he went mad.

If there is a plausibility to John Paul II as the "man of the century," it is not because he put paid to one of the political epiphenomena of the crisis of late modernity; it is because he has advanced a proposal that cuts to the heart of the modern crisis of truth and freedom. That proposal, which has emerged from the heart of the Church, has been primarily directed toward the realm of culture because it is, first and always, an evangelical proposal: a proposal to consider the possibilities of human freedom in the light of God's freedom, which led to the Cross. To account for the life of Karol Wojtyla, his stewardship of the office of Peter in the Church, and his impact on the history of our time means taking seriously the Pope's conviction that reality is cruciform, and that the story of the world is, in the final analysis, the story of the Paschal Mystery.

*Kwitny traces the intellectual origins of this political stance to what he presents as a hitherto-undiscovered book by Karol Wojtyla, *Social Ethics,* published underground in 1953. The problem is that the "book" isn't a book, and Wojtyla wasn't the principal author. *Social Ethics,* as scholars have known for some time, is the text of Wojtyla's lectures for a social ethics course in the Krakow seminary. When Wojtyla was assigned to teach this course, he adapted the lecture notes of his predecessor, Father Jan Piwowarczyk. The notes are in fact a rather conventional exposition of Catholic social doctrine (with which Kwitny seems to be unfamiliar) in the period after Pius XI's 1931 encyclical *Quadragesimo Anno*. One of the Pope's closest associates has confirmed that Father Wojtyla, for whom social ethics had not been a major intellectual interest prior to his assignment to teach the course, used the Piwowarczyk lecture notes with "some elaborations." But "the material was not his own."

20

Modern Individualism

Pierre Manent

On the last page of the final chapter of *Democracy in America*, Tocqueville summarizes the comparison he has just drawn between the new democracy and the old order as follows: "They are like two distinct humanities."

This is very much the feeling experienced by the partisans as well as the opponents of the modern democratic and individualist movement: a new humanity emerges from the old, separates itself from the former, and distances itself ever more. This common impression is more important than the contradictory judgments made by the two sides. It suggests that there is here something like a radical change in the situation, in the state of humanity.

Both the partisans and opponents are right. The democratic movement does mean, as its opponents affirm, a dissolution of communities and bonds. To the extent that other communities and attachments are reconstituted in democracy, it is on the basis of the individual consent that is the generative principle of the new regime. Likewise, the partisans of democracy are also correct: there is a liberation in this dissolution, since henceforth no individual can have an obligation to which he has not consented. The hopes of the partisans have perhaps been deceived, the fears of the others have no doubt not been confirmed. But the fact of the liberation which is a dissolution, or of the dissolution which is a liberation, the fact of emancipation, is there.

The communities to which men belong in the democratic world no longer command them. In the family, law has abolished the power of the male head of the household, and parents—from now on equals—demand less and less the obedience of their children, whom they perceive as more and more their equals and as similar. In the

---

First published in *Crisis*, October 1995. [Adapted and translated from *Commentaire*, no. 70, Summer 1995 by Daniel Mahoney and Paul Seaton.]

nation, the legitimately elected government no longer dares to other citizen-soldiers to die for the country. If it undertakes a military operation involving some risks, it turns it over to the military professionals and to what are called volunteers.

In the Church, the Roman Magisterium, while retaining intact the place of the "last things" in official documents, has ceased, since the last Council, in its actual pastoral activity to invoke the urgency of salvation while it agrees to come together in congress with other religions. Finally, the past itself, as the community of those who are dead, has lost all commanding authority, whether in the social, moral, political or religious order: it is now only the ensemble of "places of memory" open to a kind of historical tourism.

Let us consider the domain in which modern humanity registers its intimate life: literature. It would be vain to summarize its movement in a formula, and I do not have in my possession any "theory of literature," but it seems to me that from Proust and Céline to the theater of the absurd and to the new novel, it unmasks the deception of human bonds, the lie of love, the inanity or deceptiveness of language. It explores what it means to *become an individual*. It pursues this enterprise with an obstinacy and fervor that explains the obsessive concern of the literary *avant-garde*, and of the novelty which characterizes it, much more than does simple "fashion."

A desire to know is here at work, a desire which elaborates a sort of negative anthropology, supported not by faith, but by distrust. This movement opposes and substitutes itself for the two great authorities which previously nourished literature: the Greek and Roman models, on one hand, and the Christian Scriptures on the other. There is no longer heroic conduct, no path towards wisdom, no journey of the soul towards God, but quite exactly a "voyage at the end of the night" in which it is a matter of discovering finally what it is to be a pure individual, beyond any social bond or even any language.

I am going to do here what I had promised not to do: I am going to summarize briefly this movement. What is going on, in the state of society, and by means of literature—literary investigation, the instrument of literature—is the return to what the philosophers formerly called *the state of nature*, the state in which there are only individuals. We see civilization perfecting itself and the democratic nations throwing over the world an ever more ample network bound together by technological, judicial and political artifices, in order to make coexist—or rather, to foster "communication" between—peoples whose geography and history inhibited them from living together.

At the same time the human mind in these same societies gives itself the task of undoing, of "deconstructing," in the element of literature and perhaps more generally in the element of art, all bonds. This double movement—of artificial construction and of deconstruction—contains nothing contradictory; its two aspects obey the same principle: men do not have any natural connections. They therefore are the authors—the artists—of all their attachments. That is why, while the highways of communication traverse the planet, literature stubbornly says that it is impossible to say anything.

This situation of democracy, this experience of the liberating dissolution of bonds, contains a mission for each individual. His situation contains his mission: he is "condemned to be free." Recognizable in many different rhetorics, such is the specific pathos of modern individualism. Just as for Kierkegaard, to be a Christian is to become a Christian, for the modern man conscious of himself, to be an individual means to become an individual, and to become *more and more* an individual.

Certainly the development of modern individualism has not been a simple triumphal march, no matter how victorious liberalism appears to be today. It provoked extremely resolute opposition, especially in our century. It was against it that the two great revolutionary projects of our century, communism and nazism, were unleashed.

Instructed by the horrible lesson of this century, are we bound to accept both docilely and resolutely the task contained in our situation as individuals? Are we really "condemned to be free" without being able to assume some distance from our situation in order to judge it? I do not believe so. We are and want to be individuals; so be it. But that means that we are and we want to be *human* individuals. Now, as men, what do we have in common? This simple, prosaic, even flat question, modern politics does not even succeed in raising. As human individuals, what is proper to each of us and what is common to all? The doctrines which found our political regimes never confront this question because they affirm that all legitimacy has its unique source in the individual; whatever is added to the individual—and first of all the political body or state—is only a more or less unfortunate necessity, something that does not have meaning for man. However, the political order, the political regime, including the liberal political regime that we are familiar with, is a certain way of putting things in common.

What are we to put in common? To answer this question it would be necessary to use the entire edifice of political philosophy, but I can give perhaps a suggestive example. To establish a political order, before consulting individual wills, is, first of all, to have a territory in common. Certainly, a territory is the lowliest determination, but in a sense it is the most necessary. The proof of this is in "the construction of Europe." We must ask: what construction—and of what Europe—when from year to year the latter's territory is always expanding? What is this political body, this "political Europe" as one calls it, which is incapable of defining this minimal common thing, territory?

Western Europeans often feel themselves justified in their indifference to territory by the savage eruption of territorial revindication in the east of Europe, in particular by the events in Yugoslavia. In truth, however, the lesson is the reverse. The territorial hypersensitivity of the ethnic cleansers is the reverse-image, and in part the effect, of our territorial insouciance. If we do not accept the first political responsibility which is the definition of a common territory, if we do not resist the fatal notion of an indefinite extension of Europe, what we call the political construction of Europe will be in fact its dissolution, before its dislocation.

It is understood that this substitution of civilization for politics is not a simple aberration or moment of weakness. One even can invoke strong reasons in its favor. If the political order consists in putting things in common, in organizing the "common good," one cannot overlook that what unites the most is also what most separates men. In particular, the more what is common is of an elevated order, the more it is susceptible to separate men. The highest truth, religious truth, was the most active principle of unity and of community before becoming the most corrosive principle of division. It is for this reason that one finally had to subtract religious truth from the domain of the common—from public command—in order to make it something private.

It was then that the nation became the great common thing, the next context for human association in Europe. But there were several nations, and they did not delay in making terrible war on each other. Many well-intentioned and reasonable men judged that it was time to renounce this political form in Europe and to have European peoples live in the element of civilization alone. It is in this sense, that one speaks most frequently today of "Europe," which is then only the framework for the exercise of the democratic individualism, which serves as the point of departure of my exposition. I admit, without any difficulty on the plane of principle, that one can reject the nation as a practical form, but I do not believe that one can live for very long in "civilization" alone, without some political attachment, without some definition of what is common.

It might be suggested that I have neglected a particularly precious possibility, that of a human bond affirmed as such. It will be said that we can affirm a principle of action which is at the same time individualist and communitarian by starting from the observation that what is common is humanity itself, the fact of being human, and by leaving this fact indeterminate.

This, in fact, is a tempting avenue because it circumvents the awkward obligation to seek what is common. It is said that one must respect the humanity of the other man. Kant already had given this procedure its most rigorous formulation: I must respect in the other the respect he has—or that he, as a rational being, ought to have—for the moral law. However, the modern individual hardly loves the law. In truth he hates it, and it is hard to see how hatred of and respect for the law can combine in him. Then, from the respect for the other man, we create a sentimental version founded on compassion. Our humanism becomes humanitarian. Alas, pity as a political principle quickly encounters its limits. I would like to underline them below.

As Rousseau, its first great promoter, had noticed already, pity as compassion before suffering or physical misery hardly distinguishes between man and the animals—which is why in the West today the defense of "animal rights" assumes a growing vehemence. For this reason pity cannot be a sufficient principle for a properly human community.

Pity as such is in emotion, or a passion. It therefore is very dependent on images, and is exposed to their possible manipulation. Pity is egotistical: since its condition of possibility is that I myself am not suffering and that I am aware of this exemption, it causes me to feel the pleasure of not suffering. Pity is indeterminate: every suffering solicits it, and it by itself does not contain any principle of evaluation or of comparison. The crybaby draws tears from us as we pass by, indifferent, to the suffering of the courageous man. One might say that the urgency of action is a sufficiently clear principle. On the contrary, it is clear that this is not the case, since one must choose among the urgencies.

Moreover, pity in itself doesn't contain the idea of the action aimed at putting an end to the pitiable situation. Confronted with the torturer tormenting the victim, I can kill the torturer, interpose myself "peacefully" between the torturer and the victim, appear to interpose myself (precisely to give witness to my pity), ask myself if the victim doesn't have some responsibility for the fortune that afflicts him, remember that fifty years ago the grandparents of the victim were torturers and the torturer's grandparents were victims, etc.

One can define briefly the limits of pity: it doesn't make us leave the state of nature. Between two individual humans considered outside of any political order, it is a possible sentiment. There is no immediate evidence of being *human*, no immediate experience of "the other" which dispenses us from the necessity and obligation of building a political order and therefore of asking ourselves, what is common, of posing in all its amplitude *the* political question, the question of justice.

But doesn't our society marry individual liberty and social obligations thanks to a specific bond which defines a very characteristic form of justice: the contract? By the contracts he concludes with his fellow human beings, each individual is the author of all his bonds. At the same time he places limits on his good pleasure, since *pacta sunt servanda*, contracts are to be kept.

In truth, though, both in its reality and in its meaning, the contract is indeterminate, or at least under-determined. It depends on a context. In its poorest, but often most determinative definition, it is the relationship of forces. The socialist tradition has underscored repeatedly how much the contract for work between the worker and the employer was in itself an unequal relationship, under the appearance of a free agreement between two equal individuals. As precious as this instrument of human association may be, the contract leaves undetermined the question of what is common.

To remain with this example, what is common in the relationship between the worker and the employer? The business enterprise? The social class? The market? If one were to consider attentively another type of contract, the marriage contract, where what is most one's own, the body, becomes in some way common, one would be led to even more interesting reflections.

The justice of the contract is necessary, but it does not suffice. We certainly cannot abstain from posting the question: what is common? This, however, contains an ambiguity that I would like to expose in concluding. What is common can be the common denominator, that is, what each individual possesses and which all the others possess, for example, a body. All individuals have a body—the body is a common denominator—but the body is nothing that is common, in fact it is what is most one's own.

The distinction is of decisive importance when one considers the "rights of man" which, contrary to what certain of their most stirring defenders believe or hope, do not derive from what is common, but from the common denominator. In the strong, full, almost sacred sense of the term, the common is something which, appropriated or embraced by the individual, transforms him while enlarging him. Can we see, or discover, or somehow recognize that there is something—this would be precisely, the "public thing"—greater than us? And is it legitimate to hope that this public thing would render us greater than ourselves? By these two questions we take the measure of the amplitude and the gravity of the question: what is common?

21

The Liberal Paradox: Might Religion Have an Answer?

Thomas L. Pangle

In this chapter I want to try to help articulate some of the dangers, some of the requirements, and some of the opportunities presented by the puzzling spiritual condition in which our political life finds itself, as we enter a historical period that I think it may be useful to conceive of as "the postmodern political era." The word *postmodern* is today used so often, in so many differing contexts, and for so many varying purposes, that it risks becoming a buzzword that obscures more than it clarifies. Nonetheless, I think the term can have a reasonably precise and powerful significance when applied to contemporary politics and political philosophy.

To put it briefly: with the end of the Cold War, we live in a liberal-democratic civic culture whose principal institutions and mores—the free market, unhampered technology, human rights, checked and balanced representative constitutionalism—stand unchallenged by any serious rival. At the same time, however, we find that the underlying theological and philosophic foundations upon which this modern culture was built ("the laws of nature and of nature's God," or History conceived as both a logical and quasi-divine progressive unfolding of truth) are widely regarded as incredible or indefensible; we find, moreover, that the West is pervaded by a vague but profound sense that its modern, liberal self-consciousness lacks an adequately rich conception of the human personality in its full dignity, diversity, and versatility; and, most troubling of all, we hear a growing chorus of intellectual voices condemning the foundations of liberalism, together with much of liberal culture itself, as constituting covertly hegemonic or privileged sources of prejudice, discrimination, and oppression of so-called "marginalized" groups and cultures. These condemners proudly label themselves the "postmodernists."

First published in *Crisis,* May 1992.

We don't have to accept their postmodern-"ism" in order to acknowledge that they are symptomatic of something new. And the term "postmodern" signals well, it seems to me, what is new or different about our situation. The term signals the paradoxical spiritual condition of liberal democracy today. We feel ourselves the uneasy heirs of a great legacy, the Enlightenment, which in our hands has somehow lost the magic of its invincible convictions and begun to distrust itself morally as well as intellectually. We seem to have arrived too late to share wholeheartedly in the modern spirit, and yet we are not, as the moderns once were in relation to the scholastics, marching to a clear and distinct new drummer or spiritual dispensation; we lack—and it seems we do not even strongly long for—an alternative way of life, an alternative vision or goal. We appear to be resigned to modernity on almost every level except the most fundamental. We are defined by our *dis*enchantment rather than by our enchantment, by our loss of faith rather than by any new faith.

In saying that we appear to be resigned to modernity on almost every level except the most fundamental, I do not for a minute mean to suggest that contemporary political life is not adversely affected by the loss of conviction, the self-doubt, I have just sketched. It seems to me that the most massive political manifestation of the weakness of liberal principles is the contemporary crisis of legitimacy of the state, or nation. The nation-state is *the* political expression of liberal modernity; the articulation of the moral principles of human or individual rights in theorists like Hobbes and Spinoza goes together with the articulation of the supreme moral legitimacy of state sovereignty. The nation-state, conceived morally as the political entity that most deserves our allegiance, is *the* distinctive creation of modernity, in explicit and self-conscious contrast to the complex political structures of Christian feudalism and to the *polis* and empire of the pagan world. And today the nation-state is in serious trouble—serious moral trouble. The claim of the nation-state to deserve supreme political allegiance is increasingly contested.

It is perhaps easier for someone living in Canada to recognize this crisis than it is for a resident of the United States. But the situation of Canada, a country literally on the brink of breaking up, appears all too typical as we look around the world, from Czechoslovakia to India and then to Malaysia further east. It is not merely the Soviet empire that is coming apart; the states liberated from the Soviet grasp are themselves struggling to hold themselves together, or to reconstitute and redefine viable political entities. In Western Europe, the pressure on the independence and legitimacy of the state comes from a different direction: less from disintegrative forces and more from the imperatives of transnational *integrative* forces. Even in the United States and countries like it, where patriotism and national unity remain comparatively strong, the same forces are at work, raising moral challenges to national unity. Speaking generally, one may say that the state is today being torn from below and above, by the forces of localism and of globalism.

THE GLOBAL CHALLENGE

Let's consider first the challenges from above, the global challenges. These include not only military threats (including of course nuclear proliferation), and not only the imperatives of the international economic system, but also the scope and scale of environmental problems, the recurrence of mass famine and disease, and the grim tides of refugees and needy Third World immigrants. These latter human fears and sufferings, brought home by the media, put in lurid focus the all-too-frequent narrowness and heartlessness that seem to characterize sovereign states. These challenges compel us to reflect in discomfort on our unwillingness or incapacity to give adequate relief to our suffering planetary partners.

Yet there seems to result from these concerns little serious talk today of "world government," or of a search for solutions through larger, continental superstates or "co-prosperity spheres." We have learned hard lessons not only from the colonial era and the fascist lunges at domination, but more recently from the Soviet empire. The coming decades appear to hold out the promise of experimentation with confederacy and multilateral organization, in which the present states would not be superseded, but instead limited and guided by stable networks of contractual agreements with other states, issuing in policies implemented by nonsovereign administrators. It seems reasonable to hope that insofar as ideologically or religiously based conflict recedes, such confederate organization and action will indeed become more possible and more effective.

We must not forget, however, an unhappy historical fact: confederacies do not have a very successful track record. There are many reasons for the inefficacy of confederate government, some of which we may hope have been reduced in significance by modern developments in technology and so forth. But I believe that the deepest reason for the great difficulties confederate arrangements have tended to encounter is moral; and that, as such, has not changed. I would explain the difficulty as follows.

A viable political society must from time to time demand real, and sometimes ultimate, but always unequal, sacrifices from individuals and groups within the society. Indeed, to some extent every political society must make such demands routinely and constantly. For if societies are not always at war, they must always be prepared for war and hence must ask a substantial number of the young to train and prepare for the risk of life and welfare; besides, policemen, firemen, emergency relief workers—in short, heroes and heroism—are required literally every day. Now it will not quite do to tell those who must make or risk sacrifice that they do so in order to preserve the goods of the others, especially when the society defines itself in terms of reasonable or prudential collective self-interest. For the question obviously arises, why should the interest for whose protection we erected or entered upon the organization be given up for the sake of the organization, or for the sake of the other self-interested partners?

To demand real risk or sacrifice, a society must be able to claim to stand for something that *transcends* collective self-interest or security. A society must hold out the promise that the individual or group who sacrifices will be ennobled by contributing to some whole or community that, because of its nature or because of its specific, high ends, counts for more than the sum of its individual parts and interests. A society that demands sacrifices has to present itself as a whole in which the individual can find a significance and a permanence that overshadows his or her poor mortal self. Now confederacies have great difficulty making such a case, because almost by definition the members of a confederacy are each all more significant than the whole of which they form the partners or parts. When individuals or groups are asked to sacrifice, they must therefore be shown not only how they will advance the purpose of the confederacy, but how their sacrifice will advance or protect the concerns of their own primary group, the group which authorized and created the confederacy, and to which they naturally and reasonably feel a deeper sense of belonging and a higher dedication.

To apply this to our emerging world of multilateral hope and promise, it seems likely that the concerns of the partner states will always trump, in cases of conflict, the concerns of the confederate wholes. It may be, of course, that the cause of Humanity, embodied in the United Nations and kindred multilateral organizations, will counter the centrifugal force of national loyalty. But the United Nations, precisely because it is so all-inclusive, tends to be capable of uniting only on a very few issues, and remains in any case a rather distant and abstract, not to say dubious, embodiment of the moral cause of mankind.

I am inclined to judge, therefore, that while transnational problems, and multilateral authorities created to meet those problems, will become much stronger in the years to come, the nation-states will remain more decisive than any supranational organizations. The most serious challenges to the moral supremacy of the nation-state will arise, and already are arising, from below, from concerns that I have lumped together, rather crudely, under the rubric "localism." Here the same moral challenge that the nation poses to the confederacy returns, as a still more stern challenge to the nation from more intimate and local subgroupings—communities or communitarianism constituted by linguistic, ethnic, and religious homogeneity rooted in shared histories of suffering and achievement. The intensity of identity with and dedication to one's cultural group gains added strength from the fact that these groupings are often smaller than the national grouping, and thus hold out the promise of an independent political life that would be more participatory, or that would produce governments closer to the people both in spirit and in scale.

The challenge can be put as follows: what makes the liberal state more than a confederacy of cultures? Because if this is all that the liberal state truly is, does not the claim of each cultural group necessarily trump, in cases of conflict, and for the individuals who belong to the group, any claim the confederate state can make? If the liberal state tries to overcome this trump, not by invoking superior moral principles, but instead by claiming to stand for "neutrality" and even "relativism," by invoking positivistic laws or procedural "rules of the game" that eschew any moral supremacy but claim somehow to take precedence, must we not begin to grow suspicious? Do the people who invoke and enforce these "neutral procedures" have no interest in them? Do they belong to no identifiable culture? Did they come from Mars? Must we not perceive in this apparent denial or purported honesty a self-deluding or hypocritical manipulation of principles which prove on inspection, "coincidentally," to serve very clearly the interest of a subtly hegemonic cultural group— for example, secular, rationalist, Eurocentric white males who tend to share a remarkably similar and remarkably barren cultural pattern, in which *Homo economicus* tends to predominate as the model human type? This, of course, is the argument presented by leading postmodernist multiculturalists such as Stanley Fish, who has summarized this position with brevity, clarity, and candor in an article entitled "Liberalism Doesn't Exist," published in the *Duke Law Journal* in 1987.

As we observe the battering the liberal state and the liberal ideal is taking, from religious fundamentalism in Africa and Asia, from ethnic nationalism in Europe, from multiculturalism in America, we are impelled to rethink the response to these communitarian challenges, to try to bring back into vivid clarity the moral claim to legitimacy of the liberal state. But in doing so we cannot help but become aware, simultaneously, of certain deep difficulties in the liberal answer or claim. Do these difficulties justify the contemporary disenchantment with the fundamental liberal principles and the liberal-democratic state? That they need not, I think, will be most evident if we survey very briefly the history of the liberal conception, doing so under the guidance of liberal democracy's greatest friendly critic, Alexis de Tocqueville.

The liberal conception does indeed come to sight as a kind of confederacy, or compact, by which human beings create the state in order to achieve collective security for their individual lives, liberties, and properties. But this is a confederacy, not of groups, whose claims to loyalty would then remain preeminent, but of *individuals* who are conceived in principle to be in a condition—the "state of nature"— stripped of all important group loyalties (with the notable exception of spousehood and parenthood) and characterized instead by (in Locke's words) an "uncontrolled liberty," and an equality in this total independence or liberty. The basic argument is that what makes human beings universally the same—the passionate quest for material security and the capacity both to threaten and to reason with one another— outweighs in importance, for the human beings themselves, whatever differentiates them into groups.

Now from the outset, the modern liberal stress on individual rights, and on the creation, by contract, of a new kind of government dedicated to protecting those rights, found itself compelled to fight against regional, tribal, ethnic, and local loyalties of all sorts. But the big fight was against an opponent of an altogether different kind. The big fight was against an opposing universalism, the universalism of Christianity, allied with classical political philosophy as a subordinate partner. This pre-liberal, Christian universalism had argued that what counts, above all, is the universal goal of human aspiration and fulfillment, a goal which can be glimpsed only rarely or dimly in its complete version.

In criticizing this old universalism, the new, liberal universalism observed that precisely the difficulty of glimpsing or making clear the goal of human happiness means that discussion of it remains always controversial, the source of endless disagreement. To make so debatable a concern the anchoring principle of public life is to guarantee a public life of strife and, all too often, of bitter and hateful religious warfare. To end the strife, in practice, the old universalism had to institutionalize some conception of the good or the good life under the rigid, hierarchical authority of a few purported knowers who were in fact hidebound mumblers of formulae who squelched or severely discouraged the independent, critical reflection that is the matrix of all genuine belief. It was in the name, then, not only of peace and prosperity, but also of freedom and philosophy, that thinkers like Spinoza and the French *philosophes* rose up, in a rebellion aimed at the overthrow of both Aristotelian (or classical) political thought and revealed, organized religion. As Tocqueville puts it in his *Old Regime and the French Revolution*, "the Philosophy of the eighteenth century," which was "one of the principal causes of the Revolution," was profoundly irreligious; the *philosophes* "opposed the Church with a sort of fury" and "wished to rip up the very foundations of Christianity."

This great and relentless antagonism between liberal-democratic modernity and the Christian tradition has both enriched and blighted the spiritual history of the modern European continent. While the opposition between reason and revelation led the greatest thinkers to depths of reflection never achieved in England or America, the consequences for civic culture were deleterious. Critics on the left and right came to associate liberal rationalism and universalism with dogmatic, godless scientism, and hence with a homogeneous shallowness of soul, with loveless commercialism and the reduction of human relationships to calculation and the cash nexus. Tocqueville discerned with clarity the first stages in this development, and foresaw with prescient trepidation something of the outcome. He strove through his writings to convince his fellow Europeans that the American experience revealed a very different, far richer, and more symbiotic relationship between religion and liberal-democratic modernity. He strove, that is, to show that the American experience was not necessarily unique, but could serve as a model to be imitated, *mutatis mutandis*, as democracy spread throughout the world and encountered, inevitably, the opposing force of traditional religion or religiosity.

Now how exactly is this Tocquevillian perspective useful or necessary for us here and now? The postmodernist or multiculturalist critique of liberalism and rationalism that we see and hear all around us is in large measure the result of the importation into America of the late-modern radical criticisms of modernity and of rationalism carried out from left and right by thinkers such as Nietzsche and Heidegger and Marx. To be sure, contemporary multiculturalism and postmodernism has abandoned the frightening political alternatives which these great philosophic critics proposed as replacements for liberalism. But contemporary multiculturalism and postmodernism retain, in a more lighthearted, playful, and therefore in a sense more contemptuous spirit, much of the fundamental negative interpretation of the true meaning of rationalism and liberalism in human life. Yet this interpretation springs from perspectives that view liberal democracy through the prism of the experience of continental Europe.

While none of the thinkers at the source of postmodernism and multiculturalism can be called religious, all of them promulgated doctrines that evince an unmistakable longing for a substitute for religiosity. Each of these radical critics forged a curiously idealistic atheism that attempted to secularize the spiritual, moral, and artistic depths they had found missing or dying out in liberal modernity and that they had found overwhelmingly alive in the emphatically theistic biblical and Greco-Roman cultures. Each of them carried forward in some sense—to be sure in highly original and deeply reflective ways—the critique of liberalism born in the religious reaction to what was perceived to be the godless and loveless philosophies of thinkers like Spinoza, Hobbes, Locke, Hume, and Adam Smith. And our contemporary postmodernists continue this critique, while showing themselves more blithely willing to accept or live within the spiritual desert of nihilism and vulgar power struggle that they diagnose to be the outcome of the triumph of liberalism. Now Tocqueville tries to show that the American experience exhibits a viable version of liberal democracy and rationalism that is, if not immune, then at any rate resistant to this criticism. Might not a rethinking of the American experience, along Tocquevillian lines, and then a drawing on and reviving of that experience, so rethought, afford us a basis for defending liberal democracy as a model that does not necessarily imply the spiritual barrenness, the closeness to religion, that the multiculturalist and postmodernist indictment suggests?

POSTMODERN MARRIAGE BELLS

Tocqueville's argument for the symbiosis of religion and liberalism is emphatically *not* an argument that is very flattering to either of the marriage partners. In fact, the reason why the two can go well together, in his view, is because each desperately needs the other as a supplement or compensation. This means that each of the partners has to be made aware of, has to admit and seek remedies for, those deficiencies which the other can ameliorate. So if we are to follow Tocqueville, we must begin from a clear-eyed assessment of certain specific dangers to freedom and spirituality presented by modern democracy left to itself.

As is well known, Tocqueville identifies the "tyranny of the majority" as the primary threat to the human spirit in the age of democracy. When the individual compares himself to all those who surround him, Tocqueville says, "he feels with pride that he is equal to each of them"; *but*, "when he comes to contemplate the collectivity of his fellows, and to place himself alongside this great body, he is overwhelmed by his own insignificance and weakness." In other words, to continue with the words of Tocqueville, "the same equality that renders him independent of each of his fellow citizens taken one by one leaves him isolated and defenseless in the face of the majority."

This sapping of the individual's capacity to think in genuine independence from public opinion goes hand in hand with a shrinking of the citizen's belief in and inclination to significant involvement in public life. Tocqueville discerns in the democratic way of life a specific new behavioral and emotional syndrome for which he invents a word: *individualism*. Individualism is something different from selfishness or egoism. Individualism, in Tocqueville's words, "is a quiet and considered sentiment which disposes each citizen to isolate himself from the mass of his fellows and retire into the circle of family and friends." Modern democratic society, with its antitraditionalism, its opening of opportunity, its restless mobility, its stress on individual initiative and autonomy grounded in the moral principles of universal rights, uproots and detaches citizens one from another, steadily constricting the avenues and possibilities for any one person to shape or care for the lives of others.

The powerful tendency of the democratic personality to withdraw into the narrow circle of immediate acquaintances is intensified by the inordinate taste for physical comfort that is yet a third dangerous proclivity of modern democratic society. To grasp the peculiar character and intensity of this passion in modern democracy, Tocqueville insists we need to begin from this premise: "what most vividly seizes the human heart is not by any means the quiet possession of a precious object, it is the imperfectly satisfied desire to possess it, accompanied by the incessant fear of losing it." Now in modern democracy, Tocqueville observes, when "the ranks are blurred and privileges destroyed, when patrimonies are divided and enlightenment and liberty spread, the longing to acquire well-being presents itself to the imagination of the poor and the fear of losing it haunts the spirit of the rich." What is more, "a multitude of middling fortunes are established, whose possessors have enough material enjoyments to acquire a taste for them, but not enough to be contented; they never procure the material enjoyments without effort and do not indulge in them without anxiety." Accordingly, "they ceaselessly attach themselves to pursuing or to retaining these material enjoyments that are so precious, so incomplete, and so fugitive." As a further result, the democratic soul tends to be characterized by an unprecedented truncation of its conception of the future, in terms both of responsibility and of regard for long-term consequences.

From the combination of all these peculiarly democratic debilitations grows what Tocqueville calls "the secret anxiety which reveals itself in the actions of Americans." "He who has constricted his heart to the sole quest for the goods of this world is always in a hurry," Tocqueville writes; "the recollection of the brevity of life goads him on continually"; "apart from the goods he already possesses, he imagines at every moment a thousand others that death will prevent him from enjoying, if he doesn't hurry." Yet the passion for physical pleasure, while feverish, is at the same time easily discouraged: since the goal is enjoyment, the means must be prompt and easy or they contradict the goal. As a consequence, Tocqueville argues, in modern democracy there is a tendency for the souls to be "at one and the same time ardent and soft, violent and enervated."

RELIGIOUS VIRTUES

It is religion, Tocqueville insists, that can most contribute to remedying these specific ills of modern democracy. To begin with, religion counteracts in manifold ways the "secret anxiety" to which democratic man is prey. "Most religions," Tocqueville submits, "are only general, simple, and practical means for teaching to men the immortality of the soul." In worship that inspires and is inspired by belief in the immortality of one's soul, the inhabitant of democracy is momentarily liberated "from the petty passions which agitate his life and from the evanescent interests which preoccupy it." Moreover, "religions instill a general habit of behaving with the future in view"; "in this respect," Tocqueville adds, "they work as much in favor of happiness in this world as of felicity in the next."

Religion does not merely counter the anxiety peculiar to democratic man; it goes to the root causes of that anxiety by opposing both materialism and individualism. It is this, Tocqueville judges, that is "the greatest advantage of religions" for democracy. "There is no religion," Tocqueville writes, "that does not place the goal of the desires of the human being beyond and above earthly goods, and that does not naturally elevate his soul toward regions far superior to those of the senses. Nor is there any that does not impose on each certain duties toward the human species, or in common with it, and that does not thus draw one, from time to time, away from the contemplation of oneself. Religious peoples are, then, naturally strong precisely where democratic peoples are weak; this shows clearly how important it is that men preserve their religion in becoming equal."

One of Tocqueville's great themes is the way in which Americans combat the effects of individualism through "the doctrine of self-interest rightly understood." In an oft-quoted passage, Tocqueville says that this enlightened utilitarianism or egoism "does not inspire great sacrifices, but every day it prompts some small ones; by itself it cannot make a man virtuous, but its discipline shapes a lot of orderly, temperate, moderate, careful, and self-controlled citizens." But he adds, in a passage that is often overlooked, that if this doctrine "had in view this world only, it would be far from sufficient; because there are a great number of sacrifices which cannot find their recompense except in the other world."

Precisely because the private sphere assumes such importance in the lives of modern democrats, it is crucial, Tocqueville argues, that in their domestic lives they experience an oasis of order, tranquility, love, decency, and trust. The family is more likely to provide such an oasis if it is grounded on and elevated by some sort of religious sanction.

THE FIRST POLITICAL INSTITUTION

In short, the Americans' religious denominations, though they do not directly intervene in politics, must nevertheless "be considered," Tocqueville says, "as the first of their political institutions." The various denominations and priesthoods make no claim to participate in earthly legislation, but they remind citizens of supramundane limits that the citizens, even when gathered together in the majority, are obliged to heed, in thought as well as in action. "Thus," Tocqueville says, "the human spirit never sees an unlimited field before itself; however great its audacity, it feels from time to time that it must arrest itself before insurmountable barriers." "Up until now," Tocqueville adds with some caution, "no one has ever been found, in the United States, who has dared to advance this maxim: that everything is permitted in the interests of society—an impious maxim, which seems to have been invented in a century of liberty in order to legitimate all the tyrants to come." For "what can be done with a people that is master of itself, if it is not subject to God?" Christianity, Tocqueville observes, has "preserved a great empire over the spirit of the Americans, and—this is the point I wish to emphasize [he says]—it does not at all reign only as a philosophy adopted after examination, but as a religion that is believed without discussion." Religion, precisely because or insofar as its basic teachings are authoritative, and thus not subject to the arbitration of public opinion, provides a powerful counterweight to the sway of public opinion.

On the strictly political level, Tocqueville thus helps us appreciate the advantages derived from the fact that the churches or religious denominations in modern democracy, and especially the Roman Catholic Church, are institutions whose authority and structure are neither dictated by, nor intermingled with, nor simply subordinate to, the constituted political authorities. The churches do not directly compete with democratic political authority, but they do stand apart, reminding all citizens of a higher law and a higher legal authority.

This brings into view the other side of the coin: that is, the way in which liberal democracy saves religion from some of its own worst political impulses. Tocqueville argues fervently and repeatedly that the strict but friendly separation of church and state in American democracy, so far from representing a compromise of religion's influence and strength, in fact creates the condition under which religion's true strength and influence can flourish. "Considering religions from a purely human point of view," Tocqueville argues, their real strength lies in the overwhelming natural human desire for immortality. When a religion founds itself on this, "it can aspire to universality"; "it can draw to itself the heart of the human species." But when it allies itself to political powers or governments, religion mortgages its universal and permanent appeal to the limited and temporary prop of a specific regime. "It augments its strength over some but forfeits the hope of reigning over all." In addition, "it is sometimes constrained to defend allies who are such from interest rather than love; and it has to repulse as adversaries men who still love religion, although they are fighting religion's allies." In the long run, religion allied with any specific political authority is compelled to share in some measure the mortality and ultimate fragility of any such specific regime.

These general considerations take on heightened significance in democracy, where the struggle of parties, factions, and individuals produces a natural agitation and restless instability in political life. Moreover, Tocqueville adds, since "in times of enlightenment and of equality, the human spirit is loath to receive dogmatic beliefs, and senses vividly the need for them only in religion," it flows that "in these centuries, religions ought to restrict themselves more discretely than in other ages to the limits which are proper to them"; "for, in wishing to extend their power beyond religious matters, they risk not being believed in any matter."

Reminding his readers that he speaks "as a practicing Catholic," Tocqueville concedes that what he describes as the felicitous situation of religion in modern democracy is contrary to the historical practice and, what is more, the traditional spirit of Roman Catholicism. But "I think," he avers with uncustomary hesitation, that the experience of American Catholicism shows that "one is mistaken in regarding the Catholic religion as a natural enemy of democracy." In fact, Tocqueville goes on to argue, a wise Catholicism would see in liberal democracy its greatest political friend, precisely because liberal religious pluralism saves Catholicism from its own self-destructive proclivities. "Every religion has some political opinion linked to it by affinity," Tocqueville declares, and for Catholicism the affinity is with absolute monarchy; but in politics as in life generally, it is our affinities that reveal our temptations.

Catholics "are not," Tocqueville admits, "strongly drawn by the nature of their beliefs toward democratic and republican opinions." But at least they aren't naturally opposed to democracy, and in a pluralist society "their social position, as well as their being in a minority, make it a law for them to embrace those opinions." In America, Catholics "are led, perhaps in spite of themselves, toward political doctrines which, maybe, they would adopt with less zeal were they rich and predominant." Catholics ought to bless the fate that throws them in with powerful Protestant sects in a pluralist republican society. In such a society they can discover that they share with their Protestant fellow citizens the recognition that the practice of "civil liberty" affords "a noble exercise of the human faculties, the world of politics being a field opened up by the Creator to the efforts of intelligence." Catholics can discover, in other words, that obedience to authority in the highest sphere—that of revelation and concern for the life to come—can in practice harmonize with, can even help provide the healthy basis for, a proud spirit of independence and self-government in the political sphere.

ROUNDABOUT PATH TO FAITH

Tocqueville is keenly aware of the grave difficulties that attend his project. He does not suppose that the complementarity of religion and liberal democracy is natural or even easy to bring about. He worries about powerful democratic tendencies to skepticism, to vacuous pantheism, and to febrile revivalism. Above all, he recognizes a threat to religious belief that arises from his own argument. For this argument tends to value religion, not for its truth, but for its usefulness in remedying or limiting the secular ills of a secular society. But to thus esteem religion for its service to worldly political ends is to risk denying what is, from the religious point of view, the supreme value of the essentially otherworldly ends of religion itself. As Tocqueville repeatedly remarks, he is viewing religion "from a purely human point of view," and in that perspective, "what is most important for society is not that all citizens should profess the true religion but that they should profess religion." Insofar as the democratic citizenry come more and more to share this perspective, Tocqueville admits, "religion is loved, supported, and honored, and only by looking into the depths of men's souls will one see what wounds it has suffered."

"I do not know," confesses Tocqueville, "what is to be done to give back to European Christianity the energy of youth: God alone could do that." Yet Tocqueville cannot shirk the duty of attempting to discern how government might foster religious faith without violating religious liberty. "I think," he declares, "that the only effective means which governments can use to make the doctrine of the immortality of the soul respected is daily to act as if they believed it themselves. I think that it is only by conforming scrupulously to religious mortality in great affairs that they can flatter themselves that they are teaching the citizens to understand it and to love and respect it in little matters." But Tocqueville knows that this is not enough. "Governments," he adds, "must study means to give men back that interest in the future which neither religion nor social conditions any longer inspire"; "in accustoming the citizens to think of the future in this world, they will gradually be led without noticing it themselves toward religious beliefs. Thus the same means that, up to a certain point, enable men to manage without religion are perhaps, after all, the only means we still possess for bringing mankind back, by a long and roundabout path, to a state of faith."

Tocqueville's discussion leaves us wondering which of the two partners—religion, or democracy—is the more in need of the other, or which partner's health Tocqueville is himself more concerned with fostering. But is not this ambiguity part of the virtue of his analysis? Is not this ambiguity an essential, and profound, aspect of the model—of citizenship, of statesmanship, of political commentary—that he means to provide for us?

22

True and False Tolerance

Philippe Bénéton

Tolerance is an ambiguous word greatly valued by the zeitgeist. Who dares to declare himself against tolerance? There would be nothing left to say, however, if the contemporary idea of tolerance was not fundamentally distorted. Properly understood, tolerance implies respect for people but not agreement with their error or fault. Thus, ideas do not have to be "tolerant"—it is enough if they are correct.

Real tolerance, in other words, is not incompatible with either firm convictions or the desire to persuade others. Tolerance simply rejects force and intimidation toward those who think differently. But today tolerance generally signifies something else—initially it tends to be equated with relativism and then it is identified with new norms in human life and thought. Put differently, tolerance now speaks a double language.

THE REDUCTION OF TRUTH TO OPINION

The prevalent idea of tolerance is connected to relativism: "each one has his truth"; "each individual is autonomous"; "the self is the source of meaning." To be tolerant in this view is to cling to the opinion that everything is a matter of opinion and of equal opinions at that. Each person must take his bearings from his sovereign subjectivity, and no one has the right to put forth a universal standard. To affirm that a particular proposition is true by itself, apart from mere opinion, is considered an attack on tolerance.

What does this reign of universal tolerance, or dogmatic relativism, in fact mean? It has as its effect the undermining of all authority and vital knowledge, depriving

---

First published in *Crisis*, April 1996. Translated by Daniel J. Mahoney and Paul Seaton.

all meaning from liberty and toleration. It finally destroys liberty and tolerance themselves. Taken to its logical conclusion, the reign of opinion means the end of all intellectual and moral authority, whether it be the great minds whose dialogue forms culture or the institutions—Church, family, school—that traditionally have transmitted rules of conduct. The reign of opinion means the attenuation of every form of knowledge. In the kingdom of opinion, there is no place for knowledge that engages one's being.

What is opinion? It is something I possess, which depends upon my sovereign liberty; it is in no sense consubstantial with what I am. Indeed, profound experience rebels against opinion—would a survivor of a Nazi concentration camp say, for example, "Here's my opinion on what I lived through"? On the contrary, the witness is *engaged* with his experience. As long as being is implicated, *what is* does not depend on my sovereign liberty. I participate, I attest to something that does not depend on me, and, as a result, I am no longer master. The reign of the self requires one to remain at the surface, on the outside. The autonomous man—the "tolerant" man is finally emptied of substance. The tolerant man is emptied of further substance as the reign of opinion deprives liberty of all meaning. When subjectivism rules, there are no longer good reasons for genuine reflection about life. What good is it, after all, to use one's reason when the choice grounded in reason is worth the same as the most irrational one? Choices then lose all meaning; they engage nothing that counts and are no longer serious. "To be or not to be," Hamlet's famous question, is of the same order as "White or red wine?" and it calls for the same response: it does not matter, every one does what he wants, the choice is—in every sense of the term—insignificant. Absurdity reigns.

It is necessary to distinguish the freedom to choose from the freedom to determine the value of one's choice. Pure liberty implies both: I am free to decide that my life's meaning consists in bungee jumping or in doing cartwheels or pumping up my biceps or any other idiosyncratic pursuit. What is meaningful depends on the individual will. I am the master of which questions count. As Charles Taylor has underscored forcefully, under these conditions nothing is intrinsically meaningful. Freedom is deprived of significance.

In order for the exercise of my freedom to have meaning, my choices must be related to rules independent of my will: I can choose between cowardice and courage, but the value of my choice does not depend on me. To state this more emphatically, freedom of choice has no meaning unless I am not the master of meaning. Contemporary thought, of course, does not share this view; rather, opinion rules the value of things. Each person is himself the master of meaning, the master of a meaning that paradoxically means nothing. Pure freedom and universal tolerance are not just devoid of meaning—they ultimately self-destruct.

If all choices are equal, I am not able rationally to justify the choice for liberty, equality, or democracy. All "values" being equal, by what virtue can I attribute a special status to the "value" of liberty or equality? By what standard can I prefer democracy to another regime? Since opinions are equal, opinions hostile to liberty, equality, and democracy are worth the same as those that are favorable. Moreover, if opinions are equal, the opinion according to which opinions are unequal is worth the same as the opinion according to which opinions are equal. We are literally caught in a spinning wheel with no hope of extricating ourselves.

If all choices are equal, I am free to alienate my freedom. Pure freedom is defenseless against itself. The free man is free to sell his body or his soul. John Stuart Mill rightly observed that a man is not free to renounce his freedom because, if he were, he would be in a position to annihilate what justified freedom itself. Mill's proposition is meaningful, however, only if one admits that liberty is something other than an indeterminate freedom. Pure freedom can abolish itself freely, in the same way that procedural democracy can abolish itself democratically. If democracy is reduced to procedures by which the majority-will of the people is expressed, a majority vote suffices to abolish democracy as was done in 411 B.C. when the Assembly of the people at Athens enacted an end to their democracy.

If all choices are equal, logically I must deny the universal character of the rights of man. Since each "culture" is held to be irreducible, none can be said to be superior to any other. But how can one extol such cultural relativism without abandoning the universality of rights? Of all the contradictions in which dogmatic relativism is ensnared, this one is the most visible in practice. On the one hand, the universalism of rights inspires modern man to act in order for these rights to be respected everywhere; on the other, cultural relativism imposes passivity in the name of respect for the sovereign particularity of each "culture." Taken to its conclusion, this relativism leads to the claim that no one can prefer, take care, or protect any culture except his own. The cannibal has "the right to be different" by following the norm of his culture.

"These are my values," say the brutal, the violent, the sadistic. If all "values" are equal, how can I answer them? Pure freedom knows no limit. Pure liberty subverts everything, including liberty itself.

The relativism of choices, values, and opinions thus has for its effect a comprehensive leveling: if everything is worthy, nothing is. This position does not truly inspire respect for conscience. The modern man who wishes to be the creator of his own "values" experiences a feeling of power, but he cannot experience any sentiment of respect, either for himself or others. Psychology operates in the same way as logic—pure freedom tends to subvert liberty.

THE UNEQUAL EQUALITY OF OPINIONS

Thus the modern world—what we call late modernity—bases itself on principles that it cannot follow to their conclusion without destroying itself. What accounts for this contradiction? Doubtless it is a matter of blindness, but it is also one of duplicity. Its logical incoherence has its own logic that relativizes dogmatic relativism. Put another way, late modernity affirms more than it says it does.

On the one hand, modernity wants to be beyond good and evil; on the other, it redefines good and evil. On the one hand, it proclaims the equality of opinions; on the other, it defines what opinions are suitable. This way of speaking is contradictory, but it is also coherent. It is contradictory because its argument continues to violate logic, but it is coherent because what it forbids, requires, and inspires essentially cohere to change in the same direction the rule of human conduct.

The operation proceeds in three stages that are logically distinct. First, the dominant opinion, basing itself on the equality of opinions, discredits the idea of the good. Then, basing itself on egalitarian-libertarian dogmas, it redefines which opinions and attitudes are appropriate, which are more or less unsuitable, and which, finally, are execrable. Finally, basing itself on the prejudices of modern historicism and upon the appearance of being a "democratic" opinion, it gives to the new orthodoxy the seal of incontestability.

In the first stage, the recognition of the equality of opinions plays a subversive role. It disqualifies the idea of the "good life" as it has been understood by the philosophic and religious tradition of the West. The inherited norms and models of civilization henceforth are placed under the rubric of opinion, as were the multiplicity of individual opinions. Dogmatic relativism and dogmatic scientism join together to maintain that there is no intrinsic good. Consequently it is good to renounce the good. The new virtues have recognizable names—"authenticity," "tolerance," "self-expression," "openness." In other words, these are "values" that (despite the contradiction in terms) present themselves as "value free" and at the service of the pure freedom of oneself and others. It is implicitly understood that relativism stops at the principle that grounds it—the equality of opinions is not a matter of opinion but of *dogma*.

In its second stage, the dominant discourse leaves behind its professed relativism in order to present as self-evident the opinions and attitudes that define appropriate ways of being. This new version of the "good life" has two essential components: selfishness and egalitarian-humanitarian moralism. On the plane of "private morality," the golden rule is that man is innocent by nature, free from moral responsibility. Egoism is therefore a good thing. Where is pure freedom, consisting in liberating oneself from every idea of the good, better revealed than where it is most distant from the traditional notion of the good? "Free yourself," says the dominant opinion. "Reject all taboos, think of yourself first of all and cultivate pleasures, especially physical ones." To live means to cultivate "each for himself" and to strive ceaselessly for the most desirable goods of all: comfort, health, youth, irresponsible sex, entertainment, the various symbols of success. Tolerance in no way demands that one keep a balance between the traditional virtues and the modern "virtues." This practical egoism goes hand in hand with an invasive social moralism. Invited to yield to one's appetites, one is also required to cultivate the appropriate feelings. The misfortunes of those nearby count little, but those of the world demand a vigilant eye and a bleeding heart. Here relativism gives way completely, to be replaced by moral imperatives: the denunciation of evil and compassion for suffering mankind. In the

Christian moral world, evil takes a thousand forms and pierces the heart of each. In the new moral world, evil is clearly circumscribed; it is concentrated, it is incarnate entirely in certain attitudes, particularly those that violate or run counter to the new "values": racism, sexism, elitism, and all that detracts from the cult of human rights. The idea of sin is denied ex cathedra. The one who has the right opinion belongs ipso facto on the side of the just.

This accusatory moralism is also a compassionate moralism. The chattering classes resonate with emotion before the world's unhappiness. Compassion belongs to the obligatory sentiments—provided that it takes the appropriate form. The love of humanity does not concern itself with the family circle or the neighborhood. Rather, it concerns itself with the anonymous victims of "exclusion," discrimination, and persecution as well as those of natural disasters. Consequently, to flaunt these fine sentiments costs nothing: love is liberated from the labors of love. It requires only an emotion, a gesture, not a true engagement.

In its third stage, the dominant opinion employs two other arguments—one historicist, the other "democratic"—to enjoin us to rally to its cause. It demands that we submit to the authority of the present because it is the present, to submit to the reigning view because it is the general view. That more fundamental issues might be at stake is simply denied, and discussion is held to be superflous. These are orders to submit to authorities other than reason, to abdicate all genuine freedom of thought.

The dominant opinion congratulates itself on being modern and takes pride in expressing the general opinion. In large measure the dominant discourse presents itself as the spokesman of common opinion bringing to bear on everyone the weight of the supposed majority. The media present the new norms of conduct as normal, banal, self-evident, and present themselves as the representatives of public opinion, with polls ready at hand. Through the airwaves it is the entire society that seems to speak.

This norm, presented as banal or common, and thus legitimate or suitable, is itself largely fabricated by those who shape the dominant opinion. In other words, the dominant opinion is not identical with the common opinion it claims to express, but rather tends to shape the latter from the outside. It is not ordinary men who have forged the new tablets of good and evil and who orchestrate it by means of the media and in the schools. Who could deny the central role of political and intellectual elites in the moral revolution of the 1960s? The progress of equality by default is first and foremost the work of activists of equality: philosophers of absolute freedom, radical social scientists, immoderate partisans of rights, radical feminists, militant multiculturalists.

Here, too, opinions are not equal. These activists who play upon the keyboard of the new "values" had an impact disproportionate with their number. The benevolence of the men in the media counts much here, since their milieu is especially well disposed toward so-called modern ideas. Its logic levels the world, its agents orchestrate the dominant "values." On this point, Tocqueville's famous interpretation of majority tyranny is wrong in that it overestimates the role of the common man. If, as he says, opinion is the ruler in democratic societies, this opinion today does not come from the people. It is above all the work of an intellectual avant-garde and its mediatized amplifiers. Thus the dominant opinion advances masked, affecting a fictitious moral neutrality. Appealing to our autonomy, we are enclosed within a circle of suitable beliefs. The success of this maneuver is undeniable: with all the appeal of liberation, it controls the way we see and think. With the semblance of autonomy, conformity reigns. Young people especially are caught in the net, and it is very difficult for them to think that one can have a free mind and think differently, they believe they are autonomous while in fact they are profoundly conditioned. Young people are conditioned to a way of seeing and thinking that flattens and lowers life. For the Greeks, life was a tragedy; for Christians, life is a drama; for moderns deceived by ideology life was a melodrama, where the happy ending was guaranteed. For late moderns, life is but a soap opera with miserable stakes. The way of life to which the dominant opinion invites us is the one Tocqueville feared when he saw on the horizon "an innumerable crowd of equal and similar men who focus endlessly on themselves in order to procure the small, vulgar pleasures with which they fill their souls." Late modernity does not address itself to free men. Its motto can be formulated as follows: "Be a master, to be sure, but a domesticated one."

23

Law and Liberty in *Veritatis Splendor*

Russell Hittinger

One of the most curious and disturbing trends of our culture is the belief that the chief purpose of law is to annul the law itself. When authority is used to divest the community of its obligations under law, or when authority is used to recognize rights as so many immunities against the law—indeed when authority is used to subvert authority—then we tend to say that law is good, which is to say that it is accomplishing humane ends. Our ecclesial culture does not remain unaffected by this attitude.

Issues of moral theology are invariably reduced to questions of authority. When the pope said that he has no authority to ordain women, many Catholics and non-Catholics alike were shocked by the suggestion that the pope cannot use law for any purpose he so pleases. Whether we are speaking of marriage tribunals, altar girls, holy days of obligation, contraception, public policy on abortion, or whatever, people inside and outside the Church want apostolic authority used to ratify the liberty of individual choice. Law, it seems, is but a maleable tool in the hands of an interpreting community.

When law binds, it is called legalism; when it loosens, it is praised as humane. The pope speaks to this problem at the very outset of *Veritatis Splendor*, when he recounts the colloquy between Jesus and the rich young man in Matthew 19:

> Then someone came to him and said, "Teacher, what good must I do to have eternal life?" And he said to him, "Why do you ask me about what is good? There is only one who is good. If you wish to enter into life, keep the commandments." He said to him, "Which ones?" And Jesus said, "You shall not murder; You shall not commit adultery; You shall not steal; You shall not bear false witness; Honour your father and mother;

First published in *Crisis*, May 1995.

also, You shall love your neighbour as yourself." The young man said to him, "I have kept all these; what do I still lack?" Jesus said to him, "If you wish to be perfect, go, sell your possessions and give the money to the poor, and you shall have treasure in heaven; then come, follow me." (VS 6)

The pope explains that the first and ultimate question of morality is not a lawyerly question. Unlike the Pharisees, the rich young man does not ask what the bottom line is, from a legal standpoint. Rather, he asks what must be done in order to achieve the unconditional good, which is communion with God. Christ takes the sting out of law, not by annulling it, but by revealing the Good to which it directs us. Remove or forget the Good and it is inevitable that law becomes legalism. Legalism is nothing other than law without its context.

The scripture relates that the young man went away sad, for he had many possessions. But the modern audience is more apt to turn away sad when faced with the teaching that there is a moral law that is indispensable, and indeed which binds authority itself. John Paul II sometimes is treated like a simpleton, an ecclesiastical version of Dan Quayle, when he points out that all issues of circumstance, culture, place, and time notwithstanding, certain actions can never be made right, and that no human "law" can make them right. Just as from the scales and axiomatic measures of music there can come a Beethoven sonata, or a Penderecki 12-tone composition, so, too, from obedience to the commandments there opens the possibility of a creative, fluid, and completely realized human liberty. The point of learning the scales is not mindless repetition; the point is to make beautiful music. No doubt, a piano teacher who only focused upon the scales would be a simpleton, a legalist as it were. But a piano teacher who neglected to call the pupil's attention to the scalar rudiments would not be worthy of the name teacher. Musical order does not, and indeed cannot, begin merely with human spontaneity and creative improvisation. The same is true in the domain of moral action. Any one who would set up an opposition between law and freedom, and then take the side of freedom, not only underestimates the need for law, but misrepresents the nature of freedom.

The story of the rich young man, of course, shows the essential unity of the Law and Gospel. In *Veritatis* the pope also spends considerable effort dealing with a related theme: namely, the unity of the two tables of the Decalogue. "Acknowledging the Lord as God," he says, "is the very core, the heart of the law, from which the particular precepts flow and toward which they are ordered" (VS 11). Each precept, he continues, "is the interpretation of what the words 'I am the Lord your God' mean for man" (VS 13).

The issue of the two tables situates the theme of law and freedom, but it also stands at the center of the dispute between the pope and the dissenting moral theologians. The ground of the problem is actually quite simple, so simple in fact that it is easy to overlook it, or to mistake it for some other kind of problem.

II.

Upon creation, did God give to our first parents a kind of plenary authority over "ethics"—over a sphere of this worldly conduct that more or less corresponds to the second table of the Decalogue? In *Veritatis*, the pope has this to say about the answer often given by moral theologians:

> Some people . . . disregarding the dependence of human reason on Divine Wisdom . . . have actually posited a "complete sovereignty of reason" in the domain of moral norms regarding the right ordering of life in this world. Such norms would constitute the boundaries for a merely "human" morality; they would be the expression of a law which man in an autonomous manner lays down for himself and which has its source exclusively in human reason. In no way could God be considered the Author of this law, except in the sense that human reason exercises its autonomy in setting down laws by virtue of a primordial and total mandate given to man by God. These trends of thought have led to a denial, in opposition to Sacred Scripture (cf. Mt. 15:3–6) and the Church's constant teaching, of the fact that the natural moral law has God as its author, and that man, by the use of reason, participates in the eternal law, which it is not for him to establish. (VS 36)

"[C]ertain moral theologians," the pope continues, "have introduced a sharp distinction, contrary to Catholic doctrine, between an 'ethical order,' which would be human in origin, and of value for 'this world' alone, and an 'order of salvation' for which only certain intentions and interior attitudes regarding God and neighbor would be significant. This has then led to an actual denial that there exists, in Divine Revelation, a specific and determined moral content, universally valid and permanent. The word of God would be limited to proposing an exhortation . . . which the autonomous reason alone would then have the task of completing with normative directives which are truly 'objective,' that is, adapted to the concrete historical situation" (VS 37).

Notice that the pope does not accuse these (unnamed) theologians of proposing that some moral norms are naturally known, even by people who are ignorant of revelation. The Catholic Church has always held that some rudimentary precepts of the natural law are known naturally, without instruction afforded by divine positive law. Instead, the pope accuses certain unnamed theologians of constructing a sphere of human moral choice independent of, and immune from, divine governance. The fact that the human mind is naturally competent to make moral judgments is construed to mean that human practical reason has dominion. From the premise that the human mind has a natural, jurisdictional dominion over "ethics," it would seem to flow that the Church ought to butt out, and use its offices only as a kind of bully pulpit for exhorting the otherwise autonomous human agent. However, for the Church to butt out of "ethics," it would be necessary to get God out of the picture. Some theologians remove God from the picture by arguing that, at creation,

God removed Himself. It was God, after all, who created human practical reason, endowing it with a natural competence over moral conduct. By emphasizing human jurisdictional authority over ethics, these theologians perhaps do not go so far as Marcion, for they do not posit an absolute dualism between creation and salvation, or between Law and Gospel. Their opinion more resembles the modern deistic theology, according to which God indeed creates, and what he creates is good; but He hands over jurisdiction of creation to the human mind.

Thus, we find Father Joseph Fuchs contending in his most recent book that: "When in fact, nature-creation does speak to us, it tells us only what it is and how it functions on its own. In other words, the Creator shows us what is divinely willed to exist, and how it functions, but not how the Creator wills the human being *qua* person to use this existing reality." Fuchs goes on to assert that: "Neither the Hebrew Bible nor the New Testament produces statements that are independent of culture and thus universal and valid for all time; nor can these statements be given by the church or its magisterium. Rather, it is the task of human beings—of the various persons who have been given the requisite intellectual capacity—to investigate what can and must count as a conviction about these responsibilities." In other words, God creates, but he gives no operating instructions. The natural norm will have to be drawn from human reason; or, as Fuchs suggests, those "who have been given the requisite intellectual capacity." I take this to mean academic ethicians and moral theologians.

We should not overlook the fact that this kind of theology was prominent in the dissent of the theologians against *Humanae Vitae*. The majority of Paul VI's Commission for the Study of Problems of the Family, Population, and Birth Rate issued a report urging that the Church change her teaching on contraception. The authors of the majority report at least had the honesty to clearly state their theological premise. They reasoned that although the sources of human life are from created nature, the rules for the choice and administration of that natural value fall to human jurisdiction. "To take his own or another's life is a sin," the Majority Report contended, "not because life is under the exclusive dominion of God but because it is contrary to right reason unless there is question of a good or a higher order."

Similarly, Father Fuchs asserts that, "One cannot . . . deduce, from God's relationship to creation, what the obligation of the human person is in these areas or in the realm of creation as a whole." Regarding *Gaudium et Spes*, where the human conscience is spoken of as a *sacrarium* in which we find ourselves responsible before God—*solus cum solo*—Father Fuchs states that the notion that "the human person is illuminated by a light that comes, not from one's own reason . . . but from the wisdom of God in whom everything is created . . . cannot stand up to an objective analysis nor prove helpful in the vocabulary of Christian believers." Father Fuchs's rejection of the Council's teaching on the nature of conscience at least has the virtue of consistency. It follows from his own doctrine that while God creates, he does not govern the human mind. The human mind is a merely natural light, to which there corresponds a merely natural jurisdiction over ethics. In this way, Fuchs and other moral theologians have made it clear that the current debate is not merely an in-house controversy between different schools of ethics. The debate reaches the ground of the possibility of any moral theology. The pope clearly understands the seriousness of the challenge.

Turning to the injunction in Genesis 2:17, the pope writes: "By forbidding man to 'eat of the tree of the knowledge of good and evil,' God makes it clear that man does not originally possess such 'knowledge' as something properly his own, but only participates in it by the light of natural reason and of Divine Revelation, which manifest to him the requirements and promptings of eternal wisdom. Law must therefore be considered an expression of divine wisdom . . ." (41). The natural condition of man is one of participation in a higher norm. Man has liberty to direct himself because he is first directed by another.

The pope makes use of a number of authorities to express the idea of natural law as "participated theonomy." He refers to Ps. 4:6 ("Let the light of your face shine upon us, O Lord"), emphasizing that moral knowledge derives from a divine illumination; from Rom. 2:14 ("The Gentiles who had not the Law, did naturally the things of the Law"), he calls attention to the idea that it is not just by positive law that humans are directed in the moral order. From Gregory of Nyssa, he cites the passage that autonomy is predicated only of a king; from St. Bonaventure, he cites the dictum that conscience does not bind on its own authority, but is rather the "herald of a king." The very existence of conscience, the pope argues, indicates that we are under a law that we did not impose upon ourselves. Conscience is not a witness to a human power, it is a witness to the natural law. And this is only to say that the natural law is a real law which cannot be equated with our conscience. It was precisely this equation, the pope notes, that beguiled our first parents, when the serpent in Genesis 3:5 said they could be as gods. What does it mean to be as gods? It means that the human mind is a measuring measure, having authority to impact the measures of moral good and evil.

If there is anything in moral theology on which the Fathers held a unanimous opinion it was that the injunction in Genesis 2:17 summarizes the natural law. As early as the second century, Tertullian characterized this injunction "as the womb of all the precepts of God"—a "law unwritten, which was habitually understood naturally." Law did not begin with the law of the Jewish state; though the Decalogue is a divine positive law, it reiterates (in the relation between the two tables) the original ordering reported in Genesis. There never was a sphere of lawless ethics; that is to say, a sphere in which the created mind posits moral norms without any antecedent rule of law. God governed men from the very outset. Indeed, the idea that there is a lawless morality, possessed by men as a kind of natural right, is precisely the sin committed by our first parents. The first law establishes the rule of law itself, which is that men govern only by sharing in divine governance.

Throughout the Scriptures, this rule of law is reiterated. We can have rectitude in matters of ethics only insofar as the mind adheres to God (first by natural law, then through the Law, and finally through grace). Thus, in Mark 12:28, we read: "And one of the scribes . . . asked him, 'Which commandment is the first of all?'

Jesus answered (quoting Deut 6:4), "The first is, 'Hear O Israel: The Lord our God, the Lord is one; and you shall love the Lord your God with all your heart, and with all your soul, and with all your mind, and with all your strength." The second is this "You shall love your neighbor as yourself."

In his commentary on *Genesis against the Manicheans*, Augustine insisted that the sin of our first parents was a violation of the very core of the natural law. "This is what they were persuaded to do; to love to excess their own power. And, since they wanted to be equal to God, they used wrongly, that is, against the Law of God, that middle rank by which they were subject to God and held their bodies in subjection. This middle rank was like the fruit of the tree placed in the middle of paradise. Thus they lost what they had received in wanting to seize what they had not received. For the nature of man did not receive the capability of being happy by its own power without God ruling it. Only God can be happy by his own power with no one ruling."

And the very last of the Fathers, St. Bernard, in his sermons on the Canticle of Canticles, referred to the field in Genesis 2, "He claims our earth not as his fief but as his motherland. And why not? He receives from it his Bride and his very body . . . as Lord he rules over it; as Creator, he controls it; as Bridegroom, he shares it." God has dominion over the vineyard, and it is by participating in that dominion that human beings are properly ordered. Given this rule, God goes on to make us shareholders in a more profound way, through a wedding. The mystery hidden for the ages in God is that the human participation in divine governance through law was but a preparation for a wedding feast.

By organizing his discussion of natural law around the injunction in Genesis 2:17, the pope might seem to be indulging a rather abstract meditation. But this is the bottom line. The pope understands very clearly that the contemporary dispute over law and liberty is not a dispute merely over this or that vexed issue; what is really at stake today is the effort to claim theological warrant for a principle that is essentially antitheological: namely, the principle that the human mind has a justifiable claim of jurisdiction over the vineyard. This is why the Church cannot make people happy by loosening the law over this or that area of conduct. A loosened law is not what men crave. They want jurisdiction; not liberty, but plenary authority. This antitheology is at the heart of that curious phenomenon I mentioned earlier. When theologians, clergy, and laity make the plea for authority to be used to annul the law, and in effect to cancel out authority itself, what they are really requesting is for you to hand back authority which they believe is rightfully theirs. This is why the disputes today over moral theology are so nasty. They resemble nothing so much as ruthless litigation over real estate.

III.

Indeed, real estate is the favorite scriptural metaphor for the problem. The request for dominion rather than convenantal participation, along with the illusion that God is an absentee landlord, is the oldest story on the books. This desire for absolute jurisdictional authority amounts to the same story every time. Consider, for example, the parable of the wicked tenants, which is told in each of the synoptic gospels. In Matthew 21, it is told just before the parable of the marriage feast; in Mark 12, it is given just after the chief priests and the scribes ask Jesus by whose authority he teaches; and in Luke 20, it is given once again after Jesus' credentials are questioned. In Mark 12:1 and following, the parable is told in this way:

> A certain man planted a vineyard and made a hedge around it and dug a place for the winefat and built a tower and let it to tenants; and went into a far country. And at the season he sent to the tenants a servant to receive of them the fruit of the vineyard. Who, having laid hands on him, beat him and sent him away empty. And again he sent to them another servant; and him they wounded in the head and used him reproachfully. And again he sent another and him they killed; and many others, of whom some they beat, and others they killed. Therefore, having yet one son, most dear to him, he also sent him unto them last of all, saying: They will reverence my son. But the tenants said to one another: this is the heir. Come let us kill him and the inheritance will be ours. And, laying hold of him, they killed him and cast him out of the vineyard. What therefore will the Lord of the vineyard do? He will come and destroy those tenants and will give the vineyard to others.

This parable is often associated with the canticle of the vineyard in Is. 5. Every Jew of course knew by heart the song of Isaiah: "Let me sing to my friend the song of his love for his vineyard. My friend had a vineyard on a fertile hillside. He dug the soil, cleared it of stones, and planted choice vines in it." But let us consider the parable in connection with the story of that earlier vineyard in Genesis 2–3.

Just as in Genesis 2, where God plants and irrigates the plantation, and in Isaiah 5, where God is said to have established Israel as a vineyard, in Mark 12, once again, it is the owner who plants and establishes the field. The parable makes it clear that he has the strong claim to ownership—*dominium* not a mere *ius*. We notice an important difference between the original plantation and the one in the parable. Adam and Eve were given a most attractive lease over the garden: in exchange for minimal upkeep, they were entitled to enjoy all of its pleasures—provided that they not usurp ownership. This deal or protoconvenant is symbolized by the two trees. Whereas in Genesis 2 the plantation is perfect; in the parable, the vineyard is new and untried. The tenants in this parable will have to work. It is a post-Edenic situation.

According to Jewish law, a new vineyard is not recognized as profitable until four whole harvests. The produce of the fourth year are legally "first fruits." Prior to the year of first fruits, tenants perhaps were entitled to a fixed portion of the produce, usually along with some rent. Now, the servant is sent to take the rent. As the parable relates, the tenants beat him and sent him away empty. In ancient Semitic law, giving up of a garment, or the casting off of a shoe, legally signifies releasing a right or a claim. The question is, a right to what? Perhaps the tenants are at first only driving a hard bargain. Until the vineyard is shown to be fruitful, the tenants do not want to pay more than their fair share in a still risky project. Unfortunately, the rights claim seems to escalate.

It was typical in Jewish law that when a thing happens three times it is presumed to be normal. For three successive harvests, no rent was paid: hence a precedent is about to be set. The owner has to come back, lest he forfeit his ownership. In other words, what began as a hard bargain—rights to less rent—ends in a claim over the entire farm. It ends, in fact, in a plot to usurp dominion. They kill the heir. Adam stole dominion and ruined the original partnership; but things have gotten much nastier in the meantime. Adam merely hid—later, his progeny will be more aggressive. Expelled from the garden, and cast into the world, his progeny now figure that they have a more or less permanent lease, with no strings attached. We should not overlook the fact that the scribes and pharisees are the object of the parable. Although the prophets warned about this, the scribes and pharisees believed that God had given them the vineyard, and had left it to them to call the shots. The scribes and pharisees were like deists: they dug in their heels for the long haul. Everything is fine so long as He doesn't come back. And when the Lord of the vineyard returned, they killed him.

IV.

The meaning of the parable for moral theology ought to be clear. Moral theologians must not be lawyers for the tenants. John Paul II writes in *Veritatis Splendor*:

> Even if moral-theological reflection usually distinguishes between the positive or revealed law of God and the natural law, and, within the economy of salvation, between the "old" and the "new" law, it must not be forgotten that these and other useful distinctions always refer to that law whose author is the one and the same God and which is always meant for man. The different ways in which God, acting in history, cares for the world and for mankind are not mutually exclusive; on the contrary, they support each other and intersect. . . . God's plan poses no threat to man's genuine freedom; on the contrary, the acceptance of God's plan is the only way to affirm that freedom. (VS 45)

Beginning in Genesis 2, and then with the election of Israel, and continuing with the establishment of the Church, and ending in Revelation 22, where the vineyard is finally transfigured by the Tree of Life, God asserts authority over the field. Father de Lubac points out that although God makes "fresh starts in his work and devises fresh methods to bring it to a successful conclusion, it is by no means a fresh work that he undertakes." Even if, according to the parable of the treasure hidden in the field, God eventually had to stop negotiating and buy back the property, repurchasing it with the blood of his own Son, at each stage in this history God offers something covenantal to the tenants. God always makes participation the terms of the deal; men always want unilateral authority.

At every stage, the lease included ample scope for the liberty and creativity of the tenants. Our first parents could eat of every tree but one; they were permitted to name the beasts. They were not permitted, however, to claim absolute dominion. Why? Because what is at stake in the convenant, including that proto-covenant with created nature in Genesis 2, is not merely a deal regarding the administration of external properties. These things were always meant for man. Over them man always had enormous freedom. What was at stake was something internal, the order of justice according to which men act in communion with God. But we cannot act in communion with God if we unilaterally claim the law for ourselves. Again, the prophets warned the rabbinical establishment not to make the Law a mere interpretive tool to be used for their own convenience. And we must admit that this story of the wicked tenants, and the lessons to be drawn from it, is relevant to the life of the Church, and will continue to be relevant until the final reconciliation.

C. S. Lewis urges us to recall the parable of the prodigal son, which reiterates the story of Genesis:

> As a young man wants a regular allowance from his father which he can count on as his own, within which he makes his own plans (and rightly, for his father is a fellow creature) so they desired to be on their own, to take care for their own future, to plan for pleasure and for security, to have a *meum* for which, no doubt, they would pay some reasonable tribute to God in the way of time, attention, and love, but which nevertheless, was theirs not His. They wanted, as we say, to "call their souls their own." But that means to live a lie, for our souls are not, in fact, our own. They wanted some corner in the universe of which they could say to God, "This is our business, not yours."

As the pope notes at the outset of *Veritatis*, a "new situation" has come about. Opposition, even within the seminaries, to Catholic moral doctrine is "no longer a matter of limited and occasional dissent, but of an overall and systematic calling into question of traditional moral doctrine" (VS 4). Whenever we see men demand that authority be used to subvert authority, and that law be used to annul the law, we know that we are close to the heart of the story. Rights claims escalate into a claim over the entire farm.

The message for moral theologians is that they must never pervert their craft by being lawyers for the tenants against the Lord. When they act like lawyers for the tenants, they play the role of the scribes and pharisees, who also wanted to call the shots by turning the law into their own interpretive tool. Whereas the scribes and pharisees laid hold of the positive law, twisting it to their own purposes, our moral theologians are more tempted to use the rubric of natural law. The pope, however, is not going to turn the farm over to the tenants. The farm does not belong to him. The moral theologians insist that he must. Indeed, they threaten to take it anyway. But we already know how this story must end.

24

Against the Adversary Culture

Michael Novak

> Nowadays, there is a tendency to claim that agnosticism and skeptical relativism are the philosophy and basic attitude which correspond to democratic forms of political life. Those who are convinced that they know the truth and firmly adhere to it are considered unreliable from a democratic point of view, since they do not accept that truth is determined by the majority, or that it is subject to variation according to different political trends. It must be observed in this regard that if there is no ultimate truth to guide and direct political activity, then ideas and convictions can easily be manipulated for reasons of power. As history demonstrates, a democracy without values easily turns into open or thinly disguised totalitarianism.
>
> *Centesimus Annus*, 46

AGAINST NIHILISM

The moral-cultural system is crucial to the health of the capitalist democracies, and easily overlooked. By "system" I mean more than the "ethos," the complex of social values that guides human activities. I mean *institutions* and *habits*. I mean institutions such as the churches, schools, families, universities, and media of communication. These institutions tell citizens which of their behaviors will receive social approval or disapproval. These institutions help to form the inner life of individual citizens—their imaginations, aims, desires, and fears. These institutions inculcate habits, good and (sometimes, alas) bad. Such institutions are crucial because the

---

Reprinted from *The Catholic Ethic and the Spirit of Capitalism* (New York: Free Press, 1993), pp. 195–220.

primary form of capital is the human spirit, which is subject to decline as well as progress.

In any one generation, the moral life runs deeper than the busy mind easily discerns. Because the habits of the heart are learned in childhood, supplying reasons of which reason is not conscious, each generation lives off the spiritual capital of its inheritance, and may not even notice when it is squandering this treasure. By dint of habits of hard work and attentiveness parents sometimes grow successful, remain preoccupied, and leave their children barren of spiritual instruction. The moral and spiritual life of nations depends, therefore, on sequences of at least three generations. The habits inculcated by the first generation may be significantly abandoned by the second, and almost nonexistent in the third. Conversely, we do not always understand the treasures that, all unknowing, we have inherited from the hard experience of several faithful generations. In this ignorance lie the seeds of tragedy.

And such tragedy haunts the free society. A generation may not grasp until too late the full implications of altering the traditions of the past. Forgetting the principles on which their society has been constructed, any new generation may slide into behaviors and ways of thinking that set in motion its destruction. For example, the founders of the American experiment announced "We hold these truths to be self-evident," and took as a model Republican Rome, with its civic virtue. But a recent generation may brush aside this model, forget the truths once held to be self-evident, and abandon the daily disciplines that once kneaded such truths into civic virtues. A people that does let go like that of the intellectual and moral habits that hold its social system together is quite likely to fly apart. Is this not, indeed, the present greatest threat to the free societies of Western Europe and the United States?

The specific moral challenges to free societies today are perhaps too obvious to need elaboration. Precisely because such societies are affluent and free, they supply many allurements. Especially through the new technology of television, the solicitations of popular culture have come to occupy unprecedented space in the inner lives of the young—rock video, films of violence, sexual license, and the cultivation of passion and desire. Although counterbalanced by abiding moral seriousness on the part of many, there is, nonetheless, considerable evidence of mounting behavioral dysfunction among us: drugs, crime, births out of wedlock, children disoriented by divorce, teenage pregnancy, and a truly staggering number of abortions. Many of these behavioral dysfunctions result in various forms of social dependency. Thus a widespread loss of moral virtue creates larger and larger numbers of uncivic-minded hedonists on the one hand, and clients wanting to be supported by society on the other.

Indeed, although the phrase "liberal democracy" has a certain validity, there are now serious reasons for investigating whether there is a contradiction between "liberalism" (or at least a certain kind of liberalism) and democracy. In recent decades especially, at least in the United States, "liberal" has come to be associated both with a radical (and ultimately self-centered) individualism and with an insistence on doing not what one ought to do, but what one feels like doing. Radical individualism would be defective enough; it would destroy those bonds of sympathy, fellow-feeling, self-sacrifice, and sense of mutual obligation that nourish a lively community and civic responsibility. "Looking out for number one" would become a dagger in the heart of brotherhood, friendship, marriage, and family life. Worse, however, if the center of the self should slide away from its sense of duty, responsibility to others, and respect for the laws of nature and nature's God, and if it should come to pivot instead, on personal whim, feelings, or passions, the reflective self would no longer be the governor of its own behavior. When enough citizens can no longer govern their own passions and feelings, it is chimerical to imagine that they can maintain a self-governing republic.

Should this happen, a profound disorientation of intellectual habits would further undermine the truths a people once held to be self-evident, until such truths could no longer be intellectually defended. Thus Richard Rorty has propounded a "cheerful nihilism," in which any claim to "truth" independent of pragmatic social preference is to be joshingly brushed aside,[1] while Arthur M. Schlesinger Jr., once argued—but has somewhat revised his view—that America was founded on "relativism."[2] Rorty would have us be kind and tolerant to one another, while happily refusing to offer an intellectual ("metaphysical") defense of our system.

Indeed, Rorty has become perhaps the best-known philosopher in America even while rejecting both "metaphysics" and the search for "foundations." His work, he thinks, constitutes a thoroughgoing rejection not only of Plato's ideal types (which Aristotle also rejected) but also a repudiation of any object "out there" which represents an "objective" (eternal, absolute) moral standard by which human deeds should be measured. Put another way, Rorty thinks it a waste of time (and an illusion) to search for an objective ground, standard, or mirror to which humans should look for nature's verdict on their beliefs or actions. There is no "mirror of nature."[3] All is flux; history, contingency, and random events go "all the way down." We have to accustom ourselves to this unanchored standpoint (or, rather, driftpoint). There are no foundations "out there" on which to base ourselves, no lighthouses by which to orient ourselves.

Some persons find this view liberating; it frees them from the preoccupations of the traditions they learned at home and at church. Others find it shocking, silly, or nihilistic.

To surprise the latter, Rorty denies that if there is no God, "everything is permitted." Those who hold to no objective standard, and claim no foundation in universal reason or nature or God, he insists, nevertheless experience moral indignation about injustices that cause human beings to suffer. His nonbelieving "ironists" are quite capable of drawing lines to mark off what is morally unacceptable (to them), about which they can say with a certain kind of absoluteness: "Here I stand, I can do no other." He even notes that many people in the West have learned as much from Christ as from philosophy, including concern for the suffering of the vulnerable, a sort of kindness and gentleness, and a sense of solidarity with all humankind.[4]

These protestations, of course, don't satisfy those who find Rorty's rejection of objective standards, supplied by nature and nature's God, perilous and irresponsible.

In adjudicating this matter, I want to note that Rorty makes these points in response to Central Europeans such as Václav Havel and Jan Patočka, respectively the president (1990–1992) of Czechoslovakia and Czechoslovakia's most important philosopher (1907–1977). Havel and Patočka maintained under persecution that a commitment to objective "truth" was essential in the struggle against the "lie" of totalitarian communism. Rorty argues that "we" Americans do not talk the language of "being" and "consciousness" that Havel, Patočka, and other Europeans have learned from Husserl, Heidegger, and ultimately Plato. "We" are not much troubled about rooting our actions in "foundations," "we" do not talk such "metaphysics," or try to figure out how to use "being" language. But this does not mean that "we" are indifferent to tyranny, regimes of the lie, or moral cowardice. On the contrary, even without metaphysics, simply with our humble pragmatism, "we" too know that there are some things we would not do, and some forms of politics we would resist.

Of course, it is easy for Rorty to boast about the heroic way in which he and others who hold his views would conduct themselves under totalitarian pressure; he has not been put to the test. Moreover, in his case, no matter of "truth" or "universal standard" or "nature" or "divine command" could be at stake. On his own intellectual premises, he could in Havel's place have found a pragmatic reason for treating totalitarian power with "irony," all the while conforming his behavior to its demands. He could have done so out of "temporary" necessity, absorbing one more contingency among the other absurd contingencies in life. No doubt, of course, Rorty would himself be willing to become a martyr; I do not doubt his own moral integrity. Yet even he must concede that not all those who hold his views would *in principle* feel obliged to do so.

Some would surely find it possible to argue that their former liberal convictions were dependent on a quite different social context, which no longer exists, and that to adapt to another social system is no better and no worse, from a moral point of view, than to fail to adapt. After all, there is no "objective standard" compelling their consciences. They have nothing to lose, morally, in adjusting pragmatically to a new standard, even while maintaining a sense of irony and being as kind as possible to their loved ones. Social systems do differ, and one must survive as best one can. This vein of thought is especially compelling if, like Michel Foucault, one imagines that words are only a mask for power.

However such speculations may go, there are many of us in America who do not feel included under Rorty's "we." We *do* speak the language of moral foundations, being, and "laws of nature and nature's God." We do hold some truths to be foundational for a worthy social experiment ("testing whether this nation, or any nation so conceived and so dedicated, can long endure.") In distancing himself from such language, Rorty is not speaking for us. One may be quite sure that he does not speak for a majority of Americans. The moral views of the American public diverge significantly from those of humanists in our universities.

But is Rorty right? In a way, he can hardly be wrong, since he wants things both ways. He says there are no permanent, objective foundations "out there" in reality, independent of and authoritative for his consciousness. Nonetheless, he is conscious of holding certain moral standards that he will not violate. He is also confident that many others hold these standards now, and many will continue to do so. So it is false to hold that, in their case, "Without God, everything is permitted." He claims to have learned from Jerusalem as well as from Athens, from Christ as well as from Plato. Moreover, he speaks of such lessons from the past as though they constitute a more or less continuing tradition.

So what, really, does Rorty lack that would distinguish him from being a believer, say, in the Christian social gospel? Looking one way, he talks like a nihilist. Looking another, he acts more or less like the rest of us, except with a slight hint of moral superiority in his wan, ironic smile. If we pay attention to what he does, rather than to what he says, he behaves rather like a not very devout Christian, no better or worse than most others, and somewhat less dramatically than (say) Graham Greene, Albert Camus, or Gabriel Marcel. To take him seriously as a philosopher is not easy. Not even he acts as his theories would predict.

The same goes for Arthur Schlesinger Jr. He sowed relativism, yet when the same relativism grew as high as his eye in the fields of academe under the guise of multiculturalism, and when young professors began to denigrate *his* values and loves, he tried desperately to uproot what he had sown.[5] Schlesinger cannot have it both ways. If "the truths we hold" are not "true" but merely "work well for us," they may be legitimately rejected by those who judge that they do not "work for them." (I much admire Schlesinger's elegant critique of recent racialist posturings and pretensions, and applaud his defense of our common culture. But I cannot share his insistence on cultural homogenization, on the one hand, as an answer to cultural relativism, on the other. Each of these two represents an extreme and dangerous position.) It is not so easy for Rorty and Schlesinger to get along without the word "true" as they think; they pay—and the country pays—a heavy price for their reliance on preference rather than truth.

The conception of "unalienable rights" on which the American experiment rests is intelligible only in terms of truth, nature, and nature's God. Against a background of "cheerful nihilism" this experiment makes no sense at all; it is only an assertion of arbitrary will. Cheerful nihilism would render the American experiment philosophically vulnerable to any adversarial will exercised with superior power and popular consent.

Quite unlike Rorty, others have argued that the philosophical background in which the American experiment was historically placed *is* congenial to the traditions of Christian philosophy and Christian belief. Among those who champion this view are John Courtney Murray, S.J., and Jacques Maritain.[6] Indeed, a large majority of American citizens shares the Christian intellectual tradition still today and understands the American experiment in its light. Rooted in a sense of transcendence, what

Walter Lippmann has called "the public philosophy"[7] gives individual citizens an intellectual basis for resisting public expressions of arbitrary will and for vindicating their rights against aggression from any quarter. They believe these rights to be rooted not in human preference, will, or custom but in the intellect and will of God. This was the sort of belief from which the moral heroes in Eastern Europe—such as Orlov, Scharansky, Havel, Bratinka, and millions of their followers—drew the strength to overturn the most extreme totalitarian power in history.

Parallel to the task of renewing the moral foundation of free societies, therefore, is a further task of deepening their intellectual foundations. Certain classically inspired students of political philosophy, quite aware of the Enlightenment's deficiencies, have already engaged in a secular version of such a project; viz., such scholars as Leo Strauss, Allan Bloom, Francis Fukuyama, and, in his own fashion, Harry Jaffa.[8] It may even be the case that liberal institutions cannot be defended on the basis of the secular philosophies of the Enlightenment, but must be recast in more ancient terms, consistent with Jewish and Christian intellectual traditions.[9]

Furthermore, since democratic capitalist societies bring to the fore a new set of moral and intellectual virtues to complement the classical virtues, some new Aristotle should describe their actual practice today. Fresh thinking is needed on a whole range of traditional moral concepts, whose concrete embodiment is now quite different from that of the past. For example, such concepts as person, community, dignity, equality, rights, responsibilities, and common good are today enfleshed in new settings. Thus individuals today are citizens rather than subjects; they are expected to act for themselves, with initiative and enterprise, and not simply to wait for orders. In this respect, they require new virtues scarcely required of their ancestors in the classical period, such as civic responsibility, enterprise, free association, and social justice. In the closing pages of this inquiry, we will return to the new virtues required of modern citizens.

Whether they always *act* as citizens, accepting their proper civic responsibility, is another matter. Americans being interviewed on television during presidential campaigns often speak as if they think of themselves primarily as workers and consumers, worried about "pocketbook issues." These considerations are not insignificant nor, given today's vast governmental intrusions into the economy, wholly irrelevant; but they are by no means the whole of citizenship. Of course, television journalists often act as if the chief responsibility for economic performance rests not with citizens acting in a free market as they will, but with the president and his economic policies. In public discourse, therefore, the language of citizenship has fallen into disuse—or, at least, more so than in the past.[10]

Reflection on other characteristics of moral life today suggests significant additions to our working concepts of community. Even with respect to purely economic activities, for example, large and broad markets work through voluntary choice, consent, and cooperation to achieve beneficial outcomes too complex for any one agency to direct, and such outcomes give rise to a new concept of common good quite unlike the simple common good defined by a tribal chief of yore.[11] Markets serve communities, even link and unify communities; to be excluded from them is more alienating than to be included within them.

Second, from infancy our young children—erroneously described as suffering from excessive individualism—are in fact immersed in social practices, group activities, cooperative projects, and group memberships of so many sorts that scarcely any human beings in history have been so thoroughly and complexly socialized.

Thus the work to be done in reform of our civilization's moral foundation—and even in our *ideas* about it—is quite immense.[12] For the main point of culture is to give character a shape.

CULTURE AND CHARACTER

We can imagine the white-haired Pope John Paul II, as he neared the end of *Centesimus Annus*, turning his attention from political and economic problems to matters closer to his own philosophical interests—those deeper (and more influential) questions of character, culture, and truth. "Of itself," he wrote, "an economic system does not possess criteria for correctly distinguishing new and higher forms of satisfying needs from artificial new needs that hinder the formation of a mature personality. *Thus a great deal of educational and cultural* work is urgently needed."[13]

Redoubtable social thinkers such as Joseph Schumpeter and Daniel Bell have also seen that the weakest link in the threefold system of the democratic republic and the capitalist economy is its moral and cultural system. Schumpeter in *Capitalism, Socialism, and Democracy* and Bell in *The Cultural Contradictions of Capitalism* both argue that, in the long run, the American experiment is doomed,[14] and that this self-destruction will begin among the spiritual and intellectual elites. Both give long and vivid descriptions of the occupational vulnerabilities that promote this self-destruction. Both fear that this betrayal will spread outward rapidly, through the cinema and music, through magazines and newspapers, and through other fibers of the nation's spiritual nervous system.

What ultimately determine the character of a culture are its choices. As the Pope observed, "A given culture reveals its understanding of life through the choices it makes in production and consumption."[15] And again, "It is not wrong to want to live better; what is wrong is a style of life presumed to be better when directed towards 'having' rather than 'being.'"[16] Individuals, like cultures, reveal what they understand of life through their choices. A woman's inmost identity, like a man's, comes from the qualities of character revealed in her actions—from her very being, as she has shaped it by daily acts—and not from her possessions. "Even the decision to invest in one place rather than another, in one productive sector rather than another, is always a *moral and cultural choice*. The decision to invest, that is, to offer people an opportunity to make good use of their own labor, is also determined by an attitude of human sympathy and trust in Providence that reveals the human quality of the person making such decisions."[17] "The first and most important cultural task is accomplished within man's heart. The way in which he builds his future depends on the understanding he has of himself and his destiny."[18]

The Pope's emphasis here on *being* (rather than having) represents another characteristic of the Catholic ethic. The dramatist and existentialist philosopher Gabriel Marcel dedicated a whole book to this topic,[19] and devoted considerable attention to it as well in many other books.[20] The insight into being, the fact of existence, is often held to be, in fact, a distinguishing trait of the perennial philosophy—that sharp sense of the difference between existing and not existing that one sometimes glimpses in those moments of exhilaration atop a mountain or in a boat on a still lake, when one is glad to be alive and poignantly aware of the swift slipping-away of life. To *ex-sist*, to stand out from nothingness if only for a moment, is not only to glimpse one's own fragility and dependency, and not only to give thanks for an unrequested and undeserved gift, but also to perceive a dimension of life that is often obscured in the rush and distraction of everyday pragmatism. It is to be overcome (momentarily) by wonder. The habit of making such moments more frequent during one's days is a habit important to Catholic life. It is reinforced by moments of frequent prayer and occasions of gratitude. (One meaning of "eucharist," indeed, is "gratitude.")

The insight into being draws attention to what is truly central in life, uniquely and ultimately important, one's responsibility for saying "yes" to life, to the will of God Who created us to be where we are and to achieve all that we are capable of: Who gave us a vocation to wonder at His creation and to bring it to its latent perfection, so far as in us lies. From this attitude of wonder, reverence, and sense of vocation spring responsibilities for action and character development. The kind of person we become is far more important to God than the positions or possessions we may attain. This, in part, is "the truth about man."

The Pope praises democracy, the rule of law, and the separation of powers,[21] as well as the market economy and the virtues it nourishes. But always in his eyes is the pursuit of "the truth about man." Rejecting this search, socialism doomed itself to self-destruction. The same thing could happen to market democracies. Decadence, decline, and internal disintegration are latent possibilities. "From the open search for truth *the culture of a nation* derives its character," the Pope writes, adding: "when a culture becomes inward-looking, and tries to perpetuate obsolete ways of living by rejecting any exchange or debate with regard to the truth about man, then it becomes sterile and is heading for decadence."[22]

One can see why this Pope worries about the West, particularly America. We have already discussed what leading Americans today think of "truth." The nation's founding documents hold that the American experiment rests upon certain truths of nature and nature's God—that is, on a foundation beyond the power of any dictator to alter or to erase, a foundation worth giving one's life to uphold. Yet for many today "truth" is essentially a matter of taste and what "feels good for me." Others hold that *nothing* is either moral or immoral but personal opinion makes it so. Moral confusion is widespread (perhaps especially among the highly educated).

Those who welcome the Ten Commandments as a law beyond their power to wish away are sometimes ridiculed. Many who call themselves "liberal" cannot bear to call *anything* either "good" *or* "evil"; they seek every evasion possible. It has even become common to hear the essence of liberalism identified with relativism.[23] Thus an observer at a recent annual meeting of the American Academy of Religion in Kansas City had no difficulty citing many examples of the most rampant (and unchallenged) relativism.[24] Despite this *traison des clercs*, international survey data indicate that few peoples in the world are more religious than the people of the United States, both in belief and in activity.[25]

Nonetheless, the moral rot evident among Hollywood, television, and rock star elites, and the moral confusion evident in the professoriat seem steadily to be corroding the morals of ordinary people. It is not easy to explain away the extraordinarily high murder rates in U.S. cities; the prevalence of sex out of wedlock; the large proportion of female-headed households; and the moral equivalence asserted in public speech between homosexual acts and heterosexual married love. By traditional Jewish and Christian standards, certain features of current American culture bring to mind Sodom and Gomorrah, not "the city on a hill." Both on the intellectual and on the moral front, battle lines in a major cultural war are shaping up between those who cherish perennial truths and values and those who hold those truths and values in contempt.

In examining a nation's moral health, one must scrutinize especially the cultural elites who create the stories, images, and symbols of the nation's self-understanding and moral direction. The new frontier of the twenty-first century is likely to be contestation for the souls of both cultural and moral systems. Pope John Paul II calls for such criticism, both for its own sake and because U.S. culture, in particular, now exercises massive moral influence around the world.

AMERICAN FOUNDING PRINCIPLES, CURRENT PRACTICE

Like our own elites, most of the world still neglects the American Revolution. The failed French Revolution of 1789 is seized upon as the great symbolic center of the modern era of liberty. Even Cardinal Ratzinger ignored the American (and cited only the French) Revolution in his second "Instruction on Christian Freedom and Liberation."[26] "The sad truth of the matter," Hannah Arendt has written, "is that the French Revolution, which ended in disaster, has made world history, while the American Revolution, so triumphantly successful, has remained an event of little more than local importance."[27] How sad this really is becomes clear from Professor Arendt's earlier line: "The colonization of North America and the republican government of the United States constitute perhaps the greatest, certainly the boldest, enterprise of European mankind."

Intellectually isolated from Europe, and separated from it by hundreds of tacit understandings, customs, habits, laws, and institutions, the United States is still the world's most original and most profound counterculture. Its underlying presuppositions are unknown to, or left inarticulate by, even the larger part of its own intellectual elite—that "adversary culture—which Lionel Trilling was the first to analyze.[28] "It is odd indeed," Arendt writes, "to see that twentieth-century *American* even more than European learned opinion often inclined to interpret the American Revolution in the light of the French Revolution, or to criticize it because it so obviously did not conform to the lessons learned from the latter."[29]

The U.S. system was in its beginnings unlike the European, and the Framers were quite aware of their originality.[30] Do not deny to us, James Madison in effect wrote in *Federalist* 14, the originality of our *novus ordo seclorum*, through which the American people "accomplished a revolution which has no parallel in the annals of human society. They reared the fabrics of governments which have no model on the face of the globe."[31] One of the original features of the new system erected by the people of the United States was the primacy it afforded to the institutions of conscience, information, and ideas—precisely to its moral culture—over the realms of politics (limited government) and economics (the least statist in history).

Another (and at first more striking) novelty, Prof. Arendt writes, is that the American experiment drew Europe's long-slumbering attention to "the social question." "America," she wrote, "had become the symbol of a society without poverty.... And only after this had happened and had become known to European mankind could *the social question* and the rebellion of the poor come to play a truly revolutionary role."[32] The American example awakened the conscience of Europe. Poverty no longer being inevitable or irreparable, its continued existence became for the first time in history a problem for human conscience.

Indeed, long after one Frenchman, Crèvecoeur, had reported back to Europe the amazing prosperity of those Americans who had long since departed from Europe bitterly poor,[33] and about the same time as another, Alexis de Tocqueville, was describing the systemic prosperity and ordered liberty that "the hand of Providence"[34] had launched in the world through the American experiment, Victor Hugo was still able to describe the dejection and virtual hopelessness of *Les Misérables* in the France of 1832. The poverty of the poor in France already had shocked Jefferson some forty years earlier, and the French Revolution had done little to mitigate that poverty. Only gradually did the example of the United States, in moving so many millions of the poor out of poverty, awaken Europe to the social condition of its own poor.

In 1886 the Liberal party of France (the party of Tocqueville), seeking to awaken the world again to the difference that the United States had made to the history of liberty, commissioned and executed a magnificent gift to the United States: the Statue of Liberty. Imagine the work of its planning committee. "How shall we symbolize the specifically American idea of liberty?" they must have asked themselves. Being French, they decided the symbol would be in the shape of a woman, not a warrior. In this, they followed a tradition as old as the image of Lady Philosophy in Boethius's

The Consolation of Philosophy: Woman as wisdom, bearing aloft in one hand the torch of understanding against the swirling mists of passion and the darkness of ignorance. In her other hand, they placed a book of the law, inscribed "1776" to signify the truths Americans hold dear. Her face would be resolute, serious, purposive. This Lady symbolized not the French *Liberté* (the prostitute on the altar of the Black Mass), but rather that "ordered liberty" to which Pope John Paul II was to call attention in Miami exactly 101 years later.[35] Thus the primacy of morals in the American idea was fully and rightly grasped by the Liberal party of France, heirs of Tocqueville.

Virtue is the pivotal and deepest American idea. Indeed, "Virtue" was the inscription (later supplanted by *Novus Ordo Seclorum*) at first inserted as the motto on the Great Seal of the United States. To imagine an experiment in republican government without virtue, Madison had told the Virginia Assembly, is "chimerical."[36] For how could a people, unable severally to govern their own passions, combine to govern their own body politic? Tied together in the then-novel conception of "political economy," neither a free polity nor a free economy can long survive an incapacity among the people for the virtues that make liberty possible.

According to the American idea (learned from Jerusalem, Athens, Rome, Paris, and London),[37] liberty springs from the human capacities for *reflection* and *choice*. These human capacities reflect the *Light* and *Love* that are the very names of God in Whose image humans are made, and by Whom they are endowed with "unalienable rights." Habits such as temperance, fortitude, justice, and prudence provide the calm that makes human acts of *reflection* and *choice* possible. The first paragraph of *The Federalist*[38] was addressed exactly to these capacities as the American people were making the precedent-shattering decision whether to constitute the new American republic or no.

The Framers appealed again and again to the primacy of morals, and indeed to God and to Providence (that is, the wise and knowing—"provident"—Creator) in whose image they believed the human capacities of reflection and choice were stamped. "The God who made us, made us free," Jefferson said. Hannah Arendt quotes John Adams (and could as well have quoted George Washington, Benjamin Franklin, James Madison, Alexis de Tocqueville, Abraham Lincoln, and others): "I always consider the settlement of America as the opening of a grand scheme and design in Providence for the illumination of the ignorant and the emancipation of the slavish part of mankind all over the earth."[39]

It is important to underline such a powerful stream of thought as this, and its embodiment in a thousand institutional and ritual ways, for it helps to understand how, to Americans, it is somehow fundamental to stand under the judgment of God. Like the ancient Israelites (to whom, John Adams said,[40] Americans owe more than to any other people), they know that no achievement of material prosperity or of military might would spare them a yet more demanding judgment. And this judgment would be rendered by a transcendent, almighty, and unswervingly *just* God, whose judgment was to be dreaded as "a terrible swift sword." The primacy of morals is written into America's very soul.

For this reason, Americans gave a privileged place to institutions of morals and culture: to churches preaching to the faithful, to universities (in whose support, more than any other people before or since, they have invested so many of their private and public energies), to learning, and to the press. Had he to choose between having a free government or a free press (and God forbid the choice, Jefferson said), he would prefer a free press.[41] If these moral and cultural institutions go sour, if that salt loses its savor, all the rest of ordered liberty is lost: The polity is doomed to division and self-destruction, the economy to hedonism and raw self-interest.

It is absolutely critical to the American experiment, therefore, that the institutions of conscience, information, culture, and moral reflection retain this primacy. Should there ever be a "treason of the clergy," all is lost.

We began with predictions of doom for American culture by Joseph Schumpeter and Daniel Bell. However accurate and penetrating their comments may be, their pessimism need not be paralyzing. For if the primary flaw in our political economy lies not so much in our political system (democracy being a flawed and poor type of governance, until compared to the alternatives), and not so much in our economic system (capitalism being a flawed and poor organization of economy, except compared to the alternatives), *but in our moral-cultural system*, then their prognosis may in the end be more hopeful than it first appears. For if the fatal flaw lies most of all in our ideas and morals, then its source lies not in our stars but in ourselves. And there, by the grace of God, we have a chance to mend our ways. Good ideas can (and often do) drive out bad ideas. If the flaw lies in ourselves—especially in our moral, intellectual, and cultural behavior—then we ourselves have a magnificent opportunity to do something about it. That is all that free women and men can ask. A chance. No guarantee, but a chance.

THE POPE'S CHALLENGE TO THE U.S.

If I am not mistaken, this is more or less the diagnosis that Joseph Cardinal Ratzinger and Pope John Paul II have for several years now been applying to the United States. They appeal to our elites, most of all, on the plane of ideas and on the terrain of morals and of faith. They call us to step back from ourselves and to look at ourselves as others abroad see us. They ask us to look at the moral decadence visible to outsiders in American films, videotapes, music, television shows, magazines, newspapers, novels, and books, all of which our culture sends as emissaries across the world. Are we not embarrassed by *Dallas*, spoof through it may be, a series (at last count) being shown in seventy-seven different nations of the earth? Just recently a young Korean-American attorney in Washington, D.C., wrote that the young people of his nation of origin, just two decades ago wildly pro-American, have come to hold our nation in contempt for its inconstancy and changeability, and for its public immorality. He begged the proper authorities to take American Armed Forces television off the airwaves, where it is shocking to South Koreans; but if we mean to keep it, at least to keep it on restricted cable lines which only Americans can watch, in quarantined self-corruption.[42]

In many ways, of course, U.S. culture is a much-admired model and pacesetter. Our films, our music, and even many of our books are both appreciated and imitated in every corner of the world. Nonetheless, it is also widely recognized that public exposure to various of the products of American pop culture do tend to generate a loosening of morals.

I do not think that our mass media are quite as decadent as some in our midst often say. Any well-told story requires the dramatization of the essential components of human moral action. Drama and narrative, even in the most attenuated forms, necessarily pay testimony to the basic capacities of the human soul for reflection and choice, and for the courage necessary to sustain both. Nonetheless, it can hardly be said that ours is an age of moral toughness, or that our public media of communication typically (or even often) present fully Christian or Jewish visions of the moral life. Such visions would have a great deal to say about our falls into temptation, about human sinfulness, and about the human weakness to which all of us are prey. It is not the portrayal of weakness and sinfulness that constitutes decadence; it is, rather, giving in to weakness and calling it virtue. It is not weakness that makes for decadence, but moral dishonesty. A fully Christian—or Jewish—vision certainly would be much less likely than much of what we see today to call sin virtue, and virtue sin.

On a more profound level, the level of "serious" culture, Lionel Trilling—America's preeminent critic of culture—noted the detached (even hostile) point of view deeply embedded in today's cultural elites. It is not unusual for art to assume that at least some persons may "extricate themselves from the culture into which they were born." It is not odd in literature to take virtually for granted "the adversary intention, the actually subversive intention, that characterizes modern writing." There is not even anything surprising in its clear purpose of "detaching the radar form the habits of thought and feeling that the larger culture imposes, of giving him a ground and a vantage point from which to judge and condemn, and perhaps revise, the culture that produced him."[43]

This adversary intention in modern art is more than a century old, Trilling continues, but

> the circumstances in which it has its existence have changed materially.... The difference can be expressed quite simply in numerical terms—there are a great many more people who adopt the adversary program than there formerly were. Between the end of the first quarter of the century into the present time there has grown up a populous group whose members take for granted the idea of the adversary culture. This group is to be described not only by its increasing size but by its increasing coherence. It is possible to think of it as a class. As such, it of course has its internal conflicts and contradictions but also its common interests and presuppositions and a considerable efficiency of organization, even of an institutional kind.[44]

Trilling notes that "Three or four decades ago, the university figured as the citadel of conservatism, even of reason." The phrase "ivory tower" suggested its safe removal from the acids of modernism. Taste, however, "has increasingly come under the control of criticism, which has made art out of what is not art and the other way around," and now this "making and unmaking of art is in the hands of university art departments and the agencies which derive from them, museums and professional publications."[45]

Trilling's is the classic text identifying a specific "adversary culture" within U.S. culture, a culture that now governs the mainstream in the universities, the magazines, movies, and television. Coincident with its rise is the gradual collapse of the prestige of scientific and technical elites, and even of the idea of progress. This adversary culture celebrates the antibourgeois virtues. By its own innermost intention, it defines itself *against* the common culture. It has increasingly lost its connection with ordinary people, whom it is inclined to score. *They* are religious, but the adversary culture is not. More than 100 million Americans attend church or synagogue every weekend, but the so-called popular culture of Hollywood and television is ignorant of this powerful vein of popular life.

The literature concerning the existence of this "new adversary class" is already vast.[46] Critics have long since linked Eastern European discussions of the new class in socialist societies, such as are found in the work of Milovan Djilas, with the adversary culture in Western societies.

Indeed, the hardest part of the moral task we now face is the immense power of that adversary culture. To oppose that power is to risk excommunication from the mainstream. Nonetheless, as Trilling (who loved modernist works) was compelled by intellectual honesty to state, the intention of the modernist project is to subvert the classic Jewish, Christian, and natural (as well as "bourgeois") virtues. It is to perform a massive transvaluation of values, to turn the moral world upside down. It is to insinuate that what Jews and Christians have for centuries called sin is actually a high form of liberation, and that what for centuries Jews and Christians have thought to be virtuous is actually vicious. It is to hate what Jews and Christians love, and to love what Jews and Christians hate.

Ironically, the very virtue of progressivism that is its most endearing quality—namely, its openmindedness—stands here defenseless. In trying to be broad-minded about the modernist subversion, even many Christians give it the best possible interpretation, and ascribe to the traditional Jewish and Christian agenda the most negative and hostile associations. Thus it happens that, in the name of launching a counterculture, some progressives baptize the worst features of the contemporary modernist project. In the name of openness, they try to shock the bourgeois middle class by collaborating in this deliberate transvaluation of values.

The truth is, there is all too little resistance to both the modernist project and the adversary culture. To oppose these would cause one to seem to be unsophisticated, backward, and unwashed. Thus does the treason of the intellectuals proceed as silently and effectively—and for the most part as undetectably—as a cloud of invisible but deadly gas.

To the extent that the Catholic Church is and must be countercultural, will it wish to link its criticism of U.S. culture with the criticism of that culture made by the new adversary class? This is certainly a temptation. It has tempted many socialists—particularly those in Latin cultures such as Southern Europe and Latin America who have become enamored of the project launched by the Italian communist Antonio Gramsci (1891–1937).[47] According to Gramsci, it is a mistake to understand socialism as an economic doctrine, and thus to tie socialism to the outmoded economic theories of the Marxists of the nineteenth century. On the contrary, democratic and capitalist societies have proven that they can raise up the proletariat into the middle class rather quickly. Therefore, Gramsci argued, the true socialist project lies not in the realm of economics, but in the realm of culture. The true socialist is an adversary of Western culture, both in its Christian and in its bourgeois aspects. A "long march through the institutions" (to borrow a later phrase) must be undertaken to subvert Western culture and its fundamental values.

In reviewing Michael Barone's book *Our Country: The Shaping of America from Roosevelt to Reagan*,[48] James Q. Wilson asked: "Why did the American elite, which seemed so confident of its own policies and of the basic goodness of our system of governance at the beginning of the 1960s, turn so violently against it in the years centering on 1967 and 1968?" I know that *I* did, in "The Secular Saint" (1967) and *A Theology for Radical Politics* (1969),[49] too much moved by the war in Vietnam, the rise of "black power," the moral arrogance of liberal technocrats on the campuses, the assassinations of John F. Kennedy, Robert F. Kennedy, and Martin Luther King Jr. In any case, from pride in government service and optimism about "new frontiers," Jeff Bell points out, "Around 1967, the balance of powerful political and journalistic elites began to tip toward the views of society's harshest critics."[50]

Michael Barone, reviewing those events, writes: "The liberal elites, so smug and confident at the beginning of the decade, turned their face away from events that were in most cases the consequences of their own acts and found fault with the larger society instead."[51] Thus, the "adversary culture" of the 1950s became the "counterculture," a "movement" suddenly swollen by journalists, movie producers, TV stars, and radicalized professors whose favorite passion became rage—contempt for our own system.

As Jeff Bell shows, a great gap opened up between the elite and the people; a larger gap than ever. (This split is what worried me, and made me draw back, even in the last chapter of *A Theology for Radical Politics*.) It was particularly marked in the Democratic party, whose strength had theretofore come from close cooperation between the intellectual elites and the people of the neighborhoods, unions, and city "machines." The party split asunder, and the "Reagan Democrats" began to emerge. The key differences were moral. Moral relativism and equality of result held primacy in the counterculture; the great bulk of the population retained traditional values. This was the theme of *The Rise of the Unmeltable Ethnics*.

Is the adversary culture the counterculture that the Catholic Church ought to join? The Gramsci project is aimed specifically at intellectual elites not only in the universities but also in the organs of mass culture and in the governmental bureaucracies that have administrative powers over the works of culture, wherever radio, television, and the arts are supported by the state. In this respect, the term "intellectuals" is to be understood in a very broad sense; it signifies the whole range of intellectual workers in the realm of symbol-making and the propagation of values. Both politically and intellectually, therefore, the central debate of our time has switched increasingly from politics and economics to culture. Christian and Jewish intellectuals will need to be very careful in choosing where and how to direct their efforts in this more general debate. As the Church arrives on the field, the battles have already been joined. The question now appears to be: Having at last reached this crucial battleground, what should we do?

PROTECTING THE MORAL ECOLOGY

In the Jewish community, Irving Kristol has pointed out,[52] there has long been a division of labor. Receiving most notice down the ages have been the Jewish prophets of the Old Testament. But the prophets, Kristol notes, were relatively few in number and of considerably less than immediate relevance to the daily lives of most ordinary people. To meet these ordinary needs, the rabbinic tradition has nurtured the custom of practical commentary, carried through in the Talmud and in associated practical writings. The rabbis greatly outnumbered the prophets, not only in raw numbers but also in the magnitude of their daily influence.

In the Catholic tradition, by analogy, there have also been two major lines of development—one incarnational, the other eschatological. More than typical Protestant communities, the Catholic community has tried to emphasize the presence of Christ in daily physical life, the incarnation of Christ in culture. It has blessed harvests, tools, and objects of daily living. It has tried to awaken the baptized to the reality that the kingdom of God has already begun in them and among them. Catholic faith welcomes ordinary life, even blesses it; this is, so to speak, its priestly or rabbinic work.

On the other hand, not only through its tradition of celibacy and the "setting aside" of a special way of life for nuns, priests, and brothers, the Catholic tradition has also tried to maintain an eschatological witness, a sense of rupture with this world and its ordinary demands, an anticipation of the kingdom to come. This witness is akin to that of the prophets of old. It is not a gnostic witness. Consistently, the Catholic Church has set its face against the "spiritualizers" and the "enthusiasts"[53]— that is, against those who would interpret Christianity as a project for fleeing from the world, for rejecting the world, or for merely condemning the world. Since "God so loved the world that he gave his only Son" (John 3:16), it affirms the goodness of each being and every event within the providential order. In every aspect of being, it has seen mystery, fruitfulness, and the presence of God.

In one moment, then, the Catholic tendency is to affirm every culture in which it finds itself. In another moment, it has always called every culture beyond itself and toward the kingdom yet to come and, thus, has set itself up as a counterculture. For the Catholic community to be truly Catholic, both moments are indispensable. Every Christian should represent in his or her own project in life both of these emphases. Each should be at home in the world, and work within it with affirmation and love; simultaneously, each should be in the world as a stranger.

But not so much as a stranger that one falls into uncritical lockstep with a treacherous ally. By now, the new adversary class has more than fulfilled its adversary intention. Hardly any aspect of the U.S. system—political, economic, and moral-cultural—escapes withering criticism, often unfair and inaccurate criticism. Much of this criticism serves the self-interest of those who want to expand the powers and expenditures of the state. (There is profit in this prophet motive.) That such criticism is self-interested would matter little if it were accurate and fair. Most often, the appetite for prosecution outweighs the appetite for fair rebuttal. The sense of possessing a superior moral standing often overpowers a willingness to see the other side.

No democratic capitalist regime should pretend to be the kingdom of God. The U.S. regime, in particular, has been deliberately contrived to operate within a world of sin and fallibility, supplying to every ambition a counterambition. Such a political economy is self-consciously imperfect, flawed, and resolved to make the best out of the weak materials of human nature. "If men were angels, no government would be necessary," Madison wrote in *Federalist* 51. But men are not angels. Thus, criticism and prophecy do not of themselves injure a democratic capitalist regime. Even false prophecy and misplaced criticism may be put to creative use. Still, criticism and prophetic claims need to be assessed according to how accurately and creatively they are launched. Critics—and in particular the adversary culture—must in turn carry the burden of being *self*-critical. They must, if they are to be taken seriously, make sure that the interests they serve are truly just.

During the last sixty years or so, in interpreting the social doctrine of the Church, a great deal has been written about politics and (more recently) economics. No doubt this work has been necessary and valuable. It is surprising, however, to note the lack of sustained criticism regarding the culture of liberty. Neither a sound economy nor sound politics can be maintained for long in an atmosphere of decadence.

Pope John Paul II particularly has called upon U.S. Catholics to question our nation's widely diffused public morality as it is witnessed in the international media of communication that have so dramatic an effect upon the rest of the world. In raising this challenge, the Pope goes to the heart of our system's most glaring weakness (just when, ironically, many "progressive" Catholic theologians have been complaining that Rome does not understand U.S. culture). The Pope even raises the complementary question: Do American Catholic theologians *themselves* understand American culture? He has opened a debate about the true moral standing of U.S.

culture: Is it really something that the rest of the world—including Rome—should emulate?

A distinction may be useful. There are certain virtues inherent in the successful practice of democratic polities and capitalist economies. These may be thought of as those parts of public morality that are embodied in *institutional* practices, and are accordingly thought of as the specifically "democratic" and "capitalist" virtues. But there are other virtues—equally necessary for the successful practice of democracy and capitalism—proper to the moral-cultural sphere itself.

When "progressive" Catholic theologians speak admiringly of the high moral standards of the U.S. experience, often they have in mind the panoply of virtues associated with democratic *institutions*: open inquiry, due process, judgment by a jury on one's peers, and the like. This, too, is a form of public morality. Both the political institutions and the economic institutions of the free society implicitly contain hidden references to the specific new virtues required to make these institutions function according to their own inner rules. Too seldom do we make these underlying virtues explicit in our thinking, despite the fact that they are quite different from the virtues as the responsibilities of free, sovereign citizens, self-reliance, cooperativeness, openness, and personal economic enterprise. They are acquired during that long process of learning the habits of democratic living to which Tocqueville often refers.[54]

By comparison, the virtues proper to the moral-cultural system are distinct (but not separate) from the virtues proper to the political system. The founders of the U.S. order, such as Thomas Jefferson and James Madison, understood quite clearly the connection between the virtues of the moral order and those of the political order.

Thus, when Pope John Paul II suggests that the U.S. media of communication may be undercutting the practice of the moral virtues, he is implying, as well, a threat to the survival of democratic institutions. If true, this is a devastating criticism. It suggests that the very qualities of U.S. institutions that the "progressive" Catholic theologians profess to admire are being undermined by the widely broadcast public morality of our country's major media of communication. This would represent a form of pollution in the moral order even more destructive than the pollution of the physical environment. There is, so to speak, an ecology in morals as well as in the biosphere.[55]

The analysis offered by the Pope seems to be well aimed. Many important moral virtues *are* required to make a free and democratic society function according to its own inner logic; there is a set of moral virtues without which democratic institutions *cannot* be made to work. The fundamental premise of republican life is the concept of *ordered* liberty.[56]

The phrase "ordered liberty" follows the classical definition of practical wisdom, *recta ratio agendi* (the ordered reason in action). To hit the mark exactly, Aristotle observed, practical reason must be governed by (*recta,* corrected by) a good will. To do the truth, we must first love the truth—and love it well and accurately. In a similar way, to be truly free, our passions and appetites must be governed by a well-ordered love of the inner law of our humanity. In this sense, the exercise of freedom is a form of obedience to the truth—the truth about our own human nature.[57] For Christians, this truth is revealed only in Christ, the Logos "in whom, by whom, and with whom" were made all the things that were made. For those who are not Christian believers, the outlines of an analogous truth are also revealed in "the things that were made"—the habitual weakness of humans, combined with possibilities of love and renewal.[58]

THE INSTITUTIONAL TASK

All around the world people who have suffered under socialist and traditionalist institutions are longing for a freer life. They dream of living under institutions that would liberate their human capacities for reflection and for choice. There is a longing in the human heart to live under a system of natural liberty—that is, under those sorts of institutions that allow the human soul to express itself naturally in all three major fields of life: political, economic, and moral-cultural. The vast majority of peoples on this planet, in the past and still today, have not lived under such institutions. But the broad outlines of these institutions are now fairly well known to most of the peoples of the world. They have glimpsed these outlines through their own harsh experiences under meaner alternatives.

Thus, with Pope John Paul II, most people seem to understand today that their best protection from torture, tyranny, and other forms of political oppression derives from living under institutions that are (a) subject to the consent of the governed, (b) protective of minority rights, and (c) designed around internal sets of checks and balances. We have in fact been hearing a great deal more about "democracy," even in cultures in which the very word has long been spoken of (as in "bourgeois democracy") with much disdain.

Similarly, since neither communist nor traditionalist societies seem to be capable of producing the goods which the poor of the world need and desire, the reputation of the hitherto much-scorned system, capitalism, is growing. In an ever-increasing number of countries one hears the demand for freer markets, for private property, and for incentives that reward greater labor and superior skills. Human beings can scarcely help desiring to express in their institutions and daily practices their God-given capacities for personal economic initiative and creativity.

Finally, in such places as the former Soviet Union and the People's Republic of China, in South Africa and throughout Black Africa, in Latin America and elsewhere, the cry of most people is for "openness"—for institutions that permit the free exercise of liberty of conscience, inquiry, and expression.

In sum, most citizens of the world seek the three basic institutional liberations of human life: a free polity, a free economy, and a free moral-cultural system. This is seldom today a matter of ideology; it has arisen from harsh lessons of trial and error.

One cannot speak of these three liberations without also speaking of *institutions*. And one can hardly speak of institutions without speaking of the *moral virtues* that sustain them.

For human rights are not protected by words on parchment. They are protected by habits, free associations, and independent judicial institutions. Moreover, the institutions that protect human rights do not *coerce* conscience, or *force* citizens to develop their individual moral and spiritual capacities. Those institutions create space for those achievements—but do not automatically produce them. Thus, the mere achievements of the basic institutions of political and economic liberty will not itself fulfill human moral and spiritual longing. Politics and economics are not enough. That is why the next frontier for those who think counterculturally concerns the moral and spiritual dimension of culture.

We come around then to the theme that Pope John Paul II set forth in the beginning as the *leitmotif* of his pontificate: the primacy of morals. Here is where the next and most important battles lie.

> Solving serious national and international problems is not just a matter of economic production or of juridical or social organization, but calls for ethical and religious values. There is hope that the many people who profess no religion will also contribute to providing the necessary ethical foundation. But the Christian churches and the world religions will have a preeminent role in . . . building a society worthy of man.[59]

Building up civilizations that respect the true and nature-fulfilling "moral ecology" in which the virtues of ordered liberty flourish is a demanding task which will occupy the human race throughout the coming ages.

In this task, the institutions of the mass media—the much-vaunted "entertainment industry"—incur very high responsibilities, which they have barely begun to face. They, too, must be held to account. Because their influence upon the moral air we breathe and on the moral ecology we inhabit is vast, the prospects of the free society, and the virtues proper to ordered liberty, depend on their performance. The moral nobility of their task is far greater than they seem yet to recognize.

NOTES

1. Of one of his intellectual predecessors Rorty approvingly notes: "Wittgenstein . . . cheerfully tosses out half-a-dozen incompatible metaphilosophical views in the course of the *Investigations.*" *Consequences of Pragmatism* (Minneapolis: University of Minnesota Press, 1982), 23. Rorty draws an explicitly historicist consequence from this: "We Deweyan historicists . . . think that 'first principles' are abbreviations of, rather than justifications for, a set of beliefs about the desirability of certain concrete alternatives over others; the source of those beliefs is not 'reason' or 'nature', but rather the prevalence of certain institutions or modes of life in the past." Richard Rorty, "That Old-Time Philosophy," *New Republic* (April 4, 1988): 30. See also: "No specific doctrine is much of a danger, but the idea that democracy

depends on adhesion to some such doctrine is." Richard Rorty, "Taking Philosophy Seriously," *New Republic* (April 11, 1988): 33.
  2. Schlesinger once wrote:

  The American mind is by nature and tradition skeptical, irreverent, pluralistic and relativistic. . . . Our relative values are not matters of whim and happenstance. History has given them to us. They are anchored in our national experience, in our great national documents, in our national heroes, in our folkways, traditions, standards. Some of these values seem to us so self-evident that even relativists think they have, or ought to have, universal application: the right to life, liberty and the pursuit of happiness, for example; the duty to treat persons as ends in themselves; the prohibition of slavery, torture, genocide. People with different history will have different values. But we believe that our own are better for us. They work for us; and, for that reason, we live and die by them (Arthur Schlesinger Jr., "The Opening of the American Mind," *New York Times Book Review* [July 23, 1989]: 26).

  See my reply, "Relativism or Absolutes: Which Is the American Way?" *National Catholic Register* (October 29, 1989).
  3. Richard Rorty, *Philosophy and the Mirror of Nature* (Princeton: Princeton University Press, 1979).
  4. Richard Rorty, "The Seer of Prague," *The New Republic* (July 1, 1991): 39.
  5. For Schlesinger's second thoughts, see his *Disuniting of America: Reflections of a Multicultural Society* (New York: Norton, 1992).
  6. See the following remarks of Murray and Maritain:

  Because it was conceived in the tradition of natural law the American Republic was rescued from the fate, still not overcome, that fell upon the European nations in which Continental Liberalism, a deformation of the liberal tradition, lodged itself. . . . It is indeed one of the ironies of history that the tradition [of natural law] should have so largely languished in the so-called Catholic nations of Europe at the same time that its enduring vigor was launching a new Republic across the broad ocean. There is also some paradox in the fact that a nation which has (rightly or wrongly) thought of its own genius in Protestant terms should have owed its origins and the stability of its political structure to a tradition whose genius is alien to current intellectualized versions of the Protestant religion, and even to certain individualistic exigencies of Protestant religiosity. . . . Catholic participation in the American consensus has been full and free, unreserved and unembarrassed, because the contents of this consensus—the ethical and political principles drawn from the tradition of natural law—approve themselves to the Catholic intelligence and conscience (John Courtney Murray, S.J., *We Hold These Truths* [New York: Sheed & Ward, 1960], 31, 41).

  Note only does the democratic state of mind stem from the inspiration of the Gospel, but it cannot exist without it. To keep faith in the forward march of humanity despite all the temptations to despair of man that are furnished by history, and particularly contemporary history; to have faith in the dignity of the person and of common humanity, in human rights and in justice—that is, in essentially spiritual values; to have, not in formulas but in reality, the sense of and respect for the dignity of the people, which is a spiritual dignity and is revealed to whoever knows how to love it; to sustain and revive the sense of equality without sinking into egalitarianism; to respect authority, knowing that its wielders are only men, like those they rule, and derive their trust from the consent or the will of the people whose vicars or representatives they are; to believe in the sanctity of law and in the efficacious virtue—efficacious at long range—of political justice in face of the scandalous triumphs of falsehood and violence; to have faith in liberty and in fraternity, an heroical inspiration and an heroical belief are needed which fortify and vivify reason, and which none other than Jesus of Nazareth brought forth in the world (Jacques Maritain, *Christianity and Democracy* [New York: Charles Scribner's Sons, 1950], 59–60).

7. See Lippmann's remarks on public philosophy:

Freedom of religion and of thought and of speech were achieved by denying both to the state and to the established church a sovereign monopoly in the field of religion, philosophy, morals, science, learning, opinion and conscience. The liberal constitutions, with their bill of rights, fixed the boundaries past which the sovereign—the King, the Parliament, the Congress, the voters—were forbidden to go.
Yet the men of the seventeenth and eighteenth centuries who established these great salutary rules would certainly have denied that a community could do without a general public philosophy. They were themselves the adherents of a public philosophy— of the doctrine of natural law, which held that there was law "above the ruler and the sovereign people . . . above the whole community of morals" (Walter Lippmann, *The Public Philosophy* [New York: New American Library, 1956], 76, 77–78).

8. Leo Strauss, *The Rebirth of Classical Political Rationalism* (Chicago: University of Chicago Press, 1989); Allan Bloom, *The Closing of the American Mind* (New York: Simon & Schuster, 1987); Allan Bloom, ed., *Confronting the Constitution: The Challenge to Locke, Montesquieu, Jefferson, and the Federalists from Utilitarianism, Historicism, Marxism, Freudianism, Pragmatism, Existentialism* (Washington, D.C.: AEI Press, 1990); Francis Fukuyama, *The End of History and the Last Man* (New York: Free Press, 1992); Harry V. Jaffa, *American Conservatism and the American Founding* (Winston-Salem, N.C.: Carolina Academic Press, 1984); and Harry V. Jaffa, *How to Think about the American Revolution* (Winston-Salem, N.C.: Carolina Academic Press, 1978).

9. One such reconstruction has been attempted by Hollenbach:

The thesis proposed here is that Catholic teaching on human rights today presupposes a reconstruction of the classical liberal understanding of what these rights are. The pivot on which this reconstruction turns is the traditional natural law conviction that the human person is an essentially social being. Catholic thought and action in the human rights sphere, in other words, are rooted in a communitarian alternative to classical liberal human rights theory. At the same time, by adopting certain key ideas about constitutional democracy originally developed by classical liberalism, recent Catholic thought has brought about a notable new development of the longer tradition of the church while simultaneously offering an alternative to the standard liberal theory of democratic government (David Hollenbach, S.J., "A Communitarian Reconstruction of Human Rights: Contributions from Catholic Tradition," 2 [paper prepared for a project on "Liberalism, Catholicism, and American Public Philosophy" at the Woodstock Theological Center, Georgetown University, forthcoming in a book by Fr. Hollenbach]).

Some objections, however, to this synthesis have been raised:

For centuries, the cornerstone of Catholic moral theology was not the natural or human *rights* doctrine but something quite different, called the natural *law*. Rights, to the extent that they were mentioned at least by implication, were contingent on the fulfillment of prior duties. . . . Simply stated, what the church taught and tried to inculcate was an ethic of virtue as distinct from an ethic of rights. . . .

The bishops may have confused some of their readers by using language that looks in two different directions at once: that of rights or freedom on the one hand, and of virtue, character formation, and the common good on the other. They would certainly be ill-advised to give up their vigorous defense of rights, especially since the pseudomorphic collapse of Neo-Thomism in the wake of Vatican II has left them without any alternative on which to fall back; but they have yet to tell us, or tell us more clearly, how the two ends are supposed to meet (Ernest L. Fortin, "The Trouble with Catholic Social Thought," *Boston College Magazine* [Summer 1988]: 38, 42).

10. E. J. Dionne has remarked:

Because of our flight from public life, our common citizenship no longer fosters a sense of community or common purpose. Social gaps, notably the divide between blacks and whites, grow wider. The very language and music heard in the inner city is increasingly estranged from the words and melodies of the affluent suburbs. We have less and less to do with each other, meaning that we feel few obligations to each other and are less and less inclined to vindicate each other's rights (E. J. Dionne Jr., *Why Americans Hate Politics* [New York: A Touchstone Book published by Simon & Schuster, 1991]).

11. Michael Novak, *Free Persons and the Common Good* (Lanham, Md.: Madison Books, 1989). See also *Centesimus Annus*, 11, 17, 40. See esp. 43:

The Church offers her social teaching as an *indispensable and ideal orientation*, a teaching which, as already mentioned, recognizes the positive value of the market and of enterprise, but which at the same time points out that these need to be oriented towards the common good. This teaching also recognizes the legitimacy of workers' efforts to obtain full respect for their dignity and to gain broader areas of participation in the life of industrial enterprises so that, while cooperating with others and under the direction of others, they can in a certain sense "work for themselves" through the exercise of their intelligence and freedom.

12. Even so, Jacques Maritain reminds us that we need not be completely despairing. Every age sees itself as falling off in morals ("*O Tempora, O Mores*"). In a chapter called "The Old Tag of American Materialism," Maritain says:

The American people are the least materialist among the modern peoples which have attained the industrial stage. . . . Americans like to give. . . . The ancient Greek and Roman idea of the *civis praeclarus*, the dedicated citizen who spends his money in the service of the common good, plays an essential part in American consciousness. And let me observe that more often than not the gifts in question are made for the sake of education and knowledge. . . .

There is no materialism, I think, in the astonishing countless initiatives of fraternal help which are the daily bread of the American people. . . .

There is no materialism in the fact that the American charities, drawing money from every purse, and notably to assist people abroad, run every year into such enormous sums that charity ranks among the largest American industries, the second or third in size, according to statisticians. . . . Let us not forget what an immense amount of personal attention to one's neighbor and what personal effort is increasingly put forth in all the groups which exist in this country, and which spring up every day, to meet some particular human misfortune or some particular social maladjustment. . . .

There is a perpetual self-examination and self-criticism going on everywhere and in every sphere of American life; a phenomenon incomprehensible without a quest for truth of which a materialist cast of mind is incapable (Jacques Maritain, *Reflections on America* [New York: Charles Scribner's Sons, 1958], 29–30, 34–36, 38).

13. *Centesimus Annus*, 36.
14. Joseph A. Schumpeter, *Capitalism, Socialism, and Democracy*, 3d ed. (New York: Harper & Row, 1975); and Daniel Bell, *The Cultural Contradictions of Capitalism* (New York: Basic Books, 1976).
15. *Centesimus Annus*, 36.
16. Ibid.
17. Ibid.
18. Ibid., 51.
19. Gabriel Marcel, *Being and Having* (New York: Harper & Row, 1965).
20. Gabriel Marcel, *The Mystery of Being*, 2 vols. (Chicago: Regnery, 1960) and also Gabriel Marcel, *Creative Fidelity* (New York: Farrar, Straus, 1964).
21. *Centesimus Annus*, 44-47. See Russell Hittinger, "The Problem of the State in *Centesimus Annus*," *Fordham International Law Journal* 15, no. 4 (August 1992).
22. *Centesimus Annus*, 50.
23. "It would be difficult to find in contemporary political debate an issue position regarded as distinctively liberal that does not trace back either to equality of result or to relativism, which at root are the same thing." Jeffrey Bell, *Populism and Elitism: Politics in the Age of Equality* (Washington, D.C.: Regnery Gateway, 1992), 185.
24. Paul V. Mankowski, "What I Saw at the American Academy of Religion," *First Things* (March 1992): 36–41.
25. Gallup Cross-National Surveys, 1981. Cf. James Davison Hunter, *Culture Wars: The Struggle to Define America* (New York: Basic, 1991).
26. Congregation for the Doctrine of the Faith, "Instruction on Christian Freedom and Liberation" (Vatican City: Vatican Polyglot Press, 1986), 7.
27. Hannah Arendt, *On Revolution* (New York: The Viking Press, 1965), 49.
28. Lionel Trilling, *Beyond Culture: Essays on Literature and Learning* (New York: The Viking Press, 1968).
29. Arendt, 49 (italics added).
30. At a critical point in the Constitutional Convention on June 28, 1787, Franklin suggested the depths of the Framers' struggle to concur on a new order:

We indeed seem to feel our own want of political wisdom, since we have been running about in search of it. We have gone back to ancient history for models of Government, and examined the different forms of those Republics which having been formed with the seeds of their own dissolution now no longer exist. And we have viewed Modern States all round Europe, but find none of their Constitutions suitable to our circumstances (Speech of Benjamin Franklin to the Federal Convention, June 28, 1787, cited in James Madison, *Notes of Debates in the Federal Convention of 1787* [New York: W. W. Norton & Co., 1987], 209).

31. *The Federalist Papers*, No. 14.
32. Arendt, 15.
33. Crèvecoeur describes the new prosperity:

The American ought therefore to love this country much better than that wherein either he or his forefathers were born. Here the rewards of his industry follow with equal steps the progress of his labour; his labour is founded on the basis of nature, *self-interest*; can it want a stronger allurement? Wives and children, who before in vain demanded of him a morsel of bread, now, fat and frolicsome, gladly help their father to clear those fields whence exuberant crops are to arise to feed and to clothe them all; without any part being claimed, either by a despotic prince, a rich abbot, or a mighty lord (Hector St. John Crèvecoeur, *Letter from an American Farmer* [1782; reprint ed., New York: Fox, Duffield & Co., 1904], 55).

34. In Tocqueville's words:

If patient observation and sincere meditation have led men of the present day to recognize that both the past and the future of their history consist in the gradual and measured advance of equality, the discovery in itself gives this progress the sacred character of the will of the Sovereign Master. In that case effort to halt democracy appears as a fight against God Himself, and nations have no alternative but to acquiesce in the social state imposed by Providence (Alexis de Tocqueville, *Democracy in America*, trans. George Lawrence, ed. J. P. Mayer [Garden City: Anchor Books, 1969], 12).

35. "The Miami Meeting with President Reagan," *Origins* 17 (September 24, 1987): 238.
36. "Is there not virtue among us?" asked Madison defiantly. "If there be not, we are in a wretched situation. No theoretical checks, no form of government, can render us secure. To suppose any form of government will secure liberty or happiness without any virtue in the people, is a chimerical idea." Jonathan Elliot, ed., *Debates in the Several State Conventions on the Adoption of the Federal Constitution* (Philadelphia: Lippincott, 1907), Virginia, June 20, 1788.
37. Russell Kirk, *The Roots of American Order* (Washington, D.C.: Regnery Gateway, 1992).
38. Hamilton wrote as follows (except for the italicizations) to the people of the United States, in *Federalist* 1:

You are called upon to deliberate on a new Constitution for the United States of America. . . . It has frequently been remarked that it seems to have been reserved to the people of this country, by their conduct and example, to decide the important question, whether societies of men are really capable or not of establishing good government from *reflection* and *choice*, or whether they are forever destined to depend for their political constitutions on accident and force.

39. Arendt, 15.
40. John Adams wrote in 1809:

I will insist that the Hebrews have done more to civilize men than any other nation. If I were an atheist, and believed in blind eternal fate, I should still believe that fate had ordained the Jews to be the most essential instrument for civilizing the nations. If I were an atheist of the other sect, who believe or pretend to believe that all is ordered by chance, I should believe that chance had ordered the Jews to preserve and propagate to all mankind the doctrine of a supreme, intelligent, wise, almighty sovereign of the universe, which I believe to be the great essential principle of all morality, and consequently of all civilization (John Adams to F. A. Vanderkemp, February 16, 1809, in C. F. Adams, ed., *The Works of John Adams* [Boston: Little, Brown, 1854], 9: 609–10).

41. "The basis of our governments being the opinion of the people, the very first object should be to keep that right [a free press]; and were it left to me to decide whether we should have a government without newspapers, or newspapers without a government, I should not hesitate a moment to prefer the latter." Letter to Edward Carrington, January 16, 1787, in *Thomas Jefferson* (New York: Literary Classics of the United States, Inc., 1984), 880.

42. Sung-Chull Junn, "Why Koreans Think We're Jerks," *Washington Post*, "Outlook," April 9, 1989.

43. Trilling, xii. Irving Kristol adds an important clarification, which is that the new class is adversarial not just to the practices of the nation but to its ideals:

We are so used to this fact of our lives, we take it so for granted, that we fail to realize how extraordinary it is. Has there ever been in all of recorded history, a civilization whose culture was at odds with the values and ideals of that civilization itself? It is not uncommon that a culture will be critical of the civilization that sustains it—and always critical of the failure of this civilization to realize perfectly the ideals that it claims as inspiration. Such criticism is implicit or explicit in Aristophanes and Euripides, Dante and Shakespeare. But to take an adversary posture toward the ideals themselves? That is unprecedented. . . . The more "cultivated" a person is in our society, the more disaffected and malcontent he is likely to be—a disaffection, moreover, directed not only at the actuality of our society but at the ideality as well. Indeed, the ideality may be more strenuously opposed than the actuality (Irving Kristol, *Reflections of a Neoconservative: Looking Back, Looking Ahead* [New York: Basic Books, 1983], 27–28).

44. Trilling, xii.
45. Ibid., xiv–xv.
46. A useful introduction to the "new class" may be found in B. Bruce-Briggs, *The New Class?* (New Brunswick: Transaction Books, 1979). In *Beyond Culture*, Lionell Trilling showed the influence of the new class in literature; for the influence of the new class on politics and economics see, respectively, Jeane J. Kirkpatrick, "Politics and the 'New Class'," *Dictatorship and Double Standards: Rationalism and Reason in Politics* (New York: American Enterprise Institute and Simon and Schuster, 1982), 186–203; and Irving Kristol, *Two Cheers for Capitalism* (New York: Basic Books, 1978), ch. 2, "Business and the 'New Class'," 25–31.

In Marxist countries the danger of a new class was discerned as early as 1939 by Bruno Rizzi; see his *The Bureaucratization of the World*, trans. with intro. by Adam Westoby (New York: The Free Press, 1986). Almost simultaneously, James Burnham discerned an equivalent to the new class in *The Managerial Revolution* (New York: John Day Co., 1941). The concept became prominent on the left with the publication of Milovan Djilas's *The New Class* (New York: Praeger, 1957). In the United States writers on the left, such as John Kenneth Galbraith, David T. Bazelon, and Michael Harrington began to point to the "new class" as a potential ally of—if not a replacement for—the proletariat. See Galbraith, *The Affluent Society* (Boston: Houghton Mifflin, 1967), and Harrington, *Toward a Democratic Left* (New York: Macmillan, 1968), 265–97.

47. See *Antonio Gramsci: Selections from Political Writings, 1910–1920*, trans. John Mathews (Ann Arbor: Books on Demand, UMI, 1976). See also Jaime Antunez, "Socialism Chic," *Crisis* 7 (April 1989): 38–40.

48. See Bell, xvi.

49. Michael Novak, "The Secular Saint," *Illinois State University Journal* 30 (September 1967): 3–35; id., *A Theology for Radical Politics* (New York: Herder & Herder, 1969).

50. Bell, xvi.

51. Ibid., xvii.

52. Kristol distinguishes two poles in the tradition:

The terms "prophetic" and "rabbinic" which come, of course, from the Jewish tradition, indicate the two poles within which the Jewish tradition operates. They are not two equal poles: The rabbinic is the stronger pole, always. In an Orthodox Hebrew school, the prophets are read only by those who are far advanced. The rest of the students read the first five books of the Bible, and no more. They learn the Law. The prophets are only for people who are advanced in their learning and not likely to be misled by prophetic fever (Kristol, *Reflections of a Neoconservative*, 316–17).

53. See Ronald A. Knox, *Enthusiasm* (Westminster, Md.: Christian Classics, 1983).

54. "It cannot be repeated too often: nothing is more fertile in marvels than the art of being free, but nothing is harder than freedom's apprenticeship. . . . But liberty is generally born in stormy weather, growing with difficulty amid civil discords, and only when it is already old does one see the blessings it has brought." Tocqueville, 240.

Living on the boundary between the traditional society and the democratic society, Tocqueville himself saw more clearly than most the differences in the virtues required in the democratic, as opposed to aristocratic, societies. (He saw these as differences more clearly with respect to political institutions than he did with respect to economic institutions.)

55. "Yet more serious is the destruction of the *human environment*. People are rightly worried about the extinction of animal species, but too little effort is made to *safeguard the moral conditions for an authentic 'human ecology.'*" *Centesimus Annus*, 38.

56. "There is," writes Cotton Mather, "a *liberty* of corrupt nature, which is affected by *men* and *beasts* to do what they list; and this *liberty* is inconsistent with *authority*, impatient of all restraint; by this *liberty*, *Sumus Omnes Deteriores*, 'tis the grand enemy of *truth* and *peace*, and all the *ordinances* of God are bent against it. But there is a civil, a moral, a federal *liberty* . . . for that only which is *just* and *good*; for this *liberty* you are to stand with the hazard of your very *lives*." Cited in Tocqueville, 46.

57. This is clearly recognized in the recent encyclical:

A person who is concerned solely or primarily with possessing and enjoying, who is no longer able to control his instincts and passions, or to subordinate them by obedience to the truth, cannot be free: *obedience to the truth* about God and man is the first condition of freedom, making it possible for a person to order his needs and desires and to choose the means of satisfying them according to a correct scale of values, so that the ownership of things may become an occasion of growth for him (*Centesimus Annus*, 41).

For the inseparability of obedience and freedom as understood by the Pope, see Karol Cardinal Wojtyla, "The Eucharist and Man's Hunger for Freedom," Homily given at the Forty-first International Eucharistic Congress in Philadelphia, August 3, 1976 (Daughters of St. Paul Pamphlets, 1978):

> Freedom has been given to him by his Creator not in order to commit what is evil (cf. Gal. 5:13), but to do good. God also bestowed upon man understanding and conscience to show him what is good and what ought to be done, what is wrong and what ought to be avoided. God's commandments help our understanding and our conscience on their way. The greatest commandment—that of love—leads the way to the fullest use of liberty (cf. 1 Cor. 9:19–22; 13:1–13). Freedom has been given to man in order to love, to love true good: to love God above all, to love man as his neighbor and brother (cf. Dt. 6:5; Lv. 19:18; Mk. 12:30–33). Those who obey this truth, this Gospel, the real disciples of eternal Wisdom, achieve thus, as the Council puts it, a state of "royal freedom," for they follow "that King whom to serve is to reign."
>
> Freedom is therefore offered to man and given to him as a task. He must not only possess it, but also conquer it. He must recognize the work of his life in a good use, in an increasingly good use of his liberty. This is the truly essential, the fundamental work on which the value and the sense of his whole life depend (7–8).

On this same occasion in Philadelphia, the Pope noted the common aspirations of the colonial Americans and his own Polish compatriots:

> This year is the bicentennial of the day when the hunger for freedom ripened in the American society and revealed itself in liberation and the Declaration of Independence of the United States. Tadeusz Kosciuszko and Kazimierz Pulaski, my compatriots, participated in this fight for independence. The heroes of the Polish nation became heroes of American independence. And all this took place at the time when the Polish Kingdom, a big state consisting of three nations, the Poles, the Lithuanians and the Ruthenians, was beginning to lose its independence, and by degrees became the prey of its rapacious neighbors, Russia, Germany and Austria. At the same time while the United States of America was gaining independence, we were losing it for a period of more than a hundred years. And many heroic efforts and sacrifices, similar to those of Kosciuszko and Pulaski, had been necessary to ripen anew the freedom of the nation, to test it before all the world and to express it in time by the independence of our country (10–11).

58. See Michael Novak, "Christ: The Great Divide," *Crisis* (July–August 1992): 2–3.
59. *Centesimus Annus*, 60.

25
Truth and Liberty: The Present Crisis in Our Culture

Michael Novak

Few centuries have been as sanguinary as the twentieth. Leaving behind as their monuments the ruins of concentration camps and the work camps of the Gulag Archipelago, temporarily discredited, fascism and communism may have slouched into the shadows. Still, the forces of liberty have not succeeded in laying the foundations for a world of free republics. During the twentieth century, both in Europe and in the United States, the moral life of the free societies has been severely weakened. Families are a shadow of what they used to be. Traditional virtues and decencies, a sense of honor, and respect for moral character have given way to vulgar relativism. Thus, the dark underground river of the twentieth century has not been fascism nor communism but their presupposition: nihilism. And nihilism has not yet been abandoned.

THE PROBLEM OF NIHILISM

Even before fascism and communism arrived, many in Europe began to hold that humans may make themselves and the world around them whatever they wish. Gradually they denied that the human intellect has purchase on moral reality. *Choosing* matters, they insisted: *will*, not intellect. Such convictions made political nihilism plausible.

This vulgar nihilism systematically infected the souls of the "sensitive spirits"—artists, social critics, journalists, professors; in general, those who set standards, the guardians of culture. Even among liberals in the twentieth century who rejected dictatorship and the state-directed economy, many accepted (and still today accept) two

First published in *The Review of Politics*, vol. 59, no. 1, Winter 1997.

nihilist claims: that there are no constraints rooted in creation, nature, or intellect that the will must heed; and that to be free is to exercise pure will, even apart from the guidance of the intellect.

As Woody Allen still today summarizes these claims: "The heart wants what it wants."[1] The U.S. Supreme Court exemplified them in *Casey*: "At the heart of liberty is the right to define one's own concept of existence, of meaning, of the universe, and the mystery of human life."[2] This is pure nihilism. If I am free to make up my own universe, no law binds me. Nihilism means never having to be judged, and in this it gives the illusion of total freedom and unfettered autonomy. It allows one to indulge whatever desires pull one's heart.

Under Nazism and communism, these were powerful allurements. Not to have a judge (not even an inner "impartial spectator") felt, at first, like "liberation." To follow one's imperious desires wherever they listed yielded a feeling of mastery. One felt that one belonged to a master race, privy to a secret knowledge, those who know about the nothingness. Even Albert Camus found that his own early nihilism, fashionable in the cafes of the 1930s, deprived him of any arguments against the Gestapo agent who strangled one of his friends with a piano wire.[3] For to yield to nihilism was to give up the concept and criterion of truth.

That may not seem like much. Many sober liberals, from Arthur M. Schlesinger, Jr., to Richard Rorty, today recommend it.[4] Only on the basis of relativism, they say, is democracy safe. On the other hand, Václav Havel and other heroes of the struggle against totalitarianism attest that only on the basis of personal fidelity to truth, at great cost, were they able to overcome the oppressive public Lie.[5] Solzhenitsyn wrote that one word of truth is more powerful than all the arms of the most heavily armed regime.[6]

Which is it, then? Does liberty need relativism, or does liberty need truth?

THREE CONCEPTS OF LIBERTY

Political philosophers commonly use the term liberty to signify a relation between the individual and the regime in which the individual lives and acts. In this political context, the term may signify the degree to which the regime is not coercive, the space that it allows to the individual for self-determination. Isaiah Berlin in his famous essay "Two Concepts of Liberty" defined this way of thinking about liberty as "negative liberty."[7] The regime merely does not coerce, gets out of the way, stays within its own limits. At first blush, this might appear to be the liberal approach to liberty.

By contrast, Berlin's second concept of liberty appertains to state-oriented political philosophies of the communist, socialist, social democratic, and national socialist types; in other words—the nonliberal regimes. Here the governing insight is that individuals left to their own devices may in many cases be *formally* free to do something (not coerced otherwise by the regime) but not at all *able* to do it—lacking money, training, or other means and assistance. At least in certain fundamental areas and up to certain general standards of decency, proponents of this view argue, individuals need to be *enabled* to do things before they can be said to be truly free. Moreover, it is the duty of the regime so to enable them. The state must play a positive role. True freedom comes from this positive enablement, and hence true freedom is called "positive liberty," that is, state-enabled liberty.

Between the two world wars, many liberals in Britain and America were tempted to abandon the classical liberal ideal of negative liberty, in favor of the socialist ideal of positive liberty; and in this widespread cultural crisis of conscience Isaiah Berlin's essay shed much-needed light. Nonetheless, to Berlin's two concepts of liberty a third must be added,[8] if we are to properly understand the project of republican politics—the project of self-government.

By the project of self-government is meant government of the people, by the people, for the people, exercised chiefly through civil associations, but also through representative government, and a freely constituted state properly limited, divided, and checked. As distinguished from positive liberty and negative liberty, this republican project calls forth a concept of liberty as self-government. This third concept of liberty, further, forms a bridge between political philosophy and moral philosophy. "Self-government," for example, refers both to a type of regime and to the internal organization of personal moral life.

This third concept of liberty also forms a bridge between modern and ancient concepts of liberty, which to some influential political philosophers seem otherwise separated by a wide chasm. Ancient philosophers such as Aristotle, Plato, Seneca, and Cicero believed that a sound republic is "man writ large," a reflection of human nature, premised on a virtuous citizenry. By contrast, it is said, modern regimes are based not on virtue—which they judge to be too high and unrealistic an aim—but on lower and humbler bases more likely to be realized, such as interest and utility. If in the ancient view statecraft is a kind of soulcraft, the modern regime is designed to appeal very little to the soul, and perhaps not at all.[9]

Those who draw this contrast between ancient and modern political science have strong evidence on their side. Nonetheless, political reality and political thought move through history like wandering rivers and on many levels at once, maintaining continuities not always apparent on the surface. Honest atheists have often been obliged to confess that they hold today to certain Jewish and Christian concepts despite themselves—such as compassion, the idea of progress, conscience, and the unparalleled worth of the human individual. Bertrand Russell, Jean-Paul Sartre, Albert Camus, Leo Strauss, and others have observed such buried movements near the bottom of their thoughts.[10] Alexis de Tocqueville wrote that religion—and he clearly meant Judaism and Christianity—is the primary political institution of democracy.[11] Without religion, he held, belief in the inviolable rights and transcendent worth of individuals would not be indefinitely sustainable. I take his point to be not that in any one generation the masses need religion, while the intellectually strong do not, but that even the latter would over time begin to doubt whether human beings have rights in any sense that does not also apply to animals and trees and rocks, and so for democracy atheism is an untrustworthy support.

Thus, I want to suggest that in the twenty-first century we shall see a new departure in political philosophy, which is at the same time something of a return to something older than the modern. In those parts of the world in which democratic regimes and capitalist economies have been imperfectly achieved, the crisis of the coming century will be experienced, at least at first, as primarily moral and cultural. For democratic and capitalist regimes are not sustainable except under certain moral conditions and among citizens to specifiable moral habits. For their survival, they will have to tend again to central virtues.

Consider just a few: When telling falsehoods and untruths becomes the fashion, when cheating and goldbricking grow in ascendancy; when loyalty, honesty, and fidelity to promises lose point; when rules are routinely violated as long as violators can get away with it; when judges are susceptible to bribes or threats, and officials make no ruling on its merits but only on what it is worth to them; when nepotism, familism, and favoritism overpower justice and fairness; when citizens (as in many countries today) prefer to yield all their responsibilities to leaders, even if they are rogues and thugs; when no one takes pride in their daily work, and all essentially pretend to work; when no one trusts anyone else, nor accepts another man's word, nor cooperates with others except while exercising the strictest watchfulness—in such cases of moral degradation, the institutions of the commercial republic sputter and fail, and self-government dissolves.

THE SOCIAL ECOLOGY OF SELF-GOVERNMENT

Because republican self-government and the free economy grew up among a religious and moral people, political philosophers and economists took for granted the existence of such tacit moral preconditions—the functioning of specifiable moral dispositions, tendencies, and habits such as those just noted (by their absence) above. So pervasive were these habits that they seemed natural, rather than merely second-nature—that is, part of a learned social inheritance, shaped painstakingly over many centuries by populations willing to correct their bad instincts, inclinations, and habits over time and to replace them with better, in lifelong struggles of self-improvement. Dramatic personal efforts, multiplied throughout millions of families, made the institutions of democracy and the inventive economy practicable.

To allude to Reinhold Niebuhr's great line: The moral strengths of citizens make democracy (and capitalism) possible; their moral weaknesses make democracy (and capitalism) necessary.[12] Such "modern" institutions of republican self-government as checks and balances, bicameral legislatures, divided powers, and the like (though many of these, also, have ancient and medieval precedents) are not constructed in such a way that they depend on the perfect virtue of citizens. Recognizing the realism of the Jewish and Christian teaching on "original sin," the only Christian doctrine (Niebuhr also suggested) that one does not learn by belief but by experience, the American Founders in particular took pains to line up self-interest against self-interest and power against power, so that the self-love of each would become a sentinel over that of others. According to a twelfth-century monastic maxim, "Self-love dies a quarter-hour after the self."

In a word, political philosophers need to explore again the moral preconditions of democracy and capitalism, and to specify in practical detail the moral habits indispensable to their functioning. Though indispensable, these moral habits are not, given human weaknesses, sufficient; and, therefore, the checks and balances, division of offices, and other remedies for human weakness devised by our American Founders (and subsequent generations) also have their role. But institutional arrangements alone cannot keep the machinery of self-government functioning, apart from the quite substantial virtues learned and practiced by citizens. It is chimerical to think, James Madison once wrote, that without virtue in its citizens a republic can long survive.[13]

But how, as Madison asked, can a people incapable of governing its appetites in its private life possibly be capable of self-government in its public life? This is likely to be the central political problem of the twenty-first century: How to arrest the declining moral habits of our peoples. Put otherwise, how are we to instruct our children, and ourselves, in the virtues required for the survival and prospering of republican and capitalist institutions—the virtues required, secondly, to make the free society worthy, attractive, and morally delightful in itself? (Displaying this task in two steps rather than in one makes evident that virtue is also an end in itself, not merely an instrumental means to the survival of a free society.)

Liberty in this sense consists in an act of self-government by which we restrain our *desires* by temperance and related habits, and curb our *fears* by courage, steadfastness, and related habits. We do so *in order to reflect soberly, deliberate well, and choose dispassionately and justly* on the merits of the case under consideration, in such a way that others can count on our commitment and our long-term purpose. Such practices of self-government are found in a recurrent and habitual way only in persons of considerable character. It is the great fortune of the United States that our first president, George Washington, was understood by all who knew him to be the prototype of this sort of liberty—the man of character, a man one could count on, decisive, self-starting, a leader, by his very virtues worthy of the admiration and affection of his countrymen, a model for the liberty the nation promised to all who would wish to earn it.[14]

Liberty of this sort comes neither by the positive nor the negative actions of the state, although the Constitution of the American Republic allows it scope and depends upon its widespread realization. The liberty of self-government must be acquired, one person at a time. This personal task is rendered easier when the whole surrounding public ethos teaches it, encourages it, and proffers many examples of it—as well as proffering many examples of the self-destruction wrought by its absence. In this sense, personal liberty is much favored or impeded, depending upon the social ecology of liberty.

But it is fruitless to talk of a recovery of virtue if our society has lost all concept of truth. As the ancient proverb says, it is, in fact, the truth that sets us free (John 8:31–32). No truth, no liberty.

BUT WHAT IS TRUTH?

I will insist that the Hebrews have done more to civilize men than any other nation. If I were an atheist, and believed in blind eternal fate, I should still believe that *fate* had ordained the Jews to be the most essential instrument for civilizing the nations. If I were an atheist of the other sect, who believe or pretend to believe that all is ordered by chance, I should believe that *chance* had ordered the Jews to preserve and propagate to all mankind the doctrine of a supreme, intelligent, wise, almighty sovereign of the universe, which I believe to be the great essential principle of all morality, and consequently of all civilization.

—John Adams[15]

John Adams, the second president of the United States, here makes a profound point: Civilization depends on truth, and so does morality. If (contrary to Moses) there is only opinion—your opinion, my opinion, everybody else's opinion—but no truth, then there is no inherent reason why slavery is not equal to liberty, or coercion to equality. If all opinions are equal, Mussolini's are equal to Jefferson's and Adolf Hitler's to Bertrand Russell's.

By contrast, if (as Moses teaches) there is a Creator who understands all of us, who knows all things, who loves all things, who created all things, and who is also an undeceivable Judge, then however rich or powerful some persons might become, they still cannot escape God's judgment. Put another way, against power and wealth and position, other persons can appeal to truth—and to justice. More strongly still, if God is our judge, then civilization is possible. Since in that case truth counts, then human beings have the possibility of entering into rational conversation with one another, trying to persuade one another in the light of truth. As Thomas Aquinas commented, civilization is constituted by conversation.[16] Barbarians club one another; civilized people persuade one another by argument.

The reality of God, from this point of view, provides a barrier against relativism, the cult of power, and the influence of money. God sees through all these things, and humans are thereby encouraged to do the same.

On the other hand, if there is no God, as Adams insists on underlining, if Western civilization is rooted in the biblical God of the Jews (and through the Jews, the Christians) only by mere contingency, we are a quite fortunate civilization, sheerly by chance. Whether by chance or design, our liberty from power, wealth, deception, position, and tyranny in all their forms derives from our commitment to the priority of truth, even if that commitment has come about by chance. (To hold that it does come about by chance, however, is of course to render this commitment absurd—useful, but absurd.)

At this point, I want to make my point crystal clear. As readers of my earlier books *Belief and Unbelief* and *The Experience of Nothingness* will corroborate, I have long resisted making the argument that belief in God is a necessary prerequisite for the defense of the free society. I took this position in order to prevent the use of the idea of God as a mere means, that is, an instrument of worldly ambition. I did so even though the ambition in question seeks the noblest political end of all: the slow and patient pursuit of the ideal of the free republic, the only political ideal worthy of the liberty endowed in human nature. Therefore, I am not arguing here that only a theist—but no atheist or agnostic—can justify his or her commitment to the cause of a free society. The fact is, such self-proclaimed individual atheists as Sidney Hook and others have done so, both before the bar of their philosophical peers and (one supposes) to the satisfaction of their own consciences.

Admiration for Sidney Hook, Milton Friedman, and others has led me, therefore, to frame for myself the following distinctions: (1) Experience shows that atheists as individuals, in association, or as a category of citizens are often good, loyal, and even outstanding citizens. Many have served the common good of the nation in exemplary fashion. (2) Since the Constitution declares the state incompetent in the realm of conscience, there is no contradiction between being an atheist and being a good citizen. (3) Some atheists are stalwart defenders of truth, against relativism; of reason, against emotivism, bigotry, and ignorance; and of responsible and ordered liberty, against libertinism and license—and more effective in this defense than many religious people. (4) Some atheists have followed Hobbes, Locke, and others in offering an intellectual defense of "natural rights" against totalitarianism, brute power, and nihilism. They do so entirely on atheistic grounds. Nonetheless, (5) experience also shows that this defense is a Maginot Line which the swirling tides of history easily overwhelm. On the one side, atheistic arguments fail to convince religious people (a not inconsiderable constituency on the side of liberty). On the other side, for many atheists such arguments crumble before the Nietzschean critique of reason.

For such reasons, it does not seem to me likely that a *whole society over several generations* can find a sustainable intellectual basis for the free society on an atheistic premise. Atheism unsupported by Jewish and Christian tradition can tell us neither why individual rights are inviolable, nor why each individual person is of incommensurable value. It can, at best, supply a rationale based upon utility; but that defense was easily turned by Hitler into "Truth is determined by the victors." In this sense, Western atheists and agnostics have been more dependent than they have ever wanted to admit upon Jewish and Christian convictions, narratives, and dramatic forms. That was Friedrich Nietzsche's point in showing that rationalism without God is an absurdity.[17]

As if to verify Nietzsche's point, the calm rationalism of Sidney Hook, not only comfortable but reigning victorious in American universities for the first three-quarters of the twentieth century, did not survive the century. Hook's students, before the century's end, were nearly everywhere dethroned, ridiculed, and mocked by "postmodernists." The great-grandchildren of the Enlightenment, alas, suddenly abandoned reason. With it, they also abandoned respect for truth and ordered liberty.

The history of liberty, Lord Acton found, is coincident with the history of Judaism and Christianity.[18] In no other world religions does one find the view that the human person should be valued above all other creatures in the universe. No other has taught that the responsible liberty of the human person is the central drama of the universe and the bright red thread of human history.

RELATIVISM—ONCE AGAIN

Nonetheless, surveying the wreckage of the twentieth century, in which the Jewish-Christian narrative line of history was overthrown, Pope John Paul II noted in his two recent encyclicals *The Hundredth Year* (1991) and *The Splendor of Truth* (1993) that cultural elites again today are promoting relativism, skepticism, and agnosticism. This time their argument is that these are the best foundation for democratic forms of political life. In rebuttal, the pope notes how often in the first nine decades of the twentieth century the turn to relativism led to capitulation to superior power. "If there is no ultimate truth to guide and direct political activity, then ideas and convictions can easily be manipulated for reasons of power. As history demonstrates, a democracy without values easily turns into open or thinly disguised totalitarianism."[19] People who reject the fiction that truth is whatever a majority says it is root freedom in truth, not fashion. Far from being unreliable from a democratic point of view, such persons are the granite on which democracy is based.

The pope makes a further useful point: In actual practice, the concept of truth is appealed to again and again in concrete democratic life; namely, in appeals to "truthfulness in the relations between those governing and those governed, openness in public administration, impartiality in the service of the body politic, respect for the rights of political adversaries, safeguarding the rights of the accused against summary trials and convictions, the just and honest use of public funds, the rejection of equivocal or illicit means in order to gain, preserve or increase power at any cost," and the like.[20] Even from a pragmatic point of view, the concept of truth is indispensable to democratic habits. This is observable fact. Without a people's commitment to truth in all these senses, liberty is unsustainable.

Still, several questions remain. When confronted with the pope's words about truth and liberty, Milton Friedman wrote sharply and to the point in *National Review:* "Whose truth?"[21] More fully, Friedman wrote:

> As a non-Catholic classical liberal, I find much to praise and to agree with in this letter addressed to the members of the Catholic faith. My stress on its political character, on the dominance of good will and high motives over substantive content is not a

criticism. For the Church is a political as well as a religious institution, and this is a political document. But I must confess that one high-minded sentiment, passed off as if it were a self-evident proposition, sent shivers down my back: "*Obedience to the truth about God and man is the first condition of freedom.*" Whose "truth"? Decided by whom? Echoes of the Spanish Inquisition?

"*Whose* truth?" might be a relativist's question, meaning (or implying) that "your" truth is different from "my" truth, and that truth is always just somebody or other's perception. In other words, there really is not any truth; no objective standards measure which opinions are closer to or further from the reality of things. In that case, nothing exists but subjective perceptions and values. The human subject is not mastered by evidence; the subject is sovereign over the evidence. It would not be easy to discern this purely relativist view at work in Milton Freidman's expositions of evidence in economics.[22]

It is possible, of course, to make a distinction between the truths known through the use of scientific method and the "truths" known through moral reason or (more commonly today) moral "perception." For some authors, the term "reason" is restricted to the use of the mind under the rules of scientific method. Beyond that narrow range, they say, the rest is subjective. Everything else reflects merely private values, personal perception, and choice. This view, once widespread but now thought naive, is called positivism.

In the theoretical order, the impossibility of formulating the positivist position in a positivist way brought its early formulations into disrepute. More importantly, in the practical order, the universal condemnation of Nazi war criminals shows that positivism is in practice untenable. What the Nazis did may have been legal and under orders—that is, positivistically correct—but even a moral cretin should have come upon the knowledge that it was morally intolerable.

Pascal, of course, had tried to make a related claim in his aphorism: "The heart has its reasons which the reason knows not of."[23] But that is too weak a version of a stronger point: Human reason has many more uses than the two uses beloved of positivists, logic and scientific method. These include important uses in politics, practical daily life, the arts, conversation, friendship, and the moral life. In such contexts, good uses of reason can be distinguished from bad (rationalization, for instance), and some statements are understood by those with experience to ring true, while others do not ring true. Without an understanding of the distinction between truth and falsehood in these contexts, we could not use the word "realism" or distinguish it from "foolishness" or "illusion." But we do use these words, every day; and even apart from using the words, we quietly make the discriminations they express amid the many things we see and hear.

For example, we observe that some people are more expert in their observations and behaviors than others. We judge leaders and statesmen—de Gaulle, Churchill—by the perspicuity of their reason in political matters. We know some people who regularly manifest bad judgment, and lack common sense.

As is clear, Milton Friedman is neither a relativist nor a positivist. Yet his question, "Whose truth?" does bring out an important point. What we look to when we use the term *truth* is a standard that is in no one's possession. No one "holds" the truth in his grasp. On the contrary, a person may be possessed *by* the truth, in the grip of the evidence in such a way that he or she cannot deny it, once having taken it in. Indeed, such a person cannot, perhaps, be shaken from the evidence, even under torture. Truth possesses us, we do not possess it. We come under it, not it under us.

Such reflections show why writers concerned with discovering the truth, such as John Stuart Mill, have expressed confidence in appeals to tolerance, civil discourse, and an open marketplace of ideas. They believe that the truth about any particular matter, great or small, is likely to elude the grasp of any one seeker. Each seeker may be moved by one fragment of truth; other fragments emerge in the open contestation of ideas, under fair rules of argument. As Reinhold Neibuhr used to warn himself: There is always some truth in the errors of others and some error in my truth.[24] The standard of evidence is beyond all of us. We need to listen hard—even where we would rather not listen—to learn all that we might learn about reality, especially moral reality.

It is obvious that the term *truth* can be used in many different senses, not all of them acceptable. In the context of a moral and political concept such as human liberty, classically considered, the word *truth* is commonly used by religious people (Jews and Christians notably) in three senses. Consider, for example, the familiar refrain beloved of Americans, "The truth shall make you free." On the first level, this means that fidelity to the Almighty is fidelity to the very light that infuses everything that is and makes it intelligible (*i.e.,* intelligible in itself and in its relation to all other things). The practical payoff is this: fidelity to the evidence of things is the only way to avoid being ensnared by power, money, or other seductions that would turn one's eyes away from evidence. One might not always know in any particular dilemma exactly what *is* true, good, just, right; but one does wish to avoid being swayed by improper partiality.

An atheist, of course, can interpret all this more simply by appealing to a commitment to honest inquiry (or, in the language of some, "the impartial spectator" theory). The Jewish or Christian believer can be that simple, too, but in fact holds that such a commitment is not simply to a methodological principle. It is a commitment to a Person with Whom humans are in covenant, to the One-who-*is,* whose name (for Jews) it is better not to speak or write, lest it be taken to be like all other names rather than above all names. It is a commitment to an undeceivable but loving Judge.

On the second level, "The truth shall make you free" is taken as an operational axiom: Be alert for deception and illusion; seek to understand rightly; beware of the Evil Spirit whose name is the Prince of Lies; know that there are many more insights than there are sound insights. The former come frequently to the top of the head, especially among bright people; the latter are grounded in a virtually unconditioned review of all the evidence. In other words, be of steady and sober judgment, develop habits that strengthen one's ability to perceive quickly and keenly, deliberate wisely, and judge in a manner that is far more often than not (no one is perfect) "spot on," right in the bull's-eye. People under illusions or driven by errant passions are distant from reality, and their freedom is thereby diminished.

On a third level, "The truth shall make you free" signifies what is implicit on the first two levels; namely, that if one is to be ruled by evidence, not go off half-cocked, then one must deploy all the habits and dispositions necessary to act by self-mastery (by self-government, not by momentary passion or whim). To be free does not mean for humans what it means for the other animals—at least, as Tocqueville points out, not in America.[25] Two cats that frisk, run, bat each other, roll over and run again may seem to be free, but they are in fact doing no more than following the law of their own instincts. Cats do what their instincts tell them, when they tell them. They do what they want, when they want. The trouble is that humans have a far more complicated set of instincts.

From the earliest days, American preachers (Tocqueville notes) drew the distinction between animal freedom and human freedom. Humans must *order* all their instincts, get them into a proper harmony and alignment, order them "sweetly," if they can, in the order laid out for them by the Creator; and if one or another of their wants, desires, or instincts is out of order, ornery, recalcitrant, they must take it by the horns, if necessary, in as many of the little battles of daily life as it takes until it learns by second nature, if not first, where it belongs. Such battles are likely to continue all through a pilgrim's life, as *Pilgrim's Progress* taught millions.[26] In any case, the American conception of liberty is "ordered liberty," a liberty of self-mastery, self-discipline, self-government.

George Washington was a model of this new type of liberty, recognized by all, as were many other Founders: Franklin, Madison, Jefferson, Charles Carroll and, four generations later, Abraham Lincoln. These were men who went through many struggles, but came out at the end men whose word you could trust; whose commitments you could count on; whose judgments about men and affairs were shrewd and often startlingly profound (for all their plainness of statement); whose deliberations showed the work of reason in a great repertoire of various movements and a great range of mood and observations; and whose decisions hewed closely to enduring truths about the human person. Tocqueville called theirs "the new science of politics," and this science of theirs was both ancient and original (as is man himself).

In other words, the third meaning of "the truth shall make you free" is that liberty is constituted by acts of sober reflection and well-deliberated choice. Such acts spring from persons of serious and trustworthy character, whose commitments may be counted on. These acts are free because they are directed by the compass of enduring moral realism, as best these agents can discern it. To live by moral realism (the full truth about humans) is to live an examined and deliberate life. No other, such persons hold, is worth living. To be a slave to illusions is to lose touch with reality, and no longer to be either a sensible or a free person.

Liberty apart from enduring moral truth is illusion. Truth that does not issue in responsible action is sterile.

CONCLUSION

Thus, our argument has come full circle. Liberty and truth form a beneficent circle. The truth makes us free. And the one thing a free person is not free to do—unless in betrayal—is to turn his or her face against the evidence. The evidence binds, and makes us free from all else. This, at least, is how I read Jefferson, who implies that our minds must be free from every coercion except one: the coercion effected upon the mind by evidence. The mind that is coerced by nothing but the evidence is free; the mind coerced by anything but truth is unfree.

The rationale for defending liberty—especially "the free marketplace of ideas"—is to come closer to the truth. The rationale for defending truth is that it makes us free.

Without such moral foundations—without, that is, a commitment by a preponderance of citizens to the moral habits that make "liberty" and "truth" more than words on paper; that make them, that is, dependable dispositions in the moral life of the nation—it is hard to see how a republic, any republic, can long endure. Our rights are not protected by words on paper, but by habits that exhibit respect for truth and love for ordered liberty.

Keeping the meaning of truth and liberty clean and clear, like white stones in a sparkling stream of the Montana Rockies, is the task of every generation. It is, we might say, a matter of moral ecology.

NOTES

1. See Michael Lewis on Woody Allen, "The Very Last Lover," *The New Republic*, 28 September 1992, p. 11.

2. *Planned Parenthood v. Casey*, 505 U.S. 120 L Ed 2d 674 (1992). Russell Hittinger parsed the destructive notion of liberty at the heart of *Casey*: "One would seem to have a right to do or not do whatever one pleases" ("What Really Happened in the Casey Decision," *Crisis* [September 1992], pp. 16–22).

3. In view of his earlier defense of nihilism, Camus sets forth, with some difficulty, his argument against Nazism in "Letters to a German Friend: Second Letter," *Resistance, Rebellion and Death* (New York: Alfred A. Knopf, 1961).

4. Schlesinger wrote, "The American mind is by nature and tradition skeptical, irreverent, pluralistic and relativistic. . . . People with different history will have different values. But we believe that our own are better for us. They work for us; and, for that reason, we live and die by them" ("The Opening of the American Mind," *New York Times Book Review*,

23 July 1989, p. 26). A good statement of Rorty's views on democracy can be found in "Taking Philosophy Seriously," *New Republic,* 11 April 1988, p. 22, where Rorty writes, "No specific doctrine is much of a danger, but the idea that democracy depends on adhesion to some such doctrine is."

5. For the testimony of Václav Havel and other East and Central European dissidents on the culture of the Lie, see Havel et al., *The Power and the Powerless: Citizens against the State in Central and Eastern Europe* (Armark, N.Y.: M. E. Sharpe, 1990).

6. Solzhenitsyn was quoting, in his 1970 Nobel Prize lecture, an old Russian proverb: "One word of truth outweighs the world." *Nobel Lecture* (New York: Farrar, Straus & Giroux, 1970), p. 34.

7. Berlin defined negative liberty as "not being interfered with by others. The wider the area of non-interference the wider my freedom." See Berlin's famous "Two Concepts of Liberty," in *Four Essays on Liberty* (Oxford: Oxford University Press, 1969), pp. 118–72.

8. See my *Morality, Capitalism, and Democracy* (London: IEA Health and Welfare, 1990), originally delivered as an IEA Health and Welfare Unit lecture in the Queen Elizabeth II Conference Centre in 1990. The lecture's original title was "Christianity, Capitalism, and Democracy," and it so appears in the Czech and Polish translations.

9. Still, note the neat connection between the third concept of liberty and the liberal concept of "negative liberty." The American regime *permits* liberty even to those who do not practice self-government, but are slaves (as all of us are in part) to their own passions. But it cannot survive unless a sufficient proportion of its citizens do practice self-government in their private lives, and so are prepared to practice it in public as well. If all are slaves to passion and interest, free institutions cannot stand. The state cannot command or coerce self-government in private life, but it can do two things: (a) it can avoid undermining it by its laws, its regulations, and its taxes; and (b) it can support it by structures of incentives and punishments.

10. For Russell, see *Why I Am Not a Christian* (New York: Simon & Schuster, 1957), particularly pp. 14–15; Sartre's views are developed in *The Words* (New York: George Braziller, 1964); on Strauss's relationship to Judaism, see David Novak, ed., *Leo Strauss and Judaism: Jerusalem and Athens Critically Revisited* (Lanham, Md.: Rowman and Littlefield, 1996).

11. Tocqueville wrote: "While the law allows the American people to do everything, there are things which religion prevents them from imagining and forbids them to dare. Religion, which never intervenes directly in the government of American society, should therefore be considered as the first of their political institutions, for although it did not give them the taste for liberty, it singularly facilitates their use thereof" (*Democracy in America,* ed. J. P. Mayer, trans. G. Lawrence [New York: Anchor Books, 1966], p. 292).

12. In Niebuhr's words, "Man's capacity for justice makes democracy possible; but man's inclination to injustice makes democracy necessary" (*The Children of Light and the Children of Darkness: A Vindication of Democracy and a Critique of Its Traditional Defense* [New York: Charles Scribner's Sons, 1944], p. xi).

13. During the constitutional debate of 1788, Madison asked: "Is there no virtue among us? If there be not, we are in a wretched situation. No theoretical checks, no form of government, can render us secure. To suppose any form of government will secure liberty or happiness without any virtue in the people, is a chimerical idea. If there be sufficient virtue and intelligence in the community, it will be exercised in the selection of these men; so that

we do not depend on their virtue, or put confidence in our rulers, but in the people who are to choose them" (Jonathan Elliot, ed., *Debates in the Several State Conventions on the Adoption of the Federal Constitution* [Philadelphia: Lippincott, 1907], Virginia, 20 June 1788).

14. Washington declared that "Virtue and morality is a necessary spring of popular government" ("Farewell Address," 19 September 1796, in *The Early Republic, 1789–1828*, ed. Noble E. Cunningham, Jr. [Columbia, S.C.: University of South Carolina Press, 1968], p. 53). For two recent studies of Washington's exemplary character, see Richard Brookhiser, *Founding Father: Rediscovering George Washington* (New York: Free Press, 1996), and Harrison Clark, *All Cloudless Glory: The Life of George Washington from Youth to Yorktown* (Washington, D.C.: Regnery, 1996).

15. C. F. Adams, ed., *The Works of John Adams*, vol. 9 (Boston: Little-Brown, 1854), pp. 609–60. (emphasis added)

16. See St. Thomas Aquinas, I *Politics*, lect. 1; *Aristotle*, 1252b5; see also Thomas Gilby, *Between Community and Society: A Philosophy and Theology of the State* (London: Longmans, Green and Co., 1953), p. 93.

17. See Friedrich Nietzsche, *The Will to Power*, ed. Walter Kaufmann (New York: Random House, 1967).

18. Lord Acton, *Selected Writings of Lord Acton*, ed. J. Rufus Fears, vol. 3 (Indianapolis: Liberty Classics, 1988), p. 491. See also pp. 29–30.

19. Pope John Paul II, *Centesimus Annus* (Boston: Daughters of St. Paul, 1991), 46.

20. Pope John Paul II, *Veritatis Splendor* (Boston: Daughters of St. Paul, 1991), 101.

21. Friedman's comments were part of a symposium on *Centesimus Annus* in *National Review* (24 June 1991). They were reprinted as "Goods in Conflict?" in *A New Worldly Order: John Paul II and Human Freedom*, ed. George Weigel (Washington, D.C.: Ethics and Public Policy, 1992), p. 77.

22. During the conference at which this paper was presented (at the Henry Salvatori Center of Claremont McKenna College, 18–20 April 1996), Professor Friedman emphatically renounced relativism: "I have no doubt that there is an absolute standard of truth, and that in any particular matter there is a truth to be recognized. But I don't know what it is. The overlooked element here is humility. We have to know we don't know." And later, "I am not an atheist. I see the importance of religion, I respect it, I believe it has an important place in life, but I just do not see, I do not have belief myself, open as I am to it." (Conversation with the author.)

23. Blaise Pascal, *Pensées*, with an introduction by T. S. Eliot (New York: Dutton, 1958), #277.

24. See, e.g., Niebuhr's discussion on "Having, and Not Having the Truth" in *The Nature and Destiny of Man* (New York: Macmillan, 1943), p. 243: "The truth remains subject to the paradox of grace. We may have it; and yet we do not have it. And we will have it the more purely in fact if we know that we have it only in principle. Our toleration of truths opposed to those which we confess is an expression of the spirit of forgiveness in the realm of culture. Like all forgiveness, it is possible only if we are not too sure of our own virtue."

25. Tocqueville quotes Cotton Mather: "Nor would I have you mistake in the point of your own liberty. There is a liberty of corrupt nature, which is affected by men and beasts to do what they list; and this liberty is inconsistent with authority, impatient of all restraint.... But there is a civil, a moral, a federal liberty, which is the proper end and object of authority; it is a liberty for that only which is just and good" (*Democracy in America*, p. 46).

In the succinct formulation of Lord Acton, liberty is not to be defined as "the power of doing what we like, but the right of being able to do what we ought" (*Selected Writings of Lord Acton*, p. 613).

26. John Bunyan, *Pilgrim's Progress* (New York: Viking Penguin, 1965).

Part V
DOCUMENTATION

Introduction to *The Federalist*

The Federalist *is a series of eighty-five newspaper articles published in two New York newspapers from October 1787 until May 1788—during the period of debate about whether New Yorkers, like residents in other states, ought to ratify the newly proposed Federal Constitution of 1787. New York was a key state. New York's rejection of the Constitution would have split New England from the southern states so that the new nation would have emerged fatally divided. If New York rejected the Constitution, the union between the New England states and the southern states would have been militarily and economically unsustainable.*

For New Yorkers, there were many attractions to remaining an independent state. Powerful families in New York would become ambassadors to Paris and France, commander in chief, secretary of state. Only sober thinking about the long-range common good of the whole nation promoted unification.

All eighty-five articles were signed with the pen name "Publius," a good name for a writer defending the Republican principles of the new Constitution. Fifty-two of the letters were written by Alexander Hamilton, twenty-eight by James Madison, and five by John Jay. All three men were destined to become important leaders of the new nation: Madison became the third president of the United States; Jay the first chief justice of the U.S. Supreme Court; and Hamilton the first secretary of the treasury, who laid down the main lines of the national economy.

This collection of founding articles has been cherished as a classic, and still stands as the best practical exposition of the principles of Republican government ever set to paper. Its authors were not interested in utopian visions or ideological manifestos. They wanted to describe the practical measures, embodied in the text of the Constitution, that would enable sinful human beings to conduct a sustained experiment in self-government. A regime of the sort they envisaged had never yet existed on earth. As Madison wrote wist-

fully in Number 39, they had "no model" to consult; they were forced to exercise a certain originality of mind.

In the texts that follow, we have tried to highlight some strands of the moral vision that informed the practical working of the Constitution.

In the first paragraph of Number 1, Publius defines what he means by liberty: those actions taken after deliberate reflection *and* choice. *Cats, dogs, cattle, and other animals do not rise to the level of these two activities; but human beings do. Therein lie human dignity, responsibility, and duty. Whether a government can be founded on reflection and choice is an experiment now to be decided.*

The United States had no munitions factory when they went to war against the greatest army and navy in the world. Its citizens, therefore, had a keen sense of their reliance on Providence, *including the many gifts of Providence already manifest in the nation's history. Not the least of these was a universal commitment to the* Union *of all states in one nation, all citizens in one people. (Number 2)*

To keep themselves capable of sober reflection and deliberate choice, citizens require certain mental habits (virtues). But it must also be expected—all history is testimony to it—that every human being sometimes sins. (Number 6)

Publius understood that, human nature being what it is, factions *naturally arise in any free society; people disagree. (Number 10) To deal with the political problems engendered by faction, Publius chose not to diminish freedom, but to control the negative effects of multiple factions by (a) increasing their number and (b) setting them in mutual opposition, each a check upon the other.*

The machinery of republican government provides for a systematic division of powers, *running through the whole articulation of government, so that at every point and at every level,* "ambition is made to counter ambition." *Instead of expecting utopia on earth, the American framers placed their reliance upon the* division of powers *and the establishment of* checks and balances *to each and every power. (Number 51)*

The Federalist Papers

James Madison et al.

NUMBER 1
INTRODUCTION

After an unequivocal experience of the inefficacy of the subsisting federal government, you are called upon to deliberate on a new Constitution for the United States of America. The subject speaks its own importance; comprehending in its consequences nothing less than the existence of the UNION the safety and welfare of the parts of which it is composed, the fate of an empire in many respects the most interesting in the world. *It has been frequently remarked that it seems to have been reserved to the people of this country, by their conduct and example, to decide the important question, whether societies of men are really capable or not of establishing good government from reflection and choice, or whether they are forever destined to depend for their political constitutions on accident and force.* If there be any truth in the remark, the crisis at which we are arrived may with propriety be regarded as the era in which that decision is to be made; and a wrong election of the part we shall act may, in this view, deserve to be considered as the general misfortune of mankind.

This idea will add the inducements of philanthropy to those of patriotism, to heighten the solicitude which all considerate and good men must feel for the event. Happy will it be if our choice should be directed by a judicious estimate of our true interests, unperplexed and unbiased by considerations not connected with the public good. But this is a thing more ardently to be wished than seriously to be expected. The plan offered to our deliberations affects too many particular interests, innovates upon too many local institutions, not to involve in its discussion a variety of objects foreign to its merits, and of views, passions, and prejudices little favorable to the discovery of truth.

Among the most formidable of the obstacles which the new Constitution will have to encounter may readily be distinguished the obvious interest of a certain class of men in every State to resist all changes which may hazard a diminution of the power, emolument, and consequence of the offices they hold under the state establishments; and the perverted ambition of another class of men, who will either hope to aggrandize themselves by the confusions of their country, or will flatter themselves with fairer prospects of elevation from the subdivision of the empire into several partial confederacies than from its union under one government.

It is not, however, my design to dwell upon observations of this nature. I am well aware that it would be disingenuous to resolve indiscriminately the opposition of any set of men (merely because their situations might subject them to suspicion) into interested or ambitious views. Candor will oblige us to admit that even such men may be actuated by upright intentions; and it cannot be doubted that much of the opposition which has made its appearance, or may hereafter make its appearance, will spring from sources, blameless at least if not respectable—the honest errors of minds led astray by preconceived jealousies and fears. So numerous indeed and so powerful are the causes which serve to give a false bias to the judgment, that we, upon many occasions, see wise and good men on the wrong as well as on the right side of questions of the first magnitude to society. This circumstance, if duly attended to, would furnish a lesson of moderation to those who are ever so thoroughly persuaded of their being in the right in any controversy. And a further reason for caution, in this respect, might be drawn from the reflection that we are not always sure that those who advocate the truth are influenced by purer principles than their antagonists. Ambition, avarice, personal animosity, party opposition, and many other motives not more laudable than these, are apt to operate as well upon those who support as those who oppose the right side of a question. Were there not even these inducements to moderation, nothing could be more ill-judged than that intolerant spirit which has at all times characterized political parties. For in politics, as in religion, it is equally absurd to aim at making proselytes by fire and sword. Heresies in either can rarely be cured by persecution.

And yet, however just these sentiments will be allowed to be, we have already sufficient indications that it will happen in this as in all former cases of great national discussion. A torrent of angry and malignant passions will be let loose. To judge from the conduct of the opposite parties, we shall be led to conclude that they will mutually hope to evince the justness of their opinions, and to increase the number of their converts by the loudness of their declamations and by the bitterness of their invectives. An enlightened zeal for the energy and efficiency of government will be stigmatized as the offspring of a temper fond of despotic power and hostile in the principles of liberty. An over-scrupulous jealousy of danger to the rights of the people, which is more commonly the fault of the head than of the heart, will be represented as mere pretense and artifice, the stale bait for popularity at the expense of public good. It will be forgotten, on the one hand, that jealousy is the usual concomitant of violent love, and that the noble enthusiasm of liberty is too apt to be infected with a spirit of narrow and illiberal distrust. On the other hand, it will be equally forgotten that the vigor of government is essential to the security of liberty; that, in the contemplation of a sound and well-informed judgment, their interests can never be separated; and that a dangerous ambition more often lurks behind the specious mask of zeal for the rights of the people than under the forbidding appearance of zeal for the firmness and efficiency of government. History will teach us that the former has been found a much more certain road to the introduction of despotism than the latter, and that of those men who have overturned the liberties of republics, the greatest number have begun their career by paying an obsequious court to the people, commencing demagogues and ending tyrants.

In the course of the preceding observations, I have had an eye, my fellow-citizens, to putting you upon your guard against all attempts, from whatever quarter, to influence your decision in a matter of the utmost moment to your welfare by any impressions other than those which may result from the evidence of truth. You will, no doubt, at the same time have collected from the general scope of them that they proceed from a source not unfriendly to the new Constitution. Yes, my countrymen, I own to you that after having given it an attentive consideration, I am clearly of opinion it is your interest to adopt it. I am convinced that this is the safest course for your liberty, your dignity, and your happiness. I affect not reserves which I do not feel. I will not amuse you with an appearance of deliberation when I have decided. I frankly acknowledge to you my convictions, and I will freely lay before you the reasons on which they are founded. The consciousness of good intentions disdains ambiguity. I shall not, however, multiply professions on this head. My motives must remain in the depository of my own breast. My arguments will be open to all and may be judged of by all. They shall at least be offered in a spirit which will not disgrace the cause of truth.

I propose, in a series of papers, to discuss the following interesting particulars:— *The utility of the* UNION *to your political prosperity—The insufficiency of the present Confederation to preserve that Union—The necessity of a government at least equally energetic with the one proposed, to the attainment of this object—The conformity of the proposed Constitution to the true principles of republican government—Its analogy to your own State constitution*—and lastly, *The additional security which its adoption will afford to the preservation of that species of government, to liberty, and to property.*

In the progress of this discussion I shall endeavor to give a satisfactory answer to all the objections which shall have made their appearance, that may seem to have any claim to your attention.

It may perhaps be thought superfluous to offer arguments to prove the utility of the UNION, a point, no doubt, deeply engraved on the hearts of the great body of the people in every State, and one which, it may be imagined, has no adversaries. But the fact is that we already hear it whispered in the private circles of those who oppose the new Constitution, that the thirteen States are of too great extent for any general system, and that we must of necessity resort to separate confederacies of distinct portions of the whole.[1] This doctrine will, in all probability, be gradually propagated, till it has votaries enough to countenance an open avowal of it. For nothing can be more evident to those who are able to take an enlarged view of the subject than the alternative of an adoption of the new Constitution or a dismemberment of the Union. It will therefore be of use to begin by examining the advantages of that Union, the certain evils, and the probable dangers, to which every State will be exposed from its dissolution. This shall accordingly constitute the subject of my next address.

PUBLIUS [Hamilton]

NUMBER 2
CONCERNING DANGERS FROM FOREIGN FORCE AND INFLUENCE

When the people of America reflect that they are now called upon to decide a question, which in its consequences must prove one of the most important that ever engaged their attention, the propriety of their taking a very comprehensive, as well as a very serious, view of it will be evident.

Nothing is more certain than the indispensable necessity of government; and it is equally undeniable that whenever and however it is instituted, the people must cede to it some of their natural rights, in order to vest it with requisite powers. It is well worthy of consideration, therefore, whether it would conduce more to the interest of the people of America that they should, to all general purposes, be one nation, under one federal government, than that they should divide themselves into separate confederacies and give to the head of each the same kind of powers which they are advised to place in one national government.

It has until lately been a received and uncontradicted opinion that the prosperity of the people of America depended on their continuing firmly united, and the wishes, prayers, and efforts of our best and wisest citizens have been constantly directed to that object. But politicians now appear who insist that this opinion is erroneous, and that instead of looking for safety and happiness in union, we ought to seek it in a division of the States into distinct confederacies or sovereignties. However extraordinary this new doctrine may appear, it nevertheless has its advocates; and certain characters who were much opposed to it formerly are at present of the number. Whatever may be the arguments or inducements which have wrought this change in the sentiments and declarations of these gentlemen, it certainly would not be wise in the people at large to adopt these new political tenets without being fully convinced that they are founded in truth and sound policy.

It has often given me pleasure to observe that independent America was not composed of detached and distant territories, but that one connected, fertile, widespreading country was the portion of our western sons of liberty. *Providence* has in a particular manner blessed it with a variety of soils and productions and watered it with innumerable streams for the delight and accommodation of its inhabitants. A succession of navigable waters forms a kind of chain round its borders, as if to bind it together; while the most noble rivers in the world, running at convenient distances, present them with highways for the easy communication of friendly aids and the mutual transportation and exchange of their various commodities.

With equal pleasure I have as often taken notice that *Providence* has been pleased to give this one connected country to one united people—a people descended from the same ancestors, speaking the same language, professing the same religion, attached to the same principles of government, very similar in their manners and customs, and who, by their joint counsels, arms, and efforts, fighting side by side throughout a long and bloody war, have nobly established their general liberty and independence.

This country and this people seem to have been made for each other, and it appears as if it was the *design of Providence that an inheritance so proper and convenient for a band of brethren, united to each other by the strongest ties*, should never be split into a number of unsocial, jealous, and alien sovereignties.

Similar sentiments have hitherto prevailed among all orders and denominations of men among us. To all general purposes *we have uniformly been one people; each individual citizen everywhere enjoying the same national rights, privileges, and protection*. As a nation we have made peace and war; as a nation we have vanquished our common enemies; as a nation we have formed alliances, and made treaties, and entered into various compacts and conventions with foreign states.

A strong sense of the value and blessings of union induced the people, at a very early period, to institute a federal government to preserve and perpetuate it. They formed it almost as soon as they had a political existence; nay, at a time when their habitations were in flames, when many of their citizens were bleeding, and when the progress of hostility and desolation left little room for those calm and mature inquiries and reflections which must ever precede the formation of a wise and well-balanced government for a free people. It is not to be wondered at that a government instituted in times so inauspicious should on experiment be found greatly deficient and inadequate to the purpose it was intended to answer.

This intelligent people perceived and regretted these defects. Still continuing no less attached to union than enamored of liberty, they observed the danger which immediately threatened the former and more remotely the latter; and being persuaded that ample security for both could only be found in a national government more wisely framed, they, as with one voice, convened the late convention at Philadelphia to take that important subject under consideration.

This convention, composed of men who possessed the confidence of the people, and many of whom had become highly distinguished by their patriotism, virtue, and wisdom, in times which tried the minds and hearts of men, undertook the arduous task. In the mild season of peace, with minds unoccupied by other subjects, they passed many months in cool, uninterrupted, and daily consultation; and finally, without having been awed by power, or influenced by any passions except love for their country, they presented and recommended to the people the plan produced by their joint and very unanimous councils.

Admit, for so is the fact, that this plan is only *recommended*, not imposed, yet let it be remembered that it is neither recommended to *blind* approbation, nor to *blind* reprobation; but to that sedate and candid consideration which the magnitude and importance of the subject demand, and which it certainly ought to receive. But, as has been already remarked, it is more to be wished than expected than it may be so considered and examined. Experience on a former occasion teaches us not to be too sanguine in such hopes. It is not yet forgotten that well-grounded apprehensions of imminent danger induced the people of America to form the memorable Congress of 1774. That body recommended certain measures to their constituents, and the event proved their wisdom; yet it is fresh in our memories how soon the press began to teem with pamphlets and weekly papers against those very measures. Not only many of the officers of govenrment, who obeyed the dictates of personal interest, but others, from a mistaken estimate of consequences, from the undue influence of ancient attachments or whose ambition aimed at objects which did not correspond with the public good, were indefatigable in their endeavors to persuade the people to reject the advice of that patriotic Congress. Many, indeed, were deceived and deluded, but the great majority of the people reasoned and decided judiciously; and happy they are in reflecting that they did so.

They considered that the Congress was composed of many wise and experienced men. That, being convened from different parts of the country, they brought with them and communicated to each other a variety of useful information. That, in the course of the time they passed together in inquiring into and discussing the true interests of their country, they must have acquired very accurate knowledge on that head. That they were individually interested in the public liberty and prosperity, and therefore that it was not less their inclination than their duty to recommend only such measures as, after the most mature deliberation, they really thought prudent and advisable.

These and similar considerations then *induced the people to rely greatly on the judgment and integrity* of the Congress; and they took their advice notwithstanding the various arts and endeavors used to deter and dissuade them from it. But if the people at large had reason to confide in the men of that Congress, few of whom had been fully tried or generally known, still greater reason have they now to respect the judgment and advice of the convention, for it is well known that some of the most distinguished members of that Congress, who have been since tried and justly approved for patriotism and abilities, and who have grown old in acquiring political information, were also members of this convention, and carried into it their accumulated knowledge and experience.

It is worthy of remark that not only the first, but every succeeding Congress, as well as the late convention, have invariably joined with the people in *thinking that the prosperity of America depended on its Union*. To preserve and perpetuate it was the great object of the people in forming that convention, and it is also *the great object of the plan* which the convention has advised them to adopt. With what propriety, therefore, or for what good purposes, are attempts at this particular period made by some men to depreciate the importance of the Union? Or why is it suggested that three or four confederacies would be better than one? I am persuaded in my own mind that the people have always thought right on this subject, and that their universal and uniform attachment to the cause of the Union rests on great and weighty reasons, which I shall endeavor to develop and explain in some ensuing papers. They who promote the idea of substituting a number of distinct confederacies in the room of the plan of the convention seem clearly to foresee that the rejection of it would put the continuance of the Union in the utmost jeopardy. That certainly would be the case, and I sincerely wish that it may be as clearly foreseen by every good citizen that whenever the dissolution of the Union arrives, America will have reason to exclaim, in the words of the poet: "FAREWELL! A LONG FAREWELL TO ALL MY GREATNESS."[2]

PUBLIUS [Jay]

NUMBER 6
CONCERNING DANGERS FROM WAR BETWEEN THE STATES

The three last numbers of this paper have been dedicated to an enumeration of the dangers to which we should be exposed, in a state of disunion, from the arms and arts of foreign nations. I shall now proceed to delineate dangers of a different and, perhaps, still more alarming kind—those which will in all probability flow from dissensions between the States themselves and from domestic factions and convulsions. These have been already in some instances slightly anticipated; but they deserve a more particular and more full investigation.

A man must be far gone in Utopian speculations who can seriously doubt that if these States should either be wholly disunited, or only united in partial confederacies, the subdivisions into which they might be thrown would have frequent and violent contests with each other. To presume a want of motives for such contests as an argument against their existence would be to forget that men are ambitious, vindictive, and rapacious. To look for a continuation of harmony between a number of independent, unconnected sovereignties situated in the same neighborhood would be to disregard the uniform course of human events, and to set at defiance the accumulated experience of ages.

The causes of hostility among nations are innumerable. There are some which have a general and almost constant operation upon the collective bodies of society. Of this description are the love of power or the desire of pre-eminence and dominion—the jealousy of power, or the desire of equality and safety. There are others which have a more circumscribed though an equally operative influence within their spheres. Such are the rivalships and competitions of commerce between commercial nations. And there are others, not less numerous than either of the former, which take their origin entirely in private passions; in the attachments, enmities, interests, hopes, and fears of leading individuals in the communities of which they are members. Men of this class, whether the favorites of a king or of a people, have in too many instances abused the confidence they possessed; and assuming the pretext of some public motive, have not scrupled to sacrifice the national tranquility to personal advantage or personal gratification.

The celebrated Pericles, in compliance with the resentment of a prostitute,[3] at the expense of much of the blood and treasure of his countrymen, attacked, vanquished, and destroyed the city of the *Samnians*. The same man, stimulated by private pique against the *Megarensians*,[4] another nation of Greece, or to avoid a prosecution with which he was threatened as an accomplice in a supposed theft of the statuary of Phidias,[5] or to get rid of the accusations prepared to be brought against him for dissipating the funds of the state in the purchase of popularity,[6] or from a combination of all these causes, was the primitive author of that famous and fatal war, distinguished in the Grecian annals by the name of the *Peloponnesian* war; which, after various vicissitudes, intermissions, and renewals, terminated in the ruin of the Athenian commonwealth.

The ambitious cardinal, who was prime minister to Henry VIII, permitting his vanity to aspire to the triple crown,[7] entertained hopes of succeeding in the acquisition of that splendid prize by the influence of the Emperor Charles V. To secure the favor and interest of this enterprising and powerful monarch, he precipitated England into a war with France, contrary to the plainest dictates of policy, and at the hazard of the safety and independence, as well of the kingdom over which he presided by his counsels as of Europe in general. For if there ever was a sovereign who bid fair to realize the project of universal monarchy, it was the Emperor Charles V, of whose intrigues Wolsey was at once the instrument and the dupe.

The influence which the bigotry of one female,[8] the petulancies of another,[9] and the cabals of a third,[10] had in the contemporary policy, ferments, and pacifications of a considerable part of Europe, are topics that have been too often descanted upon not to be generally known.

To multiply examples of the agency of personal considerations in the production of great national events, either foreign or domestic, according to their direction, would be an unnecessary waste of time. Those who have but a superficial acquaintance with the sources from which they are to be drawn will themselves recollect a variety of instances; and those who have a tolerable knowledge of human nature will not stand in need of such lights to form their opinion either of the reality or extent of that agency. Perhaps, however, a reference, tending to illustrate the general principle, may with propriety be made to a case which has lately happened among ourselves. If Shays had not been a *desperate debtor*, it is much to be doubted whether Massachusetts would have been plunged into a civil war.

But notwithstanding the concurring testimony of experience, in this particular, there are still to be found visionary or designing men, who stand ready to advocate the paradox of perpetual peace between the States, though dismembered and alienated from each other. The genius of republics (say they) is pacific; the spirit of commerce has a tendency to soften the manners of men, and to extinguish those inflammable humors which have so often kindled into wars. Commercial republics, like ours, will never be disposed to waste themselves in ruinous contentions with each other. They will be governed by mutual interest, and will cultivate a spirit of mutual amity and concord.

Is it not (we may ask these projectors in politics) the true interest of all nations to cultivate the same benevolent and philosophic spirit? If this be their true interest, have they in fact pursued it? Has it not, on the contrary, invariably been found that momentary passions, and immediate interests, have a more active and imperious control over human conduct than general or remote considerations of policy, utility, or justice? Have republics in practice been less addicted to war than monarchies? Are not the former administered by men as well as the latter? Are there not aversions, predilections, rivalships, and desires of unjust acquisitions that affect nations as well as kings? Are not popular assemblies frequently subject to the impulses of rage, resentment, jealousy, avarice, and of other irregular and violent propensities? Is it not well known that their determinations are often governed by a few individuals in whom they place confidence, and are, of course, liable to be tinctured by the passions and views of those individuals? Has commerce hitherto done any thing more than change the objects of war? Is not the love of wealth as domineering and enterprising a passion as that of power or glory? Have there not been as many wars founded upon commercial motives since that has become the prevailing system of nations, as were before occasioned by the cupidity of territory or dominion? Has not the spirit of commerce, in many instances, administered new incentives to the appetite, both for the one and for the other? Let experience, the least fallible guide of human opinions, be appealed to for an answer to these inquiries.

Sparta, Athens, Rome, and Carthage were all republics; two of them, Athens and Carthage, of the commercial kind. Yet were they as often engaged in wars, offensive and defensive, as the neighboring monarchies of the same times. Sparta was little better than a well-regulated camp; and Rome was never sated of carnage and conquest.

Carthage, though a commercial republic, was the aggressor in the very war that ended in her destruction. Hannibal had carried her arms into the heart of Italy and to the gates of Rome, before Scipio, in turn, gave him an overthrow in the territories of Carthage and made a conquest of the commonwealth.

Venice, in later times, figured more than once in wars of ambition, till, becoming an object to the other Italian states, Pope Julius the Second found means to accomplish that formidable league,[11] which gave a deadly blow to the power and pride of this haughty republic.

The provinces of Holland, till they were overwhelmed in debts and taxes, took a leading and conspicuous part in the wars of Europe. They had furious contests with England for the dominion of the sea, and were among the most persevering and most implacable of the opponents of Louis XIV.

In the government of Britain the representatives of the people compose one branch of the national legislature. Commerce has been for ages the predominant pursuit of that country. Few nations, nevertheless, have been more frequently engaged in war; and the wars in which that kingdom has been engaged have, in numerous instances, proceeded from the people.

There have been, if I may so express it, almost as many popular as royal wars. The cries of the nation and the importunities of their representatives have, upon various occasions, dragged their monarchs into war, or continued them in it, contrary to their inclinations, and sometimes contrary to the real interests of the state. In that memorable struggle for superiority between the rival houses of *Austria* and *Bourbon*, which so long kept Europe in a flame, it is well known that the antipathies of the English against the French, seconding the ambition, or rather the avarice, of a favorite leader,[12] protracted the war beyond the limits marked out by sound policy, and for a considerable time in opposition to the views of the court.

The wars of these two last-mentioned nations have in a great measure grown out of commercial considerations—the desire of supplanting and the fear of being supplanted, either in particular branches of traffic or in the general advantages of trade and navigation, and sometimes even the more culpable desire of sharing in the commerce of other nations without their consent.

The last war but two between Britain and Spain sprang from the attempts of the English merchants to prosecute an illicit trade with the Spanish main. These unjustifiable practices on their part produced severity on the part of the Spaniards towards the subjects of Great Britain which were not more justifiable, because they exceeded the bounds of a just retaliation and were chargeable with inhumanity and cruelty. Many of the English who were taken on the Spanish coast were sent to dig in the mines of Potosi; and by the usual progress of a spirit of resentment, the innocent were, after a while, confounded with the guilty in indiscriminate punishment. The complaints of the merchants kindled a violent flame throughout the nation, which soon after broke out in the House of Commons, and was communicated from that body to the ministry. Letters of reprisal were granted, and a war ensued, which in its consequences overthrew all the alliances that but twenty years before had been formed with sanguine expectations of the most beneficial fruits.

From this summary of what has taken place in other countries, whose situations have borne the nearest resemblance to our own, what reason can we have to confide in those reveries which would seduce us into an expectation of peace and cordiality between the members of the present confederacy, in a state of separation? Have we not already seen enough of the fallacy and extravagance of those idle theories which have amused us with promises of an exemption from the imperfections, the weaknesses, and the evils incident to society in every shape? *Is it not time to awake from the deceitful dream of a golden age and to adopt as a practical maxim for the direction of our political conduct that we, as well as the other inhabitants of the globe, are yet remote from the happy empire of perfect wisdom and perfect virtue?*

Let the point of extreme depression to which our national dignity and credit have sunk, let the inconveniences felt everywhere from a lax and ill administration of government, let the revolt of a part of the State of North Carolina, the late menacing disturbances in Pennsylvania, and the actual insurrections and rebellions in Massachusetts, declare—!

So far is the general sense of mankind from corresponding with the tenets of those who endeavor to lull asleep our apprehensions of discord and hostility between the States, in the event of disunion, that it has from long observation of the progress of society become a sort of axiom in politics that vicinity, or nearness of situation, constitutes nations natural enemies. An intelligent writer expresses himself on this subject to this effect: "NEIGHBORING NATIONS [says he] are naturally ENEMIES of each other, unless their common weakness forces them to league in a CONFEDERATE REPUBLIC, and their constitution prevents the differences that neighborhood occasions, extinguishing that secret jealousy which disposes all states to aggrandize themselves at the expense of their neighbors."[13] This passage, at the same time, points out the EVIL and suggests the REMEDY.[14]

PUBLIUS [Hamilton]

NUMBER 10
THE SAME SUBJECT CONTINUED

Among the numerous advantages promised by a well-constructed Union, none deserves to be more accurately developed than its tendency to break and control the violence of faction. The friend of popular governments never finds himself so much alarmed for their character and fate as when he contemplates their propensity to this dangerous vice. He will not fail, therefore, to set a due value on any plan which, without violating the principles to which he is attached, provides a proper cure for it. The instability, injustice, and confusion introduced into the public councils have, in truth, been the mortal diseases under which popular governments have everywhere perished, as they continue to be the favorite and fruitful topics from which the adversaries to liberty derive their most specious declamations. The valuable improvements made by the American constitutions on the popular models, both ancient and modern, cannot certainly be too much admired; but it would be an unwarrantable partiality to contend that they have as effectually obviated the danger on this side, as was wished and expected. Complaints are everywhere heard from our most considerate and virtuous citizens, equally the friends of public and private faith and of public and personal liberty, that our governments are too unstable, that the public good is disregarded in the conflicts of rival parties, and that measures are too often decided, not according to the rules of justice and the rights of the minor party, but by the superior force of an interested and overbearing majority. However anxiously we may wish that these complaints had no foundation, the evidence of known facts will not permit us to deny that they are in some degree true. It will be found, indeed, on a candid review of our situation, that some of the distresses under which we labor have been erroneously charged on the operation of our governments; but it will be found, at the same time, that other causes will not alone account for many of our heaviest misfortunes; and, particularly, for that prevailing and increasing distrust of public engagements and alarm for private rights which are echoed from one end of the continent to the other. These must be chiefly, if not wholly, effects of the unsteadiness and injustice with which a factious spirit has tainted our public administration.

By a faction I understand a number of citizens, whether amounting to a majority or minority of the whole, who are united and actuated by some common impulse of passion, or of interest, adverse to the rights of other citizens, or to the permanent and aggregate interests of the community.

There are two methods of curing the mischiefs of faction: the one, by removing its causes; the other, by controlling its effects.

There are again two methods of removing the causes of faction: the one, by destroying the liberty which is essential to its existence; the other, by giving to every citizen the same opinions, the same passions, and the same interests.

It could never be more truly said than of the first remedy that it was worse than the disease. Liberty is to faction what air is to fire, an aliment without which it instantly expires. But it could not be a less folly to abolish liberty, which is essential to political life, because it nourishes faction than it would be to wish the annihilation of air, which is essential to animal life, because it imparts to fire its destructive agency.

The second expedient is an impracticable as the first would be unwise. As long as the reason of man continues fallible, and he is at liberty to exercise it, different opinions will be formed. As long as the connection subsists between his reason and his self-love, his opinions and his passions will have a reciprocal influence on each other; and the former will be objects to which the latter will attach themselves. The diversity in the faculties of men, from which the rights of property originate, is not less an insuperable obstacle to a uniformity of interests. The protection of these faculties is the first object of government. From the protection of different and unequal faculties of acquiring property, the possession of different degrees and kinds of property immediately results; and from the influence of these on the sentiments and views of the respective proprietors ensues a division of the society into different interests and parties.

The latent causes of faction are thus sown in the nature of man; and we see them everywhere brought into different degrees of activity, according to the different circumstances of civil society. A zeal for different opinions concerning religion, concerning government, and many other points, as well of speculation as of practice; an attachment to different leaders ambitiously contending for pre-eminence and power; or to persons of other descriptions whose fortunes have been interesting to the human passions, have, in turn, divided mankind into parties, inflamed them with mutual animosity, and rendered them much more disposed to vex and oppress each other than to co-operate for their common good. So strong is this propensity of mankind to fall into mutual animosities that where no substantial occasion presents itself the most frivolous and fanciful distinctions have been sufficient to kindle their unfriendly passions and excite their most violent conflicts. But the most common and durable source of factions has been the various and unequal distribution of property. *Those who hold and those who are without property have ever formed distinct interests in society.*

Those who are creditors, and those who are debtors, fall under a like discrimination. A landed interest, a manufacturing interest, a mercantile interest, a moneyed interest, with many lesser interests, grow up of necessity in civilized nations, and divide them into different classes, actuated by different sentiments and views. The regulation of these various and interfering interests forms the principal task of modern legislation and involves the spirit of party and faction in the necessary and ordinary operations of government.

No man is allowed to be a judge in his own cause, because his interest would certainly bias his judgment, and, not improbably, corrupt his integrity. With equal, nay with greater reason, a body of men are unfit to be both judges and parties at the same time; yet what are many of the most important acts of legislation but so many judicial determinations, not indeed concerning the rights of single persons, but concerning the rights of large bodies of citizens? And what are the different classes of legislators but advocates and parties to the causes which they determine? Is a law proposed concerning private debts? It is a question to which the creditors are parties on one side and the debtors on the other. Justice ought to hold the balance between them. Yet the parties are, and must be, themselves the judges; and the most numerous party, or in other words, the most powerful faction must be expected to prevail. Shall domestic manufacturers be encouraged, and in what degree, by restrictions on foreign manufacturers? are questions which would be differently decided by the landed and the manufacturing classes, and probably by neither with a sole regard to justice and the public good. The apportionment of taxes on the various descriptions of property is an act which seems to require the most exact impartiality; yet there is, perhaps, no legislative act in which greater opportunity and temptation are given to a predominant party to trample on the rules of justice. Every shilling with which they overburden the inferior number is a shilling saved to their own pockets.

It is in vain to say that enlightened statesmen will be able to adjust these clashing interests and render them all subservient to the public good. Enlightened statesmen will not always be at the helm. Nor, in many cases, can such an adjustment be made at all without taking into view indirect and remote considerations, which will rarely prevail over the immediate interest which one party may find in disregarding the rights of another or the good of the whole.

The inference to which we are brought is that the causes of faction cannot be removed and that relief is only to be sought in the means of controlling its effects.

If a faction consists of less than a majority, relief is supplied by the republican principle, which enables the majority to defeat its sinister views by regular vote. It may clog the administration, it may convulse the society; but it will be unable to execute and mask its violence under the forms of the Constitution. When a majority is included in a faction, the form of popular government, on the other hand, enables it to sacrifice to its ruling passion or interest both the public good and the rights of other citizens. To secure the public good and private rights against the danger of such a faction, and at the same time to preserve the spirit and the form of popular government, is then the great object to which our inquiries are directed. Let me add that it is the great desideratum by which alone this form of government can be rescued from the opprobrium under which it has so long labored and be recommended to the esteem and adoption of mankind.

By what means is this object attainable? Evidently by one of two only. Either the existence of the same passion or interest in a majority at the same time must be prevented, or the majority, having such coexistent passion or interest, must be rendered, by their number and local situation, unable to concert and carry into effect schemes of oppression. If the impulse and the opportunity be suffered to coincide, we well know that neither moral nor religious motives can be relied on as an adequate control. They are not found to be such on the injustice and violence of individuals, and lose their efficacy in proportion to the number combined together, that is, in proportion as their efficacy becomes needful.

From this view of the subject it may be concluded that a pure democracy, by which I mean a society consisting of a small number of citizens, who assemble and administer the government in person, can admit of no cure for the mischiefs of faction. A common passion or interest will, in almost every case, be felt by a majority of the whole; a communication and concert results from the form of government itself; and there is nothing to check the inducements to sacrifice the weaker party or an obnoxious individual. Hence it is that such democracies have ever been spectacles of turbulence and contention; have ever been found incompatible with personal security or the rights of property; and have in general been as short in their lives as they have been violent in their deaths. *Theoretic politicians, who have patronized this species of government, have erroneously supposed that by reducing mankind to a perfect equality in their political rights, they would at the same time be perfectly equalized and assimilated in their possessions, their opinions, and their passions.*

A republic, by which I mean a government in which the scheme of representation takes place, opens a different prospect and promises the cure for which we are seeking. Let us examine the points in which it varies from pure democracy, and we shall comprehend both the nature of the cure and the efficacy which it must derive from the Union.

The two great points of difference between a democracy and a republic are: first, the delegation of the government, in the latter, to a small number of citizens elected by the rest; secondly, the greater number of citizens and greater sphere of country over which the latter may be extended.

The effect of the first difference is, on the one hand, to refine and enlarge the public views by passing them through the medium of a chosen body of citizens, whose wisdom may best discern the true interest of their country and whose patriotism and love of justice will be least likely to sacrifice it to temporary or partial considerations. Under such a regulation it may well happen, that the public voice, pronounced by the representatives of the people, will be more consonant to the public good than if pronounced by the people themselves, convened for the purpose. On the other hand, the effect may be inverted. Men of factious tempers, of local prejudices, or of sinister designs, may, by intrigue, by corruption, or by other means, first obtain the suffrages, and then betray the interests of the people. The question resulting is, whether small or extensive republics are most favorable to the election of proper guardians of the public weal; and it is clearly decided in favor of the latter by two obvious considerations.

In the first place it is to be remarked that however small the republic may be the representatives must be raised to a certain number in order to guard against the cabals of a few; and that however large it may be they must be limited to a certain number in order to guard against the confusion of a multitude. *Hence, the number of representatives in the two cases not being in proportion to that of the constituents, and being proportionally greatest in the small republic, it follows that if the proportion of fit characters be not less in the large than in the small republic, the former will present a greater option, and consequently a greater probability of a fit choice.*

In the next place, as each representative will be chosen by a greater number of citizens in the large than in the small republic, it will be more difficult for unworthy candidates to practice with success the vicious arts by which elections are too often carried; and the suffrages of the people being more free, will be more likely to center on men who possess the most attractive merit and the most diffusive and established characters.

It must be confessed that in this, as in most other cases, there is a mean, on both sides of which inconveniences will be found to lie. By enlarging too much the number of electors, you render the representative too little acquainted with all their local circumstances and lesser interests; as by reducing it too much, you render him unduly attached to these, and too little fit to comprehend and pursue great and national objects. The federal Constitution forms a happy combination in this respect; the great and aggregate interests being referred to the national, the local and particular to the State legislatures.

The other point of difference is the greater number of citizens and extent of territory which may be brought within the compass of republican than of democratic government; and it is this circumstance principally which renders factious combinations less to be dreaded in the former than in the latter. The smaller the society, the fewer probably will be the distinct parties and interests composing it; the fewer the distinct parties and interests, the more frequently will a majority be found of the same party; and the smaller the number of individuals composing a majority, and the smaller the compass within which they are placed, the more easily will they concert and execute their plans of oppression. Extend the sphere and you take in a greater variety of parties and interests; you make it less probable that a majority of the whole will have a common motive to invade the rights of other citizens; or if such a common motive exists, it will be more difficult for all who feel it to discover their own strength and to act in unison with each other. Besides other impediments, it may be remarked that, where there is a consciousness of unjust or dishonorable purposes, communication is always checked by distrust in proportion to the number whose concurrence is necessary.

Hence, it clearly appears that the same advantage which a republic has over a democracy in controlling the effects of faction is enjoyed by a large over a small republic—is enjoyed by the Union over the States composing it. Does this advantage consist in the substitution of representatives whose enlightened views and virtuous sentiments render them superior to local prejudices and to schemes of injustice? It will not be denied that the representation of the Union will be most likely to possess these requisite endowments. Does it consist in the greater security afforded by a greater variety of parties, against the event of any one party being able to outnumber and oppress the rest? In an equal degree does the increased variety of parties comprised within the Union increase this security? Does it, in fine, consist in the greater obstacles opposed to the concert and accomplishment of the secret wishes of an unjust and interested majority? Here again the extent of the Union gives it the most palpable advantage.

The influence of factious leaders may kindle a flame within their particular States but will be unable to spread a general conflagration through the other States. A religious sect may degenerate into a political faction in a part of the Confederacy; but the variety of sects dispersed over the entire face of it must secure the national councils against any danger from that source. *A rage for paper money, for an abolition of debts, for an equal division of property, or for any other improper or wicked project, will be less apt to pervade the whole body of the Union than a particular member of it, in the same proportion as such a malady is more likely to taint a particular county or district than an entire State.*

In the extent and proper structure of the Union, therefore, we behold a republican remedy for the diseases most incident to republican government. And according to the degree of pleasure and pride we feel in being republicans ought to be our zeal in cherishing the spirit and supporting the character of federalists.

PUBLIUS [Madison]

NUMBER 51
THE SAME SUBJECT CONTINUED WITH THE SAME VIEW
AND CONCLUDED

To what expedient, then, shall we finally resort, for maintaining in practice the necessary partition of power among the several departments as laid down in the Constitution? The only answer that can be given is that as all these exterior provisions are found to be inadequate the defect must be supplied, by so contriving the interior structure of the government as that its several constituent parts may, by their mutual relations, be the means of keeping each other in their proper places. Without presuming to undertake a full development of this important idea I will hazard a few general observations which may perhaps place it in a clearer light, and enable us to form a more correct judgment of the principles and structure of the government planned by the convention.

In order to lay a due foundation for that separate and distinct exercise of the different powers of government, which to a certain extent is admitted on all hands to be essential to the preservation of liberty, it is evident that each department should have a will of its own; and consequently should be so constituted that the members of each should have as little agency as possible in the appointment of the members of the others. Were this principle rigorously adhered to, it would require that all the appointments for the supreme executive, legislative, and judiciary magistracies should be drawn from the same fountain of authority, the people, through channels having no communication whatever with one another. Perhaps such a plan of constructing the several departments would be less difficult in practice than it may in contemplation appear. Some difficulties, however, and some additional expense would attend the execution of it. Some deviations, therefore, from the principle must be admitted. In the constitution of the judiciary department in particular, it might be inexpedient to insist rigorously on the principle: first, because peculiar qualifications being essential in the members, the primary consideration ought to be to select that mode of choice which best secures these qualifications; second, because the permanent tenure by which the appointments are held in that department must soon destroy all sense of dependence on the authority conferring them.

It is equally evident that the members of each department should be as little dependent as possible on those of the others for the emoluments annexed to their offices. Were the executive magistrate, or the judges, not independent of the legislature in this particular, their independence in every other would be merely nominal.

But the great security against a gradual concentration of the several powers in the same department consists in giving to those who administer each department the necessary constitutional means and personal motives to resist encroachments of the others. The provision for defense must in this, as in all other cases, be made commensurate to the danger of attack. Ambition must be made to counteract ambition. The interest of the man must be connected with the constitutional rights of the place. It may be a reflection on human nature that such devices should be necessary to control the abuses of government. But what is government itself but the greatest of all reflections on human nature? If men were angels, no government would be necessary. If angels were to govern men, neither eternal or internal controls on government would be necessary. In framing a government which is to be administered by men over men, the great difficulty lies in this: you must first enable the government to control the governed; and in the next place oblige it to control itself. A dependence on the people is, no doubt, the primary control on the government; but experience has taught mankind the necessity of auxiliary precautions.

This policy of supplying, by opposite and rival interests, the defect of better motives, might be traced through the whole system of human affairs, private as well as public. We see it particularly displayed in all the subordinate distributions of power, where the constant aim is to divide and arrange the several offices in such a manner as that each may be a check on the other—that the private interest of every individual may be a sentinel over the public rights. These inventions of prudence cannot be less requisite in the distribution of the supreme powers of the State.

But it is not possible to give to each department an equal power of self-defense. In republican government, the legislative authority necessarily predominates. The remedy for this inconveniency is to divide the legislature into different branches; and to render them, by different modes of election and different principles of action, as little connected with each other as the nature of their common functions and their common dependence on the society will admit. It may even be necessary to guard against dangerous encroachments by still further precautions. As the weight of the legislative authority requires that it should be thus divided, the weakness of the executive may require, on the other hand, that it should be fortified. An absolute negative on the legislature appears, at first view, to be the natural defense with which the executive magistrate should be armed. But perhaps it would be neither altogether safe nor alone sufficient. On ordinary occasions it might not be exerted with the requisite firmness, and on extraordinary occasions it might be perfidiously abused. May not this defect of an absolute negative be supplied by some qualified connection between this weaker department and the weaker branch of the stronger department, by which the latter may be led to support the constitutional rights of the former, without being too much detached from the rights of its own department?

If the principles on which these observations are founded be just, as I persuade myself they are, and they be applied as a criterion to the several State constitutions, and to the federal Constitution, it will be found that if the latter does not perfectly correspond with them, the former are infinitely less able to bear such a test.

There are, moreover, two considerations particularly applicable to the federal system of America, which place that system in a very interesting point of view.

First. In a single republic, all the power surrendered by the people is submitted to the administration of a single government; and the usurpations are guarded against by a division of the government into distinct and separate departments. *In the compound republic of America, the power surrendered by the people is first divided between two distinct governments, and then the portion allotted to each subdivided among distinct and separate departments. Hence a double security arises to the rights of the people. The different governments will control each other, at the same time that each will be controlled by itself.*

Second. It is of great importance in a republic not only to guard the society against the oppression of its rulers, but to guard one part of the society against the injustice of the other part. Different interests necessarily exist in different classes of citizens. If a majority be united by a common interest, the rights of the minority will be insecure. There are but two methods of providing against this evil: the one by creating a will in the community independent of the majority—that is, of the society itself; the other, by comprehending in the society so many separate descriptions of citizens as will render an unjust combination of a majority of the whole very improbable, if not impracticable. The first method prevails in all governments possessing an hereditary or self-appointed authority. This, at best, is but a precarious security; because a power independent of the society may as well espouse the unjust views of the major as the rightful interests of the minor party, and may possibly be turned against both parties. *The second method will be exemplified in the federal republic of the United States. Whilst all authority in it will be derived from and dependent on the society, the society itself will be broken into so many parts, interests and classes of citizens, that the rights of individuals, or of the minority, will be in little danger from interested combinations of the majority. In a free government the security for civil rights must be the same as that for religious rights. It consists in the one case in the multiplicity of interests, and in the other in the multiplicity of sects. The degree of security in both cases will depend on the number of interests and sects; and this may be presumed to depend on the extent of country and number of people comprehended under the same government. This view of the subject must particularly recommend a proper federal system to all the sincere and considerate friends of republican government, since it shows that in exact proportion as the territory of the Union may be formed into more circumscribed Confederacies, or States, oppressive combinations of a majority will be facilitated; the best security, under the republican forms, for the rights of every class of citizen, will be diminished; and consequently the stability and independence of some member of the government, the only other security, must be proportionally increased. Justice is the end of government. It is the end of civil society. It ever has been and ever will be pursued until it be obtained, or until liberty be lost in the pursuit. In a society under the forms of which the stronger faction can readily unite and oppress the weaker, anarchy may as truly be said to reign as in a state of nature, where the weaker individual is not secured against the violence of the stronger; and as, in the latter state, even the stronger individuals are prompted, by the uncertainty of their condition, to submit to a government which may protect the weak as well as themselves; so, in the former state, will the more powerful factions or parties be gradually induced, by a like motive, to wish for a government which will protect all parties, the weaker as well as the more powerful.* It can be little doubted that if the State of Rhode Island was separated from the Confederacy and left to itself, the insecurity of rights under the popular form of government within such narrow limits would be displayed by such reiterated oppressions of factious majorities that some power altogether independent of the people would soon be called for by the voice of the very factions whose misrule had proved the necessity of it. *In the extended republic of the United States, and among the great variety of interests, parties, and sects which it embraces, a coalition of a majority of the whole society could seldom take place on any other principles than those of justice and the general good; whilst there being thus less danger to a minor from the will of a major party, there must be less pretext, also, to provide for the security of the former, by introducing into the government a will not dependent on the latter, or, in other words, a will independent of the society itself. It is no less certain than it is important, notwithstanding the contrary opinions which have been entertained, that the larger the society, provided it lie within a practicable sphere, the more duly capable it will be of self-government. And happily for the* republican cause, *the practicable sphere may be carried to a very great extent by a judicious modification and mixture of the* federal principle.

PUBLIUS [Madison]

NOTES

1. The same idea, tracing the arguments to their consequences, is held out in several of the late publications against the new Constitution.
2. The poet is Shakespeare, *King Henry VIII*, III, ii. [Ed.]
3. Aspasia, *vide* Plutarch's *Life of Pericles*.
4. Ibid.
5. Ibid. Phidias was supposed to have stolen some public gold, with the connivance of Pericles, for the embellishment of the statue of Minerva.
6. Ibid.
7. Worn by the popes.
8. Madame de Maintenon.
9. Duchess of Marlborough.
10. Madame de Pompadour.
11. The League of Cambray, comprehending the Emperor, the King of France, the King of Aragon, and most of the Italian princes and states.
12. The Duke of Marlborough.
13. *Vide Principes des Négociations* par l'Abbé de Mably.
14. Gabriel Bonnet de Mably (1709–85) was a French historian and writer on international law. [Ed.]

Introduction to *Democracy in America*

Alexis de Tocqueville, a young French aristocrat born in 1805, traveled in America during the year 1831, and three years later finished writing the first part of his report, Democracy in America.

Tocqueville believed that Providence itself had arranged that this new experiment in democracy should first be launched under the favorable conditions of the United States, and gradually sweep back upon Europe (and eventually the whole world). This new form of government, he believed, was so suited to the nature of humans and to the needs of the times that Europeans—and especially Frenchmen—had best begin preparing themselves for it.

In the passages selected below, we have drawn special attention to points of philosophical and theological interest often overlooked in discussions of the democratic experiment. Indeed, since "democracy" means majority rule, and since the form of American government is by way of representatives, who are in some measure insulated from direct pressures by the people, the form of government established in the United States is more accurately described as a "republic" than as a democracy. Since the American system mixes the democratic with the republican principle in interesting ways, the term "democratic republic" is also used.

Tocqueville is a profound student of the practical reality of democracy. He understands that state despotism and selfish passions are constant threats to freedom. In this light, he analyzes the novel "moral ecology" that sustains the existence of democracy.

In the chapters of volume 1 selected below, Tocqueville identified the emerging modern trait of individualism, as opposed to egoism (chapters 2 and 3).

Americans combat individualism through many means. One way is by associations (chapters 4 and 5). Tocqueville considers the habit of forming associations of such importance that he calls it "the first law of democracy."

313

Another way is through the doctrine of self-interest properly understood (chapter 8). Note carefully his distinction between self-interest wrongly understood and self-interest properly understood.

Finally, Tocqueville perceives a new and dangerous form of despotism, whose origins lie in loving equality more than liberty (chapter 6).

Democracy in America

Alexis de Tocqueville

CHAPTER 2
OF INDIVIDUALISM IN DEMOCRACIES

I have shown how, in ages of equality, every man finds his beliefs within himself, and I shall now go on to show that all his feelings are turned in on himself.

"Individualism" is a word recently coined to express a new idea. Our fathers only knew about egoism.

Egoism is a passionate and exaggerated love of self which leads a man to think of all things in terms of himself and to prefer himself to all.

Individualism is a calm and considered feeling which disposes each citizen to isolate himself from the mass of his fellows and withdraw into the circle of family and friends; with this little society formed to his taste, he gladly leaves the greater society to look after itself.

Egoism springs from a blind instinct; individualism is based on misguided judgment rather than depraved feeling. It is due more to inadequate understanding than to perversity of heart.

Egoism sterilizes the seeds of every virtue; individualism at first only dams the spring of public virtues, but in the long run it attacks and destroys all the others too and finally merges in egoism.

Egoism is a vice as old as the world. It is not peculiar to one form of society more than another.

Individualism is of democratic origin and threatens to grow as conditions get more equal.

Among aristocratic nations families maintain the same station for centuries and often live in the same place. So there is a sense in which all the generations are contemporaneous. A man almost always knows about his ancestors and respects them; his imagination extends to his great-grandchildren, and he loves them. He freely does his duty by both ancestors and descendants and often sacrifices personal pleasures for the sake of beings who are no longer alive or are not yet born.

Moreover, aristocratic institutions have the effect of linking each man closely with several of his fellows.

Each class in an aristocratic society, being clearly and permanently limited, forms, in a sense, a little fatherland for all its members, to which they are attached by more obvious and more precious ties than those linking them to the fatherland itself.

Each citizen of an aristocratic society has his fixed station, one above another, so that there is always someone above him whose protection he needs and someone below him whose help he may require.

So people living in an aristocratic age are almost always closely involved with something outside themselves, and they are often inclined to forget about themselves. It is true that in these ages the general conception of *human fellowship* is dim and that men hardly ever think of devoting themselves to the cause of humanity, but men do often make sacrifices for the sake of certain other men.

In democratic ages, on the contrary, the duties of each to all are much clearer but devoted service to any individual much rarer. The bonds of human affection are wider but more relaxed.

Among democratic peoples new families continually rise from nothing while others fall, and nobody's position is quite stable. The woof of time is ever being broken and the track of past generations lost. Those who have gone before are easily forgotten, and no one gives a thought to those who will follow. All a man's interests are limited to those near himself.

As each class catches up with the next and gets mixed with it, its members do not care about one another and treat one another as strangers. Aristocracy links everybody, from peasant to king, in one long chain. Democracy breaks the chain and frees each link.

As social equality spreads there are more and more people who, though neither rich nor powerful enough to have much hold over others, have gained or kept enough wealth and enough understanding to look after their own needs. Such folk owe no man anything and hardly expect anything from anybody. They form the habit of thinking of themselves in isolation and imagine that their whole destiny is in their own hands.

Thus, not only does democracy make men forget their ancestors, but also clouds their view of their descendants and isolates them from their contemporaries. Each man is forever thrown back on himself alone, and there is danger that he may be shut up in the solitude of his own heart.

CHAPTER 3
HOW INDIVIDUALISM IS MORE PRONOUNCED AT THE END OF A DEMOCRATIC REVOLUTION THAN AT ANY OTHER TIME

It is just at the moment when a democratic society is establishing itself on the ruins of an aristocracy that this isolation of each man from the rest and the egoism resulting therefrom stand out clearest.

Not only are there many independent people in such a society, but their number is constantly increasing with more and more of those who have just attained independence and are drunk with their new power. These latter have a presumptuous confidence in their strength, and never imagining that they could ever need another's help again, they have no inhibition about showing that they care for nobody but themselves.

There is usually a prolonged struggle before an aristocracy gives way, and in the course of that struggle implacable hatreds have been engendered between the classes. Such passions last after victory, and one can see traces of them in the ensuing democratic confusion.

Those who once held the highest ranks in the subverted hierarchy cannot forget their ancient greatness at once and for a long time feel themselves strangers in the new society. They regard all those whom society now makes their equals as oppressors whose fate could not concern them; they have lost sight of their former equals and no longer feel tied by common interests to their lot; each of them, in his separate retreat, feels reduced to taking care of himself alone. But those formerly at the bottom of the social scale and now brought up to the common level by a sudden revolution cannot enjoy their newfound independence without some secret uneasiness: there is a look of fear mixed with triumph in their eyes if they do meet one of their former superiors, and they avoid them.

Therefore it is usually at the time when democratic societies are taking root that men are most disposed to isolate themselves.

There is a tendency in democracy not to draw men together, but democratic revolutions make them run away from each other and perpetuate, in the midst of equality, hatreds originating in inequality.

The Americans have this great advantage, that they attained democracy without the sufferings of a democratic revolution and that they were born equal instead of becoming so.

CHAPTER 4
HOW THE AMERICANS COMBAT THE EFFECTS OF INDIVIDUALISM BY FREE INSTITUTIONS

Despotism, by its very nature suspicious, sees the isolation of men as the best guarantee of its own permanence. So it usually does all it can to isolate them. Of all the vices of the human heart egoism is that which suits it best. A despot will lightly forgive his subjects for not loving him, provided they do not love one another. He does not ask them to help him guide the state; it is enough if they do not claim to manage it themselves. He calls those who try to unite their efforts to create a general prosperity "turbulent and restless spirits", and twisting the natural meaning of words, he calls those "good citizens" who care for none but themselves.

Thus vices originating in despotism are precisely those favored by equality. The two opposites fatally complete and support each other.

Equality puts men side by side without a common link to hold them firm. Despotism raises barriers to keep them apart. It disposes them not to think of their fellows and turns indifference into a sort of public virtue.

Despotism, dangerous at all times, is therefore particularly to be feared in ages of democracy.

It is easy to see that in such ages men have a peculiar need for freedom.

Citizens who are bound to take part in public affairs must turn from the private interests and occasionally take a look at something other than themselves.

As soon as common affairs are treated in common, each man notices that he is not as independent of his fellows as he used to suppose and that to get their help he must often offer his aid to them.

When the public governs, all men feel the value of public goodwill and all try to win it by gaining the esteem and affection of those among whom they must live.

Those frigid passions that keep hearts asunder must then retreat and hide at the back of consciousness. Pride must be disguised; contempt must not be seen. Egoism is afraid of itself.

Under a free government most public officials are elected, so men whose great gifts and aspirations are too closely circumscribed in private life daily feel that they cannot do without the people around them.

It thus happens that ambition makes a man care for his fellows, and, in a sense, he often finds his self-interest in forgetting about himself. I know that one can point to all the intrigues caused by an election, the dishonorable means often used by candidates, and the calumnies spread by their enemies. These do give rise to feelings of hatred, and the more frequent the elections, the worse they are.

Those are great ills, no doubt, but passing ones, whereas the benefits that attend them remain.

Eagerness to be elected may, for the moment, make particular men fight each other, but in the long run this same aspiration induces mutual helpfulness on the part of all; and while it may happen that the accident of an election estranges two friends, the electoral system forges permanent links between a great number of citizens who might otherwise have remained forever strangers to one another. Liberty engenders particular hatreds, but despotism is responsible for general indifference.

The Americans have used liberty to combat the individualism born of equality, and they have won.

The lawgivers of America did not suppose that a general representation of the whole nation would suffice to ward off a disorder at once so natural to the body social of a democracy and so fatal. *They thought is also right to give each part of the land its own political life so that there should be an infinite number of occasions for the citizens to act together and so that every day they should feel that they depended on one another.*

That was wise conduct.

The general business of a country keeps only the leading citizens occupied. It is only occasionally that they come together in the same places, and since they often lose sight of one another, no lasting bonds form between them. But when the people who live there have to look after the particular affairs of a district, the same people are always meeting, and they are forced, in a manner, to know and adapt themselves to one another.

It is difficult to force a man out of himself and get him to take an interest in the affairs of the whole state, for he has little understanding of the way in which the fate of the state can influence his own lot. *But if it is a question of taking a road past his property, he sees at once that this small public matter has a bearing on his greatest private interests, and there is no need to point out to him the close connection between his private profit and the general interest.*

Thus, far more may be done by entrusting citizens with the management of minor affairs than by handing over control of great matters, toward interesting them in the public welfare and convincing them that they constantly stand in need of one another in order to provide for it.

Some brilliant achievement may win a people's favor at one stroke. But to gain the affection and respect of your immediate neighbors, a long succession of little services rendered and of obscure good deeds, a constant habit of kindness and an established reputation for disinterestedness, are required.

Local liberties, then, which induce a great number of citizens to value the affection of their kindred and neighbors, bring men constantly into contact, despite the instincts which separate them, and force them to help one another.

In the United States the most opulent citizens are at pains not to get isolated from the people. On the contrary, they keep in constant contact, gladly listen and themselves talk any and every day. They know that the rich in democracies always need the poor and that good manners will draw them to them more than benefits conferred. For benefits by their very greatness spotlight the difference in conditions and arouse a secret annoyance in those who profit from them. But the charm of simple good manners is almost irresistible. Their affability carries men away, and even their vulgarity is not always unpleasant.

The rich do not immediately appreciate this truth. They generally stand out against it as long as a democratic revolution is in progress and do not admit it at once even after the revolution is accomplished. They will gladly do good to the people, but they still want carefully to keep their distance from them. They think that this is enough, but they are wrong. They could ruin themselves in that fashion without warming their neighbors' hearts. What is wanted is not the sacrifice of their money but of their pride.

It would seem as if in the United States every man's power of invention was on the stretch to find new ways of increasing the wealth and satisfying the needs of the public. The best brains in every neighborhood are constantly employed in searching for new secrets to increase the general property, and any that they find are at once at the service of the crowd.

If one takes a close look at the weaknesses and vices of many of those who bear sway in America, one is surprised at the growing prosperity of the people, but it is a mistake to be surprised. It is certainly not the elected magistrate who makes the American democracy prosper, but the fact that the magistrates are elected.

It would not be fair to assume that American patriotism and the universal zeal for the common good have no solid basis. Though private interest, in the United States as elsewhere, is the driving force behind most of men's actions, it does not regulate them all.

I have often seen Americans make really great sacrifices for the common good, and I have noticed a hundred cases in which, when help was needed, they hardly ever failed to give each other trusty support.

The free institutions of the United States and the political rights enjoyed there provide a thousand continual reminders to every citizen that he lives in society. At every moment they bring his mind back to this idea, that it is the duty as well as the interest of men to be useful to their fellows. Having no particular reason to hate others, since he is neither their slave nor their master, the American's heart easily inclines toward benevolence. At first it is of necessity that men attend to the public interest, afterward by choice. What had been calculation becomes instinct. By dint of working for the good of his fellow citizens, he in the end acquires a habit and taste for serving them.

There are many men in France who regard equality of conditions as the first of evils and political liberty as the second. When forced to submit to the former, they strive at least to escape the latter. But for my part, I maintain that there is only one effective remedy against the evils which equality may cause, and that is political liberty.

CHAPTER 5
ON THE USE WHICH THE AMERICANS MAKE OF ASSOCIATIONS IN CIVIL LIFE

I do not propose to speak of those political associations by means of which men seek to defend themselves against the despotic action of the majority or the encroachments of royal power. I have treated that subject elsewhere. It is clear that unless each citizen learned to combine with his fellows to preserve his freedom at a time when he individually is becoming weaker and so less able in isolation to defend it, tyranny would be bound to increase with equality. *But here I am only concerned with those associations in civil life which have no political object.*

In the United States, political associations are only one small part of the immense number of different types of associations found there.

Americans of all ages, all stations in life, and all types of disposition are forever forming associations. There are not only commercial and industrial associations in which all take part, but others of a thousand different types—religious, moral, serious, futile, very general and very limited, immensely large and very minute. Americans combine to give fêtes, found seminaries, build churches, distribute books, and send missionaries to the antipodes. Hospitals, prisons, and schools take shape in that way. Finally, if they want to proclaim a truth or propagate some feeling by the encouragement of a great example, they form an association. In every case, at the head of any new undertaking, where in France you would find the government or in England some territorial magnate, in the United States you are sure to find an association.

I have come across several types of association in America of which, I confess, I had not previously the slightest conception, and I have often admired the extreme skill they show in proposing a common object for the exertions of very many and in inducing them voluntarily to pursue it.

Since that time I have traveled in England, a country from which the Americans took some of their laws and many of their customs, but it seemed to me that the principle of association was not used nearly so constantly or so adroitly there.[1]

A single Englishman will often carry through some great undertaking, whereas Americans form associations for no matter how small a matter. Clearly the former regard association as a powerful means of action, but the latter seem to think of it as the only one.

Thus the most democratic country in the world now is that in which men have in our time carried to the highest perfection the art of pursuing in common the objects of common desires and have applied this new technique to the greatest number of purposes. Is that just an accident, or is there really some necessary connection between associations and equality?

In aristocratic societies, while there is a multitude of individuals who can do nothing on their own, there is also a small number of very rich and powerful men, each of whom can carry out great undertakings on his own.

In aristocratic societies men have no need to unite for action, since they are held firmly together.

Every rich and powerful citizen is in practice the head of a permanent and enforced association composed of all those whom he makes help in the execution of his designs.

But among democratic peoples all the citizens are independent and weak. They can do hardly anything for themselves, and none of them is in a position to force his fellows to help him. They would all therefore find themselves helpless if they did not learn to help each other voluntarily.

If the inhabitants of democratic countries had neither the right nor the taste for uniting for political objects, their independence would run great risks, but they could keep both their wealth and their knowledge for a long time. But if they did not learn some habits of acting together in the affairs of daily life, civilization itself would be in peril. A people in which individuals had lost the power of carrying through great enterprises by themselves, without acquiring the faculty of doing them together, would soon fall back into barbarism.

Unhappily, the same social conditions that render associations so necessary to democratic nations also make their formation more difficult there than elsewhere.

When several aristocrats want to form an association, they can easily do so. As each of them carries great weight in society, a very small number of associates may be enough. So, being few, it is easy to get to know and understand one another and agree on rules.

But that is not so easy in democratic nations, where, if the association is to have any power, the associates must be very numerous.

I know that many of my contemporaries are not the least embarrassed by this difficulty. They claim that as the citizens become weaker and more helpless, the government must become proportionately more skillful and active, so that society should do what is no longer possible for individuals. They think that answers the whole problem, but I think they are mistaken.

A government could take the place of some of the largest associations in America, and some particular states of the Union have already attempted that. But what political power could ever carry on the vast multitude of lesser undertakings which associations daily enable American citizens to control?

It is easy to see the time coming in which men will be less and less able to produce, by each alone, the commonest bare necessities of life. The tasks of government must therefore perpetually increase, and its efforts to cope with them must spread its net ever wider. *The more government takes the place of associations, the more will individuals lose the idea of forming associations and need the government to come to their help. That is a vicious circle of cause and effect.* Must the public administration cope with every industrial undertaking beyond the competence of one individual citizen? And if ultimately, as a result of the minute subdivision of landed property, the land itself is so infinitely parceled out that it can only be cultivated by associations of laborers, must the head of the government leave the helm of state to guide the plow?

The morals and intelligence of a democratic people would be in as much danger as its commerce and industry if ever a government wholly usurped the place of private associations.

Feelings and ideas are renewed, the heart enlarged, and the understanding developed only by the reciprocal action of men one upon another.

I have shown how these influences are reduced almost to nothing in democratic countries; they must therefore be artificially created, and only association can do that.

When aristocrats adopt a new idea or conceive a new sentiment, they lend it something of the conspicuous station they themselves occupy, and so the mass is bound to take notice of them, and they easily influence the minds and hearts of all around.

In democratic countries only the governing power is naturally in a position so to act, but it is easy to see that its action is always inadequate and often dangerous.

A government, by itself, is equally incapable of refreshing the circulation of feelings and ideas among a great people, as it is of controlling every industrial undertaking. Once it leaves the sphere of politics to launch out on this new track, it will, even without intending this, exercise an intolerable tyranny. For a government can only dictate precise rules. It imposes the sentiments and ideas which it favors, and it is never easy to tell the difference between its advice and its commands.

Things will be even worse if the government supposes that its real interest is to prevent the circulation of ideas. It will then stand motionless and let the weight of its deliberate somnolence lie heavy on all.

It is therefore necessary that it should not act alone.

Among democratic peoples associations must take the place of the powerful private persons whom equality of conditions has eliminated.

As soon as several Americans have conceived a sentiment or an idea that they want to produce before the world, they seek each other out, and when found, they unite. Thenceforth they are no longer isolated individuals, but a power conspicuous from the distance whose actions serve as an example; when it speaks, men listen.

The first time that I heard in America that one hundred thousand men had publicly promised never to drink alcoholic liquor, I thought it more of a joke than a serious matter and for the moment did not see why these very abstemious citizens could not content themselves with drinking water by their own firesides.

In the end I came to understand that these hundred thousand Americans, frightened by the progress of drunkenness around them, wanted to support sobriety by their patronage. They were acting in just the same way as some great territorial magnate who dresses very plainly to encourage a contempt of luxury among simple citizens. One may fancy that if they had lived in France each of these hundred thousand would have made individual representations to the government asking it to supervise all the public houses throughout the realm.

Nothing, in my view, more deserves attention than the intellectual and moral associations in America. American political and industrial associations easily catch our eyes, but the others tend not to be noticed. And even if we do notice them we tend to misunderstand them, hardly ever having seen anything similar before. However, we should recognize that the latter are as necessary as the former to the American people; perhaps more so.

In democratic countries knowledge of how to combine is the mother of all other forms of knowledge; on its progress depends that of all the others.

Among laws controlling human societies there is one more precise and clearer, it seems to me, than all the others. If men are to remain civilized or to become civilized, the art of association must develop and improve among them at the same speed as equality of conditions spreads.

CHAPTER 8
HOW THE AMERICANS COMBAT INDIVIDUALISM BY THE DOCTRINE OF SELF-INTEREST PROPERLY UNDERSTOOD

When the world was under the control of a few rich and powerful men, they liked to entertain a sublime conception of the duties of man. It gratified them to make out that it is a glorious thing to forget oneself and that one should do good without self-interest, as God himself does. That was the official doctrine of morality at that time.

I doubt whether men were better in times of aristocracy than at other times, but certainly they talked continually about the beauties of virtue. Only in secret did they study its utility. But since imagination has been taking less lofty flights, and every man's thoughts are centered on himself, moralists take fright at this idea of sacrifice and no longer venture to suggest it for consideration. So they are reduced to inquiring whether it is not to the individual advantage of each to work for the good of all, and when they have found one of those points where private advantage does meet and coincide with the general interest, they eagerly call attention thereto. Thus what was an isolated observation becomes a general doctrine, and in the end one comes to believe that one sees that by serving his fellows man serves himself and that doing good is to his private advantage.

I have already shown elsewhere in several places in this book how the inhabitants of the United States almost always know how to combine their own advantage with that of their fellow citizens. What I want to point out now is the general theory which helps them to this result.

In the United States there is hardly any talk of the beauty of virtue. But they maintain that virtue is useful and prove it every day. American moralists do not pretend that one must sacrifice himself for his fellows because it is a fine thing to do so. But they boldly assert that such sacrifice is as necessary for the man who makes it as for the beneficiaries.

They have seen that in their time and place the forces driving man in on himself are irresistible, and despairing of holding such forces back, they only consider how to control them.

They therefore do not raise objections to men pursuing their interests, but they do all they can to prove that it is in each man's interest to be good.

I do not want to follow their arguments in detail here, as that would lead too far from my subject. It is enough for my purpose to note that they have convinced their fellow citizens.

Montaigne said long ago: "If I did not follow the straight road for the sake of its straightness, I should follow it having found by experience that all things considered, it is the happiest and the most convenient."

So the doctrine of self-interest properly understood is not new, but it is among the Americans of our time that it has come to be universally accepted. It has become popular. One finds it at the root of all actions. It is interwoven in all they say. You hear it as much from the poor as from the rich.

The version of this doctrine current in Europe is much grosser but at the same time less widespread and, especially, less advertised. Every day men profess a zeal they no longer feel.

The Americans, on the other hand, enjoy explaining almost every act of their lives on the principle of self-interest properly understood. It gives them pleasure to point out how an enlightened self-love continually leads them to help one another and disposes them freely to give part of their time and wealth for the good of the state. I think that in this they often do themselves less than justice, for sometimes in the United States, as elsewhere, one sees people carried away by the disinterested, spontaneous impulses natural to man. But the Americans are hardly prepared to admit that they do give way to emotions of this sort. They prefer to give the credit to their philosophy rather than to themselves.

I might drop the argument at this point without attempting to pass judgment on what I have described. The extreme difficulty of the subject would be my excuse. But I do not want to plead that. I would rather that my readers, seeing clearly what I mean, refuse to agree with me than that I should leave them in suspense.

Self-interest properly understood is not at all a sublime doctrine, but it is clear and definite. It does not attempt to reach great aims, but it does, without too much trouble, achieve all it sets out to do. Being within the scope of everybody's understanding, everyone grasps it and has no trouble in bearing it in mind. It is wonderfully agreeable to human weaknesses, and so easily wins great sway. It has no difficulty in keeping its power, for it turns private interest against itself and uses the same goad which excites them to direct passions.

The doctrine of self-interest properly understood does not inspire great sacrifices, but every day it prompts some small ones; by itself it cannot make a man virtuous, but its discipline shapes a lot of orderly, temperate, moderate, careful, and self-controlled citizens. If it does not lead the will directly to virtue, it establishes habits which unconsciously turn it that way.

If the doctrine of self-interest properly understood ever came to dominate all thought about morality, no doubt extraordinary virtues would be rarer. But I think that gross depravity would also be less common. Such teaching may stop some men from rising far above the common level of humanity, but many of those who fall below this standard grasp it and are restrained by it. Some individuals it lowers, but mankind it raises.

I am not afraid to say that the doctrine of self-interest properly understood appears to me the best suited of all philosophical theories to the wants of men in our time and that I see it as their strongest remaining guarantee against themselves. Contemporary moralists therefore should give most of their attention to it. Though they may well think it incomplete, they must nonetheless adopt it as necessary.

I do not think, by and large, that there is more egoism among us than in America; the only difference is that there it is enlightened, while here it is not. Every American has the sense to sacrifice some of his private interests to save the rest. We want to keep, and often lose, the lot.

I see around nothing but people bent publicly on proving, by word and deed, that what is useful is never wrong. Is there no chance of finding some who will make the public understand that what is right may be useful?

No power on earth can prevent increasing equality from turning men's minds to look for the useful or disposing each citizen to get wrapped up in himself.

One must therefore expect that private interest will more than ever become the chief if not the only driving force behind all behavior. But we have yet to see how each man will interpret his private interest.

If citizens, attaining equality, were to remain ignorant and coarse, it would be difficult to foresee any limit to the stupid excesses into which their selfishness might lead them, and no one could foretell into what shameful troubles they might plunge themselves for fear of sacrificing some of their own well-being for the prosperity of their fellow men.

I do not think that the doctrine of self-interest as preached in America is in all respects self-evident. But it does contain many truths so clear that for men to see them it is enough to educate them. Hence it is all-important for them to be educated, for the age of blind sacrifice and instinctive virtues is already long past, and I see a time approaching in which freedom, public peace, and social stability will not be able to last without education.

CHAPTER 6
WHAT SORT OF DESPOTISM DEMOCRATIC NATIONS HAVE TO FEAR

I noticed during my stay in the United States that a democratic state of society similar to that found there could lay itself peculiarly open to the establishment of a despotism. And on my return to Europe I saw how far most of our princes had made use of the ideas, feelings, and needs engendered by such a state of society to enlarge the sphere of their power.

I was thus led to think that the nations of Christendom might perhaps in the end fall victims to the same sort of oppression as formerly lay heavy on several of the peoples of antiquity.

More detailed study of the subject and the new ideas which came into my mind during five years of meditation have not lessened my fears but have changed their object.

In past ages there had never been a sovereign so absolute and so powerful that he could by himself alone, without the aid of secondary powers, undertake to administer every part of a great empire. No one had ever tried to subject all his people indiscriminately to the details of a uniform code, nor personally to prompt and lead every single one of his subjects. It had never occurred to the mind of man to embark on such an undertaking, and had it done so, inadequate education, imperfect administrative machinery, and above all the natural obstacles raised by unequal conditions would soon have put a stop to so grandiose a design.

When the power of the Roman emperors was at its height, the different peoples of the empire still preserved very various customs and mores. Although they obeyed the same monarch, most provinces had a separate administration. There were powerful and active municipalities in profusion, and though the whole government of the empire was concentrated in the hands of the emperor alone and he could, if necessary, decide everything, yet the details of social life and personal everyday existence normally escaped his control.

It is true that the emperors had immense and unchecked power, so that they could use the whole might of the empire to indulge any strange caprice. They often abused this power to deprive a man arbitrarily of life or property. The burden of their tyranny fell most heavily on some, but it never spread over a great number. It had a few main targets and left the rest alone. It was violent, but its extent was limited.

But if a despotism should be established among the democratic nations of our day, it would probably have a different character. It would be more widespread and milder; it would degrade men rather than torment them.

Doubtless, in such an age of education and equality as our own, rulers could more easily bring all public powers into their own hands alone, and they could impinge deeper and more habitually into the sphere of private interests than was ever possible in antiquity. But that same equality which makes despotism easy tempers it. We have seen how, as men become more alike and more nearly equal, public mores becomes more humane and gentle. When there is no citizen with great power or wealth, tyranny in some degree lacks both target and stage. When all fortunes are middling, passions are naturally restrained, imagination limited, and pleasures simple. Such universal moderation tempers the sovereign's own spirit and keeps within certain limits the disorderly urges of desire.

Apart from these reasons, based on the nature of the state of society itself, I could adduce many others which would take me outside the range of my subject, but I prefer to remain within these self-imposed limits.

Democratic governments might become violent and cruel at times of great excitement and danger, but such crises will be rare and brief.

Taking into consideration the trivial nature of men's passions now, the softness of their mores, the extent of their education, the purity of their religion, their steady habits of patient work, and the restraint which they all show in the indulgence of both their vices and their virtues, I do not expect their leaders to be tyrants, but rather schoolmasters.

Thus I think that the type of oppression which threatens democracies is different from anything there has ever been in the world before. Our contemporaries will find no prototype of it in their memories. I have myself vainly searched for a word which will exactly express the whole of the conception I have formed. Such old words as "despotism" and "tyranny" do not fit. The thing is new, and as I cannot find a word for it, I must try to define it.

I am trying to imagine under what novel features despotism may appear in the world. In the first place, I see an innumerable multitude of men, alike and equal, constantly circling around in pursuit of the petty and banal pleasures with which they glut their souls. Each one of them, withdrawn into himself, is almost unaware of the fate of the rest. Mankind, for him, consists in his children and his personal friends. As for the rest of his fellow citizens, they are near enough, but he does not notice them. He touches them but feels nothing. He exists in and for himself, and though he still may have a family, one can at least say that he has not got a fatherland.

Over this kind of men stands an immense, protective power which is alone responsible for securing their enjoyment and watching over their fate. That power is absolute, thoughtful of detail, orderly, provident, and gentle. It would resemble parental authority if, fatherlike, it tried to prepare its charges for a man's life, but on the contrary, it only tries to keep them in perpetual childhood. It likes to see the citizens enjoy themselves, provided that they think of nothing but enjoyment. It gladly works for their happiness but wants to be sole agent and judge of it. It provides for their security, foresees and supplies their necessities, facilitates their pleasures, manages their principal concerns, directs their industry, makes rules for their testaments, and divides their inheritances. Why should it not entirely relieve them from the trouble of thinking and all the cares of living?

Thus it daily makes the exercise of free choice less useful and rarer, restricts the activity of free will within a narrower compass, and little by little robs each citizen of the proper use of his own faculties. Equality has prepared men for all this, predisposing them to endure it and often even regard it as beneficial.

Having thus taken each citizen in turn in its powerful grasp and shaped him to its will, government then extends its embrace to include the whole of society. It covers the whole of social life with a network of petty, complicated rules that are both minute and uniform, through which even men of the greatest originality and the most vigorous temperament cannot force their heads above the crowd. It does not break men's will, but softens, bends, and guides it; it seldom enjoins, but often inhibits, action; it does not destroy anything, but prevents much being born; it is not at all tyrannical, but it hinders, restrains, enervates, stifles, and stultifies so much that in the end each nation is no more than a flock of timid and hardworking animals with the government as its shepherd.

I have always thought that this brand of orderly, gentle, peaceful slavery which I have just described could be combined, more easily than is generally supposed, with some of the external forms of freedom, and that there is a possibility of its getting itself established even under the shadow of the sovereignty of the people.

Our contemporaries are ever a prey to two conflicting passions: they feel the need of guidance, and they long to stay free. Unable to wipe out these two contradictory instincts, they try to satisfy them both together. *Their imagination conceives a government which is unitary, protective, and all-powerful, but elected by the people. Centralization is combined with the sovereignty of the people. That gives them a chance to relax. They console themselves for being under schoolmasters by thinking that they have chosen them themselves. Each individual lets them put the collar on, for he sees that it is not a person, or a class of persons, but society itself which holds the end of the chain.*

Under this system the citizens quit their state of dependence just long enough to choose their masters and then fall back into it.

A great many people nowadays very easily fall in with this brand of compromise between administrative despotism and the sovereignty of the people. They think they have done enough to guarantee personal freedom when it is to the government of the state that they have handed it over. That is not good enough for me. I am much less interested in the question who my master is than in the fact of obedience.

Nevertheless, I freely admit that such a constitution strikes me as infinitely preferable to one which, having brought all powers together, should then hand them over to one irresponsible man or body of men. Of all the forms that democratic despotism might take, that assuredly would be the worst.

When the sovereign is elected, or when he is closely supervised by a legislature which is in very truth elected and free, he may go to greater lengths in oppressing the individual citizen, but such oppression is always less degrading. For each man can still think, though he is obstructed and reduced to powerlessness, that his obedience is only to himself and that it is to one of his desires that he is sacrificing all the others.

I also appreciate that, when the sovereign represents the nation and is dependent on it, the powers and rights taken from each citizen are not used only for the benefit of the head of state, but for the state itself, and that private persons derive some advantage from the independence which they have handed over to the public.

To create a national representation of the people in a very centralized country does, therefore, diminish the extreme evils which centralization can produce but does not entirely abolish them.

I see clearly that by this means room is left for individual intervention in the most important affairs, but there is still no place for it in small or private matters. It is too often forgotten that it is especially dangerous to turn men into slaves where details only are concerned. For my part, I should be inclined to think that liberty is less necessary in great matters than in tiny ones if I imagined that one could ever be safe in the enjoyment of one sort of freedom without the other.

Subjection in petty affairs, is manifest daily and touches all citizens indiscriminately. It never drives men to despair, but continually thwarts them and leads them to give up using their free will. It slowly stifles their spirits and enervates their souls, whereas obedience demanded only occasionally in matters of great moment brings servitude into play only from time to time, and its weight falls only on certain people. It does little good to summon those very citizens who have been made so dependent on the central power to choose the representatives of that power from time to time. However important, this brief and occasional exercise of free will will not prevent them from gradually losing the faculty of thinking, feeling, and acting for themselves, so that they will slowly fall below the level of humanity.

I must add that they will soon become incapable of using the one great privilege left to them. Those democratic peoples which have introduced freedom into the sphere of politics, while allowing despotism to grow in the administrative sphere, have been led into the strangest paradoxes. For the conduct of small affairs, where plain common sense is enough, they hold that the citizens are not up to the job. But they give these citizens immense prerogatives where the government of the whole state is concerned. They are turned alternatively into the playthings of the sovereign and into his masters, being either greater than kings or less than men. When they have tried all the different systems of election without finding one to suit them, they look surprised and go on seeking for another, as if the ills they see did not belong much more to the constitution of the country itself than to that of the electoral body.

It really is difficult to imagine how people who have entirely given up managing their own affairs could make a wise choice of those who are to do that for them. One should never expect a liberal, energetic, and wise government to originate in the votes of a people of servants.

A constitution republican in its head and ultramonarchial in all its other parts has always struck me as an ephemeral monstrosity. The vices of those who govern and the weakness of the governed will soon bring it to ruin. Then the people, tired of its representatives and of itself, will either create freer institutions or soon fall back at the feet of a single master.

Introduction to *Centesimus Annus*

Modern papal social thought began with Leo XIII's Rerum Novarum *in 1891, whose hundredth anniversary John Paul II celebrated with* Centesimus Annus *in May 1991. This last is without question the greatest of the papal social encyclicals, for it not only sums up the lessons learned from a century of tumultuous human experience. It also reaches down to new philosophical depths in all three major realms of human liberty—political, economic, and moral/cultural.*

Read from a Catholic Whig perspective, the following important passages of Centesimus Annus *stand out; they also add new and original dimensions to Catholic social thought:*

> *The nature and development of Catholic social thought:*
> Introduction, section 3; Chapter I, sections 4–11.
> *The fatal flaws in Socialism: Chapter II, sections 13–15.*
> *The cause of the wealth of nations; human capital; the corporation:*
> Chapter IV, sections 31–32.
> *The limits of markets and faults in errant capitalism: Ibid., sections 33–38.*
> *The three liberties—economic, political, ethical/religious: Ibid., section 42.*
> *Serious flaws of the welfare state: Chapter V, section 48.*
> *Principles of the free polity: Ibid., sections 45–47.*
> *The cultural ecology of liberty: Ibid., sections 50–51.*

To a remarkable degree, Centesimus Annus *embodies insights about both human capital and the cause of wealth (IV. 32) usually attributed to the Austrian School of economics, in particular to Friedrich Hayek. In its emphasis on the central importance of human action and the acting subject, it calls to mind the work of Ludwig von Mises. The philosophical anthropology of Wojtyla is different from that of such Austrian thinkers.*

331

However, it may be significant that the phenomenological method, from which the Pope borrows so much, also had its origins in the same intellectual milieu in Vienna that stimulated Austrian economics.

Its political vision (V. 48ff) owes much to democratic experience of the American type, rather than to the intellectual currents of the French Revolution of 1789.

Its concepts of the cultural ecology of liberty is quite new and profound.

The weaving of all three of these strands—political, economic, and cultural—into one holistic vision is, perhaps, the encyclical's greatest accomplishment.

Centesimus Annus

John Paul II

ENCYCLICAL LETTER
CENTESIMUS ANNUS
ADDRESSED BY THE SUPREME PONTIFF
JOHN PAUL II
TO HIS VENERABLE BROTHERS
IN THE EPISCOPATE
THE PRIESTS AND DEACONS
FAMILIES OF MEN AND WOMEN RELIGIOUS
ALL THE CHRISTIAN FAITHFUL
AND TO ALL MEN AND WOMEN OF GOOD WILL
ON THE HUNDREDTH ANNIVERSARY
OF RERUM NOVARUM

Venerable Brothers,
Beloved Sons and Daughters,
Health and the Apostolic Blessing!

INTRODUCTION

1.1 The centenary of the promulgation of the Encyclical which begins with the words "*Rerum Novarum*,"[1] by my Predecessor of venerable memory Pope Leo XIII, is an occasion of great importance for the present history of the Church and for my own Pontificate. It is an Encyclical that has the distinction of having been commemorated by solemn papal documents from its fortieth anniversary to its ninetieth. It may be said that its path through history has been marked by other documents which paid tribute to it and applied it to the circumstances of the day.[2]

1.2 In doing likewise for the hundredth anniversary, in response to requests from many Bishops, Church institutions, and study centers, as well as business leaders and workers, both individually and as members of associations, I wish first and foremost to satisfy the debt of gratitude which the whole Church owes to this great Pope and his "immortal document."[3] I also mean to show that the vital energies rising from that root have not been spent with the passing of the years, but rather have increased even more. This is evident from the various initiatives which have preceded, and which are to accompany and follow the celebration, initiatives promoted by Episcopal Conferences, by international agencies, universities and academic institutes, by professional associations and by other institutions and individuals in many parts of the world.

2.1 The present Encyclical is part of these celebrations, which are meant to thank God—the origin of "every good endowment and every perfect gift" (Jas 1:17)—for having used a document published a century ago by the See of Peter to achieve so much good and to radiate so much light in the Church and in the world. Although the commemoration at hand is meant to honor *Rerum Novarum*, it also honors those Encyclicals and other documents of my Predecessors which have helped to make Pope Leo's Encyclical present and alive in history, thus constituting what would come to be called the Church's "social doctrine," "social teaching" or even "social Magisterium."

2.2 The validity of this teaching has already been pointed out in two Encyclicals published during my Pontificate: *Laborem Exercens* on human work, and *Sollicitudo Rei Socialis* on current problems regarding the development of individuals and peoples.[4]

3.1 I now wish to propose a "rereading" of Pope Leo's Encyclical by issuing an invitation to "look back" at the text itself in order to discover anew the richness of the fundamental principles which it formulated for dealing with the question of the condition of workers. But this is also an invitation to "look around" at the "new things" which surround us and in which we find ourselves caught up, very different from the "new things" which characterized the final decade of the last century. Finally, it is an invitation to "look to the future" at a time when we can already glimpse the third millennium of the Christian era, so filled with uncertainties but also with promises—uncertainties and promises which appeal to our imagination and creativity, and which awaken our responsibility, as disciples of the "one teacher" (cf. Mt 23:8), to show the way, to proclaim the truth and to communicate the life which is Christ (cf. Jn 14:6).

3.2 A rereading of this kind will not only confirm the permanent value of such teaching, but will also manifest the true meaning of the Church's Tradition which, being ever living and vital, builds upon the foundation laid by our fathers in the faith, and particularly upon what "the Apostles passed down to the Church"[5] in the name of Jesus Christ, who is her irreplaceable foundation (cf. 1 Cor 3:11).

3.3 It was out of an awareness of his mission as the Successor of Peter that Pope Leo XIII proposed to speak out, and Peter's Successor today is moved by that same awareness. Like Pope Leo and the Popes before and after him, I take my inspiration from the Gospel image of "the scribe who has been trained for the Kingdom of heaven," whom the Lord compares to "a householder who brings out of his treasure what is new and what is old" (Mt 13:52). The treasure is the great outpouring of the Church's Tradition, which contains "what is old"—received and passed on from the very beginning—and which enables us to interpret the "new things" in the midst of which the life of the Church and the world unfolds.

3.4 Among the things which become "old" as a result of being incorporated into Tradition, and which offer opportunities and material for enriching both Tradition and the life of faith, there is the fruitful activity of many millions of people, who, spurred on by the social Magisterium, have sought to make that teaching the inspiration for their involvement in the world. Acting either as individuals or joined together in various groups, associations and organizations, these people represent a great movement for the defense of the human person and the safeguarding of human dignity. Amid changing historical circumstances, this movement has contributed to the building up of a more just society or at least to the curbing of injustice.

3.5 The present Encyclical seeks to show the fruitfulness of the principles enunciated by Leo XIII, which belong to the Church's doctrinal patrimony and, as such, involve the exercise of her teaching authority. But pastoral solicitude also prompts me to propose an analysis of some events of recent history. It goes without saying that part of the responsibility of Pastors is to give careful consideration to current events in order to discern the new requirements of evangelization. However, such an analysis is not meant to pass definitive judgments, since this does not fall per se within the Magisterium's specific domain.

I
CHARACTERISTICS OF RERUM NOVARUM

4.1 Toward the end of the last century the Church found herself facing an historical process which had already been taking place for some time, but which was by then reaching a critical point. The determining factor in this process was a combination of radical changes which had taken place in the political, economic and social fields, and in the areas of science and technology, to say nothing of the wide influence of the prevailing ideologies. In the sphere of politics, the result of these changes was a new conception of society and of the State, and consequently of authority itself. A traditional society was passing away and another was beginning to be formed—one which brought the hope of new freedoms but also the threat of new forms of injustice and servitude.

4.2 In the sphere of economics, in which scientific discoveries and their practical application come together, new structures for the production of consumer goods had progressively taken shape. A new form of property had appeared—capital; and a new form of labor—labor for wages, characterized by high rates of production which lacked due regard for sex, age or family situation, and were determined solely by efficiency, with a view to increasing profits.

4.3 In this way labor became a commodity to be freely bought and sold on the market, its price determined by the law of supply and demand, without taking into account the bare minimum required for the support of the individual and his family. Moreover, the worker was not even sure of being able to sell "his own commodity," continually threatened as he was by unemployment, which, in the absence of any kind of social security, meant the specter of death by starvation.

4.4 The result of this transformation was a society "divided into two classes, separated by a deep chasm."[6] This situation was linked to the marked change taking place in the political order already mentioned. Thus the prevailing political theory of the time sought to promote total economic freedom by appropriate laws, or, conversely, by a deliberate lack of any intervention. At the same time, another conception of property and economic life was beginning to appear in an organized and often violent form, one which implied a new political and social structure.

4.5 At the height of this clash, when people finally began to realize fully the very grave injustice of social realities in many places and the danger of a revolution fanned by ideals which were then called "socialist," Pope Leo XIII intervened with a document which dealt in a systematic way with the "condition of the workers." The Encyclical had been preceded by others devoted to teachings of a political character; still others would appear later.[7] Here, particular mention must be made to the Encyclical *Libertas Praestantissimum*, which called attention to the essential bond between human freedom and truth, so that freedom which refused to be bound to the truth would fall into arbitrariness and end up submitting itself to the vilest of passions, to the point of self-destruction. Indeed, what is the origin of all the evils to which *Rerum Novarum* wished to respond, if not a kind of freedom which, in the area of economic and social activity, cuts itself off from the truth about man?

4.6 The Pope also drew inspiration from the teaching of his Predecessors, as well as from the many documents issued by Bishops, from scientific studies promoted by members of the laity, from the work of Catholic movements and associations, and from the Church's practical achievements in the social field during the second half of the nineteenth century.

5.1 The "new things" to which the Pope devoted his attention were anything but positive. The first paragraph of the Encyclical describes in strong terms the "new things" (rerum novarum) which gave it its name: "That the spirit of revolutionary change which has long been disturbing the nations of the world should have passed beyond the sphere of politics and made its influence felt in the related sphere of practical economics is not surprising. Progress in industry, the development of new trades, the changing relationship between employers and workers, the enormous wealth of a few as opposed to the poverty of the many, the increasing self-reliance of the workers and their closer association with each other, as well as a notable decline in morality: all these elements have led to the conflict now taking place."[8]

5.2 The Pope and the Church with him were confronted, as was the civil community, by a society which was torn by a conflict all the more harsh and inhumane because it knew no rule or regulation. It was the conflict between capital and labor, or—as the Encyclical puts it—the worker question. It is precisely about this conflict, in the very pointed terms in which it then appeared, that the Pope did not hesitate to speak.

5.3 Here we find the first reflection for our times as suggested by the Encyclical. In the face of a conflict which set man against man, almost as if they were "wolves," a conflict between the extremes of mere physical survival on the one side and opulence on the other, the Pope did not hesitate to intervene by virtue of his "apostolic office,"[9] that is, on the basis of the mission received from Jesus Christ himself to "feed his lambs and tend his sheep" (cf. Jn 21:15–17), and to "bind and loose" on earth for the Kingdom of heaven (cf. Mt 16:19). The Pope's intention was certainly to restore peace, and the present-day reader cannot fail to note his severe condemnation, in no uncertain terms, of the class struggle.[10] However, the Pope was very much aware that peace is built on the foundation of justice: what was essential to the Encyclical was precisely its proclamation of the fundamental conditions for justice in the economic and social situation of the time.[11]

5.4 In this way, Pope Leo XIII, in the footsteps of his Predecessors, created a lasting paradigm for the Church. The Church, in fact, has something to say about specific human situations, both individual and communal, national and international. She formulates a genuine doctrine for these situations, a corpus which enables her to analyze social realities, to make judgments about them and to indicate directions to be taken for the just resolution of the problems involved.

5.5 In Pope Leo XIII's time such a concept of the Church's right and duty was far from being commonly admitted. Indeed, a twofold approach prevailed: one directed to this world and this life, to which faith ought to remain extraneous; the other directed toward a purely other-worldly salvation, which neither enlightens nor directs existence on earth. The Pope's approach in publishing *Rerum Novarum* gave the Church "citizenship status" as it were, amid the changing realities of public life, and this standing would be more fully confirmed later on. In effect, to teach and to spread her social doctrine pertains to the Church's evangelizing mission and is an essential part of the Christian message, since this doctrine points out the direct consequences of that message in the life of society and situates daily work and struggles for justice in the context of being witness to Christ the Savior. This doctrine is likewise a source of unity and peace in dealing with the conflicts which inevitably arise in social and economic life. Thus it is possible to meet these new situations without degrading the human person's transcendent dignity, either in oneself or in one's adversaries, and to direct those situations toward just solutions.

5.6 Today, at a distance of a hundred years, the validity of this approach affords me the opportunity to contribute to the development of Christian social doctrine. The "new evangelization," which the modern world urgently needs and which I have emphasized many times, must include among its essential elements a proclamation of the Church's social doctrine. As in the days of Pope Leo XIII, this doctrine is still suitable for indicating the right way to respond to the great challenges of today, when ideologies are being increasingly discredited. Now, as then, we need to repeat that there can be no genuine solution of the "social question" apart from the Gospel, and that the "new things" can find in the Gospel the context for their correct understanding and the proper moral perspective for judgment on them.

6.1 With the intention of shedding light on the conflict which had arisen between capital and labor, Pope Leo XIII affirmed the fundamental rights of workers. Indeed, the key to reading the Encyclical is the dignity of the worker as such, and, for the same reason, the dignity of work, which is defined as follows: "to exert oneself for the sake of procuring what is necessary for the various purposes of life, and first of all for self-preservation."[12] The Pope describes work as "personal, inasmuch as the energy expended is bound up with the personality and is the exclusive property of him who acts, and, furthermore, was given to him for his advantage."[13] Work thus belongs to the vocation of every person; indeed, man expresses and fulfills himself by working. At the same time, work has a "social" dimension through its intimate relationship not only to the family, but also to the common good, since "it may truly be said that it is only by the labor of working-men that States grow rich."[14] These are themes that I have taken up and developed in my Encyclical *Laborem Exercens*.[15]

6.2 Another important principle is undoubtedly that of the right to "private property."[16] The amount of space devoted to this subject in the Encyclical shows the importance attached to it. The Pope is well aware that private property is not an absolute value, nor does he fail to proclaim the necessary complementary principles, such as the universal destination of the earth's goods.[17]

6.3 On the other hand, it is certainly true that the type of private property which Leo XIII mainly considers is land ownership.[18] But this does not mean that the reasons adduced to safeguard private property or to affirm the right to possess the things necessary for one's personal development and the development of one's family, whatever the concrete form which that right may assume, are not still valid today. This is something which must be affirmed once more in the face of the changes we are witnessing in systems formerly dominated by collective ownership of the means of production, as well as in the face of the increasing instances of poverty or, more precisely, of hindrances to private ownership in many parts of the world, including those where systems predominate which are based on an affirmation of the right to private property. As a result of these changes and of the persistence of poverty, a deeper analysis of the problem is called for, an analysis which will be developed later in this document.

7.1 In close connection with the right to private property, Pope Leo XIII's Encyclical also affirms other rights as inalienable and proper to the human person. Prominent among these, because of the space which the Pope devotes to it and the importance which he attaches to it, is the "natural human right" to form private associations. This means above all the right to establish professional associations of employers and workers, or of workers alone.[19] Here we find the reason for the Church's defense and approval of the establishment of what are commonly called trade unions: certainly not because of ideological prejudices or in order to surrender to a class mentality, but because the right of association is a natural right of the human being, which therefore precedes his or her incorporation into political society. Indeed, the formation of unions "cannot . . . be prohibited by the State," because "the State is bound to protect natural rights, not to destroy them; and if it forbids its citizens to form associations, it contradicts the very principle of its own existence."[20]

7.2 Together with this right, which—it must be stressed—the Pope explicitly acknowledges as belonging to workers, or, using his own language, to "the working class," the Encyclical affirms just as clearly the right to the "limitation of working hours," the right to legitimate rest and the right of children and women[21] to be treated differently with regard to the type and duration of work.

7.3 If we keep in mind what history tells us about the practices permitted or at least not excluded by law regarding the way in which workers were employed, without any guarantees as to working hours or the hygienic conditions of the workplace, or even regarding the age and sex of apprentices, we can appreciate the Pope's severe statement: "It is neither just nor human so to grind men down with excessive labor as to stupefy their minds and wear out their bodies." And referring to the "contract" aimed at putting into effect "labor relations" of this sort, he affirms with greater precision that "in all agreements between employers and workers there is always the condition expressed or understood" that proper rest be allowed, proportionate to "the wear and tear of one's strength." He then concludes: "To agree in any other sense would be against what is right and just."[22]

8.1 The Pope immediately adds another right which the worker has as a person. This is the right to a "just wage," which cannot be left to the "free consent of the parties, so that the employer, having paid what was agreed upon, has done his part and seemingly is not called upon to do anything beyond."[23] It was said at the time that the State does not have the power to intervene in the terms of these contracts, except to ensure the fulfillment of what had been explicitly agreed upon. This concept of relations between employers and employees, purely pragmatic and inspired by a thoroughgoing individualism, is severely censured in the Encyclical as contrary to the twofold nature of work as a personal and necessary reality. For if work as something personal belongs to the sphere of the individual's free use of his own abilities and energy, as something necessary it is governed by the grave obligation of every individual to ensure "the preservation of life." "It necessarily follows," the Pope concludes, "that every individual has a natural right to procure what is required to live; and the poor can procure that in no other way than by what they can earn through their work."[24]

8.2 A workman's wages should be sufficient to enable him to support himself, his wife and his children. "If through necessity or fear of a worse evil the workman accepts harder conditions because an employer or contractor will afford no better, he is made the victim of force and injustice."[25]

8.3 Would that these words, written at a time when what has been called "unbridled capitalism" was pressing forward, should not have to be repeated today with the same severity. Unfortunately, even today one finds instances of contracts between employers and employees which lack reference to the most elementary justice regarding the employment of children or women, working hours, the hygienic condition of the workplace and fair pay; and this is the case despite the International Declarations and Conventions on the subject[26] and the internal laws of States. The Pope attributed to the "public authority" the "strict duty" of providing properly for the welfare of the workers, because a failure to do so violates justice; indeed, he did not hesitate to speak of "distributive justice."[27]

9.1 To these rights Pope Leo XIII adds another right regarding the condition of the working class, one which I wish to mention because of its importance: namely, the right to discharge freely one's religious duties. The Pope wished to proclaim this right within the context of the other rights and duties of workers, notwithstanding the general opinion, even in this day, that such questions pertained exclusively to an individual's private life. He affirms the need for Sunday rest so that people may turn their thoughts to heavenly things and to the worship which they owe to Almighty God.[28] No one can take away this human right, which is based on a commandment; in the words of the Pope: "no man may with impunity violate that human dignity which God himself treats with great reverence," and consequently, the State must guarantee to the worker the exercise of this freedom.[29]

9.2 It would not be mistaken to see in this clear statement a springboard for the principle of the right to religious freedom, which was to become the subject of many solemn International Declarations and Conventions,[30] as well as of the Second Vatican Council's well-known Declaration and of my own repeated teaching.[31] In this regard, one may ask whether existing laws and the practice of industrialized societies effectively ensure in our own day the exercise of this basic right to Sunday rest.

10.1 Another important aspect, which has many applications to our own day, is the concept of the relationship between the State and its citizens. Rerum Novarum criticizes two social and economic systems: socialism and liberalism. The opening section, in which the right to private property is reaffirmed, is devoted to socialism. Liberalism is not the subject of a special section, but it is worth noting that criticisms of it are raised in the treatment of the duties of the State.[32] The State cannot limit itself to "favoring one portion of the citizens," namely the rich and prosperous, nor can it "neglect the other," which clearly represents the majority of society. Otherwise, there would be a violation of that law of justice which ordains that every person should receive his due. "When there is question of defending the rights of individuals, the defenseless and the poor have a claim to special consideration. The richer class has many ways of shielding itself, and stands less in need of help from the State; whereas the mass of the poor have no resources of their own to fall back on, and must chiefly depend on the assistance of the State. It is for this reason that wage-earners, since they mostly belong to the latter class, should be specially cared for and protected by the government."[33]

10.2 These passages are relevant today, especially in the face of the new forms of poverty in the world, and also because they are affirmations which do not depend on a specific notion of the State or on a particular political theory. Leo XIII is repeating an elementary principle of sound political organization, namely, the more that individuals are defenseless within a given society, the more they require the care and concern of others, and in particular the intervention of governmental authority.

10.3 In this way what we nowadays call the principle of solidarity, the validity of which both in the internal order of each nation and in the international order I have discussed in the Encyclical Sollicitudo Rei Socialis,[34] is clearly seen to be one of the fundamental principles of the Christian view of social and political organization. This principle is frequently stated by Pope Leo XIII, who uses the term "friendship," a concept already found in Greek philosophy. Pope Pius XI refers to it with the equally meaningful term "social charity." Pope Paul VI, expanding the concept to cover the many modern aspects of the social question, speaks of a "civilization of love."[35]

11.1 Rereading the Encyclical in the light of contemporary realities enables us to appreciate the Church's constant concern for and dedication to categories of people who are especially beloved to the Lord Jesus. The content of the text is an excellent testimony to the continuity within the Church of the so-called "preferential option of the poor," an option which I defined as a "special form of primacy in the exercise of Christian charity."[36] Pope Leo's Encyclical on the "condition of the workers" is thus an Encyclical on the poor and on the terrible conditions to which the new and often violent process of industrialization had reduced great multitudes of people. Today, in many parts of the world, similar processes of economic, social and political transformation are creating the same evils.

11.2 If Pope Leo XIII calls upon the State to remedy the condition of the poor in accordance with justice, he does so because of his timely awareness that the State has the duty of watching over the common good and of ensuring that every sector of social life, not excluding the economic one, contributes to achieving that good, while respecting the rightful autonomy of each sector. This should not however lead us to think that Pope Leo expected the State to solve every social problem. On the contrary, he frequently insists on necessary limits to the State's intervention and on its instrumental character, inasmuch as the individual, the family and society are prior to the State, and inasmuch as the State exists in order to protect their rights and not stifle them.[37]

11.3 The relevance of these reflections for our own day is inescapable. It will be useful to return later to this important subject of the limits inherent in the nature of the State. For now the points which have been emphasized (certainly not the only ones in the Encyclical) are situated in continuity with the Church's social teaching, and in the light of a sound view of private property, work, the economic process, the reality of the State and, above all, of man himself. Other themes will be mentioned later when we examine certain aspects of the contemporary situation. From this point forward it will be necessary to keep in mind that the main thread and, in a certain sense, the guiding principle of Pope Leo's Encyclical, and of all of the Church's social doctrine, is a correct view of the human person and of his unique value, inasmuch as man "... is the only creature on earth which God willed for itself."[38] God has imprinted his own image and likeness on man (cf. Gen 1:26), conferring upon him an incomparable dignity, as the Encyclical frequently insists. In effect, beyond the rights which man acquires by his own work, there exist rights which do not correspond to any work he performs, but which flow from his essential dignity as a person.

II
TOWARD THE "NEW THINGS" OF TODAY

12.1 The commemoration of Rerum Novarum would be incomplete unless reference were also made to the situation of the world today. The document lends itself to such a reference, because the historical picture and the prognosis which it suggests have proved to be surprisingly accurate in the light of what has happened since then.

12.2 This is especially confirmed by the events which took place near the end of 1989 and at the beginning of 1990. These events, and the radical transformations which followed, can only be explained by the preceding situations which, to a certain extent, crystallized or institutionalized Leo XIII's predictions and the increasingly disturbing signs noted by his Successors. Pope Leo foresaw the negative consequences—political, social and economic—of the social order proposed by "socialism," which at that time was still only a social philosophy and not yet a fully structured movement. It may seem surprising that "socialism" appeared at the beginning of the Pope's critique of solutions to the "question of the working class" at a time when "socialism" was not yet in the form of a strong and powerful State, with all the resources which that implies, as was later to happen. However, he correctly judged the danger posed to the masses by the attractive presentation of this simple and radical solution to the "question of the working class" of the time—all the more so when one considers the terrible situation of injustice in which the working classes of the recently industrialized nations found themselves.

12.3 Two things must be emphasized here: first, the great clarity in perceiving, in all its harshness, the actual condition of the working class—men, women and children; secondly, equal clarity in recognizing the evil of a solution which, by appearing to reverse the positions of the poor and the rich, was in reality detrimental to the very people whom it was meant to help. The remedy would prove worse than the sickness. By defining the nature of the socialism of his day as the suppression of private property, Leo XIII arrived at the crux of the problem.

12.4 His words deserve to be reread attentively: "To remedy these wrongs (the unjust distribution of wealth and the poverty of the workers), the socialists encourage the poor man's envy of the rich and strive to do away with private property, contending that individual possessions should become the common property of all . . . ; but their contentions are so clearly powerless to end the controversy that, were they carried into effect, the working man himself would be among the first to suffer. They are moreover emphatically unjust, for they would rob the lawful possessor, distort the functions of the State, and create utter confusion in the community."[39] The evils caused by the setting up of this type of socialism as a State system—which would later be called "Real Socialism"—could not be better expressed.

13.1 Continuing our reflections, and referring also to what has been said in the Encyclicals *Laborem Exercens* and *Sollicitudo Rei Socialis*, we have to add that the fundamental error of socialism is anthropological in nature. Socialism considers the individual person simply as an element, a molecule within the social organism, so that the good of the individual is completely subordinated to the functioning of the socioeconomic mechanism. Socialism likewise maintains that the good of the individual can be realized without reference to his free choice, to the unique and exclusive responsibility which he exercises in the face of good or evil. Man is thus reduced to a series of social relationships, and the concept of the person as the autonomous subject of moral decision disappears, the very subject whose decisions build the social order. From this mistaken conception of the person there arise both a distortion of law, which defines the sphere of the exercise of freedom, and an opposition to private property. A person who is deprived of something he can call "his own," and of the possibility of earning a living through his own initiative, comes to depend on the social machine and on those who control it. This makes it much more difficult for him to recognize his dignity as a person, and hinders progress toward the building up of an authentic human community.

13.2 In contrast, from the Christian vision of the human person there necessarily follows a correct picture of society. According to Rerum Novarum and the whole social doctrine of the Church, the social nature of man is not completely fulfilled in the State, but is realized in various intermediary groups, beginning with the family and including economic, social, political and cultural groups which stem from human nature itself and have their own autonomy, always with a view to the common good. This is what I have called the "subjectivity" of society which, together with the subjectivity of the individual, was canceled out by "Real Socialism."[40]

13.3 If we then inquire as to the source of this mistaken concept of the nature of the person and the "subjectivity" of society, we must reply that its first cause is atheism. It is my responding to the call of God contained in the being of things that man became aware of his transcendent dignity. Every individual must give this response, which constitutes the apex of this humanity, and no social mechanism or collective subject can substitute for it. The denial of God deprives the person of his foundation, and consequently leads to a reorganization of the social order without reference to the person's dignity and responsibility.

13.4 The atheism of which we are speaking is also closely connected with the rationalism of the Enlightenment, which views human and social reality in a mechanistic way. Thus there is a denial of the supreme insight concerning man's true greatness, his transcendence in respect to earthly realities, the contradiction in his heart between the desire for the fullness of what is good and his own inability to attain it and, above all, the need for salvation which results from this situation.

14.1 From the same atheistic source, socialism also derives its choice of the means of action condemned in Rerum Novarum, namely, class struggle. The Pope does not, of course, intend to condemn every possible form of social conflict. The Church is well aware that in the course of history conflicts of interest between different social groups inevitably arise, and that in the face of such conflicts Christians must often take a position, honestly and decisively. The Encyclical *Laborem Exercens* moreover clearly recognized the positive role of conflict when it takes the form of a "struggle for social justice"; [41] *Quadragesimo Anno* had already stated that "if the class struggle abstains from enmities and mutual hatred, it gradually changes into an honest discussion of differences founded on a desire for justice."[42]

14.2 However, what is condemned in class struggle is the idea that conflict is not restrained by ethical or juridical considerations, or by respect for the dignity of others (and consequently of oneself); a reasonable compromise is thus excluded, and what is pursued is not the general good of society, but a partisan interest which replaces the common good and sets out to destroy whatever stands in its way. In a word, it is a question of transferring to the sphere of internal conflict between social groups the doctrine of "total war," which the militarism and imperialism of that time brought to bear on international relations. As a result of this doctrine, the search for a proper balance between the interests of the various nations was replaced by attempts to impose the absolute domination of one's own side through the destruction of the other side's capacity to resist, using every possible means, not excluding the use of lies, terror tactics against citizens, and weapons of utter destruction (which precisely in those years were beginning to be designed). Therefore class struggle in the Marxist sense and militarism have the same root, namely, atheism and contempt for the human person, which place the principle of force above that of reason and law.

15.1 *Rerum Novarum* is opposed to State control of the means of production, which would reduce every citizen to being a "cog" in the State machine. It is not less forceful in criticizing a concept of the State which completely excludes the economic sector from the State's range of interest and action. There is certainly a legitimate sphere of autonomy in economic life which the State should not enter. The State, however, has the task of determining the juridical framework within which economic affairs are to be conducted, and thus of safeguarding the prerequisites of a free economy, which presumes a certain equality between the parties, such that one party would not be so powerful as practically to reduce the other to subservience.[43]

15.2 In this regard, *Rerum Novarum* points the way to just reforms which can restore dignity to work as the free activity of man. These reforms imply that society and the State will both assume responsibility, especially for protecting the worker from the nightmare of unemployment. Historically, this has happened in two converging ways: either through economic policies aimed at ensuring balanced growth and full employment, or through unemployment insurance and retraining programs capable of ensuring a smooth transfer of workers from crisis sectors to those in expansion.

15.3 Furthermore, society and the State must ensure wage levels adequate for the maintenance of the worker and his family, including a certain amount for savings. This requires a continuous effort to improve workers' training and capability so that their work will be more skilled and productive, as well as careful controls and adequate legislative measures to block shameful forms of exploitation, especially to the disadvantage of the most vulnerable workers, of immigrants and of those on the margins of society. The role of trade unions in negotiating minimum salaries and working conditions is decisive in this area.

15.4 Finally, "humane" working hours and adequate free-time need to be guaranteed, as well as the right to express one's own personality at the workplace without suffering any affront to one's conscience or personal dignity. This is the place to mention once more the role of trade unions, not only in negotiating contracts, but also as "places" where workers can express themselves. They serve the development of an authentic culture of work and help workers to share in a fully human way in the life of their place of employment.[44]

15.5 The State must contribute to the achievement of these goals both directly and indirectly. Indirectly and according to the principle of subsidiarity, by creating favorable conditions for the free exercise of economic activity, which will lead to abundant opportunities for employment and sources of wealth. Directly and according to the principle of solidarity, by defending the weakest, by placing certain limits on the autonomy of the parties who determine working conditions, and by ensuring in every case the necessary minimum support for the unemployed worker.[45]

15.6 The Encyclical and the related social teaching of the Church had far-reaching influence in the years bridging the nineteenth and twentieth centuries. This influence is evident in the numerous reforms which were introduced in the areas of social security, pensions, health insurance and compensation in the case of accidents, within the framework of greater respect for the rights of workers.[46]

16.1 These reforms were carried out in part by States, but in the struggle to achieve them the role of the workers' movement was an important one. This movement, which began as a response of moral conscience to unjust and harmful situations, conducted a widespread campaign for reform, far removed from vague ideology and closer to the daily needs of workers. In this context its efforts were often joined to those of Christians in order to improve workers' living conditions. Later on, this movement was dominated to a certain extent by the Marxist ideology against which Rerum Novarum had spoken.

16.2 These same reforms were also partly the result of an open process by which society organized itself through the establishment of effective instruments of solidarity, which were capable of sustaining an economic growth more respectful of the values of the person. Here we should remember the numerous efforts to which Christians made a notable contribution in establishing producers', consumers' and credit cooperatives, in promoting general education and professional training, in experimenting with various forms of participation in the life of the workplace and in the life of society in general.

16.3 Thus, as we look at the past, there is good reason to thank God that the great Encyclical was not without an echo in human hearts and indeed led to a generous response on the practical level. Still, we must acknowledge that its prophetic message was not fully accepted by people at the time. Precisely for this reason there ensued some very serious tragedies.

17.1 Reading the Encyclical within the context of Pope Leo's whole Magisterium,[47] we see how it points essentially to the socioeconomic consequences of an error which has even greater implications. As has been mentioned, this error consists in an understanding of human freedom which detaches it from obedience to the truth, and consequently from the duty to respect the rights of others. The essence of freedom then becomes self-love carried to the point of contempt for God and neighbor, a self-love which leads to an unbridled affirmation of self-interest and which refuses to be limited by any demand of justice.[48]

17.2 This very error had extreme consequences in the tragic series of wars which ravaged Europe and the world between 1914 and 1945. Some of these resulted from militarism and exaggerated nationalism, and from related forms of totalitarianism; some derived from the class struggle; still others were civil wars or wars of an ideological nature. Without the terrible burden of hatred and resentment which had built up as a result of so many injustices both on the international level and within individual States, such cruel wars would not have been possible, in which great nations invested their energies and in which there was no hesitation to violate the most sacred human rights, with the extermination of entire peoples and social groups being planned and carried out. Here we recall the Jewish people in particular, whose terrible fate has become a symbol of the aberration of which man is capable when he turns against God.

17.3 However, it is only when hatred and injustice are sanctioned and organized by the ideologies based on them, rather than on the truth about man, that they take possession of entire nations and drive them to act.[49] Rerum Novarum opposed ideologies of hatred and showed how violence and resentment could be overcome by justice. May the memory of those terrible events guide the actions of everyone, particularly the leaders of nations in our own time, when other forms of injustice are fueling new hatreds and when new ideologies which exalt violence are appearing on the horizon.

18.1 While it is true that since 1945 weapons have been silent on the European continent, it must be remembered that true peace is never simply the result of military victory, but rather implies both the removal of the causes of war and genuine reconciliation between peoples. For many years there has been in Europe and the world a situation of non-war rather than genuine peace. Half of the continent fell under the domination of a Communist dictatorship, while the other half organized itself in defense against this threat. Many peoples lost the ability to control their own destiny and were enclosed within the suffocating boundaries of an empire in which efforts were made to destroy their historical memory and the centuries-old roots of their culture. As a result of this violent division of Europe, enormous masses of people were compelled to leave their homeland or were forcibly deported.

18.2 An insane arms race swallowed up the resources needed for the development of national economies and for assistance to the less developed nations. Scientific and technological progress, which should have contributed to man's well-being, was transformed into an instrument of war: science and technology were directed to the production of ever more efficient and destructive weapons. Meanwhile, an ideology, a perversion of authentic philosophy, was called upon to provide doctrinal justification for the new war. And this war was not simply expected and prepared for, but was actually fought with enormous bloodshed in various parts of the world. The logic of power blocs or empires, denounced in various Church documents and recently in the Encyclical *Sollicitudo Rei Socialis*,[50] led to a situation in which controversies and disagreements among Third World countries were systematically aggravated and exploited in order to create difficulties for the adversary.

18.3 Extremist groups, seeking to resolve such controversies through the use of arms, found ready political and military support and were equipped and trained for war; those who tried to find peaceful and humane solutions, with respect for the legitimate interests of all parties, remained isolated and often fell victim to their opponents. In addition, the precariousness of the peace which followed the Second World War was one of the principal causes of the militarization of many Third World countries and the fratricidal conflicts which afflicted them, as well as of the spread of terrorism and of increasingly barbaric means of political and military conflict. Moreover, the whole world was oppressed by the threat of an atomic war capable of leading to the extinction of humanity. Science used for military purposes had placed this decisive instrument at the disposal of hatred, strengthened by ideology. But if war can end without winners or losers in a suicide of humanity, then we must repudiate the logic which leads to it: the idea that the effort to destroy the enemy, confrontation and war itself are factors of progress and historical advancement.[51] When the need for this repudiation is understood, the concepts of "total war" and "class struggle" must necessarily be called into question.

19.1 At the end of the Second World War, however, such a development was still being formed in people's consciences. What received attention was the spread of Communist totalitarianism over more than half of Europe and over other parts of the world. The war, which should have reestablished freedom and restored the right of nations, ended without having attained these goals. Indeed, in a way, for many peoples, especially those which had suffered most during the war, it openly contradicted these goals. It may be said that the situation which arose has evoked different responses.

19.2 Following the destruction caused by the war, we see in some countries and under certain aspects a positive effort to rebuild a democratic society inspired by social justice, so as to deprive Communism of the revolutionary potential represented by masses of people subjected to exploitation and oppression. In general, such attempts endeavor to preserve free market mechanisms, ensuring, by means of a stable currency and the harmony of social relations, the conditions for steady and healthy economic growth in which people through their own work can build a better future for themselves and their families. At the same time, these attempts try to avoid making market mechanisms the only point of reference for social life, and they tend to subject them to public control which upholds the principle of the common destination of material goods. In this context, an abundance of work opportunities, a solid system of social security and professional training, the freedom to join trade unions and the effective action of unions, the assistance provided in cases of unemployment, the opportunities for democratic participation in the life of society—all these are meant to deliver work from the mere condition of "a commodity," and to guarantee its dignity.

19.3 Then there are the other social forces and ideological movements which oppose Marxism by setting up systems of "national security," aimed at controlling the whole of society in a systematic way, in order to make Marxist infiltration impossible. By emphasizing and increasing the power of the State, they wish to protect their people from Communism, but in doing so they run the grave risk of destroying the freedom and values of the person, the very things for whose sake it is necessary to oppose Communism.

19.4 Another kind of response, practical in nature, is represented by the affluent society or the consumer society. It seeks to defeat Marxism on the level of pure materialism by showing how a free market society can achieve a greater satisfaction of material human needs than Communism, while equally excluding spiritual values. In reality, while on the one hand it is true that this social model shows the failure of Marxism to contribute to a humane and better society, on the other hand, insofar as it denies an autonomous existence and value to morality, law, culture and religion, it agrees with Marxism, in the sense that it totally reduces man to the sphere of economics and the satisfaction of material needs.

20.1 During the same period a widespread process of "decolonization" occurred, by which many countries gained or regained their independence and the right freely to determine their own destiny. With the formal reacquisition of State sovereignty, however, these countries often find themselves merely at the beginning of the journey toward the construction of genuine independence. Decisive sectors of the economy still remain de facto in the hands of large foreign companies which are unwilling to commit themselves to the long-term development of the host country. Political life itself is controlled by foreign powers, while within the national boundaries there are tribal groups not yet amalgamated into a genuine national community. Also lacking is a class of competent professional people capable of running the State apparatus in an honest and just way, nor are there qualified personnel for managing the economy in an efficient and responsible manner.

20.2 Given this situation, many think that Marxism can offer a sort of shortcut for building up the nation and the State; thus many variants of socialism emerge with specific national characteristics. Legitimate demands for national recovery, forms of nationalism and also of militarism, principles drawn from ancient popular traditions (which are sometimes in harmony with Christian social doctrine) and Marxist-Leninist concepts and ideas—all these mingle in the many ideologies which take shape in ways that differ from case to case.

21.1 Lastly, it should be remembered that after the Second World War, and in reaction to its horrors, there arose a more lively sense of human rights, which found recognition in a number of International Documents[52] and, one might say, in the drawing up of a new "right of nations," to which the Holy See has constantly contributed. The focal point of this evolution has been the United Nations Organization. Not only has there been a development in awareness of the rights of individuals, but also in awareness of the rights of nations, as well as a clearer realization of the need to act in order to remedy the grave imbalances that exist between the various geographical areas of the world. In a certain sense, these imbalances have shifted the center of the social question from the national to the international level.[53]

21.2 While noting this process with satisfaction, nevertheless one cannot ignore the fact that the overall balance of the various policies of aid for development has not always been positive. The United Nations, moreover, has not yet succeeded in establishing, as alternatives to war, effective means for the resolution of international conflicts. This seems to be the most urgent problem which the international community has yet to resolve.

III
THE YEAR 1989

22.1 It is on the basis of the world situation just described, and already elaborated in the Encyclical *Sollicitudo Rei Socialis*, that the unexpected and promising significance of the events of recent years can be understood. Although they certainly reached their climax in 1989 in the countries of Central and Eastern Europe, they embrace a longer period of time and a wider geographical area. In the course of the '80s, certain dictatorial and oppressive regimes fell one by one in some countries in Latin America and also of Africa and Asia. In other cases there began a difficult but productive transition toward more participatory and more just political structures. An important, even decisive, contribution was made by the Church's commitment to defend and promote human rights. In situations strongly influenced by ideology, in which polarization obscured the awareness of a human dignity common to all, the Church affirmed clearly and forcefully that every individual—whatever his or her personal convictions—bears the image of God and therefore deserves respect. Often, the vast majority of people identified themselves with this kind of affirmation, and this led to a search for forms of protest and for political solutions more respectful of the dignity of the person.

22.2 From this historical process new forms of democracy have emerged which offer a hope for change in fragile political and social structures weighed down by a painful series of injustices and resentments, as well as by a heavily damaged economy and serious social conflicts. Together with the whole Church, I thank God for the often heroic witness borne in such difficult circumstances by many Pastors, entire Christian communities, individual members of the faithful, and other people of good will; at the same time I pray that he will sustain the efforts being made by everyone to build a better future. This is, in fact, a responsibility which falls not only to the citizens of the countries in question, but to all Christians and people of good will. It is a question of showing that the complex problems faced by those peoples can be resolved through dialogue and solidarity, rather than by a struggle to destroy the enemy through war.

23.1 Among the many factors involved in the fall of oppressive regimes, some deserve special mention. Certainly, the decisive factor which gave rise to the changes was the violation of the rights of workers. It cannot be forgotten that the fundamental crisis of systems claiming to express the rule and indeed the dictatorship of the working class began with the great upheavals which took place in Poland in the name of solidarity. It was the throngs of working people which foreswore the ideology which presumed to speak in their name. On the basis of a hard, lived experience of work and of oppression, it was they who recovered and, in a sense, rediscovered the content and principles of the Church's social doctrine.

23.2 Also worthy of emphasis is the fact that the fall of this kind of "bloc" or empire was accomplished almost everywhere by means of peaceful protest, using only the weapons of truth and justice. While Marxism held that only by exacerbating social conflicts was it possible to resolve them through violent confrontation, the protests which led to the collapse of Marxism tenaciously insisted on trying every avenue of negotiation, dialogue, and witness to the truth, appealing to the conscience of the adversary and seeking to reawaken in him a sense of shared human dignity.

23.3 It seemed that the European order resulting from the Second World War and sanctioned by the Yalta Agreements could only be overturned by another war.

Instead, it has been overcome by the non-violent commitment of people who, while always refusing to yield to the force of power, succeeded time after time in finding effective ways of bearing witness to the truth. This disarmed the adversary, since violence always needs to justify itself through deceit, and to appear, however falsely, to be defending a right or responding to a threat posed by others.[54] Once again I thank God for having sustained people's hearts amid difficult trials, and I pray that this example will prevail in other places and other circumstances. May people learn to fight for justice without violence, renouncing class struggle in their internal disputes, and war in international ones.

24.1 The second factor in the crisis was certainly the inefficiency of the economic system, which is not to be considered simply as a technical problem, but rather a consequence of the violation of the human rights to private initiative, to ownership of property and to freedom in the economic sector. To this must be added the cultural and national dimension: it is not possible to understand man on the basis of economics alone, nor to define him simply on the basis of class membership. Man is understood in a more complete way when he is situated within the sphere of culture through his language, history, and the position he takes toward the fundamental events of life, such as birth, love, work and death. At the heart of every culture lies the attitude man takes to the greatest mystery: the mystery of God. Different cultures are basically different ways of facing the question of the meaning of personal existence. When this question is eliminated, the culture and moral life of nations are corrupted. For this reason the struggle to defend work was spontaneously linked to the struggle for culture and for national rights.

24.2 But the true cause of the new developments was the spiritual void brought about by atheism, which deprived the younger generations of a sense of direction and in many cases led them, in the irrepressible search for personal identity and for the meaning of life, to rediscover the religious roots of their national cultures, and to rediscover the person of Christ himself as the existentially adequate response to the desire in every human heart for goodness, truth and life. This search was supported by the witness of those who, in difficult circumstances and under persecution, remained faithful to God. Marxism had promised to uproot the need for God from the human heart, but the results have shown that it is not possible to succeed in this without throwing the heart into turmoil.

25.1 The events of 1989 are an example of the success of willingness to negotiate and of the Gospel spirit in the face of an adversary determined not to be bound by moral principles. These events are a warning to those who, in the name of political realism, wish to banish law and morality from the political arena. Undoubtedly, the struggle which led to the changes of 1989 called for clarity, moderation, suffering and sacrifice. In a certain sense, it was a struggle born of prayer, and it would have been unthinkable without immense trust in God, the Lord of history, who carries the human heart in his hands. It is by uniting their own sufferings, for the sake of truth and freedom, to the sufferings of Christ on the Cross that man is able to accomplish the miracle of peace and is in a position to discern the often narrow path between the cowardice which gives in to evil and the violence which, under the illusion of fighting evil, only makes it worse.

25.2 Nevertheless, it cannot be forgotten that the manner in which the individual exercises his freedom is conditioned in innumerable ways. While these certainly have an influence on freedom, they do not determine it; they make the exercise of freedom more difficult or less difficult, but they cannot destroy it. Not only is it wrong from the ethical point of view to disregard human nature, which is made for freedom, but in practice it is impossible to do so. Where society is so organized as to reduce arbitrarily or even suppress the sphere in which freedom is legitimately exercised, the result is that the life of society becomes progressively disorganized and goes into decline.

25.3 Moreover, man, who was created for freedom, bears within himself the wound of original sin, which constantly draws him toward evil and puts him in need of redemption. Not only is this doctrine an integral part of Christian revelation, it also has great hermeneutical value insofar as it helps one to understand human reality. Man tends toward good, but he is also capable of evil. He can transcend his immediate interest and still remain bound to it. The social order will be all the more stable, the more it takes this fact into account and does not place in opposition personal interest and the interests of society as a whole, but rather seeks ways to bring them into fruitful harmony. In fact, where self-interest is violently suppressed, it is replaced by a burdensome system of bureaucratic control which dries up the wellsprings of initiative and creativity. When people think they possess the secret of a perfect social organization which makes evil impossible, they also think that they can use any means, including violence and deceit, in order to bring that organization into being. Politics then becomes a "secular religion" which operates under the illusion of creating paradise in this world. But no political society—which possesses its own autonomy and laws[55]—can ever be confused with the Kingdom of God. The Gospel parable of the weeds among the wheat (cf. Mt 13:24–30; 36–43) teaches that it is for God alone to separate the subjects of the Kingdom from the subjects of the Evil One, and that this judgment will take place at the end of time. By presuming to anticipate judgment here and now, man puts himself in the place of God and sets himself against the patience of God.

25.4 Through Christ's sacrifice on the Cross, the victory of the Kingdom of God has been achieved once and for all. Nevertheless, the Christian life involves a struggle against temptation and the forces of evil. Only at the end of history will the Lord return in glory for the final judgment (cf. Mt 25:31) with the establishment of a new heaven and a new earth (cf. 2 Pet 3:13; Rev 21:1); but as long as time lasts, the struggle between good and evil continues even in the human heart itself.

25.5 What Sacred Scripture teaches us about the prospects of the Kingdom of God is not without consequences for the life of temporal societies, which, as the adjective indicates, belong to the realm of time, with all that this implies of imperfection and impermanence. The Kingdom of God, being in the world without being of the world, throws light on the order of human society, while the power of grace penetrates that order and gives it life. In this way the requirements of a society worthy of man are better perceived, deviations are corrected, the courage to work for what is good is reinforced. In union with all people of good will, Christians, especially the laity, are called to this task of imbuing human realities with the Gospel.[56]

26.1 The events of 1989 took place principally in the countries of Eastern and Central Europe. However, they have worldwide importance because they have positive and negative consequences which concern the whole human family. These consequences are not mechanistic or fatalistic in character, but rather are opportunities for human freedom to cooperate with the merciful plan of God who acts within history.

26.2 The first consequence was an encounter in some countries between the Church and the workers' movement, which came about as a result of an ethical and explicitly Christian reaction against a widespread situation of injustice. For about a century the workers' movement had fallen in part under the dominance of Marxism, in the conviction that the working class, in order to struggle effectively against oppression, had to appropriate its economic and materialistic theories.

26.3 In the crisis of Marxism, the natural dictates of the consciences of workers have reemerged in a demand for justice and a recognition of the dignity of work, in conformity with the social doctrine of the Church.[57] The workers' movement is part of a more general movement among workers and other people of good will for the liberation of the human person and for the affirmation of human rights. It is a movement which today has spread to many countries, and which, far from opposing the Catholic Church, looks to her with interest.

26.4 The crisis of Marxism does not rid the world of the situations of injustice and oppression which Marxism itself exploited and on which it fed. To those who are searching today for a new and authentic theory and praxis of liberation, the Church offers not only her social doctrine and, in general, her teaching about the human person redeemed in Christ, but also her concrete commitment and material assistance in the struggle against marginalization and suffering.

26.5 In the recent past, the sincere desire to be on the side of the oppressed and not to be cut off from the course of history has led many believers to seek in various ways an impossible compromise between Marxism and Christianity. Moving beyond all that was short-lived in these attempts, present circumstances are leading to a reaffirmation of the positive value of an authentic theology of integral human liberation.[58] Considered from this point of view, the events of 1989 are proving to be important also for the countries of the Third World, which are searching for their own path to development, just as they were important for the countries of Central and Eastern Europe.

27.1 The second consequence concerns the peoples of Europe themselves. Many individual, social, regional and national injustices were committed during and prior to the years in which Communism dominated; much hatred and ill will have accumulated. There is a real danger that these will reexplode after the collapse of dictatorship, provoking serious conflicts and casualties, should there be a lessening of the moral commitment and conscious striving to bear witness to the truth which were the inspiration for past efforts. It is to be hoped that hatred and violence will not triumph in people's hearts, especially among those who are struggling for justice, and that all people will grow in the spirit of peace and forgiveness.

27.2 What is needed are concrete steps to create or consolidate international structures capable of intervening through appropriate arbitration in the conflicts which arise between nations, so that each nation can uphold its own rights and reach a just agreement and peaceful settlement vis-à-vis the rights of others. This is especially needed for the nations of Europe, which are closely united in a bond of common culture and an age-old history. A great effort is needed to rebuild morally and economically the countries which have abandoned Communism. For a long time the most elementary economic relationships were distorted, and basic virtues of economic life, such as truthfulness, trustworthiness and hard work were denigrated. A patient material and moral reconstruction is needed, even as people, exhausted by longstanding privation, are asking their governments for tangible and immediate results in the form of material benefits and an adequate fulfillment of their legitimate aspirations.

27.3 The fall of Marxism has naturally had a great impact on the division of the planet into worlds which are closed to one another and in jealous competition. It has further highlighted the reality of interdependence among peoples, as well as the fact that human work, by its nature, is meant to unit peoples, not divide them. Peace and prosperity, in fact, are goods which belong to the whole human race: it is not possible to enjoy them in a proper and lasting way if they are achieved and maintained at the cost of other peoples and nations, by violating their rights or excluding them from the sources of well-being.

28.1 In a sense, for some countries of Europe the real post-war period is just beginning. The radical reordering of economic systems, hitherto collectivized, entails problems and sacrifices comparable to those which the countries of Western Europe had to face in order to rebuild after the Second World War. It is right that in the present difficulties the formerly Communist countries should be aided by the united effort of other nations. Obviously they themselves must be the primary agents of their own development, but they must also be given a reasonable opportunity to accomplish this goal, something that cannot happen without the help of other countries. Moreover, their present condition, marked by difficulties and shortages, is the result of an historical process in which the formerly Communist countries were often objects and not subjects. Thus they find themselves in the present situation not as a result of free choice or mistakes which were made, but as a consequence of tragic historical events which were violently imposed on them, and which prevented them from following the path of economic and social development.

28.2 Assistance from other countries, especially the countries of Europe which were part of that history and which bear responsibility for it, represents a debt in justice. But it also corresponds to the interest and welfare of Europe as a whole, since Europe cannot live in peace if the various conflicts which have arisen as a result of the past are to become more acute because of a situation of economic disorder, spiritual dissatisfaction and desperation.

28.3 This need, however, must not lead to a slackening of efforts to sustain and assist the countries of the Third World, which often suffer even more serious conditions of poverty and want.[59] What is called for is a special effort to mobilize resources, which are not lacking in the world as a whole, for the purpose of economic growth and common development, redefining the priorities and hierarchies of values on the basis of which economic and political choices are made. Enormous resources can be made available by disarming the huge military machines which were constructed for the conflict between East and West. These resources could become even more abundant if, in place of war, reliable procedures for the resolution of conflicts could be set up, with the resulting spread of the principle of arms control and arms reduction, also in the countries of the Third World, through the adoption of appropriate measures against the arms trade.[60] But it will be necessary above all to abandon a mentality in which the poor—as individuals and as peoples—are considered a burden, as irksome intruders trying to consume what others have produced. The poor ask for the right to share in enjoying material goods and to make good use of their capacity for work, thus creating a world that is more just and prosperous for all. The advancement of the poor constitutes a great opportunity for the moral, cultural and even economic growth of all humanity.

29.1 Finally, development must not be understood solely in economic terms, but in a way that is fully human.[61] It is not only a question of raising all peoples to the level currently enjoyed by the richest countries, but rather of building up a more decent life through united labor, of concretely enhancing every individual's dignity and creativity, as well as his capacity to respond to his personal vocation, and thus to God's call. The apex of development is the exercise of the right and duty to seek God, to know him and to live in accordance with that knowledge.[62] In the totalitarian and authoritarian regimes, the principle that force predominates over reason was carried to the extreme. Man was compelled to submit to a conception of reality imposed on him by coercion, and not reached by virtue of his own reason and the exercise of his own freedom. This principle must be overturned and total recognition must be given to the rights of the human conscience, which is bound only to the truth, both natural and revealed. The recognition of these rights represents the primary foundation of every authentically free political order.[63] It is important to reaffirm this latter principle for several reasons:

29.2 a) because the old forms of totalitarianism and authoritarianism are not yet completely vanquished; indeed there is a risk that they will regain their strength. This demands renewed efforts of cooperation and solidarity between all countries;

29.3 b) because in the developed countries there is sometimes an excessive promotion of purely utilitarian values, with an appeal to the appetites and inclinations toward immediate gratification, making it difficult to recognize and respect the hierarchy of the true values of human existence;

29.4 c) because in some countries new forms of religious fundamentalism are emerging which covertly, or even openly, deny to citizens of faiths other than that of the majority the full exercise of their civil and religious rights, preventing them from taking part in the cultural process, and restricting both the Church's right to preach the Gospel and the rights of those who hear this preaching to accept it and to be converted to Christ. No authentic progress is possible without respect for the natural and fundamental right to know the truth and live according to that truth. The exercise and development of this right includes the right to discover and freely to accept Jesus Christ, who is man's true good.[64]

IV
PRIVATE PROPERTY AND THE UNIVERSAL DESTINATION OF MATERIAL GOODS

30.1 In *Rerum Novarum*, Leo XIII strongly affirmed the natural character of the right to private property, using various arguments against the socialism of his time.[65] This right, which is fundamental for the autonomy and development of the person, has always been defended by the Church up to our own day. At the same time, the Church teaches that the possession of material goods is not an absolute right, and that its limits are inscribed in its very nature as a human right.

30.2 While the Pope proclaimed the right to private ownership, he affirmed with equal clarity that the "use" of goods, while marked by freedom, is subordinated to their original common destination as created goods, as well as to the will of Jesus Christ as expressed in the Gospel. Pope Leo wrote: "those whom fortune favors are admonished . . . that they should tremble at the warnings of Jesus Christ . . . and that a most strict account must be given to the Supreme Judge for the use of all they possess"; and quoting Saint Thomas Aquinas, he added: "But if the question be asked, how must one's possessions be used? the Church replies without hesitation that man should not consider his material possessions as his own, but as common to all . . . ," because "above the laws and judgments of men stands the law, the judgment of Christ."[66]

30.3 The Successors of Leo XIII have repeated this twofold affirmation: the necessity and therefore the legitimacy of private ownership, as well as the limits which are imposed on it.[67] The Second Vatican Council likewise clearly restated the traditional doctrine in words which bear repeating: "In making use of the exterior things we lawfully possess, we ought to regard them not just as our own but also as common, in the sense that they can profit not only the owners but others too"; and a littler later we read: "Private property or some ownership of external goods affords each person the scope needed for personal and family autonomy, and should be regarded as an extension of human freedom. . . . Of its nature private property also has a social function which is based on the law of the common purpose of goods."[68] I have returned to this same doctrine, first in my address to the Third Conference of the Latin American Bishops at Puebla, and later in the Encyclicals *Laborem Exercens* and *Sollicitudo Rei Socialis*.[69]

31.1 Rereading this teaching on the right to property and the common destination of material wealth as it applies to the present time, the question can be raised concerning the origin of the material goods which sustain human life, satisfy people's needs and are an object of their rights.

31.2 The original source of all that is good is the very act of God, who created both the earth and man, and who gave the earth to man, so that he might have dominion over it by his work and enjoy its fruits (Gen 1:28). God gave the earth to the whole human race for the sustenance of all its members, without excluding or favoring anyone. This is the foundation of the universal destination of the earth's goods. The earth, by reason of its fruitfulness and its capacity to satisfy human needs, is God's first gift for the sustenance of human life. But the earth does not yield its fruits without a particular human response to God's gift, that is to say, without work. It is through work that man, using his intelligence and exercising his freedom, succeeds in dominating the earth and making it a fitting home. In this way, he makes part of the earth his own, precisely the part which he has acquired through work; this is the origin of individual property. Obviously, he also has the responsibility not to hinder others from having their own part of God's gift; indeed, one must cooperate with others so that together all can dominate the earth.

31.3 In history, these two factors—work and the land—are to be found at the beginning of every human society. However, they do not always stand in the same relationship to each other. At one time the natural fruitfulness of the earth appeared to be, and was in fact, the primary factor of wealth, while work was, as it were, the help and support for this fruitfulness. In our time, the role of human work is becoming increasingly important as the productive factor both of nonmaterial and of material wealth. Moreover, it is becoming clearer how a person's work is naturally interrelated with the work of others. More than ever, work is work with others and work for others: it is a matter of doing something for someone else. Work becomes ever more fruitful and productive to the extent that people become more knowledgeable of the productive potentialities of the earth and more profoundly cognizant of the needs of those for whom their work is done.

32.1 In our time, in particular, there exists another form of ownership which is becoming no less important than land: the possession of know-how, technology and skill. The wealth of the industrialized nations is based much more on this kind of ownership than on natural resources.

32.2 Mention has just been made of the fact that people work with each other, sharing in a "community of work" which embraces ever widening circles. A person who produces something other than for his own use generally does so in order that others may use it after they have paid a just price, mutually agreed upon through free bargaining. It is precisely the ability to foresee both the needs of others and the combinations of productive factors most adapted to satisfying those needs that constitutes another important source of wealth in modern society. Besides, many goods cannot be adequately produced through the work of an isolated individual; they require the cooperation of many people in working toward a common goal. Organizing such a productive effort, planning its duration in time, making sure that it corresponds in a positive way to the demands which it must satisfy, and taking the necessary risks—all this too is a source of wealth in today's society. In this way, the role of disciplined and creative human work and, as an essential part of that work, initiative and entrepreneurial ability becomes increasingly evident and decisive.[70]

32.3 This process, which throws practical light on a truth about the person which Christianity has constantly affirmed, should be viewed carefully and favorably. Indeed, besides the earth, man's principal resource is man himself. His intelligence enables him to discover the earth's productive potential and the many different ways in which human needs can be satisfied. It is his disciplined work in close collaboration with others that makes possible the creation of ever more extensive working communities which can be relied upon to transform man's natural and human environments. Important virtues are involved in this process, such as diligence, industriousness, prudence in undertaking reasonable risks, reliability and fidelity in interpersonal relationships, as well as courage in carrying out decisions which are difficult and painful but necessary, both for the overall working of a business and in meeting possible setbacks.

32.4 The modern business economy has positive aspects. Its basis is human freedom exercised in the economic field, just as it is exercised in many other fields. Economic activity is indeed but one sector in a great variety of human activities, and like every other sector, it includes the right to freedom, as well as the duty of making responsible use of freedom. But it is important to note that there are specific differences between the trends of modern society and those of the past, even the recent past. Whereas at one time the decisive factor of production was the land, and later capital—understood as a total complex of the instruments of production—today the decisive factor is increasingly man himself, that is, his knowledge, especially his scientific knowledge, his capacity for interrelated and compact organization, as well as his ability to perceive the needs of others and to satisfy them.

33.1 However, the risks and problems connected with this kind of process should be pointed out. The fact is that many people, perhaps the majority today, do not have the means which would enable them to take their place in an effective and humanly dignified way within a productive system in which work is truly central. They have no possibility of acquiring the basic knowledge which would enable them to express their creativity and develop their potential. They have no way of entering the network of knowledge and intercommunication which would enable them to see their qualities appreciated and utilized. Thus, if not actually exploited, they are to a great extent marginalized; economic development takes place over their heads, so to speak, when it does not actually reduce the already narrow scope of their old subsistence economies. They are unable to compete against the goods which are produced in ways which are new and which properly respond to needs, needs which they had previously been accustomed to meeting through traditional forms of organization. Allured by the dazzle of an opulence which is beyond their reach, and at the same time driven by necessity, these people crowd the cities of the Third World where they are often without cultural roots, and where they are exposed to situations of violent uncertainty, without the possibility of becoming integrated. Their dignity is not acknowledged in any real way, and sometimes there are even attempts to eliminate them from history through coercive forms of demographic control which are contrary to human dignity.

33.2 Many other people, while not completely marginalized, live in situations in which the struggle for a bare minimum is uppermost. These are situations in which the rules of the earliest period of capitalism still flourish in conditions of "ruthlessness" in no way inferior to the darkest moments of the first phase of industrialization. In other cases the land is still the central element in the economic process, but those who cultivate it are excluded from ownership and are reduced to a state of quasi-servitude.[71] In these cases, it is still possible today, as in the days of *Rerum Novarum*, to speak of inhuman exploitation. In spite of the great changes which have taken place in the more advanced societies, the human inadequacies of capitalism and the resulting domination of things over people are far from disappearing. In fact, for the poor, to the lack of material goods has been added a lack of knowledge and training which prevents them from escaping their state of humiliating subjection.

33.3 Unfortunately, the great majority of people in the Third World still live in such conditions. It would be a mistake, however, to understand this "world" in purely geographic terms. In some regions and in some social sectors of that world, development programs have been set up which are centered on the use not so much of the material resources available but of the "human resources."

33.4 Even in recent years it was thought that the poorest countries would develop by isolating themselves from the world market and by depending only on their own resources. Recent experience has shown that countries which did this have suffered stagnation and recession, while the countries which experienced development were those which succeeded in taking part in the general interrelated economic activities at the international level. It seems therefore that the chief problem is that of gaining fair access to the international market, based not on the unilateral principle of the exploitation of the natural resources of these countries but on the proper use of human resources.[72]

33.5 However, aspects typical of the Third World also appear in developed countries, where the constant transformation of the methods of production and consumption devalues certain acquired skills and professional expertise, and thus requires a continual effort of retraining and updating. Those who fail to keep up with the times can easily be marginalized, as can the elderly, the young people who are incapable of finding their place in the life of society and, in general, those who are weakest or part of the so-called Fourth World. The situation of women too is far from easy in these conditions.

34.1 It would appear that, on the level of individual nations and of international relations, the free market is the most efficient instrument for utilizing resources and effectively responding to needs. But this is true only for those needs which are "solvent," insofar as they are endowed with purchasing power, and for those resources which are "marketable" insofar as they are capable of obtaining a satisfactory price. But there are many human needs which find no place on the market. It is a strict duty of justice and truth not to allow fundamental human needs to remain unsatisfied, and not to allow those burdened by such needs to perish. It is also necessary to help these needy people to acquire expertise, to enter the circle of exchange, and to develop their skills in order to make the best use of their capacities and resources. Even prior to the logic of a fair exchange of goods and the forms of justice appropriate to it, there exists something which is due to man because he is man, by reason of his lofty dignity. Inseparable from that required "something" is the possibility to survive and, at the same time, to make an active contribution to the common good of humanity.

34.2 In Third World contexts, certain objectives stated by Rerum Novarum remain valid, and, in some cases, still constitute a goal yet to be reached, if a man's work and his very being are not to be reduced to the level of a mere commodity. These objectives include a sufficient wage for the support of the family, social insurance for old age and unemployment, and adequate protection for the conditions of employment.

35.1 Here we find a wide range of opportunities for commitment and effort in the name of justice on the part of trade unions and other workers' organizations. These defend workers' rights and protect their interests as persons, while fulfilling a vital cultural role, so as to enable workers to participate more fully and honorably in the life of their nation and to assist them along the path of development.

35.2 In this sense, it is right to speak of a struggle against an economic system, if the latter is understood as a method of upholding the absolute predominance of capital, the possession of the means of production and of the land, in contrast to the free and personal nature of human work.[73] In the struggle against such a system, what is being proposed as an alternative is not the socialist system, which in fact turns out to be State capitalism, but rather a society of free work, of enterprise and of participation. Such a society is not directed against the market, but demands that the market be appropriately controlled by the forces of society and by the State, so as to guarantee that the basic needs of the whole of society are satisfied.

35.3 The Church acknowledges the legitimate role of profit as an indication that a business is functioning well. When a firm makes a profit, this means that productive factors have been properly employed and corresponding human needs have been duly satisfied. But profitability is not the only indicator of a firm's condition. It is possible for the financial accounts to be in order, and yet for the people—who make up the firm's most valuable asset—to be humiliated and their dignity offended. Besides being morally inadmissible, this will eventually have negative repercussions on the firm's economic efficiency. In fact, the purpose of a business firm is not simply to make a profit, but is to be found in its very existence as a community of persons who in various ways are endeavoring to satisfy their basic needs, and who form a particular group at the service of the whole of society. Profit is a regulator of the life of a business, but it is not the only one; other human and moral factors must also be considered which, in the long term, are at least equally important for the life of a business.

35.4 We have seen that it is unacceptable to say that the defeat of so-called "Real Socialism" leaves capitalism as the only model of economic organization. It is necessary to break down the barriers and monopolies which leave so many countries on the margins of development, and to provide all individuals and nations with the basic conditions which will enable them to share in development. This goal calls for programmed and responsible efforts on the part of the entire international community. Stronger nations must offer weaker ones opportunities for taking their place in international life, and the latter must learn how to use these opportunities by making the necessary efforts and sacrifices and by ensuring political and economic stability, the certainty of better prospects for the future, the improvement of workers' skills, and the training of competent business leaders who are conscious of their responsibilities.[74]

35.5 At present, the positive efforts which have been made along these lines are being affected by the still largely unsolved problem of the foreign debt of the poorer countries. The principle that debts must be paid is certainly just. However, it is not right to demand or expect payment when the effect would be the imposition of political choices leading to hunger and despair for entire peoples. It cannot be expected that the debts which have been contracted should be paid at the price of unbearable sacrifices. In such cases it is necessary to find—as in fact is partly happening—ways to lighten, defer or even cancel the debt, compatible with the fundamental right of peoples to subsistence and progress.

36.1 It would now be helpful to direct our attention to the specific problems and threats emerging within the more advanced economies and which are related to their particular characteristics. In earlier stages of development, man always lived under the weight of necessity. His needs were few and were determined, to a degree, by the objective structures of his physical make-up. Economic activity was directed toward satisfying these needs. It is clear that today the problem is not only one of supplying people with a sufficient quantity of goods, but also of responding to a demand for quality: the quality of the goods to be produced and consumed, the quality of the services to be enjoyed, the quality of the environment and of life in general.

36.2 To call for an existence which is qualitatively more satisfying is of itself legitimate, but one cannot fail to draw attention to the new responsibilities and dangers connected with this phase of history. The manner in which new needs arise and are defined is always marked by a more or less appropriate concept of man and of his true good. A given culture reveals its overall understanding of life through the choices it makes in production and consumption. It is here that the phenomenon of consumerism arises. In singling out new needs and new means to meet them, one must be guided by a comprehensive picture of man which respects all the dimensions of his being and which subordinates his material and instinctive dimensions to his interior and spiritual ones. If, on the contrary, a direct appeal is made to human instincts—while ignoring in various ways the reality of the person as intelligent and free—then consumer attitudes and lifestyles can be created which are objectively improper and often damaging to the person's physical and spiritual health. Of itself, an economic system does not possess criteria for correctly distinguishing new and higher forms of satisfying human needs from artificial new needs which hinder the formation of a mature personality. Thus a great deal of educational and cultural work is urgently needed, including the education of consumers in the responsible use of their power of choice, the formation of a strong sense of responsibility among producers and among people in the mass media in particular, as well as the necessary intervention by public authorities.

36.3 A striking example of artificial consumption contrary to the health and dignity of the human person, and certainly not easy to control, is the use of drugs. Widespread drug use is a sign of a serious malfunction in the social system; it also implies a materialistic and, in a certain sense, destructive "reading" of human needs. In this way the innovative capacity of a free economy is brought to a one-sided and inadequate conclusion. Drugs, as well as pornography and other forms of consumerism which exploit the frailty of the weak, tend to fill the resulting spiritual void.

36.4 It is not wrong to want to live better; what is wrong is a style of life which is presumed to be better when it is directed toward "having" rather than "being," and which wants to have more, not in order to be more but in order to spend life in enjoyment as an end in itself.[75] It is therefore necessary to create lifestyles in which the quest for truth, beauty, goodness and communion with others for the sake of common growth are the factors which determine consumer choices, savings and investments. In this regard, it is not a matter of the duty of charity alone, that is, the duty to give from one's "abundance," and sometimes even out of one's needs, in order to provide what is essential for the life of a poor person. I am referring to the fact that even the decision to invest in one place rather than another, in one productive sector rather than another, is always a moral and cultural choice. Given the utter necessity of certain economic conditions and of political stability, the decision to invest, that is, to offer people an opportunity to make good use of their own labor, is also determined by an attitude of human sympathy and trust in Providence, which reveal the human quality of the person making such decisions.

37.1 Equally worrying is the ecological question which accompanies the problem of consumerism and which is closely connected to it. In his desire to have and to enjoy rather than to be and to grow, man consumes the resources of the earth and his own life in an excessive and disordered way. At the root of the senseless destruction of the natural environment lies an anthropological error, which unfortunately is widespread in our day. Man, who discovers his capacity to transform and in a certain sense create the world through his own work, forgets that this is always based on God's prior and original gift of the things that are. Man thinks that he can make arbitrary use of the earth, subjecting it without restraint to his will, as though the earth did not have its own requisites and a prior God-given purpose, which man can indeed develop but must not betray. Instead of carrying out his role as a cooperator with God in the work of creation, man sets himself up in place of God and thus ends up provoking a rebellion on the part of nature, which is more tyrannized than governed by him.[76]

37.2 In all this, one notes first the poverty or narrowness of man's outlook, motivated as he is by a desire to possess things rather than to relate them to the truth, and lacking that disinterested, unselfish and aesthetic attitude that is born of wonder in the presence of being and of the beauty which enables one to see in visible things the message of the invisible God who created them. In this regard, humanity today must be conscious of its duties and obligations toward future generations.

38.1 In addition to the irrational destruction of the natural environment, we must also mention the more serious destruction of the human environment, something which is by no means receiving the attention it deserves. Although people are rightly worried—though much less than they should be—about preserving the natural habitats of the various animal species threatened with extinction, because they realize that each of these species makes its particular contribution to the balance of nature in general, too little effort is made to safeguard the moral conditions for an authentic "human ecology." Not only has God given the earth to man, who must use it with respect for the original good purpose for which it was given, but man too is God's gift to man. He must therefore respect the natural and moral structure with which he has been endowed. In this context, mention should be made of the serious problems of modern urbanization, of the need for urban planning which is concerned with how people are to live, and of the attention which should be given to a "social ecology" of work.

38.2 Man receives from God his essential dignity and with it the capacity to transcend every social order so as to move toward truth and goodness. But he is also conditioned by the social structure in which he lives, by the education he has received and by his environment. These elements can either help or hinder his living in accordance with the truth. The decisions which create a human environment can give rise to specific structures of sin which impede the full realization of those who are in any way oppressed by them. To destroy such structures and replace them with more authentic forms of living in community is a task which demands courage and patience.[77]

39.1 The first and fundamental structure for "human ecology" is the family, in which man receives his first formative ideas about truth and goodness, and learns what it means to love and to be loved, and thus what it actually means to be a person. Here we mean the family founded on marriage, in which the mutual gift of self by husband and wife creates an environment in which children can be born and develop their potentialities, become aware of their dignity and prepare to face their unique and individual destiny. But it often happens that people are discouraged from creating the proper conditions for human reproduction and are led to consider themselves and their lives as a series of sensations to be experienced rather than as a work to be accomplished. The result is a lack of freedom, which causes a person to reject a commitment to enter into a stable relationship with another person and to bring children into the world, or which leads people to consider children as one of the many "things" which an individual can have or not have, according to taste, and which compete with other possibilities.

39.2 It is necessary to go back to seeing the family as the sanctuary of life. The family is indeed sacred: it is the place in which life—the gift of God—can be properly welcomed and protected against the many attacks to which it is exposed, and can develop in accordance with what constitutes authentic human growth. In the face of the so-called culture of death, the family is the heart of the culture of life.

39.3 Human ingenuity seems to be directed more toward limiting, suppressing or destroying the sources of life—including recourse to abortion, which unfortunately is so widespread in the world—than toward defending and opening up the possibilities of life. The Encyclical *Sollicitudo Rei Socialis* denounced systematic antichildbearing campaigns which, on the basis of a distorted view of the demographic problem and in a climate of "absolute lack of respect for the freedom of choice of the parties involved," often subject them "to intolerable pressures . . . in order to force them to submit to this new form of oppression."[78] These policies are extending their field of action by the use of new techniques, to the point of poisoning the lives of millions of defenseless human beings, as if in a form of "chemical warfare."

39.4 These criticisms are directed not so much against an economic system as against an ethical and cultural system. The economy in fact is only one aspect and one dimension of the whole of human activity. If economic life is absolutized, if the production and consumption of goods become the center of social life and society's only value, not subject to any other value, the reason is to be found not so much in the economic system itself as in the fact that the entire sociocultural system, by ignoring the ethical and religious dimension, has been weakened, and ends by limiting itself to the production of goods and services alone.[79]

39.5 All of this can be summed up by repeating once more that economic freedom is only one element of human freedom. When it becomes autonomous, when man is seen more as a producer or consumer of goods than as a subject who produces and consumes in order to live, then economic freedom loses its necessary relationship to the human person and ends up by alienating and oppressing him.[80]

40.1 It is the task of the State to provide for the defense and preservation of common goods such as the natural and human environments, which cannot be safeguarded simply by market forces. Just as in the time of primitive capitalism the State had the duty of defending the basic rights of workers, so now, with the new capitalism, the State and all of society have the duty of defending those collective goods which, among others, constitute the essential framework for the legitimate pursuit of personal goals on the part of each individual.

40.2 Here we find a new limit on the market: there are collective and qualitative needs which cannot be satisfied by market mechanisms. There are important human needs which escape its logic. There are goods which by their very nature cannot and must not be bought or sold. Certainly the mechanisms of the market offer secure advantages: they help to utilize resources better; they promote the exchange of products; above all they give central place to the person's desires and preferences, which, in a contract, meet the desires and preferences of another person. Nevertheless, these mechanisms carry the risk of an "idolatry" of the market, an idolatry which ignores the existence of goods which by their nature are not and cannot be mere commodities.

41.1 Marxism criticized capitalist bourgeois societies, blaming them for the commercialization and alienation of human existence. This rebuke is of course based on a mistaken and inadequate idea of alienation, derived solely from the sphere of relationships of production and ownership, that is, giving them a materialistic foundation and moreover denying the legitimacy and positive value of market relationships even in their own sphere. Marxism thus ends up by affirming that only in a collective society can alienation be eliminated. However, the historical experience of socialist countries has sadly demonstrated that collectivism does not do away with alienation but rather increases it, adding to it a lack of basic necessities and economic inefficiency.

41.2 The historical experience of the West, for its part, shows that even if the Marxist analysis and its foundation of alienation are false, nevertheless alienation—and the loss of the authentic meaning of life—is a reality in Western societies too. This happens in consumerism, when people are ensnared in a web of false and superficial gratifications rather than being helped to experience their personhood in an authentic and concrete way. Alienation is found also in work, when it is organized so as to ensure maximum returns and profits with no concern whether the worker, through his own labor, grows or diminishes as a person, either through increased sharing in a genuinely supportive community or through increased isolation in a maze of relationships marked by destructive competitiveness and estrangement, in which he is considered only a means and not an end.

41.3 The concept of alienation needs to be led back to the Christian vision of reality, by recognizing in alienation a reversal of means and ends. When man does not recognize in himself and in others the value and grandeur of the human person, he effectively deprives himself of the possibility of benefitting from his humanity and of entering into that relationship of solidarity and communion with others for which God created him. Indeed, it is through the free gift of self that one truly finds oneself.[81] This gift is made possible by the human person's essential "capacity for transcendence." Man cannot give himself to a purely human plan for reality, to an abstract ideal or to a false utopia. As a person, he can give himself to another person or to other persons, and ultimately to God, who is the author or our being and who alone can fully accept our gift.[82] Man is alienated if he refuses to transcend himself and to live the experience of self-giving and of the formation of an authentic human community oriented toward his final destiny, which is God. A society is alienated if its forms of social organization, production and consumption make it more difficult to offer this gift of self and to establish this solidarity between people.

41.4 Exploitation, at least in the forms analyzed and described by Karl Marx, has been overcome in Western society. Alienation, however, has not been overcome as it exists in various forms of exploitation, when people use one another, and when they seek an ever more refined satisfaction of their individual and secondary needs, while ignoring the principal and authentic needs which ought to regulate the manner of satisfying the other ones too.[83] A person who is concerned solely or primarily with possessing and enjoying, who is no longer able to control his instincts and passions, or to subordinate them by obedience to the truth, cannot be free: obedience to the truth about God and man is the first condition of freedom, making it possible for a person to order his needs and desires and to choose the means of satisfying them according to a correct scale of values, so that the ownership of things may become an occasion of personal growth. This growth can be hindered as a result of manipulation by the means of mass communication, which impose fashions and trends of opinion through carefully orchestrated repetition, without its being possible to subject to critical scrutiny the premises on which these fashions and trends are based.

42.1 Returning now to the initial question: can it perhaps be said that, after the failure of Communism, capitalism is the victorious social system, and that capitalism should be the goal of the countries now making efforts to rebuild their economy and society? Is this the model which ought to be proposed to the countries of the Third World which are searching for the path to true economic and civil progress?

42.2 The answer is obviously complex. If by "capitalism" is meant an economic system which recognizes the fundamental and positive role of business, the market, private property and the resulting responsibility for the means of production, as well as free human creativity in the economic sector, then the answer is certainly in the affirmative, even though it would perhaps be more appropriate to speak of a "business economy," "market economy" or simply "free economy." But if by "capitalism" is meant a system in which freedom in the economic sector is not circumscribed within a strong juridical framework which places it at the service of human freedom in its totality and sees it as a particular aspect of that freedom, the core of which is ethical and religious, then the reply is certainly negative.

42.3 The Marxist solution has failed, but the realities of marginalization and exploitation remain in the world, especially the Third World, as does the reality of human alienation, especially in the more advanced countries. Against these phenomena the Church strongly raises her voice. Vast multitudes are still living in conditions of great material and moral poverty. The collapse of the Communist system in so many countries certainly removes an obstacle to facing these problems in an appropriate and realistic way, but it is not enough to bring about their solution. Indeed, there is a risk that a radical capitalistic ideology could spread which refuses even to consider these problems, in the a priori belief that any attempt to solve them is doomed to failure, and which blindly entrusts their solution to the free development of market forces.

43.1 The Church has no models to present; models that are real and truly effective can only arise within the framework of different historical situations, through the efforts of all those who responsibly confront concrete problems in all their social, economic, political and cultural aspects, as these interact with one another.[84] For such a task the Church offers her social teaching as an indispensable and ideal orientation, a teaching which, as already mentioned, recognizes the positive value of the market and of enterprise, but which at the same time points out that these need to be oriented toward the common good. This teaching also recognizes the legitimacy of workers' efforts to obtain full respect for their dignity and to gain broader areas of participation in the life of industrial enterprises so that, while cooperating with others and under the direction of others, they can in a certain sense "work for themselves"[85] through the exercise of their intelligence and freedom.

43.2 The integral development of the human person through work does not impede but rather promotes the greater productivity and efficiency of work itself, even though it may weaken consolidated power structures. A business cannot be considered only as a "society of capital goods"; it is also a "society of persons" in which people participate in different ways and with specific responsibilities, whether they supply the necessary capital for the company's activities or take part in such activities through their labor. To achieve these goals there is still need for a broad associated workers' movement, directed toward the liberation and promotion of the whole person.

43.3 In the light of today's "new things," we have reread the relationship between individual or private property and the universal destination of material wealth. Man fulfills himself by using his intelligence and freedom. In so doing he utilizes the things of this world as objects and instruments and makes them his own. The foundation of the right to private initiative and ownership is to be found in this activity. By means of his work man commits himself, not only for his own sake but also for others and with others. Each person collaborates in the work of others and for their good. Man works in order to provide for the needs of his family, his community, his nation, and ultimately all humanity.[86] Moreover, a person collaborates in the work of his fellow employees, as well as in the work of suppliers and in the customers' use of goods, in a progressively expanding chain of solidarity. Ownership of the means of production, whether in industry or agriculture, is just and legitimate if it serves useful work. It becomes illegitimate, however, when it is not utilized or when it serves to impede the work of others, in an effort to gain a profit which is not the result of the overall expansion of work and the wealth of society, but rather is the result of curbing them or of illicit exploitation, speculation or the breaking of solidarity among working people.[87] Ownership of this kind has no justification, and represents an abuse in the sight of God and man.

43.4 The obligation to earn one's bread by the sweat of one's brow also presumes the right to do so. A society in which this right is systematically denied, in which economic policies do not allow workers to reach satisfactory levels of employment, cannot be justified from an ethical point of view, nor can that society attain social peace.[88] Just as the person fully realizes himself in the free gift of self, so too ownership morally justifies itself in the creation, at the proper time and in the proper way, of opportunities for work and human growth for all.

V
STATE AND CULTURE

44.1 Pope Leo XIII was aware of the need for a sound theory of the State in order to ensure the normal development of man's spiritual and temporal activities, both of which are indispensable.[89] For this reason, in one passage of Rerum Novarum he presents the organization of society according to the three powers—legislative, executive and judicial—something which at the time represented a novelty in Church teaching.[90] Such an ordering reflects a realistic vision of man's social nature, which calls for legislation capable of protecting the freedom of all. To that end, it is preferable that each power be balanced by other powers and by other spheres of responsibility which keep it within proper bounds. This is the principle of the "rule of law," in which the law is sovereign, and not the arbitrary will of individuals.

44.2 In modern times, this concept has been opposed by totalitarianism, which, in its Marxist-Leninist form, maintains that some people, by virtue of a deeper knowledge of the laws of the development of society, or through membership of a particular class or through contact with the deeper sources of the collective consciousness, are exempt from error and can therefore arrogate to themselves the exercise of absolute power. It must be added that totalitarianism arises out of a denial of truth in the objective sense. If there is no transcendent truth, in obedience to which man achieves his full identity, then there is no sure principle for guaranteeing just relations between people. Their self-interest as a class, group or nation would inevitably set them in opposition to one another. If one does not acknowledge transcendent truth, then the force of power takes over, and each person tends to make full use of the means at his disposal in order to impose his own interests or his own opinion, with no regard for the rights of others. People are then respected only to the extent that they can be exploited for selfish ends. Thus, the root of modern totalitarianism is to be found in the denial of the transcendent dignity of the human person who, as the visible image of the invisible God, is therefore by his very nature the subject of rights which no one may violate—no individual, group, class, nation or State. Not even the majority of a social body may violate these rights, by going against the minority, by isolating, oppressing, or exploiting it, or by attempting to annihilate it.[91]

45.1 The culture and praxis of totalitarianism also involve a rejection of the Church. The State or the party which claims to be able to lead history toward perfect goodness, and which sets itself above all values, cannot tolerate the affirmation of an objective criterion of good and evil beyond the will of those in power, since such a criterion, in given circumstances, could be used to judge their actions. This explains why totalitarianism attempts to destroy the Church, or at least to reduce her to submission, making her an instrument of its own ideological apparatus.[92]

45.2 Furthermore, the totalitarian State tends to absorb within itself the nation, society, the family, religious groups and individuals themselves. In defending her own freedom, the Church is also defending the human person, who must obey God rather than men (cf. Acts 5:29), as well as defending the family, the various social organizations and nations—all of which enjoy their own spheres of autonomy and sovereignty.

46.1 The Church values the democratic system inasmuch as it ensures the participation of citizens in making political choices, guarantees to the governed the possibility both of electing and holding accountable those who govern them, and of replacing them through peaceful means when appropriate.[93] Thus she cannot encourage the formation of narrow ruling groups which usurp the power of the State for individual interests or for ideological ends.

46.2 Authentic democracy is possible only in a State ruled by law, and on the basis of a correct conception of the human person. It requires that the necessary conditions be present for the advancement both of the individual through education and formation in true ideals, and of the "subjectivity" of society through the creation of structures of participation and shared responsibility. Nowadays there is a tendency to claim that agnosticism and skeptical relativism are the philosophy and the basic attitude which correspond to democratic forms of political life. Those who are convinced that they know the truth and firmly adhere to it are considered unreliable from a democratic point of view, since they do not accept that truth is determined by the majority, or that it is subject to variation according to different political trends. It must be observed in this regard that if there is no ultimate truth to guide and direct political activity, then ideas and convictions can easily be manipulated for reasons of power. As history demonstrates, a democracy without values easily turns into open or thinly disguised totalitarianism.

46.3 Nor does the Church close her eyes to the danger of fanaticism or fundamentalism among those who, in the name of an ideology which purports to be scientific or religious, claim the right to impose on others their own concept of what is true and good. Christian truth is not of this kind. Since it is not an ideology, the Christian faith does not presume to imprison changing sociopolitical realities in a rigid schema, and it recognizes that human life is realized in history in conditions that are diverse and imperfect. Furthermore, in constantly reaffirming the transcendent dignity of the person, the Church's method is always that of respect for freedom.[94]

46.4 But freedom attains its full development only be accepting the truth. In a world without truth, freedom loses its foundation and man is exposed to the violence of passion and to manipulation, both open and hidden. The Christian upholds freedom and serves it, constantly offering to others the truth which he has known (cf. Jn 8:31–32), in accordance with the missionary nature of his vocation. While paying heed to every fragment of truth which he encounters in the life experience and in the culture of individuals and of nations, he will not fail to affirm in dialogue with others all that his faith and the correct use of reason have enabled him to understand.[95]

47.1 Following the collapse of Communist totalitarianism and of many other totalitarian and "national security" regimes, today we are witnessing a predominance, not without signs of opposition, of the democratic ideal, together with lively attention to and concern for human rights. But for this very reason it is necessary for peoples in the process of reforming their systems to give democracy an authentic and solid foundation through the explicit recognition of those rights.[96] Among the most important of these rights, mention must be made of the right to life, an integral part of which is the right of the child to develop in the mother's womb from the moment of conception; the right to live in a united family and in a moral environment conducive to the growth of the child's personality; the right to develop one's intelligence and freedom in seeking and knowing the truth; the right to share in the work which makes wise use of the earth's material resources, and to derive from that work the means to support oneself and one's dependents; and the right freely to establish a family, to have and to rear children through the responsible exercise of one's sexuality. In a certain sense, the source and synthesis of these rights is religious freedom, understood as the right to live in the truth of one's faith and in conformity with one's transcendent dignity as a person.[97]

47.2 Even in countries with democratic forms of government, these rights are not always fully respected. Here we are referring not only to the scandal of abortion, but also to different aspects of a crisis within democracies themselves, which seem at times to have lost the ability to make decisions aimed at the common good. Certain demands which arise within society are sometimes not examined in accordance with criteria of justice and morality, but rather on the basis of the electoral or financial power of the groups promoting them. With time, such distortions of political conduct create distrust and apathy, with a subsequent decline in the political participation and civic spirit of the general population, which feels abused and disillusioned. As a result, there is a growing inability to situate particular interests within the framework of a coherent vision of the common good. The latter is not simply the sum total of particular interests; rather it involves an assessment and integration of those interests on the basis of a balanced hierarchy of values; ultimately, it demands a correct understanding of the dignity and the rights of the person.[98]

47.3 The Church respects the legitimate autonomy of the democratic order and is not entitled to express preferences for this or that institutional or constitutional solution. Her contribution to the political order is precisely her vision of the dignity of the person revealed in all its fullness in the mystery of the Incarnate Word.[99]

48.1 These general observations also apply to the role of the State in the economic sector. Economic activity, especially the activity of a market economy, cannot be conducted in an institutional, juridical or political vacuum. On the contrary, it presupposes sure guarantees of individual freedom and private property, as well as a stable currency and efficient public services. Hence the principal task of the State is to guarantee this security, so that those who work and produce can enjoy the fruits of their labors and thus feel encouraged to work efficiently and honestly. The absence of stability, together with the corruption of public officials and the spread of improper sources of growing rich and of easy profits deriving form illegal or purely speculative activities, constitutes one of the chief obstacles to development and to the economic order.

48.2 Another task of the State is that of overseeing and directing the exercise of human rights in the economic sector. However, primary responsibility in this area belongs not to the State but to individuals and to the various groups and associations which make up society. The State could not directly ensure the right to work for all its citizens unless it controlled every aspect of economic life and restricted the free initiative of individuals. This does not mean, however, that the State has no competence in this domain, as was claimed by those who argued against any rules in the economic sphere. Rather, the State has a duty to sustain business activities by creating conditions which will ensure job opportunities, by stimulating those activities where they are lacking or by supporting them in moments of crisis.

48.3 The State has the further right to intervene when particular monopolies create delays or obstacles to development. In addition to the tasks of harmonizing and guiding development, in exceptional circumstances the State can also exercise a substitute function, when social sectors or business systems are too weak or are just getting under way, and are not equal to the task at hand. Such supplementary interventions, which are justified by urgent reasons touching the common good, must be as brief as possible, so as to avoid removing permanently from society and business systems the functions which are properly theirs, and so as to avoid enlarging excessively the sphere of State intervention to the detriment of both economic and civil freedom.

48.4 In recent years the range of such intervention has vastly expanded, to the point of creating a new type of State, the so-called "Welfare State." This has happened in some countries in order to respond better to many needs and demands, by remedying forms of poverty and deprivation unworthy of the human person. However, excesses and abuses, especially in recent years, have provoked very harsh criticisms of the Welfare State, dubbed the "Social Assistance State." Malfunctions and defects in the Social Assistance State are the result of an inadequate understanding of the tasks proper to the State. Here again the principle of subsidiarity must be respected: a community of a higher order should not interfere in the internal life of a community of a lower order, depriving the latter of its functions, but rather should support it in case of need and help to coordinate its activity with the activities of the rest of society, always with a view to the common good.[100]

48.5 By intervening directly and depriving society of its responsibility, the Social Assistance State leads to a loss of human energies and an inordinate increase of public agencies, which are dominated more by bureaucratic ways of thinking than by concern for serving their clients, and which are accompanied by an enormous increase in spending. In fact, it would appear that needs are best understood and satisfied by people who are closest to them and who act as neighbors to those in need. It should be added that certain kinds of demands often call for a response which is not simply material but which is capable of perceiving the deeper human need. One thinks of the condition of refugees, immigrants, the elderly, the sick, and all those in circumstances which call for assistance, such as drug abusers: all these people can be helped effectively only by those who offer them genuine fraternal support, in addition to the necessary care.

49.1 Faithful to the mission received from Christ her Founder, the Church has always been present and active among the needy, offering them material assistance in ways that neither humiliate nor reduce them to mere objects of assistance, but which help them to escape their precarious situation by promoting their dignity as persons. With heartfelt gratitude to God it must be pointed out that active charity has never ceased to be practiced in the Church; indeed, today it is showing a manifold and gratifying increase. In this regard, special mention must be made of volunteer work, which the Church favors and promotes by urging everyone to cooperate in supporting and encouraging its undertakings.

49.2 In order to overcome today's widespread individualistic mentality, what is required is a concrete commitment to solidarity and charity, beginning in the family with the mutual support of husband and wife and the care which the different generations give to one another. In this sense the family too can be called a community of work and solidarity. It can happen, however, that when a family does decide to live up fully to its vocation, it finds itself without the necessary support from the State and without sufficient resources. It is urgent therefore to promote not only family policies, but also those social policies which have the family as their principal object, policies which assist the family by providing adequate resources and efficient means of support, both for bringing up children and for looking after the elderly, so as to avoid distancing the latter from the family unit and in order to strengthen relations between generations.[101]

49.3 Apart from the family, other intermediate communities exercise primary functions and give life to specific networks of solidarity. These develop as real communities of persons and strengthen the social fabric, preventing society from becoming an anonymous and impersonal mass, as unfortunately often happens today. It is in interrelationships on many levels that a person lives, and that society becomes more "personalized." The individual today is often suffocated between two poles represented by the State and the marketplace. At times it seems as though he exists only as a producer and consumer of goods, or as an object of State administration. People lose sight of the fact that life in society has neither the market nor the State as its final purpose, since life itself has a unique value which the State and the market must serve. Man remains above all a being who seeks the truth and strives to live in that truth, deepening his understanding of it through a dialogue which involves past and future generations.[102]

50.1 From this open search for truth, which is renewed in every generation, the culture of a nation derives its character. Indeed, the heritage of values which has been received and handed down is always challenged by the young. To challenge does not necessarily mean to destroy or reject a priori, but above all to put these values to test in one's own life, and through this existential verification to make them more real, relevant and personal, distinguishing the valid elements in the tradition from false and erroneous ones, or from obsolete forms which can be usefully replaced by others more suited to the times.

50.2 In this context, it is appropriate to recall that evangelization too plays a role in the culture of the various nations, sustaining culture in its progress toward the truth, and assisting in the work of its purification and enrichment.[103] However, when a culture becomes inward-looking, and tries to perpetuate obsolete ways of living by rejecting any exchange or debate with regard to the truth about man, then it becomes sterile and is heading for decadence.

51.1 All human activity takes place within a culture and interacts with culture. For an adequate formation of a culture, the involvement of the whole man is required, whereby he exercises his creativity, intelligence, and knowledge of the world and of people. Furthermore, he displays his capacity for self-control, personal sacrifice, solidarity and readiness to promote the common good. Thus the first and most important task is accomplished within man's heart. The way in which he is involved in building his own future depends on the understanding he has of himself and of his own destiny. It is on this level that the Church's specific and decisive contribution to true culture is to be found. The Church promotes these aspects of human behavior which favor a true culture of peace, as opposed to models in which the individual is lost in the crowd, in which the role of his initiative and freedom is neglected, and in which his greatness is posited in the arts of conflict and war. The Church renders this service to human society by preaching the truth about the creation of the world, which God has placed in human hands so that people may make it fruitful and more perfect through their work; and by preaching the truth about the Redemption, whereby the Son of God has saved mankind and at the same time has united all people, making them responsible for one another. Sacred Scripture continually speaks to us of an active commitment to our neighbor and demands of us a shared responsibility for all of humanity.

51.2 This duty is not limited to one's own family, nation or State, but extends progressively to all mankind, since no one can consider himself extraneous or indifferent to the lot of another member of the human family. No one can say that he is not responsible for the well-being of his brother or sister (cf. Gen 4:9; Lk 10:29–37; Mt 25:31–46). Attentive and pressing concern for one's neighbor in a moment of need—made easier today because of the new means of communication which have brought people closer together—is especially important with regard to the search for ways of resolving international conflicts other than by war. It is not hard to see that the terrifying power of the means of destruction—to which even medium and small-sized countries have access—and the ever closer links between the peoples of the whole world make it very difficult or practically impossible to limit the consequences of a conflict.

52.1 Pope Benedict XV and his successors clearly understood this danger.[104] I myself, on the occasion of the recent tragic war in the Persian Gulf, repeated the cry: "War—never again!" No, never again war, which destroys the lives of innocent people, teaches how to kill, throws into upheaval even the lives of those who do the killing and leaves behind a trail of resentment and hatred, thus making it all the more difficult to find a just solution of the very problems which provoked the war. Just as the time has finally come when in individual States a system of private vendetta and reprisal has given way to the rule of law, so too a similar step forward is now urgently needed in the international community. Furthermore, it must not be forgotten that at the root of war there are usually real and serious grievances: injustices suffered, legitimate aspirations frustrated, poverty, and the exploitation of multitudes of desperate people who see no real possibility of improving their lot by peaceful means.

52.2 For this reason, another name for peace is development.[105] Just as there is a collective responsibility for avoiding war, so too there is a collective responsibility for promoting development. Just as within individual societies it is possible and right to organize a solid economy which will direct the functioning of the market to the common good, so too there is a similar need for adequate interventions on the international level. For this to happen, a great effort must be made to enhance mutual understanding and knowledge, and to increase the sensitivity of consciences. This is the culture which is hoped for, one which fosters trust in the human potential of the poor, and consequently in their ability to improve their condition through work or to make a positive contribution to economic prosperity. But to accomplish this, the poor—be they individuals or nations—need to be provided with realistic opportunities. Creating such conditions calls for a concerted worldwide effort to promote development, an effort which also involves sacrificing the positions of income and of power enjoyed by the more developed economies.[106]

52.3 This may mean making important changes in established lifestyles, in order to limit the waste of environmental and human resources, thus enabling every individual and all the peoples of the earth to have a sufficient share of those resources. In addition, the new material and spiritual resources must be utilized which are the result of the work and culture of peoples who today are on the margins of the international community, so as to obtain an overall human enrichment of the family of nations.

VI
MAN IS THE WAY OF THE CHURCH

53.1 Faced with the poverty of the working class, Pope Leo XIII wrote: "We approach this subject with confidence, and in the exercise of the rights which manifestly pertain to us. . . . By keeping silence we would seem to neglect the duty incumbent on us."[107] During the last hundred years the Church has repeatedly expressed her thinking, while closely following the continuing development of the social question. She has certainly not done this in order to recover former privileges or to impose her own vision. Her sole purpose has been care and responsibility for man, who has been entrusted to her by Christ himself: for this man, whom, as the Second Vatican Council recalls, is the only creature on earth which God willed for its own sake, and for which God has his plan, that is, a share in eternal salvation. We are not dealing here with man in the "abstract," but with the real, "concrete," "historical" man. We are dealing with each individual, since each one is included in the mystery of Redemption, and through this mystery Christ has united himself with each one forever.[108] It follows that the Church cannot abandon man, and that "this man is the primary route that the Church must travel in fulfilling her mission . . . the way traced out by Christ himself, the way that leads invariably through the mystery of the Incarnation and the Redemption."[109]

53.2 This, and this alone, is the principle which inspires the Church's social doctrine. The Church has gradually developed that doctrine in a systematic way, above all in the century that has followed the date we are commemorating, precisely because the horizon of the Church's whole wealth of doctrine is man in his concrete reality as sinful and righteous.

54.1 Today, the Church's social doctrine focuses especially on man as he is involved in a complex network of relationships within modern societies. The human sciences and philosophy are helpful for interpreting man's central place within society and for enabling him to understand himself better as a "social being." However, a man's true identity is only fully revealed to him through faith, and it is precisely from faith that the Church's social teaching begins. While drawing upon all the contributions made by the sciences and philosophy, her social teaching is aimed at helping everyone on the path of salvation.

54.2 The Encyclical Rerum Novarum can be read as a valid contribution to socioeconomic analysis at the end of the nineteenth century, but its specific value derives from the fact that it is a document of the Magisterium and is fully a part of the Church's evangelizing mission, together with many other documents of this nature. Thus the Church's social teaching is itself a valid instrument of evangelization. As such, it proclaims God and his mystery of salvation in Christ to every human being, and for that very reason reveals man to himself. In this light, and only in this light, does it concern itself with everything else: the human rights of the individual, and in particular of the "working class," the family and education, the duties of the State, the ordering of national and international society, economic life, culture, war and peace, and respect for life from the moment of conception until death.

55.1 The Church receives "the meaning of man" from divine revelation. "In order to know man, authentic man, man in his fullness, one must know God," said Pope Paul VI, and he went on to quote Saint Catherine of Siena, who, in prayer, expressed the same idea: "In your nature, O eternal Godhead, I shall know my own nature."[110]

55.2 Christian anthropology therefore is really a chapter of theology, and for this reason, the Church's social doctrine, by its concern for man and by its interest in him and in the way he conducts himself in the world, "belongs to the field . . . of theology and particularly of moral theology."[111] The theological dimension is needed both for interpreting and solving present-day problems in human society. It is worth noting that this is true in contrast both to the "atheistic" solution, which deprives man of one of his basic dimensions, namely the spiritual one, and to permissive and consumerist solutions, which under various pretexts seek to convince man that he is free from every law and from God himself, thus imprisoning him within a selfishness which ultimately harms both him and others.

55.3 When the Church proclaims God's salvation to man, when she offers and communicates the life of God through the sacraments, when she gives direction to human life through the commandments of love of God and neighbor, she contributes to the enrichment of human dignity. But just as the Church can never abandon her religious and transcendent mission on behalf of man, so too she is aware that today her activity meets with particular difficulties and obstacles. That is why she devotes herself with ever new energies and methods to an evangelization which promotes the whole human being. Even on the eve of the third millennium she continues to be "a sign and safeguard of the transcendence of the human person,"[112] as indeed she has always sought to be from the beginning of her existence, walking together with man through history. The Encyclical *Rerum Novarum* itself is a significant sign of this.

56.1 On the hundredth anniversary of that Encyclical I wish to thank all those who have devoted themselves to studying, expounding and making better known Christian social teaching. To this end, the cooperation of the local Churches is indispensable, and I would hope that the present anniversary will be a source of fresh enthusiasm for studying, spreading and applying that teaching in various contexts.

56.2 In particular, I wish this teaching to be made known and applied in the countries which, following the collapse of "Real Socialism," are experiencing a serious lack of direction in the work of rebuilding. The Western countries, in turn, run the risk of seeing this collapse as a one-sided victory of their own economic system and thereby failing to make necessary corrections in that system. Meanwhile, the countries of the Third World are experiencing more than ever the tragedy of underdevelopment, which is becoming more serious with each passing day.

56.3 After formulating principles and guidelines for the solution of the worker question, Pope Leo XIII made this incisive statement: "Everyone should put his hand to the work which falls to his share, and that at once and straightway, lest the evil which is already so great become through delay absolutely beyond remedy," and he added, "in regard to the Church, her cooperation will never be found lacking."[113]

57.1 As far as the Church is concerned, the social message of the Gospel must not be considered a theory, but above all else a bias and a motivation for action. Inspired by this message, some of the first Christians distributed their goods to the poor, bearing witness to the fact that, despite different social origins, it was possible for people to live together in peace and harmony. Through the power of the Gospel, down the centuries monks tilled the land, men and women Religious founded hospitals and shelters for the poor, Confraternities as well as individual men and women of all states of life devoted themselves to the needy and to those on the margins of society, convinced as they were that Christ's words "as you did it to one of the least of these my brethren, you did it to me" (Mt 25:40) were not intended to remain a pious wish, but were meant to become a concrete life commitment.

57.2 Today more than ever, the Church is aware that her social message will gain credibility more immediately from the witness of actions than as a result of its internal logic and consistency. This awareness is also a source of her preferential option for the poor, which is never exclusive or discriminatory toward other groups. This option is not limited to material poverty, since it is well known that there are many other forms of poverty, especially in modern society—not only economic but cultural and spiritual poverty as well. The Church's love for the poor, which is essential for her and a part of her constant tradition, impels her to give attention to a world in which poverty is threatening to assume massive proportions in spite of technological and economic progress. In the countries of the West, different forms of poverty are being experienced by groups which live on the margins of society, by the elderly and the sick, by the victims of consumerism, and even more immediately by so many refugees and migrants. In the developing countries, tragic crises loom on the horizon unless internationally coordinated measures are taken before it is too late.

58 Love for others, and in the first place love for the poor, in whom the Church sees Christ himself, is made concrete in the promotion of justice. Justice will never be fully attained unless people see in the poor person, who is asking for help in order to survive, not an annoyance or a burden, but an opportunity for showing kindness and a chance for greater enrichment. Only such an awareness can give the courage needed to face the risk and the change involved in every authentic attempt to come to the aid of another. It is not merely a matter of "giving from one's surplus," but of helping entire peoples which are presently excluded or marginalized to enter into the sphere of economic and human development. For this to happen, it is not enough to draw on the surplus goods which in fact our world abundantly produces; it requires above all a change of lifestyles, of models of production and consumption, and of the established structures of power which today govern societies. Nor is it a matter of eliminating instruments of social organization which have proved useful, but rather of orienting them according to an adequate notion of the common good in relation to the whole human family. Today we are facing the so-called "globalization" of the economy, a phenomenon which is not to be dismissed, since it can create unusual opportunities for greater prosperity. There is a growing feeling, however, that this increasing internationalization of the economy ought to be accompanied by effective international agencies which will oversee and direct the economy to the common good, something that an individual State, even if it were the most powerful on earth, would not be in a position to do. In order to achieve this result, it is necessary that there be increased coordination among the more powerful countries, and that in international agencies the interests of the whole human family be equally represented. It is also necessary that in evaluating the consequences of their decisions, these agencies always give sufficient consideration to peoples and countries which have little weight in the international market, but which are burdened by the most acute and desperate needs, and are thus more dependent on support for their development. Much remains to be done in this area.

59.1 Therefore, in order that the demands of justice may be met, and attempts to achieve this goal may succeed, what is needed is the gift of grace, a gift which comes from God. Grace, in cooperation with human freedom, constitutes that mysterious presence of God in history which is Providence.

59.2 The newness which is experienced in following Christ demands to be communicated to other people in their concrete difficulties, struggles, problems and challenges, so that these can then be illuminated and made more human in the light of faith. Faith not only helps people to find solutions; it makes even situations of suffering humanly bearable, so that in these situations people will not become lost or forget their dignity and vocation.

59.3 In addition, the Church's social teaching has an important interdisciplinary dimension. In order better to incarnate the one truth about man in different and constantly changing social, economic and political contexts, this teaching enters into dialogue with the various disciplines concerned with man. It assimilates what these disciplines have to contribute, and helps them to open themselves to a broader horizon, aimed at serving the individual person who is acknowledged and loved in the fullness of his or her vocation.

59.4 Parallel with the interdisciplinary aspect, mention should also be made of the practical and as it were experiential dimension of this teaching, which is to be found at the crossroads where Christian life and conscience come into contact with the real world. This teaching is seen in the efforts of individuals, families, people involved in cultural and social life, as well as politicians and statesmen, to give it a concrete form and application in history.

60.1 In proclaiming the principles for a solution of the worker question, Pope Leo XIII wrote: "This most serious question demands the attention and the efforts of others."[114] He was convinced that the grave problems caused by industrial society could be solved only be cooperation between all forces. This affirmation has become a permanent element of the Church's social teaching, and also explains why Pope John XXIII addressed his Encyclical on peace to "all people of good will."

60.2 Pope Leo, however, acknowledged with sorrow that the ideologies of his time, especially Liberalism and Marxism, rejected such cooperation. Since then, many things have changed, especially in recent years. The world today is ever more aware that solving serious national and international problems is not just a matter of economic production or of juridical or social organization, but also calls for specific ethical and religious values, as well as changes of mentality, behavior and structures. The Church feels a particular responsibility to offer this contribution and, as I have written in the Encyclical *Sollicitudo Rei Socialis*, there is a reasonable hope that the many people who profess no religion will also contribute to providing the social question with the necessary ethical foundation.[115]

60.3 In that same Encyclical I also addressed an appeal to the Christian Churches and to all the great world religions, inviting them to offer the unanimous witness of our common convictions regarding the dignity of man, created by God.[116] In fact I am convinced that the various religions, now and in the future, will have a preeminent role in preserving peace and in building a society worthy of man.

60.4 Indeed, openness to dialogue and to cooperation is required of all people of good will, and in particular of individuals and groups with specific responsibilities in the areas of politics, economics and social life, at both the national and international levels.

61.1 At the beginning of industrialized society, it was "a yoke little better than that of slavery itself" which led my Predecessor to speak out in defense of man. Over the past hundred years the Church has remained faithful to this duty. Indeed, she intervened in the turbulent period of class struggle after the First World War in order to defend people from economic exploitation and from the tyranny of the totalitarian systems. After the Second World War, she put the dignity of the person at the center of her social messages, insisting that material goods were meant for all, and that the social order ought to be free of oppression and based on a spirit of cooperation and solidarity. The Church has constantly repeated that the person and society need not only material goods but spiritual and religious values as well. Furthermore, as she has become more aware of the fact that too many people live, not in the prosperity of the Western world, but in the poverty of the developing countries amid conditions which are still "a yoke little better than that of slavery itself," she has felt and continues to feel obliged to denounce this fact with absolute clarity and frankness, although she knows that her call will not always win favor with everyone.

61.2 One hundred years after the publication of *Rerum Novarum*, the Church finds herself still facing "new things" and new challenges. The centenary celebration should therefore confirm the commitment of all people of good will and of believers in particular.

62.1 The present Encyclical has looked at the past, but above all it is directed to the future. Like Rerum Novarum, it comes almost at the threshold of a new century, and its intention, with God's help, is to prepare for that moment.

62.2 In every age the true and perennial "newness of things" comes from the infinite power of God, who says: "Behold, I make all things new" (Rev 21:5). These words refer to the fulfillment of history, when Christ "delivers the Kingdom to God the Father . . . that God may be everything to everyone" (1 Cor 15:24, 28). But the Christian well knows that the newness which we await in its fullness at the Lord's second coming has been present since the creation of the world, and in a special way since the time when God became man in Jesus Christ and brought about a "new creation" with him and through him (2 Cor 5:17; Gal 6:15).

62.3 In concluding this Encyclical I again give thanks to Almighty God, who has granted his Church the light and strength to accompany humanity on its earthly journey toward its eternal destiny. In the third millennium too, the Church will be faithful in making man's way her own, knowing that she does not walk alone, but with Christ her Lord. It is Christ who made man's way his own, and who guides him, even when he is unaware of it.

62.4 Mary, the Mother of the Redeemer, constantly remained beside Christ in his journey toward the human family and in its midst, and she goes before the Church on the pilgrimage of faith. May her maternal intercession accompany humanity toward the next millennium, in fidelity to him who "is the same yesterday and today and for ever" (cf. Heb 13:8), Jesus Christ our Lord, in whose name I cordially impart my blessing to all.

Given in Rome, at Saint Peter's, on May 1, the Memorial of Saint Joseph the Worker, in the year 1991, the thirteenth of my Pontificate.

NOTES

1. Leo XIII, Encyclical Letter *Rerum Novarum* (May 15, 1891): Leonis XIII P. M. Acta, XI, Rome, 1892, 97–144.
2. Pius XI, Encyclical Letter *Quadragesimo Anno* (May 15, 1931): AAS 23 (1931), 177–228; Pius XII, Radio Message (June 1, 1941): AAS 33 (1941), 195–205; John XXIII, Encyclical Letter *Mater et Magistra* (May 15, 1961): AAS 53 (1961), 401–464; Paul VI, Apostolic Letter *Octogesima Adveniens* (May 14, 1971): AAS 63 (1971), 401–441.
3. Cf. Pius XI, Encyclical Letter *Quadragesimo Anno* (May 15, 1931), III: AAS 23 (1931), 228.
4. Encyclical Letter *Laborem Exercens* (September 14, 1981): AAS 73 (1981), 577–647; Encyclical Letter *Sollicitudo Rei Socialis* (December 30, 1987): AAS 80 (1988), 513–586.
5. Cf. Saint Irenaeus, *Adversus Haereses*, I, 10, 1; III, 4, 1: PG 7, 549–550; 855–856; SCh 264, 154–155; SCh 211, 44–46.
6. Leo XIII, Encyclical Letter *Rerum Novarum* (May 15, 1891): Leonis XIII P. M. Acta, XI, Rome, 1892, 132.
7. Cf., for example, Leo XIII, Encyclical Epistle *Arcanum Divinae Sapientiae* (February 10, 1880): Leonis XIII P. M. Acta, II, Rome, 1882, 10–40; Encyclical Epistle Diuturnum Illud (June 29, 1881): Leonis XIII P. M. Acta, II, Rome, 1882, 269–287; Encyclical Letter *Libertas Praestantissimum* (June 20, 1888): Leonis XIII P. M. Acta, VIII, Rome, 1889, 212–246; Encyclical Epistle Graves de Communi (January 18, 1901): Leonis XIII P. M. Acta, XXI, Rome, 1902, 3–20.
8. Encyclical Letter Rerum Novarum (May 15, 1891): Leonis XIII P. M. Acta, XI, Rome, 1892, 97.
9. Ibid.: loc. cit., 98.
10. Cf. ibid.: loc. cit., 109–110.
11. Cf. ibid.: description of working conditions; anti-Christian workers' associations: loc. cit., 110–111, 136–137.
12. Ibid.: loc. cit., 130; cf. also 114–115.
13. Ibid.: loc. cit., 130.
14. Ibid.: loc. cit., 123.
15. Cf. Encyclical Letter *Laborem Exercens* (September 14, 1981), 1–2, 6: AAS 73 (1981), 578–583, 589–592.
16. Cf. Encyclical Letter *Rerum Novarum* (May 15, 1891): Leonis XIII P. M. Acta, XI, Rome, 1892, 99–107.
17. Cf. ibid.: loc. cit., 102–103.
18. Cf. ibid.: loc. cit., 101–104.
19. Cf. ibid.: loc. cit., 134–135, 137–138.
20. Ibid.: loc. cit., 135.
21. Cf. ibid.: loc. cit., 128–129.
22. Ibid.: loc. cit., 129.
23. Ibid.: loc. cit., 129.
24. Ibid.: loc. cit., 130–131.
25. Ibid.: loc. cit., 131.
26. Cf. Universal Declaration of Human Rights (1948).
27. Cf. Encyclical Letter *Rerum* Novarum (May 15, 1891): Leonis XIII P. M. Acta, XI, Rome, 1892, 121–123.

28. Cf. ibid.: loc. cit., 127.
29. Ibid.: loc. cit., 126–127.
30. Cf. Universal Declaration of Human Rights (1948); Declaration on the elimination of every form of intolerance and discrimination based on religion or convictions.
31. Cf. Second Vatican Ecumenical Council, Declaration on Religious Freedom Dignitatis Humanae; John Paul II, Letter to Heads of State (September 1, 1980): AAS 72 (1980), 1252–1260; Message for the 1988 World Day of Peace (January 1, 1988): AAS 80 (1988), 278–286.
32. Cf. Encyclical Letter *Rerum Novarum* (May 15, 1891): Leonis XIII P. M. Acta, XI, Rome, 1892, 99–105, 130–131, 135.
33. Ibid.: loc. cit., 125.
34. Cf. Encyclical Letter *Sollicitudo Rei Socialis* (December 30, 1987), 38–40: AAS 80 (1988), 564–569; cf. also John XXIII, Encyclical Letter *Mater et Magistra* (May 15, 1961), I: AAS 53 (1961), 407.
35. Cf. Leo XIII, Encyclical Letter *Rerum Novarum* (May 15, 1891): Leonis XIII P. M. Acta, XI, Rome, 1892, 114–116; Puis XI, Encyclical Letter *Quadragesimo Anno* (May 15, 1931), III: AAS 23 (1931), 208; Paul VI, Homily for the Closing of the Holy Year (December 25, 1975): AAS 68 (1976), 145; Message for the 1977 World Day of Peace (January 1, 1977): AAS 68 (1976), 709.
36. Encyclical Letter *Sollicitudo Rei Socialis* (December 30, 1987), 42: AAS 80 (1988), 572.
37. Cf. Encyclical Letter *Rerum Novarum* (May 15, 1891): Leonis XIII P. M. Acta, XI, Rome, 1892, 101–102, 104–105, 130–131, 136.
38. Second Vatican Ecumenical Council, Pastoral Constitution on the Church in the Modern World Gaudium et Spes, 24.
39. Encyclical Letter *Rerum Novarum* (May 15, 1891): Leonis XIII P. M. Acta, XI, Rome, 1892, 99.
40. Cf. Encyclical Letter *Sollicitudo Rei Socialis* (December 30, 1987), 15, 28: AAS 80 (1988), 530, 548–550.
41. Cf. Encyclical Letter *Laborem Exercens* (September 14, 1981), 11–15: AAS 73 (1981), 602–618.
42. Pius XI, Encyclical Letter *Quadragesimo Anno* (May 15, 1931), III: AAS 23 (1931), 213.
43. Cf. Encyclical Letter *Rerum Novarum* (May 15, 1891): Leonis XIII P. M. Acta, XI, Rome, 1892, 121–125.
44. Cf. Encyclical Letter *Laborem Exercens* (September 14, 1981), 20: AAS 73 (1981), 629–632; Address to the International Labor Organization (ILO), Geneva (June 15, 1982): Insegnamenti V/2 (1982), 2250–2266; Paul VI, Address to the International Labor Organization (June 10, 1969): AAS 61 (1969), 491–502.
45. Cf. Encyclical Letter *Laborem Exercens* (September 14, 1981), 8: AAS 73 (1981), 594–598.
46. Cf. Pius XI, Encyclical Letter *Quadragesimo Anno* (May 15, 1931), I: AAS 23 (1931), 178–181.
47. Cf. Encyclical Epistle *Arcanum Divinae Sapientiae* (February 10, 1880): Leonis XIII P. M. Acta, II, Rome, 1882, 10–40; Encyclical Epistle *Diuturnum Illud* (June 29, 1881): Leonis XIII P. M. Acta, II, Rome, 1882, 269–287; Encyclical Epistle *Immortale Dei* (November 1, 1885): Leonis XIII P. M. Acta, V, Rome, 1886, 118–150; Encyclical Letter

Sapientiae Christianae (January 10, 1890): Leonis XIII P. M. Acta, X, Rome, 1891, 10–41; Encyclical Epistle *Quod Apostolici Muneris* (December 28, 1878): Leonis XIII P. M. Acta, I, Rome, 1881, 170–183; Encyclical Letter *Libertas Praestantissimum* (June 20, 1888): Leonis XIII P. M. Acta, VIII, Rome, 1889, 212–246.

48. Cf. Leo XIII, Encyclical Letter *Libertas Praestantissimum* (June 20, 1888), 10: Leonis XIII P. M. Acta, VIII, Rome, 1889, 224–226.

49. Cf. Message for the 1980 World Day of Peace (January 1, 1980): AAS 71 (1979), 1572–1580.

50. Cf. Encyclical Letter *Sollicitudo Rei Socialis* (December 30, 1987), 20: AAS 80 (1988), 536–537.

51. Cf. John XXIII, Encyclical Letter *Pacem in Terris* (April 11, 1963), III: AAS 55 (1963), 286–289.

52. Cf. Universal Declaration of Human Rights, issued in 1948; John XXIII, Encyclical Letter Pacem in Terris (April 11, 1963), IV: AAS 55 (1963), 291–296; "Final Act" of the Conference on Cooperation and Security in Europe, Helsinki, 1975.

53. Cf. Paul VI, Encyclical Letter Populorum Progressio (March 26, 1967), 61–65: AAS 59 (1967), 287–289.

54. Cf. Message for the 1980 World Day of Peace (January 1, 1980): AAS 71 (1979), 1572–1580.

55. Cf. Second Vatican Ecumenical Council, Pastoral Constitution on the Church in the Modern World Gaudium et Spes, 36, 39.

56. Cf. Post-Synodal Apostolic Exhortation *Christifideles Laici* (December 30, 1988), 32–44; AAS 81 (1989), 451–481.

57. Cf. Encyclical Letter *Laborem Exercens* (September 14, 1981), 20: AAS 73 (1981), 629–632.

58. Cf. Congregation for the Doctrine of the Faith, Instruction on Christian Freedom and Liberation Libertatis Conscientia (March 22, 1986): AAS 79 (1987), 554–599.

59. Cf. Address at the Headquarters of the Economic Community of Western Africa on the Occasion of the Tenth Anniversary of the "Appeal for the Sahel," Ouagadougou, Burkina Faso (January 29, 1990): AAS 82 (1990), 816–821.

60. Cf. John XXIII, Encyclical Letter *Pacem in Terris* (April 11, 1963), III: AAS 55 (1963), 286–288.

61. Cf. Encyclical Letter *Sollicitudo Rei Socialis* (December 30, 1987), 27–28: AAS 80 (1988), 547–550; Paul VI, Encyclical Letter *Populorum Progressio* (March 26, 1967), 43–44: AAS 59 (1967), 278–279.

62. Cf. Encyclical Letter *Sollicitudo Rei Socialis* (December 30, 1987), 29–31: AAS 80 (1988), 550–556.

63. Cf. Helsinki Final Act and Vienna Accord; Leo XIII, Encyclical Letter *Libertas Praestantissimum* (June 20, 1888), 5: Leonis XIII P. M. Acta, VIII, Rome, 1889, 215–217.

64. Cf. Encyclical Letter *Redemptoris Missio* (December 7, 1990), 7: AAS 83 (1991), 255–256.

65. Cf. Encyclical Letter *Rerum Novarum* (May 15, 1891): Leonis XIII P. M. Acta, XI, Rome, 1892, 99–107, 131–133.

66. Ibid.: loc. cit., 111, 113–114.

67. Cf. Pius XI, Encyclical Letter *Quadragesimo Anno* (May 15, 1931), II: AAS 23 (1931), 191; Pius XII, Radio Message (June 1, 1941): AAS 33 (1941), 199; John XXIII,

Encyclical Letter *Mater et Magistra* (May 15, 1961), II: AAS 53 (1961), 428–429; Paul VI, Encyclical Letter *Populorum Progressio* (March 26, 1967), 22–24: AAS 59 (1967), 268–269.

68. Second Vatican Ecumenical Council, Pastoral Constitution on the Church in the Modern World Gaudium et Spes, 69, 71.

69. Cf. Address at the Opening of the Third General Conference of the Latin American Bishops (January 28, 1979), III, 4: AAS 71 (1979), 199–201; Encyclical Letter *Laborem Exercens* (September 14, 1981), 14: AAS 73 (1981), 612–616; Encyclical Letter *Sollicitudo Rei Socialis* (December 30, 1987), 42: AAS 80 (1988), 572–574.

70. Cf. Encyclical Letter *Sollicitudo Rei Socialis* (December 30, 1987), 15: AAS 80 (1988), 528–531.

71. Cf. Encyclical Letter *Laborem Exercens* (September 14, 1981), 21: AAS 73 (1981), 632–634.

72. Cf. Paul VI, Encyclical Letter *Populorum Progressio* (March 26, 1967), 33–42: AAS 59 (1967), 273–278.

73. Cf. Encyclical Letter *Laborem Exercens* (September 14, 1981), 7: AAS 73 (1981), 592–594.

74. Cf. ibid., 8: loc. cit., 594–598.

75. Cf. Second Vatican Ecumenical Council, Pastoral Constitution on the Church in the Modern World *Gaudium et Spes*, 35; Paul VI, Encyclical Letter *Populorum Progressio* (March 26, 1967), 19: AAS 59 (1967), 266–267.

76. Cf. Encyclical Letter *Sollicitudo Rei Socialis* (December 30, 1987), 34: AAS 80 (1988), 559–560; Message for the 1990 World Day of Peace (January 1, 1990): AAS 82 (1990), 147–156.

77. Cf. Post-Synodal Apostolic Exhortation *Reconciliatio et Paenitentia* (December 2, 1984), 16: AAS 77 (1985), 213–217; Pius XI, Encyclical Letter *Quadragesimo Anno* (May 15, 1931), III: AAS 23 (1931), 219.

78. Encyclical Letter *Sollicitudo Rei Socialis* (December 30, 1987), 25: AAS 80 (1988), 544.

79. Cf. ibid., 34: loc. cit., 559–560.

80. Cf. Encyclical Letter *Redemptor Hominis* (March 4, 1979), 15: AAS 71 (1979), 286–289.

81. Cf. Second Vatican Ecumenical Council, Pastoral Constitution on the Church in the Modern World *Gaudium et Spes*, 24.

82. Cf. ibid., 41.

83. Cf. ibid., 26.

84. Cf. Second Vatican Ecumenical Council, Pastoral Constitution on the Church in the Modern World Gaudium et Spes, 36; Paul VI, Apostolic Letter *Octogesima Adveniens* (May 14, 1971), 2–5: AAS 63 (1971), 402–405.

85. Cf. Encyclical Letter *Laborem Exercens* (September 14, 1981), 15: AAS 73 (1981), 616–618.

86. Cf. ibid., 10: loc. cit., 600–602.

87. Ibid., 14: loc. cit., 612–616.

88. Cf. ibid., 18: loc. cit., 622–625.

89. Cf. Encyclical Letter *Rerum Novarum* (May 15, 1891): Leonis XIII P. M. Acta, XI, Rome, 1892, 126–128.

90. Ibid.: loc. cit., 121–122.

91. Cf. Leo XIII, Encyclical Letter *Libertas Praestantissimum* (June 20, 1888): Leonis XIII P. M. Acta, VIII, Rome, 1889, 224–226.
92. Cf. Second Vatican Ecumenical Council, Pastoral Constitution on the Church in the Modern World *Gaudium et Spes*, 76.
93. Cf. ibid., 29; Pius XII, Christmas Radio Message (December 24, 1944): AAS 37 (1945), 10–20.
94. Cf. Second Vatican Ecumenical Council, Declaration on Religious Freedom *Dignitatis Humanae*.
95. Cf. Encyclical Letter *Redemptoris Missio* (December 7, 1990), 11: AAS 83 (1991), 259–260.
96. Cf. Encyclical Letter *Redemptor Hominis* (March 4, 1979), 17: AAS 71 (1979), 270–272.
97. Cf. Message for the 1988 World Day of Peace (January 1, 1988): AAS 80 (1988), 1572–1580; Message for the 1991 World Day of Peace (January 1, 1991): AAS 83 (1991), 410–421; Second Vatican Ecumenical Council, Declaration on Religious Freedom Dignitatis Humanae, 1–2.
98. Cf. Second Vatican Ecumenical Council, Pastoral Constitution on the Church in the Modern World Gaudium et Spes, 26.
99. Cf. ibid., 22.
100. Cf. Pius XI, Encyclical Letter *Quadragesimo Anno* (May 15, 1931), I: AAS 23 (1931), 184–186.
101. Cf. Apostolic *Exhortation Familiaris Consortio* (November 22, 1981), 45: AAS 74 (1982), 136–137.
102. Cf. Address to UNESCO (June 2, 1980): AAS 72 (1980), 735–752.
103. Cf. Encyclical Letter *Redemptoris Missio* (December 7, 1990), 39, 52: AAS 83 (1991), 286–287, 299–300.
104. Cf. Benedict XV, Exhortation *Ubi Primum* (September 8, 1914): AAS 6 (1914), 501–502; Pius XI, Radio Message to the Catholic Faithful and to the Entire World (September 29, 1938): AAS 30 (1938), 309–310; Pius XII, Radio Message to the Entire World (August 24, 1939): AAS 31 (1939), 333–335; John XXIII, Encyclical Letter Pacem in Terris (April 11, 1963), III: AAS 55 (1963), 285–289; Paul VI, Address to the General Assembly of the United Nations (October 4, 1965): AAS 57 (1965), 877–885.
105. Cf. Paul VI, Encyclical Letter *Populorum Progressio* (March 26, 1967), 76–77: AAS 59 (1967), 294–295.
106. Cf. Apostolic Exhortation *Familiaris Consortio* (November 22, 1981), 48: AAS 74 (1982), 139–140.
107. Encyclical Letter *Rerum Novarum* (May 15, 1891): Leonis XIII P. M. Acta, XI, Rome, 1892, 107.
108. Cf. Encyclical Letter *Redemptor Hominis* (March 4, 1979), 13: AAS 71 (1979), 283.
109. Ibid., 14: loc. cit., 284–285.
110. Paul VI, Homily at the Final Public Session of the Second Vatican Ecumenical Council (December 7, 1965): AAS 58 (1966), 58.
111. Encyclical Letter *Sollicitudo Rei Socialis* (December 30, 1987), 41: AAS 80 (1988), 571.
112. Second Vatican Ecumenical Council, Pastoral Constitution on the Church in the Modern World *Gaudium et Spes*, 76; cf. John Paul II, Encyclical Letter *Redemptor Hominis* (March 4, 1979), 13: AAS 71 (1979), 283.

113. Encyclical Letter *Rerum Novarum* (May 15, 1891): Leonis XIII P. M. Acta, XI, Rome, 1892, 143.
114. Ibid.: loc. cit., 107.
115. Cf. Encyclical Letter *Sollicitudo Rei Socialis* (December 30, 1987), 38: AAS 80 (1988), 564-566.
116. Ibid., 47: loc. cit., 582.

What Freedom Is:
Homily in Orioles Park at Camden Yards

In Baltimore, the Holy Father recalls the past achievements of the Church in the United States and challenges today's Catholics to engage in the new evangelization with increased vitality and courage. Because democracy demands a commitment to certain moral truths about the human person and human society, His Holiness encourages America's Catholics to let their faith illumine their contribution to the future of their country.

"Oh, that today you would hear his voice: harden not your hearts" (Psalms 95:7–8).

Dear Brothers and Sisters in Christ,

1. Each day, the Church begins the Liturgy of the Hours with the Psalm which we have just prayed together: "Come, let us sing joyfully to the Lord" (Ps 95:1). In that call, ringing down the centuries and echoing across the face of the globe, the Psalmist summons the People of God to sing the praises of the Lord and to bear great witness to the marvelous things God has done for us. Priests, women and men religious, and increasing numbers of lay people daily recite the Liturgy of the Hours, giving rise to a powerful mobilization of praise to God—officium laudis—to God who, through his Word, created the world and all that is in it: "In his hands are the depths of the earth, and the tops of the mountains are his. His is the sea, for he has made it, and the dry land, which his hands have formed" (Psalms 95:4–5).

Not only are we God's creatures. In his infinite mercy, God has chosen us as his beloved people: "For he is our God, and we are the people he shepherds, the flock he guides" (Psalms 95:7). He chose us in Christ, the Good Shepherd, who gave his life for his sheep and who calls us to the banquet of his Body and Blood, the Holy Eucharist which we are celebrating together this morning.

2. The Psalmist's call to hear the Lord's voice has particular significance for us as we celebrate this Mass in Baltimore. Maryland was the birthplace of the Church in colonial America. More than three hundred and sixty years ago, a small band of Catholics came to the New World to build a home where thy could "sing joyfully to the Lord" (Psalms 95:1) in freedom. They established a colony whose hallmark was religious tolerance, which would later become one of the cultural cornerstones of American democracy. Baltimore is the senior Metropolitan See in the United States. Its first bishop, John Carroll, stands out as a model who can still inspire the Church in America today. Here were held the great Provincial and Plenary Councils which guided the Church's expansion as waves of immigrants came to these shores in search of a better life. Here in Baltimore, in 1884, the bishops of the United States authorized the "Baltimore Catechism," which formed the faith of tens of millions of Catholics for decades. In Baltimore, the country's Catholic school system began under the leadership of Saint Elizabeth Ann Seton. The first seminary in the United States was established here, under the protection of the Virgin Mother of God, as was America's first Catholic college for women. Since those heroic beginnings, men and women of every race and social class have built the Catholic community we see in America today, a great spiritual movement of witness, of apostolate, of good works, of Catholic institutions and organizations.

With warm affection therefore I greet your archbishop, Cardinal Keeler, and thank him for his sensitive leadership in this local Church and his work on behalf of the Bishops' Conference. With esteem I greet the other cardinals and bishops present here in great numbers, the priests, deacons, and seminarians, the women and men religious, and all God's people, the "living stones" (1 Peter 2:5) whom the Spirit uses to build up the Body of Christ. I gladly greet the members of the various Christian churches and ecclesial communities. I assure them of the Catholic Church's ardent desire to celebrate the Jubilee of the Year 2000 as a great occasion to move closer to overcoming the divisions of the second millennium (cf. *Tertio Millennio Adveniente*, 34). I thank the civil authorities who have wished to share this sacred moment with us.

[In Castillan:] Doy gracias a los fieles de lengua espanola presentes aqui y a todos los que siguen esta misa por radio o television. La Iglesia es su casa espiritual. Sus parroquias, asociaciones, escuelas y programas educativos religiosos necesitan su cooperacion y el entusiasmo de su fe. Con especial afecto, les exhorto a transmitir sus tradiciones catolicas a las generaciones jovenes.

I greet the Spanish-speaking faithful present here and all those following this Mass on radio or television. The Church is your spiritual home. Your parishes, associations, schools, and religious education programs need your cooperation and the enthusiasm of your faith. With special affection, I encourage you to transmit your Catholic traditions to the younger generations.

3. Our celebration today speaks to us not only of the past. The Eucharist always makes present anew the saving mystery of Christ's Death and Resurrection, and points to the future definitive fulfillment of God's plan of salvation. Two years ago,

at Denver, I was deeply impressed by the vitality of America's young people as they bore enthusiastic witness to their love of Christ and showed that they were not afraid of the demands of the Gospel. Today, I offer this Mass for a strengthening of that vitality and Christian courage at every level of the Church in the United States: among the laity, among the priests and Religious, among my brother bishops. The whole Church is preparing for the third Christian millennium. The challenge of the great Jubilee of the Year 2000 is the new evangelization: a deepening of faith and a vigorous response to the Christian vocation to holiness and service. This is what the Successor of Peter has come to Baltimore to urge upon each one of you: the courage to bear witness to the Gospel of our Redemption.

In today's Gospel reading, the Apostles ask Jesus: "Increase our faith" (Luke 17:5). This must be our constant prayer. Faith is always demanding because faith leads us beyond ourselves. It leads us directly to God. Faith also imparts a vision of life's purpose and stimulates us to action. The Gospel of Jesus Christ is not a private opinion, a remote spiritual ideal, or a mere program for personal growth. The Gospel is the power which can transform the world! The Gospel is no abstraction: it is the living person of Jesus Christ, the Word of God, the reflection of the Father's glory (cf. Hewbrews 1:2), the Incarnate Son who reveals the deepest meaning of our humanity and the noble destiny to which the whole human family is called (cf. *Gaudium et Spes*, 22). Christ has commanded us to let the light of the Gospel shine forth in our service to society. How can we profess faith in God's word, and then refuse to let it inspire and direct our thinking, our activity, our decisions, and our responsibilities toward one another?

4. In America, Christian faith has found expression in an impressive array of witnesses and achievements. We must recall with gratitude the inspiring work of education carried out in countless families, schools, and universities, and all the healing and consolation imparted in hospitals and hospices and shelters. We must give thanks for the practical living out of God's call in devoted service to others, in commitment to social justice, in responsible involvement in political life, in a wide variety of charitable and social organizations, and in the growth of ecumenical and interreligious understanding and cooperation. In a more global context, we should thank God for the great generosity of American Catholics whose support of the foreign missions has greatly contributed to the spiritual and material well-being of their brothers and sisters in other lands. The Church in the United States has sent brave missionary men and women out to the nations, and not a few of them have borne the ultimate witness to the ancient truth that the blood of martyrs is the seed of Christianity. In my visits to Catholic communities around the world I often meet American missionaries, lay, religious, and priests. I wish to make an appeal to young Catholics to consider the missionary vocation. I know that the "spirit of Denver" is alive in many young hearts. Christ needs many more committed men and women to take that "spirit" to the four corners of the world.

5. Today though, some Catholics are tempted to discouragement or disillusionment, like the Prophet Habakkuk in the first reading. They are tempted to cry out

to the Lord in a different way: why does God not intervene when violence threatens his people; why does God let us see ruin and misery; why does God permit evil? Like the Prophet Habakkuk, and like the thirsty Israelites in the desert at Meribah and Massah, our trust can falter; we can lose patience with God. In the drama of history, we can find our dependence upon God burdensome rather than liberating. We too can "harden our hearts."

And yet the Prophet gives us an answer to our impatience: "If God delays, wait for him; he will surely come, he will not be late" (cf. Habakkuk 2:3). A Polish proverb expresses the same conviction in another way: "God takes his time, but he is just." Our waiting for God is never in vain. Every moment is our opportunity to model ourselves on Jesus Christ—to allow the power of the Gospel to transform our personal lives and our service to others, according to the spirit of the Beatitudes. "Bear your share of the hardship which the gospel entails," writes Paul to Timothy in today's second reading (2 Timothy 1:8). This is no idle exhortation to endurance. No, it is an invitation to enter more deeply into the Christian vocation which belongs to us all by Baptism. There is no evil to be faced that Christ does not face with us. There is no enemy that Christ has not already conquered. There is no cross to bear that Christ has not already borne for us and does not now bear with us. And on the far side of every cross we find the newness of life in the Holy Spirit, that new life which will reach its fulfillment in the resurrection. This is our faith. This is our witness before the world.

6. Dear Brothers and Sisters in Christ: openness to the Lord—a willingness to let the Lord transform our lives—should produce a renewed spiritual and missionary vitality among American Catholics. Jesus Christ is the answer to the question posed by every human life, and the love of Christ compels us to share that great good news with everyone. We believe that the Death and Resurrection of Christ reveal the true meaning of human existence; therefore nothing that is genuinely human fails to find an echo in our hearts. Christ died for all, so we must be at the service of all. "The Spirit God has given us is no cowardly spirit. . . . Therefore, never be ashamed of your testimony to our Lord" (2 Timothy 1:7–8). Thus wrote Saint Paul to Timothy, almost two thousand years ago; thus speaks the Church to American Catholics today.

Christian witness takes different forms at different moments in the life of a nation. Sometimes, witnessing to Christ will mean drawing out of a culture the full meaning of its noblest intentions, a fullness that is revealed in Christ. At other times, witnessing to Christ means challenging that culture, especially when the truth about the human person is under assault. America has always wanted to be a land of the free. Today, the challenge facing America is to find freedom's fulfillment in the truth: the truth that is intrinsic to human life created in God's image and likeness, the truth that is written on the human heart, the truth that can be known by reason and can therefore form the basis of a profound and universal dialogue among people about the direction they must give to their lives and their activities.

7. One hundred thirty years ago, President Abraham Lincoln asked whether a nation "conceived in liberty and dedicated to the proposition that all men are created equal" could "long endure." President Lincoln's question is no less a question for the present generation of Americans. Democracy cannot be sustained without a shared commitment to certain moral truths about the human person and human community. The basic question before a democratic society is: "how ought we to live together?" In seeking an answer to this question, can society exclude moral truth and moral reasoning? Can the Biblical wisdom which played such a formative part in the very founding of your country be excluded from that debate? Would not doing so mean that America's founding documents no longer have any defining content, but are only the formal dressing of changing opinion? Would not doing so mean that tens of millions of Americans could no longer offer the contribution of their deepest convictions to the formation of public policy? Surely it is important for America that the moral truths which make freedom possible should be passed on to each new generation. Every generation of Americans needs to know that freedom consists not in doing what we like, but in having the right to do what we ought.

8. How appropriate is Saint Paul's charge to Timothy! "Guard the rich deposit of faith with the help of the Holy Spirit who dwells within us" (2 Timothy 1:14). That charge speaks to parents and teachers; it speaks in a special and urgent way to you, my brother bishops, successors of the Apostles. Christ asks us to guard the truth because, as he promised us: "You will know the truth and the truth will make you free" (John 8:32). *Depositum custodi!* We must guard the truth that is the condition of authentic freedom, the truth that allows freedom to be fulfilled in goodness. We must guard the deposit of divine truth handed down to us in the Church, especially in view of the challenges posed by a materialistic culture and by a permissive mentality that reduces freedom to license. But we bishops must do more than guard this truth. We must proclaim it, in season and out of season; we must celebrate it with God's people, in the sacraments; we must live it in charity and service; we must bear public witness to the truth that is Jesus Christ.

9. Catholics of America! Always be guided by the truth—by the truth about God who created and redeemed us, and by the truth about the human persons, made in the image and likeness of God and destined for a glorious fulfillment in the Kingdom to come. Always be convincing witnesses to the truth. "Stir into a flame the gift of God" that has been bestowed upon you in baptism. Light your nation—light the world—with the power of that flame! Amen.

John Paul II on the American Experiment

> In receiving the credentials of the Honorable Lindy Boggs as Ambassador to the Holy See on December 16, 1997, Pope John Paul II offered some pointed comments on the "credibility" of the United States and its world leadership. Herewith the complete text of a statement that bears close reading.
> —The Editors

It gives me great pleasure to welcome you to the Vatican for presentation of the Letters of Credence by which you are appointed Ambassador Extraordinary and Plenipotentiary of the United States of America to the Holy See. I am grateful for the greetings which you convey from President Clinton, and I reciprocate with good wishes to him and the American people.

You represent a nation that plays a crucial role in world events today. The United States carries a weighty and far-reaching responsibility, not only for the well-being of its own people, but for the development and destiny of peoples throughout the world. With a deep sense of participation in the joys and hopes, the sorrows, anxieties, and aspirations of the entire human family, the Holy See is a willing partner in every effort to build a world of genuine peace and justice for all. I am certain that, following upon the good work of your predecessors, you will apply your many personal talents and your long experience of public life to strengthening understanding and cooperation between us.

The Founding Fathers of the United States asserted their claim to freedom and independence on the basis of certain "self-evident" truths about the human person: truths which could be discerned in human nature, built into it by "nature's God." Thus they meant to bring into being, not just an independent territory, but a great

---

Copyright (c) 1998 *First Things* 82 (April 1998): 36–37.

experiment in what George Washington called "ordered liberty": an experiment in which men and women would enjoy equality of rights and opportunities in the pursuit of happiness and in service to the common good. Reading the founding documents of the United States, one has to be impressed by the concept of freedom they enshrine: a freedom designed to enable people to fulfill their duties and responsibilities toward the family and toward the common good of the community. Their authors clearly understood that there could be no true freedom without moral responsibility and accountability, and no happiness without respect and support for the natural units or groupings through which people exist, develop, and seek the higher purpose of life in concert with others.

The American democratic experiment has been successful in many ways. Millions of people around the world look to the United States as a model in their search for freedom, dignity, and prosperity. But the continuing success of American democracy depends on the degree to which each new generation, native-born and immigrant, makes its own the moral truths on which the Founding Fathers staked the future of your Republic. Their commitment to build a free society with liberty and justice for all must be constantly renewed if the United States is to fulfill the destiny to which the Founders pledged their "lives . . . fortunes . . . and sacred honor."

I am happy to take note of your words confirming the importance that your government attaches, in its relations with countries around the world, to the promotion of human rights and particularly to the fundamental human right of religious freedom, which is the guarantee of every other human right. Respect for religious conviction played no small part in the birth and early development of the United States. Thus John Dickinson, Chairman of the Committee for the Declaration of Independence, said in 1776: "Our liberties do not come from charters; for these are only the declaration of preexisting rights. They do not depend on parchments or seals; but come from the King of Kings and the Lord of all the earth." Indeed it may be asked whether the American democratic experiment would have been possible, or how well it will succeed in the future, without a deeply rooted vision of divine providence over the individual and over the fate of nations.

As the year 2000 draws near and Christians prepare to celebrate the bi-millennium of the birth of Christ, I have appealed for a serious examination of conscience regarding the shadows that darken our times. Nations and states too can make this a time of reflection on the spiritual and moral conditions of their success in promoting the integral good of their people. It would truly be a sad thing if the religious and moral convictions upon which the American experiment was founded could now somehow be considered a danger to free society, such that those who would bring these convictions to bear upon your nation's public life would be denied a voice in debating and resolving issues of public policy. The original separation of church and state in the United States was certainly not an effort to ban all religious conviction from the public sphere, a kind of banishment of God from civil society. Indeed, the vast majority of Americans, regardless of their religious persuasion, are convinced that religious conviction and religiously informed moral argument have a vital role in public life.

No expression of today's commitment to liberty and justice for all can be more basic than the protection afforded to those in society who are most vulnerable. The United States of America was founded on the conviction that an inalienable right to life was a self-evident moral truth, fidelity to which was a primary criterion of social justice. The moral history of your country is the story of your people's efforts to widen the circle of inclusion in society, so that all Americans might enjoy the protection of law, participate in the responsibilities of citizenship, and have the opportunity to make a contribution to the common good. Whenever a certain category of people—the unborn or the sick and old—are excluded from that protection, a deadly anarchy subverts the original understanding of justice. The credibility of the United States will depend more and more on its promotion of a genuine culture of life, and on a renewed commitment to building a world in which the weakest and most vulnerable are welcomed and protected.

As they have done throughout your country's history, the Catholic people in the United States will continue to make an important contribution to the development of American culture and society. The recently completed Special Assembly of the Synod of Bishops for America has highlighted the range and variety of activity which Catholics, out of commitment to Christ, undertake for the betterment of society. May this transforming and elevating work continue to flourish for the good of individuals, the strengthening of families, and the benefit of the American people as a whole.

Your Excellency, these are some of the thoughts prompted by your presence here as your country's diplomatic representative. These reflections evoke a prayer: that your country will experience a new birth of freedom, freedom grounded in truth and ordered to goodness. Thus will the American people be able to harness their boundless spiritual energy in service of the genuine good of all humanity. Be assured that the various Offices of the Holy See will be ready to assist you in the fulfillment of your mission. Upon you and upon the people of the United States of America I cordially invoke abundant divine blessings.

Letter to the National Prayer Breakfast

"Christ yesterday and today, the beginning and the end, Alpha and Omega; all time belongs to him and all the ages; to him be glory and power through every age for ever. Amen."

1. With this ancient invocation to the Lord of History, I greet all of you and thank you for the gracious invitation extended to me through Senator Connie Mack to address the *Forty-Eighth National Prayer Breakfast sponsored by the Congress of the United States*. Although it is not possible for me to be present in person, I am grateful for this opportunity to share some thoughts with you through my representative in the United States, Archbishop Gabriel Montalvo.

We are now at the dawn of the new millennium, when Christians throughout the world are celebrating the Great Jubilee of the Year 2000—the 2000th anniversary of Christ's taking flesh and dwelling among us, the central event of history and the key to the meaning of human existence. This great anniversary invites believers everywhere to rejoice in the grace poured out upon mankind in the fullness of time, and encourages us to look to the future with renewed hope in the power of the Spirit to make all things new.

An evocative part of the Jubilee celebrations in the City of Rome involved the ceremonial opening of a Holy Door in each of the four Major Basilicas. This ritual symbolizes the passage which believers are called to make, through faith in Christ, from sin to grace, from spiritual death to salvation. Two weeks ago, leaders from Christian denominations worldwide joined me in opening the Holy Door at the Basilica of Saint Paul, and together we crossed its threshold. That was an eloquent sign of our commitment to ensure that, in the millennium just beginning, Christians will give ever fuller expression to that unity which is Christ's gift to his Church, so that together we may cross the threshold of hope in openness to the future which God in his providence holds out to us.

2. The beginning of a millennium evokes reflection on the passage of time, especially when we are convinced that humanity is at a crossroads and must make important decisions regarding the epoch that is opening up before us. This is a time to reaffirm our belief that the God who created the universe and fashioned human beings in his own image and likeness continues to guide and sustain human history: The Great Jubilee of the Year 2000 obliges us Christians to renew our faith in Christ, the key, the center and the goal of all history, the new Adam who reveals man to himself, unlocks the mystery of his origin and goal, and sheds light on the path that leads to humanity's true destiny.

This great vision of faith has *an authentically public dimension*: for the deeper understanding of the truth about human nature and human fulfillment given to us by faith naturally inspires efforts to build a better and more humane world. The century just ended has shown clearly that immense suffering results when *economic and political systems do not respect the full truth about man*, his spiritual nature, and his quest for the transcendent in his search for truth and freedom. Where this kind of vision is lacking, Scripture tells us, "the people perish" (*Proverbs* 29:18). Is not the quest for a social order in which all members of the human family can flourish and live in a manner worthy of their innate dignity the great moral challenge of this new millennium? As believers, we are convinced that the light of faith is an indispensable source of vision and strength in our efforts to meet this challenge. And the light of faith, in leading us to acknowledge the truth of God's word, helps us to know the liberating and transforming power of this truth, and inspires us to place all our talents, our intellectual resources, our persuasive ability, our experience and our skill at the service of God, our neighbor and the common good of the human family.

3. This great project—the building of a world more worthy of the human person, a society which can foster a renaissance of the human spirit—calls also for *that sense of moral responsibility which flows from commitment to truth*: "walking the path of truth", as the Apostle John puts it (3 *Jn* 3). And such a moral responsibility, by its very nature, cannot be reduced to a purely private matter. The light of Christ should illumine every thought, word and action of believers; there is no area of personal or social life which it is not meant to penetrate, enliven and make fruitful. The spread of a purely utilitarian approach to the great moral issues of public life points to the urgent need for a rigorous and reasoned public discourse about the moral norms that are the foundation of any just society. A living relationship with the truth, Scripture teaches, is the very source and condition of authentic and lasting freedom (cf. *Jn* 8:32).

Your nation was built as an experiment in ordered freedom, an experiment in which the exercise of individual freedom would contribute to the common good. The American separation of Church and State as institutions was accompanied from the beginning of your Republic by the conviction that strong religious faith, and the public expression of religiously-informed judgments, contribute significantly to the moral health of the body politic. Within the fabric of your national life *a particular moral authority has been entrusted to you who are invested with political responsibility* as representatives of the American people. In the great Western democratic tradition, men and women in political life are servants of the *polis* in its fullest sense— as a moral and civil commonwealth. They are not mere brokers of power in a political process taking place in a vacuum, cut off from private and public morality. Leadership in a true democracy involves much more than simply the mastering of techniques of political "management": your vocation as "representatives" calls for vision, wisdom, a spirit of contemplation, and a passion for justice and truth.

4. Looking back on my own lifetime, I am convinced that the epoch-making changes taking place and the challenges appearing at the dawn of this new millennium call for just such a "prophetic" function on the part of religious believers in public life. And, may I say, this is particularly true of you who represent the American people, with their rich heritage of commitment to freedom and equality under the law, their spirit of independence and commitment to the common good, their self-reliance and generosity in sharing their God-given gifts. In the century just ended, *this heritage became synonymous with freedom itself* for people throughout the world, as they sought to cast off the shackles of totalitarianism and to live in freedom. As one who is personally grateful for what America did for the world in the darkest days of the twentieth century, allow me to ask: Will America continue to inspire people to build a truly better world, a world in which freedom is ordered to truth and goodness? Or will America offer the example of a pseudo-freedom which, detached from the moral norms that give life direction, and fruitfulness, turns in practice into a narrow and ultimately inhuman self-enslavement, one which smothers people's spirits and dissolves the foundations of social life? These questions pose themselves in a particularly sharp way when we confront the urgent issue of protecting every human being's inalienable right to life from conception until natural death. This is the great civil rights issue of our time, and the world looks to the United States for leadership in cherishing every human life and in providing legal protection for all the members of the human community, but especially those who are weakest and most vulnerable.

5. For religious believers who bear political responsibility, our times offer a daunting yet exhilarating challenge. *I would go so far as to say that their task is to save democracy from self-destruction.* Democracy is our best opportunity to promote the values that will make the world a better place for everyone, but a society which exalts individual choice as the ultimate source of truth undermines the very foundations of democracy. If there is no objective moral order which everyone must respect, and if each individual is expected to supply his or her own truth and ethic of life, there remains only the path of contractual mechanisms as the way of organizing our living together in society. In such a society the strong will prevail and the weak will be swept aside. As I have written elsewhere, "if there is no ultimate truth to guide and direct political action, then ideas and convictions can easily be ma-

nipulated for reasons of power. As history demonstrates, a democracy without values easily turns into open or thinly disguised totalitarianism" (Encyclical Letter *Centesimus Annus*, No. 46).

Faith compels Christians in the public arena in your country to promote a new political culture of service, based on the vision of life and civilization that has sustained the American people in the positive character and outlook that has nourished their optimism, their hope, their willingness to be generous in the service of others, and will protect them from the cynicism which dissipates the very energies needed for building the future. Today this optimism is being tested, but *the Gospel of Jesus Christ remains the sturdy foundation of hope for the future.*

I am convinced that, precisely at this crossroads in history, the Christian message of truth and justice, and of our universal brotherhood as God's beloved children, has the power to emerge once again as the "good news" for our times, *a compelling invitation to real hope.* It will do so if "the power of God leading to salvation" (cf. *Rom* 1:16) is seen in the transformed lives of those who profess the Gospel as the pole-star of their lives and the deepest source of their commitment to others. To build a future of hope is, to use a favorite expression of the late Pope Paul VI, to build a "civilization of love". Love, as Scripture teaches, casts out fear: fear of the future, fear of the other, fear that there is not enough room at the banquet of life for the least of our brothers and sisters. Love does not tear down but is rather the virtue that "builds up". And this is my prayer for you: that as men and women involved in public life, you will truly be builders of a civilization of love, of a society which, precisely because it embodies the highest values of truth, justice and freedom for all, is also a sign of the presence of God's Kingdom and its peace.

May God grant you this in your personal lives, in your families and in the country you are privileged to serve!

From the Vatican, January 29, 2000

Index

abortion, 32, 158–59
absolutism, 120–21
acting person, 45, 80–81, 103
Acting Person, The (John Paul II), 42–43, 47
Action Française, 207
Acton, Lord, 21, 287n25; and Catholic Whig tradition, 144, 156; and liberty coincident with Judaism and Christianity, 281
Adam and Eve, story of, 241, 242, 243
Adams, John, 95–96, 256, 270n40, 279
Adenauer, Konrad, 147
adversary culture, 255, 258–61, 262, 271n43, 271n46
Agnelli, U., 89
agnosticism: and democratic forms of political life, 246; and individual commitment to cause of free society, 280; and public discourse, 37
Allen, Woody, 275
American Constitutional Law (Tribe), 138
American Ecclesiastical Review and church/state theory, 150
American experiment, 18, 254–57; and Christian philosophy and belief, 250; predictions of its end, 252, 257. *See also* Founders, American; United States

ancien régime, 127, 128, 141, 143, 145, 160, 207
Anderson, Brian, xvi
Anthony of Florence, Saint, 60
anthropology: Christian, 83; and crisis of liberal democracy and Communism, 3; of the free market, 65
apoliticism, 131–32
Aquinas, Thomas, 42, 43, 60, 144, 187, 189, 279; and God's mercy, 97, 99; prudence of, 95
Arendt, Hannah, 254
Aristotle, xviii, 90, 113, 131, 248, 276; and ordered liberty, 263–64; and superior empowered or excluded, 113–14
atheism, 34, 277, 280
Augustine, 242
authority: and the law, 237; and relativism, 231–32
automation, myth of, 88

Barone, Michael, 260
Bauman, Zygmut, 177
Bayle, Pierre, 167
"Beautiful Stranger, A" (Zieba), 64–66
being, 253
Belief and Unbelief (Novak), 280

399

Bell, Daniel, 252, 257
Bell, Jeff, 260
Benéton, Philippe, 231–36
Berger, Peter, 75, 104
Berlin, Isaiah, 275–76, 286n7
Bernard, St., 242
Bernstein, Carl, 40, 201, 211
"Bill for Establishing Religious Freedom" in Virginia, 133, 137
birth control, 195
bonds, dissolution of, 214–15
Bossuet, Jacques, 122–23
Bouyer, Louis, 208
Branicki, Jdrzej, 67
Burke, Edmund, 149
Buttiglione, Rocco: and Christian economics, 83–90; *Karol Wojtyla*, 47; study and counsel with John Paul II, xiii–xiv

Calas, Jean, 167
Calvinism, American, and original sin, 130
Camus, Albert, 275, 276, 285n3
capitalism, 13, 103; argument for superiority of on economic grounds, 88; and definition of word "capital," 75; different modes of, 25–26, 65; market prerequisites for, 26; monopoly, 26, 86–87; and the poor, 102, 103–4
Capitalism, Socialism, and Democracy (Schumpeter), 252
Capitalist Resolution, The: Fifty Propositions about Prosperity, Equality, and Liberty (Berger), 75
Capitalist Revolution, The (Berger), 104
caritas, 99–105
Carroll, John, 145
Casey v. Planned Parenthood, 5, 275, 285n2
Catholic human rights movement, 150–60
Catholic Social Thought and Liberal Institutions (Novak), 191
Catholic Whig tradition, 144, 156, 331

celibate clergy, 46
Centesimus Annus (John Paul II), xvi, 6–24, 29, 157, 158, 246; and capitalism and the market, 12–14, 25–28, 65–66; and divine governance and the state, 188; and the free market and solidarity, 90, 191; and free society including economic freedom, 32; and freedom, 6–7; and human rights, 8, 193–98; and ideology and Christianity, 52; introduction and text of, 331–98; and just wages, 73–74; and the liberal state, 185–98; and the limited state, 36; and natural law, 193–95; and private property, 68; and relativism, 281; and *Rerum Novarum*, 32, 186; resonance to Americans, xiv, 6; and Revolution of 1989, 8–12, 201–2; and totalitarianism, 187–88, 192, 281
Central and Eastern Europe: economic circumstance of, 61–62; years of contact cut off with rest of world, xv
"Chapter 77" (Havel), 16
character and culture, 252–54
Charles, Maxim, 208
Chesterton, G.K., 31
Christian Democratic movement, 147, 162n15
Christian Marxism, 207
Christianity: and changes to political economy, 91–97; and equality-uniqueness of persons, 93–94; and God as Creator, 92, 95; ideology, 52–59; and incarnate God, 95; injustices done by, 51–52; and necessity of ideas of in modern world, xix; and Truth, 95–97
Christianity and Democracy (Maritain), 147
Church, Roman Catholic. *See* Roman Catholic Church
Churchill, Winston, 102
citizenship, language of, 251
civic religion and transcendent source of human existence, 35

Civil Constitution of the Clergy, 111, 121
civil society: reconstructing of, 16–17; and religious freedom, 151
civilization and Truth, 95–96
clergy, non-participation of in politics, 57–58
Codex Iuris Canonici (John Paul II), 193
collectivism and Marx, 85–86
Commentary on the Letter of Saint John (Augustine), 61
Commission for the Study of Problems of the Family, Population, and Birth Rate, 240
common, the, 217–18
communio, xvii, 34; versus liberty, 83–84
Communio magazine, 30
Communione e Liberazione, xiv
Communism: as "an act against man," 10; Church siding with against democracy, 112; collapse of, 3–4, 9, 11, 21n2; condemnation of by Church, 112; as perverse imitation of Christianity, 132; silence of the Church relative to, 128–29
community: and independence of each person, 93; and John Paul II, 45; religion as affair of, 130; and universal family, 95
compassion, 92, 94–95, 276
computer and world as manifestation of consciousness, 77
condoms, distribution of, 46
confederacy: democracy as, 223; of nations, 221–22
Congregation for the Doctrine of the Faith, 153–54
Connell, Francis, 150
conservatism, 29, 32
Consolation of Philosophy, The (Boethius), 255–56
Constant, Benjamin, 114, 115
Constitution of the United States: and introduction of God, 130; and majority rule, 135–36

consumerism, 27; and liberal democracy, 31–32; and libertinism, 87–89; and the person, 80
cooperation and *caritas*, 101
counterculture, 260
creation, reason for, 99–100
creativity: of God as original source, 69; and property, 68–82
Creator God, 92–93, 95, 239–40
Crèvecoeur, Hector St. John, 255, 270n33
Crisis magazine, 45
Crisis of Modern Times (Roepke), 66–67
Critique of Pure Tolerance, A (Marcuse), 170
Crosby, John, 45
Cross, Derek, xv
Cultural Contradictions of Capitalism, The (Bell), 252
culture: adversary, 255, 258–61, 262, 271n43, 271n46; as central debate of our time, 261, 265, 278; and character, 252–54; and health of capitalist democracies, 246–47, 257, 262–64, 277; and the market, 15, 27; as means to serve truth, 34; as prior to politics and economics, 160; priority of and John Paul II, 201–12; reconversion of in France by Lustiger group, 207–9; religion as key to, 197; and society's dependence on public morals, 205–6

Dahrendorf, Ralf, 66
Dante, 98, 114
de Gasperi, Alcide, 147
de Lubac, Henri, 29, 44
de Maistre, Joseph, 110, 115, 120
de Vittoria, Francesco, 60
Decalogue, 238, 241
Declaration of Independence: and natural law as higher law, 194; theistic nature of, 34
Declaration on Religious Freedom (*Dignitatis Humanae*), 145, 150–51, 182

democracy, 3–4, 102; according to
  Tocqueville, 116–19, 276; and
  emancipation of the will, 116–17; and
  ending of plans to destroy Christianity, 109; health of and moral-cultural
  system, xix, 4–5, 21, 246–47, 257,
  262–64, 277; and individualism, 213;
  internal critique of by John Paul II,
  156–60; internal critique of by
  modern Church, 156–60; legitimate
  autonomy of recognized by Church,
  17, 58, 59; and meaninglessness, 132;
  and Paul VI, 147; religious political
  history of, 109–25; support by post-
  Christendom Church, 17; survival of
  and virtue, 256, 270n36, 277, 278;
  totalitarian, 143; and truth, 157–58.
  See also liberal democracy
Democracy in America (Tocqueville):
  introduction and text of, 313–30;
  study of at Institute, xvi; and two
  distinct humanities, 231
d'Entreves, A. P., 195
Derrida, Jacques, 171
*Desire of Nations, The: Rediscovering the
  Roots of Political Theology*
  (O'Donovan), 31
Dewey, John, 135
Dignitatis Humanae (Declaration on
  Religious Freedom), 145, 150, 152–
  53, 182, 192, 194, 207
dignity: of the individual, 34, 38; and
  work, 7, 69–70
Djilas, Milovan, 259
domestic church, 47
Dominican monastery in Krakow, xv–xvi
Dostoyevsky, Feodor, 99, 184
duty and religious freedom, 139–40
Dworkin, Ronald, 30, 197

Economical-Philosophical Manuscripts
  (Marx), 85
economics: autonomy of, 63; and *caritas*,
  101–2, 105; and *Centesimus Annus*,
  25–28; and Christian evangelization,
  64; culture of, 75; and determinism,
  80; and ethics, 90; experience as
  teacher of, xviii; and human person,
  101, 103; Japanese system of, 89–90;
  organization of and consciousness,
  85–86; and political changes and
  Christianity, 91–97. *See also* consumerism
Ecrasez l'infame (Voltaire), 168–69
ecumenism, 180–81
Edict of Nantes, revocation of, 120
education: needed for moral foundation
  in market economy, 15; need for in
  liberal democracy, 252
Elizabeth I, 120
employment, 79, 82n4
English Glorious Revolution, 120
Enlightenment, 110–12, 220, 251
entrepreneurship, 86–87
equality of income or wealth, 72–74
ethos and democracy, 4
Europe: culture of and natural law, 194–
  95, 197; as a political territory, 215–16
euthanasia, 158–59
Evangelium Vitae (John Paul II), 38, 157
evangelization: of culture in France of
  1997, 207–9; new, 51; and realistic
  Christian view of practical matters,
  64; use of Church's power, 210
evil, intrinsic, 158
experience and economic and practical
  wisdom, xviii
Experience of Nothingness, The (Novak),
  280

faith as opposed to ideology, 51–59
fanaticism, 173–74
fear, facing down of, 10–12
federalism and subsidiarity, 163n17
Federalist, The, 256; and human flaws,
  97, 262; introduction and text of,
  291–312; and originality of U.S.
  system, 255; study of at Institute, xvi
feelings, 42
Fenton, Joseph Clifford, 150
Feuerbach, Ludwig, 85
Fifty-Five Years' War, 3

First Amendment to the Constitution, 21, 137–40
First Vatican Council, 142, 144
Fish, Stanley, 223
Flaubert, Gustave, 132
Fogarty, Gerald, 146
Foucault, Michel, 171, 249
Founders, American, 268n30; and constitutional order based on religious morality, 34, 37, 139, 256; and human flaws, 97; and new order for the ages, 133; and providential history, 93; and representational governance, 135. See also American experiment
France: and post-World War II Christian Democracy, 147; and Statue of Liberty, 255–56; and World Youth Day of 1997, 206–9
free economy and *Centesimus Annus*, 12–14
free society: and cultural necessities in, xviii; moral-cultural foundations of, 16–17; problems of, xvii; three liberties in, xiii
freedom: and *Centesimus Annus*, 6–8; and choice, 232–33; and John Paul II, 43, 156, 272n57; and the law, 238; as liberty to pursue one's personal gratification, 4; as means to truth and love, 4, 28, 34, 84; and obedience, 272n57; and property, 85; and solidarity, 190–91; and truth, 28, 101, 264, 272n57, 279, 283–85. See also religious freedom
French Revolution, 33, 142, 161n4, 207; and American Revolution, 254, 255; and freedom, 7, 22n8; political viewpoints in wake of, 114–15
Friedman, Milton, 189–90, 280, 281–82, 283, 287n22
From Enlightenment to Revolution (Voegelin), 67
Fuchs, Joseph, 240–41
Fukuyama, Francis, 3, 21n1, 251
fun and business, 78–79

fundamentalism: liberal, 64; and "possession" of the truth, 53

Gaudium et Spes (Pastoral Constitution on the Church in the Modern World), 45, 145, 151–52, 207, 210
Gelasius I and Gelasian tradition, 150–51, 152, 154
Genesis against the Manicheans (Augustine), 242
gentlemen, 94–95
Gibbons, James, 145–46, 147
Gilder, George, 77
Gilson, Etienne, 43
globalism and the modern state, 221–22
God: adherence to as basis for ethics, 241–42; and authority, 244–45; as basis for government, 256, 270n40, 279; Christian as incarnate, 95; as Creator, 92; as Creator only, 239–40; as giver of moral law, 239–40; idea of and Marx, 85–86; and mercy, 97; as sovereign over nations and individuals, 19, 35; as a trinity, 93; and truth versus ideology, 53–54; and the United States Constitution, 130
Gorbachev, Mikhail, xviii, 11
Gospel and unity with Law, 238
governance, capacity as God-given, 19–20
grace and John Paul II, 43–44
Gramsci, Antonio, 260, 261
Grant, George, 31
Gregory XVI, 109, 141, 142, 160n2
Guardini, Romano, 63–64
Gutierrez, Gustavo, 192

Haire, R. M., 172–73
Hamilton, Alexander, 291
Hauerwas, Stanley, 30–31
Havel, Václav, 16, 198, 249, 251, 275
Hayek, Friedrich, xvii, 66, 331
Heart of the World, Center of the Church (Schindler), 29–30
Hebblethwaite, Peter, 40
hedonism, 247, 253

Hegel, Georg Wilhelm Friedrich, xix, 85
Heidegger, Martin, 224, 249
Helsinki Accords, 194
His Holiness: John Paul II and the History of Our Time (Bernstein and Politi), 201
history and Creator God, 92–93
Hitler, Adolf, 280
Hittinger, Russell, 185–98, 237–45, 285n2
Hobbes, Thomas, 127, 225, 280
Hoeffner, Cardinal, 58
Holy See, 76
homo ludens, 78
Hook, Sidney, 280–81
Hopkins, Gerald Manley, 95
Howard, Michael, 141
Hugo, Victor, 103, 255
human person: as core of Christian social doctrine, 83–84; and economics, 101, 103; idea of nature of, 3–4; made in "image and likeness" of God, 7
human rights: Catholic revolution of, 7, 150–60, 210; and *Centesimus Annus*, 8, 193–98; John Paul II's list of, 193; and liberal state, 223; as limit upon state, 195–97; and link to obligations and truth, 8; and modern constitutionalism, 192; and natural law, 193–95
human sovereignty as foundation of democracy, 124–25
Humanae Vitae (Paul VI), 195
Hume, David, 225
Husserl, Edmund, 249

ideology and Christianity, 51–59
incarnation and God in Christianity, 95
individualism: and Catholicism, 33–34; and John Paul II, 33; and literature, 214; modern, 213–18; "radical," 7, 247–48; and Tocqueville, 226
Industrial Revolution, 7
Ingarden, Roman, 41
Innocent XI, 120
institutions, democratic, 263, 264–65
"Instruction on Certain Aspects of the 'Theology of Liberation,'" 153–55

"Instruction on Christian Freedom and Liberation" (Ratzinger), 154–55, 254
intellect as God-given, 95–96
International Academy of Philosophy, xiv

Jacobinism, 142–43, 161n4, 195
Jadwiga, Blessed Queen, 204
Jagiellonian University, 204–5
Japanese economic system, 89–90
Jay, John, 291
Jefferson, Thomas, 92, 93, 103, 139, 256, 271n41, 285; and "Bill for Establishing Religious Freedom" in Virginia, 133, 137
Jesus Christ, 184; on adherence to God, 241–42; *communio*, 84; on compassion, 92; John Paul II and, 44; the parable of the wicked tenants, 243; on the rich man in Matthew 19, 237–38
Jews: division of labor in community of, 261, 272n52; and peace in the United States, 130; and sovereign God as basis for government, 256, 270n40, 279
John XXIII: opening Church to modern world, 180; *Pacem in Terris*, 8, 187
John of the Cross, St., 43
John Paul II, xiii; and abortion and euthanasia, 158–59; and acting person and economic choices, 80–81; and celibate clergy, 46; and Christianity not as an ideology, 52–53; and colonial Americans and Polish compatriots, 272n57; comparison to Leo XIII, 47, 185; and culture, 160, 252–53; and "domestic church" of husband and wife, 47; and the free economy, 12–14, 185; and freedom, 28, 43, 156, 182, 279; and grace, 43–44; and human rights, 8, 153–56, 158–59, 193–98; and internal critique of democracy, 156–60; and Jesus Christ, 44; and the liberal state, 185–98; liberalism of, 29–39; as man of the century, 211; moral and cultural challenge to U.S., 257, 262–63; and natural law versus divine law, 241–42;

and need for education and cultural work in liberal democracies, 252; and non-fanaticism and non-fundamentalism, 37–38; and person as subjective agent, 46–47; personal qualities of, 41; philosophy of, 40–47; as a poet and dramatist, 41; and primacy of morals, 265; and private property, 68, 69; and profit and just wage, 70, 72–74; and religious freedom, 151–52; and Revolution of 1989, 8–12, 15; and suggestion of Poland as location for Institute, xv; support of democratic governments, 141, 155–56; teachings on sexual ethics, 45–46; and the Third World, 155–56; and totalitarianism, 211; and "truth about man," 253; visit to Poland of 1997, 202–6; and World Youth Day of 1997 in Paris, 206–10. *See also* Acting Person, The; Centesimus Annus; Evangelium Vitae; Gaudium et Spes; Lumen Gentium; Sollicitudo Rei Socialis; Veritatis Splendor
John Paul II Institute, 29
Judaism: and equality-uniqueness of persons, 93–94; and idea of Creator God, 92; and incarnate God, 95; necessity ideas of in modern world, xix; and Truth, 95–97
Judgment Day, 97
junk bonds, 71
justice: as inherent in people, 20–21; in liberal democracy, 56

Kant, Immanuel, 41, 42, 216
Karol Wojtyla (Buttiglione), 47
Kennedy, Anthony, 4–5
King, Martin Luther, Jr., 32, 194, 201, 260
Kingdom of God and political society, 36
Kolbe, Maximilian, 43
Königswinterer Kreis, 149
Kristol, Irving, 102, 261, 272n5
Kulturkampf, 4–5, 18
Kupczak, Jaroslav, 42
Kwasniewski, Alexander, 203

Kwitny, Jonathan, 201, 211

laity and participation in politics, 57–58
land, ownership of, 68–69
Latin America and capitalism, 25
law: and human discretion versus divine establishment, 239–45; and liberty in *Veritatis Splendor*, 237–45; of "nature and nature's God," 249; rule of, 189, 196, 198, 237–38, 239, 241–42; and scriptures, 237–38, 239, 241–42
legalism, 237–38
Legutko, Ryszard, xvi, 166–78
Leo XIII, xiv, 6, 7; and America, 145, 146; Christian personalism, 7, 8; and church/state theory, 150; comparison to John Paul II, 47, 185; and economic liberalism, 30; and liberal state, 187; and natural law and rights, 192, 194; and private property, 68, 69, 185, 187; and proposed French republic, 127; and the state as participator in divine governance, 186–87; and work, 81
Les Miserables (Hugo), 103, 255
Letter Concerning Toleration, A (Locke), 167, 169
"Letter from Birmingham Jail" (King), 194
Lewandowski, Janusz, 67
Lewis, C. S., 245
liberal democracy: attitude of Church from 1864–1965, 145–50; *Centesimus Annus* as magisterial legitimation for, 29; crisis in, 3–4, 55–56; criticism of consumerism of, 31–32; and materialism, 226–27; modern contradictions in use of term, 247; and religion as a matter of private opinion, 54; and religious freedom, 152; and subsidiary principle, 149. *See also* democracy
liberalism: criticisms of, 30–32; and development on grounds of Christianity, 66; and freedom, 38–39; fright of and French Revolution, 114; as fundamentalism, 64; historical

condemnation of by the Church, 112, 142–44; of John Paul II, 29–39; and the liberal tradition, 32, 33; Paul VI's criticism of, 192; and postmodern symbiosis with religion, 225, 227–30; postmodernist or multiculturalist critique of, 219, 224–25; religious answers to paradox of, 219–30; Schindler's criticism of, 29–30; as a term, 30
"Liberalism Doesn't Exist" (Fish), 223
liberation theology, 129, 153–54, 183, 192
libertarianism, 30, 73
libertinism: and consumerism, 87–89; and the market, 27
liberty: and Acton's association with Judaism and Christianity, 281; versus *communio*, 83–84; and exercise of free will, 275; and lack of constraints, 275; and law in *Veritatis Splendor*, 237–45; longing for, 264; negative and positive, 275–76, 286n7, 286n9; ordered, 263–64; and reflection and choice, 256, 270n38; and religion according to Tocqueville, 117–18; and right to define one's existence, 4; of spirit, 101; three concepts of, 275–77; threefold, xiii, 100–101, 264; and virtuous action, 277–79
Lincoln, Abraham, 18, 133, 135, 136–37
Lippmann, Walter, 251, 267n7
literature and individualism, 214
Locke, John, 127, 130, 167, 169, 223, 225, 280
logical deduction and practical wisdom, xviii
Longinqua Oceani (Leo XIII), 146, 150
Louis XIV, 120
love: and *caritas*, 99–102, 105; five types of, 98–99
Lublin lectures of Karol Wojtyla (John Paul II), 42
Lumen Gentium (John Paul II), 45, 210
Lustiger, Jean-Marie, 206–9

Machiavelli, 118, 127

MacIntryre, Alasdair, 31
Madison, G. B., 172, 177
Madison, James, 135, 139, 153, 163n17, 262; and *The Federalist*, 291; and *Memorial and Remonstrance*, 140; and multiplicity of rights, 129–30; and originality of U.S. system, 255; and virtue, 256, 270n36, 278, 286n13
Man of the Century (Kwitny), 201, 211
Manent, Pierre: and Christianity and democracy, 109–25; and modern individualism, 213–18
Marcel, Gabriel, 253
Marcuse, Herbert, 88, 170
Maréchal, Joseph, 42
Maritain, Jacques, 41, 147, 162n13, 192; and American experiment, 250, 266n6, 268n12
markets: and communities, 251–52; and culture, 27; as generator of goods, 61; and human creativity, 79–80; non-sustainability of without moral environment, 66; workability of from experience not logic, xviii
Marsilius of Padua, 114
Marx, Karl, 224
Marxism, 143; Christian, 207; and collectivism, 85–86; and definition of capitalism, 102; and economic structure determining consciousness, 85–86; and Revolution of 1989, 9
Marxist–Leninist theory, failures of, 4
media and role in determining moral-cultural virtues, 263, 265
Memorial and Remonstrance (Madison), 140
Mercier, Désiré, 42
mercy, 97, 99–100
metapolitical sphere, 57
Milken, Michael, 71, 72, 73
Mill, John Stuart, 170, 176, 233, 283
Mirari Vos (Gregory XVI), 109, 142
modernity: and dignity of the individual, 33; and freedom, 211; and loss of conviction and self-doubt, 220; and opinions, 233–34; and will's emancipation, 114

monarchy, national, 119, 126
monopoly capitalism, 26, 86–87
Montesquieu, 127
Montini, Giovanni Battista. *See* Paul VI
moral: claim of liberal state, 223; ecology, 261–65; life depends on three generations, 247
Moral Sense, The (Wilson), 42
morality: and adversary culture, 259–60; as central political debate of twenty-first century, 278; Christian or Jewish vision of, 258; crisis of, xviii, 247, 254, 257–58; decay of public in Central and Eastern Europe, 62–63; and founding of United States, 255–57; as framework for market economy, 15; grounded in law, 237–38; and health of capitalist democracies, 103, 104, 246–47, 257, 262–64, 277; and human reason versus Divine law, 239–42; necessity for in democracy, 158–59; and relativism, 234–35; and truth, 284–85; and widespread loss of virtue in modern society, 247. *See also* law
Moro, Aldo, 147
Morris, Charles R., 40
multiculturalism and critique of liberalism, 224–25
Murray, Charles, 30
Murray, John Courtney, 18–21, 161n4, 182, 250, 266n6; and *Centesiumus Annus*, 38; and church/state theory, 150–51; and liberalism and Catholic truth, 30; and neoconservatives, 29; and religious freedom, 152–53; *We Hold These Truths*, 18–21, 194–95

"naked square" postulate, 54–55
Napoleonic persecution of Church, 142, 144
narrow infinity, 5, 22n6
nation: appearance of and uniting of Empire and Church, 121–22; localism and globalism undermining of, 220; modern demand for allegiance to, 220
national life and the holy, 57, 58

national monarchies, 119–20
natural law, 193–95, 239
Neibuhr, Reinhold, 277, 283, 286n12, 287n24
Nell-Breuning, Oswald von, 149
neoconservatives, 29
Neuhaus, Richard John, 14; and the Catholic moment, 179–84; and liberalism of John Paul II, 29–39; and property and creativity, 68–82; and United States style of religious freedom, 133–40
Nietzsche, Friedrich, 132, 224, 280; and Christianity as Platonism for the people, 92; and Christianity bringing about feminization of the male, 95
nihilism: cheerful, 248, 250; political, 274–75, 280
non-establishment clause of First Amendment, 137–40
Nous, 93
Novak, Michael, xiii–xix, 26, 191; against the adversary culture, 246–73; and *caritas*, 98–105; and Christianity and political economy, 91–97; and cultural crisis of truth and liberty, 274–88; and philosophy of John Paul II, 40–47

obligations and rights, 8
O'Connor, Sandra Day, 4–5
Octogesima Adveniens (Paul VI), 192
O'Donovan, Oliver, 31
Old Regime and the French Revolution (Tocqueville), 224
opinion, 231–36, 279
original sin, 12, 97, 130, 278
Our Country: The Shaping of America from Roosevelt to Reagan (Barone), 260
ownership, right and wrong, 70–71
Ozanam, Frederick, 209

Pacem in Terris (John XXIII), 8, 187, 192
Pangle, Thomas L., 219–30
Paris, and World Youth Day of 1997, 206–10
Paris Commune of 1870, 143, 144

Pascal, Blaise, 282
Pascendi (Pius X), 111
Patocka, Jan, 92, 249
Paul, St., 58
Paul VI: and criticism of liberalism, 192; and democracy, 147; and Jacques Maritain, 41; and *Populorum Progressio*, 155; and Second Vatican Council proclamation on liberty, 45
Peace of Westphalia, 144
Péguy, Charles, 97, 102, 132
person: acting, and economics, 80–81, 103; and John Paul II, 45
personalism, Christian, 7, 8
phenomenology, 41
pilgrimages, student, in France, 208
pity, 216–17
Pius VI, 145
Pius VII, 142, 148, 161n5
Pius IX, 141, 149, 187; and opposition to secular liberalism, 142–43, 146
Pius X, 110
Pius XI, 128, 147, 188
Pius XII, 128, 149–50, 187
Piwowarczyk, Jan, 211–12
Plato, 93, 248, 249, 276
Platonism, 92, 93, 94
pluralism, 136, 181
Poland, xvi, 44, 103; John Paul II's 1997 visit to, 202–6; Revolution of 1989, 10, 11
Politi, Marco, 40, 201, 211
Politics (Aristotle), 113
politics: as argument about good person, good society, and freedom, 10; and economic changes brought by Christianity, 91–97; and history of religion, 119–23, 126–27; as way of putting things in order, 215–16
Pope John Paul II: The Biography (Szulc), 202
Populorum Progressio (Paul VI), 155
positivism, 282
postmodernism: and critique of liberalism, 224–25; definition of, 219–20

poverty, 61, 72; causes of, 74–75; and Christian economic system, 101; in Europe versus United States in nineteenth century, 255; and the free market, 14, 61
Power/Knowledge (Foucault), 171
practical, necessity of, xvii–xviii
profit, 70
progress and time, 92
progressivism, 129
property, 68–82; definition and right of, 84–85; lack of respect for in Central and Eastern Europe, 62–63
Protestant Reformation and human capital, 102–3
Protestants: and pluralist republican society, 229; and situation in United States, 130–31
Proudhon, Pierre-Joseph, 68
Psalms and private property, 68
public discourse and agnosticism, 37
public philosophy, 251, 267n7
"public square" postulate, 133–34; formulation of, 54–55; foundations of, 55–56
Puritanism, 121

Quadragesimo Anno (Pius XI), 148, 149
Quanta Cura (Pius IX), 112
Qu'est-ce que la Propriéte (Proudhon), 68
Quod Aliquantum, 111

Ratzinger, Joseph, 54, 57, 180, 182, 254; and common economic minimum, 67; moral-cultural call to the U.S., 257; and natural law, 195; and non-return to politicized Christianity, 63
Rawls, John, 30, 31, 135, 197
"reactionary" school of nineteenth-century Catholicism, 110, 114–15
real estate metaphors for discussion of liberty, 242–45
reason, 96–97
Redemptoris Missio (John Paul II), 35
relativism, 96, 231–32, 233, 246; America founded on, 248; and liberty, 275; and Schlesinger, 248, 250; and truth, 281–85

Index

religion: and democracy according to Tocqueville, 116–19, 123, 276, 286n11; and First Amendment, 137–40; free exercise of, 137–38; as key to culture, 197; political history of, 119–23, 126–27; and postmodern symbiosis with liberalism, 225, 227–30; as a private affair, 63; social power of, 117–18
religious freedom, 8, 191; nature of, 151–53, 163n26, 164n29
religious truth, 216; three forms of, 283–85
representational governance, 135
Republic (Plato), 93
Rerum Novarum (Leo XIII), xiv, 6, 209; and capitalist monopoly, 86–87; and criticism of economic liberalism, 30; and freedom, 7; metaphysical scheme of, 197; and natural law, 194; and political state, 186, 188; and private property, 68, 185, 187; and rights, 193; and work, 81
resources, human creativity as principal, 75, 77–78
Revolution, American, and *Centesimus Annus*, 33
Revolution, Polish, of 1989, 8–12, 15, 156; and John Paul II as a seminal figure in, 201–2; and rights, 193, 197
rights. *See* human rights
Rise of the Unmeltable Ethnics, The (Novak), 260
Risorgimento, Italian, 142, 143
Roepke, Wilhelm, 66–67
Rokita, Jan Maria, 61–62
Roman Catholic Church: and apoliticism, 131–32; and Aristotle, 113; centralization in mid-nineteenth century, 143; and charity, 61; and crisis of unbelief, 180; cultural contribution to poor, 76–77; as defender of human rights, 141; and desirability of separation from state according to Tocqueville, 118; distinction between lay and clerical vocations, 57–58; and economics, 60–67; and ecumenism, 180–81; encounter with and embrace of democracy, xix, 57–58, 126–33, 157; and faith as opposed to ideology, 53–59; and gap between Europe and North America, xiv; and the Gospel, 179, 180; hostility toward in post-Enlightenment period, 52; hostility toward secular liberalism, 142–44; incarnational and eschatological traditions in, 261–62; influence of America on from 1864 to 1965, 145–47; metapolitical status of, 57–59; and monarchical regimes, 126; and necessity of moral political actions, 183; past failures to respect dignity and freedom of others, 38, 51–52; as perfect society or republic, 113, 119; and political history of religion, 119–23, 126–27; and power and Lustiger group, 206–7; and proposing rather than imposing, 35; and religion as a private matter, 123–24; selling of its wealth, 76–77; status of in United States, 131; and temple in the polis, 58; and Tocqueville, 228–29; totalitarianism pushing it towards democracy, 147; and truth, 54; utopias of, 127–29
Rorty, Richard, 30, 31, 44, 175, 265n1, 285n4; and "cheerful nihilism," 248, 275; and democracy and philosophy, 171; and influence of Christian charity, 91–92; and lack of objective moral standard, 248–50
Rousseau, Jean Jacques, 113, 127, 216
rule of law. *See* law, rule of
Russell, Bertrand, 44, 92, 276

sacrifices and political society, 221–22
Sarte, Jean-Paul, 276
Scheler, Max, 41–42
Schindler, David, 29
Schlesinger, Arthur M., 248, 250, 266n2, 275, 285n4

Schumpeter, Joseph, 60, 252, 257
science, and Christian intelligibility, 95
Scriptures and rule of law, 237–38, 239, 241–42
Second Vatican Council, 29, 40, 44, 45, 111; and church/state relations, 150–51; and Declaration on Religious Freedom (*Dignitatis Humanae*), 145, 150–51, 182; and ecumenism, 181; as end of Constantinian epoch, 210; and lack of condemnation of communism, 112; and opening to the Church, 180; and religious freedom, 151–53
"Secular Saint, The" (Novak), 260
secularization, 63–64, 66
self-government: and liberty, 276; and right morality, 277–78
sexual ethics, John Paul VI's teachings on, 45–46
Siefert, Josef, xiv, xv
sin and the human Church, xvii, 41
Singulari Nos (Gregory XVI), 142
Smith, Adam, 66, 74, 90, 225
social: contract, 31, 217, 223; doctrine as opposed to social teaching, 83; justice, 46–47; life and the holy, 57, 58
Social Contract (Rousseau), 113
Social Ethics (Wojtyla), 211–12
socialism: and Christian notion of equality, 94; Church's silence relative to, 128–29; and collectivism, 7; condemnation of by Church, 112; errors of as anthropological, 8–9; Gramsci's view as a cultural matter, 260; practical problems in, xviii; and private property, 68
society: as prior to the state, 21; subjectivity of, 36, 37
Socrates, 96
solidarity, 46, 148, 190–91, 196; and the free market, 90; and property, 70
Solidarity movement, 11, 16, 203
Sollicitudo Rei Socialis (John Paul II), 155–56, 160, 190–91
Solzhenitsyn, Aleksandr, 275
Souter, David, 4–5

speculation, illicit, 71, 72, 73–74
Spinoza, Baruch, 224, 225
spiritual: crisis of, xviii; life of nations depends on three generations, 247. *See also* morality; religion
Stalin, Josef, 75, 167
state: and agnosticism versus atheism, 110; check upon power of, 189; crisis of legitimacy of, 220; existence to serve society, 21; individual, family, and society prior to, 36; liberal and John Paul II, 185–98; liberal and religious answer to paradoxes of, 219–30; limited, 35–36; and religious freedom, 151; rights-based limits upon, 195–97; and separation from Church according to Tocqueville, 118; and separation of religion from public life, 54; social assistance or welfare, 16, 104, 185, 188
state of nature, 214, 223
Statue of Liberty, 255–56
Strategic Defense Initiative (SDI), 11
Sturzo, Don Luigi, 147
subjectivity: and human person as agent, 46–47; of society, 36, 37
subsidiarity, 46, 141, 148–50, 163n17, 188–89
sumptuary laws, 72
Swiezawski, Stefan, 210
Syllabus of Errors (Pius IX), 142, 145, 146, 187
Szulc, Tad, 40, 202, 211

Talmon, J. R., 143
Tawney, R. H., 102
Taylor, Charles, 232
temple in polis, image of, 58–59
Teresa of Avila, St., 43
territory, 215
Tertio Millennio Adveniente (John Paul II), 38
Tertullian, 241
theological-political problem, solutions to, 119–23
theology and academe and the Church, 182

Theology for Radical Politics, A (Novak), 260
theory, inadequacies of, xvii–xviii
Thérèse of Lisieux, St., 43, 209
Thomism, 42, 186
time and progress, 92
Tinque, Henri, 67
Tischner, Josef, 44
Tocqueville, Alexis de, 132, 255, 263, 270n34, 272n54; and argument for symbiosis of religion and liberalism, 225, 227–30; and civil society, 16; democracy and religion according to, 116–19, 123, 276, 286n11; and free-market society, 88; and history of liberal-democratic state, 223–30; and human versus animal freedom, 284, 287n25; and individualism, 226, 227; and materialism, 226–27; and Puritanism, 121
tolerance: and *homo liberalis*, 176; ideology of, 174–75; and James Madison, 130; and philosophical legitimacy, 171–72, 174; problems with, 166–78; and relativism, 231–32, 233; true and false, 231–36
totalitarianism, 161n4, 211, 249, 280; and *Centesimus Annus*, 187–88, 192, 281; as factor pushing Church toward democracy, 147; and *Quadragesimo Anno*, 149; and rights-based approach to the political order, 196; and separation of religion from public life, 37
Traite sur la tolerance (Voltaire), 167, 168
tree of knowledge, 241
Tribe, Lawrence, 138
Trilling, Lionel, 255, 258–59
Trinity, 93, 99
Trump, Donald, 71
truth: and culture, 34; and current Americans, 250–51, 253–54; and democracy, 157–58; discrediting of absolute, 129; and freedom, 28, 101, 264, 272n57, 279, 283–85; and human reason and civilization, 95–96; and link to human rights, 8; and meaninglessness in modern democracy, 132; "possession of," 52–53; reduction of to opinion, 231–33; as "a regime," 171, 174; and relativism, 249–50, 281–85; religious, and separation of humans, 216; and tolerance, 169
"truth about man," 9, 11, 17, 253
truths, five foundational of American culture war, 19–21
Two Cheers for Capitalism (Kristol), 102
"Two Concepts of Liberty" (Berlin), 275–76

United Nations, 192, 222
United States: and "capitalism," 25; and Christian majority, 136; and crisis of morality, xviii, 247, 254, 257–58; culture war in, 4–5, 18; and discrediting of absolute truth, 129; immigration into, 104; influence on the Church between 1864 and 1965, 145–47; originality of system of government of, 255; and public sentiment, 136–37; and Puritanism, 121; and religion as a social power, 118; and religious freedom, 133–40; and sovereignty higher than state, 19, 35. *See also* American experiment; Founders, American
U.S. Supreme Court: and *Casey v. Planned Parenthood*, 5, 275, 285n2; and definition of liberty, 4–5
"universal destination of goods," 69
universalism of Christianity, 223–24
utopias of the Church, 127–29

Vatican II. *See* Second Vatican Council
Vattimo, Gianni, 171
Vehementer Nos (Pius X), 110
Veritatis Splendor (John Paul II), 33, 157–58, 238; law and liberty in, 237–45; and relativism and truth, 281
vineyard, parable of, 243–44
virtue, 78, 256; moral-cultural versus political, 263; required of citizens, 251, 263; and survival of democracy, 256, 270n36, 277, 278

vocation, 66
Voegelin, Eric, 67
Voltaire, 123, 167, 168
von Balthasar, Hans Ur, 7, 22n7, 53–54

Walesa, Lech, 203
Washington, George, 278, 284, 287n14
We Hold These Truths (Murray), 18–21, 194–95
Wealth and Poverty (Gilder), 77
Wealth of Nations, The (Smith), 74
Weber, Max, 102
Weigel, George, xvi
welfare state, 16, 104, 185, 188
Whitehead, Alfred North, 95
Why I Am Not a Christian (Russell), 92
Wiegel, George, 3–24, 141–65
will of the human individual, 129; emancipation of and modern democracy, 117; liberty as exercise of, 275; and national monarchies, 120; notion of sovereignty of, 112–13
Wilson, James Q., 42, 260
Wojtyla, Karol. *See* John Paul II
Wolff, Robert Paul, 166
work: and dignity, 69–70; and fun, 78–79; need for ethic of, 88–90
workers' versus producers' mentality, 88–89
world government, 221
World Youth Day, 12th in Paris in 1997, 206–10
Wyszynski, Stefan, 10, 203

Yalta Agreement, 9–10
yuppies, 88

Zieba, Maciej, xv, 51–67

About the Contributors

Philippe Benéton is professor of political science at the University of Rennes in France.

Alain Besançon is an emeritus professor at l'École des Hautes Études en Sciences Sociales in Paris and a member of the prestigious Institut. He is the author of numerous books including *The Rise of the Gulag: The Intellectual Origins of Leninism* (Continuum), *L'Image Interdit* (Fayard), and *Les Trois Tentations de L'Eglise* (Calmann-Levy). He is a contributing editor to *Commentaire*.

Rocco Buttiglione is Pro-rector at the International Academy of Philosophy in Liechtenstein. He has been a philosophical collaborator with the Pope for many years. For several years he also has been consultor of the Pontifical Commission for Justice and Peace. He is the author of many books and articles on Catholic social thought and the thought of Pope John Paul II. He is presently a member of the Italian Parliament for the United Christian Democrats.

Russell Hittinger is incumbent of the Warren Chair of Catholic Studies, at the University of Tulsa, where he is also a research professor in the School of Law. He specializes in issues of theology and law. From 1991 to 1996, he was a research scholar at the American Enterprise Institute for Public Policy Research, in Washington, D.C., where he worked on issues of law and religion. His books and articles have appeared in such places as the University of Notre Dame Press, Oxford University Press, the *Review of Metaphysics*, the *Review of Politics*, and the *International Philosophical Quarterly*, as well as in several law journals. He is on the editorial boards of *First Things* and the *American Journal of Jurisprudence*. He is presently working on a book entitled *The Popes and the Desacralized Caesar: Roman Theories of the Modern State 1800–1989*.

About the Contributors

Ryszard Legutko is professor of philosophy at the Jagiellonian University of Krakow, where he teaches ancient and political philosophy, and is the president of the Center for Political Thought. He is a contributor to and columnist of many dailies, weeklies, and monthlies, including *Czas Krakowski, Tygodnik Powszechny, Znak Monthly, Critical Review, Reason, Partisan Review*, and others. For many years he was editor-in-chief of *Arka*.

Pierre Manent is professor at l'École des Hautes Études en Sciences Sociales, Paris. He is the author of many books, including *An Intellectual History of Liberalism* (Princeton), *Tocqueville and the Nature of Democracy* (Rowman & Littlefield), *Modern Liberty and Its Discontents* (Rowman & Littlefield), and *The City of Man* (Princeton). He is a contributing editor to the French journal *Commentaire*. He has written extensively on the relationship of religion and politics in modern thought.

Richard John Neuhaus is president of the Institute on Religion and Public Life, a nonpartisan interreligious research and education institute in New York City. He is the editor-in-chief of the institute's publication, *First Things*, and the author of many books.

Michael Novak, theologian, author, former U.S. ambassador, presently holds the George Frederick Jewett Chair in religion and public policy at The American Enterprise Institute for Public Policy in Washington, D.C., where he also serves as the director of social and political studies. Mr. Novak is the author of many books, articles, essays, and reviews in newspapers and magazines worldwide. Most recently he coauthored with his daughter Jana, *Tell Me Why: A Father Answers His Daughter's Questions about God.*

Thomas L. Pangle has been professor, department of political science, at the University of Toronto since 1979. He is currently also a fellow of St. Michael's College. He has been a visiting professor at Dartmouth College, the University of Chicago, and the l'École des Hautes Études en Sciences Sociales in Paris. Most recently he published *The Learning of Liberty* with Lorraine Smith Pangle.

George Weigel is former president and a current senior fellow of the Ethics and Public Policy Center, a Washington, D.C., research institute. Mr. Weigel has produced a volume of articles at the intersection of religious values and American public life and is one of the country's leading authorities on ethics, war, and peace. He is the author and editor of numerous books, most recently *Witness to Hope: The Biography of John Paul II.*

Maciej Zieba, a Polish Dominican priest, is former director of the publishing house "w drodze" in Poznan, Poland, and one of the founders of the Center for Political Thought in Krakow. He has recently launched a think tank dedicated to Catholic social thought, The Tertio Millennio Institute. In addition to these duties he lectures at the University of Poznan and is a columnist and contributing editor for *Tygodnik Powszechny*. He is the author of several books, and his articles have been translated into English in *Crisis* and *First Things*.